The HighScope Preschool Curriculum

The HighScope Preschool Curriculum

Ann S. Epstein, PhD
Mary Hohmann

HIGHSCOPE PRESS®

Ypsilanti, Michigan

Published by
HighScope® Press

A division of the
HighScope Educational Research Foundation
600 North River Street
Ypsilanti, Michigan 48198-2898
734.485.2000, FAX 734.485.0704
Orders: 800.40.PRESS; Fax: 800.442.4FAX; www.highscope.org
E-mail: *press@highscope.org*

Copyright © 2012 by HighScope Educational Research Foundation. All rights reserved. Except as permitted under the Copyright Act of 1976, no part of this book may be reproduced or distributed in any form or by any means, electronic or mechanical, including photocopy, recording, or any information storage-and-retrieval system, without either the prior written permission from the publisher, or authorization through payment of the appropriate per-copy fee to the Copyright Clearance Center, Inc., 222 Rosewood Drive, Danvers, MA 01923, 978.750.8400, fax 978.646.8600, or on the web at www.copyright.com. The name "HighScope" and its corporate logos are registered trademarks and service marks of the HighScope Foundation.

Editors: Nancy Brickman, Jennifer Burd, Joanne Tangorra, Marcella Weiner
Cover design, text design: Judy Seling, Seling Design LLC
Production: Judy Seling, Seling Design LLC; Kazuko Sacks, Profit Makers LLC

Library of Congress Cataloging-in-Publication Data
Epstein, Ann S.
  The HighScope preschool curriculum / Ann S. Epstein and Mary Hohmann.
      p. cm.
   ISBN 978-1-57379-650-7 (soft cover : alk. paper) 1. Education, Preschool--Curricula. 2. Active learning.
 I. Hohmann, Mary. II. High/Scope Educational Research Foundation. III. Title.
   LB1140.4.E79 2012
   372.19--dc23
                              2012019672

Printed in the United States of America
10 9 8 7 6 5 4

To generations of educators
and the young children
who inspire them

Contents

Foreword xi

Acknowledgments xv

Introduction: The HighScope Approach to Preschool Education 1

    Origin of the HighScope Preschool Curriculum 2

    The Central Principles of the HighScope Preschool Curriculum 3

        Active participatory learning 4

        Adult-child interaction 5

        Learning environment 5

        Daily routine 5

        Assessment 6

    Evidence of Effectiveness 7

        Findings of the HighScope Perry Preschool Study 7

        Findings of the HighScope Preschool Curriculum Comparison Study 8

        Findings of the HighScope Training of Trainers Evaluation 9

        Findings from independent investigators 10

        Why the HighScope Preschool Curriculum works 11

Chapter 1. Active Participatory Learning: The Way Children Construct Knowledge 13

    Human Development As a Framework for Education 14

        Learning as developmental change 14

        Active participatory learning — A complex process 16

        Adults as supporters of active learners 20

    Key Developmental Indicators — A Framework for Understanding Active Learning 25

        What happens in an active learning setting 26

        What children do in the active learning setting 26

        What adults do in the active learning setting 37

        How adults and children interact in the active learning setting 46

        The effects of active learning 48

    The Practical Ingredients of Active Learning 51

        Using the ingredients of active participatory learning 51

        Active participatory learning: The foundation of the HighScope Curriculum 53

Chapter 2. Adult-Child Interaction: Establishing a Supportive Climate 55

    Understanding Supportive Climates 56

        The child's sense of self: Development through interaction 56

        Building blocks of human relationships 58

        Who is in control? Contrasting social climates for children 62

        The effects of a supportive climate 65

    Strategies for Creating Supportive Climates: Six Key Elements 67

        Sharing of control between adults and children 68

        Focusing on children's strengths 70

        Forming authentic relationships with children 72

        Making a commitment to supporting children's play 75

        Using encouragement instead of praise 78

        Adopting a problem-solving approach to social conflict 79

        Using the elements of support: Moving a group of children from place to place guided by the key elements of support 83

        How the elements of support relate to the rest of the curriculum 86

        How the elements of support relate to program quality 86

Chapter 3. Involving Families in Active Learning Settings 91

The Benefits of Family Involvement 92

The HighScope Framework for Family Involvement 94

    Family as a frame for understanding children 95

    Active learning in support of family involvement 96

    A supportive climate for family involvement 100

    The effects of valuing families 102

Strategies for Supporting Family Involvement: Four Key Elements 103

    Knowing yourself, and your family's roots, beliefs, and attitudes 103

    Learning from children and families about their styles and traditions 104

    Creating positive relationships between yourself and others 110

    Anticipating excellence from each child 113

    Using the elements of family support: Two examples 114

    The elements of family support and the rest of the curriculum 116

Chapter 4. Working in Teams: Adult Collaboration to Promote Active Learning 119

Understanding Teamwork 120

    Teamwork: An interactive process 120

    The effects of teamwork 122

    Forming the team 123

Strategies for Daily Teamwork: Five Key Elements 125

    Establishing supportive relationships among adults 126

    Gathering accurate information about children 129

    Making group decisions about children: Interpreting observations and planning what to do next 131

    Planning lessons: Using the elements of the curriculum to plan the program day 134

    Making group decisions about teamwork 138

    Using the elements of daily teamwork: Involving a new team member 142

    Staff support and supervision 143

    Looking ahead: The relationship of adult teamwork to the rest of the HighScope Curriculum 148

Chapter 5. Child and Program Assessment 151

Child Assessment 153

    Authentic assessment of children 153

    COR Advantage 155

Program Assessment 162

    Valid program quality assessment 162

    The Preschool Program Quality Assessment (PQA) 164

Chapter 6. The Learning Environment: Arranging and Equipping Spaces for Active Learners 171

Ideas That Shape Settings for Active Learning 172

    Environments for children and the active learning ingredients 172

    General guidelines for organizing space and materials 174

    Modifying the learning environment to accommodate children with special needs 187

    The effects of arranging and equipping space according to HighScope guidelines 190

Strategies for Arranging Active Learning Settings 190

    Arranging and equipping specific interest areas 190

    The relationship of arranging and equipping space to the rest of the curriculum 221

Chapter 7. The HighScope Daily Routine: A Framework for Active Learning 223

Understanding the Daily Routine 224

The daily routine supports child initiative 224

The daily routine provides a social framework 225

The daily routine provides a flexible structure 227

The daily routine supports curriculum values 227

General Guidelines for Organizing a Daily Routine 228

A variety of active learning periods provides children with a range of experiences and interactions 228

Active learning periods occur in a reasonable, predictable sequence that meets the particular needs of the setting 236

Experiences take place in an appropriate physical setting 239

Each period involves children in active learning experiences within a supportive climate 239

The daily routine provides a range of learning experiences 240

The daily routine flows smoothly from one interesting experience to the next 241

Chapter 8. The HighScope Plan-Do-Review Process 243

Understanding Planning Time 244

What is planning? 245

Why is planning important? 249

What children do as they plan 251

How Adults Support Children's Planning 258

Adults plan with children in an intimate setting 259

Adults provide materials and experiences to maintain children's interest at planning time 260

Adults converse with individual children about their plans 261

Adults anticipate changes in children's planning over time 271

Understanding Work Time 275

What is work time and why is it important? 275

What children do at work time 278

How Adults Support Children at Work Time 282

Adults scan the interest areas to find out what children are doing 282

Adults choose children to observe, gain children's perspectives, and form on-the-spot interaction plans 285

Adults offer children comfort and contact 286

Adults participate in children's play 289

Adults converse with children 293

Adults encourage children's problem solving 300

Adults bring work time to an end 304

Understanding Recall Time 307

What is recall and why is it important? 307

What children do as they recall 310

How Adults Support Children at Recall Time 313

Adults recall with children in a calm, cozy setting 315

Adults provide materials and experiences to maintain children's interest at recall time 316

Adults converse with children about their work-time experiences 316

Adults anticipate changes in the way children recall over time 322

Chapter 9. Group Times, Outside Times, Transitions 325

Special Features of Group Times 326

Scaffolding Children's Learning at Group Times 327

Understanding Small-Group Time 328

What is small-group time? 331

Why is small-group time important? 333

Where small groups meet 338

What children do at small-group time 338

How Adults Support Children at Small-Group Time 341

Adults prepare for small groups *before* children arrive 341

Adults set small groups in motion: The beginning 341

Adults scaffold children's ideas and use of materials: The middle 342

Adults bring small-group time to a close: The end 345

Understanding Large-Group Time 353

What is large-group time? 353

Why is large-group time important? 357

Where large groups meet 360

What children do at large-group time 360

How Adults Support Children at Large-Group Time 363

Adults prepare for large-group time *before* children arrive 363

Adults set large groups in motion: The beginning 363

Adults scaffold children's ideas and initiatives: The middle 364

Adults bring large-group time to a close: The end 366

Understanding Outside Time 374

What is outside time? 374

Why is outside time important? 375

Where children play outside 376

What children do at outside time 376

How Adults Support Children at Outside Time 377

Adults help children obtain the materials they need 377

Adults use work-time support strategies 378

Adults observe nature with children 380

Adults bring outside time to a close 381

How Adults Support Children During Transitions 381

Adults adjust transition times to suit children's developmental needs 382

Adults plan for transitions with individual children in mind 383

Adults plan for cleanup, the longest transition 384

Understanding Other Group Times 387

Meal- and snacktime 387

Greeting and departure time 387

Message board 388

Chapter 10. Introduction to HighScope's Curriculum Content 391

KDIs — Guideposts for Child Development 393

The Significance of the KDIs 397

KDIs focus adults' observations and interpretations of children's actions 397

KDIs serve as a cross-cultural reference for observing and interpreting children's actions 397

KDIs help adults maintain reasonable expectations for children 397

KDIs answer questions about the legitimacy of children's play 398

KDIs guide decisions about materials and the daily routine 398

KDIs enable adults to recognize and support children's emerging capacities 399

Using the KDIs to Support Teaching and Learning 399

Use the KDIs as a basis for assessing the materials available to children 399

Use the content areas and KDIs to organize and interpret observations of children 401

Use KDI-based child observations as a basis for daily team planning 404

Use the KDIs as a guide to planning small-group and large-group times 404

Use the content areas and KDIs to guide on-the-spot interactions with children 405

Use the curriculum-based planning and assessment tool, COR Advantage 405

References 407

Photo Credits 413

Index 415

Foreword

The foundation of early childhood education and developmentally appropriate practice is knowledge of child development. Those of us who approach the world from a developmental perspective recognize and embrace the value of *both* continuity *and* change. This highly anticipated fourth version of the HighScope Preschool Curriculum — contained in a nine-book set — is firmly grounded in this developmental principle. Not surprisingly, the revised curriculum provides the assurance of continuity by building on the base of the HighScope Educational Research Foundation's widely respected research. The essential components of the curriculum have not changed, because they have been proven to lead to lasting positive consequences for children, families, and society. At the same time, this revised version fully reflects our evolving knowledge base, including the most current research on child development, learning, and effective teaching practices.

In recent decades, we have seen an explosion of interest in and support for early childhood education. Widespread recognition of the power of early experience to change lives is due in large part to dissemination of the results of the Perry Preschool Project (which later became a part of the HighScope Educational Research Foundation). This landmark experimental study demonstrated that high-quality early childhood programs not only have positive, long-lasting educational and economic consequences for the individual children who participate but also are enormously cost-effective for society as a whole.

Data from the Perry Preschool Project continue to lift all boats in the early childhood arena. But it is important to remember that Perry was not just any preschool. Unlike many programs before or since, it operated with a well-defined, *validated* curriculum — that is, one that has been evaluated and had its effectiveness demonstrated. The essential elements of the curriculum, then and now, include active learning, comprehensive whole-child goals, and child-guided as well as teacher-guided learning experiences. The well-known cornerstone of the curriculum is engaging children in the *plan-do-review* process. This teaching strategy, which promotes the development of self-regulation and executive function, undoubtedly contributed to the Perry graduates being more likely to achieve in school, be employed, earn higher wages, and own their own homes while being less likely to be dependent on welfare or engage in criminal behavior. The pillars of the curriculum remain, and are clearly described and illustrated in this book, the core volume and trusted component of continuity in the revised curriculum; they are also reflected in the companion set of volumes covering each of the curriculum's eight content areas (Epstein, 2012a–h).

So how is this latest version of the HighScope Curriculum different? What has changed? Although many of these practices were present in some form previously, this version is significantly expanded, updated, and more explicit. The "new and improved" HighScope model includes several features that will benefit children and also make teachers' work easier and more fulfilling.

The curriculum is based on a newly revised set of key developmental indicators (KDIs). These content goals address all domains of child development and are organized into eight key areas: Approaches to Learning; Social and

Emotional Development; Physical Development and Health; Language, Literacy, and Communication; Mathematics; Creative Arts; Science and Technology; and Social Studies. Moreover, the KDIs are aligned with the Head Start Child Development and Early Learning Framework, the Common Core Standards, and state early learning standards. The KDIs assist teachers in many ways, such as focusing their observations and interpretations of children's actions, helping them maintain reasonable expectations for children, and enabling them to recognize and support children's emerging capacities.

The HighScope Curriculum emphasized children's approaches to learning — initiative, planning, engagement, problem solving, and reflection — well before the rest of the educational world recognized the predictive power of these capabilities. In addition, the curriculum addresses the key competencies that children need to be prepared for success in kindergarten, such as language, early literacy, and mathematics skills. In this way, using the HighScope Curriculum has been demonstrated to help close the achievement gap that is already present at entrance to preschool between children from low-income families and their more affluent peers. Given that we have a special responsibility to our nation's most vulnerable children, it is essential that publicly funded programs use a validated curriculum, such as HighScope's, that has been proven effective in achieving that goal.

Among the most exciting and useful components of the revised curriculum are the eight KDI companion books, one for each of the HighScope content areas listed above (Epstein, 2012a–h). These tools guide teachers in their most important, but difficult, task — scaffolding children's learning. Even very experienced teachers find it difficult to teach in each child's *zone of proximal development* — as Vygotsky called it — to provide just the right kind and amount of support to help a child continue to make progress. The wide range of individual differences in every group makes this an especially daunting task. These books help teachers identify approximately where children are on a continuum of learning — providing examples of behaviors a child might demonstrate at early, middle, and later levels for each of the KDIs. Then, teachers will find specific examples of what they can do to support children at each of these levels and to gently extend and challenge them to move forward. Just as children need scaffolding, teachers need scaffolding. Teaching young children can be as exhausting as it is rewarding. Such scaffolding for teachers frees them to be more responsive to the individual strengths and needs of children and to take advantage of the inevitable teachable moments.

The HighScope Curriculum is still organized around *both* child-guided or child-initiated experiences *and* teacher-guided or teacher-initiated experiences. However, the revised curriculum is now more explicit — early childhood teachers must be intentional in everything they do. In teacher-guided learning, teachers take the lead during a planned experience determined by their goals. In child-guided learning, children gain knowledge and skills through their own interaction and exploration. In either situation, teachers are intentional — both children and teachers are actively engaged mentally and physically. This new set of publications clearly illustrates such intentional teaching in action.

The revised curriculum also guides teachers in how to use various learning contexts and formats — areas or centers, whole or small groups, routines and transitions, and the outdoors. We know from large-scale studies that too much time is wasted in preschool while children wait to move from one activity to another or fidget during extended whole-group times. Children in Head Start and public pre-K programs — in fact, all children — have no time to waste. There are too many missed opportunities for learning in our early childhood programs. The HighScope Curriculum helps teachers take advantage of every part of the environment and the daily schedule. Guidance for effectively using whole-group activities is especially welcome. Even though small groups are one of the most effective formats for learning, they rarely occur in any classroom setting. HighScope has always included small-group time in its daily routine, but now these groups will be even more valuable, given the scaffolding support for teachers provided in the KDI companion books.

A validated curriculum is a core component of an effective early childhood program, but another essential element is an aligned, authentic, developmentally appropriate assessment system. HighScope has COR Advantage (Epstein et al., 2014) to help teachers track child progress, communicate with families, and meet data gathering and reporting requirements. Implementing a comprehensive curriculum with fidelity requires knowledgeable, intentional teachers, which is why HighScope also provides ongoing professional development.

HighScope's curriculum developers work with and directly observe children and teachers on a daily basis. Their work is carried out in an on-site demonstration preschool as well as in programs across the country and around the world. Therefore, the curriculum is sensitive and responsive to the realities of cultural and linguistic diversity, and adaptable for children with disabilities and special needs.

The reality and joy of teaching young children leap off the pages of these materials with enchanting vignettes and true-to-life examples that experienced teachers will easily recognize. Just as the leadership of HighScope and the Perry Preschool Project made possible the respect and support that early childhood education enjoys today, the "new and improved" research-based HighScope Preschool Curriculum will lead early childhood education programs into the future.

— Sue Bredekamp, PhD
Early Childhood Education
Consultant and Author

Acknowledgments

Since the publication in 1971 of HighScope's first preschool manual, adults in early childhood programs throughout the United States and around the world have used the HighScope Preschool Curriculum to guide their interactions with young children. Integrating the insights and experiences of teachers and trainers with current research on child development and teaching practices, staff at the HighScope Educational Research Foundation have updated the curriculum over the decades, maintaining a balance between continuity and change. We have held firm to the active learning principles that longitudinal research shows prepare children to succeed in school and in life. At the same time, we have embraced the ever-astounding emerging knowledge about how young children think, learn, and engage with the world.

To accommodate the major additions we've made to the curriculum since the publication of the last curriculum manual, this version is presented as a set of nine books, with new titles and a fresh format. The ingredients of active participatory learning, and the classroom and assessment practices to implement them, are presented in this volume. Our teaching practices, while built around the same core principles as before, have been updated to better meet the needs of today's teachers and children. The curriculum content, or key developmental indicators (KDIs), presented in the eight KDI companion books (Epstein, 2012a–h), has been wholly revised to reflect new information about what and how young children learn, and how adults support their early development. We are indebted to those who make the study of children their life's work. They contribute to the body of knowledge we have incorporated in the up-to-date curriculum, making it contemporary while remaining true to the enduring characteristics of young children worldwide.

The late David Weikart, who initiated the development of the HighScope Curriculum with the Perry Preschool Study and later established the HighScope Foundation, played a central role in the publication of previous versions of our curriculum. His work continues to shape our thinking about the best ways to encourage young children's learning and development, and help them create lives that are individually fulfilling and contribute to the well-being of their families, communities, and society as a whole.

We are indebted to our current and former colleagues at the HighScope Foundation who played an active role in the multiyear process of revising the preschool curriculum. First and foremost are the early childhood specialists and associated staff who collaborated on the development of the KDIs that are the heart of the new curriculum content. We extend special thanks to the following for reviewing and re-reviewing the manuscript to make sure we "got it right" for children and adults: Beth Marshall, Sue Gainsley, Shannon Lockhart, Polly Neill, Kay Rush, Julie Hoelscher, Emily Thompson, and Karen Sawyers. Others whose work contributed to our curriculum development include Phyllis Weikart, Charles Hohmann, and Andrea DeBruin-Parecki. Linda Horne was invaluable in helping us stay organized and on the same page as we worked our way through multiple iterations of the curriculum content.

Staff in other departments also lent their support and challenged us to produce the best publication possible. Larry Schweinhart was an early advocate of updating HighScope's curriculum content to reflect concurrent changes in national and state early learning standards. Clay Shouse not only monitored the production process but made us reflect on how to make the publication of maximum use to practitioners in the field. Likewise, Kathy Woodard helped us think about how to communicate the central messages we wanted to get across about the proven effectiveness, feasibility, and adaptability of the HighScope Curriculum in different settings. Marijata Daniel-Echols and other researchers asked the tough "How do you know?" questions that kept us on our toes in performing the dance between research and practice — a distinguishing feature of the HighScope approach.

HighScope talks about the importance of learning through all the senses and this book fulfills that precept. Under the direction of Nancy Brickman, the editorial and production staff created a publication that lets educators absorb the words in their minds and hearts while attending to the evocative images on the page. Our appreciation goes to Jennifer Burd, Joanne Tangorra, and Marcella Weiner for their editorial wizardry; and to Kevin McDonnell, whose eye and ear for capturing children and adults on videotape awakens our vision and hearing to what is and what can be. Thanks also go to Katie Bruckner, whose technical expertise, exceeded only by her good spirits, kept the production process running smoothly. Others who contributed their considerable skills were photographers Bob Foran and Gregory Fox; book designer Judy Seling; and production specialist Kazuko Sacks.

Many people outside the foundation contributed to the development and implementation of the HighScope Preschool Curriculum presented in this publication. Our thanks to Sue Bredekamp for her active interest in the revision process and for writing a thoughtful foreword. The early childhood field relies on people like her to remind us what is important. HighScope field consultants and certified trainers connected us to the practitioners who use the curriculum in their programs on a daily basis. We are also grateful to teachers and staff of HighScope programs who invited us to photograph their classrooms in action, including the staff of Hazel Park Head Start in Hazel Park, Michigan, and Perry Nursery School in Ypsilanti, Michigan. Finding out from teachers, child care providers, and parents what was working — and what additional support they needed — guided us in the organic process of curriculum refinement and renewal. It is for you that this publication is written. We hope you find it not only helpful but also inspiring. It inspires us to imagine you planning, doing, and reflecting every day about what children learn and how important you, and by extension we, are to their development.

Most of all, our thanks go to the children and their families whose participation in a vast array of programs over the decades has encouraged us to create and re-create the HighScope Preschool Curriculum. Observing and sharing in your efforts and accomplishments has enriched our lives. We hope that the ideas, strategies, words, and images in this book continue to enrich yours.

INTRODUCTION

The HighScope Approach to Preschool Education

The word *curriculum* comes from the Latin word for the course in a running or chariot race. The HighScope Preschool Curriculum advances students along a course of development as they gain essential knowledge and skills. The essence of this "course" is the dynamic interaction of an educational philosophy, a body of research, a series of teaching practices, and a set of meaningful learning goals for children. *The HighScope Preschool Curriculum* and the eight companion books in this set (Epstein, 2012a–h) represent the HighScope Educational Research Foundation's progress to date in the ongoing work of curriculum development. This introduction describes the curriculum's origins, its basic principles, and the evidence of its effectiveness for children, families, and society.

> "Families and communities shape the context in which children grow, framing children's most important early experiences and encounters with their environments."
>
> — National Education Goals Panel (Kagan, Moore, & Bredekamp, 1995, p. 6)

Origin of the HighScope Preschool Curriculum

Although the HighScope Curriculum is now used in settings serving the full range of preschool-age children, it was originally developed to serve children at risk of school failure from poor neighborhoods in Ypsilanti, Michigan. In 1962, David P. Weikart, director of special services for the city's public schools, initiated what later became known as the HighScope Perry Preschool Study. He designed this project in response to the persistent failure of high school students from the poorest neighborhoods. Over the years, these students consistently scored in the lower ranges on intelligence tests and academic achievement tests. Alarmed by these trends, Weikart searched for causes and cures. He concluded that the low IQ scores reflected inadequate learning opportunities in the schools these students attended rather than limited innate intelligence.

A series of committees including elementary school principals, social workers, and psychologists looked for practical programs that the Division of Special Services could implement to counteract this pattern of school failure. A review of child development research published in the landmark book *Intelligence and Experience* (Hunt, 1961) suggested that early intervention with three- and four-year-old children held the promise of reversing this negative trend. Influenced by this view, committee members eventually proposed a preschool education program for the at-risk children. Typical nursery schools of the day focused

Learning in the HighScope Preschool Curriculum begins with children's direct and immediate experiences with people, materials, events, and ideas.

on social and emotional growth. However, committee members believed that the curriculum in the proposed program should also address children's intellectual development to better prepare them to succeed in school.

Because this was an innovative proposition, there was some question as to whether and how such a program would work. To test the program's efficacy right from the start, Weikart and his team randomly assigned children from the target low-income neighborhood to two groups, one who would have the preschool experience and another who would have no preschool experience. In a subsequent project, the HighScope Preschool Curriculum Comparison Study, the program's effectiveness was also compared to two other models — the traditional nursery school approach and a direct instruction program. (See "Evidence of Effectiveness," on p. 7 for results from both studies.)

The team further agreed on three basic criteria for the development of an effective preschool curriculum:

- A coherent theory about teaching and learning must guide the curriculum development process.
- Curriculum theory and practice must support each child's capacity to develop individual talents and abilities through ongoing opportunities for active learning.
- The teachers, researchers, and administrators must work as partners in all aspects of curriculum development to ensure that theory and practice receive equal consideration.

For half a century, the HighScope Preschool Curriculum has held true to these founding criteria, even as it evolves to encompass the latest knowledge from theory, research, and practice. The curriculum was originally based on the writings of Jean Piaget and his colleagues (Piaget & Inhelder, 1966/1969), and the progressive educational philosophy of John Dewey (1938/1963).

Action plus reflection equals learning — HighScope teachers create opportunities in the daily routine for children to reflect on and talk about their play experiences.

Since then, HighScope has drawn on the work of Lev Vygotsky (1934/1962) and other "constructivist" models, which maintain that children actively "construct" their understanding of the world based on their experiences and social interactions, rather than just passively receiving knowledge and skills from adults. The curriculum has also been updated using findings from contemporary cognitive-developmental research and recent brain research (see chapter 1).[1]

The Central Principles of the HighScope Preschool Curriculum

The diagram on the next page, "The HighScope Preschool Wheel of Learning," illustrates the curriculum principles that guide HighScope preschool teachers in their daily work with children. This section briefly introduces each component of the wheel; subsequent chapters discuss each of these principles in greater detail.

---

[1] For a complete description of the history and evolution of the HighScope Preschool Curriculum, see Hohmann, Weikart, and Epstein (2008, pp. 3–5).

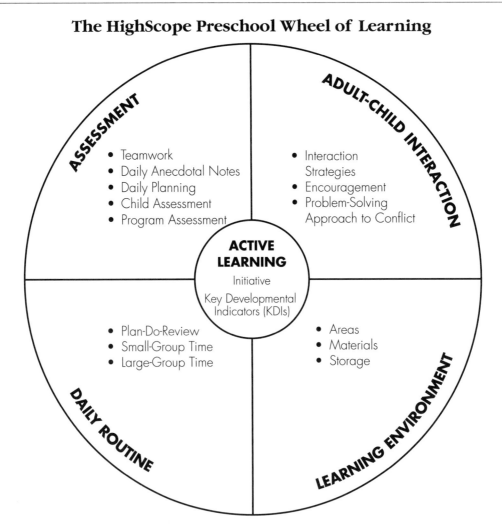

Active participatory learning

Through **active participatory learning** — having *direct experiences* and deriving meaning from them through *reflection* — young children construct knowledge that helps them make sense of their world. The power of active learning comes from **initiative.** Young children act on their innate desire to explore; they ask and search for answers to questions about people, materials, events, and ideas that arouse their curiosity; they solve problems that stand in the way of their goals; and they generate new strategies to try.

As children follow their intentions, they engage with the curriculum's content as identified in the **key developmental indicators (KDIs)**. KDIs are child behaviors that reflect developing mental, emotional, social, and physical abilities.

(See pp. 28–29 for the full list of preschool KDIs.) KDIs occur during children's creative, ongoing interactions with people, materials, events, and ideas, for example, when they are *planning* (KDI 2), expressing *emotions* (KDI 9), using *gross-motor skills* (KDI 16), *speaking* with adults and peers (KDI 22), *measuring* (KDI 36), involved in *pretend play* (KDI 43), exploring the *natural and physical world* (KDI 51), and participating in classroom *decision making* (KDI 55).

The extent to which adults support children's initiative and understand children's actions in terms of the KDIs determines the adults' success in implementing the HighScope Curriculum. Clearly, active learning experiences influence every aspect of our work with children and form the core of the preschool curriculum.

Adult-child interaction

Active learning depends on positive **adult-child interactions**. Mindful of the importance of providing a psychologically safe climate for young learners, adults using the HighScope preschool approach strive to be supportive as they converse and play with children. Throughout the day, guided by an understanding of how preschool children think and reason, they practice positive **interaction strategies** — sharing control with children, focusing on children's strengths, forming authentic relationships with children, supporting children's play, and adopting a problem-solving approach to social conflict. This interaction style enables the child to freely and confidently express thoughts and feelings, and to experience true partnerships with adults in play and conversation. Adults rely on **encouragement** and use a **problem-solving approach** to deal with everyday classroom situations rather than a child-management system based on praise, punishment, and reward.

Learning environment

Because the physical environment has a powerful impact on the behavior of children and adults, the HighScope Curriculum places a strong emphasis on planning the layout of the program setting and selecting appropriate materials. This **active learning environment** provides children with ongoing opportunities to make choices and decisions. Thus, adults organize the play space into specific **interest areas** to support preschool children's abiding interest in such activities as sand and water play, building, solving puzzles, pretend play, drawing and painting, reading and writing, counting, sorting, climbing, singing, and moving. The interest areas contain a wide and plentiful assortment of easily accessible **materials** children can use to carry out their play ideas. Natural, found, commercial, and homemade materials provide many opportunities each day for children to engage with curriculum content in creative and purposeful ways. Adults arrange **storage**

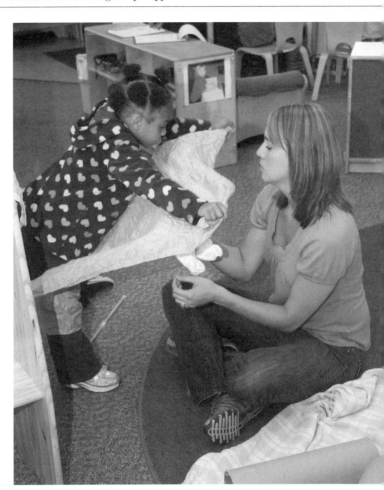

Rather than manage *children from a distance, adults in HighScope programs* interact *with them wherever they are and at their level.*

for materials using low shelves, clear boxes, and labels children can understand (using pictures and simple words), so they can independently find, use, and return the items they need.

Daily routine

In addition to arranging the setting, adults also plan a consistent **daily routine** that supports active learning. The routine enables young children to anticipate what happens next and gives them a great deal of control over what they do during each part of their preschool day. The HighScope preschool daily routine includes the **plan-do-review** process, which enables children to express their intentions, carry them out,

The layout of the classroom, and the materials in it, are carefully planned because of their strong impact on what children learn.

and reflect on what they have done. Adults set this process in motion by asking an appropriate question, such as "What would you like to do?" Children indicate their plans, then carry them out — for just a few minutes or for as long as an hour. Pretending, building block structures, and drawing are common child-initiated activities during the "do" period, after which adults encourage children to review their experiences. The children may talk about what they have done or express themselves by demonstrating, drawing, or writing. Opportunities for adult-guided group experiences are another consistent feature of the routine. At **small-group time** children explore and experiment with new or familiar materials adults have selected based on their daily observations of children's interests, the KDIs, and local events. During **large-group time** both children and adults initiate movement and music activities, story reenactments, and cooperative play and projects. Through a common daily routine focused around opportunities for active learning, children and adults build a sense of community.

Assessment

In HighScope settings, assessment includes a range of tasks to observe, document, evaluate, and continually strive to improve interactions with children, families, and coworkers. **Teamwork** built on supportive adult relationships forms a solid base for adults doing this work together. Each day the teaching team members gather accurate information by observing and interacting with children and taking **daily anecdotal notes** based on what they see and hear. Before the children arrive, after the children leave, or while the children are napping, teaching team members engage in daily **planning** sessions in which they share their observations of children, analyze the observations in terms of the KDIs, and make plans for the next day. Periodically, the team uses the observations recorded in their daily anecdotal notes to complete individual **child assessments** with COR Advantage (Epstein et al., 2014). Supervisors and teachers also periodically complete a **program assessment** using the Preschool Program Quality Assessment (PQA; HighScope, 2003a) to look at the effectiveness of their curriculum implementation, relationships with families, professional development, and overall program management.

These five basic principles — active learning, positive adult-child interactions, a child-friendly learning environment, a consistent daily routine, and team-based assessment — form the framework of the HighScope Curriculum. This book elaborates on each of these principles. The other eight books in this set, the KDI companion books, provide detailed information on how adults can use these principles as they support the development of the knowledge and skills identified by the KDIs in each of the eight curriculum content areas.

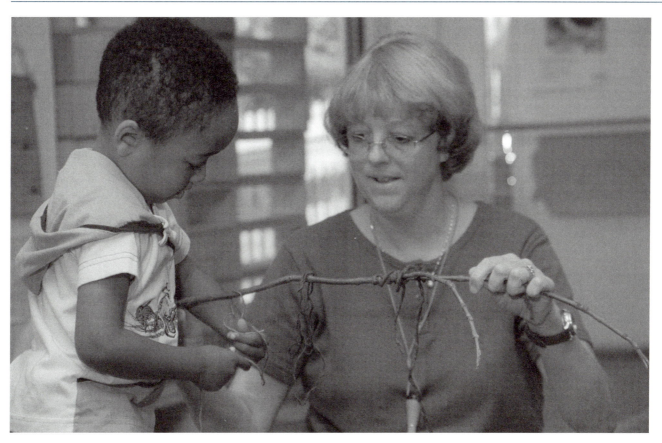

Assessment that is grounded in children's everyday experiences in the classroom is a key element of HighScope programs. This teacher observes carefully as the child ties another length of twine to his stick creation. Later she will add an anecdotal note and a photo of the finished project to his assessment portfolio.

Evidence of Effectiveness

Over the years, researchers have tested the validity of the HighScope approach to preschool education, gathering longitudinal data in both the HighScope Perry Preschool Study and the HighScope Preschool Curriculum Comparison Study. Between 1989 and 1992, HighScope researchers also investigated the effectiveness and outcomes of the HighScope teacher-training model in the HighScope Training of Trainers Evaluation. In addition, independent studies have looked at the effectiveness of the HighScope Curriculum relative to other program models. This section reviews the results of these research initiatives and explains how the HighScope approach to preschool education produces lasting benefits for children, families, educators, and society.

Findings of the HighScope Perry Preschool Study

Data on the effects of the curriculum in the HighScope Perry Preschool Study come from interviewing and reviewing the records of the 123 students who participated in the preschool intervention project from 1962 to 1967 (Schweinhart et al., 2005). In addition to information gathered directly from the students over the years (participants were age 40 at the time of their most recent interviews), research staff also examined their school, social services, and arrest records. They found major differences favoring the 40-year-olds who had been enrolled in the active learning preschool program (see graph, opposite page).

- **Social responsibility.** By age 40, 36 percent of preschool program group members had been arrested five or more times as compared with 55 percent of the no-preschool program group, and fewer had been arrested for violent crimes (32 percent vs. 48 percent), property crimes (36 percent vs. 58 percent), and drug crimes (14 percent vs. 34 percent).

- **Earnings and economic status.** At age 40, more of the program group than the no-program group were employed (76 percent vs. 62 percent), and the program group had higher median annual earnings than the no-program group ($20,800 vs. $15,300). At age 40, more of the program group owned their own homes (37 percent vs. 28 percent), owned their own cars (82 percent vs. 60 percent), and had savings accounts (76 percent vs. 50 percent).

- **Educational performance.** Almost a third again as many preschool program group members as no-preschool program group members graduated from regular or adult high school or received General Education Development certification (77 percent vs. 60 percent). Earlier in the study, the preschool program group had significantly higher average achievement scores at age 14 and literacy scores at age 19 than the no-preschool program group.

- **Marriage and family life.** At age 40, more program males than no-preschool males took responsibility for raising their children (57 percent vs. 30 percent); more program males were married (71 percent vs. 54 percent); and more had second or third marriages (29 percent vs. 8 percent). At age 40, more of the program group than the no-program group said they were getting along very well with their families (75 percent vs. 64 percent).

These findings indicate that a high-quality preschool program such as the HighScope Curriculum can significantly increase children's future school and life success and their contributions to family and community life. A cost-benefit analysis shows that society saves more than $16 for every dollar invested in this high-quality program (Schweinhart et al., 2005).

A central tenet of HighScope's educational philosophy is that children "construct" an understanding of the world through their own initiatives.

Findings of the HighScope Preschool Curriculum Comparison Study

Data on the 68 students who were randomly assigned to attend one of three preschool curriculum models from 1967 to 1970 were also gathered over the years, most recently when they reached the age of 23 (Schweinhart & Weikart, 1997). Some had attended the *HighScope program,* in which children engaged in active participatory learning across all areas of development; a second group participated in a *traditional nursery school approach* (Sears & Dowley, 1963), where children engaged in child-initiated activities and teachers focused on social and emotional development; and a third group was enrolled in a *direct instruction curriculum* (Bereiter & Engelmann, 1966), in which adults led small groups of children in learning academic subjects.

Both the initial evaluation and longitudinal follow-up found no significant group differences in academic achievement or measured intelligence. However, significant differences appeared in the area of *social responsibility*, favoring the two programs in which children took more initiative over the adult-directed curriculum. This included differences in acts of crime and misconduct; as shown in the graph of mean arrests, on the next page, the direct instruction group experienced over twice as many lifetime arrests, including over twice as many adult arrests, as either of the other two curriculum groups (Schweinhart & Weikart, 1997).

Findings of the HighScope Training of Trainers Evaluation

In the multipart national HighScope Training of Trainers evaluation (Epstein, 1993), researchers surveyed 203 HighScope trainers, observed and interviewed 366 teachers in HighScope and non-HighScope early childhood settings, and assessed 200 preschool children in HighScope and comparison classrooms operating under different auspices and serving diverse populations. In programs that had HighScope training, there were significantly better supervisory and teaching practices than in non-HighScope settings (Epstein, 1993). Independent observers rated the HighScope classrooms as higher on the following dimensions:

- Overall program quality

Major Findings: HighScope Perry Preschool Study at Age 40

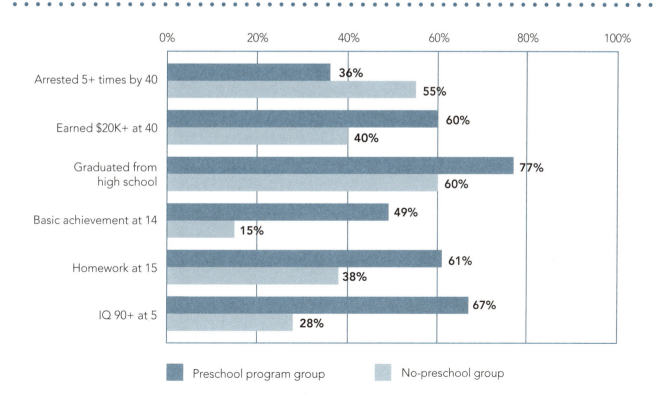

- Organizing and labeling the room to promote children's independence
- Providing diverse materials that were easily accessible to children
- Encouraging children to plan activities based on their interests
- Encouraging children to review and reflect on their actions and experiences
- Using observations and open-ended questions to extend children's play

Children in HighScope programs also outscored their non-HighScope peers in initiative, social relations, cognitive development, motor development, and overall development (Epstein, 1993). The findings especially showcased the importance of the plan-do-review sequence in children's learning. The more teachers provided opportunities for children to plan and review activities of their own choice — a hallmark of the HighScope Curriculum — the higher children scored on measures of the academic and social skills needed for school success (Epstein, 1993).

Findings from independent investigators

Independent studies confirm that preschool children attending well-run HighScope programs do better than those in other program settings. Studies in the United Kingdom (Sylva, 1992) and the Netherlands (Veen, Roeleveld, & Leseman, 2000) found that when children plan, carry out, and review their own learning activities, they play with more purpose and perform better on measures of language and intellectual development. The Head Start Family and Child Experiences Survey (Zill, Resnick, Kim, O'Donnell, & Sorongon, 2003) found that those attending HighScope programs improved significantly more from fall to spring on measures of literacy and social development than

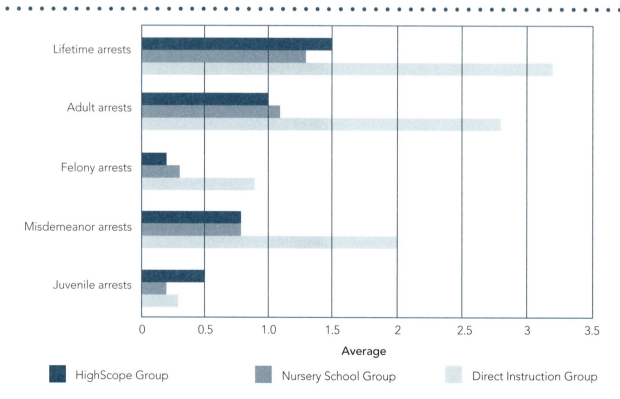

HighScope Preschool Curriculum Comparison Study: Mean Arrests Through Age 23 by Curriculum Groups

> **Developmental Differences Between Children in HighScope and Comparison Programs**
>
> - Children in HighScope programs significantly outperformed children in comparison programs in the following areas:
>   - **Initiative**, including complex play, joining in program activities
>   - **Social relations**, including relating to peers, social problem solving
>   - **Motor development**, including music and movement, focusing energies during physical activities
>   - **Overall development**
>
> - Children in HighScope programs tended to outscore children in comparison programs in **cognitive development**, including representation, classification, and language skills
>
> - Comparison children showed no significant advantages over HighScope children on any of the assessments.
>
> — Adapted from Epstein (1993, p. xx)

children attending classrooms using the Creative Curriculum or other curriculum models.

Why the HighScope Preschool Curriculum works

Looking at the research findings, we can conclude that the reason the HighScope Preschool Curriculum works is this: Participating as active learners within a supportive classroom community, children develop a sense of initiative and prosocial dispositions that positively affect their subsequent learning and life decisions.

Since its beginnings, the HighScope preschool approach has encouraged children to develop initiative within a supportive social context. During the daily plan-do-review process, children express, carry out, and reflect on their intentions. Throughout the day, children pursue their own interests, generate ways to answer their own questions, and share ideas with others. Supported by adults who are genuinely interested in what they say and do, young children are able to construct their own understanding of the world around them and gain a sense of control and personal satisfaction. The curriculum works because its unflagging attention to children's strengths and abilities empowers them to follow through on their interests purposefully and creatively. In the process, children develop trust, initiative, curiosity, resourcefulness, independence, and responsibility — habits of mind that will serve them well throughout their lives.

CHAPTER 1

Active Participatory Learning: The Way Children Construct Knowledge

Human Development as a Framework for Education

The cornerstone of the HighScope approach to early childhood education is the belief that **active participatory learning** is fundamental to the full development of human potential and that active learning occurs most effectively in settings that provide *developmentally appropriate learning opportunities*. Therefore, the overarching goal of our early childhood work is to establish an operational model that supports active learning in diverse settings. In doing so, we have made the following basic assumptions about human growth and development:

- Human beings develop capacities in predictable sequences throughout their life span. As people mature, new capabilities emerge.
- Despite the general predictability of human development, each person displays unique characteristics from the time of birth, which through everyday interactions progressively differentiate into a unique personality. Learning always occurs in the context of each person's unique characteristics, abilities, and opportunities.
- There are times during the life cycle when certain kinds of things are learned best or most efficiently, and there are teaching methods that are more appropriate at certain times in the developmental sequence than at others.

Given that developmental change is a basic fact of human existence but that each person is also developmentally unique, and that there are optimal times for particular kinds of learning, developmentally appropriate education can be defined by three criteria. An educational experience, procedure, or method — whether adult- or child-initiated — is developmentally appropriate if it

- Exercises and challenges the capacities of the learner that are emerging at a given developmental level

> "The active learning philosophy holds that learning is a process of engagement with resources and ideas, involves people solving problems and discovering new things, contributes to personal development and social change, occurs sometimes in isolation but more often in collaboration with others, and ignites creativity."
> — Piscatelli (2000, p. 40)

- Encourages and helps the learner to develop a unique pattern of interests, talents, and goals
- Presents learning experiences when learners are best able to master, generalize, and retain what they learn and can relate it to previous experiences and future expectations

Furthermore, in the HighScope approach, learning is viewed as a *social experience* involving meaningful interactions among children and adults. Since children learn at different rates and have unique interests and experiences, they are more likely to reach their full potential for growth when they are encouraged to interact and communicate freely with peers and adults. These social experiences occur in the context of real-life activities that children have planned and initiated themselves, or within adult-initiated experiences that afford ample opportunity for children's choice, leadership, and individual expression.

Learning as developmental change

The HighScope Curriculum originally drew extensively on the work of Jean Piaget and his colleagues (Piaget & Inhelder, 1966/1969) and the progressive educational philosophy of John Dewey (1938/1963). Since then, it has been updated according to the results of ongoing cognitive-developmental research (Clements, 2004; Gelman & Baillargeon, 1983; Gelman & Brenneman, 2004; Gelman & Gallistel, 1978/1986; Goswami, 2002; National Research Council, 2005;

Active learning takes place when children explore in a way that builds on their interests and abilities.

Necombe, 2002; Smith, 2002), and brain research (Shore, 2003; Thompson & Nelson, 2001; Smith, 2002). While Piaget and Dewey explained learning in terms of broad developmental *stages,* today's cognitive-developmental researchers study children's *learning pathways* or *developmental trajectories* as they relate to specific content and tasks (for example, vocabulary and counting).

Many HighScope teaching practices, particularly the notion that development occurs within sociocultural settings where adults scaffold children's learning, were first derived from the work of Lev Vygotsky (1934/1962). Vygotsky saw the social or cultural environment as being particularly crucial to the development of language and thought processes. The HighScope teaching practices that come from this view also continue to be updated, based on the theory and research of those who have followed Vygotsky's lead (Rowe & Wertsch, 2002).

Interestingly, current brain research validates the active learning approach favored by cognitive-developmental researchers and theorists (Shore, 2003; Thompson & Nelson, 2001). In the view of all these experts, learning depends on **interaction**. By interaction, they mean a child's encounters with people, objects, events, or activities, and later, ideas. In other words, without experiences, the brain has nothing to work with.

In a cognitive-developmental model such as HighScope's, learning is seen as a process of *developmental change* — that is, a process in which we learn by relating and adding new information to what we already know and, if necessary, even

> **Brain Research Supports Active Learning**
>
> •
>
> "Neuroscientists stress the fact that interaction with the environment is not simply an interesting feature of brain development; it is an absolute requirement….Early experiences have a decisive impact on the architecture of the brain, and on the nature and extent of adult capacities. They directly affect the way the brain is 'wired.'"
>
> — Shore (2003, pp. 15 and 18)

changing the way we thought before. For example, if we know how to care for a pet guinea pig — to give it certain kinds of food and clean water — then we have a knowledge base to care for other pets, such as a cat or dog. However, a conscientious pet owner still has more to learn — such as what cats and dogs eat and drink that is different from what guinea pigs eat and drink. This ongoing process of developmental change, first identified by Piaget and upheld by current research, is called *assimilation* (using our existing knowledge and behaviors to explore new things) and *accommodation* (changing our mental models of how the world works to take new and sometimes contradictory information into account). It often takes many experiences of assimilation and accommodation before changes in thinking are fully formed and consistently applied in our actions.

Active participatory learning — A complex process

The learning process in the HighScope model is seen as an *interaction* between the goal-oriented actions of the learner and the environmental realities that affect those actions. Children construct their own models of reality, which develop over time in response to new experiences and exposure to other viewpoints.

In embracing the view of learning as a process of developmental change, HighScope adopted the term *active participatory learning* to describe the central process of the HighScope Curriculum. This

Children are natural explorers, experimenters, and problem solvers.

is defined as learning in which the child, by acting on objects and interacting with people, ideas, and events, constructs new understanding. No one else can have experiences for the child or construct knowledge for the child. Children must do this for themselves.

In this book, "active participatory learning" stands for four critical elements in the activities of preschool children: (1) direct action on objects, (2) reflection on actions, (3) intrinsic motivation, invention, and generativity, and (4) problem solving. Each of these elements is discussed here. Later in this chapter we discuss how adults support these elements through the materials and daily activities they provide and their interactions with young children. All these components are captured in the five ingredients of active learning, described in the last section of the chapter.

Direct actions on objects

Active learning depends on the use of *materials* — natural and found materials, household objects, toys, equipment, and tools. Active learning begins as young children manipulate objects, using their bodies and all their senses to find out about the objects. Acting on objects gives children something "real" to think about and discuss with others. Through these types of concrete experiences with materials and people, children gradually begin to form abstract concepts. As developmental psychologist John H. Flavell (1963) puts it, "Children perform real actions on materials which form the learning base, actions as concrete and direct as the materials can be made to allow" (p. 367).

Reflection on actions

Action alone is not sufficient for learning. To understand their immediate world, children must interact *thoughtfully* with it. Children's understanding of the world develops as they carry out actions arising from the need to test ideas or find answers to questions. A young child reaching for a ball is pursuing an internal question, such as "Hmm… wonder what this thing does?" By acting (grasping, tasting, chewing, dropping, pushing, and rolling) and then reflecting on these actions, the child begins to answer the question and to construct

---

The Importance of Independent Problem Solving

Experiences in which the preschool child produces some effect on the world (in contrast with, say, watching television) are crucial to the development of thought processes because the child's logic develops from the effort to interpret the information gained through such experiences; interpretation of new information modifies the interpretative structures themselves as the child strives for a more logical internal model of reality. Therefore, if we want children to become intelligent problem solvers, the best way to do so is to give them many opportunities to work on problems of interest to them — that is, problems that arise from their own attempts to comprehend the world.

Children as Active Participatory Learners

Active participatory learning — the direct and immediate experiencing of objects, people, ideas, and events — is a necessary condition for cognitive restructuring and hence for development. Put simply, young children learn concepts, form ideas, and create their own symbols or abstractions through self-initiated activity — moving, listening, searching, feeling, manipulating. Such activity, carried on within a social context in which an alert and sensitive adult is a *participant-observer*, makes it possible for the child to be involved in intrinsically interesting experiences that may produce contradictory conclusions and a consequent reorganization of the child's understanding of his or her world.

These children try different ways of manipulating objects in the water table.

a personal understanding of what balls do. Put another way, the child's actions, and reflections on those actions, result in the development of thought and understanding. Thus, active learning involves both the *physical activity* of interacting with objects to produce effects and the *mental activity* of interpreting these effects and fitting the interpretations into a more complete understanding of the world.

Intrinsic motivation, invention, and generativity

In this perspective, the impetus to learn clearly arises from within the child. The child's personal interests, questions, and intentions lead to exploration, experimentation, and the construction of new knowledge and understanding. Active learners are questioners and inventors. They generate

By pursuing an internal motivation and reflecting on her actions as she goes, this child builds a tower.

Young Children and Adults Think Differently

Learning to understand the world is a slow and gradual process in which children try to fit new observations to what they already know or think they understand about reality. As a result, they often come to their own unique conclusions, conclusions that, from the standpoint of adult thinking, may seem erroneous. Adults interacting with children should recognize that this type of thinking is part of the active learning process and should accept children's nonadult reasoning — in time, children's thinking will become more like adult thinking. Below are some of the ways preschool children think differently from adults:

It's alive! "It's running after me!" four-year-old Erin exclaims as she runs away from a trickle of water. Erin is not being silly or cute. She is trying to understand her direct experience. At ages three and four, children are only beginning to distinguish between living and nonliving things. They sometimes equate movement with life ("The butter's running! It's alive!") and wonder when dead pets or relatives will be alive again.

Interpreting words correctly. "I'm beside myself with excitement!" exclaims Mrs. Cantu.

"How you do that?" James asks, looking at her curiously.

"Do what?" Mrs. Cantu asks.

"You…be…be…beside you. How you do it?"

Young children base the meanings of words on their own experiences. To James, "beside" means "next to." He is trying to figure out how Mrs. Cantu can be next to herself.

Blending intuitive and scientific thought. "Look, my magnet catches nails," Wanda says to her friend, Topher.

"We catch nails 'cause our magnets have strong powers."

"But we can't catch these sticks. They don't have powers."

Wanda and Topher have constructed their ideas from careful observation (the magnets pick up nails but not sticks) and intuition or fantasy (the magnet "catches" some things because of special "powers").

One thing at a time. Because they generally focus on one thing at a time, young children usually don't make "both… and" statements. For example, when Corey asks his friend Vanessa if she has any pets, she says she doesn't. This doesn't stop Corey from asking her whether she has any cats (even though cats are included in the larger class of pets). When Vanessa says she doesn't have a cat, Corey asks her if she has a dog. Vanessa replies that she does have a dog, and Corey confides that he has a dog, too. Neither child is aware that Vanessa's dog is both a dog *and* a pet.

Judging by appearances. Young children tend to make judgments about "how much" and "how many" based on appearances. For example, young children reason that a nickel is more than a dime because it's bigger. They might also think that a cup (8 ounces) of juice in a small glass is more than a cup of juice in a bigger glass simply because the smaller glass is fuller.

hypotheses — "I wonder how I can get this block that I want to be my scuba diving air tank to stay on my back?" — and test them out by using and combining materials in a way that makes sense to *them*. As inventors, children create unique solutions and products: "I tried tying the block on with string, and it kept falling off, but the tape made it work." While children's creations may sometimes be messy, unstable, or unrecognizable to adults, the *process* by which children think about and produce these creations is the way they come to understand their world. It is also important to recognize that the errors children make ("The string won't hold the block on") are as important as their successes in providing them with essential information about their original hypotheses. Thus, active learning is an ongoing, inventive process in which children combine materials, experiences, and ideas to generate effects that are new to them. Although adults may take for granted the laws of nature and logic, each child discovers them as if for the first time.

This child keeps trying the different puzzle pieces until he finds the shape that fits into each cutout.

Problem solving

Experiences in which children produce an effect they may or may not anticipate are crucial to the development of their ability to think and reason. When children encounter real-life problems — unexpected outcomes or barriers to fulfilling their intentions — the process of reconciling the unexpected with what they already know about the world stimulates learning and development. For example, Roberto, a child pretending to cook soup, tries to cover the pot of "soup" (water) with a lid. He expects the lid to cover the pan, but instead it falls into the soup and water splashes on his hand. Roberto knows from experience that the lid is supposed to stay on top of the pan, so he decides to place several other lids on the pot until he finds one that fits properly and does not fall into the soup. Through repeated experiences like this, he will learn to consider the size of any cover in relation to the size of an opening.

Adults as supporters of active learners

Given that children learn through their own experiences and discoveries, what is the role of adults in the active learning environment? In the broadest sense, adults are *supporters of development,* and as such, their primary goal is to encourage active learning on the part of the child. Adults both attend to what children learn and how they learn it, and they *empower* children to take control of their own learning. In carrying out this role, adults are not only active and participatory but also observational and reflective; *they are conscious participant-observers*.

While children interact with materials, people, ideas, and events to construct their own understanding of reality, *adults observe and interact with children to discover how each child thinks and reasons*. Adults strive to recognize each child's particular interests and abilities, and to offer the child appropriate support and challenges. This adult role is complex and develops gradually as the adult becomes more adept at recognizing

Examining Our Beliefs About How Children Learn

Early childhood programs open up a world of learning for young children. How teachers set up the classroom and plan the program day affects what and how children learn. As you begin to create your HighScope classroom, ask yourself the questions listed below. Are there other beliefs you are aware of in yourself or those with whom you work? Which of your beliefs support children's learning and which ones would you like to work on changing?

Do you believe…?		
Children are not interested in learning on their own; they need to be motivated by adults.	or	Children come to school eager to learn; they can and should take responsibility for their own learning.
Children learn when adults show and tell them what to do and think.	or	Children construct knowledge through exploration, observation, and reflection.
Children learn concepts such as letters, numbers, colors, shapes, and days of the week through drill and practice, including recitations and ditto sheets.	or	Children learn concepts through hands-on interactions with materials, people, events, and ideas, in activities and contexts that are meaningful to them.
Children's identical art projects (or their attempts to copy them) make a cute and colorful wall display that impresses parents and administrators.	or	Children's unique and individual artwork should be displayed (even a piece of paper covered with an indeterminate color of paint and a hole made by the brush).
Children learn by following adults; children are neither ready nor responsible enough to act as leaders.	or	Children learn by acting as leaders as well as followers; they enjoy giving directions and seeing others carry them out.
Children given choices about what they want to do will run around the classroom; their behavior will be out of control.	or	Children given choices engage in purposeful activity as they attempt to achieve the goals they set for themselves.
Children left to their own devices will do the same thing over and over again; they will not advance their learning.	or	Children practice a skill or test their own knowledge until they are sure of it; they approach the next level when they are ready.
Children need to learn their ABCs and 123s or else they will not be ready for school; academics should take precedence over social and emotional skills.	or	Children need to learn and develop in all domains; social and emotional skills underlie children's ability to acquire knowledge in other content areas.

The Adult's Role in Supporting Active Learning

- **Organizing environments**

Play areas are clearly defined and stocked with interesting, age-appropriate materials.

- **Organizing routines**

The sequence of the day's events is carefully planned. Here, the teacher uses a message board to help children learn about variations in the day's routine.

- **Establishing a supportive social climate**

Relationships among adults and children are relaxed and positive.

- **Encouraging children's intentional actions, problem solving, and verbal reflections**

  The adult focuses on the children's actions and goals.

- **Interpreting children's actions in terms of the curriculum content**

  Teams meet daily to discuss and interpret observations in terms of the curriculum content areas and key developmental indicators (KDIs).

- **Planning experiences**

  The adults planned this activity to build on children's emerging writing skills.

In an active learning setting, adults support and empower children in their learning.

and meeting each child's developmental needs. Basically, adults in HighScope settings support children by

- Organizing environments and routines for active learning
- Establishing a climate for positive social interactions
- Encouraging children's intentional actions, problem solving, and verbal reflection
- Observing and interpreting the actions of each child in terms of the developmentally based curriculum content domain and the key developmental indicators (KDIs)
- Planning experiences that build on the child's actions and interests

It is the major purpose of this book to describe in detail these aspects of the adult's role; therefore, specific examples of how adults support children appear throughout the text. Before undertaking this mission, adults should examine — and if necessary reconsider — their beliefs about how children learn. To truly support children as active participatory learners, adults must be willing to relinquish their need for control, applaud children's initiative and independence, and commit themselves to being active and attentive partners with children in the learning process.

Key Developmental Indicators — A Framework for Understanding Active Learning

If a set of beliefs about how children learn and how adults support learning form the *process* of the HighScope approach, then the **key developmental indicators (KDIs)** provide the *content* by which we can measure the progress of active learning as it takes place. The preschool KDIs are a series of statements that form the curriculum for social, cognitive, and physical development of children from the ages of three to five years. Each statement highlights an active child behavior that is essential for the development of the fundamental abilities that emerge during early childhood. The KDIs are not a set of specific topics and learning objectives; instead, they are basic concepts and skills that young children naturally use repeatedly, given the opportunity. Together, the KDIs define the kind of knowledge young children are acquiring as they interact with materials, people, ideas, and events.

Since the KDIs describe activities that young children readily engage in, the role of adults is to create an environment in which these behaviors can occur and then to recognize, support, and build on them when they do. HighScope uses the term "scaffolding" to describe how adults support children at their current developmental level and gently extend their thinking and reasoning to the next level when children are ready. *The creation of an environment rich with opportunities for KDIs, together with appropriate adult support, are critical elements in educating young children.*

Children engage with numerous KDIs as they interact with people, materials, events, and ideas.

> ### The Adult's Role in Scaffolding Children's Active Learning
>
> HighScope uses the term **scaffolding** to describe the process whereby adults support and gently extend children's thinking and reasoning. *Scaffolding* is a term introduced by developmental psychologist Jerome Bruner (1986) and is based on the work of Lev Vygotsky (1978). Vygotsky referred to the *zone of proximal development* as the area between what children can accomplish on their own and what they can do with the help of an adult or another child who is more developmentally advanced. HighScope teachers carefully observe children so they know when and how to enter this zone. Children must be secure and confident in what they already know before they are ready to move to the next level. When HighScope says adults support and extend children's learning, it means that the adults first validate, or support, what children already know, and then, when the time is right, gently encourage them to extend their thinking to the next level.
>
> This carefully calibrated adult role is also captured in these statements from noted educational thinkers Jean Piaget and John Dewey:
>
> "To understand is to discover, or reconstruct by rediscovery, and such conditions must be complied with if in the future individuals are to be formed who are capable of production and creativity and not simply repetition.... Above all, the adult must continually find fresh ways to stimulate the child's activity and be prepared to vary his or her approach as the child raises new questions or imagines new solutions."
>
> — Piaget (1972, pp. 20–21)
>
>
>
> "The educator is responsible for a knowledge of individuals and for a knowledge of subject-matter that will enable activities to be selected which lend themselves to social organization in which all individuals have an opportunity to contribute something, and in which the activities in which all participate are the chief carrier of control.... When education is based upon experience and educative experience is seen to be a social process...the teacher loses the position of external boss or dictator but takes on that of leader of group activities."
>
> — Dewey (1933, pp. 56, 59, 71)

The HighScope KDIs are organized around these eight content areas: **Approaches to Learning; Social and Emotional Development; Physical Development and Health; Language, Literacy, and Communication; Mathematics; Creative Arts; Science and Technology; and Social Studies.** These content areas, and the 58 KDIs that comprise them, are discussed in the KDI books that accompany this manual (Epstein, 2012a–h).

What happens in an active learning setting

So far in this chapter we have outlined the perspective that underlies the HighScope Curriculum. We have introduced the concept of active participatory learning and briefly described the adult's role in supporting the active learning process. The next section illustrates how an active learning approach is implemented in early childhood settings. We describe what children typically do, what adults do, and how adults and children interact. We also present the beneficial short- and long-range effects — for both adults and children — of participating in an active learning program.

What children do in the active learning setting

Children initiate activities that grow from personal interests and intentions

How can we tell when children are truly engaged in active learning? One of the defining characteristics of active learners is that they are focused on their own actions and thoughts. At the art table, Jeff goes over to the easel to get the green paint; Vanessa stands up to press her elbows into her play dough; Craig places his picture on the floor to have more room to work on it. These actions evoke discussion:

Craig: Hey, Jeff. You didn't clean up.

Jeff: I'm still painting. I need some green.

Craig: I'm still painting too, and I need all the colors.

Vanessa: Look! Look! Holes! I did it!

Active learners find plenty of things to do and often talk about what they intend to do. At first glance, adults who are expecting to see quiet groups of children doing the same thing at the same time may view an active learning setting as disorganized. But adults who understand the importance of supporting active learners realize that a child's *internal motivation* creates an effective organizing force both within the child and in the classroom or center. For example, if a child needs green paint, a smock, another block, or a friend to help, he or she can generally meet the need independently because an active learning environment supports this type of decision making. Because children in active learning settings make choices based on their own interests and questions, and then have time to follow through on their plans, they are intensely involved with people and materials and freely share their ideas, findings, and observations. With appropriate adult support, they thus become active agents of their own learning rather than passive recipients of adult-directed learning.

Children choose materials and decide what to do with them

One of the hallmarks of programs based on active learning is the many opportunities they provide for children to make choices. Young children are quite able and eager to choose materials and decide how to use them. Many materials are new to young children, so they often do not use the materials according to their intended function. Instead, children are inventive — manipulating the materials according to their own interests and

In an active learning setting, children follow and develop their own internal motivation.

abilities. One child might use tape, for example, to fasten pieces of paper together, while another might take the tape outside and use it for fastening acorns, flower petals, sticks, and stones together. Consider a group of children working with similar materials — paper, glue, yarn, and paper towel tubes — at an art table. It is likely that each child will choose to do something different with the materials:

Della cuts a piece of paper into little bits, which she puts inside a paper towel tube. "Still need more," she says, getting up to peer down into the tube to see how full it is.

Dan wraps yarn around his paper towel tube and then puts glue on top of the yarn "to make the string stick."

HighScope Preschool Curriculum Content
Key Developmental Indicators

A. Approaches to Learning
1. **Initiative:** Children demonstrate initiative as they explore their world.
2. **Planning:** Children make plans and follow through on their intentions.
3. **Engagement:** Children focus on activities that interest them.
4. **Problem solving:** Children solve problems encountered in play.
5. **Use of resources:** Children gather information and formulate ideas about their world.
6. **Reflection:** Children reflect on their experiences.

B. Social and Emotional Development
7. **Self-identity:** Children have a positive self-identity.
8. **Sense of competence:** Children feel they are competent.
9. **Emotions:** Children recognize, label, and regulate their feelings.
10. **Empathy:** Children demonstrate empathy toward others.
11. **Community:** Children participate in the community of the classroom.
12. **Building relationships:** Children build relationships with other children and adults.
13. **Cooperative play:** Children engage in cooperative play.
14. **Moral development:** Children develop an internal sense of right and wrong.
15. **Conflict resolution:** Children resolve social conflicts.

C. Physical Development and Health
16. **Gross-motor skills:** Children demonstrate strength, flexibility, balance, and timing in using their large muscles.
17. **Fine-motor skills:** Children demonstrate dexterity and hand-eye coordination in using their small muscles.
18. **Body awareness:** Children know about their bodies and how to navigate them in space.
19. **Personal care:** Children carry out personal care routines on their own.
20. **Healthy behavior:** Children engage in healthy practices.

D. Language, Literacy, and Communication[1]
21. **Comprehension:** Children understand language.
22. **Speaking:** Children express themselves using language.
23. **Vocabulary:** Children understand and use a variety of words and phrases.
24. **Phonological awareness:** Children identify distinct sounds in spoken language.
25. **Alphabetic knowledge:** Children identify letter names and their sounds.
26. **Reading:** Children read for pleasure and information.
27. **Concepts about print:** Children demonstrate knowledge about environmental print.
28. **Book knowledge:** Children demonstrate knowledge about books.
29. **Writing:** Children write for many different purposes.
30. **English language learning:** (If applicable) Children use English and their home language(s) (including sign language).

---

[1] Language, Literacy, and Communication KDIs 21–29 may be used for the child's home language(s) as well as English. KDI 30 refers specifically to English language learning.

E. Mathematics

31. **Number words and symbols:** Children recognize and use number words and symbols.

32. **Counting:** Children count things.

33. **Part-whole relationships:** Children combine and separate quantities of objects.

34. **Shapes:** Children identify, name, and describe shapes.

35. **Spatial awareness:** Children recognize spatial relationships among people and objects.

36. **Measuring:** Children measure to describe, compare, and order things.

37. **Unit:** Children understand and use the concept of unit.

38. **Patterns:** Children identify, describe, copy, complete, and create patterns.

39. **Data analysis:** Children use information about quantity to draw conclusions, make decisions, and solve problems.

F. Creative Arts

40. **Art:** Children express and represent what they observe, think, imagine, and feel through two- and three-dimensional art.

41. **Music:** Children express and represent what they observe, think, imagine, and feel through music.

42. **Movement:** Children express and represent what they observe, think, imagine, and feel through movement.

43. **Pretend play:** Children express and represent what they observe, think, imagine, and feel through pretend play.

44. **Appreciating the arts:** Children appreciate the creative arts.

G. Science and Technology

45. **Observing:** Children observe the materials and processes in their environment.

46. **Classifying:** Children classify materials, actions, people, and events.

47. **Experimenting:** Children experiment to test their ideas.

48. **Predicting:** Children predict what they expect will happen.

49. **Drawing conclusions:** Children draw conclusions based on their experiences and observations.

50. **Communicating ideas:** Children communicate their ideas about the characteristics of things and how they work.

51. **Natural and physical world:** Children gather knowledge about the natural and physical world.

52. **Tools and technology:** Children explore and use tools and technology.

H. Social Studies

53. **Diversity:** Children understand that people have diverse characteristics, interests, and abilities.

54. **Community roles:** Children recognize that people have different roles and functions in the community.

55. **Decision making:** Children participate in making classroom decisions.

56. **Geography:** Children recognize and interpret features and locations in their environment.

57. **History:** Children understand past, present, and future.

58. **Ecology:** Children understand the importance of taking care of their environment.

Katie, spreading glue on her paper, watches Dan. "No, no," she tells Dan when he tries to roll his tube and string on her gluey paper.

"I'm gonna make a long spying thing," announces Joey as he cuts holes in two paper towel tubes and ties them together.

Kim Wan cuts a tube into rings and glues the rings in a row on his paper.

The freedom to make choices like these is essential to active learning because it is by making choices that children learn more about what interests them, what questions to answer, what contradictions to resolve, and what explanations to accept. Because adults in active learning settings understand the important role that children's choices play in learning, they strive to incorporate an element of choice in all of children's activities, even those — such as washing one's hands or zipping one's coat — that many adults might see as incidental to the "real program." Children, after all, do not make distinctions between the regular program and incidental events. They approach most situations with a desire for active involvement. By making choices available in all parts of a program, not just during "free play" or "free-choice" times (what HighScope calls "work time"), adults increase children's active involvement and thus broaden their opportunities to learn.

Children explore materials actively with all their senses

The active learning process involves all the senses. A young child learns what an object is by experimenting with it — holding, squeezing, climbing on, crawling under, dropping, poking, smelling, and tasting it; viewing it from many angles; and listening to the sounds it makes.

When children explore an object and discover its attributes, they begin to understand how the different parts function and fit together, how the object "works," and what the object is really like rather than how it appears. When children discover that the outside part of a pineapple is hard and prickly while the inside part is sweet and juicy, they are beginning to understand that an object that looks forbidding may taste good. Even if they are told this, they still do not *learn* it unless they make their own discoveries.

Through exploration, children answer their own questions and satisfy their curiosity. In active learning settings, adults respect children's desire to explore, recognizing that exploration is one of the most important ways young children learn.

When children are able to choose their own materials and what they will do with them, their involvement in play increases.

Children discover relationships through direct experience with objects

As children become familiar with the objects around them and continue to experiment with them, they discover for themselves how each object works, how it compares and relates to other objects, and how objects work together. Children learn about the relationships between objects by finding out the answers to their own questions, such as, "What happens when you put a long necklace on the teddy bear?" "Add a wooden block to the cardboard block tower?" "Pour sand from the milk jug into the strainer?" Two-year-old Barnie, for example, is not yet able to look at two cardboard boxes and tell which one is bigger, wider, deeper, or taller. To gain a sense of their relative proportions, he has to work with the boxes, fitting them together, stacking them, getting into them, and standing them next to each other.

Adults in active learning settings give children like Barnie the time and space they need to discover relationships on their own. They resist the temptation to help children do something "right" or to show children what to do, knowing that this can deprive children of valuable opportunities for learning and discovery. Children need time to work at their own pace with materials to discover for themselves the relationships between things.

Many early childhood educators today feel pressured to directly "teach" children how things work. For example, they drill them on combining sounds to make related words *(bat, cat, hat)* or directly teach them simple addition combinations (1+1, 1+2). They may tell them the properties of shapes (triangles have three sides) or scientific facts (ice melts when it gets warm). Such direct instruction replaces time that used to be devoted to exploration, inquiry, and discovery through play. While young children may learn specific information directly from adults, research shows it may be at the expense of curiosity and creativity and the possibility for deeper learning (Gopnik, 2011). High-pressure instruction may also deprive children of the "fun" of discovery and make them — as well as teachers and parents — anxious about how, what, and how much preschoolers are learning.

Children transform and combine materials

Changing the consistency, shape, or color of a material — transforming it in some way — is

These children practice the many ways they can play with scarves.

Discovering How Objects Relate to Each Other

As they explore objects, children learn about relationships — that one box fits inside another, that juice can overflow a cup, that one block can be placed on top of another, that a truck fits inside a hollow block, that one tower is taller than another, that one truck goes faster than another. Simple discoveries like these are the foundations for children's emerging understanding of mathematical concepts connected to shapes, spatial awareness, and measuring. Adults need to stand back and let children discover such relationships for themselves. This takes patience and an understanding of children's social and emotional as well as cognitive developmental needs:

> Bonnie is fitting together large Lego blocks. One of the pieces is upside-down so that it won't fit on the one below it. As Mr. Bloom reaches over to help her, Bonnie pushes his hand away. "I do it. I do it," she insists. After considerable trial and error, she manages to fit the Lego block on top of the one below and then reaches for another block.

These children learn about the properties of materials and cause-and-effect relationships as they take apart and manipulate pieces of old cell phones (with batteries removed).

Why Preschool Shouldn't Be Like School

Child development researcher Alison Gopnik acknowledges that ours is a highly anxious era in which parents instruct their children at younger and younger ages and pressure administrators and teachers to make preschool more like elementary school. There are skeptics, however, and research is bearing out their claims that direct instruction is not an effective educational substitute for play time in young children. Below is an excerpt of what Gopnik had to say on a blog post for Slate about why direct instruction may "backfire" when it comes to early learning:

"Perhaps direct instruction can help children learn specific facts and skills, but what about curiosity and creativity — abilities that are even more important for learning in the long run? [Studies] suggest that the doubters are on to something. While learning from a teacher may help children get to a specific answer more quickly, it also makes them less likely to discover new information about a problem and to create a new and unexpected solution....

"Adults often assume that most learning is the result of teaching and that exploratory, spontaneous learning is unusual. But actually, spontaneous learning is more fundamental. It's this kind of learning, in fact, that allows kids to learn from teachers in the first place.

"Learning from teachers first requires you to learn about teachers. For example, if you know how teachers work, you tend to assume that they are trying to be informative....These assumptions lead children to narrow in, and to consider just the specific information a teacher provides. Without a teacher present, children look for a much wider range of information and consider a greater range of options.

"Knowing what to expect from a teacher is a really good thing, of course: It lets you get the right answers more quickly than you would otherwise.... But there is an intrinsic trade-off between that kind of learning and the more wide-ranging learning that is so natural for young children. Knowing this, it's more important than ever to give children's remarkable, spontaneous learning abilities free rein. That means a rich, stable, and safe world, with affectionate and supportive grown-ups, and lots of opportunities for exploration and play. Not school for babies."

— Gopnik (2011, para. 2 and 10–12)

another example of how children work with materials in the active learning setting. Consider Ahmed, who is playing in the sandbox. As he presses down on the sand to make a level panful, the sand becomes compacted and will no longer pour. When Ahmed adds some water to his pan of sand, he notices that the hard, dry, compacted sand has turned into a soupy liquid. As Ahmed molds the wet sand, the smooth, flat surface becomes a series of mounds and craters.

Sand play is just one of countless activities in which young children manipulate, combine, and thereby transform materials. As children engage in this type of activity, they are learning about the less obvious, but essential, properties of materials. In the process, they begin to construct many scientific concepts. A child learns, for example, that the quantity of clay remains the same, whether it is clumped together in a ball or flattened out in a thin layer. Children are also learning about cause-and-effect relationships. For example, a child who ties a knot at the end of a string (cause) learns that this action keeps the beads on the string (effect). By providing materials that can take many forms and by valuing children's efforts to transform and combine the materials, adults in active learning settings are encouraging these kinds of important discoveries.

> ### The Essentials of Discovery
>
> For the young child, *access* to materials, *freedom* to manipulate, combine, and thereby transform them in his or her own way, and *time* to do so are the essentials of the process of discovery. Adults in active learning settings provide these essentials.

> ### Preschoolers' Typical Transformations
>
> - Mixing paints
> - Adding food coloring to water
> - Blowing bubbles
> - Wringing out a wet sponge
> - Making a paper chain
> - Folding a doll blanket
> - Cracking open nuts
> - Sawing wood
> - Drilling holes
> - Shaking a tambourine
> - Fitting oneself into a doll cradle
> - Printing a mask created at the computer
> - Rolling a play dough ball into a long coil
> - Putting on a wig
> - Twisting wire around a stick

This child uses a variety of tools in his sand play.

Children use age-appropriate tools and equipment

Opportunities to use tools and equipment designed for specific purposes are abundant in the active learning setting. By age three, children can coordinate two or more actions and thus are capable of using a wide range of tools and equipment. These include both equipment designed for children — wheeled toys, climbers, swings — and such adult items as computers, eggbeaters, food grinders, and staplers. As children use simple tools and technology, they are developing a range of movement and coordination skills. Consider the actions involved in riding a tricycle: the child must simultaneously grasp the handlebars, turn them to steer, and pedal. Similarly, when hammering, the child must grasp the hammer, steady the nail, aim, and pound. As they work with tools and equipment, children are developing gross-motor, fine-motor, and body-awareness skills. The determination to master these physical abilities also reflects the development of dispositions — approaches to learning — that will enable them to do more things on their own and to solve more complex problems.

Clearly, opportunities for problem solving are plentiful when children work with tools and technology: One child searches for a nail that is long enough to connect two pieces of wood; another tries to find a piece of wood that is the right size to form one side of a birdhouse. Children also experience cause-and-effect relationships: sawing fast makes lots of sawdust and takes more effort; turning the handle of the eggbeater faster makes more bubbles; touching an arrow icon on the screen makes the picture flip upside down.

Initially, just *using* a tool may be more important to the child than its intended function. For example, turning a vacuum cleaner on and off, pushing and pulling it, steering it, managing the cord, and fitting the machine under a table may be more important to a youthful vacuumer than actually cleaning the carpet.

Children use their large muscles

Active learning for a preschooler means learning with the whole body. Children are eager to stretch their physical strengths and capacities. They love to climb on top of blocks; move chairs and tables; lift up their friends; roll across the floor; mash clay with their elbows; turn around until they're dizzy; and run, hop, jump, push, crawl, shout, whisper, sing, wiggle, throw, pound, kick, climb, and twist. Such movements are an undeniable part of their youthful nature. Expecting young children not to move is like expecting them not to breathe. Therefore, in the active learning environment, adults provide space and time for children to engage in activities that exercise the large muscles and also provide lots of things for children to push, throw, lift, kick, and carry.

Exploring materials, discovering relationships, transforming and combining materials, acquiring

Even while playing with blocks, this child feels a natural urge to move his body in many other ways!

skills with tools and equipment, and using the large muscles are vital manipulative processes.

Through such daily opportunities children gain a basic knowledge of the physical world — what it is made of, how it works, and the effect their actions have upon it.

Children talk about their experiences

In active learning settings, children talk about what they are doing (or plan to do or have just done) throughout the day. Children are encouraged to set the agenda in conversations with adults, and as a result, what the child says often takes the adult by surprise. Listen to Jerry talking to Mrs. Gibbs about their field trip to a farm: "I left my lunch on the bus, and I had to share some of Toni's. His sandwich was flat. This flat! He sat on it 'cause his dad was late. Boy, was his dad mad, so Toni didn't tell him. It was in the bag, so it was okay."

Clearly, Mrs. Gibbs didn't plan a trip to the farm so Jerry could have an experience with a flat sandwich. She thought he might talk about the goat he milked or the chicken feathers he collected, and she was mildly surprised that Jerry was so captivated by Toni's flat sandwich. Paula, on the other hand, describes the egg she found

When children are allowed to converse freely in their own way, they connect language with personally meaningful experiences.

in the hayloft: "It was way down in there. It didn't break. The other one did." Whether children talk about sandwiches or eggs, however, the process of putting actions into words is the same. But — conscientious adults might ask — who learned more, Jerry or Paula? Each child was particularly interested in a different aspect of the trip. Perhaps Paula learned more about eggs and hay while Jerry learned more about what happens when one sits on a sandwich. What we can say with assurance is that both children were involved in memorable experiences that caused them some surprise, both had the opportunity to consciously reflect on their findings, and both were free to describe these reflections in their own words.

When children are free to converse about personally meaningful experiences, they use language to deal with ideas and problems that are real and important to them. As the children communicate their thoughts through language and listen to one another's ideas and comments, they learn that their personal way of speaking is effective and respected. In the active learning setting, where children's language reflects their personal perceptions, thoughts, and concerns, each child's voice is heard.

Children talk about what they are doing in their own words

What children say in the active learning setting reflects their own experiences and understanding and is often characterized by a logic that differs from adult thinking:

> "I didn't put any animals in my barn," Melissa says about a farm she made with blocks. "Just horses and cows."

> "That car can't go," Max giggles, pointing to a side-view picture of a car in a storybook. "It's got only two wheels!" "The other two wheels are on the other side," his dad points out. "No they're not!" Max exclaims, as he turns the page to look.

Why should an adult encourage children to say things in their own words when what they say is often incorrect? Because young children like Melissa and Max are using the best reasoning powers at their disposal. No matter how many times an adult tells Melissa that horses and cows are animals, until she develops the capacity to understand class inclusion, to her "a horse is a horse is a horse." Period. Max sees a car with two wheels. Since he is not yet able to imagine another spatial perspective, he thinks his father is joking when he explains to Max that the other two wheels are on the other side of the car. When Max looks on the "other side," he finds another picture, not the other side of the car. According to Melissa's and Max's best reasoning, their views and perceptions are correct. *They need the opportunity to share their observations so that talking about what they think and see becomes a natural part of their lives.* As they mature and experience new contradictions, their thinking will develop along with their self-confidence, and their observations will become increasingly more logical and realistic. In the meantime, they are developing the habit of talking about what they understand and what's important to them.

What adults do in the active learning setting

Adults provide a variety of materials for children to work with

Observers new to active learning settings may be surprised by the wide range of materials that are available to children. Adults provide such a variety of materials to assure that there are plentiful opportunities for children to make choices and manipulate materials — key aspects of the active learning process. Materials may include any familiar or unfamiliar objects of interest to young children, except for things that are clearly dangerous (such as metal cans with sharp edges) or too difficult for this age group (such as a Monopoly game). In chapter 6 we describe specific materials and the play and learning they support, but

In the active learning classroom, adults make sure that materials are plentiful so several children can use them at once.

following are some general types of materials that are typically offered to stimulate young children's active participatory learning:

- **Practical everyday objects useful to adults.** Children enjoy using the same things that the important people in their lives use — a lunch box like dad's, hair curlers like big sister's, earrings like mom's, shaving cream like grandpa's.

- **Natural and found materials.** Natural materials like shells, acorns, and pine cones and found materials like cardboard boxes and toilet-paper tubes appeal to children because they can be used in many different ways for many different purposes. And they appeal to adults because they are easily accessible, plentiful, and often free.

- **Tools.** Tools are important to children for the same reason they are important to adults — they help "get the job done." Therefore, provide real tools — scissors, hole punches, and construction tools, such as hammers and screwdrivers. (It is important that tools be in good condition and that safety procedures be followed consistently by both children and adults.) Computers with appropriate software can also serve as tools to help children accomplish their intentions, such as making a mask or decorating a place mat to use in pretend play.

- **Messy, sticky, gooey, drippy, squishy materials.** Touchable materials like sand, water, paste, paint, and play dough appeal strongly to many children because of the interesting sensory experiences they provide.

> **Some Materials for Active Participatory Learning**
>
> It is important to stock your early childhood setting with a wide variety of materials of interest to young children. The materials listed here are just a few examples of the kinds of materials that will support active participatory learning experiences. See chapter 6 for more details on selecting materials for an active learning environment.
>
> **Practical Everyday Objects**
> Pots and pans, eggbeaters, spatulas, food grinders, empty and clean food containers, pieces of wood, sheets, tires, boxes, plastic milk crates, baskets, books, paper, writing materials
>
> **Natural and Found Materials**
> Stones, shells, leaves, acorns, pine cones, sand, carpet scraps, paper towel tubes, empty and clean plastic squeeze bottles, newspaper
>
> **Tools**
> Brooms, dustpans, mops, buckets, sponges, hammers, saws, hand drills, vices, nails, screws, staplers, tape, hole punches, scissors, paper clips, car jacks, bicycle pumps, shovels, hoes, trowels, wheelbarrows, hoses, watering cans, computers with appropriate software
>
> **Messy Materials**
> Water, soap bubbles, paste, dough, glue, paint
>
> **Heavy or Bulky Materials**
> Boxes, tree stumps, wagons, shovels, piles of dirt, wooden planks, climbing structures, large blocks
>
> **Easy-to-Handle Materials**
> Blocks, beads, buttons, playing cards, dry beans or rice or pasta,[2] toy cars, stuffed animals, ink pads and stamps
>
> ---
> [2] Some programs have a policy of not using dried food as play items. Follow the policies of your program.

- **Heavy, large materials.** Children use their whole bodies, exercise their muscles, and gain a sense of their physical capacities when using large wooden blocks, shovels, wheeled toys, and other sturdy, heavy materials.

- **Easy-to-handle materials.** Materials that fit in their hands — buttons, toy figures, Lego blocks, and so forth — give children a sense of control because they can use such small objects successfully without adult assistance.

Adults provide space and time for children to use materials

To take full advantage of the materials in the active learning setting, children need an organized environment. Two key aspects of the adult's role in the active learning setting, therefore, are to **arrange and equip play areas** and to **plan a daily routine.** The specifics of planning the environment and routine are covered in detail in later chapters, but a few key elements of the environment and routine will be introduced here.

First, adults divide the environment into distinct spaces organized around specific kinds of experiences, for example, house, art, block, toy, and sand-and-water areas. Each space is stocked with abundant materials related to that type of play.

Second, adults plan a consistent daily routine so that children have opportunities for many different kinds of interactions with people and materials. **Plan-work-recall time** is a lengthy segment of the day allotted for children to work throughout the classroom or center with materials of their own choosing. **Small-group time** is the segment of the day in which children work in groups of six to eight in one location with similar sets of materials. (Even though the adult chooses a set of materials for children to use at small-group time and a content focus for the activity, children are free to make choices among the materials provided, to add materials, and to use the materials in individual ways.) **Large-group time** is a segment of the day in which the whole group comes together for songs, movement activities, and other

Common Materials in Active Learning Settings

• Found materials

• Practical everyday objects useful to adults

• Natural materials

Active Participatory Learning: The Way Children Construct Knowledge   *41*

• Easy-to-handle materials

• Heavy or bulky materials

Adults divide the classroom space into distinct learning areas and stock each space with abundant materials related to that type of play.

group experiences. **Outside time** is usually the segment of the day allotted for children to play outside with swings, wheeled toys, outdoor art materials, materials from nature, and so forth.

By choosing materials, planning the arrangement of space, and offering a consistent daily routine, adults are able to set the stage for children's active participatory learning. Once the stage is set, adults continue to be active and involved — observing children and supporting and extending their initiatives throughout the day.

Adults seek out children's intentions

In active learning settings, adults believe that understanding children's intentions and encouraging children to follow through on them is essential to the learning process. By seeking out children's intentions, adults strengthen children's sense of initiative and control.

Adults are careful to *acknowledge children's choices and actions*. This lets children know that what they are doing is valued. Adults often let themselves be guided by the child's example, thereby demonstrating the importance they place on children's intentions. For example, Stony is crawling, so Mrs. Lewis crawls beside him. When Stony stops, Mrs. Lewis stops. When he crawls fast, she crawls fast to keep up with him. Stony laughs with delight at the game he has created, and Mrs. Lewis laughs right along with him.

Similarly, it is common for adults in active learning settings to *use materials in the same ways children are using them* — for example, stacking blocks, flattening play dough, packing sand. In this way they are nonverbally communicating to children that their activities are important, as

This adult gets down on the children's level to support them as they work on resolving a conflict.

well as offering opportunities for children to make thought-provoking comparisons.

To ascertain the intentions behind children's actions, adults *watch what children do with materials without preconceptions* because children often use materials in unexpected ways. In the detailed example on page 52, three-year-old Callie is deeply involved in labeling envelopes with people's initials and then sealing them. Rather than assuming Callie will use envelopes in the conventional way — enclosing something in them before sealing them — the adult observes Callie closely to discern her intention, then encourages her to use the envelopes *her* way.

In addition to seeking out children's intentions through observation, adults also *ask children about their intentions.* This gives children the opportunity to put their intentions into words and reflect on them. For example, an adult sees Scott sitting on the floor and sanding wood scraps, but she will not be able to tell whether Scott is sanding for its own sake or for some other purpose unless she talks with him. She sits down next to Scott and picks up several wood scraps he has sanded. Then she makes this observation:

Adult: You've been doing a lot of work, Scott.

Scott: Yep...sanding...it's my job.

Adult: Oh, sanding is your job.

Scott: (Continues sanding) I sand these (tosses sanded piece in a bucket). Then I put 'em here, in the bucket. Billy's the wrapper. He's not here right now.

Adult: Oh, you sand and Billy wraps.

Scott: But he's getting more tape.

For more on conversing with children about their intentions and plans, see the discussion of planning with children in chapter 8.

Adults listen for and encourage children's thinking

Children's **reflections** on their actions are a fundamental part of the learning process. Listening for and encouraging each child's particular way of thinking strengthens the child's emerging thinking and reasoning abilities. Adults *listen to children as they work and play* so they can understand from children's spontaneous comments how they are thinking about what they are doing. Markie, for example, chants, "One for you...one for you...one for you" as he puts a block on each opening of his tower. His chant indicates that he is thinking out loud about matching blocks and openings in one-to-one correspondence.

Another way adults encourage children to reflect is to *converse with children about what they are doing and thinking.* In programs based on the HighScope Curriculum, relaxed conversation between adults and children occurs throughout the day. As they converse with children, adults *focus on the child's actions and ideas* rather than

Adults encourage children to reflect on their actions by talking about what they are thinking and doing.

introduce unrelated topics. Instead of lecturing children or asking a lot of questions, adults make frequent comments that repeat, amplify, and build on what the child says. In the course of these conversations, adults pause frequently to give children ample time to think and gather their thoughts into words. Note, for example, how Mrs. Foster encourages Kurt's thinking in this conversational exchange:

Kurt: I like that music. It's real fast.

Mrs. Foster: I think it's helping us put these blocks away real fast.

Kurt: I'm gonna put them on this truck and go really fast.

Mrs. Foster: All the way to the block shelf?

Kurt: Yep. Here I go, just like my daddy. (Drives off to block shelf, unloads blocks, returns for more.)

Mrs. Foster: I saw your daddy's truck when he brought you this morning.

Kurt: (Laughs) But my daddy's truck is…big…too big for this room…. It wouldn't even fit in the door!

Mrs. Foster: No it wouldn't fit in the door.

Kurt: The doors are big enough for…for…this one! (Drives truck loaded with blocks to the door and then to the block shelf.)

Strategies for conversing with children are covered throughout this book. In particular, see the section in chapter 8 on conversing with children at work time.

As noted earlier, adults in active learning settings understand that encouraging children's thinking means accepting children's answers and explanations — even when they are "wrong." Because children's thinking and reasoning skills are still developing, the conclusions children draw are often faulty by adult standards. However, if adults continually correct children, they encourage children to keep their thoughts to themselves. On the other hand, by accepting children's conclusions, adults encourage children to test their ideas. For example, consider Karla, a child who made a play dough ball and expected it to bounce. Karla finally concluded that the ball would not bounce because it was not round enough. The teacher accepted this conclusion, and Karla made another "very round" ball to test her idea. Many very round play dough balls later, Karla finally decided, "This play dough is too squishy to bounce." Again, the adult accepted Karla's idea. By accepting each new hypothesis Karla offered, the adult encouraged Karla's further reflection and testing:

This adult converses with children at work time, focusing on their actions and ideas.

Teacher: It *is* squishy. Can you think of some way to change that?

Karla: Well…if I leaved it. Leaved it out…'til tomorrow!

Teacher: If you left the ball out of the container?

Karla: Yeah! It would get hard!

Teacher: Would it bounce if it were hard?

Karla: Yeah! Then it would bounce. Leave it right here 'til tomorrow. Okay? (Karla puts a work-in-progress sign next to the ball of play dough so no one will touch it in the meantime.)

Adults encourage children to do things for themselves

Adults in active learning settings are guided by a belief that encouraging children to solve the problems they encounter offers them more learning opportunities than doing things for them or attempting to provide a problem-free environment. Therefore, they stand by patiently and wait while children take care of things independently — zipping a jacket, fastening a buckle, stirring juice, wiping up spills, moving the waste can, fitting the tricycle through the door, or finding a board that spans the space between two blocks. Adults can do most such things far more easily and efficiently than children can, but by waiting for children to do these things for themselves, adults allow children to think of and practice ways of solving the everyday problems they encounter.

In an active learning environment, where children are constantly involved with materials and are encouraged to do things for themselves, spills and messes are inevitable and are actually important opportunities for learning. Dallas, for example, finds out what happens when he keeps pouring juice past the top of his cup. Juice gets on the table, the chair, the floor. To clean it up he has to get enough paper towels to soak up all the liquid. He also has to figure out a way to get the juice-soaked paper towels to the trash. In the active learning setting, *adults show understanding of such mishaps* because they view them as

> ### Give Children Time to Solve Problems Themselves
>
> Mr. Mulla saw that Chad and Anil were having trouble cutting the long pieces of masking tape they needed for a box structure because the tape kept getting stuck to itself. Although he could have come to their aid, Mr. Mulla waited while the boys came up with a number of ideas on their own. When one didn't work, they simply tried something else. Finally, Chad taped one end of the tape to the table edge and held it there while Anil pulled the tape out as long as they needed it. Anil then cut the tape and each boy held on to an end until they could attach it to their box structure in the place they wanted it. While it took quite a while for the boys to solve this problem, their solution worked, and in the process of solving the problem they found out something about the properties of tape. The boys felt good about their idea, especially when other children began to notice and copy it.

opportunities for children to gain the satisfaction of solving their own problems.

Another way adults encourage children to solve their own problems is to *refer children to one another for ideas, assistance, and conversation* so that children come to rely on one another, rather than always turning to adults for assistance. For example, when Tess can't remember how to print out the mask she just made on her computer screen, Mr. Wills suggests that she ask Mia (another child who had just printed out a mask) to show her how to do it.

Adults in active learning settings also *encourage children to ask and answer their own questions*. Generally, if a child knows enough to ask a particular question, he or she knows enough to have some idea of an answer. For example, following the incident with Tess and Mia, Tess came to Mr. Wills the next day with the same problem. Here's how Mr. Wills handled it:

Mr. Wills: What did you do yesterday when Mia helped you?

Tess: Pushed this (points to the printer button).

Mr. Wills: That's exactly what you did. What happened when you pushed that button?

Tess: It came out! (She pushes the printer button and watches the printer print out her mask.)

Providing a variety of materials, planning the play space and routine, seeking out children's intentions, listening for and encouraging children's thinking, and encouraging children to do things for themselves are key to the adult's role in active learning programs. More of these types of strategies are provided throughout this manual and the KDI guides (Epstein, 2012a–h) that accompany it.

How adults and children interact in the active learning setting

Children and adults are active and interactive

In an active learning environment, both children and adults act, think, and solve problems throughout the day. Children are active in choosing

In an active learning setting, adults show understanding for the inevitable mishaps that occur as children explore materials and how they work.

materials, activities, and playmates. Adults are active in supporting and participating in the learning experiences initiated by children as well as in planning group experiences and setting them in motion. Both children and adults take initiative and respond to one another's initiatives, building on one another's ideas, suggestions, and actions. These reciprocal, give-and-take, relationships are what drive both teaching and learning.

Adults and children form partnerships

In active learning settings, adults and children form partnerships. Whether joining in a child's play, working with a child to solve a problem, or conversing with a child about his or her experiences, the adult relates to the child as a *partner*, seeking out the child's intentions and helping the child carry out and expand upon his or her intended activity. Sita, for example, is rolling tennis balls under a chair. Mr. Bloom stretches out on his stomach on the other side of the chair, holding a tennis ball. "Wait," Sita instructs. "They have to go here," she says, indicating a path under the chair, "not out there." "Oh, in here," responds Mr. Bloom, rolling his ball along the path indicated by Sita.

The reciprocal give-and-take of a partnership relationship is more supportive of children's development than its alternatives — in which the adult assumes either a dominant or a passive role by directing, lecturing, diverting, or simply watching or ignoring the child's work and play. To form partnerships with children, adults in active learning settings **position** *themselves at the children's physical level,* **follow** *children's ideas and interests,* and **converse** *with children in a give-and-take style.*

By using these strategies to form a partnership with Sita, Mr. Bloom is letting her know that what she is doing is valued and accepted, and that he will be there to provide support as she expands on her explorations.

Children and adults invent and discover

Active learning is a process that *unfolds*, not a set of prescribed directives to be followed. In the active learning setting, children and adults invent, explore, and make unexpected discoveries. Although adults have set up the environment to support children's interests and activities, they cannot predict with accuracy what children will do or say or how they themselves will respond. Mr. Garcia, for example, is very pleased that he has finally been able to add a color printer to the computer system his preschoolers are using. He expects the children to print out the masks they are making on the computer screen in many different colors. Instead, they use the computer and printer exactly as they often use the easel — filling

Adults play as partners with children, for example, by imitating what they are doing.

the whole piece of paper (computer screen) with one color. "Of course," Mr. Garcia realizes upon seeing the children excitedly clutching their pieces of paper filled with one color, "why didn't I think of that!" In the active learning setting, children and adults share the surprises and pleasures of teaching and learning.

The effects of active learning

Choices for children provide an alternative to adult-child conflict

When children are free to make choices and decisions, potential adult-child conflicts are often avoided and are replaced with cooperative learning experiences. When adults understand children's need to be active, they become involved in supporting and extending children's self-initiated activities rather than trying to control children's behavior. For example, since adults expect children to talk about their choices and decisions, children who speak freely and express their intentions are not labeled "disruptive." When children are free to decide how to use materials, adults are as willing to support the child who uses a material in an exploratory way (smearing paste on paper and arms, touching it, and smelling it) as they are to support the child who uses the materials in the expected way (using paste to fasten pieces of paper together in the course of making something). When adults eliminate long periods of waiting and listening in favor of active learning experiences, children direct their energies toward working with the materials they have selected rather than engaging in disruptive behavior.

By accepting children's exploratory behaviors as normal and desirable, rather than attempting to dispute or eliminate them, adults make their own lives and children's lives more enjoyable, less contentious, and more conducive to learning.

Children and adults develop confidence

In an active learning setting, children are free to pursue their own interests. Adults stock the environment with developmentally appropriate materials and interact with children to support them in pursuing their intentions. Children are free to make errors as they gain an understanding of their world; adults do not correct children's errors, but, when appropriate, they challenge children's thinking about what they are doing so that children can begin to construct a more complete picture of reality. In this atmosphere, young children develop feelings of competence because they receive encouragement and support for their actions, choices, exploratory behaviors, and emerging thoughts and explanations. Adults feel more competent too, because they find themselves supporting, rather than disputing, more of children's actions, and because each day they learn something new about the children in their group. As one adult put it, "I'm not yelling at the children any more. I'm paying attention to *their* interests instead of trying to get them to sit still and pay attention to *me*."

Children draw on early active learning experiences in later school settings

Some adults worry that an "active learning" early childhood setting will put children at a disadvantage when they enter elementary school. What happens to active learners when they must remain seated at desks, follow detailed instructions, speak only when permitted to do so, and concentrate on paper-and-pencil tasks?

Active learners tend to adjust well to elementary school because they identify themselves as

When children are free to choose play materials and adults acknowledge their choices, children remain more engaged.

"can-do" people who take care of their own needs and solve problems. In the best of circumstances, the elementary school setting will also encourage active learning. However, in settings that do not, children tend to use their problem-solving skills to adapt to the new style of teaching and learning, and continue to function as active learners outside of school. Since active learners have developed into self-confident decision makers, they often carry these attributes into whatever school settings they encounter.

Regardless of the setting or form of instruction in elementary schools, children continue to learn best by doing, thinking, speaking, and solving problems independently. Therefore, it is imperative that early childhood settings support active learning practices. Through their experiences in such active learning settings, children develop a strong sense of their own ability to affect and understand their world, a capacity that will serve them well throughout their lives.

Denver Project Follows HighScope Children Into Non-HighScope Settings

From 1987 to 1995, the Clayton Foundation (now Clayton Early Learning) in Denver, Colorado, operated a HighScope kindergarten program (Clayton Kids) and a HighScope after-school program (Clayton Thinkers) for its kindergarten graduates in grades 1–3 in public schools across the city.[3] In response to the question, "How well do Clayton Kids fare once they are in the public school system?" Clayton staff asked each elementary school for progress reports that included teacher comments on the 41 children who had graduated from the Clayton Kids kindergarten program and were currently enrolled in the Clayton Thinkers after-school program. Clayton staff were able to collect school progress reports and teacher comments on 34 of their 41 enrollees (Dalton, 1991). They found that the elementary school teachers rated 88 percent of the Clayton after-school group as average or higher in standard school subject areas (reading, writing, math, cooperation, and so forth); 38 percent were rated as average; 29 percent as above average; and 21 percent as well-above-average. The teachers also commented favorably on the children's social and intellectual abilities. For example, consider these excerpts taken from teacher reports on children's progress:

D. is always willing to help on any project.

I appreciate M.'s enthusiasm and creativity.

J. is a real hard worker.

T. is one of the best readers in the class.

W. often sees unique solutions to problems.

N. has many good ideas.

E. has made great strides in her skills as a reader, writer, and leader this year.

I'm enjoying watching A. grow and become more responsible and independent.

C. is a pleasure to have in class.

R. is a good group member and a hard worker.

S. puts a lot into her assignments.

V. is spontaneous, enthusiastic, straightforward in her thoughts, and lets everyone know what she is thinking. She enjoys learning and asking questions.

It is apparent from these findings that Clayton's active learners continued to do well in traditional elementary school settings. (For an account of a prekindergarten program based on the HighScope Curriculum whose children's success in kindergarten and third grade has been researched and documented, see Hauser-Cram, Pierson, Walker, & Tivnan, 1991.)

---

[3]The program later became the first charter school in Denver, but has since closed.

The Practical Ingredients of Active Learning

To provide a practical frame of reference for adults interested in implementing programs based on an active learning philosophy, we have developed five **ingredients of active learning.** These ingredients capture the essence of the active learning process in summary form. They are easily understood and can be used by adults in any early childhood setting to evaluate whether an activity for children is truly a developmentally appropriate, active experience and to plan for activities that meet these criteria. As we explore the details of the HighScope educational approach throughout the rest of this book, we will return again and again to the following active learning ingredients:

- **Materials** — There are abundant, age-appropriate materials that the child can use in a variety of ways. Learning grows out of the child's direct actions on the materials.

- **Manipulation** — The child has opportunities to explore, manipulate, combine, and transform the materials chosen.

- **Choice** — The child chooses what to do. Since learning results from the child's attempts to pursue personal interests and goals, the opportunity to choose activities and materials is essential.

- **Child language and thought** — The child communicates verbally and nonverbally, describing what he or she is seeing and doing. The child reflects on actions, integrating new experiences into existing knowledge, and modifies his or her thinking accordingly.

- **Adult scaffolding** — Adults support the child's current level of development and offer gentle extensions as he or she moves to the next developmental stage.

Using the ingredients of active participatory learning

Anyone caring for young children — parents, teachers, home visitors, caregivers in child care centers and child care homes, grandparents, other family and friends — can use the active learning ingredients to provide developmentally appropriate experiences for young children. The active learning ingredients apply to experiences and activities involving one child or two children as well as activities for small groups and large groups of children. Active learning opportunities are present throughout a formally structured day as well as in other daily events, such as trips in a car or visits to a park. *In the HighScope Curriculum, the ingredients of active learning guide every experience and activity adults and children engage in during their time together.*

Adults implementing the HighScope Curriculum use the ingredients of active learning as a guide to observing children, planning experiences, and interacting with children in any curriculum area. In the example on page 52, we show how this framework is applied in the context of a writing activity undertaken by three-year-old Callie. We describe how each active learning ingredient shapes the general decisions adults make in

---

Why Children Need to Make Choices

"The intrinsic motivation argument leads to perhaps the most common-sense rationale for allowing children to select learning experiences. A child will, like anyone else, learn best what he is interested in learning. If you allow him to choose, he will select what interests him. If he is interested in something, he will be an active agent in developing his understanding rather than a passive consumer of knowledge. Piaget's 50 years of research on children's thinking has led him to postulate that a child's active involvement in learning is at the heart of the developmental process. The child, Piaget says, 'is the chief architect of his own mental model of the world.'"

— Lickona (1973, p. 7)

An Active Learning Experience: Observing and Supporting Callie

Materials. The adults in Callie's classroom have provided a wide range of materials to encourage and support young children's developing writing abilities. The materials available include writing tools and materials, three-dimensional materials for letter play and letter-making, and a variety of print materials. The availability of a wide range of writing materials seemed to have the stimulating effect intended by the adults, and they noted that Callie and several other children have chosen to work with them:

> Callie got out some envelopes and markers.

Manipulation. The adults expect Callie and her classmates to manipulate the reading and writing materials in a variety of ways. For example, children might turn pages, point to and circle letters, draw, paint, print, and so on, as they explore the shape and feel of letters, or they might transform a variety of materials into letters. In addition, since most of the children have observed that writing is used for important purposes in the world around them — for lists, taking restaurant orders, letter-writing, and so forth — the adults expect that some children will want to use (or pretend to use) writing for some of these same functions. Callie's use of the writing materials has the active, physical quality that we associate with young children's manipulations; it also shows her growing understanding of some of the functions of writing:

> Callie seemed to be repeating a sequence of actions:
> - Put an envelope in front of herself on the table
> - Picked up the envelope in both hands
> - Licked it thoroughly three or four times
> - Pounded the envelope shut with her fist
> - Turned it over and drew on the front
> - Gave it to someone

Choice. In this classroom, the children are free to use any of the writing materials they want to during the plan-work-recall (plan-do-review) segment of the daily routine.

> None of the other children at the art table were working with envelopes and markers. (One was drawing, two were working with stickers; one was playing with wooden letters.) Working with the envelopes was obviously Callie's choice.

Child language and thought. As children work with writing materials, the teachers observe them and listen attentively, waiting for the child to initiate conversation about what he or she is doing and taking care not to use language to dominate or control the child's experience.

> Callie was very quiet as she worked, but when she completed each envelope, she would give it to someone, saying "This is for you." I sat for a while at Callie's table, and soon she gave one to me, saying "Here, Ann, I made this for you."

Adult scaffolding. The adults recognize that preschoolers are beginning to make a connection between spoken and written language and to realize that they can write things down for themselves. They understand that children's writing starts out as scribbles and drawings, and gradually, through trial and error, emerges as recognizable script. The adults in Callie's classroom therefore encourage children's early, creative interest in the writing process and support all children's attempts at writing, whether or not they use conventional forms:

> I sat down at the art table to see what children were doing. When Callie saw that she had written lots of A's, I wanted to recognize her accomplishment so I said, "Callie, you made A's on my envelope!"
>
> "That's your name!" she told me.
>
> "A's for Ann," I replied." "A is the first letter in my name."
>
> When Callie gave Linda an envelope, Linda threw it down on the floor saying, "That's not how you write my name. It's L-I-N-D-A."
>
> Linda is five and has been writing her name and other words for some time. I wanted to acknowledge both Linda's skill and Callie's, so I said, "That is the way you spell your name, Linda. Callie wrote the first letter of Linda. She used the letter L to stand for your whole name."
>
> I also found when I started to open my envelope that Callie stopped me, saying, "No, I already did that!" Since I wanted to respect her intentions, I pressed down the part of the flap I had lifted and turned the envelope over so I could see the front again.
>
> "Is this what you wanted me to have?" I asked, looking at the front of the envelope.
>
> "Yep. That's what I made for you," Callie replied, before turning to another envelope and beginning the process again. Clearly what was important to Callie was sealing the envelope and writing on the outside. She had no intention of putting anything inside the envelope.

preparing for children's writing experiences as well as specific decisions about how to interact with and support Callie. The teachers' observations of Callie are presented in italic type.

Active participatory learning: The foundation of the HighScope Curriculum

In the chapters that follow and in the KDI books accompanying this manual, the concept of active learning will continue to guide our discussions. In particular, the concept of active learning comes into play throughout discussions of how adults interact with children to create a supportive climate (chapter 2); work with families (chapter 3); work as teaching teams to make the active learning process effective in their particular setting and with their particular children (chapter 4); authentically assess children's development and monitor program quality (chapter 5); select and arrange materials for children to choose and manipulate (chapter 6); develop the daily routine so children have opportunities to initiate, plan, carry out, and discuss their actions and ideas individually and in groups (chapters 7 to 9); and use the HighScope KDIs as a framework for planning the content of learning (chapter 10 and the KDI books that accompany this manual, Epstein, 2012a–h).

When all the active learning ingredients are present, children are able to pursue their interests, explore ideas and materials, and relate their experiences to others.

Essential Ingredients of Active Learning: A Summary

Choice: The child chooses what to do.
- Children initiate activities that grow from personal interests and intentions.
- Children choose materials.
- Children decide what to do with materials.

Materials: There are abundant materials that children can use in many ways.
- Children use a variety of materials.
  - Practical everyday objects
  - Natural and found materials
  - Tools
  - Messy, sticky, gooey, drippy, squishy materials
  - Heavy or bulky materials
  - Easy-to-handle materials
- Children have space to use materials.
- Children have time to use materials.

Manipulation: Adults encourage children to manipulate objects freely.
- Children explore actively with all their senses.
- Children discover relationships through direct experience.
- Children transform and combine materials.

- Children use age-appropriate tools and equipment.
- Children use their large muscles.

Child language and thought: The child describes what he or she is thinking and doing.
- Children talk about their experiences.
- Children talk about what they are seeing and doing in their own words.

Adult scaffolding: Adults recognize and encourage children's intentions, reflections, problem solving, and creativity.
- Adults form partnerships with children.
  - Put themselves on children's physical level
  - Follow children's ideas and interests
  - Converse in a give-and-take style
- Adults seek out children's intentions.
  - Acknowledge children's choices and actions
  - Use materials in the same way children are using them
  - Watch what children do with materials
  - Ask children about their intentions
- Adults listen for and encourage children's thinking.
  - Listen to children as they work and play
  - Converse with children about what they are doing and thinking
  - Focus on children's actions and ideas
  - Make comments that repeat, amplify, and build on what the child says
  - Pause frequently to give children time to think and gather their thoughts into words
- Adults encourage children to do things for themselves.
  - Stand by patiently and wait while children take care of things independently
  - Show understanding of children's mishaps
  - Refer children to one another for ideas, assistance, and conversation
  - Encourage children to ask and answer their own questions
  - Accept children's answers and explanations even when they are "wrong"

CHAPTER

Adult-Child Interaction: Establishing a Supportive Climate

Understanding Supportive Climates

A supportive interpersonal climate is essential for active learning, because active learning is a social, interactive process. Therefore, one of the HighScope Curriculum's major goals is to assist adults in establishing and maintaining settings where they can interact positively with children so that children can work and play free of fear, anxiety, boredom, and neglect. This goal stems from the findings of psychological theory, research, and practice that **active learning** is the primary means by which children construct social, emotional, intellectual, and physical knowledge.

In an active learning setting children are free to manipulate materials, to make choices, plans, and decisions; to talk about and reflect on what they are doing; and to accept support from adults and peers as needed. Children who engage in these kinds of active learning experiences grow in their ability to think and reason and also in their ability to understand themselves and relate well to others.

The purpose of this chapter is to clarify the meaning of **adult support** in an active learning classroom or center by defining the **building blocks of human relationships,** examining **contrasting interpersonal climates** and their effects on children, and focusing on the **elements of adult support** that contribute to a supportive active learning climate.

The child's sense of self: Development through interaction

From infancy, children's experiences with the significant people in their lives affect how they view themselves and consequently how they interact with people in various situations. A young child's **sense of self** — how the child sees him- or herself as a distinct human being apart from others — develops gradually during these interactions. The series of stages that children progress through during this process have been described in a variety of ways.

> "In practice, each child's self-understanding develops in collaboration with others. What, after all, is a child's real self? As adults, we have our views of the child's real self; the child, too, has views. Sometimes the child knows better than we do; other times we know better than the child. The goal is to collaborate with the child in the development of a self that is both valued and true."
>
> — Curry and Johnson (1990, p. 8)

From psychoanalyst Erik Erikson's perspective (1950), children from infancy to preschool age negotiate three major stages of social and emotional development — *trust versus mistrust, autonomy versus shame and doubt,* and *initiative versus guilt.* When children's experiences with adults lead to the development of trust, autonomy, and initiative rather than mistrust, shame, doubt, and guilt, children develop lasting feelings of hope, acceptance, willpower, and purpose.

Clinical infant researchers Stanley and Nancy Greenspan (1985) regard the period from infancy to age four as a time of six emotional milestones — *self-regulation and interest in the world, falling in love, developing intentional communication, emergence of an organized sense of self, creating emotional ideas,* and *emotional thinking.* The Greenspans believe that two basic tendencies guide children's development: *regulation and harmony,* and *exploration of new experience and practice.* Furthermore, they maintain that adult support of children's age-appropriate experiences is essential for building a social and emotional climate conducive to children's health and learning. In such a learning climate, children feel a sense of full emotional engagement, mastery, and control.

Classical child development studies conducted by psychoanalyst John Bowlby (1969) and psychologist Mary Ainsworth and colleagues (Ainsworth, Salter, Blehar, Walters, & Wall, 1978), as well as by contemporary researchers (Honig, 2002; Waters & Cummings, 2000), revolve around

Research shows that children's learning flourishes in environments where adults are warm and caring, and interact with children in nondirective ways.

the importance of **attachment** — the process by which a child becomes emotionally attached to parent(s) or other significant caregivers. Attachment directly affects key aspects of the child's personality, including emotional self-regulation, empathy, sympathy, problem solving, playfulness, and sociability. Michael Lewis (1986) describes the process this way: "Through the establishment of reciprocal and responsive interactions and the emergence of a sense of self, children are able to establish relationships that provide them with a secure base from which to explore their environment" (p. 15). Once young children are firmly attached to parent(s) or significant caregivers, their main emotional task, according to psychologist Margaret Mahler and colleagues (Mahler, Pine, & Bergman, 1975), is to gain a sense of themselves as individuals who are separate and distinct from others yet are still able to maintain their strong emotional attachments.

Clearly, the ongoing support of attentive adults enables children to flourish — to grow, to learn, and to construct a working knowledge of the physical and social world. Research shows that when adults are warm and friendly, and interact in nondirective ways, children exhibit "high task involvement, language comprehension, social participation, constructive use of materials, spontaneity, creativity, sympathy, and independence" (Phyfe-Perkins & Shoemaker, 1986, p. 186). Furthermore, research shows that how adults interact with children is directly reciprocated by the children themselves. When adults act as partners, children turn to them for *interaction*. By contrast, adults who act as managers socialize children to turn to them for *management*. Moreover, adults who interact as partners rather than managers also enhance young children's ability to communicate effectively with others (Wood, McMahon, & Cranstoun, 1980).

In sum, adults support children when they express pleasure in children's initiative and autonomy, share the children's excitement about their discoveries, join as partners without dominating children's play, and know when to stand by versus when and how to gently step in to facilitate children's problem solving and extend their learning. To support young children's emerging sense of self, adults need to be knowledgeable and reflective about all these aspects of adult-child interaction.

Building blocks of human relationships

While **sense of self** is a fairly abstract concept, it becomes clearer when considered in the context of five key capacities identified in child development literature as building blocks of children's social and emotional health. These capacities for **trust, autonomy, initiative, empathy,** and **self-confidence** provide the foundation for much of the socialization that occurs as the child grows to adulthood. These capacities are particularly apt to flourish within an active learning setting that supports the growth of positive social relationships.

Trust. Trust is the confident belief in oneself and in others that allows a young child to venture forth into action knowing there are people he or she can depend on to provide support and encouragement when needed. The development of trust begins at birth as parents and caregivers respond to their infant's needs. As they feed, change, cuddle, and play with their baby, they make him or her feel safe and secure. By toddlerhood, the child's sense of trust has developed to the point where he or she can explore in the next room out of the adult's sight. But the toddler still needs to check back often to see that the significant adult is still there. Bolstered by trust, three- and four-year-olds leave home for hours at a time to play with friends or attend preschool. Learning to trust a new set of people outside the family is an important step forward for this age group. In a supportive setting, young children extend the range of their trusting relationships to new adults and peers. (For more on trusting relationships and how adults support their development, see the discussion of KDI 12. Building relationships in the companion book *Social and Emotional Development,* Epstein, 2012g.)

Autonomy. Autonomy is the capacity for independence and exploration that prompts a child to make such statements as "I wonder what's around the corner" and "Let me do it." While young children need to feel a strong attachment to their parents or primary caregivers, they also need to develop a sense of themselves as distinctly separate persons who can make their own choices and do things for themselves. An example of early independent thinking is an infant, Sam, who coos and gurgles to his stuffed bear — he has discovered a simple way to entertain himself. Saying no indiscriminately is one way toddlers express their emerging sense of autonomy. Also, with toddlers' newfound mobility comes a feeling of independence that can lead them into troublesome situations — for example, finding themselves immobilized in a tangle of clothes they have decided to take off by themselves, or being startled by the clatter of pots and pans they have pulled out of a cupboard. By the preschool years, children are able to do many things on their own without putting themselves at such risk, and adults should encourage this independence. Preschool-aged children take great pride in dressing themselves, pouring their own juice, riding bikes, carrying big boxes, and "reading" a book to a friend. These kinds of experiences enhance children's sense of autonomy, giving them the courage to reach out and explore new materials, situations, and relationships. (For more information on children's independent use of resources and interest in taking care of their own physical needs, see the discussion of KDI 5. Use of resources in the companion book *Approaches to Learning,* Epstein, 2012a; and the discussion of KDI 19. Personal care in the companion book *Physical Development and Health,* Epstein, 2012e.)

Examining Our Beliefs About How Adults Interact With Children

Young children are social beings. Much of their learning is mediated by their interactions with adults. In fact, how they feel about learning — and about themselves as learners — is shaped by their early interactions with adult family members and teachers. As you prepare to implement the HighScope Curriculum in your early childhood setting, ask yourself the questions listed below. Are there other beliefs you are aware of in yourself or those with whom you work? Which of your beliefs nurture early development, and which ones would you like to work on changing?

Do you believe…?

Adults should act authoritatively to directly teach children what they need to learn.	or	Adults should act as play partners with children because children learn and develop understanding through play.
Adults should set the learning agenda and goals for children in the classroom.	or	Adults should plan learning experiences that build on children's interests and abilities.
Adults should control and distribute classroom materials to children.	or	Adults should encourage and enable children to get materials on their own.
Adults should solve problems for children so they don't get out of hand.	or	Adults should facilitate children solving problems on their own.
Adults should do the talking in the classroom so children will learn to listen.	or	Adults should listen to children in the classroom so children will learn to talk.
Adults should ask children questions to make sure they know the right answer and correct them when they are wrong.	or	Adults should ask questions sparingly, and only to find out information that the adult does not know.
Adults should keep a firm hand in the classroom to maintain discipline and counter children's natural inclination to be disruptive.	or	Adults can avert many discipline problems by providing opportunities for children to be actively engaged in the pursuit of their own interests.
Adults should hold children accountable for their actions so children will learn there are consequences and become responsible for their behavior.	or	Adults should help children observe cause and effect so they can gradually learn to make more effective choices and regulate their own behavior.

Initiative. Initiative is children's capacity to begin and then follow through on a task — to take stock of a situation, make a decision, and act on what they have come to understand. From infancy on, initiative is evident as young children signal and act on their intentions. For example, a toddler, Francie, sees her mother's key ring on top of a stool. Her face lights up. She gurgles, then says her all-purpose word for interesting objects, "Da-boo, da-boo." She crawls to the stool and, gripping it with both hands, pulls herself to a standing position. Then, to grasp the keys, she releases her two-handed grip on the stool, but loses her balance and sits back on the floor with a thump. She then works her way back up the stool into a standing position and at this point holds onto the stool with both hands — all the while gazing at the keys. With great care, she slowly removes one hand from the stool, grasps the keys with her free hand, puts them in her mouth, and then, using both hands, works her way down the stool into a sitting position. Once seated, she joyfully shakes, mouths, throws, and retrieves the keys she has worked with such determination to possess. Preschool-aged children are even more ambitious than toddlers and much more articulate about their intentions: "Play with blocks." "I'm going to get some paper, lots of it, and cover up that box my daddy gave me, and cut some holes in it for windows, and that's going to be my fort. Me and Jamal, he's going to help." It is important for adults to encourage preschool-aged children to describe their intentions in their own words. This helps children act purposefully and feel confident in their ability to make choices and decisions — to make things happen — and to see themselves as competent, able people. (For more on children's initiative and how adults support its development, see the discussion of KDI 1. Initiative in the companion book *Approaches to Learning,* Epstein, 2012a.)

Empathy. Empathy is the capacity that allows children to understand the feelings of others by relating them to feelings that they themselves have had. Empathy helps children form friendships and

A child's developing empathy is apparent when she comforts an upset classmate.

develop a sense of belonging. The first glimmers of empathy appear in infancy. Psychologist Janet Strayer (1986) has this to say about an infant's capacity for empathy toward peers: "Although their cognitive understanding is limited, 6-month-olds react with interest and contact behaviors toward crying peers" (p. 50). In a group setting, for example, some infants and toddlers make a point of playing near peers they are especially fond of, and they will gaze sadly at their special friends if they are crying — sometimes moving even closer and patting their friends or offering a toy as comfort. Strayer also reports that infants' concern extends to siblings as well as peers: "Mothers report that by 14 months of age, 65 percent of infants show empathic concern for their siblings" (p. 50). It is also true that infants reflect the feelings of their parents and adult caregivers. Consider, for example, Tony, an infant who smiles widely, gurgles, waves his arms, and kicks his legs when his dad arrives to pick him up from child care. But, on the days when his dad arrives at the center feeling pressured and irritable, Tony's initial expressions of delight quickly become muted, mirroring his dad's irritability. By the preschool years, children are able to exhibit their concern for others in many ways. With their increasing

> ### The Beginnings of Empathy
>
> "Seeing a child fall and hurt himself, Hope, 9 months old, stared, tears welling up in her eyes, and crawled to her mother to be comforted — as though *she* had been hurt, not her friend. When 15-month-old Michael saw his friend Paul crying, Michael fetched his own teddy bear and offered it to Paul; when that didn't stop Paul's tears, Michael brought Paul's security blanket from another room.
>
> "Such small acts of sympathy and caring, observed in scientific studies, are leading researchers to trace the roots of empathy — the ability to share another's emotions — to infancy, contradicting a long-standing assumption that infants and toddlers were incapable of these feelings.
>
> "In some of the most recent and surprising findings, researchers have identified individual neurons in primates that respond primarily to specific emotional expressions, a response that could be a neural basis for empathy. These findings are opening a new research area in which scientists are searching for the specific brain circuitry that underlies the empathic impulse."
>
> — Goleman (1989, p. B20)

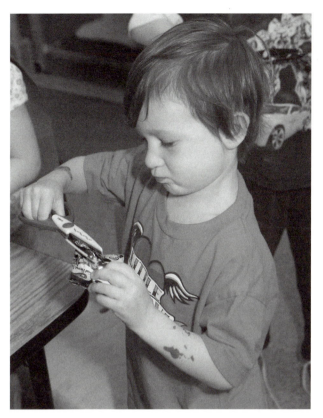

Self-confidence develops through accomplishments that are meaningful to children, like using scissors to open a food packet at snacktime.

language ability, preschool-aged children have a greater capacity to express their own feelings as well as their empathy for the feelings of others — "Your mouth is going down. Why are you so sad, little girl?" "Ricky's very sad because he tore the picture for his mom." "Oh, boy. Shane's smiling because he's going to see his daddy." (For more information on the development of empathy and how adults support it, see the discussion of KDI 10. Empathy in the companion book *Social and Emotional Development,* Epstein, 2012g.)

Self-confidence. Self-confidence is the capacity to believe in one's own ability to accomplish things. It is a core of inner pride that can sustain children through the difficulties and strife they are bound to encounter in their lives. Self-confidence develops when children spend time in supportive settings — developing their abilities and interests and having opportunities to experience success. Child development researchers Nancy Curry and Carl Johnson (1990) report that certain types of experiences influence one's self-confidence: "The available evidence suggests that it is protective to have a well-established feeling of one's own worth as a person together with a confidence and conviction that one can cope with life's challenges. The limited evidence suggests that two types of experiences are most influential: secure and harmonious love relationships, and successful accomplishment of tasks important to the individual" (p. 3).

Successful accomplishments, however, can be elusive if adults do not capitalize on children's problem-solving opportunities. It is understandable that adults may become annoyed with

> ### An Unsentimental View of Self-Esteem
>
> "Like it or not, self-esteem is very much a function of such unyielding realities as what we can do, what we've done with what we have, what we've made of ourselves....
>
> "In addressing interpersonal relations, we'd do well to make education more participatory and provide more opportunities for performance and interaction. Having students speak, discuss a story, explain a math problem, or read a paper to classmates would go a long way toward building the connections that help foster self-esteem....
>
> "For our part, the best we can do is teach children, in an atmosphere of compassion and active participation, that self-respect is earned, often with considerable difficulty, and equip them to earn it."
>
> — Schmoker (1989, p. 34)

children who manage to put themselves in troublesome situations — the infant stuck under the highchair, the toddler crying in the midst of a clutter of pots and pans, the preschooler pouring himself a glass of juice and spilling it all over a table. Ironically, however, potentially negative situations such as these often provide excellent problem-solving opportunities that can help children develop self-confidence. For example, with appropriate adult support and reassurance, the infant can find a way to remove herself from underneath the highchair, the toddler can be encouraged to put the pans back in the cupboard, and the preschooler can take responsibility for wiping up the spilled juice. When adults have the patience to look at these types of situations from the *child's* point of view, they recognize the importance of encouraging children to begin to solve their own problems, thereby laying the groundwork for learning experiences that build a child's sense of competence and self-respect. (For more information on the development of young children's problem solving with materials

and how adults support it, see the discussion of KDI 4. Problem solving in the companion book *Approaches to Learning,* Epstein, 2012a.)

Even very young children, however, are not fooled into self-confidence by adult manipulation and false praise. (See "Using Encouragement Instead of Praise" on pp. 78–79.) For example, consider David's experience: He is sitting in his highchair happily throwing his spoon on the floor every time his mom hands it back to him. When saying "Don't throw your spoon, David" does not produce the result Mom desires, she removes David from the highchair and tells him to pick up his spoon. "No!" he says firmly. "Then Mommy will help you," says his mom, taking David's hand, guiding it to the spoon, curling his fingers around the handle, and holding her hand around his. "There. David was a good boy. He picked up his spoon," says his mom in tones of praise and approval. "No, *Mommy* do it," David replies matter-of-factly. Self-confidence develops as a result of one's own actions and decisions, and children seem to understand this and expect adults to understand it as well — and to act accordingly. (For more information on how to support children's confidence in their own abilities, see the discussion of KDI 8. Sense of competence in the companion book *Social and Emotional Development,* Epstein, 2012g.)

Who is in control? Contrasting social climates for children

The qualities of supportive social climates in early childhood programs are better understood when viewed in contrast to the qualities of two other climates that are quite common in early childhood programs: the **laissez-faire climate** and the **directive climate.** We focus on these climates because many early childhood settings are distinguished by one or the other or by a combination of the two.

Laissez-faire climates. A laissez-faire, permissive climate is largely controlled by the children themselves. The daily routine and the physical

Setting up the classroom to encourage children to get and use materials independently is one of many aspects of shared control in a supportive social climate.

environment are loosely structured, giving free rein to children's play, which adults in these settings view as the primary focus of the early childhood program. Adults purposely leave children alone so that they may play with one another and with the materials provided, intervening only to respond to children's requests to impart information, or to restore order when necessary.

This type of climate works well for independent-minded children who take leadership roles with their peers and are able to obtain adult assistance when they need it. But because of the relative lack of structure and adult involvement inherent in this type of approach, some children may become frustrated. For example, they may have difficulty finding things to do; they may give up in the face of problems; or they may feel anxious, bored, confused, or out of control. On a more positive note, a laissez-faire climate offers plenty of freedom for children and respects their need for play as a primary learning activity. Some adults believe such a climate mirrors the conditions of daily life, therefore preparing children to cope with reality and develop survival skills.

Directive climates. The directive approach to teaching and learning is characterized by adult-controlled activities. The daily routine and physical setting are tightly controlled by adults so that they can lead children efficiently through adult-planned learning sequences. In short, adults talk; children listen and follow directions. Ideally, children remain still, quiet, and attentive while adults, following skill-based objectives, show and tell them what they need to know. Then children drill and practice until they can duplicate the adult model or score adequately on an assessment instrument. Children who are not able to remain still and attentive during instructional sessions are publicly corrected or separated from their peers. This climate rewards children who enjoy following directions. They experience the feeling of success that comes from meeting adult expectations. But the range of acceptable behaviors in such a climate is so narrow that most children require ongoing adult supervision to keep them on task.

Supportive climates. In the supportive climate advocated by HighScope, adults and children share control over the teaching and learning process. In this climate, adults provide a balance between the freedom children must have to explore as active learners and the limits needed to permit them to feel secure in the classroom or center. Adults create an orderly physical environment to support a broad range of children's interests, and they establish a daily routine within which children express and carry out their intentions. Throughout the day, children and adults initiate active learning experiences based on children's strengths and interests. Even during adult-initiated experiences, children make choices and decisions about materials and outcomes. Adults make their presence known by joining children as *partners* who are genuinely interested in and committed to watching, listening to, conversing with, and working with children; they encourage children and assist them as they solve problems that arise throughout the day. When conflicts arise, adults are not judgmental. Instead, they model appropriate behaviors and engage children in problem solving so that children experience the satisfaction of figuring out and being responsible for their own solutions. Adults and children alike view problems, mistakes, and conflicts as *active learning opportunities*.

We believe a supportive climate serves young children well. Children flourish because it enables them to focus on their own interests and initiatives, try out their ideas, talk about their actions, and solve child-sized problems in age-appropriate ways. At the same time, adults who are knowledgeable about early development can support children's interests and gently extend their knowledge and skills. Teachers in this type of active learning environment intentionally balance child-guided and adult-guided instruction (Epstein, 2007) to create a true partnership in the learning process. Through this partnership, a supportive climate stimulates and strengthens children's ongoing development of trust, autonomy, initiative, empathy, and self-confidence.

Shifting from climate to climate. In many early childhood settings, the locus of control shifts back and forth from one climate to another, from laissez-faire, to supportive, to directive, without conscious thought on the part of adults. Here is an example of a shifting climate in an imaginary child care center:

Tall Timbers Center

*A **supportive climate** prevails as the day begins with greeting time. The children cluster around Miss Beale and Miss Lee, eagerly sharing tales about what they did at home, special outings, surprising occurrences, their pets, their siblings, their friends, and the important things that have happened to them recently.*

*Next it's time for free play, and the climate becomes **laissez-faire**. The children play with materials, alone and together, while Miss Beale and Miss Lee work at record keeping and prepare the daily lesson. The adults take turns reminding the children to use their "indoor" voices and walking feet, and they intervene to settle disputes, such as restraining Max and Billy from throwing blocks.*

*At one point, Miss Beale summons five children over to a small table for the letter lesson of the day, and the climate shifts to **directive**. Since Miss Beale views this time as her true "teaching" time with the children, she directs this session like "real" school. She expects children to watch and listen as she explains and demonstrates how to print the letter G. Next she passes out worksheets and pencils*

> ### In the Eye of the Beholder: Dressing in Two Different Social Climates
>
> *Below are two real-life stories about how two young children — Lyle and Gus — get ready for child care. As you read the stories, consider which social climate each story represents. Then decide what effect each climate has on these two children:*
>
> It's almost time to leave for the day care center. Four-year-old Lyle, still in his pajamas, is playing with his racing cars.
>
> "Hurry up, Lyle," his dad calls, "or I'll be late for work."
>
> "I'm waiting for mom to pick out my clothes," Lyle calls back. This brings his mom, who selects his clothes, dresses him, brushes his hair, and buttons his sweater.
>
> "Don't you look smart," she says. And he does.
>
> Meanwhile, down the block, Lyle's best friend, Gus, is also getting ready for day care. He opens his shirt drawer and finds his favorite shirt with cars all over it. He hesitates because it has buttons that are hard to fasten, but he decides to wear it anyway. He manages to get three buttons buttoned, and that seems like enough. "See," he says to his mom with pride.
>
> "Those are hard to button," she comments "and you did them all by yourself!"
>
> Next, he opens his pants drawer. But he can't see his pants because his pants drawer is underneath his shirt drawer, which is still open. When he tries to close his shirt drawer, only one side will go in; so he pulls the drawer all the way out. It falls into his pants drawer. Luckily, the handles are pointing up, so Gus pulls the shirt drawer out and most of the shirts stay in.
>
> "Do you need some help, Gus?" his mother asks.
>
> "Nope. I can do it myself." Gus picks out his favorite red plaid pants his grandma sent him for his birthday last year. They're a little short, but that's okay, he reasons, because then he can see his yellow Big Bird socks better. "Look, I'm all ready," Gus announces a few minutes later.
>
> "Yes, you certainly are," his mom agrees.

so they can practice filling the whole page with G's. *"Oh, Thomas. You can do better than that," she says, pausing to guide his hand.*

While climate shift is a common occurrence in many early childhood settings and may at times be unavoidable, in the HighScope approach adults consciously strive to maintain a consistently supportive climate throughout the day.

The effects of a supportive climate

When adults maintain a consistently supportive climate for active learners, everyone benefits from the partnerships that emerge.

Children and adults are free to learn

When children and adults work together in an active learning setting with a supportive social climate, children are motivated to carry out their own intentions. Adults encourage children to use what they know to solve problems and to initiate new experiences from which they gain new insights. In this open-ended approach, children learn through experience and construct their own understanding of the world. Adults also learn — about the capacities of individual children, about how to interact in a genuine way to support each child's development, and about their own potential for providing appropriate support.

Children gain experience in forming positive relationships

When adults in an active learning setting share control, encourage problem solving, and invest a genuine part of themselves in their interactions with children, they model a positive interpersonal style. When adults are kind and patient, children learn to appreciate these qualities and, in dealing with others, may exhibit these same qualities. When adults greet children with pleasure and respect, children often respond in kind. Of course, even in a supportive climate in which adults

Contrasting Climates for Children

Laissez-Faire Climate	Supportive Climate	Directive Climate
• Children are in control most of the time, with adults as bystanders who provide supervision.	• Children and adults share control.	• Adults are in control.
• Adults intervene to respond to children's requests, offer information, restore order.	• Adults observe children's strengths, form authentic partnerships with children, support children's intentional play.	• Adults give directions and information.
• Curriculum content comes from children's play.	• Curriculum content comes from children's initiatives; adults plan ways to support children's learning with key developmental indicators in mind.	• Curriculum content comes from learning objectives set by adults.
• Adults highly value children's play.	• Adults highly value children's active learning.	• Adults highly value drill and practice for children.
• Adults use various approaches to child management.	• Adults take a problem-solving approach to social conflict.	• Adults use correction and separation as predominant child management strategies.

and children share control, positive interactions between individuals are not automatic. Rather, such relationships form over time under the influence of understanding and caring adults who model warm and empathic behavior and support its development in young learners.

Adults see children's behaviors in terms of development

In a supportive, active learning climate, adults view children's behavior in terms of *development*. For example, like individuals of all ages, young children experience social conflicts. In settings where adults and children share control, adults tend to view social conflict as resulting from young children's tendency to focus on their own intentions, rather than from their being naughty or mean. To explain this point more fully, let's consider the behavior of Vanessa, a very young three-year-old. When Vanessa entered preschool, she often hit children who intruded into "her" play space. Observing this behavior and understanding the partnership role of adults in supportive learning climates, Vanessa's teachers helped her find verbal alternatives to hitting. But because they also understood Vanessa's strong desire to carry out her intentions, they studied the play activities she was attempting to defend — lining up rubber animals, balancing blocks, filling and emptying sand containers — and helped her find more protected spaces to play in until she was ready to play with others.

Seeing behavior in terms of development rather than deficits, this adult does not push the child to "hold the pencil right." Instead she focuses on the literacy skills that are emerging as the child writes her name in her own way on the sign-in sheet.

Children grow in their capacity to trust, be autonomous, take initiative, and feel both empathy and self-confidence

In a supportive climate, these building blocks for a healthy sense of self have a greater opportunity to flourish than in the other two social climates. In a directive climate, adults are in control and children have limited opportunities to interact with either people or materials. In a laissez-faire climate, children are largely on their own and, while some children thrive, others are apt to feel lost or controlled by their more outgoing peers. In a supportive climate, adults strive to support each child's initiatives so that the child gains a sense of self-control and competence. Since children are permitted to make and then discuss choices and decisions that affect themselves and the people around them, they develop a sense of their own powers and their own limits. Very early on, they come to understand that they do not have to wait for things to happen to them — they can make things happen themselves.

Strategies for Creating Supportive Climates: Six Key Elements

By using six key elements of support as guidelines for working with children, adults create supportive climates that encourage the development of young children's capacities for trust, autonomy, initiative, empathy, and self-confidence. In the HighScope Curriculum, these elements come into play throughout the day whenever adults and children are interacting. The elements of support are the following:

- Sharing of control between adults and children
- Focusing on children's strengths
- Forming authentic relationships with children
- Making a commitment to supporting children's play
- Using encouragement instead of praise
- Adopting a problem-solving approach to social conflict

Adults can establish a supportive climate by incorporating these elements of support into any setting, program, or activity they share with children — homes, home visits, classrooms, child care centers, before- and after-school settings, recreation centers, playgrounds, field trips, and other outings. The following sections provide specific strategies adults can use to establish and maintain a supportive learning climate.

Sharing of control between adults and children

Sharing of control in a supportive climate calls for *reciprocity* — a mutual give-and-take between children and adults. In their interactions with each other, both children and adults take turns being leader and follower, teacher and learner, speaker and listener. Adults can share control with children by adopting the following four strategies:

Take cues from children

Following children's cues in play and conversation gives children the opportunity to express their own ideas and follow through on them in the company of an attentive, cooperative adult partner — someone who can assist them without taking control of the experience or diverting them from their original quest. Here are three examples of adults sharing control by taking cues from children:

Gwen, an infant lying on her back and looking up at her mom, starts to make clicking noises with her tongue. When she stops, her mother answers, making clicking noises with her tongue. Now it is Gwen's turn again, and so forth. The dialogue continues until Gwen turns away, directing her attention to a little green rattle she can just reach with her hand.

Manuel, a toddler, wants to help with a grown-up task — carrying water to the water table. "Me help. Me do it," he says, tugging at the full water bucket Mrs. Alvarez is carrying. She puts the bucket down, but it is so heavy Manuel cannot get it to budge. His eyes fill with tears.

"Manuel," she says. "You could pull the bucket in the wagon." Manuel's face brightens. He gets the wagon, they lift the bucket in together, and Manuel pulls the wagon with the bucket in it to the water table. Together they empty the bucket. "Again," Manuel says, as he heads back to the sink with his wagon and bucket.

Kimi and Reggie are the snack helpers for the day at their preschool. They bring juice, bananas, cups, and napkins to the children at the snack table. "Wait a minute," Reggie says, "These bananas can be telephones!" Reggie has caught the group's attention, but they don't quite understand what to do. Observing the children's confusion, Ruth, Reggie's teacher, puts her banana "phone" up to her ear. "Ring, ring. Hello, Ruth!" Reggie says into his banana phone, happy that someone understands his idea. "You want some juice?"

"Yes, please, and a cup too," she responds.

"Okay," he answers. While Reggie gives his teacher the juice and a cup, Kimi calls Midori. The process continues until everyone is served.

Participate with children on children's terms

Adults are open to children's intentions, feelings, and ideas. To become partners with children, adults set aside the vision of themselves as all

Cheese! Putting herself in children's hands, a teacher enjoys taking part in a pretend trip.

powerful and all knowing. As partners, they share in children's interests, delights, and creative urges. To capture and build on children's natural enthusiasms, adults put themselves in children's hands as often as possible. They follow children's directions, willingly assume the pretend roles assigned to them by children ("Your leg is broken, but I'm the doctor so I'll fix it"), and play games according to the children's rules.

Learn from children

Clearly, active learning is not a one-way street. In a climate of shared control, adults and children alike are both learners and teachers. Adults learn a lot from children's choices, behaviors, reactions, emotions, and attitudes.

For example, Mrs. Kim spent an evening learning a new computer program that involved driving a car around a town. The next day, with some anxiety, she showed a group of children what she had learned. "Let me do that," said Jason, sitting at the screen and in just a few minutes mastering the technique that had taken Mrs. Kim all evening to learn. As she watched and admired Jason's ease, she decided to try to approach the next new computer program with the same eagerness and lack of worry that Jason had exhibited.

Children can also teach adults about basic human needs. When a home day-care provider's four-year-old daughter became angry because the other children had gotten into her private things, the mother and daughter talked about what had happened. After the mother had done all she felt she could, she left her daughter, who was still somewhat upset, and went into another room. The next thing she knew, there was her daughter, saying "You can't leave me just because I'm angry." "You're right about that," her mom agreed. She remembered this experience every time one of the children in her care was angry or upset and she was tempted to walk away before the issue was resolved.

Relinquish control, consciously giving control to children

In the eyes of young children, adults are big and powerful. While there are times that call for the judicious use of this power (for example, to set and maintain reasonable limits so that children can feel safe and secure), there are also times when adults should relinquish power so that children may experience the impact and potency of their own ideas and intuitions.

Adults give control to children in conversation, for example, when they follow each *contribution* from a child with a contribution of their own or an *acknowledgment* of what the child said, rather than with a question. Most of the time when an adult asks a question, the adult retains control of the conversation because the question itself often shapes or limits the child's response. When the adult responds instead with a contribution or an acknowledgment, the child retains control of the conversation because the child is able to direct the conversation toward his or her particular interests. Consider the conversation between Karla and her teacher discussed in the previous chapter (pp. 44–45). Karla was unable to make a play dough ball bounce. Here is some more of their conversation:

Karla: It doesn't bounce!

Teacher: I see. It doesn't bounce. *(Acknowledgment)*

Karla: It sticks to the floor. It's…it's…it's flat!

Teacher: When you throw it, it doesn't bounce. It sticks to the floor and it's flat. *(Acknowledgment)*

Karla: I'm going to make another one, a very round one, because this one won't even work.

Teacher: Okay, I'll watch you make a very round one. I'm glad I came over to see what you were doing. *(Contribution)*

While many opportunities for children and adults to share control arise spontaneously throughout the day, adults can also plan some control-sharing activities. For example, at planning time (the time of day when each child decides what to do next), Miss Ricks started out the year by having each child relate their plans to her. Once the children had become very comfortable with the process of planning, Miss Ricks realized that they could ask one another about their plans. So, occasionally, the children took turns replacing Miss Ricks as the solicitor of plans. At other times, she had the children form pairs and discuss their plans with their partners. While Miss Ricks also participated in this activity by being one child's planning partner and by joining any other pair that needed her, the children shared the responsibility for listening to and acknowledging one another's plans.

Sharing control is clearly a complicated matter. Psychologist Urie Bronfenbrenner (1979) believes that as children develop in a supportive climate, the balance of power between them and the significant adults in their lives gradually shifts, with children taking increasing control of their own actions. "Learning and development are facilitated by the participation of the developing person in progressively more complex patterns of reciprocal activity with someone with whom that person has developed a strong and enduring emotional attachment and when the balance of power gradually shifts in favor of the developing person" (p. 60). Our goal is to empower children by giving them as much support and control as possible at each stage of their lives.

Focusing on children's strengths

Because learning occurs best when children are motivated by personal goals and interests, adults can create a supportive climate by discovering and building on children's interests, talents, capacities, and abilities. They start by observing young children in action so that they can capitalize on children's natural desires and interests. This contrasts with approaches in which adults look for children's weaknesses and prescribe activities designed to correct them. Generally, in such deficit-based approaches, adults must motivate children to do things they have no desire to do.

Children are more motivated to try new things when adults encourage them to follow their interests.

The more adults try to pressure children into action, the more defensive and anxious children become. By focusing on children's strengths, however, adults do not have to motivate children; the children have already motivated themselves. Discussed next are several strategies adults can use to focus effectively on children's strengths.

Look for children's interests

When adults seek out and support children's interests, children are free to follow through on activities they are already highly motivated to pursue. They are also willing to try new things that build on what they are already doing. Consider Greg, for example. He loves to play with trucks. At first glance, he seems to be doing the same thing over and over again. By watching and listening, however, the adults in his child care center discover that his repertoire of truck sounds is growing steadily and becoming increasingly elaborate. His pretend trucks have five gears, and the sounds he makes for each gear as the truck negotiates a "really steep grade" are astonishingly distinct and realistic. The adults conclude that Greg really enjoys making noises because he is so good at distinguishing and imitating sounds. This prompts them to add a music area to their child care center, in which Greg becomes very interested. He often makes up his own songs on the xylophone about trucks and "long hauls."

View situations from the child's perspective

Sometimes adults have a tendency to view children's strengths with mixed emotions because children's newfound enthusiasms can mean extra work for adults. It makes sense to look at these situations from the child's point of view, however, because the feelings of success the child gets from attempting a new activity are more important in the long run than any short-term inconvenience to adults.

Jalessa, for example, is attempting to spoon tomato soup into her mouth, but soup is dribbling down her arm and onto the floor. Mrs. Dalgato, her child care provider, could express irritation because of the mess Jalessa is making. Instead, because she knows that Jalessa's intention is to feed herself rather than make a mess, Mrs. Dalgato chooses to focus on Jalessa's newfound skill. She watches and smiles as Jalessa continues. "Look at Jalessa," her older brother, Freeman, exclaims, "she's using a spoon just like us big kids!" "Yes, she is," says Mrs. Dalgato. "She's eating her soup with a spoon all by herself." She makes a note to share this new accomplishment with Jalessa and Freeman's dad when he picks them up after work.

Share children's interests with parents and staff

The principle of attending to children's strengths and interests rather than their deficits also extends to interactions with colleagues and parents. When adults who work with children focus on all the things children cannot do or do not do very well, children and their parents often become defensive and discouraged. On the other hand, when adults focus on children's strengths, children feel successful and parents see their children as able individuals.

For example, consider Mrs. Hagen, the mother of very active twin boys. She is used to having other adults tell her what a handful the twins are, so she tries to keep a low profile when she comes to pick them up from preschool. Today, Justin and Jerome are happily digging in the sandbox when their mom arrives. Even so, when their teacher comes over to talk with her, Mrs. Hagen has a sinking feeling. "I'm so glad you're here," their teacher begins. "Justin and Jerome had such a busy work time this morning. They used boxes to make a robot and then made a house for the robot in the block area. Several other children saw what they were doing and asked Jerome and Justin to help them make robots too. They were very patient as they worked with the other children. Pretty soon we had four robots in the block area!" Mrs. Hagen is relieved, grateful, and heartened to have someone else recognize and encourage the best in her boys. "Thank you," she says. "I have some boxes in the basement they might like to use when they get home."

Plan around children's strengths and interests

Most educators and adults who care for children believe that each child is unique and, consequently, they strive to individualize or differentiate their teaching approach for each child. Since children's strengths and interests are tangible manifestations of their uniqueness, focusing on children's strengths is a key to individualization in the HighScope Curriculum. Teachers scaffold (support and gently extend) children's learning based on their interests, individual abilities, and levels of development. In daily adult planning sessions, for example, the question "What do we want to plan for Vanessa tomorrow?" is coupled with a discussion about what Vanessa was engaged in today: "Today, Vanessa took all the big farm animals off the shelf and stood them up around herself with all the heads facing toward her. But as soon as some other children came to the block area, she put all the animals away and went to the toy area. She played there for the rest of work time, making similar arrangements with the little plastic animals, sometimes making them face inward and sometimes outward. Maybe we could build on her interest in arranging and positioning animals and support her need for her own work space tomorrow by using the little plastic animals at small-group time."

Forming authentic relationships with children

Adults, like children, have strengths and interests. In a supportive climate, adults' unique capacities and enthusiasms enrich and enliven their interactions with children, laying the foundations for authentic relationships that allow honest, effective teaching and learning to occur. According to psychologist Carl Rogers (1983), authenticity is "a transparent realness in the facilitator, a willingness to be a person,

This adult's natural enthusiasm and authentic reactions to classroom situations help children see her as a partner in their explorations and discoveries.

to be and live the feelings and thoughts of the moment. When this realness includes a prizing, a caring, a trust, a respect for the learner, the climate for learning is enhanced. When it includes a sensitive and accurate empathic listening, then indeed a freeing climate, stimulative of self-initiated learning and growth, exists. The student is *trusted* to develop" (p. 133).

Since teaching and learning are social, interactive processes, it is imperative that adults share their best, most genuine selves so that their effect on children is positive and sustained. The immediate experience of the reciprocity and mutual respect inherent in authentic relationships supports and encourages **trust** ("I know Mrs. Finch is going to give me time to answer. I know she'll listen to me when I speak"); **autonomy** ("I can do it on my own because I know she'll be there to help if I need it"); **initiative** ("I can go up to Mrs. Finch and talk to her or show her something because she's interested in what I say and do"); **empathy** ("Jimmy likes to swing; so do I"); and **self-confidence** ("What I have to say is important because the people at my table listen to me"). The memories of such relationships continue to guide children long after they have moved on to other relationships with adults and peers in other learning settings.

Since no prescribed set of behaviors will work for every adult and child, each adult improvises — bringing everything she or he knows into each interaction. In the following section we describe some effective strategies that will guide adults toward authenticity.

Share yourself with children

Adults working with children in a climate of support encourage and respect children's motivation to pursue their interests. They also draw upon their own interests. A visitor to one child care center was astonished by a group of two-year-olds who sang songs together. "These little children sing so well. They're so involved they can't wait to suggest a new song! What's the secret?" he asked. "Why," answered the director, "it's simple. Mrs. Wiggens loves to sing. She sings every day with the children, so for them singing is the most natural thing in the world. With Mrs. Wiggens, even I can sing!"

Respond attentively to children's interests

Adults give children's interests their full attention out of the firm belief that what interests a child is the key to that child's learning: "Look what I found!" says Eddie, holding up a brilliant green leaf. "Well, look at that," says Mrs. Smith, squatting down to take a closer look, "there's a drop of water sliding around on it." "Where?" asks Eddie, bending very close to the leaf. "Oh, yeah. Here, let me hold it so it won't slide off. Hey, Willie, look what I got here. Look, a water drop."

Give children specific feedback

Adults speak in their own voices, sharing their own observations, laughter, and surprise: "Look at how far your airplane flew this time, Teri! I had no idea that adding one paper clip could make such a difference." They also share their honest puzzlement: "I don't know what's making the door squeak so much, Ellie. Let's take a look at it."

Adults listen very carefully and patiently, never knowing what a child will say until the child says it, or how they will respond until the child has finished: "This is my song," Sylvie says, handing Miss James a paper full of pencil marks. Without saying anything, Miss James squats down so that her head is level with Sylvie's. Holding the paper so they can both see it, she studies Sylvie's song. "See," says Sylvie, pointing to a mark in the

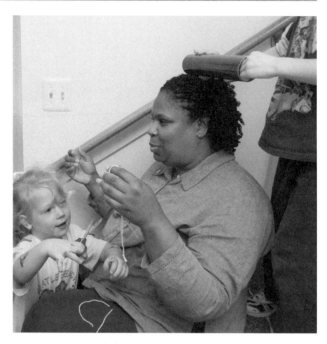

Responding to children's interests, a teacher gets her hair done in a pretend beauty shop. One "stylist" (the boy behind her) is curling her hair with a big "roller," while the other is cutting yarn to make hair bows.

middle of the paper, "it's about my dog. Here's where he's running very fast. Don't go in the road, little dog. The cars will hit you. Come back, come back! He runs to me and jumps and licks my face all over. You silly puppy. You stay with me. Stay right here. I will take care of you. Now let's sing it. Okay?" "Okay," Miss James agrees. "You start and I'll sing with you."

As Curry and Johnson (1990) remind us, "Authenticity and specificity in response to children should guide caregivers and teachers in their work with children. Honest feedback to specific behaviors helps children grow and change more than global comments such as 'good job'" (p. 3).

Adults look forward to personal conversations with children because they are unique and enjoyable. In a conversation with four-year-old Rudy about his magnet, Mr. Oser uses the words *repel* and *attract*. Rudy offers a much more graphic explanation: "Look what my magnet caught!" Mr. Oser responds using Rudy's terms. "Your magnet caught lots of nails, but my magnet isn't catching any of these toothpicks!" Through such dialogue focused on real interests and specific events, children and adults share opportunities to teach and learn. In this type of climate, children eventually develop the habit of sharing their interests with peers, as well as with adults:

Corey: We love mud, don't we Jeff!

Jeff: Yeah, we love mud.

Corey: It gets all over the place.

Jeff: I got some in my hair.

Corey: Me too. I got some on my shoe.

Jeff: I got some on both my shoes.

Ask honest questions and respond to questions honestly

When questions arise between people in authentic relationships, they are honest questions — questions, very simply, to which the person asking the question does not have the answer:

- "Where is the stapler, James? Tanika needs it to staple her crown together."
- "Teacher, how you do this?"
- "I have never seen a shell like this, Loretta. Where did you find it?"

Honest questions reflect the questioner's real interest in hearing the answer, whatever it might be.

Similarly, authenticity requires that adults respond honestly to children's honest questions:

Clarita: Miss James, why do you have that stuff up there on your eyes?

Miss James: This green eye shadow on my eyelids?

Clarita: Yeah, why do you put it up there?

Miss James: Well…because I like it. It makes my eyes look greener. And it's fun, like I'm going to a party.

Clarita: This isn't a party! This is…is…here!

Miss James: Well, I think being here with you is fun!

Clarita: Like a party?

Miss James: Yes, fun like a party with lots of people I like.

Clarita: I like Carter. He's my best friend.

There is no rush to answer honest questions. The asker pauses, waits patiently for a reply, and accepts the fact that sometimes there are no answers:

Miss James: Why did you put lots of colors on this side of your picture, LaRita, and no colors on this side?

LaRita: Because.

By being authentic with children in these ways, adults help children form their own authentic relationships with others.

Making a commitment to supporting children's play

When young children are free from illness, malnutrition, neglect, and abuse they turn their considerable energies to play. Play is pleasurable, spontaneous, creative, and unpredictable. Whether it is noisy or quiet, messy or orderly, silly or serious, strenuous or effortless, children find play deeply satisfying, challenging, enjoyable, and rewarding.

When adults are asked about their pleasant childhood memories, their minds often fill with images of play: jumping rope, playing hopscotch, making mud pies, climbing trees, feeding chickens, playing kick the can and hide and seek, picking grapes in the back garden, playing dress-up, having fun with the water hose, hiding under the drapes in the dining room. Adults remember play because it is an activity they had control over and that consequently had a strong impact on them. The learning that emerges from active involvement in play is probably one of the main reasons both children and adults keep coming back for more.

Children play out of the need to construct meaning from their lives. They need to use all their senses to find out about things: "What does this odd thing on my highchair tray taste like?

Complex play develops with adult support: First the teacher listens to and encourages the child to think through her plan to "make a ball" with the blocks. Then the child builds a dance floor (constructive play) and, with her friends and the teacher, dresses up and dances (dramatic play).

How does it feel, look, smell, sound? What will happen if I bang it or throw it on the floor?" Play is the way children explore what things do and how things work. It is also their way of making sense of personalities, social interactions, and the darker side of life: "You're dead. You can't move. We take you to the hospital and make you alive again. Now get in that ambulance, Joey."

Play in a supportive climate involves the **ingredients of active learning — materials** to play with and **manipulate**; **choices** about what, where, how, and with whom to play; **child thought and language** as they play; and **adult scaffolding** that ranges from setting up an environment for play to actually participating in it. When children play under these supportive conditions, they have many opportunities to be aware of others; to watch and imitate what others do; to be adventurous; to concentrate on things that interest them; to work near and with others; and to converse about what they are doing and feeling. Consequently, there are many opportunities for trust, autonomy, initiative, empathy, and self-confidence to flourish. In the section that follows we discuss ways adults act on their commitment to children's play in a supportive active learning setting.

Observe and understand the complexity of children's play

Since children communicate through play, it is important that adults commit themselves to learning the complex language of play. They can do this by watching and listening to children.

Adults who observe children carefully discover the many forms that play can take. Play develops in complexity as children themselves change and grow. Very young children engage in **exploratory play** — simple repetitive play experiences in which they explore the properties and functions of materials and tools, not for the purpose of making something, but simply for the pleasure of "doing it." This early play evolves into **constructive play,** the making of structures and creations, and **dramatic play,** in which children assume pretend roles and act out their own scenarios about people and animals. As they grow older, children begin to play **games with rules,** first playing by their own rather flexible rules and then by the strict rules set by the expert maker of the game. To effectively support children's play without disrupting it, adults must be able to distinguish among and accept a variety of play forms.

Be playful with children

"More [adults] need to be joyful and playful as they work with young children, ready to accept the unexpected connection or alternative with good humor and patience" (Fromberg, 1987, p. 60). Playful adults get down on the floor and build with blocks. They get "rescued" from the

---

The Other Side of Play

Sometimes children's play is disquieting. William, a shy four-year-old, is kneeling on the floor, stabbing a rubber doll in its stomach with a screwdriver. On one hand, his teacher would like to stop him because it is very painful to watch him play like this, and she doesn't want children to hurt others, even in play. On the other hand, he is playing, pretending — he isn't hurting anybody, or destroying the tough rubber doll, or interfering with other children. As he pretends, he seems to be expressing a side of himself that his shy, quiet manner generally obscures. As the teacher watches, another child comes over to William and recruits him to play with the construction tools at the workbench. William becomes completely absorbed in this new play activity with his friend. While the teacher is relieved that the direction of William's play has changed so easily and naturally, she also realizes that because William is so quiet she often overlooks him. Therefore, she resolves to observe William more carefully and to schedule a home visit, so that she can find out more about him from his mom. In this case, William's teacher has the feeling that perhaps his play is telling her much more about him than she could ever learn through more direct means.

"burning house" and rushed to the "hospital" in the "ambulance." They eat pine-cone soup and blast off in rocket ships. They tell and read stories, make up and sing songs, play catch, slide, climb, dig in the sandbox, play tag, and hide and seek. Some adults play quietly, others quite boisterously. Some love to sing, some to dance, some to play with glitter, some to make things that really work. Even adults who consider themselves to be serious people are quite able to participate in the intensity of children's play, once they give themselves permission and understand its value for children. Contradictory as it may seem, playing with children is something that adults in a supportive active learning climate do consciously, respectfully, seriously yet lightheartedly, and with great satisfaction. They play without teasing, belittling, or physical aggression. Teachers accept that sometimes children's play can be upsetting to adults, for example, as they work out troublesome situations at home or anxieties about the relationships at school. They understand that through play, adults are supporting the active learning process and children's spontaneous desire to learn.

Using encouragement instead of praise

Many adults use praise because they think it helps children feel good about themselves and their work, and inspires them to keep striving. They may also use praise as a behavior management tool, that is, to help children settle down and "act like good boys and girls." Psychologist Alfie Kohn (1993, 2001) crusades against using praise with children, because saying "good job" is manipulative, steals children's pleasure in accomplishment, makes children lose interest, creates *praise junkies* who are dependent upon receiving accolades for everything they do, and actually reduces rather than enhances children's achievement.

Research bears out these warnings. Studies show that praise can be damaging because extrinsic rewards decrease children's intrinsic motivation (Filcheck, McNeil, Greco, & Bernard, 2004). That is, using praise invites children to perform for external reinforcement rather than to embrace learning because it is self-rewarding. When adults use praise, children also learn to depend on adults to figure out what is right or wrong, instead of developing this ability themselves. Children may become afraid to try something new for fear they will not be complimented, or worse, that they will be criticized for doing something incorrectly. Some children may even come to view the absence of praise as criticism.

HighScope has long trained teachers to use **encouragement** instead of praise, a practice now increasingly advocated among early childhood practitioners (Copple & Bredekamp, 2009). By encouraging children, adults acknowledge their efforts and accomplishments. The focus is on children's actions and what they are learning, not on whether the children have pleased the adult. Try using the strategies listed below to encourage rather than praise young children.

Participate in children's play

Joining in children's play is a form of encouragement because it lets the children know their activities and ideas are important and meaningful. It also provides opportunities for the adults to introduce new experiences and expand on children's knowledge and skills. Consider this example:

Ellen, a teacher, sits at a table in the house area where several children are playing "restaurant." She asks what is on the menu and they reply, "We're cooking soup." Ellen wonders if they can make "tomato and rice soup." The children put red blocks and Styrofoam pellets in a pan, stir it up, and dish it out in a bowl. Ellen pretends to eat it and says she'd like some crackers to dunk in her soup. One of the children cuts pieces of construction paper to use as crackers. Soon other children sit at the table and ask for different types of soup, including "chicken noodle" and "monster chunk." The cooks use materials from all over the classroom to respond to these requests. When the table is full of customers, one child gets a notepad and asks the teacher for help writing down the type of soup each person wants.

In this example, the teacher could have said, "Yum, you cook good soup" when she sat down. If she had, the pretend play probably would not have taken off in so many creative directions. But by entering fully into the children's play, the teacher inspired the children's problem solving, involved others in the role play, and created an opportunity to develop literacy and social skills.

Encourage children to describe their efforts, ideas, and products

Instead of telling children that they have done a "good job" or made something "beautiful," make specific comments that encourage them to talk about what they are doing, how they are doing it, and anything else about the process that is important to them. Focus on the child's actions, not just the end result. For example, rather than saying to a child "That's a lovely painting," you might point to it and say, "I wonder how you made all the layers of color in this corner." Such a statement shows that you are interested and encourages the child to reflect on and describe what he or she did. It also leads to a natural conversation about the activity and helps you to build an authentic relationship with the child.

Repeat and restate children's words

By repeating and restating what children say, you let the children know you're truly listening and that you acknowledge their activities and efforts. These strategies can also help you clarify what a child has said, create opportunities to introduce new words, and rephrase or model the pronunciation of words children are just learning. It also prevents you from asking too many questions. Consider the following example:

Armondo, the teacher, observes Linda using the stapler and paper in the art area. Linda says, "It won't work. The 'tapler is broke." Armondo replies, "The stapler is broken?" Linda nods her head yes. She has heard the correct pronunciation and grammar without being corrected. Meanwhile, Armondo has clarified what the problem is with the material.

(For more information on building self-confidence by authentically supporting children's emerging competence rather than offering praise, see the discussion of KDI 8. Sense of competence in the companion book *Social and Emotional Development,* Epstein, 2012g.)

Adopting a problem-solving approach to social conflict

The problem-solving approach to social conflict is a long-term strategy supportive adults use with children from toddlerhood through high school graduation. As children grow in their ability to anticipate and resolve social conflicts, the conflicts they must confront become increasingly complex. However, when children practice resolving social conflicts from an early age, by the time they reach adulthood they have many of the social skills they need, the habit of using them, and the confidence gained from their years of experience and support. To help children develop these skills, use the strategies suggested below.

Approach social conflicts matter-of-factly, firmly, and patiently

In the course of children's play, conflicts arise — Jenni has the piece of wood that Tanya wants, Lyle and Hank come to blows because they both want to pretend to be the dad, and Vanessa hits anyone who invades her territory. In a supportive climate, adults know that children's desires are bound to conflict and that incidents like these are natural occurrences. They regard conflict situations as opportunities for children to develop skills in social problem solving. Although children's conflicts with peers can be annoying, adults focus their energies on enabling children to resolve the issues at hand rather than on punishing children for their immature social skills.

A problem-solving conversation happens as children get ready for a pretend play episode. The children have established that the boy dressed in a suit and construction hat will be the dad, and the teacher (wearing a "backpack") will be a child just home from school. Both girls want to be the mom. The solution they arrive at is to have two moms, one a stepmom.

Use a six-step process to help children learn how to resolve social conflicts

When social conflicts arise, what guides adults? In the supportive climate of an active learning setting — in which adults are accepting, attentive, playful, and authentic — adults use a problem-solving process to help children resolve conflicts and become more aware of themselves as capable problem solvers. This process can be broken down into the six problem-solving steps listed at right, which were developed by HighScope conflict resolution consultant Betsy Evans (2002). The steps/strategies are summarized next, illustrated with an extended example of a preschool conflict.

> **Steps in Resolving Conflicts With Preschoolers**
>
> 1. Approach calmly, stopping any hurtful actions.
> 2. Acknowledge children's feelings.
> 3. Gather information.
> 4. Restate the problem.
> 5. Ask for ideas for solutions and choose one together.
> 6. Be prepared to give follow-up support.

Approach social conflicts calmly (step 1) and acknowledge children's feelings (step 2). Adults calmly stop hurtful behavior and acknowledge children's feelings so children can let go of their emotions and clear the decks for identifying and solving the problem.

Adult: *(Kneels between Lyle and Hank with an arm around each one.)* You look angry, Lyle, and Hank, you seem really upset. *(The boys nod in agreement.)*

Gather information (step 3) and restate the problem (step 4). It is important to hear both sides of the dispute without taking sides so each child's position is heard and acknowledged.

Adult: What's the problem?

Lyle: I want to be the dad. I said so first.

Hank: Well, you're always the dad. I want to be big.

Lyle: I'm the biggest, so huh! You can't be the dad. You're too little.

Adult: So the problem is, Lyle, you want to be the dad, and Hank, *you* want to be the dad. *(Both boys nod in agreement.)*

Ask for ideas for solutions and choose one together (step 5); be prepared to give follow-up support (step 6).

Adult: What can we do to solve this problem? *(The boys look at her, thinking.)*

Lyle: I could be the dad today, and then you can be the dad the next day.

Hank: Well, I could be the dad today!

Adult: It sounds like you both want to be the dad today.

Lyle: We don't need two dads....Hank, you could be the ladder guy *and* wear the tool belt!

Hank: And the gloves!

Lyle: Okay, the gloves. *(Both boys look pleased.)*

Adult: So, Lyle, you're going to be the dad, and Hank, you're going to be the ladder guy who wears the tool belt and the gloves. *(The boys nod yes. The adult watches them get started and checks in with them as the ladder guy and dad build a "swamp boat.")*

Curry and Johnson (1990), point out that this problem-solving process puts children in control. "THEY agree on the situation, THEY figure out what to do about it, and THEY choose what happens next. Mastery and autonomy are developed here!" (p. 117). Note that the steps in problem solving are not only a connected sequence, as in the example of Hank and Lyle, but also a set of distinct strategies that, like a box of tools, may be used singly or in any combination.

Finding alternatives to hurtful behavior, naming feelings, and thinking of solutions are not easy things to do, especially for young children who live in the present and often see things from their own point of view. Children need many real-life experiences in working through conflicts with peers and much ongoing support from adults to develop the capacity to anticipate and deal effectively with the conflicts they encounter. Given the opportunity to practice working through social conflict in a supportive climate, however, children learn to trust themselves as problem solvers, to trust adults to assist them when they need it, to be empathic and helpful to others, and to have faith in their individual and collective capacities to make relationships work. The scenario "Uh-Oh, Rachel, I'm Telling on You!" on page 83 illustrates how problems become problem-solving opportunities in a supportive setting. (For further discussion of how children develop social problem-solving skills, and how adults support this aspect of social development, see the discussion of KDI 15. Conflict resolution in the companion book *Social and Emotional Development,* Epstein, 2012g.)

These, then, are the six key elements of supportive climates — sharing of control, focusing on children's strengths, forming authentic relationships, making a commitment to supporting children's play, using encouragement instead of praise, and adopting a problem-solving approach

Resolving a conflict: The teacher places herself between two fighting children (top left) to keep them from getting hurt. She acknowledges both children's feelings (top right and bottom left) and listens carefully as they each talk about the problem.

Later, even though a solution has been agreed to, this child needs further support. The teacher acknowledges his feelings again, and they discuss the problem until he is comfortable returning to his play.

Uh-Oh, Rachel, I'm Telling on You!

Rachel is carrying two jars of paint from the easel to the art table, where she is painting a boat she made at the workbench. She very carefully sets both jars down, but one is so close to the table's edge that it tips over, spilling red paint on Brandon's tennis shoes.

Billy, who is making a walkie-talkie, sounds the alarm. "Uh-oh! Look what Rachel did! Paint on Brandon's shoes. It looks like blood! Brandon, your momma's going to give you a spanking!"

Brandon bursts into tears, and Rachel hides under the table.

Mrs. Williams takes in the situation as she looks up from the house area. She walks over to the art table. "Brandon, what's the matter?" she asks.

"Billy says my momma's going to give me a spanking…because of my shoes.…It's like blood."

"Nobody's spanking me!" Rachel yells out from under the table.

"Nobody's getting a spanking," Mrs. Williams says calmly, "but it looks like there's some red paint to clean up."

"I could use the mop like I did that other day," answers Rachel, coming out from under the table.

"You could use the mop," answers Mrs. Williams. (Rachel leaves to get the sponge mop.) "What about your tennis shoes, Brandon?"

"My momma washed them in the sink when me and Jimmy played in the mud!"

"You could wash them in the sink like your momma does," Mrs. Williams says.

"Then they'll be all wet!" Rachel cries.

"I know. Put them in the sun," answers Billy. "That's what my grandma does!"

"My mom put them in the dryer," Brandon chimes in. "They made a funny noise…like thumping!" (He takes off his shoes and turns on the cold water.)

---

to social conflict. When these elements are in place, a supportive climate prevails, enabling children to grow in trust, autonomy, initiative, empathy, and self-confidence.

Using the elements of support: Moving a group of children from place to place guided by the key elements of support

Adults can use the elements of support to help shape their interactions with children and deal with many kinds of interpersonal situations positively and supportively. Here is an example of how adults use the elements of support as a framework for planning a transition experience for children.

Most adults working with groups of young children face the task of getting them safely and smoothly from one place to another. In some programs, the task of moving children takes on major importance because of the physical layout of the setting — for example, the playground is on the opposite side of the building, or the bathroom or lunchroom is down the hallway. In programs housed in more child-oriented buildings, adults face the same issue whenever they leave the building for a walk or field trip. Lining children up and having them travel single file often seems, at first glance, to be the most efficient way to handle such problems. However, since establishing and maintaining a quiet, orderly line of young children generally requires waiting on the part of children and constant adult vigilance, traveling in such a manner can quickly become a negative experience for everyone involved. By considering ways to incorporate the elements of support into the situation, however, adults can come up with some positive alternatives.

Sharing control. As much as we might think that young children ought to be able to walk in a line without talking or "bothering their neighbors," they usually show little natural inclination to do this, so if the adults choose this way of moving the group, the activity is by necessity adult-controlled. How then can adults shift the climate into a supportive one where adults and children share control? One strategy is to establish anchor points. For example, on a walk, placing one adult (or a designated child leader) at the starting point and one at the destination permits children to walk singly, with a friend, with several peers, or near an adult, as long as they stay on the path between the two adults or designated anchors. When the only sink available for hand washing is down the hall and around the corner, one adult can station herself in the bathroom while the other remains in the classroom sending and receiving small groups of travelers. What generally happens in anchored situations is that once adults shift some of the control back to children, children move quite appropriately from anchor to anchor. They know what is expected of them and enjoy the challenge of venturing between the two points on their own.

Focusing on strengths. Expecting children to line up and move silently in single file for any length of time is a policy that cannot help but highlight children's weaknesses. How can we approach the same situation with a focus on children's strengths? A good starting point is to think about what children like to do and do well. For example, they may be eager to play outside, even though it is quite a walk through and around the building to get there. They may enjoy carrying things. What if, then, they were to take things outside to play with, carrying things both singly and in pairs? This way, the journey from classroom to playground could focus on what they *can* do rather than on what they are not very good at.

Forming authentic relationships. Generally, the intent of silent lines is to prevent interactions both among the travelers themselves and between the travelers and the environments they are passing through. One way to shift toward authenticity is to think of traveling from place to place as a leisurely walk taken for pleasure and an opportunity to enjoy time with friends and acquaintances. The walk then becomes a time to chat, to notice things along the way, to stop in and say hello to neighbors. One preschool class, for example, frequently paused at the door of a neighboring class to see what they were doing and say hello. Another stopped at "Grandma Norton's" to look at her flowers and greet her if she was out on her porch or in the yard. (Once she knew their schedule, she almost always managed to be outside to greet them!) Traveling can be more than a means to an end. It can become a pleasant and rewarding process in itself, particularly for children who feel somewhat inhibited by the more formal atmosphere of the center or classroom. For these children, traveling can become a time for relaxation and intimacy.

Making a commitment to supporting children's play. A regimented line leaves no room for play. In fact, playful children in lines are generally reprimanded. How can adults shift from strict regimentation toward play, yet still provide limits within which children will be safe and secure and not disrupt others? One way to do this is to move in playful ways with anchors at either end — as a train; in wagons with some riders and some pullers; walking, holding streamers or scarves; as stealthy cats; wearing special traveling hats; not stepping on any lines or cracks; and so on. Children who are energetically focused on playful ways of moving are fun to travel with and require far fewer reprimands.

Using encouragement instead of praise. The adventure of traveling from place to place — even if it is just to see what's down the hall — is inherently interesting to young children. They don't need the promise of a reward at the end. However, adults may be concerned about maintaining standards for proper behavior on the way to the destination. They may reinforce their standards by praising children who move in a quiet and orderly manner with comments such as "I like the way you're walking." The qualities being praised — walking in a line, not talking — hold little value for children. If they stop or diverge from the path to examine something or talk excitedly about where they are going, they will not be praised and may in fact be criticized for their natural exuberance and interest. This makes going from place to place a time to please adults, instead

Walking "octopus style" along a busy street, with strings of children and adults holding hands to form the tentacles, is a safe alternative to walking in a line. How are the elements of support at work here?

of a potential learning opportunity for children. Instead, adults can encourage children to proceed from place to place by sharing their interests along the way ("I wonder what flowers will be blooming at Grandma Norton's today"), talking about where they are going ("We got new soap in the bathroom dispenser. What do you think it will smell like?"), and joining in the fun of the journey (e.g., encouraging children to walk in interesting ways and imitating their movements).

Adopting a problem-solving approach to social conflict. With encouragement, children themselves can think of ways to travel safely from place; when children are included in solving the problem, they are more committed to making the solution work. Mrs. Brads tried this at large-group time:

Mrs. Brads: Today is our day to use the gym.

Willis: Yippee!

Mrs. Brads: You like going to the gym, Willis.

Various other children: I do.... Me too.... So do I.... I really, *really* like it.... It's my best thing.

Mrs. Brads: Lots of people like to go to the gym.

Katie: My daddy goes to the gym. He has very strong muscles.

Mrs. Brads: We can all have very strong muscles if we use them. Now, here's a problem. How can we get to the gym safely and quietly?

Sarah: Walk on our tippy toes. *(She demonstrates.)*

Joey: Crawl like a puppy and just make a tiny noise like this. *(He yips very softly.)*

Beth: I want to be a kitty.

Mrs. Brads: Okay. Let's try those ideas. Mrs. Hines will go first, and I'll be last. You can tiptoe or crawl like a puppy or kitty. *(Mrs. Hines tiptoes to* *the door and everyone follows her either on tiptoes or their knees. Mrs. Brads crawls part way down the hall and then switches to tiptoeing.)*

Moving as a group from place to place can be viewed as a problem or it can be viewed as an appropriate opportunity for group problem solving. The choice is yours.

How the elements of support relate to the rest of the curriculum

The elements of support are guidelines adults use to establish and maintain supportive climates in which children generate and construct their own understanding and learning. Therefore, these key elements influence the implementation of every other aspect of the curriculum. In the next chapter, for example, we explore how the principles of sharing control, focusing on strengths, and creating authentic relationships relate to involving families in active learning settings. Similarly, the strategies for enhancing adult teamwork discussed in chapter 4 are built on the premise that adult teams work most effectively in a supportive climate. Authentic child and program assessment, covered in chapter 5, depends on observing children and teachers in natural environments instead of imposing artificial situations and standards to judge their performance. Chapter 6, which focuses on arranging and equipping an active learning setting, examines ways adults can share control of physical space with children so that children can find, use, and return the materials they need. Through the daily routine and the plan-do-review process, discussed in chapters 7, 8, and 9, children have numerous opportunities to initiate ideas and share control over teaching and learning. And finally, the HighScope key developmental indicators (KDIs), discussed in chapter 10 and the eight KDI companion books (Epstein, 2012a–h), provide adults with a clearer understanding of the general kinds of abilities and interests typical of young children, so that adults can accurately interpret and build on them. Thus, together with the ingredients of active learning, the elements of support provide a guiding framework for the discussion of the HighScope Curriculum that unfolds in the following pages.

How the elements of support relate to program quality

The elements of adult-child support, together with the other distinctive features of the HighScope Curriculum, comprise a comprehensive model of early childhood program quality. Programs striving to monitor and improve their quality often use a quality rating and improvement system (QRIS), such as the Classroom Assessment Scoring System (CLASS; Hamre & Pianta, 2007) to measure the extent to which these interrelated elements are present in the classroom. The CLASS framework examines how teachers establish an educational environment and interact with students in three broad domains: emotional support, classroom organization (management), and instructional support. Like the CLASS, the HighScope Curriculum and the Program Quality Assessment (PQA; HighScope Educational Research Foundation, 2003a; see chapter 5) recognize that children's learning depends on the comprehensive and effective integration of all these classroom elements. Thus, in addition to the specific adult-child support strategies described in this chapter, HighScope provides teachers with an overall philosophy of active learning and the comprehensive set of curriculum components described in this nine-book set. When teachers build their interactions with children around these HighScope components, they can also achieve the multiple dimensions of quality reflected in comprehensive evaluation tools such as the CLASS. (See the chart on pp. 88–89 to see how elements of the CLASS relate to the HighScope Curriculum.)

Adult-Child Interaction Strategies for Creating Supportive Climates: A Summary

Sharing of control between adults and children
- Adults take cues from children.
- Adults participate with children on children's terms.
- Adults learn from children.
- Adults relinquish control, consciously giving control to children.

Focusing on children's strengths
- Adults look for children's interests.
- Adults view situations from the child's perspective.
- Adults share children's interests with parents and staff.
- Adults plan around children's strengths and interests.

Forming authentic relationships with children
- Adults share themselves with children.
- Adults respond attentively to children's interests.
- Adults give children specific feedback.
- Adults ask honest questions and respond to questions honestly.

Making a commitment to supporting children's play
- Adults observe and understand the complexity of children's play.
- Adults are playful with children.

Using encouragement instead of praise
- Adults participate in children's play.
- Adults encourage children to describe their efforts, ideas, and products.
- Adults repeat and restate children's words.

Adopting a problem-solving approach to social conflict
- Adults approach social conflicts matter-of-factly, firmly, and patiently.
- Adults use a six-step process to help children learn how to resolve social conflicts.

The Relationship Between the CLASS Framework and the HighScope Curriculum

CLASS Areas and Dimensions	HighScope Curriculum Components				
	Adult-Child Interaction	Active Learning	Learning Environment	Daily Routine	Key Developmental Indicators
Emotional Support					
Positive climate	Focus on strengths Authentic relationships Encouragement instead of praise			Varied social interactions Appropriate settings	Approaches to Learning Physical Development & Health Social & Emotional Development Social Studies
Negative climate[1]	Focus on strengths Authentic relationships Encouragement instead of praise			Varied social interactions Appropriate settings	Approaches to Learning Physical Development & Health Social & Emotional Development Social Studies
Teacher sensitivity	Focus on strengths Encouragement instead of praise		Providing materials	Varied learning experiences Consistency & predictability Smooth transitions	Social & Emotional Development
Regard for student perspectives	Shared control Authentic relationships Supporting play	Choice Child language & thought	Providing materials	Varied learning experiences	Approaches to Learning Social Studies
Classroom Organization					
Behavior management	Conflict resolution		Organizing space	Varied social interactions Consistency & predictability Appropriate settings Smooth transitions	Social & Emotional Development
Productivity		Materials Manipulation Choice	Organizing space Establishing interest areas Providing materials	Varied learning experiences Consistency & predictability	Approaches to Learning
Instructional learning formats	Supporting play	Materials Manipulation Choice	Establishing interest areas	Varied social interactions Appropriate settings	Approaches to Learning

[1] HighScope Curriculum components aim to avoid a negative climate.

CLASS Areas and Dimensions	HighScope Curriculum Components				
	Adult-Child Interaction	Active Learning	Learning Environment	Daily Routine	Key Developmental Indicators
Classroom Organization (cont.)					
Classroom chaos[2]	Shared control Conflict resolution		Organizing space Establishing interest areas	Varied learning experiences Consistency & predictability Appropriate settings Smooth transitions	Social & Emotional Development Social Studies
Classroom management	Shared control Conflict resolution		Organizing space Establishing interest areas	Varied learning experiences Consistency & predictability Appropriate settings Smooth transitions	Social & Emotional Development Social Studies
Child responsibility	Shared control	Choice Child language & thought	Organizing space	Varied social interactions Varied learning experiences Smooth transitions	Approaches to Learning Social & Emotional Development
Instructional Support					
Concept development	Supporting play	Child language & thought Adult scaffolding	Organizing space Establishing interest areas Providing materials	Varied learning experiences	All key developmental indicators
Quality of feedback	Focus on strengths	Adult scaffolding		Varied learning experiences	All key developmental indicators
Language modeling		Adult scaffolding		Varied social interactions	Language, Literacy, & Communication
Instructional conversation	Shared control Authentic relationships	Child language & thought Adult scaffolding		Varied learning experiences Varied social interactions	Language, Literacy, & Communication Mathematics Creative Arts Science & Technology Social Studies
Literacy instruction		Child language & thought Adult scaffolding		Varied social interactions	Language, Literacy, & Communication
Richness of instructional methods	Supporting play	Adult scaffolding	Providing materials	Varied social interactions Varied learning experiences Appropriate settings	All key developmental indicators

---

[2] HighScope Curriculum components aim to prevent or reverse classroom chaos.

CHAPTER 3

Involving Families in Active Learning Settings

The Benefits of Family Involvement

Research repeatedly shows that family involvement is critical to children's overall development and success in school. For example, the Head Start Family and Child Experiences Survey (US Department of Health and Human Services, 2003) found that parent involvement was associated with many positive academic and social outcomes for children. Academically, children whose parents read to them more frequently had higher scores on early literacy assessments. Socially, the more parents participated in family activities with their children, the fewer behavioral problems children had in school. Importantly, parental involvement in their children's education moderated the negative effects of violence, depression, and other risk factors affecting children's school readiness and emotional well-being.

> "There is strong evidence to suggest that when home and school collaborate, programs tend to have many more positive outcomes that last for longer periods of time."
> — Elias et al. (1997, p. 87)

The overwhelming research evidence on the importance of families, summarized in the landmark report *Eager to Learn* (National Research Council, 2001), led the authors to recommend that early childhood programs "build alliances with parents to cultivate complementary and mutually reinforcing environments for young children at home and at the center" (p. 318). Parent educator Janice Keyser (2006) says that the relationships among the important adults in a child's life can be as important as the child's own relationships with those adults. As Keyser states, "Children's

Parental involvement can yield many positive academic and social outcomes for children, promoting their school readiness and overall emotional well-being.

emotional safety and sense of well-being are deeply affected by the adult relationships around them. Children are also taking an intense observation course on relationships; they learn how to communicate, express caring, solve problems, and work together from watching the adults around them" (p. 1).

Quite simply, the stronger the relationship between home and school, the better the care young children receive in both settings. Teachers and parents can share information and help make one another more aware of children's accomplishments and needs. By working together, the adults who care for young children also serve as positive role models for them. Consultants and authors Amy Baker and Lynn Manfredi/Petitt (2004) say that "when caregivers' own relationships are positive, they set a moral tone and teach children about responsibility, mutual respect, integrity, and human values in the way children learn best — through experience" (p. 2). They explain that friendly relationships allow teachers to share parents' delight in their child's progress. Likewise, parents are reassured that the adults with whom they entrust their child every day will value, nurture, and support their child as he or she continues to grow. When parents and teachers have confidence in one another, says child development and mental health expert Alice Honig (2002), "the child is more likely to feel confident as well" (p. 54). An added benefit is that a good relationship with parents is part of a teacher's "compensation package" and research shows that positive home-school connections can help reduce staff turnover (Center for the Child Care Workforce, 2001). This in turn results in a more stable early childhood program setting for children, with less stress for them and their parents.

The importance of the home-school connection is shown by its inclusion in virtually all state and professional early childhood program standards. For example, the accreditation criteria of the National Association for the Education of Young Children (2005) require that staff communicate with families around such issues as children's separation from parents at the start of the school day, special needs, and daily care routines. Head Start and Early Head Start Performance Standards (US Department of Health and Human Services, 2002) identify parents' relationships with teachers and caregivers as a priority, not only to share information about children, but also to solicit parent input on curriculum planning, implementation, and evaluation. The annual review of preschool education by the National Institute for Early Education Research (Barnett, Epstein, Carolan, Fitzgerald, Ackerman, & Friedman, 2010) shows parent involvement is a universal component of program quality standards, that is, it appears as a criterion in every state. Measures, such as the Program Quality Assessment (PQA; HighScope Educational Research Foundation, 2003a) and other standardized program evaluation tools used in licensing and accreditation, also include items for rating the nature of family-staff relationships.

Establishing supportive relationships between early childhood programs and families benefits everyone — children, parents, staff, and the program as a whole. Educators can foster these relationships in many ways, for example, by

When parents and teachers form strong alliances and work together, they instill confidence in children and provide a positive model of respectful and supportive relationships.

talking informally with parents at daily dropoff and pickup times, conducting scheduled home visits, sharing information in print and electronic formats, and inviting parents to visit or volunteer in the program when their schedules permit. Staff can also learn about and interact with parents by becoming involved in the local community where the program's families live. These and other strategies for building the supportive home-school bridges that foster young children's active learning are discussed in this chapter.

The HighScope Framework for Family Involvement

HighScope promotes diverse strategies to encourage family involvement in children's programs. Many of these ideas are not unique to HighScope, and are recommended as part of general "best practices." However, HighScope brings the same unique emphasis on active learning for children to its interactions with families. For example, while parent workshops are common in early childhood settings, HighScope advocates using hands-on learning activities instead of merely lecturing parents or passing out informational brochures. The HighScope approach to working with families is characterized by the following:

Interactions focus on the family. Teachers learn about the family's background and culture, discover their strengths, and identify what these elements can contribute to their child's education and the program as a whole. Teachers also support and encourage family initiative. Staff are also sensitive to issues that affect child and family well-being, and assist families in obtaining the assistance they need.

Teacher-parent partnerships are promoted. Information is shared in both directions. Parents educate teachers about their children. Teachers offer parents insights into child development and how the curriculum supports their child's learning. The relationship is characterized by mutual respect.

Interactions are guided by the plan-do-review process. Teachers and parents discuss their goals for each child and how home and school can work together to achieve them. As they carry out their respective roles, teachers and parents periodically review the child's progress and make adjustments if needed.

Teachers and parents are encouraged to share child observations with one another. Teachers share anecdotal information from COR Advantage with parents to help them understand and support their child's development. Parents are encouraged to record and share observations about what the child does and says at home.

Classrooms incorporate home-based materials and activities. Teachers include real and familiar objects from the home in the classroom. They plan activities that reflect the home and community environment. Parents are encouraged to share materials, experiences, interests, and skills with all the children in the program.

Taking time to talk with families at pickup and dropoff times helps to build positive, trusting relationships.

Staff emphasize the importance of adult-child interaction in early education. Staff help parents become better observers of their children so the parents can scaffold learning at home. Parent volunteers are also given meaningful roles in the classroom so they can interact with children and become partners in the active learning process.

Family as a frame for understanding children

From the day they are born, children live within a family that shapes their beliefs, attitudes, and actions. By striving to understand and respect each child's family, we encourage children to view themselves and others as valued, contributing members of society. Educator Carol Brunson Phillips (1988) offers a compelling argument for making schools more like homes: "To grow and thrive as adults, children need skills to operate in two cultures — one that will provide them with power and productivity in mainstream America, and one that provides them with a sense of meaning in life, a history, and a home.…We must examine the values and beliefs that underlie child-rearing practices and ways of being in the world and that influence children's learning styles. We need to figure out how to make our classrooms more like our homes" (p. 47). Janet Gonzalez-Mena (2007) says it is not just a matter of recognizing the diversity that exists in our society, but actively "honoring differences" (as she states in the subtitle of her book, *Diversity in Early Care and Education*), to build the relationships that will truly support children in all the settings where we want them to grow and thrive.

Clearly, the impact of family life — in all its complexity — affects every aspect of a child's development. Phillips (1988) defines a family system or culture as involving "all the things that families do to enable their children to know and understand their group's shared ideas about values, beliefs, and behaviors. This participation in a home culture gives the child the power to influence his or her environment and to have an impact on the world" (pp. 46–47). According to Leslie Williams and Yvonne De Gaetano (1985), who codirected a multicultural early childhood education program called "A Learning Environment Responsive to All (ALERTA)," a family's culture includes everything from food, dance, music, dress, and art to lifestyle, recreation, social customs, medicine, history, holidays, and language to religious beliefs, rules, education, attitudes toward others, and childrearing practices. In fact, culture has so many components that Gonzalez-Mena (2007) says we can best think of it as a "complex system" that affects every aspect of how we perceive ourselves and interact with others. Children grow up in a "family system" whose values and beliefs they carry with them throughout their school years and into adulthood. (For more on acknowledging the role of culture and diversity at home and in the classroom, see KDI 53. Diversity, in the *Social Studies* companion book, Epstein, 2012h.)

The HighScope approach recognizes the important role families play in young children's development. We want children to know who they are — to be well rooted in their home cultures. We also want them to know that who they will become is ultimately their responsibility — the result of the choices and decisions they will make for themselves based on the experiences and support provided by others. If we do our jobs well as parents, educators, and caring adults, we will enable children to understand their own families and learn from others. To achieve these goals, adults implementing the HighScope Curriculum support children's families by striving to

- Understand children's home cultures
- Create open relationships among adults and children involved in the early childhood setting
- Positively influence the way children see, hear, understand, and learn from their peers

Programs that understand and value each child's family and home culture encourage children to view themselves and others as valued members of the community.

- Empower all children to act confidently and with respect for others based on their own decisions and understanding

In their homes children generally adopt their family's interaction styles and customs. Outside the home, however, where people may speak a different language or dialect, follow unfamiliar customs, or exhibit unfamiliar attitudes and behaviors, children may experience the setting as confusing or even hostile. To make the child's transition from home to an early childhood setting as smooth as possible, adults using the HighScope Curriculum are guided by a belief in the active learning process, and the assumption that children develop best in a supportive climate.

Active learning in support of family involvement

The ingredients of active learning — *materials, manipulation, choice, language and thought from children,* and *adult scaffolding* — not only guide HighScope's approach to *children* but also to *families.*

Materials from home to manipulate

Children are powerfully motivated to imitate parents and family members: farm children play on hay wagons, children from fishing communities play on boats, and so forth. By knowing about each child's family, adults in early childhood settings can provide children with the tools or playing cards, for example, adults in the classroom will want to add looms, yarn, beads, drums, subway tokens, sheet music, and cards to the early childhood setting. They will also make available to children selected pictures, books, and magazines that include images of families like their own.

Choices reflecting family life

Allowing and encouraging children to choose their own ways of buttoning, fixing, mixing, building, pasting, weaving, carrying, and arranging is one way to nurture their view of themselves as people who can do things for themselves and for others. When children make choices about what to play with and how to use materials, they will often make choices that reflect experiences they have had at home and in important family situations.

At work time in the house area, Ghayda puts a vase with flowers (pipe cleaners with large wooden beads at the top end) in the middle of the table, just like her mother does "when my khala (Arabic for aunt) comes for dinner."

At outside time, Benilda (whose grandmother recently died) plays "funeral" with several other children. "Here is where we walk and carry flowers," she directs them. "Here is where we put flowers on the dirt and cry."

At work time in the art area, Chatham tears strips of colored construction paper. He lays several strips vertically, then crosses them with several strips horizontally. "I'm making a rug like my daddy," he tells his teacher.

When children become independent doers and thinkers, they are in a good position to make their own judgments about what works best for them and to withstand pressures to accept the solutions of others without trying them out for themselves. Knowing they can carry out at school

---

All Kinds of Cooking Utensils

Children's choices about using materials reflect their home experiences. This child prepares "breakfast," choosing from a selection of kitchen utensils to flip "pancakes."

baskets	mortar and pestle
bread pans	pastry molds
calabashes (gourds)	pots and pans
chopsticks	rice bowls
clay pots	rice steamers
coffee grinders	rolling pins
deep fryers	skillets
frying pans	stew pots
garlic presses	tablecloths
graters	tortilla presses
measuring spoons	woks
mixing bowls	wooden spoons

---

and materials they see people using at home. Depending on what is familiar to the particular children in their care, adults can provide appropriate food containers, clothing and accessories, music, and art. If children see adults in their homes or communities weaving, knitting, drumming, riding the subway, singing in choir,

Stocking the preschool with real items and tools children see adults using at home helps children re-create their home life in their play.

the same activities they see family members doing at home reassures them that their choices and abilities are valued and supported in both places.

Home language from children

Since young children learn best by putting their experiences into their own words, it is important that children be able to share their observations and enthusiasm in the language or dialect they already speak (including sign language). Adults in early childhood settings make every possible attempt to converse with each child in his or her home language. They can do this by

- Hiring staff who speak the children's home languages
- Drawing in parents, grandparents, and older siblings as volunteers and encouraging them to use their home language in the classroom

> ### Bringing Family Art to Early Childhood Settings
>
> When Mrs. Lukosavitz discovered that four-year-old An-Mei was learning the art of Chinese calligraphy and how to "hold the brushes very lightly," she arranged to call on An-Mei's grandmother and observe one of An-Mei's "lessons." Once Mrs. Lukosavitz found out what kinds of paper, inks, and pens were used, she added them to the art corner to support An-Mei and to encourage her to share her experiences with the other children.
>
>
>
> One day, Joseph told his child care mom, Maria, that "Uncle Tundye from Nigeria" was staying at his house with "all his big, big pictures." In talking with Joseph's mom, who was helping Tundye sell his paintings, Maria arranged to have Tundye visit. During his visit, he made the children a special painting and told them a story about Anansi, the spider. For many days after, the children enjoyed painting large "Anansi pictures" with lots of "big parts of black and red and yellow like Tundye's from Nigeria."

- Spending time with members of the children's families to learn essential words and phrases in the home language
- Learning to speak one of the languages used by non-English speakers in the classroom

Since we want children to communicate, we want to make it as easy as possible for them to talk with peers and adults in whatever language they speak. This reinforces the home-school connection. Furthermore, the more conversant young children are in their home language, the more easily they will learn a second. (For more on dual language learners, see KDI 30. English language learning, in the companion book *Language, Literacy, and Communication,* Epstein, 2012c.)

Respectful support (scaffolding) from adults

Different families have different interaction styles. By closely observing children and talking with their parents, adults can begin to answer questions such as

- How much space is enough space for each individual child?
- How close or far away do I need to be to support rather than disrupt each child's play?
- Which children rely on eye contact, body language, or stillness to gain attention?
- Which children prefer little eye contact?
- Which children seek out touch? Which children avoid being touched?
- How do different children signal distress, confusion, sorrow, delight?

When four-year-old Kera, for example, wanted Miss Kay's attention, she used the nonverbal attention-getting strategies that worked well with her family and relatives. She looked at Miss Kay and glanced down when Miss Kay looked in her direction; she moved very close to Miss Kay; she gently touched Miss Kay's clothing. Miss Kay, on the other hand, attended primarily to children's verbal requests. Often when Kera had worked patiently for five minutes to gain Miss Kay's attention, Miss Kay would turn instead to someone like Billy as soon as he called, "Miss Kay! Hey, Miss Kay! Come here. You're not gonna believe this!" Eventually, Miss Kay realized that she was spending very little time with Kera and knew very little about her. When Miss Kay talked to her team member about this, they decided she should begin observing Kera more closely. The more she watched Kera and talked with her team member about what she saw, the more Miss Kay learned to recognize, appreciate, and respond to Kera's quiet communications. She also spoke with Kera's parents about how their daughter communicated her needs at home. As Miss Kay began to attend more to Kera in the classroom, acknowledging her nonverbal cues with both physical and verbal

By observing children and talking with parents, teachers can identify and respect families' different interaction styles and respond to differences in the ways children communicate.

responses, Kera's comfort and confidence with talking increased.

It is also important to attend and respond to differences in children's conversational styles. Some children freely associate, jumping from topic to topic in their conversations: "My grandma broke her leg. I have a cut right here, wanna see it? I like getting haircuts except the hair dryer. Fire trucks are loud." Other children converse about one thing and then stop: "My brother fell on his head. He got stitches and a spider ring. I didn't get one." It is important for adults to encourage and appreciate both the vitality of the first style and the focus of the second, and to attend to what children are saying regardless of how they say it.

A supportive climate for family involvement

Achieving comfort with children's families depends on establishing a supportive climate in the educational setting. In chapter 2 we noted that a supportive climate has certain characteristics — characteristics that can be expanded to include children's families. A supportive climate for family involvement, then, is characterized by shared control between children and adults, a focus on children's and *families'* strengths, authenticity on the part of adults, and a commitment to children's *family-inspired* play.

Shared control between children and adults

To the extent that adults share control with children, they allow children both to interact in familiar ways and to learn new ways of interacting from other children and adults in the early childhood setting. Sharing control allows children to express a variety of beliefs and attitudes. This means that adults do not always have the last word, as three young children in Mr. Levy's care demonstrated during their doll-baby play:

Jana: I know where babies come from. The stork brings them and then the mommy wakes up.

Teri: Oh, that's silly. They come from the mommy's tummy.

Jana: No, from the stork. My big brother told me.

Beth: Well, it's really like this. The baby gets borned from the mommy's tummy, but then the stork comes from heaven and brings the baby's soul.

Jana: Oh!

Teri: Okay. Now let's get these babies back to bed.

Focusing on children's and families' strengths

An emphasis on children's and families' strengths promotes children's self-respect and helps counteract social stereotypes. To understand this point, consider the experiences of home visitor Sally W. who worked with a family in an isolated, rural area. Billy and Caroline M. and their children lived in a one-room wooden building with a cement floor and walls covered with newspapers. The yard was home to a variety of dogs and the rusted bodies of pickup trucks.

When I first started visiting this family," Sally tells the home visitors she trains, "I was terrified. Their lives were so different from mine, I only saw negatives. As I continued to visit them, however, I began to learn how they coped with adversities that I have never had to face. I began to admire the family's strengths — their sense of humor, the way they worked together, their gardening ability, their trapping and hunting skills, and their strong commitment to educating their children. As I saw how these strengths were reflected in their children, I began to see how much each child was capable of and how much each had to offer. I wanted the children to feel strong and proud when they went to public school, and I wanted their teachers to see them as I did.

In working with children, it is important that we focus on what they and their families *can* do. It is up to the adults who have daily contact with children to look for, inform themselves about, and promote both family strengths and individual strengths, so that children, their peers, and the other adults in their lives recognize and value them.

Authenticity on the part of adults

Rather than "brush off" or minimize children's fears and concerns about the differences they notice in people, adults discuss them honestly and directly, in a matter-of-fact tone. This provides children with both a sympathetic listener and useful information about coping with the differences they notice. Adults' genuine attention to children alerts them to children's fears and concerns about differences and provides children with an understanding conversational partner. The following scenario depicts just such a conversation between an adult and a child who is facing an unsettling situation. The adult takes this opportunity to explain another child's appearance in terms that make sense to her peers and lead to acceptance.

Lerone: I don't like that girl. She don't have no hair.

Ms. Holmes: Marla's hair came out because she was burned in a fire.

Lerone: She hurt bad?

Ms. Holmes: Yes, she was in the hospital for a long time. But now she can play with her friends again.

Lerone: She looks funny.

Ms. Holmes: We're used to seeing people with hair, but some people lose their hair.

Lerone: Hey! Chauncey [local NBA player] doesn't have hair!

Ms. Holmes: No, he doesn't, but he makes lots of baskets and has lots of friends.

Lerone: Yeah, he made a hook, then he hugged Rip and gave him five! I saw it on TV.

Ms. Holmes: Chauncey and Rip are friends.

Later that day, Ms. Holmes noticed Lerone pushing Marla on the taxi.

Commitment to children's family-inspired play

Young children's play often gets to the heart of their lives, reflecting such emotionally charged family situations as births, deaths (of pets and relatives), weddings, funerals, family gatherings, and religious observances.

Four-year-old Kalani's mother, for example, gave birth to Kalani's new brother at home.

Adults show children their commitment to family-inspired play by actively participating in it with children.

After her brother's birth, Kalani's play with dolls reflected this experience. Another child, five-year-old Bonnie Lou, whose father was in a hospital-based rehabilitation facility during an extended illness, often directed her playmates in "visiting daddy." This involved making get-well cards, baking "cookies" and a "birthday cake," taking a long car ride to the facility, walking down lots of hallways and turning corners (sometimes getting lost), taking a walk to feed the "ducks" (there was a pond on the grounds), eating "clam chowder" in the cafeteria, and falling asleep on the long ride home "in the nighttime."

At one point, Matthew asked Bonnie Lou why her dad was in the hospital. Here was their exchange:

Bonnie Lou: He has to stay in this special hospital until he gets better.

Matthew: Does he have a broken leg?

Bonnie Lou: No, he goes there to rest and get strong. He's coming home soon.

Matthew: Oh, my daddy goes to work.

The effects of valuing families

When early childhood professionals value diverse family styles and traditions, everyone in the early childhood setting benefits. Staff and family learn about one another and children feel secure as they move between the two environments. These multiple benefits are described in the section that follows.

Children talk about their families

When adults respond positively to children's family experiences and ways of communicating about them, children have the opportunity to talk freely about their families:

- "I have a special way to write my Chinese name."
- "My grandma's gonna tell about that Br'er Rabbit. Can't nobody get him."
- "I miss my daddy at the army hospital. I'm glad when he gets better and comes home."

Children explore and appreciate family differences

Ignoring differences with phrases such as "People are really all the same," distorts reality and inhibits children's natural curiosity. When respect for family traditions is embedded in the early childhood setting, children have the opportunity to explore and appreciate the differences they notice:

Aaron: We don't put a tree in our house! We light the candles and get presents for all the days we have the candles.

Talitha: Hey, I'm gonna tell my mom and dad about that. They only give us presents on one day!

Children and adults see each other in a positive light

When adults recognize children's strengths, other children do so as well.

Nealey: I know who can help us! Renata is real good at puzzles.

Villette: That little tiny girl with the long black hair down to here?

Nealey: Yeah, she can do puzzles faster than anyone. Hey, Renata…

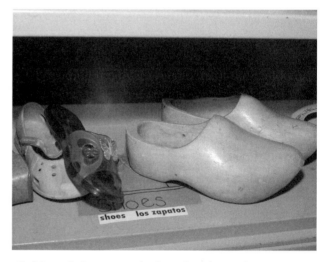

Children feel supported when their home language is represented in the learning environment. Labeling interest areas and materials in the different languages of the classroom lets children and their families know that everyone is valued.

While children are free to express their fears about one another's differences, they also have the opportunity to appreciate each person's abilities — whether for painting pictures, building towers, helping on the computer, making up songs, being the mommy, or figuring out how to fit all the large Tinkertoys back in the box.

Children are free to use their energies on growth and development

Children's anxieties are diminished when adults greet children in their home languages, when children find similarities between their homes and their early childhood settings, when adults concentrate on what children *can* do rather than on what they cannot, and when adults encourage children to observe and talk about differences matter-of-factly. In such a supportive atmosphere, they can attend fully to the matters at hand and enjoy the energy and camaraderie of the people around them.

Strategies for Supporting Family Involvement: Four Key Elements

Adults implementing the HighScope Curriculum want children to feel comfortable and secure as they move between the home and early childhood setting. The following family support strategies will help adults ease this transition for children:

- Knowing yourself and your family's roots, beliefs, and attitudes
- Learning from children and families about their styles and traditions
- Creating positive relationships between yourself and others
- Anticipating excellence from each child

As with the ingredients of active learning, the elements of a supportive climate, and other strategies in this curriculum, the strategies presented in this section apply to adults whenever and wherever they find themselves teaching and caring for children. The strategies influence every adult-child interaction in these circumstances.

Knowing yourself, and your family's roots, beliefs, and attitudes

To understand the family practices, beliefs, and attitudes of the children we serve, we need to know who *we* are and what influences *our* perceptions of other families. We have found the following strategies to be helpful in setting such an examination in motion. Using these strategies on your own or introducing them at teacher meetings, workshops, or parent get-togethers can assist you in understanding the roots of your beliefs about yourself and others.

List family origins

One way to begin is with family origins. Where were you, your parents, grandparents, and great-grandparents born? You may be surprised by the regional and national diversity within your own family tree.

Examine your "whats, hows, and whys"

To help you become aware of your own family's influence on you, Williams and De Gaetano (1985) suggest analyzing your own values, beliefs, customs, and daily lifestyle in terms of three simple categories: *what, how,* and *why.* Ask yourself the following questions:

> *What* things are really important to me? What kinds of music, food, clothing, art, and dance make me feel comfortable, secure, "at home"?
>
> *How* do I behave as a parent, family member, friend? How do I commonly act when ill, having fun, or celebrating holidays or special occasions like weddings? How do I express myself at home, at work?
>
> *Why* do I behave a certain way, believe what I believe, adopt particular attitudes? What religious, educational, historical, legal, and social beliefs are important to me?

Be aware of personal filters

When we look closely at ourselves and our family experiences, we can begin to see that who we are and what we believe influences the way we interact with both children and adults. One staff member, for example, realized that her fondness for wearing casual clothing to work so that she could play comfortably on the floor with children might be taken as a sign of disrespect or personal laziness by some parents who were expected to dress more formally for their jobs. Once she realized this, she took more care about her appearance at the beginning and end of each day. She also realized that she tended to pay more attention to children who talked a lot. Therefore, she gradually learned to attend more often to less talkative children. She also decided that she wanted to be more patient with families who were more rushed or pessimistic than she.

By recognizing and appreciating our own strengths and personal filters, we can also begin to realize that most of the people with whom we have daily contact are guided by a slightly or radically different set of "whats, hows, and whys." By identifying the beliefs that shape our own lives, we can begin to seek out and understand the beliefs that shape the lives of the children in our care, and their families.

Home visits are one of the best ways for teachers to learn about families — their values, culture, and relationships. In turn, parents learn about the adults who will be interacting with their children.

Learning from children and families about their styles and traditions

As important as it is to know ourselves, it is just as important to understand the families of the children we serve. Understanding children's "whats, hows, and whys" enables adults to provide familiar materials and adopt comfortable interaction styles that make children feel welcome and secure in early childhood settings. Here are some strategies for learning about children's families.

Conduct home visits

Visiting families in their homes is one of the best ways to learn about their values and the aspirations they have for their children. To fully appreciate the value of home visits, we return to Sally W., the home visitor introduced on page 100. Sally's visits to the M. family are part of a countywide child development program in which home visits with young children and their families are the main program activity. Each week Sally drives to the family's home and spends an hour or so talking with parents Caroline and Billy (when Billy is available) about their immediate concerns for their children. She also engages the adults and the under-school-age children in an active learning experience. The kinds of active learning experiences she chooses are increasingly shaped by what she learns about how the M. family lives and what they value.

"One of the first things I noticed," Sally recalls, "was that there were no 'typical' toys for the children to play with — no dolls, cars, crayons, wheel toys, puzzles. And yet, whenever I visited, the little ones were usually engaged in some play activity — for example, picking up rocks and stones, putting them in an old bucket, and then dumping the stones out again. Once when I arrived, the entire family were watching three-and-a-half-year-old Sammy write in the dirt. Of course, Sammy wasn't really writing, but he thought he was, just as any three-and-a-half-year-old would write by making important-looking lines and squiggles.

"Realizing that the family had no money for commercial toys and that the children had a great capacity to play contentedly with whatever was at hand, I decided to rely on 'found' materials and the children's ingenuity for my home visit activities. One day, for example, we made little dolls out of sticks and baling twine, and Caroline supplied some material scraps from her sewing basket supplies. The next week when I arrived, there were not only more stick dolls but also walnut dolls, and handkerchief dolls, and even a doll one of the older boys had whittled. We played for weeks with those dolls — building them houses out of boxes and newspaper. We added farm animals and furniture that we made from all kinds of odds and ends — matchboxes, toilet-paper tubes, cereal boxes. Billy even made a special shelf to store all these treasures.

"I also brought books for the family to read together from the county library, but the library was so far away that the family rarely got there on their own. Then, during one of my visits, the children persuaded Caroline to tell one of her stories about what she used to do when she was a little girl, so I could hear it. She told a spellbinding story about how she used to bring the cows home for her dad at milking time and how one time she was chased up a tree by the neighbor's bull. I was so excited, I asked her if I could tape-record her story during my next visit. She agreed, and after I taped her story, I took it home, typed it on my computer using a big, kindergarten-sized type, and printed it out. On my next visit, I brought watercolor paints, brushes, and paper so the children could illustrate Caroline's story. When everything was finished, we punched holes and tied the story and pictures together into a book. After that, bookmaking became a regular practice with us. Sometimes even the older children got involved between visits."

It is clear that the more Sally learned about the family from her weekly home visits, the more she was able to incorporate her knowledge of their family strengths and interests into her active learning goals.

Build home visits into home child care and center-based programs

In contrast to home visit programs like Sally W.'s, most early childhood programs are conducted outside of children's homes. In these center-based programs, it is vital that the adults who teach and care for the children make a concerted effort to visit each family before or during the child's first few weeks in the program. Such a visit allows adults to see children at home where they are most comfortable and to learn about the things they particularly enjoy.

Center-based programs generally set aside time at the beginning and end of each enrollment period for home visits. Teachers generally conduct such visits in pairs. In part, this is for safety reasons. If any problems emerge, it is good to have a backup person there. Also, since their children

Visiting children in their home environment where they are most comfortable offers insights into their interests and the activities they enjoy.

will interact with both members of the teaching team — even though one will be their child's primary small-group leader — it allows parents to meet both teachers and see how they interact with one another. If children change groups, or one teacher is unexpectedly absent for a period of time, parents already know the other adult responsible for taking care of their child.

Home visits often require scheduling flexibility, especially when children come from a distance and parents work. Sometimes parents are reluctant to have teachers visit them. There are various reasons for this, for example, in their experience a visit from a teacher meant a child was "in trouble"; they may fear their home and its furnishings will be judged; they may worry the visit will inconvenience other people who live there (such as someone who works a night shift and sleeps during the day); or they may be concerned about the teacher's safety. In such situations, the visit can occur in a neutral public setting, such as a restaurant, park, or library. While teachers may not glean as much information as they would by going to the home, at least the visit begins a relationship between the school and the family.

Once the logistics of the visit are established, it is important to build rapport, put family members at ease, and find out about each family's strengths, values, and desires for their children. Each adult will approach these goals differently, depending on who they are and the techniques they use to put other people at ease. If you are new to home visiting, or you are anxious about meeting new families for the first time, think about applying the strategies for establishing a supportive learning environment to working with families (see

Establishing a Supportive Climate With Parents

Sharing control with parents
- Take cues from parents.
- Participate with parents on parents' terms.
- Learn from parents.
- Give conversational control to parents.

Focusing on family strengths
- Look for family interests.
- Look at situations from parents' perspectives.
- Find out about children's interests from parents.
- Plan around family strengths and interests.

Forming authentic relationships with parents
- Show genuine interest in parents.
- Respond attentively to parents' interests.
- Listen carefully and respectfully to parents.
- Give parents specific feedback.
- Ask honest questions and respond to questions honestly.

Making a commitment to supporting family play
- Encourage parents' play with their children.
- Learn about families by watching and listening to parents and children play together.

Involving Families in Active Learning Settings 107

Making home visits in pairs gives parents the opportunity to meet their child's primary teacher as well as the other adult who will be caring for their child.

"Establishing a Supportive Climate With Parents," opposite page). These strategies can guide your interactions with parents as well as with children.

One HighScope teaching team, Mr. Milton and Mrs. Ernal, carried out their initial home visits by setting aside two-and-a-half days to go together to each of the homes of the 18 children in their urban, center-based program. They called each family to ask if they could visit, explaining that they wanted to meet each child and family in the setting where they were most at home in order to help ease the child's transition from home to center. Through this call they were able to set up a 30- to 45-minute visit with each family.

Because they went as a team, once they had exchanged greetings and introductions, Mr. Milton was able to focus on the child (or children) and Mrs. Ernal on the parent. After getting information and requesting help ("Can we include your address and phone number on the class list?" "Would you like to accompany us on field trips?" "Would you be able to care for the class guinea pig on weekends or holidays?"), they talked about things the family liked to do together and things the child liked to do. Whenever Mrs. Ernal made notes on a blank sheet of paper, she would say something like "Thanks for mentioning that. Let me write that down so I won't forget." When she and Mr. Milton went with the child to see where she or he usually played, Mrs. Ernal always left her page of notes out so that parents could see for themselves that she really was only writing down what she said she was and not making judgments about their home or lifestyle. Here are some of the notes Mrs. Ernal made on this series of visits:

Kestin — Has been with her family for 6 months, being adopted. Likes dolls. (Make sure dolls are immediately visible.)

Athi — Has lots of toy vehicles. Likes to build, take things apart, and fix them with real tools. (Open construction area.) Dad plays guitar and sings. (Available to play for children on Friday mornings.)

Joel — Likes to dance. (Have CDs and player available.)

Alexis — Grandmother works at Terri's Bakery (close enough for field trip).

Boomer — Noodle-maker (mother will bring and make noodles with the children).

Knut and Bjarne — Grandmother raises chicks (will bring baby chicks in a few weeks).

Tara — Came out in sari, put on Indian music, and danced for us. (Add saris to house area, Indian music CD to music area.)

Juan — Just arrived from Colombia, speaks only Spanish. Family speaks Spanish, although father speaks English (he's from New York). (Speak Spanish with Juan and help interpret messages to and from other children.)

Participate in community life

After these initial home visits, Mr. Milton and Mrs. Ernal continued to learn about their children's families through potlucks, parent get-togethers and meetings, phone calls, talking with parents as they dropped off and picked up their children, and subsequent home visits. Since they both lived in the same community as the families they served, they also had the opportunity over the course of the year to meet families at religious services, the gym, the grocery store, the farmers' market, local meetings, school meetings for their older children, the health clinic, the dentist, the library, the ice cream parlor, the bowling alley, the fishing dock, the pool, the roller rink, local restaurants, and the county fair. At the local Heritage Festival, for example, they watched Knut and Bjarne's dad and aunt dancing with a Swedish folk dance group and invited them to the early childhood center to dance with the children.

Observe children closely every day

Visiting homes and participating in community life are vital ways to learn about children's families, but they usually are not everyday activities. Observing children is something that adults who teach and care for children can do on a daily basis. Each day, adults can observe children's play and interaction styles, listen to how they express themselves and what they talk about, and learn about the things that particularly interest each child. Mrs. Lukosavitz, for example, discovered An-Mei's interest in Chinese calligraphy by watching and listening to her as she worked with art materials (see "Bringing Family Art to Early Childhood Settings," p. 98). One day An-Mei took a small watercolor brush and some black tempera paint to the table and began making very light and deliberate brush strokes. "What is

Inviting parents into the preschool setting for special gatherings and visits during their child's day makes them feel welcome and strengthens the home-school connection.

that?" asked Anthony who was sitting next to her and making a Batman mask. "That's my name," she replied. "That's not your name," laughed Anthony. "Your name starts with *A* just like *Anthony*." "No," she said quietly. "This is my Chinese name. My grandma is teaching me." "Oh," said Anthony studying the lines closely. "What's my Chinese name?" "I don't know," replied An-Mei. Anthony paused and then brightened, "Ask your grandma if she can make me one." "Okay," An-Mei smiled. When her grandmother came to visit, she translated each child's name into Chinese characters.

Reach out to families

In addition to visiting families, participating in community life, and observing children each day, adults can also reach out to families to make them feel welcome at the early childhood setting. Here are some strategies that can help staff do this:

Share anecdotes. Begin conversations with family members with an anecdote or story that illustrates their child's abilities. For example, "Mrs. Baines, let me tell you what Lynette did today. She spent all of work time in the block area building a large building with lots of rooms for animals and people."

Plan family gatherings. Invite families to an open house or family potluck. Family members can see the early childhood setting and meet staff and other families.

Publicly acknowledge families' importance to your program. One full-day program in New York City did this by filling a bulletin board with photographs of each parent or guardian accompanied by a brief descriptive caption. For example,

Gloria Galeano, mother of Maria (toddler group) and Eduardo (preschool). When she isn't working or going to nursing school, she loves to sew. She made the beautiful animal quilt in the toddlers' doll corner. Thanks, Gloria!

❖

Jack Rizzo, father of Vince (preschool). As you can see, Jack likes motorcycles and so does Vince. His job keeps him busy so he doesn't ride much anymore. Whenever he's in town he spends a few hours with us in the block area. He makes great car and truck sounds!

❖

Rayanne James, mother of twins Rayette and Rayelle (toddler group). Another set of twins at home keeps Rayanne very busy. How does she do it?! Rayette and Rayelle are very excited about their new brothers."

❖

Here is Mandy (infant group) and her mom, Gwen, at a family gathering last summer.

Another program decided to create a family book featuring each child on his or her own page. Teachers gave each family a blank page in a plastic page protector and asked them to put family photos on the page that represented the important people and events in their family. Teachers emphasized that these pictures would be handled by the children so, while every effort would be made to preserve the photos, parents should not include their most cherished or one-of-a-kind pictures. Teachers also offered to photocopy pictures to put on the family's book page.

If a child in your program does not have a photo with a parent, take a picture of the child and one of the teachers doing something together. Consider taking a camera on the home visit so you can take pictures of the children and their families.

Converse with family members at dropoff and pickup times. Make the most of the daily opportunities to speak with family members when they drop off and pick up their children. Go out of your way to welcome parents who don't often pick up or drop off their children, for example, a parent whose normal work schedule doesn't allow it or a noncustodial parent. Those parents may be less likely to enter the classroom or make initial contact with the teacher, and will appreciate a warm and welcoming outreach.

Staff members of one full-day program in Dayton, Ohio, for example, not only make a point of speaking to family members at dropoff and pickup times, but also encourage them to spend a few minutes with their child in the center at the end of the day to ease the transition from center to home. It is not unusual to see a father sitting on the floor working on one last puzzle with his daughter, a boy leading his mom to the sandbox to see his roads and bridges, and a mom in a rocking chair giving seven-month-old Jinnie her late afternoon bottle. "It makes it so much easier on both of us when I feed Jinnie here," her mother says. "When we leave, we've already spent time together. I've already been able to feed and cuddle her, and we both arrive home comfortable and relaxed — instead of Jinnie screaming with hunger and frustration."

Encourage family members to join their children on their lunch hours. In a downtown Pittsburgh center, for example, parents come for lunch hour in their work clothes and, depending on their arrival time and the schedule of their child's group, they either feed their infants, have lunch with their preschoolers, play on the playground, or read a naptime story. "I really feel lucky that I can spend lunch time with Ricky," remarks one dad. "I feel cheated when I have to miss it."

Encourage parents to join in as adults read with children at the beginning of the program day.

Send home brief anecdotal notes. One early childhood staff in Milton Keynes, England, for example, developed what they call a *Home Link Book*. Made of 8½" x 11" paper folded in half with a construction paper cover bearing the child's name, a copy of this book goes back and forth with each child each day. At one point during the day, a staff member makes a brief, dated entry:

Monday 18th January. Stephen thought up the idea of turning the house area into a fish-and-chip shop. He used straws for chips and shells as fish. The other children soon copied his idea.

Stephen's mom writes back:

Stephen has been talking about his "zipper coat" and what he has been doing there at the house area. I have a suggestion for used Christmas cards. Stick them on a thin card (piece of cardboard) and make a jigsaw puzzle by marking them in four, six, or eight sections. Cut them out.

Send home a newsletter on a regular basis. Include specific anecdotes about each child. For example:

On our field trip to the apple orchard on Tuesday, Nicole found a bird's nest and said, "It's full of sticks and prickles." Ramon caught a cricket and carefully brought it back in his apple bag....

Encourage family members to join you and the children on outings and field trips. This provides many opportunities for parents and children and parents and staff to converse, enjoy one another's company, and share an active learning experience.

(For additional ideas on practical ways to reach out to families, see "50 Ways to Connect With Parents.")

Creating positive relationships between yourself and others

Knowing yourself, the children in your program, and their families paves the way for the creation of positive relationships. Although it may be easier

50 Ways to Connect With Families

1. Newsletters (printed or online)
2. Family meetings and workshops
3. School and/or classroom website and blogs
4. Personal notes
5. Phone calls
6. E-mails and text messages
7. Activity calendars (may be posted on web page)
8. Home visits
9. Family networks
10. Field trips
11. Orientation visits
12. Family handbooks
13. Classroom volunteer opportunities
14. Family bulletin board (may be posted on web page)
15. Family library
16. Toy lending library
17. Family room
18. Family support groups
19. Continuing education (such as GED)[1]
20. Family literacy program[1]
21. Job training[1]
22. CDA training[1]
23. Links with agencies of interest to families
24. Invitations to professional meetings
25. Visits to other early childhood programs
26. Child activity logs for each part of the daily routine
27. Parent-teacher conferences
28. Child, family, and classroom photos posted in the classroom
29. Donations of materials from home
30. Advisory board or policy committee
31. Book study group
32. Family night
33. Potlucks and picnics
34. Suggestion box
35. Discount coupons for family activities

You can also connect with parents by involving them in the following:

36. Help in classroom set-up
37. Fundraising
38. Creating content for the school or classroom website
39. Building the playground
40. Repairing classroom equipment
41. Helping children transition to kindergarten
42. Preparing special snacks
43. Sharing a talent
44. Making furniture or materials
45. Getting books from the library
46. Sharing observations of children
47. Completing child assessment together
48. Conducting playground assessment
49. Completing program assessment
50. Sharing their photos of videos of the classroom

---
[1]Provided directly by the program or by referring parents to relevant community agencies

to maintain such relationships with people who have views and experiences similar to your own, it is essential that adults in early childhood settings strive to relate openly and honestly to all children and families. Here are some strategies for building such relationships:

Accept and trust others

One way to build trusting relationships is to see yourself and others as members of the human family. Think of the people in your immediate or extended family — your mate, your child, your mother, your friend, your Aunt Lou. Now, as you look at people in a parent meeting or a staff meeting, imagine each one as someone else's mate, child, mother, friend, or aunt — someone who is as important to others as your family is to you.

Involving parents and caregivers in outings and field trips is another way to build bonds with program families.

From this perspective, it makes sense to approach the families of the children in your care with the respect and care you hope others will extend to your immediate family.

Value human differences

The array of human differences is vast. It is important to realize, however, that the way we respond to difference is partly a matter of choice. We choose, for example, how we respond to families that include people who are blind or deaf, use a wheelchair, have a different skin color, shave their heads, have partners of the same sex, or eat foods we have never tasted. When we choose to fear or ignore such differences, we build barricades. But if we choose to value differences, we allow ourselves to reach out to others and learn from them.

Adults can help children learn to value the differences they notice. For example, when four-year-old Martin tried to rub all the brown off Waleed's skin, Waleed said, "No, I'm brown like my daddy." "You're right, Waleed," agreed Mrs. Rivera, supporting the interchange. "Every person's skin is its own beautiful color. Your skin color comes from your mom and dad when you're born." "Oh," said Martin, incorporating this new idea into his old way of seeing Waleed's skin.

Focus on people's strengths

When adults focus on strengths, children are encouraged to do the same. Mrs. Ernal and Mr. Milton, for example, viewed Juan, a child newly arrived from Colombia, as a lively, alert, social child. Yet Juan had become frustrated because he could not talk and joke with his preschool peers as he had done in Colombia. Mrs. Ernal and Mr. Milton wanted the English-speaking children to view Juan as an important member of their team of playmates. Therefore, in introducing him, they focused on Juan's intense desire to communicate rather than on his frustration with English. They spoke Spanish with him, translated for him, and encouraged the other children to use Juan's Spanish words and phrases. The teachers asked Juan's parents to write down a list of useful Spanish words they could use with him (for example, the parts of the daily routine and the names of the classroom areas and his favorite play materials). They also taught some simple Spanish words to the other children. Eventually, Juan became more familiar with his new setting and the English language, and as his peers became more familiar with his Spanish language, Juan's ease with and enjoyment of preschool activities grew.

Communicate clearly and honestly

We communicate with our whole bodies. Therefore, it is important for children and families that we say the same thing with our words as we say with our facial expressions and actions. By being aware of what we say and how we act we can convey positive messages to children about themselves and their peers. Monica, for example, spends a lot of time sitting on the floor playing with children, watching them, reading to them, singing, and so forth. Children often settle comfortably in her lap. Because she wants to send the message that all children are equally welcome, she is very conscious of cuddling and attending to each child she holds. Whoever sits in her lap receives the same unspoken message: "I'm glad you're here with me." In the same manner, whenever she meets parents, she gives them her full attention and lets them know she is glad to talk with them about their children.

Anticipating excellence from each child

Since children are influenced by adult expectations, it is our responsibility to anticipate the very best from each child in our care. Here are some strategies to consider in helping children excel:

Avoid labeling and stereotyping children and families

As early childhood educators, it is important that from the start we focus on, encourage, and alert others to children's strengths rather than burden children with labels that limit their own and other people's belief in their innate capacities and abilities.

Avoid referring to children as "disadvantaged," "developmentally delayed," "not ready for kindergarten," "immature," "aggressive," "language-impaired," "quiet little girl," "rowdy boy," "wild," and "deprived." Choose positive, specific, descriptive words that highlight children's strengths — words such as "active," "involved in role play," "detailed story teller," "problem solver," "effective nonverbal communicator," "interested in letters," "able planner," "rhymer," and "wagon puller."

Regard each child as competent

By regarding each child as a capable individual, adults help unlock the child's potential. It is our responsibility to look for and recognize each child's special gifts and, to the extent possible, to help each child develop his or her special skills.

Assume that each child will succeed

Expect children to be capable individuals — successful planners, decision makers, role players, explorers, block builders. Maintain a supportive active learning setting where children can succeed. In a special education class in Marysville, Michigan, some preschoolers used wheelchairs, some crawled, some wore hearing aids, and some could not or would not speak. Their teacher's initial response to the HighScope approach was skeptical: "Active learning, shared control, problem solving — these approaches will never work with my kids!" By focusing primarily on the children's disabilities, the teacher was not recognizing their potential for success. However, once she gave the children materials to manipulate, the opportunity to make choices, and to talk in whatever way they could about what they were doing, she was overwhelmed by their enthusiasm, involvement, and excitement. Language, or as close as each child could come to it, poured out of the children (whereas before, when language learning was approached mainly through drills, very few

When interacting with families, teachers give them their full attention, and they let parents know they are always glad to talk to them about their children.

children had shown much inclination to communicate verbally). Once she opened the door to active learning, the teacher learned from the children themselves about their many strengths and abilities.

Understanding our own motivations and attitudes, learning about children and families, creating positive relationships, anticipating excellence in others as well as ourselves — these are the elements of family support. These elements enable adults and children to think well of themselves and their peers, to appreciate the contributions and strengths of others, and to proceed in the knowledge that they are unique and valued members of the human family.

Using the elements of family support: Two examples

Here are two examples of how to use the elements of family support to (1) deal with *conflicting approaches to setting limits for children*, and (2) guide *observations of children*.

Example 1: Setting limits for children

In any learning environment, children need adults to set clear and reasonable limits so that they can carry out their plans and ideas safely and enjoyably. It is not unusual, given our family differences, for adults to disagree on how to set and maintain such limits. For example, a teacher may be committed to a problem-solving approach to setting limits for children, while a child's family relies on a more traditional punishment-and-reward approach. How can the elements of family support help in this type of situation?

Review your own definition of "setting limits." Recall your childhood experiences. How were limits set for you as a child? Who set them? Who enforced them? Were they consistent? Unpredictable? How did you respond? An examination of these types of childhood experiences can make you aware of the origins of your expectations about setting limits. It also enables you to reconstruct the thoughts and feelings behind the choices about limit-setting you have made as an adult and early childhood professional.

Learn how children's families set limits. On a home visit or at a parent meeting, find out from parents how *their* parents set limits for them as children, and how they responded. You will probably find that as children, the parents of the children in your program were punished, left to set their own limits, or experienced some kind of help in sorting out conflicts.

Create positive relationships with families over the issue of limit-setting. Once you recall your own experiences and have learned about the experiences of the parents of the children in your care, you are on the way to creating a positive relationship with parents around the issue of setting limits. Once you have conversed with parents and know something about their upbringing, perhaps even sharing some similar childhood experiences, parents are no longer on "the other side of the issue." Instead, you can begin to appreciate and comment on their strengths — their concern for their children's well-being, their advocacy on the children's behalf, their willingness to talk about difficult issues, their honesty in sharing their own experiences. You can also be clear and honest about why your approach to limit-setting focuses on problem solving — you want to give children opportunities to learn from their mistakes and feel good about resolving their own conflicts, cleaning up their spills, and finding alternatives to challenging behavior.

Although you and the parents may never achieve universal agreement, talking together honestly about limit-setting allows you all to share your views and the reasons behind them, and to begin to trust that both of you want what is best for the children.

Anticipate excellence from children and families. Assume that your relationship with parents will continue to develop positively. Keep them up to date on the children's interests and accomplishments. Instead of thinking of a particular parent as "difficult," or "uninformed," think about his or her strengths — a quick mind, a willingness to try new things, a sense of humor, generosity. Focus on these strengths and assume that by working closely together you will succeed in bringing out the best in his or her child. Often parents view you as the expert on child development. When you create a positive relationship with them, they appreciate your guidance.

Example 2: Observing and Supporting a Child's Family Experiences

Each time you learn about the "whats, hows, and, whys" of a child's family, write it down and share it with your team members so you can incorporate your knowledge into daily plans and interactions. Here are the notes one team made about Billy's family experiences:

8/30   Father from Nigeria. Mother and Billy born in South Carolina. Moved here so parents could teach and do graduate work at the university. Billy has traveled to Nigeria with his parents and has also lived in Washington, DC. Parents value education highly. Want Billy to be stimulated and allowed to work at his own fast pace.

9/11   Brought in recording of "drum music to play for cleanup time." This stimulated a lot of conversation about drums. Billy showed how you play these drums with your hands, not with sticks.

10/4   Although he is very verbal and imaginative, Billy is very attuned to other children's nonverbal behavior. "Hey, Mrs. Millete, Kera needs you. Look at her face looking at you that way."

10/20   Billy and Joey mixed brown, black, and white paint to get the color that was the same as their skin.

11/6   Drew a picture for his momma and dictated, "This is me eating greens. And this is my baby brother with no teeth yet. No greens for him, just milk and mushy stuff."

11/9   Billy excited about getting his Chinese name from An-Mei's grandmother. Spent a long time learning to make the Chinese characters.

12/5 *At snacktime, Billy told about how his grandma is coming in on his birthday to tell the story of* Bruh Alligator an' Bruh Rabbit. *"*Bruh *means brother in Gullah," he translated when he saw the puzzled look on Vanessa's face.*

(For more information on recording and sharing anecdotal notes with your team members to help plan supportive and challenging learning experiences for the children in your program, see chapters 4 and 5.)

The elements of family support and the rest of the curriculum

The elements of support for family involvement — *knowing yourself, learning from others, creating positive relationships,* and *anticipating excellence from each child* — expand a supportive climate and influence every other aspect of the HighScope Curriculum. Chapter 4, "Working in Teams," focuses on how teamwork is guided by these very elements: self-awareness, knowledge of others, positive relationships, and

By focusing on the strengths of each family and working closely with parents, you will bring out the best in their children.

anticipation of success based on mutual respect. As teams plan for children, they consider everything they know about each child's family, what makes her or him comfortable and secure, and what things each child enjoys doing. Chapter 5 talks about how staff and parents can share observations about children, using COR Advantage as a common tool for talking about and understanding early development. In chapter 6, "The Learning Environment: Arranging and Equipping Spaces for Active Learners," adult teams take children's families into account so that children will find familiar materials as well as pictures and books about people like themselves in the program setting. Chapters 7, 8 and 9 ("The HighScope Daily Routine," "The HighScope Plan-Do-Review Process," and "Group Times, Outside Times, Transitions") illustrate many natural opportunities for children to work and play with other children — some of whom are similar and some of whom are different. Adults learn how to support and encourage children's interest in their peers throughout the day. Chapter 10 provides an overview of the HighScope key developmental indicators and discusses how adults can support and encourage children as they pursue their own interests in the ways that make the most sense to them. These are detailed further in the eight companion volumes of curriculum content (Epstein, 2012a–h).

An understanding of the important influences of family on children's learning, along with the ingredients of active learning and the elements of support, is integral to understanding the rest of the curriculum as it unfolds in the following chapters and accompanying books.

Strategies for Supporting Family Involvement: A Summary

Knowing yourself and your family's roots, beliefs, and attitudes
- List family origins.
- Examine family "whats," "hows," and "whys."
- Be aware of personal filters.

Learning from children and families about their styles and traditions
- Conduct home visits.
- Build home visits into home child care and center-based programs.
- Participate in community life.
- Observe children closely every day.
- Reach out to families.

Creating positive relationships between yourself and others
- Accept and trust others.
- Value human differences.
- Focus on people's strengths.
- Communicate clearly and honestly.

Anticipating excellence from each child
- Avoid labeling and stereotyping children and families.
- Regard each child as competent.
- Assume that each child will succeed.

CHAPTER 4

Working in Teams: Adult Collaboration to Promote Active Learning

Understanding Teamwork

In implementing the HighScope Curriculum, adults work in teams to support children's active learning. Team members share a commitment to the educational approach and work together to exchange accurate information about children, design curriculum strategies, and evaluate the strategies' effectiveness. Team members strive to deepen their understanding of the curriculum and of individual children so they can provide a setting that is both consistent with their goals and beliefs about learning and consistent in implementation from one adult to another.

In applying the HighScope Curriculum, effective teamwork

- Creates a supportive climate for adults so that the support and trust they feel among themselves pervades their interactions with the children

- Meets adults' needs for belonging, achievement, recognition, and curriculum understanding so that when they are with children they can concentrate fully on the children's interests and intentions

- Results in a unified approach to curriculum implementation, enabling all adults working with the same group of children to provide each child with consistent, appropriate adult support

The purpose of this chapter is to look at what teamwork in a HighScope early childhood setting entails, including the nature of the teamwork process, the effects of teamwork, steps in forming the team, and the practical strategies that enable adult teams to support children's active learning on a daily basis.

Teamwork: An interactive process

Teamwork is an interactive process. In working as a team, adults use many of the same curriculum principles and strategies that they use in working with children. **At its best, teamwork is a process of active learning that calls for a supportive climate and mutual respect.** In this section we will briefly touch on some of the ways teamwork relates to the basic curriculum principles for supporting active learning, establishing supportive climates, and involving families (as discussed in chapters 1–3).

> "Adult relationships have a powerful impact on children's quality of life. When adults are uncomfortable or mistrustful with one another, children feel the tension and are less able to attend to normal developmental tasks. But when adults have trusting relationships with plenty of give-and-take and care is seamless, children reap the benefits."
>
> — Baker & Manfredi/Petitt (2004, p. 10)

Teamwork is active

As adults work closely together to implement the HighScope Curriculum, they are active learners who are constructing a new understanding of how best to support each child's development. To do this they must call upon a common set of curriculum principles and strategies as well as the knowledge gained from their individual observations of children, past experiences, and training. Team members make choices — about how to interpret what they see children doing; about when, where, and how to build on children's abilities; and about which of their current practices to shift, retain, improve upon, or discard. As they work together, team members put their observations of children and events into their own words so that, collectively, they can use and build upon what they know. Team members give and receive support, taking turns talking and listening to each other's ideas so that together they can incorporate these ideas into new strategies for working with children. Adult collaboration in a HighScope program, then, is an *active, participatory process*.

Ongoing adult teamwork sets the stage for children's participation in an active and cooperative learning community.

Teamwork is supportive

Effective teamwork draws on the same elements of support that adults use as they work with children. Team members share control — rather than follow the directives of one person. Team members share responsibility for promoting teamwork, setting curriculum goals, raising issues, and solving problems. As they talk about and plan for children, each team member takes initiative and serves the team as both a leader and a participant. Team members also focus on strengths — they look for ways to use one another's abilities and interests, and concentrate on what *can* be done rather than dwell on problems and obstacles. In addition, they strive for relationships with one another that are based on honesty, attentiveness, open dialogue, and patience. Because of their commitment to play as the primary path to early learning and development, they enjoy a sense of humor about their work together. Their adoption of a problem-solving approach to conflicts enables them to deal with one another matter-of-factly, patiently, and with kindness, in the belief that such situations are opportunities for personal and collective growth.

Teamwork is respectful

Each member of the team appreciates and respects the experiences, understanding, and beliefs of the others. Team members work hard to create mutual trust, to engage in honest communication, and to know both themselves and their collaborators. Rather than say, "She can't understand me, she's not from here!" or "I don't want *him* on my team — he's too young!" team members anticipate success, avoid labeling each other, and assume that by working diligently together they will be able

Effective teams work together to share information and ideas, ensuring a unified approach to curriculum implementation and consistent support for the children in their care.

to provide high-quality learning environments for the children in their care. Respect for one another frees team members from a fear of judgment and allows them to focus their collective energies on children.

Teamwork calls for mutual respect and an understanding of the principles of active learning and supportive climates. In the next section, we discuss some of the beneficial effects of this approach to teamwork.

The effects of teamwork

When adults work together to establish and maintain active learning environments for children, the effects are far-reaching. By working together, team members gain recognition, a sense of accomplishment, and a feeling of belonging to a group of learners. They come to value having colleagues with similar curriculum goals with whom to talk and solve problems. They find they can provide a more consistent approach to the children in their care because together they have set goals and come up with strategies for implementing them. When adults share control with their team members, they often find it easier to share control with young children.

Team members grow in curriculum understanding

By focusing on children's actions and interests, team members develop a better understanding of child development and the ways the curriculum can be used to guide their daily interactions with children. Through observation, reflective thinking, and problem solving, team members come to see themselves as people who can make and test curriculum decisions. They discover or reaffirm an adventurous sense of teaching and learning, an eagerness to learn from shared observations, and the challenge of building on and improving what they know. Team members wrestle together with curriculum and teamwork issues and enjoy the ongoing process of generating new ideas and strategies.

Team members are empowered

Team members see that they are able to solve problems and make decisions that have a positive effect on their own lives and the lives of the children in their care. They also develop the ability to welcome the challenge of change rather than be overwhelmed by it.

Team members develop a problem-solving approach to teaching and learning

"What exactly did Vanessa do with the blocks?" "What do her actions signify?" "What would happen tomorrow if…?" "How else can we support her emerging ability to stack and balance?" "What happened when we tried that strategy with Vanessa?" "What modifications can we make?" As team members discuss questions like these, they become increasingly analytical and articulate about child development issues as they *specifically* apply to individual children. They are able to voice and pursue their thoughts and intuitions so that when they find something that works, they can repeat or build on this strategy in related situations.

Team members teach and learn from one another

On a daily basis, team members share what they are learning about children and curriculum strategies. Therefore, collective learning is an ongoing process. As organizational psychologist Rensis Likert (1967) found in his studies of teams, "The important skills are not bottled up in a particular individual but are rapidly shared and cooperatively improved" (p. 57).

Forming the team

Identify daily team teaching and planning partners

Identifying team members in your particular early childhood setting is the first step toward effective teamwork. The type of setting and the agency with which it is connected influence who is readily available for daily team teaching and planning.

A Time for Planning

Staff of early childhood programs often wonder how to make time for the team to plan together as a group. In one Oklahoma day care center, staff have solved this problem by planning as children nap, in the same room with the sleeping children. It's a large room, and children sleep at one end while adults talk quietly at the other — where they can still keep an eye on the children but the children cannot overhear the adults talking about them. This teaching team reports that regular practice has made them efficient planners — they do it in 30 minutes, leaving them plenty of time for staff breaks.

If you work in a *center-based early childhood program*, you probably already work in teaching teams when children are present, although your team may not meet together regularly to plan together for children. If yours is a full-day program in which children come and go throughout the day and staff work in shifts, coordinating team efforts will be complicated because it requires communication between staff at changeover times. And, if you work in a laboratory school setting, the logistics of collaboration become even more complex. The large number of people — college students, student teachers, work-study students, regular staff — who regularly or periodically work in such settings complicates the mechanics of collaboration, calling for a firm public schedule of staff meeting time.

Home-based programs present their own special teamwork issues. You may be a home day care provider working by yourself. Finding another home day care provider, family member, or student volunteer to collaborate with will probably require you to reach into your personal store of initiative and ingenuity. On the other hand, if you are a home day care provider who employs one or two staff members, your team is already formed. If you are a home visitor, you already have an ideal circumstance in which to collaborate with parents.

Teamwork is most effective when teaching team members have designated, uninterrupted time each day to share their observations of children and to plan the next day's activities.

Other home visitors working with similar families may also be available to act as partners.

Designate a daily, uninterrupted time for the team to meet

To work most effectively, teaching team members need *daily, uninterrupted adult meeting time* so that they can share observations of children and plan what to do next. Because most early childhood programs are not initially established with adult teamwork in mind, almost everyone working with young children has to make some effort to find time to meet as a team on a daily basis. If you have not already done so, you will want to look closely at your current schedule and, with administrative support, identify a daily adult evaluation and planning time — before children arrive, after they leave, or while they are napping. This may entail starting your program for children later than it currently starts, ending it earlier, or hiring additional staff.

HighScope recognizes, however, that there are some situations where daily team planning is not feasible. Some teams therefore meet every other day, twice a week, or at a minimum, once a week. In these circumstances, team members find mechanisms other than face-to-face meetings to share observations about the children, use this information to plan for individual children and the class as a whole, and clarify which team member is responsible for preparing and carrying out each part of the daily schedule.

Include support staff on the team as needed

In an agency setting, it is also important to enlist the support staff as collaborators — the speech therapist, health coordinator, home visitor, psychologist, parent specialist, education coordinator, curriculum assistant, lead supervising teacher, student-teacher coordinator, trainer, social worker, nutritionist, and so forth. These are the people who *periodically* join the immediate staff team in training sessions, staff meetings, or "on the floor" to work with specific children or to contribute from their particular area of expertise.

The collaboration of immediate staff and support staff ensures that all the adults within the agency who come in contact with children work toward the same goals and carry out common

---

Parents Join the Team

The Montgomery County Community Action Agency (MCCAA) Head Start Program in Dayton, Ohio, not only encourages on-site parent-staff collaboration, but also conducts a formal program for interested parent volunteers called Parent Education Participation Program (PEPP). The program is designed to give parent volunteers job experience and training that will qualify them later on to apply for staff positions within the MCCAA Head Start program.

Interested parents volunteer for at least one 3-hour session per week for 32 weeks. During the 32 weeks, parents attend training sessions with staff and gradually take on increasing amounts of responsibility, according to a cumulative 10-step sequence. Step one, for example, includes four sessions of observing children using the active learning checklist and sharing these observations with staff.

Hiring Potential Collaborators

A preschool administrator in Kansas supports her staff by using a careful hiring process to look for new staff members who are philosophically compatible with the HighScope educational approach and will work well with other team members. She follows a four-step hiring process:

1. **Preliminary interview:** Talk to the candidate to gather information about his or her experiences and approach to working with children. To what extent, for example, does the candidate share control with children and other adults?

2. **Written questions:** Ask the candidate to describe in writing how he or she would respond to a typical situation such as the following: *It's cleanup time, and Joey wants to save his block building to show his mom. How might you respond?* Ask the candidate to design an early learning environment. Give the candidate a blank floor plan on which to draw in interest areas, materials, and equipment.

3. **Meet the staff:** Other staff members casually interview the candidate. This gives the candidate and staff members a chance to assess whether they might work comfortably with one another. Later, staff members who may be working closely with the candidate share their observations.

4. **Observe the candidate:** Observe the candidate with children. Does he or she tend to be supportive? Overly permissive? Highly directive?

Through this process, the director reports, she is generally able to hire staff who support the active learning program she administers.

---

strategies for reaching them. Such teamwork avoids the confusion and frustration that result when, for example, the immediate staff members are focusing on active learning and supporting children's strengths; the home visitors are focusing on children's deficits and ways to overcome them; the speech therapist is taking children to labs for drill and practice; the parent specialist is responding to parents' push for academics by advocating worksheets as preparation for kindergarten; and the psychologist is instituting a child-management system based on behavior modification. While each person may be acting independently with the best of intentions, the conflicting strategies and demands of this eclectic approach are apt to confuse the children while at the same time immobilizing staff who work with the children every day. However, when immediate staff members have a regular daily evaluation and planning time, support staff can generally arrange their schedules to join them periodically or as needed to wrestle with issues of mutual concern. This way they can work together rather than at cross-purposes.

Strategies for Daily Teamwork: Five Key Elements

Adult teams implementing the HighScope Curriculum meet to discuss their observations of children and identify general curriculum strategies. Ideally they meet daily, for example, after children have left for the day or while they are napping (especially if someone else can watch the children at this time). However, daily team planning is not always feasible, depending on the program's schedule and administrative policies. So whenever and however team members can plan, they use various strategies to *share information* (e.g., reading and talking about anecdotes in person, looking at written or online anecdotal observations about the children), *divide and clarify roles* (e.g., deciding who is responsible for which tasks, such as buying materials, interacting with a specific child or group of children), and *use the curriculum as a common guide* to plan and carry out the day. The following elements guide staff in their individual and collaborative efforts:

- Establishing supportive relationships among adults
- Gathering accurate information about children
- Making group decisions about children: Interpreting observations and planning what to do next
- Planning lessons: Using the elements of the curriculum to plan the program day
- Making group decisions about teamwork

The following sections describe the strategies for implementing each of these elements.

Establishing supportive relationships among adults

An early childhood team is a small, but complex, social system formed for the purpose of generating ways to support active learners. To be successful, team members need to build supportive relationships among themselves through open communication, respect for differences, and patience. Following are some strategies for building such relationships.

Communicate openly

Supportive relationships depend on specific, honest, straightforward communication. Psychologist Virginia Satir (1988) calls open communication *leveling*, in contrast to the four crippling patterns of communication listed next. When people feel the threat of rejection ("I'm afraid she won't like me. She'll think my field trip idea is stupid"), they often react by falling into one of these negative patterns:

- *Placating:* "No matter what I think or feel, I'll agree with whatever she wants."
- *Blaming:* "I'll find fault with her idea so she'll know that I'm not someone she can push around."
- *Computing:* "I'll use a lot of jargon so she'll be really impressed by how much I know."
- *Distracting:* "I'll change the subject so we don't have to deal with this uncomfortable issue."

On the other hand, when people choose to level with one another, they say what they mean. Their words, facial expression, body position, and voice tone are in harmony rather than in opposition to one another. According to Satir (1988), levelers are people you trust: "You know where you stand with them, and you feel good in their presence" (p. 94). Further, Satir says, "Being a leveler enables you to have integrity, commitment, honesty, intimacy, competence, creativity, and the ability to work with real problems in a real way…. People are hungry for straightness, honesty, and trust. When they become aware of leveling and are courageous enough to try it, they diminish their distance from other people" (p. 98).

Open communication occurs when team members identify issues and describe how they interpret or approach them as clearly and specifically as possible. Barriers to communication occur when one or more people withhold feelings or relevant information by placating, blaming, computing, or distracting.

Suppose, for example, that you and your team are planning to make pancakes with the children tomorrow. You are concerned that the activity as it currently stands does not include the ingredients of active learning. Here are examples of five different ways you might communicate your concerns. In our view, only the fifth one, **leveling**, is helpful:

- *Placating:* "I'm really sorry to ask such a dumb question. Promise you won't get mad at me. Making pancakes with kids is great. They each get a chance to stir the batter. Maybe I don't understand. Is this active learning?" or (Looking down at the table, sighing) "Sure, making pancakes is fine with me."
- *Blaming:* "What's the matter with you? Don't you remember anything about active learning? You've missed the boat with this pancake activity!"
- *Computing:* "The ingredients of active learning provide the parameters of any

developmentally appropriate process we engage in with preoperational children. Let us consider these critical factors. Any comments?"

- *Distracting:* "Pancakes. Granddad used to make them at our house. I'll look in the kitchen to see if we have everything we need. [Calls from the kitchen.] We're out of juice and napkins. I'll stop at the store on my way home."

- *Leveling:* "So far the only action we have children doing is stirring the pancake batter. How can we give them choices, materials to manipulate, and opportunities to talk and think about what they are doing?"

Leveling is not easy, especially if it involves breaking old communication patterns. And while leveling results in honest, useful communication, it does not shield you from being human — from making mistakes, being criticized, affecting others, and exposing your imperfections. On the other hand, leveling also allows you to grow, to learn from your mistakes without being devastated, and to respect yourself as a person and a team member.

Respect individual differences

Rather than avoid differences, supportive team members wrestle with different ideas, values, experiences, and views of the curriculum. Likert's (1967) management studies show, for example, that a major human asset in productive teams is the "capacity to use differences for purposes of innovation and improvement, rather than allowing differences to develop into bitter, irreconcilable, interpersonal conflict" (p. 135).

Similarly, human resource developer Gordon Lippitt (1980) points out that "in an effective group, persons are willing to express their differences openly. Such expressions create authentic communication and more alternatives for a quality decision" (p. 14). For example, in the team of adults planning to make pancakes with children, Sue is an experienced cook, Shawna is well-versed

In a supportive team, members of the group feel free to express their ideas and individual differences openly, choosing to collaborate and engage in authentic communication.

in the ingredients of active learning, and Melany is an engaging storyteller. Together, they come up with a sure-fire plan for the activity that includes an easy pancake recipe; materials and ingredients so that each child can make and fry his or her own batter; and plans for the group to eat the pancakes and listen to an Indian folk tale about "runaway" batter that Melany will tell using the baking tools as props.

While some individual differences may make other team members uncomfortable, each team member makes a choice about how to respond. A team member can choose to see individual characteristics as barriers to collaboration or as opportunities for growth. For example, the chart presented on page 128, "Breaking Down Barriers to Collaboration," illustrates some contrasting choices a team member might make in response to interpersonal differences.

In supportive team relationships, adults *choose to collaborate*. They view one another as valuable resources for gaining a broader perspective on educating young children and working with others.

Have patience with the teamwork process

Establishing an honest dialogue about specific curriculum issues, leveling with people, getting to know team members in a more than superficial way, learning from one another's strengths and differences — all these processes take time. Therefore, be patient with yourself, your team members, and the teamwork process. Though the process of developing supportive relationships may appear inefficient and time-consuming, in the long run it allows early childhood teams to work effectively together through the daily ups and downs of life with children. In fact, how we work with team members and with children are mirror images.

Breaking Down Barriers to Communication

Individual Characteristic	Choice to Erect Barriers	Choice to Collaborate and Grow
Speaks in dialect.	It is too hard to figure out what this person means.	It is worth the effort to try to understand this person.
Speaks negatively of women.	He is a jerk to avoid.	I can counter his negative comments firmly, matter-of-factly.
Wants everyone to do things her way.	She's a tyrant to fight.	I can propose alternatives that make sense to me.
Uses a wheelchair.	I am afraid I will do or say the wrong thing so I will not say anything.	He is a person, first of all, so I will approach him as I approach others.
Lives with her "significant other" who is a woman.	I do not want anything to do with a woman like that.	Maybe she can help us understand children who live in nontraditional families.
Believes in faith healing.	I know better than that!	Maybe his faith will help us when we are in a fix. Who knows?
Lives "on the wrong side of the tracks."	Why should I associate with her? My neighborhood is better.	We can learn from her about the children and families in her neighborhood.
Father is in jail.	Like father, like son. Stay away from him.	He has faced hard times and survived. That quality can help the team.
Never finished school.	She must not be very smart.	She can help us understand why children leave school.
Close to retirement.	Forget about him. He's leaving soon. What does he care?	How can we learn from his experience?
Unusual hair style.	She must disrespect people like me. I'll be on my guard.	She is willing to take a stand. We need risk-takers on our team.

When members of a team work together to establish supportive relationships with one another, they not only support active learning in children, they also enhance the quality of the work environment for themselves.

Gathering accurate information about children

Early childhood teams work together each day to gather accurate information about children to guide their daily interactions and plans. As team members interact with children, they are constantly observing and collecting factual information about them. Team members also briefly document findings about children as the first step in the process of deciding what to do next to support children.

Observe children throughout the day

"Observation," John Dewey (1933) reminds us, "is exploration, inquiry for the sake of discovering something previously hidden and unknown" (p. 193). Through observation and interaction, adults get to know children. They watch and listen closely to children as they work and play with them to find out what interests them, what holds their attention, and what they understand about their world. Guided by the ingredients of active learning, they ask themselves questions such as these:

— *What materials does Eli enjoy playing with?*
— *What exactly does he do with materials?*
— *What problems does he encounter? How does he solve them?*
— *What are Eli's interests? What does he like to do?*
— *What choices does he make?*
— *With whom does he like to play?*
— *What kind of play does Eli choose?*
— *How does he communicate verbally? Nonverbally?*
— *What language or dialect does he speak?*
— *What does he say?*
— *What kinds of experiences does Eli share? Reenact? Re-create in models, drawings, paintings?*
— *What kinds of questions does he ask spontaneously?*
— *Who supports him? How?*
— *With whom does he feel at ease?*

As team members learn about the HighScope plan-do-review process and the HighScope key developmental indicators (KDIs), they ask themselves additional questions, such as these:

— *What kinds of plans does Eli make?*
— *How engaged is he during each part of the day?*
— *Is Eli able to name and begin to regulate his emotions?*

Characteristics of an Effective Team

1. **Climate:** There is a positive climate of mutual sharing and trust. Staff and administrators know what is expected of them.

2. **Goal setting:** Staff work together to set goals. The goals then drive the team.

3. **Expectations:** Expectations are clear and are based on a shared philosophy and set of goals.

4. **Decision making:** Whenever possible, staff make decisions by consensus. They discuss many alternatives. Once a decision is made, everyone commits to carrying it out.

5. **Handling conflict:** Problems are viewed as a normal part of working together. Staff use conflict-resolution strategies to solve problems effectively.

6. **Regular evaluation of teamwork:** All members work together to achieve team goals. Program evaluation is based on whether the team as a whole has achieved the group's goals.

— *Does he represent his experiences through art? music? movement? pretend play?*

— *To what extent does Eli express himself using language? Is his vocabulary growing?*

— *How is he involved with classifying objects? Does he count them or arrange them in patterns?*

By asking and searching for answers to such questions, adults gradually begin to understand and anticipate how each child might act in specific situations. This information guides adults in planning experiences for children and in interacting with them from moment to moment.

Briefly note observations

It is easy to forget the details of even the most vivid experiences. Therefore, it is important for team members to document in some way what they observe about children. This enables team members to recall, report, and build on their discoveries.

There are many ways to record brief observations. Some adults jot notes on cards or sticky notes they carry in their pockets. Others make brief entries in spiral notebooks or on clipboards strategically placed around the room. Taking quick photos is another option. Setting aside a "recall prop basket" is a memory strategy that works for one day care teacher. Whenever she wants to remember something, she tosses a representative item labeled with the child's name into a basket. For example, a peg with the masking tape label "Miko and Karleen" might stand for a game these two girls devised with the pegs and pegboard. You need not include a great deal of detail in these forms of instant documentation. All you need is enough to jog your memory. You can fill in more detail later when you record a full observation and share it with your colleagues.

Whatever the documentation method, it is important for each team member to collect objective observations of individual children to share later with the rest of the team.

Suspend judgment

Team members observe and document children's actions from a neutral, matter-of-fact perspective. Here, for example, are two contrasting observations of the same situation:

- *Matter-of-fact anecdote or observation.* Lynnette stacked cardboard blocks. Next to them she stacked square, hollow blocks. Worked by herself without talking for 15 minutes.

- *Judgmental anecdote or observation.* Lynnette built a castle out of cardboard blocks and square, hollow blocks. Worked by herself for 15 minutes. Is not a sociable child.

While the first anecdote states that Lynnette stacked blocks, the second anecdote jumps to the conclusion that the stacks are a castle. The only way to confirm this, however, is to talk with or listen to Lynnette. As to whether or not Lynnette is a sociable child, neither anecdote provides enough information to draw any conclusion. Playing alone is as fundamental to children's play as playing with others. Playing alone for 15 minutes in itself may signify nothing other than Lynnette's great concentration and interest in the task at hand.

Gathering accurate and objective information about children is the first step in the daily team planning process. Team members use these anecdotes to recall, report, and build on their observations of children's interests and behaviors.

It is important that we describe children's actions as objectively as possible so that we do not unwittingly undervalue children who, for example, explore rather than build models, or who work alone rather than with others. To systematically record objective observations of children based on the HighScope Curriculum content, use COR Advantage (Epstein et al., 2014), which is described in chapter 5.

Making group decisions about children: Interpreting observations and planning what to do next

Once team members have gathered information about children, they must next decide "What does this information mean? How do we act on it?" Through collective reflection on the available information, the team generates strategies to support each child's development.

Reflect on the significance of children's actions

Reflective thinking about child observations is an open-ended process in which adults explore their observations, add overlooked details, relate new information to what they already know about the child, and speculate on possible meanings. Suspending judgment throughout this process makes it far easier for adults to fully explore alternative explanations of children's behavior and to generate a variety of corresponding support strategies.

For example, one teaching team decided they needed to observe Vanessa, a three-year-old child who had just joined their program. They gathered these observations about three of Vanessa's play episodes:

Vanessa: Play episode 1

— Piled six large hollow blocks on top of one another.

— Stacked four small hollow blocks end to end.

— Called, "Look it! Look it!"

— Stacked nine cardboard blocks end to end.

— Said, "Look it! Look it!"

— Looked at Erin's block structure.

— Climbed up the ramp, balanced, and jumped off.

— Repeated this three times until Erin said, pointing to her block structure, "My truck."

— Watched Erin pretend to drive her truck.

— When Erin left, Vanessa tried the same thing. From her seat, she saw the ramp again and slid down.

— Climbed back up on the ramp, balanced, and jumped off.

Vanessa: Play episode 2

— In the art area, got paste, piece of paper.

— Saw Eliot's box of paper scraps. Said, "I want some of that."

— Tried to take Eliot's box. He said "NO."

— Got another box from the shelf.

— Covered paper with paste. Put paper scraps on top. Left some paste areas uncovered.

— Ilana, Jeff, and Michael talked about their moms coming to get them. Vanessa said, "My mommy pick me up."

— Said, "Look it! Look it!" to Karl [adult].

— He asked her about her paper. She said, "For Mommy."

— Put away paste, got sponge, wiped off table and pants.

Vanessa: Play episode 3

— In the toy area, sat next to Karl.

— Lined up small blocks.

— Said, "Look it! Look it!"

— Moved small plastic bear along a line of blocks.

— Stacked small blocks and stood two bears on top.

— To Karl, "Look it! Look it!"

— Karl asked, "What did you make?"

— Vanessa raised her hands to the height of her stack.

— Karl said, "You stacked the blocks that high!"

— Vanessa nodded, adding, "I do it!"

After the team shared these observations, they wrestled with a number of questions: "What do these observations signify? What do they tell us about Vanessa?" Here are the conclusions they reached as they continued their discussion:

After observing this child's interest in building structures with blocks of different shapes, the adults in her program might support and extend her play by planning a small-group-time math activity around three-dimensional shapes.

What Vanessa's actions tell us about her

— Enjoys stacking blocks.

— Balances big and small, heavy and light blocks skillfully.

— Understands pasting sequence.

— Enjoys physical activities — stacking, climbing, balancing, jumping, sliding, wiping table.

— Chooses different blocks and different ways to stack them.

— Is engaged in what she is doing.

— Concentrates on materials she selects.

— Solves problems (got own paper scraps, used block structure as truck and climber).

— Uses language to call attention to her accomplishments ("Look it!"), voice her needs ("I want some of that"), and share important events ("My mommy pick me up").

— Seeks out Karl's acknowledgment; feels comfortable with him.

— Understands questions.

— Uses gestures effectively.

— Creates gestures when she needs them.

— Plays by herself.

— Is attuned to people and materials around her.

— Watches and imitates others (Erin).

— Mom is important to her.

Generate support strategies to try

After documenting what they know about children's interests and abilities, the next question for teaching teams to resolve is, "What do we do tomorrow based on what we learned today?" Here are the strategies Vanessa's team generated based on their knowledge of Vanessa, active learning, the daily routine, and the key developmental indicators. They decided to try these strategies during the following few days:

Support strategies to try with Vanessa

- **Throughout the day**
  — Be attuned to Vanessa as she plays so that when she looks for adult acknowledgment, an adult is there to converse with her.
  — Watch for further instances of Vanessa imitating other children.
  — Pause to include Vanessa in conversations.
  — Continue to give Vanessa time to solve her own problems.

- **At outside time**
  — Add loose materials Vanessa can stack and balance to the outdoor play area — boxes, boards, logs, lumber scraps, cans, plastic foam packing pieces.
  — Watch for Vanessa climbing, sliding, and jumping.
  — The stationary slide may be too high for Vanessa. Add removable sliding board and sawhorse pieces.
  — Bring out things for Vanessa to jump off of — balance beam, tree stumps, upside-down rocking boat, railroad tie.

- **At planning time**
  — Keep Vanessa in Karl's group for planning and small-group time.

- **At small-group time**
  — Use paste, paper scraps, paper towel tubes at small-group time tomorrow. Watch to see how Vanessa and others use them.
  — Plan additional small-group times around other sticky, gooey materials — play dough, real dough, finger paints, mud pies.

- **At large-group time**
  — Provide opportunities for imitation by suggesting group games: Have children take turns choosing a movement for others to imitate in "Everybody Do This."

- **At cleanup time**
  — Continue to count on Vanessa as an able cleanup person.

Try out the strategies and talk about how they are working

Strategies like those the team generated for Vanessa are a starting point. When adults try such strategies, however, they find that some work well while others do not. Some strategies do not work at first but eventually become effective as team members learn to adjust them to the actual situations they face with children. Some strategies that appear very promising, however, turn out to be useless. The only way to discover a strategy's effectiveness is to try it out. Here, for example, are highlights from a conversation the team had after trying out some of the strategies they had generated for Vanessa:

Strategy: Watch for further instances of Vanessa imitating other children. "I was surprised to see two examples of Vanessa imitating. In the block area she watched Jeff pretending to be a lion and she made her hands into claws just like he was doing. Then, at large-group time, she was the first one there. She sat down and started to pat the beat, just like we had done yesterday, so it seemed to me that she was imitating Karl from yesterday!"

Strategy: Continue to give Vanessa time to solve her own problems. "At one point this morning I was afraid this idea wasn't going to work. Vanessa went into the block area and hit Zach. But then Jeff turned around and said, 'Use your words.' So Vanessa told Zach, 'I want to play here.' Zach moved his cars away from the front of the block shelf, and Vanessa began stacking the cardboard blocks.

"That reminds me. Vanessa went to wash her hands after painting, came out of the bathroom and said to me, 'Soap.' I got the liquid-soap dispenser down off the high shelf and was ready to give her a squirt, but she stopped me. 'I do it.'

she said. I gave her the bottle so she could do it herself. And she did!"

Strategy: Add loose materials Vanessa can stack and balance to the outdoor play area — boxes, boards, logs, lumber scraps, cans, plastic foam packing pieces. "These were great strategies except that today Vanessa was on the swings the whole time we were outdoors! Ilana, Jeff, and Michael used lots of the new materials to build a great house, though. I think we should bring out some sheets and blankets tomorrow for them, because they wanted something to use to make a roof. With Vanessa, we should just keep watching. She is very active and well-coordinated."

Strategy: Be attuned to Vanessa as she plays so that when she looks for adult acknowledgment, an adult is there to converse with her. "It seemed to me that Vanessa didn't say, 'Look it! Look it!' as much today. I still heard her saying it, but not as often — probably because one of us was generally near her. I know that I was much more aware of trying to see where she was and trying to keep myself close to her if I saw that no other adult was in her vicinity."

As they review the effectiveness of the strategies they have developed on a daily basis, teams fine-tune their plans and generate further strategies to support young children's growth and development. (See teaching strategies for each key developmental indicator in the corresponding companion books to *The HighScope Preschool Curriculum*, Epstein, 2012a–h.)

Planning lessons: Using the elements of the curriculum to plan the program day

Once team members have gathered information about children, their next step is deciding what it means and how to act on it. Teachers use the HighScope KDIs and COR Advantage to reflect on the significance of their observations for a child or group of children. The teachers then generate ideas for building on individual and group interests and scaffolding development by supporting what children know and gently extending their learning. As they engage in lesson planning, team members decide on one or more strategies, try them out, and then review them afterward to see what did or did not work.

Below are the strategies you can use to make planning an effective and rewarding experience for your teaching team.

Plan together at a consistent, mutually acceptable time

Planning is most effective and efficient when it happens at the same time every day. However, while HighScope recommends daily team planning, we recognize it is not always possible due to program schedules and staffing patterns. Planning every other day or twice a week can work, but planning should happen not less than once a week. Team members think creatively about when and where they can plan, and how to exchange information about children during the times they can't meet face-to-face (e.g., sharing handwritten or computerized anecdotal notes). For example, in half-day programs, the team might plan right after the children leave and before the adults do a final cleaning up. In full-day programs, the team might plan quietly in the nap area while children are resting, close enough to keep watch but far enough so as not to disturb the children or be overheard discussing them. Occasionally, other onsite staff or parent volunteers might help watch the children at naptime while the teachers plan. Fortunately, once team members are used to the planning process, it does not take long. Teachers can go over the day's notes and make plans for individual children and lesson plans for the group as a whole in about half an hour.

Use plan-do-review strategies to plan effectively and efficiently

During planning time, team members turn the strengths and problems of one day into the plans and strategies for the next. They systematically review what happened, develop a new work plan, decide how to carry it out, and establish criteria

Creating Lesson Plans for Children

If at all possible, plan with your teaching team. Together with your teaching team, look at your observations about children, then ask yourself these questions:

- What did I see children doing today?
- What do their actions tell me about….

— Their developmental level?

— Their interests?

- How can I provide materials and interact with children to support their play and learning?

Here is an example of how this planning process can work:

First consider children's developmental levels.	Dev. level →	Jenna speaks in one- or two-word responses.
Then identify children's interests.	Interests →	The children really enjoy using the cardboard tubes that a parent donated to the classroom.
Put the two together to come up with a lesson plan idea.	Plan idea →	For the children's planning time, I'll ask them to look through a tube and tell what they want to do at work time.
Plan and use adult support strategies to make the activity appropriate for the developmental range of all the children in your group.	Dev. range →	Jenna uses one- or two-word phrases, and Henry uses a compound subject or object in sentences.
	My strategy →	With children like Jenna, who can point or say a few words about what they want to do or play with, I can use comments to acknowledge what they say.
	My strategy →	With children like Henry, I can ask them to share more details about their plan: • What else will they use? • Are they going to work with anyone else? • Do they think they'll do this for all of work time? • Do they want to make a second plan?

— Adapted from Marshall, Lockhart, & Fewson (2007, p. 152)

During planning time, teachers use the HighScope KDIs and COR Advantage to reflect on their written observations of children and to generate ideas for supporting and extending children's learning.

for evaluating its success. As adults plan, they do the following:

- *Evaluate* what did and did not work in the previous day's plan.
- *Pool the day's anecdotal observations,* adding to what each team member was able to observe children doing and saying.
- *Discuss what each anecdote reveals* about the observed child's development and make plans about how to act on that knowledge the next day. Strive for consensus on plans.
- *Plan group activities* based on observations, children's interests and developmental levels, and the curriculum's learning content as reflected in the KDIs and COR Advantage.
- *Plan for individual children* based on observations, children's interests and developmental levels, and the curriculum's learning content as reflected in the KDIs and COR Advantage.
- *Set responsibilities* for each team member and make sure everyone holds the same expectations for carrying out the next day's plan.

- *Set long-range goals for individual children* based on their particular interests and development, and plan strategies for engaging them in activities and interactions to help them accomplish these goals.
- *Discuss and resolve any group or individual problems,* for example, when and where children can run, hop, and jump in the classroom, or how to respond to a parent's concern about the food served at snacktime. Strive for consensus on solutions to problems. If team members cannot agree on one idea, they can decide to try alternative solutions and then review them later to see what did and did not work.
- *Occasionally review the team planning process itself* to identify both strengths and areas for improvement.

As they go through this plan-do-review process, team members ask themselves three questions: (1) *What do you know* (what happened today)? (2) *What does it mean* (what do you understand about children's interests, development, and learning)? and (3) *What actions will you take tomorrow* (what will you do to support children)?

Remain focused and organized during the planning session

To keep planning manageable, team members break each task into smaller parts. For example, as a source of ideas when planning large-group time, each team member might share what he or she observed children doing that day, come up with an idea for the next day's large-group time, and talk about the related KDIs and COR Advantage items. Next the team might go over the materials needed for the activity and decide which team member will be responsible for preparing which materials. After they make sure they are clear about these expectations, team members might discuss who will introduce the activity and in what way, who will do what in the middle of the activity, and which team member will use which strategy for bringing the large-group time to a close.

Margaret tells her coteacher Becky that at work time, several children were moving and making noises like their pets — cats, dogs, and a parrot. Based on this observation and thinking of KDI 43. Pretend Play (Creative Arts), they decide to do a large-group time in which the children pretend to be animals and imitate animal sounds. To begin, they will sing a favorite song, "Old MacDonald Had a Farm," and encourage the children to name an animal, then stop singing to imitate the animal's actions and sounds. As a back-up, they will have pictures of familiar animals. Margaret says she will get the pictures. They agree Becky will introduce the activity by saying "Yesterday, I heard some of you barking like dogs and chirping like birds. I thought today we'd sing "Old MacDonald" and pretend to be different animals on his farm." She will begin singing the song, stopping after the words "And on his farm he had a _____." Once a child names an animal and everyone pretends to be and make a noise like that animal, Margaret will begin the song again, then stop to call on children who volunteer animal names. For children who are reluctant to name an animal, or for variety, she will bring out the animal pictures so they can choose one by pointing. At the end of large-group time, they will tell the children the pictures will be in the house area beginning tomorrow. Becky will bring large-group time to a close by suggesting children move and make noises like an animal of their choice on their way to snacktime.

Rotating tasks helps individual team members grow as professionals. These teachers alternate taking the lead in singing and signing with children at large-group time.

Decide together on the form for planning and recording decisions

A standard form serves several purposes. It highlights what needs to be reviewed and decided. It helps team members organize and focus their discussion. Finally, when information and decisions are written down for all to see, confusion or disagreements become obvious and can be resolved.

The most convenient forms are those that simply follow the order of the daily routine. For small-group activities (such as planning, recall, and small-group time) divide that area of the form into two or more columns to correspond to the number of groups in your setting. As a guide, you can also jot down what you expect children at earlier, middle, and later levels of development might do during a small-group time activity. Another useful tool is to write down on the form the relevant KDI numbers and COR Advantage item letters that are the content focus of each part of the day. Programs might also include abbreviations for relevant early learning state standards, Head Start Child Development and Early Learning Outcomes, or other important categories being addressed in the daily plan.

Whatever planning form staff develop, it should be simple, convenient, and reflect the daily schedule and content of their particular setting. (For an example of a completed daily lesson plan, see "Sample Preschool Daily Plan.")

Rotate tasks

Take turns carrying out different parts of the plan. Dividing the labor keeps each team member attuned to each part of the day. It also makes it less likely anyone will feel he or she is regularly stuck with a difficult or less desirable task. Rotation also allows team members to grow as professionals. Even if someone is unsure of his or her ability to do something, such as leading the children in a song, colleagues can provide the support and encouragement to take a risk and try something new. When teams establish trust, anything is possible!

Take advantage of each team member's strengths

Every adult brings unique interests and talents to the team. Just as teachers acknowledge children's efforts and accomplishments, HighScope recognizes it is important to let team members know their contributions are valued. Also, as they do with children, teachers use encouragement rather than praise with one another. For example, adults feel acknowledged when their colleagues ask them to do something, observe what they do in order to learn from them, comment on how children react to the experience, and suggest ways for continuing and building on the activity in the future.

Making group decisions about teamwork

Team members should regularly ask themselves: How are we doing as a team? What expectations do we have for ourselves as team members? Who does what? When? Are we sharing responsibilities equitably?

The processes of building supportive relationships, gathering accurate information about children, and generating strategies to support children's learning call for a consciousness of how the team is functioning. This involves discussing roles and expectations, sharing responsibility for team functioning, and making curriculum decisions as a team.

Discuss team members' roles and expectations

To avoid confusion and promote harmony, it is important for all teams to consider the roles and expectations that lay the groundwork for day-to-day interdependence among the members. While each early childhood team is different, some general starter questions are useful for guiding most team discussions; these are presented in "Discussing Team Members' Roles," on page 141. Add other questions as needed to address the particular concerns of your group.

Sample Preschool Daily Plan

Adults: Shannon and Dora	**Date:** 10-4-2013

Greeting Time KDI/COR Advantage: KDIs 11, 24, 25, 26, 27/COR Advantage Items E, F, N, O, P, Q
Door: Shannon   **Books:** Dora
Child Messages: 1. Joey's turn to choose song in song book
   2. New Legos in the toy area
   3. Matthew's birthday, 4 years old   **Transition:** By children's ages

Planning Time KDI/COR: KDIs 1, 2, 56/COR Item A (Shannon) Have children drive Lego car on a map of the classroom (using area signs)	**Planning Time KDI/COR:** KDIs 1, 2, 35/COR Item A (Dora) Have children wrap a toy they want to play with in a scarf and bring it back to the table

Work Time
Support the new Legos; spend time with Anna in the art area

Cleanup
5-more-minute song, ring bell and play soft music

Recall Time KDI/COR: KDIs 6, 21, 22/COR Item L (Shannon) Have children talk to each other on play phones	**Recall Time KDI/COR:** KDIs 6, 21, 22, 25, 29, 39/COR Items O, R (Dora) Have children write their letter under the area where they played in an area chart

Snack: Milk, water, carrots, and dip   **KDI/COR:** KDIs 19, 20, 21, 22, 26/COR Items E, F, L, Q

Large-Group Time: Easy to join: Sing "I dropped my head on the floor" and ask children what other parts of the body they can drop
Activity: Song book: Joey
Activity: Give each child a scarf; play fast and slow music
Large-Group Time KDI/COR: KDIs 16, 41, 42/COR Items Y, Z
Transition: Ask children to put away scarves as we say the color of the scarves and then move to small-group time

Small-Group Time Shannon **Materials:** Blue and yellow paint, paper **Small-Group Time KDI/COR:** KDIs 40, 48/COR Items A, BB	**Small-Group Time** Dora **Materials:** Pegs and pegboards **Small-Group Time KDI/COR:** KDIs 31, 32/COR Item S

Earlier	Middle	Later	Earlier	Middle	Later
Children will paint with hands, saying it changed color	Children will paint with hands, saying it changed to green, then explain how they got green	Children will predict what will happen before they try it, then test their predictions	Children will say random numbers	Children will point and count 1–5	Children will point and count more than 5, using the last number to say the total

Outside Time KDI/COR: KDI 16/COR Items I, J
Bikes, balls, sand toys, bubbles

To Remember
Parent meeting tonight

Content -----> **Interests** -----> **Planning Ideas** -----> **Developmental Range** ----> **Support Strategies**

As team members implement the HighScope Curriculum, they continue to wrestle with curriculum issues. Together they address questions such as "How can we incorporate enough time for plan-do-review into our daily routine?"

Share responsibility for team functioning

As they work together, team members periodically take time to consider their own roles as *collaborators*. They ask and discuss such questions as the following:

— *What are our strengths as a team?*

— *To what extent are we using open communication? Relying on and valuing each other? Sharing responsibility? Collecting and designing strategies around our observations of children? Sharing decision making?*

— *To what extent are we collaborating with support staff, parents, administrators? How are we maintaining contact with all parents? Our agency? The community?*

— *To what extent do we have contact with the other programs our children are currently enrolled in? The ones they will enter when they leave our program?*

Make curriculum decisions as a team

As team members consider and implement curriculum ideas, they also address whatever issues arise as a team. Here, for example, are some general curriculum questions teams must discuss:

— *How shall we arrange our active learning environment? What changes can we make now? Later? Whose support do we need to make these changes?*

— *What materials do we want to add? Eliminate? Supplement?*

Discussing Team Members' Roles

Planning for children
- When do we meet each day as a team to discuss child observations and plan for the next day?
- How do we record our plans for ourselves? For others (parents, visitors, support staff)?

Getting ready for children
- Who opens the building?
- Who takes the chairs off the tables?
- Who restocks paint, paste, glue, tape, paper, staplers, nails, lumber scraps, sand, etc.?
- Who checks on guinea pig food? Fish food?
- Who makes sure there are enough food and utensils for snacks and meals?
- Who sets up special materials for the day?
- Who checks out and returns library books?
- Who empties, cleans, and refills the water table?
- How and when do we rotate tasks so that responsibilities are shared?

Working together for smooth transitions
- Who greets the bus?
- Who greets parents who bring their children?
- Who greets the children?
- Who deals with bumps and bruises? Children who become ill? Medications?
- Who goes outdoors with the first group of children? Waits inside with those who need more time to put on boots, coats, mittens?
- Who takes children to the bus?
- Who talks with parents as they pick up their children?
- How and when do we rotate these responsibilities?

Supporting each other while working with children
- How can team members maintain contact with one another while maintaining their focus on children?
- What if a team member needs to leave unexpectedly?
- What if a team member needs to focus all her attention on one or two children for some length of time?
- What if a team member becomes really angry or upset with a child or team member?
- What can team members do when a child's favorite adult is absent?
- How can team members support one another in the event of unexpected visitors? Last-minute plan changes?
- What can team members do when an adult expects to talk with one of them during the time they are working with children?
- How do team members divide responsibility for the group on outings and field trips?

— *What common limits and expectations do we want to set for children?*

— *How can we incorporate enough time for plan-do-review into our daily routine?*

— *To what extent do our small-group times include the ingredients of active learning?*

— *What do we understand about the key developmental indicators? How can we learn to recognize and support them?*

— *How can we incorporate opportunities for children to recall their experiences by reenacting them, talking about them, and drawing pictures?*

There are as many answers to these questions as there are teams. More important than the answers, however, is the team's willingness to wrestle with each issue in terms of the curriculum and to come up with strategies to try.

Using the elements of daily teamwork: Involving a new team member

Collaboration among early childhood team members rests on establishing supportive adult relationships, gathering accurate information about children, and making group decisions regarding curriculum-related strategies and teamwork.

While teamwork is ongoing among adults, it does not preclude individual action. In fact, collaboration strengthens each person's capacity to act: "Teamwork develops security in interpersonal relationships and better understanding of one's functions and contributions to the group. Thus, an individual gains the respect of the group for contribution, with the result that the group is better able to sanction individual action" (Lippitt, 1980, p. 15).

On the other hand, some adults are very comfortable acting alone and have little experience with collaboration. Drawing such a person into the team can be difficult but rewarding. Here is how the elements of daily teamwork might be used by an early childhood team to involve a new team member:

An early childhood agency works closely with a senior citizen's group. Recently, one of its members, Virginia Jones, has joined your early childhood team. She works with you and the children three mornings a week and on those days stays for the daily team meeting. She is energetic and warm with the children, encouraging them to call her "Grandma Jones." Recently, she made four-year-old Chris her special project. Chris has cerebral palsy, uses a wheelchair, and communicates with gestures, noises, and facial expressions. Chris and Grandma Jones clearly enjoy each other. However, in her desire to help Chris, Mrs. Jones does things for him that he can do for himself. "Chris, you're my boy," she tells him affectionately. "Grandma will do that for you." While you appreciate Mrs. Jones's enthusiasm, you are concerned about her effect on Chris's developing a sense of autonomy and initiative.

Establishing supportive relationships among adults

Open communication with Mrs. Jones during the daily team meeting is one important way to begin working on this situation. In reviewing the morning together, a team member might begin the discussion with reflections on a specific situation, in this case, for example, a small-group experience using stickers. Here is how the conversation might go:

Janet: One goal we had for small-group time today was that each child would choose colored paper, stickers, and other decorations, and decide how to arrange them. We wanted children to use the stickers any way they wanted to. I know that this was a challenge for Chris. What did he do himself?

Mrs. Jones: Well, when I asked him if he wanted green paper, he nodded and smiled. I asked him if he wanted the duck stickers and he nodded, and he nodded "Yes" again when I asked him if he wanted the ducks in a row. So he made lots of choices.

Janet: Yes, he certainly agreed with you about the paper, the duck stickers, and their position. Did he actually touch or handle any of the materials?

Mrs. Jones: No. It would have been just too hard for him.

Myron: Which part was too hard for him?

Mrs. Jones: Well, the stickers were too small, and getting the paper off the backs would have been too frustrating for him.

Myron: You know, I noticed that a number of children really struggled with getting the sticker backing off. What I did with Alyse and Ryan, who were quite frustrated, was to pull the backing off just a little way, giving it a little start so they had an edge to grab on to. That worked for them. Do you think this might work with Chris?

Mrs. Jones: Well, yes, it might. And I also think we should get some bigger stickers.

Janet: Yes! That might help a lot of the children. What if we had big and little stickers tomorrow, and for Chris and other children who have trouble, we can pull the backing just a little bit to get them started.

Mrs. Jones: That just might work with Chris!

Myron: Let's try it and see. I know where we can get some big stickers.

In addition to such open communication, it is also important for team members to seek out, understand, and respect Mrs. Jones's uniqueness, using the special resources she brings to the team. For example, she has lived through the Civil Rights Movement and the Vietnam War, events other team members may only know about from books, has persevered and remained optimistic through many personal and political changes, and has reared her own children and grandchildren. Along the way, she's collected a storehouse of stories about people she has known and places she has lived, and she loves to tell stories to anyone who will listen. In addition, she never throws anything away and makes clothing, toys, and games from everyday materials. Along with communicating openly about active learning as an alternative to doing things for children, it is equally important for team members to find as many opportunities as possible to put Mrs. Jones's storytelling and toy-making strengths to use.

Mrs. Jones, like any other adult, will probably not change overnight, or after one discussion with team members about Chris and active learning. It will take time, some successes with storytelling and toy-making, support from team members, and further discussions about active learning for her to see for herself that she can help Chris most by encouraging him to do things for himself, even though most physical acts require an enormous effort from Chris.

Gathering accurate information about children and making group decisions about strategies to try

It is important that Mrs. Jones take part in observing Chris and other children to discover their interests and abilities, especially since she may well be more accustomed to seeing what children cannot do rather than what they can do. As she participates in discussions that focus on accurate information about children and is involved in developing and testing strategies to support them, she is very apt to find examples of strategies she used or saw in the past but has never thought about before in terms of active learning. Being a member of a curriculum-centered early childhood team puts Mrs. Jones in the position of translating her experiences with children and people into a new language and culture — that of shared control. And, for Mrs. Jones or anyone else, learning a new language and way of doing things takes time, persistence, and a chance to practice and make mistakes in a supportive setting.

Making group decisions about teamwork

Scheduling periodic discussions about team members' roles and expectations, shared responsibility for team functioning, and curriculum decisions on the days Mrs. Jones is present for team meetings will enable her to become involved in understanding and contributing to team functioning. As she participates in this process, Mrs. Jones will come to realize that others value her observations and contributions, and she, in turn, will be more likely to value and attempt to implement the ideas of her teammates.

Staff support and supervision

Just as observation is essential for teachers to learn about and support children, it also helps adults learn about and improve their teaching practices. In addition to being observation based, supervision in HighScope programs is also mutual and interactive. Unlike styles of supervision that go in one direction (top-down), supervisory relationships in HighScope settings are joint problem-solving endeavors. All the players are motivated to serve the best interests of children and families. Put another way, supervisors and teachers act as a team to promote professional development in the same way that teachers work together to promote child development.

HighScope uses two techniques, both based on observation and supervisor-teacher interaction, to support curriculum implementation and solve problems in the classroom. One form of support is called observation/feedback (O/F). This process may be initiated by the supervisor or teaching team and occurs in response to a specific question or concern about curriculum implementation. The supervisor writes an extensive narrative based on the focus of the observation (e.g., the learning environment), makes the relevant curriculum notes (e.g., how well the setup of the environment encourages children to elaborate on their play and interact with others), and then discusses these in a mutual feedback process with the teachers.

The other system for supporting and supervising teachers uses the Program Quality Assessment (PQA; described in chapter 5), a tool for evaluating specific aspects of program implementation. The supervisor conducts a classroom observation using one or more PQA sections (such as "Learning Environment" or "Daily Routine") and shares the results with the teachers. Together they set goals for program improvement. In addition to identifying goals for individuals or teaching teams, the PQA can serve as an agency-wide needs assessment. The results can then be used to design a tailor-made professional development program, in which staff members can enhance existing skills and develop new ones.

Each of these observation-based procedures for supporting teachers is described below. To use them effectively, staff in supervisory positions take workshops and practice the techniques during HighScope training. For more information on training opportunities for teachers and supervisors, visit the HighScope website at www.highscope.org.

Observation/feedback (O/F)

In observation/feedback (O/F), supervisors observe children in the classroom and how teachers interact with them. Supervisors then provide feedback on teachers' strengths and areas for improvement (or "modifiable issues"). Teachers and supervisors agree on a time of day, the child(ren) to observe, and the part of the curriculum that will be the focus of the observation (for example, active learning, small-group time, adult support during work time). The observation lasts approximately 15–20 minutes. The observer uses the two-column Narrative/Notes Form to record a detailed narrative of what happens and makes notes relevant to the issue(s) in question. The supervisor and teaching team then discuss the observation, list strengths and modifiable issues, generate solutions to problems together, and make a plan for improvement that includes follow-up support.

Observation/feedback is effective for several reasons:

- *Supervisors and teachers share a commitment to understanding children.* Because they are

In programs that use HighScope, supervisors and teachers act as a team to promote professional development using observation-based tools, such as the Program Quality Assessment, to evaluate specific aspects of program implementation.

interested in providing the best program possible, supervisors and teachers are able to look objectively at what is working well and what is working less well in terms of outcomes for children, rather than viewing the session as a personal critique of the teacher. A supervisor in a HighScope training course described the value of O/F this way:

I learned some principles that will help me provide feedback in an effective, encouraging way. I have been so sensitive to the already low self-esteem of some of my staff that it was difficult for me to make suggestions for improvement in a way that wouldn't deflate them further. The principle of observing the children as the means of getting to what is happening in the classroom and leaving behind the focus on the teacher is so sensible and practical. I'm really excited about the prospects of success with this model. (Dayton Teacher-Trainer)

- *Children are the focus of the observation.* By focusing on the children, supervisors actually learn more about the quality of the program's teaching and learning than when their focus is on the adult's behavior. Supervisors can identify which elements of the curriculum are being implemented and where the gaps might be. The process is also less anxiety-provoking for teachers since the spotlight is on the children, not on them.

- *The curriculum guides observation and team discussion.* By reviewing the ingredients of active learning, the elements of adult support, and other distinctive features of the curriculum, the team can see what is working and, when necessary, develop strategies for improving teaching practices.

- *Conversation about the observation is reciprocal.* In the dialogue that follows the observation, the supervisor and teacher talk and listen, give and take. Often O/F is initiated by teachers, rather than supervisors, because teachers want a trusted and knowledgeable "third person" to help them see and hear what is going on with a particular child or group of children during a particular part of the day. For example, a teacher might say to a supervisor, "Large-group time isn't going well for some of the children lately. Jackson and Alyce, for example, lose interest after a few minutes, and it's hard to get their attention back. Can you observe our large-group time next Tuesday? We have some ideas but would really appreciate another pair of eyes and ears." The supervisor would then observe Tuesday's large-group time, complete the Narrative/Notes Form, and join the teachers for their daily team planning meeting.

- *Team discussion results in mutually agreed upon action.* Once the team has examined what's happened in terms of the curriculum — especially the ingredients of active participatory learning and KDIs — they generate solutions and decide which one(s) to try. Putting their decision into "action" is an important step in the process and follows the same principles as the "work" that children do. In O/F, the "review" results in a "plan" that the teachers "do." Later, supervisors and teachers will repeat this cycle to see if the action is working or needs adjustment. In this way, the work of the adult team follows the same principles as the work of the children in the program. Participants of all ages learn valuable lessons in the process.

Program Quality Assessment (PQA)

The Program Quality Assessment (PQA; HighScope Educational Research Foundation, 2003a) also uses observation as a tool for focusing team discussion — in this case, with a focus on the quality of program implementation. HighScope teaching practices are captured in the 39 classroom items in the PQA. (Another 24 items focus on agency-level factors.) The PQA is organized to enable the supervisor and teachers to record objective anecdotes about what they observe in the classroom. Because supervisors and teachers are both familiar with the PQA, there is nothing hidden or surprising about

Observation and Feedback

Two teachers asked their supervisor to observe a large-group time. The planned activity was to have children move their bodies in different ways to slow and fast music. After the observation, the team talked about where the teachers got the idea for the activity, the KDIs featured, which elements of active learning were present or missing, the extent to which children were engaged, and what the teachers would continue or do differently the next time they planned a similar activity.

The team's discussion developed as follows:

Supervisor (sharing her observations): Eleven of the 16 children — Jeremy, Dahlia, Noah, Patsy, Bing, Jacob, Dewan, Juan, Tiffany, Pilar, and Sasha — were engaged the whole time. During the slow music, Karl and Bella went to the house area and brought back scarves to move with.

Teacher A: We planned the activity to focus on the "music" KDI in Creative Arts. Karl and Bella added the "movement" KDI.

Teacher B: Several children called out what they were doing, which is the "speaking" KDI in Language, Literacy, and Communication. They used some interesting "vocabulary" too! I cracked up when Jeremy wiggled his bottom and said, "Look at me shake that thing!" Some of the other children used words like *bend*, *turn*, and *back-and-forth*.

Supervisor: Yes, and I heard Bing say, "Twist, twisting my arms!" I also noticed Jackson, Kate, and Bethany stopped moving to the music and went to the block area about 20 seconds after you began the slow piece. You called them back to the group, but they continued building with the blocks.

Teacher B: It bothered me that they weren't engaged. I wondered if the slow piece lasted too long to hold their attention.

Teacher A: Good point. You know, when I put on that second song, I was worried that it might be too long, but it was a part of our plan to move to the different tempos.

Teacher B: Maybe we should have switched the music back and forth between the fast music and the slow music instead of letting both songs play all the way through. We would have still had the experience of moving to the different tempos, but each would have lasted a more reasonable amount of time.

Teacher A: I like that. I think it would work.

Supervisor: So one idea is that you could switch between songs, depending on what the children's actions are telling you they need. That would certainly be following the children's lead in real time! That makes me wonder. When you were planning the large-group time, where did the idea come from?

---

the content of the observation. Teachers know what to expect during the observation and contribute as equal participants during the discussion that follows the observation.

The PQA supports teamwork and professional development in several ways. Teachers might request that the supervisor, who is knowledgeable about the curriculum, look at a specific area or set of items when they have identified a concern about the classroom or the program. For example, teachers may want to know if children have adequate time in each part of the daily routine. The items on the PQA may also serve as an impetus for team discussion around such questions as "Where do we think we are most and least effective as a classroom?" or "Room arrangement is working pretty well. Now what can we do to improve adult-child interactions?" A supervisor might also initiate a complete or partial PQA observation to pinpoint strengths and areas for improvement across the agency's classrooms. The results would then lead to ideas for a series of professional development workshops, mentoring activities, and so on.

HighScope agencies typically conduct a PQA on the four classroom-level sections (Learning

Observation and Feedback (cont'd.)

Teacher B: Driving to work yesterday, I heard a bouncy oldies tune on the radio and found myself swaying to the music. Later, when we were planning, I thought the children would enjoy moving to music. We decided to use different tempos, not just fast ones.

Teacher A: I just realized that the whole idea came from us. I wonder how we could have built more on what we observed the children doing.

Supervisor: Do the children ever sing or move to music on their own?

Teacher A: I heard Dahlia humming tunes from that new Disney movie the other day. She kind of skated around the house area and fetched dishes while she hummed.

Teacher B: Lots of kids have been to see that movie and have the CD at home. It's got a whole range of musical tempos. Maybe we could use the selection at the beginning of the CD. It plays through all the tunes and tempos, but it's instrumental — no singing, which can be distracting because the children stop moving to listen to the words.

Supervisor: So next time you do a "moving to music activity," you can use music the children are familiar with, like the tunes from the Disney movie.

Teacher A: What about Noah and Patsy? They got so excited jumping to the fast music that they began running around the room. I had to practically corral them back to the group. Any ideas on how we can support those large movements but still keep them focused on the music?

Supervisor: I noticed that when the children were moving with the scarves, they seemed to stay more focused. Can we come up with any ideas from that?

Teacher B: For right now, maybe if we do moving to music with objects, it will work better than just moving bodies. Having something in their hands seems to help some children stay focused. Or we could start with one and give children the option of doing the other once things got underway.

Supervisor: So, let's review what you'd do next time with this type of activity.

Teacher A: We'd still use slow and fast music, but it would be music the children were already familiar with, like music from the Disney movie or holiday tunes we heard the children singing.

Teacher B: Giving the children a choice of moving their bodies or moving with objects seems like a good idea. We'd also be focusing on several key developmental indicators that way.

Teacher A: And, if we are using several different songs, we'll switch back and forth between them so the children aren't listening to any one song for too long. We'll watch the children for cues on when it's time to switch.

Supervisor: Sounds like a plan to me. Try it and let me know how it goes.

Environment, Daily Routine, Adult-Child Interaction, and Curriculum Planning and Assessment) two or three times a year. Agency-level sections (Parent Involvement and Family Services, Staff Qualifications and Staff Development, and Program Management) are usually completed once or twice a year, and rely more on documents and interviews than on observations as the sources of information. (For more on the PQA, see chapter 5.)

In summary, the purpose of staff supervision and support is to gather data about what teachers do in the classroom — not to pass judgment on them but to see how well the classroom works for the children. When the class is going well, supervisors can make teachers aware of the practices they use that are effective and supportive of children's development. If something is not going well — for example, children are wandering away during the reading of the message board — the supervisor-teaching team will collaborate to find a more engaging way to share the messages.

This way of thinking is similar to the attitude HighScope encourages teachers to adopt with children. When children are focused on a task,

Teamwork, such as conducting a large-group time activity as partners, brings staff members together around the common goal of making a difference in children's lives.

teachers support and encourage their work. When children hit one of their peers during a conflict, they are not viewed as "misbehaving" but rather as not having yet learned how to behave appropriately in that type of situation. Similarly, when a classroom situation does not go well, it is not seen as stemming from "bad" behavior by the teacher, but rather that the teacher needs to examine his or her teaching practices — often with input from trusted colleagues — to learn how to handle the situation more effectively. HighScope teams assume good intentions and help teachers and supervisors achieve them. The children are the ultimate beneficiaries.

Looking ahead: The relationship of adult teamwork to the rest of the HighScope Curriculum

The five elements of daily teamwork — establishing supportive relationships among adults, gathering accurate information about children, making group decisions about children, planning lessons using the elements of the curriculum, and making group decisions about teamwork — are integral to how adults work together to implement the HighScope Curriculum. Following the next chapter on *child and program assessment*, this book describes the classroom practices adults use

Strategies for Supporting Daily Teamwork: A Summary

Forming the team
- Identify daily team teaching and planning partners.
- Designate a daily, uninterrupted time for the team to meet.
- Include support staff on the team as needed.

Establishing supportive relationships among adults
- Communicate openly.
- Respect individual differences.
- Have patience with the teamwork process.

Gathering accurate information about children
- Observe children throughout the day.
- Briefly note observations.
- Suspend judgment.

Making group decisions about children: Interpreting observations and planning what to do next
- Reflect on the significance of children's actions.
- Generate support strategies to try.
- Try out strategies and talk about how they are working.

Planning lessons: Using the elements of the curriculum to plan the program day
- Plan together at a consistent, mutually acceptable time.
- Use plan-do-review strategies to plan effectively and efficiently.
- Remain focused and organized during the planning session.
- Decide together on the form for planning and recording decisions.
- Rotate tasks.
- Take advantage of each team member's strengths.

Making group decisions about teamwork
- Discuss team members' roles and expectations.
- Share responsibility for team functioning.
- Make curriculum decisions as a team.

to carry out the curriculum's principles: *arranging and equipping spaces for active learners*, conducting the HighScope *plan-do-review* sequence, and the other elements of the *daily routine*. The eight companion books to The HighScope Preschool Curriculm describe how these practices identify and build on the HighScope *key developmental indicators*.

The ongoing daily teamwork of immediate staff and the support staff who are able to join them from time to time makes the effective implementation of this curriculum possible. Teamwork builds bridges among adults who make a difference in children's lives, uniting them as they support the development of children's strengths and emerging skills and abilities. Adult teamwork also models for children a way of interacting with others that relies on **cooperative relationships, constructive problem solving,** and **personal initiative**.

CHAPTER 5

Child and Program Assessment

In the National Association for the Education of Young Children (NAEYC) position statement quoted at right, Sue Bredekamp and Teresa Rosegrant (1992) recognize the potentials and risks of assessing children and the programs that serve them. As researcher and instrument developer Samuel Meisels (2001) reminds us, "Fundamentally, for assessment to have an enhancing rather than a corrosive impact, we need to bear in mind the root word of 'evaluation' — value. Too often, what takes place in the name of assessment does not correspond to the values by which we try to lead our professional lives or manage our professional activities" (p. 5).

So how can we conduct child and program assessment so as to match the values we uphold? Bredekamp and Rosegrant (1992) define child assessment as "the process of observing, recording, and otherwise documenting the work children do and how they do it, as a basis for a variety of educational decisions that affect the child" (p. 10). They say program evaluation and accountability addresses the question of whether the program, as implemented, meets its goals and objectives for children and families. In sum, when done appropriately, programs measure how much young children grow and learn and how well teachers support that development. Staff use the results of this ongoing assessment to continue what is working and improve what is not, for example, to expand children's experiences or provide teachers with additional training.

HighScope has two comprehensive assessment tools to carry out this systematic review and enhancement process. COR Advantage (Epstein et al., 2014) assesses children's learning across content areas. Based on their observations, teachers write daily anecdotes that objectively describe children's behavior, use

> "Assessment can be used to ensure that individual children's needs are met and that each child benefits from educational experiences; unfortunately, assessment can also be used to harm children — to label, track, or deny children opportunities. Similarly, assessment can be used to inform and enhance curriculum or to narrow and limit curriculum. Assessment has the potential to improve teaching or to impoverish it."
>
> — Bredekamp & Rosegrant (1992, p. 6)

these anecdotal notes to rate their development, and then plan activities to help individual children as well as the group have positive learning experiences. (See chapter 4 for how teaching teams carry out this process.) The Preschool Program Quality Assessment (PQA; HighScope, 2003a) evaluates whether teachers and agencies are implementing the most effective teaching and program management practices. Using the observational and interview items on the PQA, an evaluator rates a

Child assessment is meaningful if practitioners can use the findings to make sound educational decisions.

set of essential program components to identify strengths and areas for improvement.[1] Because COR Advantage reflects basic child development principles and research, and the PQA is consistent with national standards and best practices, both assessment instruments are suitable for use in any and all developmentally based programs, not just those implementing the HighScope Curriculum.

Assessment works best when it is a dynamic process that involves multiple contributors and uses data collected in different situations over several points in time. Information gathered in this way is "authentic," that is, it produces valid results that can help us accurately determine how well programs meet the needs of the children and families they serve. Conducting valid assessment requires time and money to obtain the instruments, train teachers and supervisors to use them, collect and interpret data, make changes based on the results, and then reevaluate the outcomes.

Why should programs invest their limited resources in this way? Child development professors Virginia Buysse and Lisa Boyce (2003) answer that professionals "are motivated by a genuine desire to understand how our work affects young children, families, and the programs that serve them.…Program evaluation is a worthwhile investment when information obtained through systematic data collection leads to more effective ways of identifying children and families who need services or of designing interventions that are more acceptable and effective" (p. 4). Even when no problems are identified, conscientious educators are motivated to continually improve their teaching practices based on valid assessments of how and what children are learning. Likewise, programs want to be sure their policies build on the strengths of staff members and the families they serve.

In HighScope early childhood settings, assessment is conducted with these goals for children and programs in mind. This chapter begins with an overview of the authentic assessment of children, followed by a description of the content and procedures for using COR Advantage. It then presents a discussion of effective program quality measures and describes the Preschool PQA.

Child Assessment

Authentic assessment of children

Educators assess children to measure their development and see whether the programs children attend contribute to their growth. Traditional **testing** — such as when a child is pulled out of the classroom to answer a series of predetermined questions — is one way to measure children's learning. But, as expressed by the teacher in the quotation below, this type of assessment provides only limited information. It typically looks at learning for which there is only one correct answer. It does not indicate how children initiate their own

> "If I could change one thing about teaching here, it would be to limit the busywork of evaluating children. I feel like I spend the whole first month out in the hall testing one child at a time, when I should be in the classroom with all the children. To top it off, once I've finished the testing, the information that I'm left with is not that useful in my teaching. What I need is something meaningful that doesn't take much time."
>
> — A Detroit Head Start teacher at a HighScope training workshop

---

[1] HighScope has also developed and validated comprehensive assessment tools for other program settings, including the Infant-Toddler Program Quality Assessment (Epstein et al., 2014; Hohmann, Lockhart, & Montie, 2013); the Family Child Care Program Quality Assessment (HighScope, 2009); the Youth Program Quality Assessment (HighScope, 2003c); and the Ready Schools Assessment (HighScope, 2006). Information about child and program assessments is available at www.highscope.org.

Discussing child observations right after the children leave for the day ensures that the data recorded are fresh and authentic.

learning, engage with materials, solve problems, or collaborate with others. Moreover, it only shows how young children perform in the testing situation, not how they act in real educational settings and everyday life. Given how variable children's behavior can be from day to day — depending, for example, on whether they are tired or rested, hungry or recently fed — testing is likely to yield an unreliable and invalid picture of their development (Hills, 1992).

Another way to measure children's development is with **authentic assessments**. These include observations, portfolios of children's work, and ratings of children's behavior by the adults who know them (Jablon, Dombro, & Dichtelmiller, 2007). These types of measures provide teachers with valuable and practical information to understand and plan for the developmental needs of their students. Authentic assessments are more naturalistic than traditional tests. They take place in the real world or duplicate a familiar situation, instead of creating an artificial environment. As such, they provide a more accurate picture of what children normally do and are likelier to reflect their true capabilities.

Assessments based on objective observations of children as they interact with familiar materials and people are valid and authentic. They are not biased, because they respect and accommodate

---

Advantages of Authentic Assessment

Authentic assessment of children, in contrast to testing, offers the following advantages:

- Is based on children's performance in "real" classroom activities rather than an artificial testing situation
- Can focus on a broad range of developmental areas
- Assesses thinking and problem-solving abilities, not just factual knowledge
- Produces a profile of change and development over time
- Helps adults develop objective observational skills
- Helps adults become more knowledgeable about child development
- Encourages programs to become more child-oriented (view learning from child's perspective)
- Provides child-focused information adults can use to plan activities
- Makes adults pay attention to the "invisible" child
- If done as part of regular ongoing activities, does not add to program time or cost
- Can be done by all staff, including aides and assistants, with proper training
- Provides feedback to program administration and funding agencies
- Provides valuable and meaningful information for staff and parents to share

cultural, ethnic, and linguistic differences. Comprehensive observations are also more open-ended and look at a broader range of behavior than tests, which as noted above, often focus on a single area of learning (National Education Goals Panel, 1998). Finally, when authentic measures assess children over time, the results are not distorted by how children feel or their willingness to "perform" on a particular day.

HighScope recognizes that tests can be informative and are sometimes necessary, for example, for research or diagnostic purposes. Tests may be the only feasible option in large-scale program evaluations and are often required by a funding source. However, HighScope is a strong proponent of authentic observational assessment, especially with young children, and therefore develops authentic tools to measure development in as "real" an environment as possible.

The assessment instruments HighScope develops are always validated, meaning they meet the same rigorous scientific standards for **reliability** and **validity** as do conventional tests. A reliable assessment produces the same results when completed by different observers or at two closely spaced points in time. A valid instrument measures what it claims, is consistent with findings from similar measures, and may also predict future behavior. When developed according to these strict requirements, authentic measures can and should be as *standardized* as conventional tests.

COR Advantage

COR Advantage (Epstein et al., 2014) is the most recent version of HighScope's Child Observation Record (COR) child assessment system. This validated, observation-based instrument assesses children from infancy through kindergarten in all areas of development. It is available in paper-and-pencil format and online (with appropriate security guards) at www.coradvantage.org. Next we describe the content and components of COR

The teacher's notes about this activity may relate both to the content of the computer activity as well as the children's social interactions, yielding assessment data for both children in more than one learning area.

A quick note jotted down during children's block play can be expanded and recorded as a COR entry later, as teachers discuss their observations for the day.

Advantage, and explain how to complete the tool (collect and score the data) and use the information it generates.

COR Advantage content. COR Advantage is organized into nine categories (content areas) of development. Within each category is a list of items based on the same child development framework as the key developmental indicators (KDIs). (The alignment of KDIs and COR Advantage items is posted on the HighScope website at www.highscope.org). Each content area is composed of items that address key components in early learning, for a total of 34 items plus 2 for English language learners (see list, opposite page). Based on objective anecdotal notes about the child, recorded over time by an observer (such as a teacher, caregiver, parent, or researcher), each item is scored using an eight-level scale ranging from 0 (lowest) to 7 (highest).

COR Advantage is one continuous measure from birth to kindergarten. This developmental continuum allows programs that serve children over many years to track their progress throughout their length of enrollment. Multiple levels also help assess children with special needs, whose developmental ages may differ across one or more dimensions.

COR Advantage components. COR Advantage has a number of components designed to assist observers in collecting and using the assessment data. The *User Guide* (Epstein, Marshall, & Gainsley, 2014b) provides the rationale for this tool, instructions for its completion (i.e., how to enter and score anecdotes as well as compile summary forms), and answers to frequently asked questions. The *Scoring Guide* (Epstein, Marshall, & Gainsley, 2014c) provides descriptions of all the content areas, items, and developmental levels, along with examples at each level to help users score COR Advantage reliably. However, these resources are not intended as a substitute for COR Advantage training, which HighScope strongly recommends and makes available through courses and workshops. (See the HighScope website at www.highscope.org for information on training.)

In both the online and paper-and-pencil formats of COR Advantage, the actual assessment tool is accompanied by explanatory notes and sample anecdotes that describe and clarify each of the COR Advantage categories, items, and levels. (See "Sample COR Advantage Item" on pp. 158–159.) Also available is *Information for Families* (Epstein, Marshall, & Gainsley, 2014a), a booklet intended to go to each family to explain what COR Advantage is and how family members can participate in their child's assessment by sharing home anecdotes with staff. The online version of COR Advantage includes a secure Family Network

> "In using COR Advantage to heighten their observational skills, teachers get excited about things they hadn't noticed before. This tool helps them focus and formalize the notes made on each child. Observation is good early childhood practice and should be the primary assessment tool!"
>
> — A Houston early childhood program supervisor

Content Areas and Items in COR Advantage

Approaches to Learning
A. Initiative and planning
B. Problem solving with materials
C. Reflection

Social and Emotional Development
D. Emotions
E. Building relationships with adults
F. Building relationships with other children
G. Community
H. Conflict resolution

Physical Development and Health
I. Gross-motor skills
J. Fine-motor skills
K. Personal care and healthy behavior

Language, Literacy, and Communication
L. Speaking
M. Listening and comprehension
N. Phonological awareness
O. Alphabetic knowledge
P. Reading
Q. Book enjoyment and knowledge
R. Writing

Mathematics
S. Number and counting
T. Geometry: Shapes and spatial awareness
U. Measurement
V. Patterns
W. Data analysis

Creative Arts
X. Art
Y. Music
Z. Movement
AA. Pretend play

Science and Technology
BB. Observing and classifying
CC. Experimenting, predicting, and drawing conclusions
DD. Natural and physical world
EE. Tools and technology

Social Studies
FF. Knowledge of self and others
GG. Geography
HH. History

English Language Learning (if appropriate)
II. Listening to and understanding English
JJ. Speaking English

component that connects families to the anecdotes and photos that teachers enter for their child and offers activities family members can use to support children's development in areas assessed by the tool.

Besides the instrument itself (the *Scoring Guide*), the *User Guide,* and family booklets, the paper-and-pencil version of COR Advantage also includes booklets for recording child anecdotes, reproducible child and class summary forms, and desk-size guides with COR Advantage categories and items. In the online version, COR Advantage users enter and score anecdotes on the computer. The resulting data is tabulated for individuals and the class as a whole in a number of graphic formats. A child's report, called "Your Child's Development Profile" (see sample on p. 160), is used to communicate with families in both the online and paper-and-pencil versions of COR Advantage. In addition, COR Advantage aligns with state early learning standards, including Common Core state standards; Head Start's Child Development and Early Learning Framework and Five Essential Domains for Infants and Toddlers; and other early learning standards.

Completing COR Advantage. Using COR Advantage is a continuous process. Adults record objective anecdotal notes on children throughout the year (see chapter 4) and use them to produce COR Advantage reports at periodic intervals. Raters may also use information from portfolios, photos, videos, or other types of documentation to score COR Advantage. While it is not feasible for teachers to record an anecdote on every child,

Sample COR Advantage Item

This sample item is one of seven in the Language, Literacy, & Communication category. The actual item and the indicators for its seven levels are boldfaced. Below each indicator are sample anecdotes to guide the user in assigning items and levels to their anecdotes.

M. Listening and comprehension

Listening to and comprehending spoken and written words are essential aspects of learning. Children progress from understanding simple spoken words and phrases (also signs and gestures) to more complex and detailed information. Their understanding of oral and written stories undergoes a similar development. First, they pick up individual story elements, such as a character or single event. Later, they grasp interactions among characters and the sequence and causal relationships between events. Children also begin to connect what they hear and read to people and events in their own lives.

Level 0. Child responds to a voice by turning his or her head, establishing eye contact, or smiling.

The child responds to a voice by turning, looking, or smiling in the direction of the speaker. The speaker may or may not be in view.

- 9/29 While lying on a blanket outside, Jackson smiled when Theresa (his caregiver) spoke to him.
- 12/16 Hanna was lying on a mat. She turned her head toward Kay (her caregiver) when she heard Kay's voice.

Level 1. Child responds nonverbally to simple statements or requests.

The child responds to a verbal statement or request with a simple gesture (for example, nods or shakes head, looks toward the person or object being discussed) or appropriate action (for example, brings the requested object).

- 5/28 After naptime, Charlotte (a caregiver) said to Sebastian, "Let's put your shoes on!" Sebastian handed Charlotte his shoe.
- 12/16 During choice time, Sophia (the teacher) and Marcenia were looking at a book. When Sophia said, "I wonder where the kitten went?" Marcenia pointed to the kitten hiding behind the barn.

Level 2. Child responds verbally to simple statements or questions.

The child responds to a verbal statement or question with a word or simple phrase (such as "Yes" or "No," "More milk," or "All done").

- 7/19 At dropoff time, when Molly's mother left and said, "See you later," Molly said, "Bye-bye."
- 10/4 At lunchtime, when Thomas (a caregiver) asked Damien if he wanted more crackers, Damien said, "All done."

Level 3. Child adds to a conversation by connecting the topic to his or her own experience.

The child listens to a conversation between others, has an idea of what they are talking about, and makes a connection to his or her own experiences. The child makes a comment relevant to the topic being discussed.

- 7/11 At greeting time, Bryson listened to Stella and her dad discuss an upcoming field trip to the fire station. He moved closer to them and said, "I think we will see the fire trucks with the big ladders!" [Anecdote is for Bryson]
- 8/25 During work time while playing at the water table, Hayden said, "I'm three" when he heard James and Cynthia talking about birthdays.

Level 4. Child retells (remembers) three or more details in a story or book.

In talking about a story or book with an adult or other children, the child shares at least three details that happened (images, characters, actions, or events). The child may offer this information spontaneously and/or in response to a follow-up question.

- 11/9 At greeting time, Isaiah said, "I love that book about Max. He got mad at his mom, and then he wore a wolf suit and rode a boat to the monsters."
- 3/22 During snack, Paula said, "I got a new book. It's called *Knuffle Bunny*." When Miss Darla asked her what it was about, Paula said, "It's about Trixie who has a bunny and then she loses it and goes boneless." Miss Darla asked, "Does Trixie find her bunny?" Paula said, "Yes, they left it in the washing machine."

Level 5. Child predicts what will happen next in an unfamiliar story or book and gives a reason based on what happened earlier in the book or on his or her own experience.

The child says what he or she thinks will happen next even though the child is not familiar with the story or book being discussed. The prediction is based on what has happened before in the story or a relevant experience from the child's own life. The child may offer this information spontaneously and/or in response to a question.

- 2/3 During work time in the book area, while listening to a new book that Miranda (his teacher) was reading, Hunter said, "I think the mommy is going to let the girl come back and buy the bear, because she really wants it."

- 4/16 At morning arrival, while listening to a story, Angelina said, "I think the duck will follow the piggy. He did before and got back home."

Level 6. Child shows an understanding of content information (the topic) by asking and/or answering clarifying questions about key points presented orally or in text.

The child conveys an interest in and understanding of a subject by answering and/or asking relevant questions to clarify information that is presented verbally and/or in written format (print or onscreen).

- 10/2 When Mr. Smith was reading a book about the ocean, Susannah asked whether it was safe to swim in the ocean or if there were sharks.

- 1/16 When Alvaro was talking about dinosaurs, Julian asked him if the brontosaurus was a plant eater or a meat eater. Alvaro told him that it was "a plant eater" and that "its long neck helped him reach high leaves." [Anecdote is for Alvaro and Julian]

Level 7. Child compares and contrasts relationships among characters, events, and themes in a book or story.

In discussions or representations (that map story elements or graphically represent ideas), the child says what is similar and/or different about the characters and events portrayed. The child identifies the central ideas or themes in the fiction or nonfiction text. The child may cite specific textual evidence.

- 5/15 When using a Venn diagram to explore the characters in *The Three Bears,* Isaac noticed that Papa Bear and Baby Bear both liked porridge, but Papa Bear's porridge was "too hot" and Baby Bear's porridge was "just right." He said, "That's what's different."

- 4/5 In looking at a nonfiction book about snakes, Tanya said, "On page 7 it says that some snakes lay eggs, but other ones have babies."

— Adapted from *COR Advantage 1.5: Scoring Guide* (Epstein, Marshall, & Gainsley, 2014c, pp. 34–35)

Teachers consult the explanations and examples in the COR Advantage Scoring Guide as they choose an assessment item and developmental level for each anecdote.

> **Sample Page From "Your Child's Development Profile" (family report)**
>
> **Maggie Henderson**
> Report Date: 06/02/15
> School Year 2014–2015
>
> **Approaches to Learning**
> Maggie expresses a plan with a simple sentence and follows through. She asks for help solving a problem with materials. Maggie says one thing she did soon after the event.
>
> **Supporting Anecdotes:**
>
> 4/22: During planning time, Maggie put her letter-link symbol on the house area sign and said, "House area. Hide and seek from monsters." She pointed to the children who had been monsters the day before and then went to the house area.
>
> 5/14: At snacktime, after tugging on the top of her applesauce cup, Maggie handed it to Robin and said, "Help please."
>
> 4/19: During recall time, Maggie said, "Wyatt, Kira, Abby, scaring monsters. I say, 'Stop Monsters!'"
>
> **Social and Emotional Development**
> Maggie explains the reason behind an emotion. She asks an adult to play with her or share in an activity. Maggie makes a comment directly to another child. Maggie transitions between parts of the daily routine. She attempts to deal with conflict in a simple way.
>
> **Supporting Anecdotes:**
>
> 5/1: At work time in the house area, Maggie said, "My baby crying. She sad. She bumped her head."
>
> 4/18: During outside time, Maggie got the soccer ball from the shed, brought it over to Robin, and said, "Robin, play me soccer?" They kicked the ball back and forth to each other.
>
> 5/6: At work time at the sand and water table, Maggie and Blake worked together with the frogs. She asked Blake, "Your frog gonna jump?"
>
> 4/18: After snack, Maggie put her cup and plate away and went to large-group time. When Robin reminded her to throw her napkin away, she went back to the table, threw it away, and then returned to large group.
>
> 3/28: At outside time, Maggie and another child tugged on the same swing. Maggie said, "My turn." Then she wiggled onto the seat behind the other child who was still holding the swing.
>
> — Excerpted from *COR Advantage: User Guide* (Epstein, Marshall, & Gainsley, 2014b, p. 27)

every day, in every category, they do record several observations per week per child. They regularly review their collection of anecdotes to make sure each child's behavior is documented in each of the COR Advantage categories. If they notice a gap, they pay special attention to that child and area in the next few days to record what they observe.

Using the notes or other documentary evidence relevant to each item, raters score or "level" the anecdotes on a scale of 0 to 7 to reflect each child's current level of development. Depending on a program's needs and reporting requirements, the anecdotes are used to complete and score COR Advantage two to four times a year, for example, at the beginning, midpoint, and end of the program. Less frequent measurement does not permit one to track development over time. More frequent measurement does not allow sufficient time between assessments for any changes to show up.

Using COR Advantage. COR Advantage can be used by different people and for different purposes. Anyone who is familiar with the child(ren) being assessed and who has been trained to record and score anecdotal notes can complete COR Advantage. This tool is primarily used by the teachers and caregivers who are responsible for daily planning and regular reporting on their program. It is also used extensively by researchers and evaluators studying child development and how it is affected by program participation. The assessment may also be completed by paraprofessionals, curriculum supervisors, therapists, and other program or administrative staff directly involved with the children. Training by a designated HighScope trainer guarantees all these individuals will use the tool correctly.

Of particular value to adults who use COR Advantage for planning (i.e., adults who work directly with children) are the suggested learning activities included in the online version's lesson plan activity bank. These activities help teachers scaffold (support and gently extend) early learning in all content areas. Teachers can search for activities related to particular COR Advantage items, parts of the day, or keywords, and add selected activities to their own lesson plan. Teachers can also add their own favorite activities to the bank of activity suggestions in the program.

In addition to providing teachers with the basis for daily planning, COR Advantage information can be shared with a variety of audiences. During formal conferences, as well as with COR Advantage's secure Family Network, teachers share anecdotes (but not scores) with families to involve them in their child's program experience and to educate them about how to extend their child's learning at home. Administrators use COR Advantage results to monitor their programs and identify areas for staff inservice training. Finally, policymakers and funders, interested in holding programs accountable for their effectiveness, can rely on COR Advantage to provide accurate and objective information about how children are learning and developing.

Children's deep engagement with the materials and each other is visible evidence of the commitment by program staff to monitor the elements of program quality.

The Characteristics of Effective Program Quality Measures

Effective and user-friendly program quality measures have the following characteristics:

They define quality along a continuum.
Assessment instruments that permit only yes-no (or pass-fail) responses to each item provide limited information. Such measures are often used to measure compliance with regulations, but do not allow for the fact that quality is achieved in stages. An assessment tool that rates quality along a continuum helps programs see where they are now and the steps they need to take to continue improving.

They provide users with many concrete examples.
For the assessment tool to be used accurately and objectively, it should clearly describe typical behaviors at each level of program quality. Concrete examples allow different raters to interpret and score the same behavior in the same way, which is what researchers call inter-rater reliability. Multiple examples also help the staff see what level they are at currently and know, by specific illustrations, what they are striving to achieve.

They are comprehensive.
There are two aspects of comprehensiveness necessary for effective program assessment. First, measures should look at both the *structure* and the *process* of a program. Most instruments cover structural qualities, such as safety or diversity of materials. However, many fail to pay equal, if not more attention, to processes such as adult-child and child-child interactions. Research consistently shows these process features are crucial to defining quality and promoting child development. Second, comprehensiveness also means looking at the program from *multiple perspectives*. While our top concern is children, we should also pay attention to how programs serve families and staff. A complete program assessment tool should therefore look at how teachers interact with parents, how staff work together to plan for the children, how supervisors support staff development, and how management secures adequate resources. In other words, a program quality assessment should look at the classroom, the agency, the home, and the community — and the activities and experiences of the participants in each.

They have been field-tested and validated.
Although it is tempting for programs to create their own assessment tools, homemade measures limit the ability of staff to share information inside and outside the program. Moreover, "reinventing the wheel" fails to make use of decades of valuable research identifying what components are worth evaluating and how to look at them reliably and validly. By instead using proven assessment systems built on standard best practices, programs can advance the early childhood field as a whole, and at the same time benefit themselves.

Program Assessment
Valid program quality assessment

Decades of research, summarized in the National Research Council's landmark report *Eager to Learn* (2001), make it clear that program quality is positively and significantly related to early development and learning. In order to evaluate and understand children's performance and progress, we need to measure the educational experiences that the programs they attend are providing. Put another way, *programs*, rather than children, should be held accountable for early learning. To help programs meet their obligation to nurture the growth of young children, early childhood educators need valid tools to assess how well their programs promote learning in all areas of development. Such tools are typically referred to as *program quality* measures.

Child development professors Walter Gilliam and Valerie Leiter (2003) say the primary reason to evaluate program quality is to answer the question, "Does it work?" That is, does the program meet the goals it hopes to achieve with the children and families it serves? In designing an informative evaluation, program developers are

The Uses of Effective Program Quality Measures

Good program quality measures offer the following options and benefits across a wide array of uses and in different types of settings:

They serve as training tools.
Effective evaluation highlights program strengths and identifies areas to be improved through staff recruitment and training. Concrete examples help to define good practices for novice teachers. They help experienced teachers reflect on what they do and encourage them to continue growing as professionals.

They allow supervisors to observe individual staff members and provide constructive feedback.
Assessment can be anxiety-provoking if the rules are arbitrary and the intention is meting out judgment rather than improving performance. But a well-constructed tool can provide the person being assessed with clear expectations and opportunities for growth. Properly used, a good assessment tool allows a supervisor and a teacher (or teachers) to work as a team.

They facilitate research and program evaluation.
We often evaluate our programs to meet individual funding requirements. Beyond that, practitioners share a responsibility to contribute to the field as a whole. Assessments should serve both local and broad interests. They should meet rigorous scientific standards of reliability and validity, and produce results that are clear and concise. Instruments that work for researchers and practitioners build bridges between them. Researchers can ask meaningful questions and practitioners can use the results in their programs.

They communicate with many audiences.
Good assessment tools avoid jargon. They speak clearly to professional and lay audiences, including teachers, administrators, parents, researchers, and policymakers. If all these audiences understand the language used in an assessment tool, they are in a better position to collaborate on and commit to achieving high levels of program quality.

---

forced to consider whether they have set goals that are both meaningful and realistic, and how the achievement of these goals should be defined and measured. "Desired outcomes should be attainable" (Gilliam & Leiter, 2003, pp. 8–9).

Program quality, like child development, is complex and has many dimensions. It includes the *structural* components of the classroom, that is, how the learning environment is set up and what happens during the program day. Quality is especially dependent on *process,* notably how adults interact with children, and plan and carry out meaningful learning experiences. The ways in which staff relate to parents, one another, and the community can also affect children. Finally, agency-wide factors influence what happens in the classroom and therefore indirectly impact children. These agency-wide factors include how staff are recruited and trained, and how the program is financed and managed.

While we know all these quality components are important, we are still faced with the challenge of defining and measuring them. Only valid assessment instruments can guarantee we are looking at the right ingredients of quality in an honest and accurate manner. Good evaluation tools give us the information to determine whether we are achieving high levels of quality, and if not, where and how we can improve. Effective measures recognize that quality varies along a continuum; it is not a yes-no judgment. They examine programs along many dimensions, and provide concrete examples of different levels of quality so that observers can know what to look for. Like all assessment tools, they should be properly field-tested and achieve acceptable levels of reliability and validity.

Objective program measures are also essential to encourage self-assessment and to promote communication among everyone concerned about achieving high levels of program quality that will

The detailed examples of best practices given in the PQA's indicators can help experienced teaching teams consider whether long-established practices are working.

promote early development. Objective tools — with clear examples and an absence of jargon — give us a common language to share program information with parents, administrators, researchers, and policymakers. They help us talk honestly among ourselves and communicate with many audiences.

The Preschool Program Quality Assessment (PQA)

The Preschool Program Quality Assessment (HighScope, 2003a) is a rating instrument designed to comprehensively evaluate the quality of early childhood programs and identify staff training needs. Here we describe the PQA's content and components, and explain how to complete the PQA (data collection and scoring) and use the information it produces.

PQA content and components. The PQA consists of 63 items divided into seven sections. Each item is scored on a five-point scale from a low (1) to a high (5) level of quality. Form A: Classroom Items contains 39 items in four sections: Learning Environment, Daily Routine, Adult-Child Interaction, and Curriculum Planning and Assessment. Form B: Agency Items contains 24 items in three sections: Parent Involvement and Family Services, Staff Qualifications and Staff Development, and Program Management. Each PQA item includes detailed indicators that define the levels of quality, with many examples illustrating each one. The first three sections of Form A are designed to be completed mainly through classroom observation, while the rest of the assessment is interview based. (The Preschool PQA items are listed, without indicators, on pp. 169–170. Examples of a PQA classroom item and an agency item, respectively, are shown with their indicators on pp. 166–167.)

In addition to the assessment forms, the PQA includes an *Administration Manual* (HighScope, 2003b) that describes the instrument, explains how to use it, and reviews the research demonstrating its reliability and validity. A final section aligns the items of the PQA with the Head Start Performance Standards (US Department of Health and Human Services, Administration for Children and Families, Head Start Bureau, 2002). The PQA can also be aligned with state and local program performance standards. Like COR Advantage, the PQA comes in print and electronic versions. To access the online version of the PQA (HighScope & Red-e Set Grow, 2012), go to www.onlinepqa.net.

Although the PQA's *Administration Manual* and assessment forms contain instructions for collecting anecdotal evidence and scoring the PQA, HighScope highly recommends that raters receive training in using the instrument. Training results in the most effective, reliable, and valid use of the measure. For information on training, visit the HighScope website at www.highscope.org.

Completing the PQA. To collect data to complete the PQA, raters record supporting evidence for each item (objective anecdotal notes) as they observe classrooms or interview teachers and administrative staff. Based on their notes, they assign ratings to each indicator and compute item and summary scores. When the PQA is used by teaching staff as a self-assessment, or by a supervisor to support teachers' curriculum implementation, one or more sections can be completed during a single session. If the agency is conducting a comprehensive self-assessment with the entire PQA, each section may be completed at a different time. However, to get an accurate picture of the program at a single point in time, this period should be limited to several days or a week at most. When trained outside observers administer a PQA at a multisite organization, they generally score each classroom based on a half-day visit and complete one overall rating for the agency-level items.

Using the PQA. The PQA can be completed by a trained independent rater such as a researcher, program evaluator, outside consultant, or agency administrator. It may also be used as a self-assessment by site staff such as center directors, curriculum specialists, education or parent coordinators, individual teachers or teaching teams, or parents. Students who are preparing to become early childhood teachers and caregivers may also conduct a PQA. They can do it on someone else's classroom, or as a self-assessment of their own student teaching. They can then discuss the results with their instructor as part of their training and professional development.

Uses for the PQA include training, monitoring, staff support and supervision, and research and evaluation. These multiple uses are described in the following:

Training. Both preservice and inservice training activities are enriched by the PQA. It can be used in its entirety to provide trainees with a comprehensive picture of program quality. Individual sections can be used to focus on specific program components. The detailed examples in the indicators for each item offer concrete illustrations of "best practices." Users often comment that the PQA defines the term *developmentally appropriate practice* by translating an idea or ideal into specific implementation strategies. Even experienced teachers find that the PQA's depth and specificity help them reconsider long-established practices from a new perspective.

Self-assessment and monitoring. The PQA is a valuable tool for administrators and teachers to assess their own practices and identify areas for growth. It can also be used by those responsible for quality control to monitor program implementation at a single site or across multiple sites. Because the PQA is objective and quantitative, it can be used to set program goals in one or more areas, and to provide a numerical and anecdotal record of progress. HighScope also uses the PQA to certify teachers and accredit programs according to rigorous performance standards.

Staff support and supervision. Supervision can be effective and nonthreatening when the PQA is used to conduct observations and the results are discussed as a team. A teaching team and a supervisor familiar with the curriculum and the instrument may agree to focus on a particular aspect of implementation (for example, the learning environment). The supervisor then uses the relevant PQA section(s) to observe, record anecdotes, rate the items, and discuss the results with the teaching team. Together, they identify both strengths and areas for improvement, using the PQA's concrete examples to develop a plan of action. They arrange a time for a follow-up observation to review how the plan is working.

Research and evaluation. The PQA has been used extensively as a research tool when administered by trained outside observers. Studies can be designed to document program practices, compare quality in different program settings, evaluate whether and how staff training improves quality, and examine the relationship between program quality and young children's development.

Information and dissemination. With its straightforward language and detailed examples, the PQA can be used to explain research-based

Sample Classroom Item From the Preschool PQA

This example from the Classroom Items section of the instrument (HighScope, 2003a, Form A, p. 34) is completed by observation in the classroom. Depending on which boxes are checked in the rows of each item, raters assign an item score on a scale from 1 to 5 points.

III-F. Adults participate as partners in children's play.

Level 1 Indicators	Level 3 Indicators	Level 5 Indicators	Supporting Evidence/ Anecdotes
❏ Adults do not participate in children's play.	❏ Adults sometimes participate as partners in children's play.	❏ Adults participate as partners in children's play.	
❏ Adults are not partners in children's play.	❏ Adults use some strategies as partners in children's play.	❏ Adults use a variety of strategies as partners in children's play: • Observe and listen before and after entering children's play. • Assume roles as suggested by children. • Follow the children's cues about the content and direction of play. • Imitate children.	
❏ Adults attempt to dominate children's play (e.g., by redirecting play around adult ideas, telling children what to play with, how to play, or whom to play with).	❏ Adults quickly offer suggestions or ideas after entering children's play or offer suggestions outside the children's play theme.	❏ Adults support children at their developmental level and help add complexity to their play. • Match the complexity of their play. • Offer suggestions for extending play. • Stay within the children's play theme.	

Sample Agency Item From the PQA

This example from the Agency Items section of the instrument (Epstein et al., 2013, Form B, p. 24) is completed in interviews with agency staff. Depending on which boxes are checked in the rows of each item, raters assign an item score on a scale from 1 to 5 points.

VI-F. Instructional staff are regularly observed in the program setting and provided with feedback by someone familiar with the curriculum's goals, objectives, and methods for working with children.

Level 1 Indicators	Level 3 Indicators	Level 5 Indicators	Supporting Evidence/ Anecdotes
❏ Instructional staff are not observed or given feedback.	❏ Instructional staff are observed and given feedback 1–2 times per year.	❏ Instructional staff are observed and given feedback 3 or more times per year.	
❏ The person responsible for evaluating staff is not familiar with the curriculum for any age level in the program.	❏ The person responsible for evaluating staff is moderately familiar with the curriculum used at each age level in the program. **Example:** – The person evaluating the program understands its preschool curriculum but is unfamiliar with its infant and toddler curriculum.	❏ The person responsible for evaluating staff is very familiar with the curriculum used at each age level in the program.	
❏ Staff do not participate in the evaluation process.	❏ Staff sometimes participate in the evaluation process.	❏ Staff participate as equals in the evaluation process and discuss ways to build on their strengths and improve the quality of the program based on the curriculum.	

> ### Child and Program Assessment Strategies: A Summary
>
> **Child Assessment**
> - Use a validated and authentic observation-based child assessment to measure all areas of children's development.
> - Collect objective anecdotal notes and other documentary evidence.
> - Use anecdotal information to plan daily for individual children's development and for the group as a whole.
> - Complete the child assessment two to four times a year to measure changes in children's development and learning.
> - Share and discuss the results of the child assessment with families at conferences.
> - Share the results of the child assessment with program administrators and funding agencies.
>
> **Program Assessment**
> - Use a validated and authentic program assessment to measure all areas of curriculum implementation and program management along a continuum of quality.
> - Use the program assessment to collect objective anecdotal data and other documentary evidence.
> - Complete the program assessment one or two times a year to monitor program quality, recognize areas of strength, and identify areas for improvement.
> - Use the results of the program assessment to create a plan for staff development.
> - Share and discuss the results of the program assessment among the teaching staff.
> - Share the results of the program assessment with program administrators and funding agencies.

practices to a variety of audiences. These include administrators and policymakers, particularly those who may not know the elements of high-quality programs. The PQA can also help support staff understand the actions and requests of the instructional staff. It is an effective tool to explain the program to parents and suggest ways they can carry out similar practices at home. PQA results can be easily communicated to researchers. Finally, the many concrete examples help others replicate proven practices in their own settings.

Meisels (2001) reminds us that the act of conducting valid assessment on children's progress and program delivery is only the first step in acquiring useful information. Ongoing interaction with children and families should continue to inform our knowledge base about what is and is not meeting their needs. Likewise, continuous program monitoring and reflection are needed to honestly evaluate what we are doing well and where and how we can improve curriculum implementation, support services, and program operations. Finally, valid assessment calls for examining the consequences that follow from using the data. We must constantly reassess actions and outcomes to insure that our decisions positively affect child and staff development.

Categories and Items on the Preschool PQA

Form A: Classroom Items

I. Learning Environment
A. The classroom provides a safe and healthy environment for children.
B. The space is divided into interest areas (for example, building or block area, house area, art area, toy area, book area, sand and water area) that address basic aspects of children's play and development.
C. The location of the interest areas is carefully planned to provide for adequate space in each area, easy access between areas, and compatible activities in adjacent areas.
D. An outdoor play area (at or near the program site) has adequate space, equipment, and materials to support various types of play.
E. Classroom areas and materials are systematically arranged, labeled, and accessible to children.
F. Classroom materials are varied, manipulative, open-ended, and authentic and appeal to multiple senses (sight, hearing, touch, smell, taste).
G. Materials are plentiful.
H. Materials reflect human diversity and the positive aspects of children's homes and community cultures.
I. Child-initiated work (work designed and created by children) is on display.

II. Daily Routine
A. Adults establish a consistent daily routine. Children are aware of the routine.
B. The parts of the daily routine include time for children to do the following: to plan; to carry out their plans; to recall and discuss their activities; to engage in small-group activities; to engage in large-group activities; to have snacks or meals; to clean up; to transition to other activities; to play outside; and to nap or rest (if applicable — i.e., full-day programs).
C. An appropriate amount of time is allotted for each part of the daily routine.
D. The program has time each day during which children make plans and indicate their plans to adults.
E. The program has time each day (e.g., work time, choice time, center time, free play) during which children initiate activities and carry out their intentions.
F. The program has time each day during which children remember and review their activities and share with adults and peers what they have done.
G. The program has time each day for small-group activities that reflect and extend children's interests and development.
H. The program has time each day for large-group activities that reflect and extend children's interests and development.
I. During transition times, children have reasonable choices about activities and timing as they move from one activity to the next.
J. The program has a set cleanup time with reasonable expectations and choices for children.
K. The program has time each day for snacks or meals that encourage social interaction.
L. The program has an outside time each day during which children engage in a variety of physical activities.

III. Adult-Child Interaction
A. Children's basic physical needs are met.
B. Children's separation from home and daily entry to the program are handled with sensitivity and respect.
C. Adults create a warm and caring atmosphere for children.
D. Adults use a variety of strategies to encourage and support child language and communication.
E. Adults use a variety of strategies to support classroom communication with children whose primary language is not English.
F. Adults participate as partners in children's play.
G. Adults encourage children's learning initiatives throughout the day (both indoors and outdoors).
H. Adults support and extend children's ideas and learning during group times.
I. Adults provide opportunities for children to explore and use materials at their own developmental level and pace.
J. Adults acknowledge individual children's accomplishments.
K. Adults encourage children to interact with and turn to one another for assistance throughout the day.
L. Children have opportunities to solve problems with materials and do things for themselves.
M. Adults involve children in resolving conflicts.

(continued on p. 170)

Categories and Items on the Preschool PQA (cont.)

IV. Curriculum Planning and Assessment

A. Staff use a comprehensive and documented curriculum model or educational approach to guide teaching practices.

B. Staff use a team teaching model and share responsibilities for planning and implementing program activities.

C. Staff maintain records on children and families, including the following data on each child:
- Name, birthdate, name of parent or guardian, home address, and phone number
- Child immunization records, health and disability status, accident reports
- Assessment of child's progress
- Home visit documentation, parent/teacher conference documentation
- Family goals, treatment referrals, and follow-up

D. Staff record and discuss anecdotal notes as the basis for planning for individual children.

E. Staff regularly use a child observation measure of proven reliability and validity to assess children's developmental progress.

Form B: Agency Items for Infant-Toddler and Preschool Programs

V. Parent Involvement and Family Services

A. The program provides a welcoming environment for families and a variety of opportunities for parents to become involved in the program.

B. Parents are represented on program advisory and/or policymaking committees.

C. Parents are encouraged to participate in program activities with children.

D. Staff and parents exchange information about the curriculum and its relationship to children's development.

E. Staff and parents interact informally to share information about the day's activities and children's experiences.

F. Staff form partnerships with parents and exchange information about how to promote and extend children's learning and social development at home.

G. Staff members schedule home visits and formal parent conferences to share information with parents and seek input from parents about the program and their children's development.

H. The program or its host agency provides diagnostic and special education services for children with special needs.

I. Staff provide parents with referrals and access to supportive services as needed.

J. Program activities are coordinated within the program and/or with community agencies and/or the public schools to facilitate children's smooth transitions at each age level.

VI. Staff Qualifications and Staff Development

A. The program director has the appropriate education, training, and experience.

B. Instructional staff have the appropriate education, training, and experience for the age group they are working with.

C. Support staff (e.g., cook, bus driver, secretary) and volunteers receive the appropriate orientation and supervision.

D. Staff participate in ongoing professional development activities such as conferences, inservice training, professional workshops, college-level courses and seminars, compiling or consulting a resource library, teacher exchanges, observation, mentoring, and coaching.

E. Inservice training involves participants in topics specific to young children's development and practice.

F. Instructional staff are regularly observed in the program setting and provided with feedback by someone familiar with the curriculum's goals, objectives, and methods for working with each age group of chldren in the program.

G. The director and teachers are affiliated with a local, state, and/or national early childhood professional organization.

VII. Program Management

A. The program is licensed based on regulations passed by the state and/or local licensing agencies.

B. Program policies promote continuity of care by classroom adults (paid staff who work directly with children).

C. Staff regularly conduct a program assessment and use the results to improve the program.

D. The program has a child recruitment and enrollment plan.

E. The program has a fully developed set of operating policies and procedures.

F. The program is accessible to those with disabilities.

G. The program is adequately funded.

— Excerpted from the Preschool PQA (Form A [HighScope, 2003a] and Form B [Epstein et al., 2013])

CHAPTER 6

The Learning Environment: Arranging and Equipping Spaces for Active Learners

Ideas That Shape Settings for Active Learning

Young children in action need spaces that are arranged and equipped to promote active learning. To capture the spirit of such spaces, try recalling the pleasurable things you did as a young child. Perhaps you played in water, made mud pies, curled up in a cozy chair with a picture book, climbed trees, collected bottle caps, or played hide-and-seek. Many of the activities you remember as enjoyable were probably noisy and messy. As you think about how to plan spaces for a new generation of active, inquisitive children, keep in mind your own favorite play experiences.

> "The classroom environment reflects the program's goals—at the most basic level, that children be healthy and safe....Beyond being a safe place, the developmentally appropriate environment continually invites children's initiative and active exploration of materials. Materials are well organized and physically within reach to enable children to readily find and use them. Effective teachers create a rich learning environment that... take[s] into account evolving learning needs."
>
> — Copple & Bredekamp (2006, pp. 27–28)

Young children need space to use materials, explore, create, and solve problems; space to spread out, move around in, talk freely about what they are doing; space to work alone and with others; space to store their belongings and display their inventions; and space for adults to join them in support of their intentions and interests.

Environments for children and the active learning ingredients

To understand how the physical setting contributes to the learning experiences that occur there, let us look at HighScope settings in terms of the **ingredients of active learning: materials, manipulation, choice, child language and thought, and adult scaffolding.**

Materials that interest children are essential for active learning. The setting, therefore, includes a wide variety of materials that children can explore, transform, and combine. The materials are arranged to promote **manipulation** — children's direct use of materials — as opposed to being arranged primarily for demonstration or display. To enable children to manipulate materials freely, without disturbing or being disturbed by others, the setting has enough materials for each child and plenty of work and play space.

Choice for children is another principle that governs the arrangement of the setting. The space is divided into well-defined interest areas that offer visible and accessible storage of materials so that children can see the choices available and easily reach the materials. The commitment to provide choices also implies *openness* and *flexibility* — that is, materials children can use in a variety of ways in the pursuit of different types of play and interest areas located so that children can move easily from one to another as the focus of their play dictates.

To encourage **child language and thought**, the interest areas are stocked with interesting open-ended materials that engage children and inspire them to learn and communicate in both verbal and nonverbal ways. To encourage experiences with written language, the setting is also print rich — it includes many books and other print materials as well as tools children can use to make their own written material.

Children's play is enriched by **adult scaffolding**, which can best occur when spaces are easily accessible for adults as well as children. This means there is room for adults to watch and comfortably join children's play at the children's physical levels. Adult scaffolding also implies that the environment is planned to encourage children's sense of security and control. Materials are stored in the same locations so that children can find and return materials as they need them and

Active learning settings are arranged to promote choice. Children have easy access to a wide range of interesting materials and can move easily from one interest area to another as their play activities develop and change.

also feel in control of their environment; attention is paid to keeping the setting safe, clean, and inviting, thus creating an overall feeling of warmth and welcome. Yet cleanliness and order are not overemphasized. Adults understand that action is the norm for children. While the space may look cluttered as children work, times of play and intensive use of materials are followed by cleanup times when materials are sorted and put away, and order is restored.

In summary, adults using the HighScope Curriculum promote children's active learning by establishing settings where children can

- Engage in a wide range of play, alone and with others, including exploring, building, pretending, painting and drawing, and playing simple games

- Find, use, and return materials of particular interest to them as they pursue their own plans and intentions

- Feel safe, valued, adventurous, and competent

Our purpose in this chapter is to present general guidelines for organizing space and materials for active learners, discuss the effects of such organization, and offer practical strategies for

A thoughtfully planned classroom allows children to find, use, and return materials of particular interest to them as they pursue their own plans and intentions.

arranging and equipping specific interest areas for children. While the focus is on early learning, the health and safety of adults and children are also important in setting up and furnishing the learning environment. Because licensing requirements are subject to change, programs are advised to consult the most current information provided by regulatory agencies and professional organizations.

General guidelines for organizing space and materials

Adults using the HighScope Curriculum organize space so that children have as many opportunities for active participatory learning and as much control over their environment as possible. The following guidelines influence their decisions as they arrange and equip early childhood centers and child care homes:

- The space is inviting to children.
- The space is divided into well-defined and labeled interest areas to encourage distinctive types of play.
- The space incorporates places for group activities, eating, napping, and storing children's belongings.
- Interest areas are arranged to promote visibility and easy movement between areas.
- Interest areas are flexible enough to accommodate practical considerations and children's changing interests.
- Materials are plentiful and open-ended to support a wide range of play experiences.
- Materials reflect children's family lives.
- The storage and labeling of materials promotes the find-use-return cycle.

Sources of Information for Health and Safety Standards

Program licensing requirements, which are the minimum standards for approved operation, vary by state and auspices. The suggestions in this chapter are guided by the criteria established by professional and administrative organizations including the American Academy of Pediatrics, Head Start, National Association for the Education of Young Children, and National Association for Family Child Care. Readers are advised to check the standards specific to their program's location and auspices, as well as the requirements for complying with the Americans with Disabilities Act. In addition, all equipment and furnishings should meet both the licensing standards and the guidelines of the US Consumer Product Safety Commission. For specific information on preparing, serving, and storing food, see relevant state licensing standards and the US Department of Agriculture Child and Adult Care Food Program guidelines for child care.

Design elements, such as softness, colors and textures, lighting, coziness, and sound make spaces inviting to children.

The space is inviting to children

Do children and adults respond favorably to the overall physical environment you have created? Certain design elements, which are discussed next, can make your early childhood space comfortable and welcoming.

Softness. To create comfortable play surfaces, use carpets, throw rugs, easy chairs, cushions and pillows, mattresses, beanbag chairs, futons, curtains or drapes, and wall hangings. Such soft materials are not only cozy and inviting but also absorb sound. To create a comfortable outdoor play space, provide grass, sand, shrubbery, trees, wood, water, flowers, foliage, and hammocks.

Rounded corners. Large potted plants, hanging plants, easy chairs, pillows, and fabric hangings placed or hung in corners round out sharp edges.

Pleasing colors and textures. Some colors and textures soothe and invite; others do not. Examine your walls, ceilings, and floor coverings. If they make you want to move in, they are fine; if not, you might want to consider alternatives.

Natural materials and light. The use of wood and outdoor light from windows and skylights is another way to soften the environment by bringing a bit of nature inside. Warm artificial lighting is also important. In the past, programs were advised to use incandescent rather than fluorescent lighting to seem more homelike and less institutional. However, as environmental and energy concerns mandate the use of fluorescent bulbs (regular and compact), programs can still choose those that mimic the soft lighting characteristic of incandescent bulbs. Choose "warm" rather than "cool" fluorescent bulbs, with color temperatures in the 2700–3000 K range. An added benefit of being environmentally sound is that it will also save on the program's energy costs.

Cozy places. A loft, nook, or window seat with pillows and books gives children a place to pause, be by themselves, observe, and take

Even the youngest preschool children can "read" picture labels or labels made from the objects themselves.

things in without having to respond socially (Phyfe-Perkins & Shoemaker 1986). Cozy places are especially important to children in full-day programs who need a break from ongoing interactions.

Purposeful sound. The sound in an early childhood setting should primarily be that of children, busy at work in activities of their own choice. Acoustical engineers who help to design center-based settings stress the need to balance purposeful and meaningful noise, which stimulates children's senses and learning, from background noise, which can actually interfere with their development (Manlove, Frank, & Vernon-Feagans, 2001). Unnecessary background noise or adults chattering to one another (and unrelated to what the children are doing) may especially interfere with young children's speech and language development (Maxwell & Evans, undated).

Sometimes, in a well-intended effort to sound "home-like," teachers will play background music throughout the day. They may think it is soothing or see it as an opportunity to introduce children to a variety of musical styles. However, extraneous sounds during play times can interfere with children's concentration and distract teachers from paying attention to what the children are engaged in. Music should only be played when it has a purpose, for example, when children choose to play instruments or listen at work time, or when moving to music at large-group time.

The space is divided into well-defined and labeled interest areas to encourage distinctive types of play

An active learning setting is designed to support the types of play that young children enjoy — sensory exploration, building, creating things, pretending, using books, and playing simple games. To support these pursuits, a HighScope setting is divided into areas with simple names that make sense to young children — for example, the **sand and water area, block area, house area, art area, toy area, book and writing area, woodworking area, music and movement area, computer area** (for programs with computers), and the **outdoor area.** These interest areas are defined by low boundaries and the child-accessible materials stored in them — blocks in the block area, paints in the art area, and so forth. Simple **area signs** with representative objects (for example a paintbrush in the art area), photographs, letters, and words help children identify the areas and the kinds of materials and activities that characterize their use.

While the amount of space available varies from program to program, the play spaces for children take first priority in the distribution of space. Each interest area needs adequate space for materials and for the number of children who wish to play there at any given time. Using most of the overall space for the interest areas means moving to other parts of the building such space gobblers as office desks, file cabinets, and tables used only for meals.

There are no hard and fast rules for the number of areas in the room. As a general consideration, however, it is better to have fewer areas with materials that can be used in many ways than many areas, each with a limited number of items. Too many areas can overwhelm young children and an overabundance of materials makes it hard for them to see how items are related or to use them in creative ways. For example, there is no need for a separate "math area" when children can sort and match small blocks or count and compare sets of plastic animals in the "toy area."

The number of areas also depends on practical considerations. A large space can accommodate more areas, each with ample room for materials and children. Programs in small spaces will have fewer areas, but may compensate by changing the areas now and then (if done infrequently).

> ### Designing Classroom Space
>
> "When children are in a large space, they feel small in comparison to their surroundings, and time seems to pass more slowly for them. When children are in a playhouse, in a play yard tent, or under a table, they feel large in comparison to their surroundings, and attention seems to be sustained....We have learned that the perception of the size of the space in which children play affects the quality of the play and thus the potential for learning....Altering space to make children feel large in relation to their environment may enable children to enter complex play more quickly and to continue complex play for longer periods of time."
>
> — Tegano, Moran, DeLong, Brickley, & Ramanssini (1996, pp. 136, 138)

For example, there can be permanent house, art, block, sand and water, and toy areas, with a sixth rotating area for woodworking or something else that reflects the children's current interests. Some programs begin with fewer areas (three or four) to make it easier for children to learn them. Once these become familiar, one or two areas are added. Children and teachers can then decide together which materials should be moved from the existing areas to the new ones.

Establishing well-defined interest areas is one concrete way to foster children's capacities for initiative, autonomy, and social relationships. Because the areas are accessible on a daily basis, children know what materials are available and where to find them. The consistent and therefore dependable organization of the space gives children the opportunity to anticipate where they would like to work and what they would like to do with the materials there. Since they can depend on the availability of materials, children are free to focus on the process and interactions of play. In fact, research has demonstrated that "in programs where children made choices and worked at their own pace in a variety of well-defined activity settings, children exhibited high levels of social interaction, child-initiated behavior, and child involvement in activities" (Phyfe-Perkins & Shoemaker, 1986, p. 184).

The space incorporates places for group activities, eating, napping, and storing children's belongings

In a large space, it is helpful to locate the interest areas around the perimeter. This provides an open central space for *group activities,* such as morning greeting and movement experiences, and easy access to all the areas. If your program is located in a small or oddly shaped space, or in a series of adjoining rooms, consider alternative ways of providing group meeting space and routing traffic from one area to another. For example, make the block area large enough for group meetings.

When it comes to *eating* and *napping,* child care homes have an advantage over center-based programs because they already have a table for family dining and beds and couches for sleeping. In center-based programs, it is important to incorporate spaces for eating and napping in such a way that they do not take space away from the interest areas. For example, to avoid filling up potential interest areas with tables that are used only for eating, consider eating on the tables that serve as work surfaces in the art, toy, and house areas. On the other hand, if space is plentiful, and especially if children spend the whole day in your program, designating a separate room for eating — with child-sized tables and chairs and a pleasant view — will provide a natural and beneficial change of scene. The same advice is true for napping. If naptime is part of your program, and there is space for napping removed from the interest areas, children

These children enjoy a snack and a story at their small-group table.

can rest without being distracted by toys and materials. But if space is limited, consider having children set up their cots in the meeting space or passageways between areas.

By providing *storage space for each child,* you allow children to have a space to call their own in which they can keep track of personal belongings. Along with a place to hang outdoor clothing, each child needs a personal storage container that he or she can reach independently and readily identify by "reading" the label (the child's name and symbol or his or her letter link). In some centers, for example, children's personal storage space is a shelf near the coathooks that contains an appropriately labeled tub, box, basket, or cubbyhole for each child, with the youngest children's belongings stored on the lowest shelves, and the older children's on the higher shelves.

A Label for David's Tub

One morning, David arrived wearing a new belt. After he showed it to his friends, he took it off because, as he said, "I want to keep it new." "Here, David," said Mrs. Hill, "I'll put that in your tub so you'll know where it is when it's time to go home." David gave her his new belt, she put it in his tub, and David continued to play.

When Ricky came in late and joined David in his play, the first thing David said was, "Ricky, wanna see my new belt! Mrs. Hill put it in my tub." With great anticipation, the two boys headed for the tubs, but stopped short in front of two shelves of 18 tubs each. David looked perplexed. "Which one's mine?" he wondered aloud, although all 36 tubs were clearly labeled with each child's name. David thought for a moment, then went to the first tub on the top row, pulled it out carefully to see if it held his belt, pushed it back again, and tried the next tub. After checking 20 tubs or so in this manner, David found his belt, showed it to Ricky, and put it back on. "I'm not losin' it again!" he said.

Shortly after David lost and found his belt, the adults in David's program helped each child choose a letter link – a name learning system that pairs a child's printed nametag with a letter-linked picture of an object that starts with the same letter and sound. David chose a "drum" and taped it on his tub. "This is my tub, the one with the drum. The *D* and these other letters say my name, David." He never lost his belt or any of his special things again. At least not when he remembered to put them in his tub!

Interest areas are arranged to promote visibility and easy movement between the areas

Visibility between areas. Visibility means arranging the entire space so that, when standing, children can observe their peers in other areas and adults can quickly scan the space to locate each child. Low boundaries between areas accomplish this goal. In multiroom settings, visibility from room to room is increased by keeping doors open and, when possible, cutting openings in interior walls between rooms.

Open floor plan. An **open floor plan** helps to promote easy movement between the areas of the classroom. "How children behave in their environment depends to some extent on how the space is organized and the messages the room arrangement conveys. When there is a clear path from one interest area to another, the message is 'Come and see what else there is to do'" (Copple & Bredekamp, 2009, p. 97). It is therefore important to keep the floor plan as open and uncluttered as possible instead of using every bit of space for shelves, furniture, equipment, and toys. Early childhood licensing requirements and accreditation standards generally require 35 square feet of free space per child (40 square feet for children with special needs), not including kitchens, bathrooms, furnishings, and spaces used exclusively by adults. These requirements are based on both behavioral and health considerations. "Lack of space is associated with difficult behavior and increased density of air pollution, including germs" (Aronson, 2002, p. 120).

An open and uncluttered classroom that allows children to move from interest area to interest area fosters active learning.

Children should be able to move freely from interest area to interest area — they should be able to move to the art area, for example, without going through the house area. If the block and house areas share one room, locate the areas on the sides of the room so that as people enter they can go into the block area or the house area without having to walk through either one to get to the other. If you must pass through one room to get to another, establish a passageway so that children can play in either room undisturbed by the traffic flow. Establishing passageways around the areas allows children easy access and the opportunity to play in relative peace. Wide passageways and area entrances accommodate children who are carrying blocks or their own creations. If children's play often spills over from one area into another — for example, when the pretend play in the house area continues into the block area — it makes sense to put these areas close together to encourage interrelated play and reduce traffic problems.

Interest areas are flexible enough to accommodate practical considerations and children's changing interests

In arranging the interest areas, flexibility is essential. Adults make changes in space arrangement and equipment throughout the program year to accommodate children's evolving interests, the over- or under-use of certain interest areas, unforeseen traffic patterns, field-trip experiences and reenactments, new materials, and the need for novelty. Here are some examples of how adults in one center adapted the areas and materials in response to what they saw children doing:

Dory and Sammy have been building robots in the block area, so the adults add boxes, foil, wire, and a bucket of old radio parts to the art area. Dory and Sammy use these materials to make big robots with moving parts.

❖

The adults conclude that children are not using the toy area because, if they do, they cannot see over the two tables, or get to the toy shelves, or find a place on the floor to play. Therefore, the adults decide to take out one table, move the other against the wall, and turn one shelf so that it is more visible. Children respond to these changes by playing in the area as if it were totally new.

❖

Now that the weather is nice and the sand table is just outside the door, which is next to the book area, the adults decide to move the book area to the other side of the room. As a result, children can enjoy the books without being disturbed by the traffic to and from the sand table.

❖

After a trip to the grocery store, the adults and children rearrange the house area to make room for children to build grocery store shelves and set up a checkout counter.

Involve children in changes. Regardless of why you change your play space, *involving children in making changes in the environment* gives them a sense of control over their world. Treating space arrangement and equipment issues as opportunities for problem solving involves children positively in changes that might otherwise upset their sense of consistency and security. For example, in Andrea's child care home, the children themselves wheel out toy storage carts, take down the toy storage boxes, and help set up the areas on a daily basis. In another setting, children help make the decisions about where new materials and equipment should go. In establishing an

The setup of interest areas should allow for children to elaborate on their play.

area for a new workbench and construction tools, for example, children carry the books and the bookrack to the other side of the room to make a suitable space for the workbench, which they have brought from the storage closet. After sorting the wood and Styrofoam pieces into tubs, the children make and attach their own labels.

Strategies for shared space. If your program is housed in a building that also serves another function (such as a church) or is located in your own home, the *sharing of space* that is necessary calls for another kind of flexibility. Setting up and taking down interest areas on a weekly or daily basis is an ongoing chore and calls for creative thinking and the conviction that space for active learning is well worth the effort. Here are some storage strategies for programs that use shared space:

- Casters or wheels on interest-area storage shelves that make them easy to turn and move against the wall
- Hinged storage shelves that close up like boxes
- Storage tubs that fit under beds, sofas, and easy chairs
- Storage tubs or boxes that stack behind couches or in closets, hallways, and entryways

- Toy baskets and containers stored on wheeled carts

Weather considerations. Weather changes may also require flexibility in the use of space. When rain, wind, smog, snow, or temperature extremes keep you inside, you and the children may decide to move storage shelves, tables, chairs, and sofas to convert part of the indoor space into an obstacle course or an open space for wheeled toys or running games. On the other hand, when the weather is nice, you and your hardy band of movers may decide to move entire interest areas (house, art, block, water table) outdoors.

Multiple usage. Finally, flexibility means *multiple usage.* For example, a sofa can be a comfortable place to sit with a book, a place to store things under and crawl behind, a puppet stage, a make-believe hospital bed, or a fort. A table can be an eating space, a work surface for painting or rolling play dough, a platform for a block city, a place to work under, or a structure to pretend with (covered with a blanket, it becomes a house, or pushed against another table, it becomes an obstacle-course tunnel). In the HighScope Curriculum, it is important for *both* adults and children to realize that the interest areas and the things in them can be used in many different ways, depending on children's needs and imaginations.

Materials are plentiful and open-ended to support a wide range of play experiences

Make sure materials are plentiful. "Plentiful" means there are enough materials in each area so that a number of children can play there at the same time. For example, there are enough sets of big blocks for several children to build a structure that they can play in together, and enough sets of small blocks that children can use them for filling and emptying as well as building. Whenever possible, there are at least two of everything — dump trucks, hammers, staplers, dress-up shoes. There are also many "found materials," including recycled paper and containers, corks, bottle caps, and paper-towel tubes.

Stocking multiples of materials ensures that several children at once can use them; this also helps to reduce conflicts.

Offer materials that are open ended. "Open-ended" means materials can be used in many different ways, rather than a limited or "closed" number of ways determined by the manufacturer or other adults. "When an object or environment is open to many interpretations and uses, the child holds the power to tell it what it is to be or do, rather than it giving the child some preconceived 'correct' way to perceive or act" (Talbot & Frost, 1989, p. 12). Closed-ended materials, by contrast, can constrict the child's imagination. Materials that can be used in only one or two

Dolls and Diversity

Educator Louise Derman-Sparks, author of *Anti-Bias Curriculum* (1989), uses a set of 16 dolls to tell children stories, often about things that are happening in their daily lives. In her stories, the doll Zoreisha is African-American, speaks English, and lives with her mom and grandmother. David is an American of European descent who speaks English, has weak legs because of a spinal defect, uses a wheelchair, and lives with his mom and dad. May is Chinese, speaks Cantonese, is learning English, and lives with her father and sister because her mom died. While these special dolls are always at hand for adults and children to use, children discuss their plans for playing with them with an adult because the dolls are so "real" and treated with great respect.

---

ways can quickly become tiresome and uninteresting to children (and adults!). Moreover, if children sense they are using materials "incorrectly" (by adult standards), they may become discouraged and simply not use them at all.

In HighScope settings, the materials in each area support a wide range of play suitable to the interests and emerging abilities of the children in the program — there are materials for sensory exploration, building, making things, pretending, and playing simple games; materials that encourage children's interests in art, music, pretend play, writing and storytelling, numbers, and the physical world; and materials that support the key developmental indicators (KDIs) in Approaches to Learning; Social and Emotional Development; Physical Development and Health; Language, Literacy, and Communication; Mathematics; Creative Arts; Science and Technology; and Social Studies. This calls for many materials that are fairly simple in themselves but that children can use in many different ways, depending on their interests, abilities, and experiences — materials such as balls, blocks, paper, and scarves.

Materials reflect children's family lives

Finally, materials and the images they convey reflect children's everyday family life. The way we arrange and equip spaces for children says, in effect, "This is who we are and what we value." Therefore, it is important that homelike items, books, magazines, pictures, photographs, dolls, and play figures accurately portray the realities of the families and communities of the children in the program. (See "Identifying Children's Family Cultures" on p. 148 and "Family Experiences Classroom Checklist" on p. 149).

The storage and labeling of materials promotes the find-use-return cycle

The most important idea governing how materials are stored is to make it possible for children to find and return the materials they need on their own. In a sense, the interest areas are a series of attractive, open storage units, each stocked with materials that support a certain kind of play. Children move from area to area, locating the things they need to make bottle-cap soup, write a letter, put on a show, build a boat, and so forth. As they play, children use materials freely, wherever they need them. Play dough may be carried to the house area to be used as "food for babies" and to the block area to become "snakes in the river." Blocks may be carried to the toy area to make a puppet stage. At cleanup time, however, all the blocks, all the play dough, and everything else children have used are returned to their original storage spaces so that children can find them when they need them again. While the storage of materials is consistent, the use of the materials is flexible.

Store similar things together. Storing similar materials together — the blocks in the block area, the art supplies in the art area, and so forth — helps children find and return the things they need in their play. Within each interest area, placing materials with similar functions close together helps children see alternatives and think about different ways of accomplishing tasks. In the art area,

Identifying Children's Family Cultures

Beth Marshall, HighScope Director of Early Childhood, provides some examples of how the teachers whom she and her staff work with learn about children's home experiences and then incorporate this knowledge into their early childhood settings:

"**Parents** are an invaluable source of information about their home cultures. Making a home visit is an excellent way to learn about a child's family setting and experiences. For example, when one teaching team visited Efrat's home, they discovered that although her mom is a chemist, she used to be a concert pianist. Jazz was playing in the background while they visited, and when one recording ended, Efrat went over and expertly put another CD in the CD player. After the visit, the team decided to add a CD player and music CDs to the music and movement area. They also decided to ask Efrat's mom if they could borrow some of Efrat's favorite selections.

"Talking with parents informally as they drop off and pick up their child is another way of keeping in touch with the children's families. One day, for example, a child care director told Kenneth's mom that Kenneth had been using the tools in the construction area regularly. Kenneth's mother then explained that Kenneth's dad liked to tinker in his workshop and often fixed broken appliances for friends. She also mentioned that her husband often found ways for Kenneth to help him with these activities. In a subsequent planning session, the teaching team decided to change the construction area to a 'take-apart-and-put-together area' to build on Kenneth's interests and support his home culture. In this area they placed small used appliances such as toasters and hair dryers, along with screwdrivers, pliers, and safety goggles. Kenneth and the other children enjoyed taking the appliances apart and looking at what was inside.

"The **community** may also give us important insights into children's cultures. Look at the community from the child's viewpoint. If you do not live in the community around your school or center, try to visit it often. What are the neighborhood's colors, sounds, and smells? What are people wearing? What types of goods are sold in the area stores? What occupations seem to be typical of the area? What types of vehicles do you see? Are there special events or celebrations in the community? Looking and listening as you visit the community will give you ideas for materials to add to your classroom. The teacher in Jessica's program, for example, knew that many of the children in her group lived in an urban area and sometimes rode buses around town. So she placed toy buses in the block area.

"Of course, we can also learn about culture from the **children** themselves. Adults can watch what children do with materials and listen to their comments about them. Hearing about Bradley's interest in imitating his grandfather, a baker, his teachers decided to add additional baking tools to the house area in their classroom. After hearing Corrin talk about the special letters in her home, one of the teachers relayed the anecdote to her mom. Her mom laughed and said yes, there were lots of press-on letters laying around the house right then. She had just started back to work as an architect and was able to do most of her work at home. The teachers decided to add some press-on letters to the art area — Corrin enjoyed using them and demonstrating them to the other children.

"The examples of Efrat, Kenneth, Jessica, Bradley, and Corrin illustrate how the experiences children have in their families and communities can be incorporated into the classroom or center by adding materials and making changes in the setting to encourage children to build upon those experiences. When this happens, learning about cultural diversity becomes a natural part of classroom life."

— Adapted from Marshall (1996, pp. 139, 141)

Family Experiences Classroom Checklist[1]

How well does your classroom or center reflect children's home settings? To evaluate your setting, here is a checklist that is organized by several interest areas.

Art area
- ❑ Paint, crayons, and paper mirror the skin colors of people in the school community.
- ❑ Other art materials representing the art and crafts of the community are available (for example, weaving supplies, clay).

Block area
- ❑ Toy people are multiracial and without sex-role stereotyping.
- ❑ Animal figures simulate those found in your area (for example, house pets).
- ❑ Toy vehicles represent those found in the community.

Book area
- ❑ Books written in children's home languages are included.
- ❑ Books depict a variety of racial, ethnic, and cultural groups, focusing on modern lifestyles and including natural-looking illustrations of people.
- ❑ References to color in books are nonstereotypic (avoid books that associate black with evil, white with purity and goodness).
- ❑ Books represent a variety of family situations, including single-parent families, two-parent families, gay parents, biracial couples, stepparents and blended families, multi-generation families living in the same household, children cared for by extended family members.
- ❑ Books portray women and men in realistic situations, with both girls and boys playing active roles, and both women and men seen as independent problem-solvers.
- ❑ Books show children and adults with various disabilities. Disabled characters, including the elderly, are portrayed as real people who happen to have handicaps rather than as objects of pity.

House area
- ❑ There are multiracial girl and boy dolls with appropriate skin colors, hair textures and styles, and facial features.
- ❑ Contents and arrangement of house area reflect homes found in community (for example, patio area in Southwest).
- ❑ Kitchen utensils, empty food containers reflect what children see their family members using and eating.
- ❑ Dress-up clothing is reflective of the community, including occupations of the children's parents.
- ❑ Whenever possible, child-sized wheelchairs, crutches, glasses with lenses removed, and other assistive devices, are available.

Music and movement area
- ❑ Recorded music and instruments reflect children's cultures.
- ❑ A variety of instruments are available for children's use.
- ❑ Movement games that are characteristic of the culture are played.

Toy area
- ❑ Puzzles reflect the community atmosphere (for example, rural or urban).
- ❑ Puzzles represent occupations of the parents and others in the community.
- ❑ Toy figures, puzzles, and so forth, depict multiracial people and avoid sex-role stereotyping.

— Adapted from Marshall (1996, pp. 143–144)

---

[1] Program staff should adhere to their state's licensing regulations when adding materials to the classroom. Check local licensing regulations and agencies and organizations such as the Consumer Product Safety Commission (www.cpsc.gov), the American Academy of Pediatrics (www.aap.org), and the National Resource Center for Health and Safety in Child Care and Early Education (www.nrckids.org) for current information on product safety.

for example, the various drawing tools — crayons, markers, chalk, colored pencils — might occupy one shelf, and fasteners — tape, paper clips, staplers, string, yarn, glue — might be stored on another shelf.

Use containers children can see into and handle. Open, easy-to-handle containers help children see and find what they need. These containers should be stored on low, open shelves. Clear plastic containers (shoe and sweater storage-boxes, gallon milk jugs with the upper part cut off, refrigerator storage containers, clear plastic salad bar containers) will hold small, loose materials and provide a clear view of them. Low, flat containers, such as egg cartons and silverware trays, also provide highly visible storage for small materials. Baskets with handles, dish tubs, ice cream tubs, sturdy boxes, and milk crates may be used to store larger materials. Children can handle such containers on their own. Some large materials, however — hollow blocks, boxes, buckets, boards — do not need containers and can be stored and stacked directly on the floor. These also need labels, however, so children can find and return the materials independently. You can place the labels directly on the floor and place the items on top of the labels.

Label containers in a way that makes sense to children. Labeling the container, or the place on the shelf (or floor) where the material goes, provides a regular storage space that children can count on to find what they need and then return the material, even if it is scattered during play. Labels that are understandable to young children include those made from the material itself as well as tracings of the material, drawings, catalog pictures, photographs, or photocopies, or any of these along with the word.

Picture labels provide a map that children can "read" on their own. At cleanup time, children enjoy sorting materials into their containers and matching things to their labels on the shelves. They also enjoy deciding where new materials should go and making their own labels for them. One team member, new to the idea of labeling, noted, "If I had known it would help children to be so independent of me and in control, I would have labeled the center a lot sooner!"

For very young children, labels made from the objects themselves (an actual paintbrush taped to the paintbrush storage can, for example) make the most sense. For visually impaired children, use labels made from the objects themselves or labels with a lot of texture (such as a unit-block tracing cut from sandpaper) to help them read with their fingertips. For children who show an interest in letters and words, it is appropriate to provide written labels, but always provide picture or object labels as well — for example, add the word *stapler* next to the drawing of the stapler.

Covering labels on both sides with clear contact paper or clear tape makes them easy to attach to shelves or containers with loops of masking tape, and easy to move to another shelf when it is time to make room for new materials.

Most programs also make labels for each interest area called *area signs*. (These can also be purchased from HighScope Press at www.highscpope.org.) The block area sign, for example, might be a large poster hung or displayed in the block area where children can see it. It may include the words *Block Area* along with some actual blocks and pictures, drawings, or photographs of block-area play. The *Art Area* sign might have those words with a paintbrush, crayon, or

These "labels" are ones that children at all developmental levels can understand — the materials themselves.

> **Acquainting Children With the Names of Areas and Materials**
>
> Knowing the names of things gives children a sense of control and ownership over their space. Here are some strategies to help children learn these names:
>
> - Use the interest area names as you converse with children: "Oh, Miguel, I see you're in the block area with Sanjay!"
>
> - Use the names of materials in conversation with children: "You're using the sifter, Yvette."
>
> - Play a train game in which you and a train of children travel from area to area. Have children take turns being the leader and deciding which area you will travel to next.
>
> - Play a simple version of "Simon Says" (without winners and losers). Have children take turns being Simon and deciding which area to go to and how to get there. For example, "Simon says, crawl to the art area!" "Simon says, hop to the toy area!"

photograph of a painting taped to it. Area signs help children new to the setting learn area names and see at a glance where they can find the materials they need. Once children learn the names and symbols or words that represent each area, they can also refer to them at planning and recall time (Vogel, 2001). Area signs and material labels that use letters and words are also interesting to beginning writers who enjoy copying them.

Modifying the learning environment to accommodate children with special needs

Young children with a wide range of special needs (speech and language delays, chronic illness, physical impairments, developmental disabilities) benefit from being in programs with other children without such characteristics. Staff and children without special needs are also enriched by their daily contact with these children and their families. Preschoolers are particularly well suited to accepting children of different abilities and developmental levels as a matter of course. As far as they are concerned, everyone and everything is equal when it comes to learning about a world that presents new people, objects, and events on a daily — even an hourly — basis.

The primary goals of inclusion programs (those enrolling children both with and without special needs) are to allow all children to participate fully, operate as independently as possible, and reach their maximum developmental potential. The equipment and materials in the learning environment can contribute significantly toward the accomplishment of these individual and program goals. To support children as they navigate the space, teachers should avoid a common tendency toward overprotection so that young children with special needs will develop feelings

Classrooms designed to support children without overprotecting them help children with special needs develop alongside their typically developing peers.

Accommodating Children With Special Needs

Below are several ideas for adapting materials in your setting to accommodate children with special needs. Many of these strategies will also help typically developing children to operate with greater independence, and use their senses in more diverse and interesting ways.

Ideas for adapting available materials

- To make brush handles and crayons easier to grip, wrap them with masking tape or slide them through a slit in a small rubber ball.
- Paste fabric shapes and other small materials onto a storybook to make it more tactile.
- Lower easels and coat hooks.
- For children with impaired vision, accompany vision-based activities with auditory options.
- For children with impaired hearing, accompany auditory-based activities with visual options.
- Prop children who cannot sit with bolsters or pillows.
- Raise or lower surface heights as needed (e.g., shorten table legs or add sturdy extensions.)
- Eliminate pets or plants that may aggravate respiratory problems.

Ideas for accommodating wheelchairs

- Measure traffic lanes to guarantee easy maneuverability.
- Add ramps to maximize access not only in and out of the building, but to areas children use within the building.
- Make sure wheels will not catch on the edges of rugs, tables and chairs, and other furnishings. If necessary, add padding to corners (firmly secured so children will not pull it off).
- Check table heights so wheelchairs can fit underneath. Add blocks, rubber or foam pads, or other sturdy wedges as needed. Securely fasten large trays to the arms of wheelchairs so children can use this surface to work alongside their peers.
- Position water and sand tables with ample space for wheelchairs around them.
- Explore scooter boards, or other safe and appropriate options, as mobility alternatives.

Possible specialized purchases

- Eating utensils with special grips or edges
- Puzzles with extra-large pieces or knobs
- Books with extra-large pictures
- Hypoallergenic art materials
- Foods that accommodate allergies or other nutritional problems
- Magnifying glasses, sound amplifiers, and other assistive devices

of competence alongside their typically developing peers. This entails maintaining an ongoing and open dialogue with family members as well, who naturally are concerned for their child's health and safety.

Furnishing a program that includes children with special needs presents both challenges and creative opportunities. In addition to meeting regular licensing standards, such programs must also comply with requirements in the Individuals with Disabilities Education Act (IDEA). This involves adapting policies and practices, including making various physical accommodations in the learning environment. Modifications typically involve how the space is arranged, and how the equipment and materials are chosen and used in the setting. Considerations include relevant health and safety precautions, promoting the young child's emerging self-sufficiency, and providing opportunities for learning on a par with children who do not have special needs.

Sometimes accommodations require only minor adjustments. Often, creative problem-solving and readily available supplies suffice to increase the safety, accessibility, or use of equipment and materials. Other cases entail the purchase of specialized equipment or specific assistive devices. For ideas on adapting or purchasing equipment in an active-learning setting, see *I Belong: Active Learning for Children With Special Needs* (Dowling & Mitchell, 2007). Other resources include the Division for Early Childhood of the Council for Exceptional Children, IDEA Infant and Toddler Coordination Association, and National Information Center for Children and Youth with Disabilities.

As children engage in play of their own choosing, adults partner with them to provide support and learn about their interests.

The effects of arranging and equipping space according to HighScope guidelines

When adults arrange or rearrange a space for children using the guidelines just presented, they will notice many positive effects.

Children engage in active learning

It is difficult for children to play and learn in an environment lacking materials, but children spring into action when adults organize and equip appealing interest areas. Children can explore, build, pretend, and create because they have a variety of engaging materials to choose from, manipulate, and talk about with peers and adults. In well-equipped, well-organized settings, where adults provide ongoing attention and support, children are motivated to pursue their own ideas and interests with vigor and enthusiasm.

Children take the initiative

Areas for active learning are set up so that children can be initiators, doers, and problem-solvers. They get out their own blocks, find the paints, water the plants, fill the water table, print out the masks they made on the computer, get the glue, fasten the clamp to the workbench, and drape a blanket over the house area table. By encouraging children to find, use, and return things themselves, adults foster children's independence, competence, and success. Children develop the habit of saying and believing, "I can do that!"

Adults are free to interact with children and learn from them

Areas arranged for active learning enable adults to observe and interact with children. Since the environment itself is set up to engage children in play of their own choosing, adults are freed from managing, entertaining, or directing children. Instead, they can concentrate on supporting children, learning about their interests and abilities as they partner with them in play, and helping them solve child-size problems.

Strategies for Arranging Active Learning Settings

In the first part of this chapter, we discussed the general principles and guidelines that govern the arrangement of active learning settings. In this section, we present strategies for setting up interest areas for specific kinds of play. While the number and names of these areas will vary by program, certain basic ones (house, block, art, and book area, for example) will be in virtually every setting, while one or more others (toy, woodworking, computer, music and movement) will appear in only some settings. Even if you don't have a separate area designated for each of these interests — as noted earlier, you don't want to overwhelm children with too many areas — you will still want to consider providing the materials described below in some area. For example, a front-facing book rack can go next to a comfortable chair or bean bag in the house area. Sand and water materials might go in the art area since both activities need to be near a sink and children enjoy molding with sand. Computers, if you have them, can be part of the book and writing area.

Some interests, such as mathematics and science, do not need their own area. Rather, materials to support early learning in these domains should be available throughout the room. For example, children develop spatial awareness and measurement skills (mathematics) when they build with blocks of different shapes and sizes in the block area. They experiment and predict (science) when they mix paints in the art area.

This chapter concludes by examining how the principles of arranging space and providing hands-on learning materials relate to and support the other elements of the HighScope Curriculum.

Arranging and equipping specific interest areas

The block area

Almost all children enjoy playing in the block area and can find something to do with blocks, whether or not they have ever played with them before. Young children with little prior experience enjoy taking blocks off the shelves, heaping them into piles, lining them up, stacking them, loading them into cartons, dumping them out, carrying them, and fitting them carefully back on the shelves. After they have had plenty of time to explore blocks, children begin to build all kinds of structures. With increasing thoughtfulness, they begin to experiment with balance and enclosure, patterns, and symmetry; they also combine blocks with little people, animals, and vehicles in pretend play. Structures become houses and barns; lined-up blocks become roads and fences. As children play on their own and with others, adults recognize and support their exploration, imitation, spatial problem solving, sorting, comparing, and pretending.

Space for quiet and vigorous block play. Many children play very vigorously in the block area, taking up lots of space. A road race may extend from one end of the block area to the other, for example, and hospital play may involve numerous patients, hospital staff, and beds. Such highly social play is normal and important. At the same time, other children play very quietly with blocks, exploring and arranging them by themselves in their own space. This quiet, solitary block play is equally valid and necessary. Since the vigorous, more social block players often take over the space they need at the expense of the quiet block players, it is important to provide space for both kinds of play. Here are some strategies to consider:

- Enclose part of the block area to create a nook for quiet block play.

Children's block play is often highly social and requires room for movement.

- Take blocks outside where there is more space for both quiet and vigorous block play.
- Help quiet block players find a spot outside the block area where they can take their blocks and play undisturbed — for example, under a table, in a tent, or inside a large box.

Location. Because of its popularity, the block area works best when located in a spacious area. Setting up the area so that it opens onto a central space allows block play to extend outward on particularly busy days. Locating the block area away from the area for wheeled toys and the general traffic flow allows children to balance their structures undisturbed and keeps accidental topplings to a minimum.

Since role play often extends from the house area to the block area, locating the block area next to or across from the house area allows children to use both areas simultaneously without disrupting children working in other areas. In the house area, blocks become beds, walls, telephones, dishes, and cars, while pots and pans, tablecloths, mirrors, and dolls add realistic details to the structures children build in the block area.

If your block area is small, try one or more of the following strategies to make it more spacious:

- Eliminate extra furniture (adult-sized desks, file cabinets, unused tables, storage cabinets).
- Use hallways for coats, cubbies, and extra storage.

Block Area Materials[2]

Building materials
- Large hollow blocks, ramps, boards
- Unit blocks (as many shapes and sizes as possible)
- Small blocks (multicolored and/or plain)
- Cardboard blocks
- Blocks made from boxes or milk cartons, covered with cloth or contact-paper
- Pieces of carpet, cardboard, Plexiglass, Styrofoam
- Sheets, blankets, tarps, tents
- Packing boxes
- Boards, sticks, logs, stumps, and tree-stump rounds
- Cardboard, metal, or plastic tubes
- Rope and pulleys

Take-apart-and-put-together materials
- Wooden or plastic "take-apart" trucks and cars (some that snap, some that screw)
- Large Tinkertoys
- Interlocking blocks and boards
- Clip-on wheels and blocks
- Interlocking train tracks
- Plastic plumbing pipes and connectors

Fill-and-empty materials
- Dump trucks, pickup trucks
- Boxes, cartons, baskets, cans, buckets, crates, picnic baskets
- Small blocks
- Small vehicles, people, animals
- Dollhouse furniture

- Empty sewing spools
- Stones, pea gravel

Pretend-play materials
- Cars and trucks (scaled to blocks)
- Construction and farm vehicles
- Planes, helicopters, boats, trains, buses
- Multiracial dollhouse people, dollhouse furniture
- Wooden, rubber, or plastic animals familiar to children
- Steering wheel

Reference photos
- Photographs of children's homes, neighborhoods, farms
- Photographs and drawings of children's block structures

---

[2]Program staff should adhere to their state's licensing regulations when adding materials to the classroom.

- Add a loft and move one of the interest areas from the floor level to the loft.
- Move blocks and building materials outside.

Low shelves and storage containers can create boundaries in the block area. A flat, tightly woven carpet can help to define the area, reduce noise, and provide a comfortable work surface.

Materials. Block area materials include all kinds of things to build with, put together and take apart, fill and empty, and pretend with. When space permits, the block area also includes materials children can test their strength against, such as logs, tree-stump rounds, and a real gate. Since the block area has wide appeal and a number of children often plan to play there at the same time, it is important to have plenty of materials. This often means supplementing commercially made blocks with homemade and found building materials.

Accessible storage. Big heavy blocks, large boxes, boards, carpet pieces, wooden vehicles, and large Tinkertoys can be stored on the floor in clearly labeled containers or spaces. Before you begin labeling block area materials, look at how you have arranged them and decide which materials will work best with individual labels, and which with group labels. For example, you might put all the small, multicolored blocks in a basket or tub labeled with a picture, photograph, or one or two of the blocks themselves. You might store the unit blocks by size, with one label for all the square blocks, one for all the rectangles, and so forth. You might put all the medium-sized cars on one shelf, all the trucks on another, and all the little metal cars in a tub.

The house area

The house area supports both individual and cooperative play. Many children spend time in the house area — stirring, filling, emptying, pouring, shaking, mixing, rolling, folding, zipping, buttoning, snapping, brushing, and trying things on and taking them off. They may imitate cooking sequences they have seen at home or pretend to feed a doll or stuffed animal.

Children involved in exploring, imitating, and pretending in the house area are often content to play by themselves or alongside others. Other children play there with friends, acting out familiar roles — moms, dads, stepparents, babies, brothers and sisters, aunts and uncles, grandparents, firefighters, store clerks, babysitters, and pets. Children also reenact events they have experienced or heard about — visiting the dentist, going to the emergency room, moving, going shopping, talking on the phone, cleaning up after a flood, visiting daddy, having a birthday party, dressing up to "go out," celebrating holidays, going to church, and attending weddings, funerals, picnics, and movies. By providing a setting for role play, the house area allows children to make sense of their immediate world. Children have numerous opportunities to work together, express their feelings, and use language to communicate roles and respond to one another's needs and requests.

Location. Since house area play often extends into the block area, locating the house area next to, or across from, the block area, as noted earlier, allows this interaction to occur with a minimum of distraction to children working elsewhere. Providing space for more than one kind of role play is

In the house area, children reenact important events, such as fixing breakfast in the morning.

another important consideration in arranging the house area. Allocating enough space so that one part of the house area can be defined as a kitchen, for example, while leaving another part open, allows children to set up a living room, bedroom, backyard, garage, workshop, doctor's office, spaceship, store, fire station, stage, or whatever setting they need for the particular pretend play they have in mind. One early childhood team converted a small alcove into an additional role-play space by covering the alcove opening with a piece of plywood into which they cut a door and two windows.

Low storage shelves, child-sized appliances or sinks, a refrigerator, storage boxes, and a free-standing mirror or door can all serve as house area boundaries. In one house area, a puppet stage that often becomes a store counter helps to define the area. In another, "a loft house" facing into the center of the room provides a boundary as well as a versatile role-play space. Depending on the children's play, the loft becomes a boat, a hideaway, a pet store, a castle, a spaceship, or a "gingerbread house."

Materials. House area materials include cooking and eating equipment and all kinds of materials for dramatic play. The list of house area materials includes many things adults can purchase at garage sales, flea markets, thrift shops, and discount stores. Families can also bring in items that are clean and safe but are no longer used at home. When they are aware of the need, some businesses will donate items they no longer use or have replaced with newer models. For example, a hotel that is changing to computer-card door locks may donate its old keys, and a fabric store may donate fabric remnants.

As you equip the house area, it is important to provide child-sized appliances and adult-sized utensils. A child-sized sink, stove, and refrigerator are built so that young children can comfortably reach and use them. A child-sized sink, for example, could be a real sink built on a small scale or a wooden unit including a tub for water. We recommend adult-sized utensils and dishes because they

> ### House Area Flexibility in Action
>
> One morning in the house area of a Pittsburgh preschool, some girls and boys decide to "go out." The girls dress up in pantyhose, long gloves, and big hats, and spray themselves with "perfume" from empty perfume bottles. The boys shave with real shaving cream and bladeless razors, and put on ties, colorful suspenders, vests, and hats. After the "party," the children decide to move. They pack all the dress-up clothes in boxes and suitcases; tie the refrigerator together with a rope and lift it onto a small, wheeled dolly; unscrew the knobs from the stove with a screwdriver "so they won't get knocked"; load everything that will fit into a shopping cart; move everything they have packed to the center of the room; and then move back into their "new" house. At the end of the move, one of the boys hands his "wife" a newspaper saying, "You look for the sales, honey. I'll get this stove fixed and stir us up something hot."

are generally more durable than the toy utensils made for children, they allow for larger motions, and they hold more "food." Children seem to prefer the "real thing," probably because they see adults using spoons, mixing bowls, strainers, and so forth at home and the urge to imitate adult actions is powerful.

Props — collections of materials related to particular roles — are also important house area equipment. Some props come from field trips. A farmer, for example, might contribute an empty feed sack, a piece of rope, or a bale of straw. Special role-related articles of clothing are often stored in prop boxes — the hospital box contains a lab coat; the farmer box, a pair of overalls. Other everyday dress-up clothes (hats, dresses, pants, scarves) are always available.

A child-height table with chairs in the house area accommodates real and pretend cooking, real and pretend family-style meals and snacks, and small-group projects.

House Area Materials[3]

Cooking and eating equipment
- Child-sized sink, stove, refrigerator
- Adult-sized forks, spoons, knives, chopsticks
- Cooking containers — pots, pans, wok, rice cooker
- Cooking tools
  – barbecue cooking utensils
  – slotted spoons, spatulas, ladles
  – eggbeater, whisk, food mill, mortar and pestle
  – sand timer, bell timer
  – teapot, coffeepot
  – colander, sieves
  – ice cube trays
  – cookie press and cutters
  – hamburger press, tortilla press
  – can opener
- Baking equipment
  – cake pans, muffin pans, loaf pans
  – mixing bowls and lids
  – measuring cups and spoons
  – rolling pin
  – sifter
  – canister set
- Dishes — plates, bowls, cups, saucers
- Sponges, dishcloths, towels, potholders
- Tablecloths, placemats, napkins
- Things to cook and serve[4] — seeds, seed pods, beans, nuts, shells, stones, pine cones, chestnuts, acorns, macaroni, noodles, buttons, bottle caps, poker chips, Styrofoam packing pieces, paper clips, pieces of string
- Empty food containers — boxes, cans, cartons, jars, and bags, with original labels in English, Japanese, Arabic, Spanish, and so forth to reflect children's home languages

Pretending and role-play materials
- Dolls — female and male, commercial and homemade, to reflect the skin colors, hair styles, facial features, and special needs of children in the program
- Stuffed animals
- Doll beds, blankets, stroller, front/back pack
- Baby rattles, bibs, bottles, diapers, clothes (pants and dresses)
- Broom, dustpan
- Toaster (wooden or de-electrified), clocks (wind-up or de-electrified)
- Mirror
- Two telephones
- Small stepladder
- Dress-up clothes and accessories — hats, shoes, purses, wallets, briefcases, scarves, head wraps, jewelry, masks, neckties, belts, suspenders
- Lunchboxes, picnic basket, laundry basket
- Toolbox and tools
- Envelopes, canceled stamps, seals, stickers, junk mail, newspapers, magazines
- Typewriter, computer keyboard
- Sturdy cardboard boxes
- Low, movable partitions
- Props
  – home-builders' props: toolbox, tools, empty paint cans, brushes, pipe fittings, blueprints
  – doctors' props: lab coats, Band-Aids, gauze, stethoscope, cloth bandages
  – farm props: overalls, pail, straw, animal brush, empty feedbag
  – gas-station props: empty oil can, hose, rags, empty paste-wax can, jack, lug wrench, steering wheel, hubcaps, maps
  – fire-station props: hats, raincoats, boots, hoses
  – restaurant props: chefs' hats, aprons, cups, straws, napkins, menus, order pads and pencils
  – fishing props: fishing poles, nets, heavy boots, sou'westers, buckets, oars, gas can, buoys

Homelike materials
- Rocking chair or easy chair
- Blankets, sheets, quilts, pillows, beach towels, sleeping bags
- Photos of program's children and their families
- Wall hangings reflecting local community
- Real plants, watering can

Real cooking equipment (stored out of children's reach and used only with an adult present)
- Hotplate, toaster oven
- Electric frying pan
- Popcorn popper with clear lid

Reference photos and recipes
- Cookbooks, picture recipes
- Field-trip photos (for role-play ideas)

---

[3] Program staff should adhere to their state's licensing regulations when adding materials to the classroom.
[4] If your program does not allow the use of real food (for example, pasta, rice, or beans), provide children with the other materials listed here for pretend cooking and serving.

Realness

"Children sense the difference between toys and real objects. In many situations, especially where size is not a problem, they prefer the real thing over the sham. Perhaps it has to do with physical attributes — a greater and more minute degree of its detail, its weight and heft, its strength and longevity, or its being constructed of denser materials. Or maybe it has to do with association — 'This is the hammer my dad uses' — that magically imparts attributes of the original user to the novice. Or perhaps its value, in terms of materials or time spent in creating it, gives it a quality that a mere copy can never have. It might also be its actual usefulness; i.e., it will do more things better, longer or easier.

"For instance, a real fire engine in a playground will have a much more profound impact on children than a climber made to remind children of one, especially if it has its original bell, hoses, gauges, chrome plating, tires, and other details still intact. Things that actually *do* something help so much to create its rich character. In fact, the more working or mechanical parts it actually has that children can either control or relate to, the better. This gives it a specialness that no copy can match; and by association with both its original purpose and its history, it endows the new users with special capabilities."

— Talbot & Frost (1989, p. 13)

Props relating to different roles – including dress-up clothes – are always available to children in the house area.

Making the house area homelike. You can welcome children to the house area by making it as much like children's real homes as possible. This may mean, in one center, having a brightly colored tablecloth and flowers on the table or, in another, earth-colored mats and candles. The house area might include futons, hammocks, woven mats, or quilts, depending on what children are familiar with. In some parts of the country you might see kindling, logs, and the outer casings of a wood-burning stove. Suitcases may figure prominently in the house area in a community where children move or travel a lot. Depending on the population, the empty food boxes may have original labels in Spanish, Japanese, Chinese, Thai, Korean, Arabic, or Croatian. Dress-up clothes may include saris, obis, turbans, multilayered skirts, or wide sashes.

Accessible storage. Many odd-shaped, one-of-a-kind materials in the house area present storage challenges. Here are some strategies that might help:

- Hang pots, pans, and utensils on pegboard or wall hooks, tracing their outlines as they hang, and fastening the labels behind the hanging objects.

Familiar Things From Home in the House Area

It is a cold December day. Miguel and his family have just moved to New York City from Puerto Rico, and this is Miguel's first day of preschool. He has never seen snow and ice before, or such tall buildings. Where are the beach, the ocean, the palm trees, the warm sun, he must wonder. At work time in the toy area, Miguel chooses the small lock-together blocks and takes them to the house area where a few other children are playing a CD of salsa music. He finds a seat near them at the kitchen table, which is decorated with a bright red tablecloth and a bouquet of flowers. There, surrounded at last by familiar sights and sounds, Miguel builds an "areoplano para regresar a Puerto Rico" (airplane to take me back to Puerto Rico).

- Use the space organizers people use in their homes — silverware trays, cup racks, spice racks, plate racks, and canisters. Canisters labeled with a picture or an object can be used to store loose items for pretend cooking, like stones, buttons, seeds, and beans.
- Store clothing and accessories as they are stored in people's homes — on hooks (easier than hangers), in drawers, and in boxes (with labels). Sometimes the container itself serves as its own label — a hanging shoe holder for shoes, a jewelry box for jewelry, a towel rack for towels, a bed or chest for blankets.
- Orient labels the same way an item is stored. For example, trace the outline of a coffee pot and attach the tracing to the wall right behind the spot on the shelf where the coffee pot is stored.

The art area

For some children, the art area is a place to explore materials. Here they stir, roll, cut, twist, fold, flatten, drip, blot, fit things together and take

The art area contains a plentiful variety of materials for children to explore and use to make things.

them apart, combine and transform materials, or fill up whole surfaces with color, fringes, paste, or paper scraps. Other children use art materials to make things — pictures, books, weavings, movie tickets, menus, cards, hats, robots, birthday cakes, cameras, fire trucks. In a well-stocked art area with plenty of work space, children exploring materials work alongside children who are using the same materials to make something they especially want or need.

Location. In the art area you will need water, light, easy-to-clean flooring, plenty of work surfaces, and spaces for drying and displaying projects:

Water: Children working with art materials need water for mixing paints and washing up. A low sink in the art area allows children to use water without disturbing children in other areas. If you do not have a sink in the art area, consider these alternatives: adding buckets or dishpans and a water cooler, large thermoses with spigots, or pitchers of water. If the art area is outside, try a hose and bucket. Keep a supply of towels and sponges nearby for cleanup.

Light: Putting the art area near windows or under a skylight provides children with natural light by which to work, see colors, and notice the interplay of light and color. "Hey, something changed," Michael, a preschooler, exclaimed, as a cloud passed over the sun while he was painting.

Easy-to-clean flooring: A smooth tile floor (ceramic or vinyl) or sheet of linoleum works well. If neither are possible, consider covering the art area floor each day with newspaper, a drop cloth, or a tarp. The plastic mats used under office chairs can also help to protect, as well as extend the space in, the art area. Putting down a floor covering, like putting on a smock, can become part of children's art area routine. In nice weather, try moving the art area outdoors.

Work surfaces: Children need space to spread out and work on their own art projects undisturbed: low, sturdy tables; low counter tops; smooth floor space; or easels. Think also about locating the art area so that it opens into a central area, thus allowing children to spread out on the floor with their projects if necessary.

Drying space: Children need a place to dry their artwork. Clotheslines, folding clothesracks, and flat paper racks are some of the possibilities. Hooks mounted on a wall or shelf backs can hold smocks.

Display space: Low bulletin boards (at children's eye level) and the backs of shelves can be used to display pictures, while the tops of shelves can hold structures and models.

Materials. Art area materials include all kinds of paper, painting and printing materials, fasteners, drawing and cutting tools, modeling and molding materials, and collage materials. Unlike the block and house areas, in which the same blocks and dishes can be used year after year, the art area, with its consumable supplies, must be restocked continually. Recycling is one way to ease replacement costs — putting construction scraps in a scrap box instead of throwing them away, using office and computer paper with one blank side, saving catalogs, junk mail, yarn ends, fabric scraps, Styrofoam packing bits, egg cartons, boxes, and paper towel tubes. Here are some other ideas:

- Partially fill small glue bottles so that children can squeeze all they want without using up all the glue in one day. At the same time, provide other squeezing experiences with garlic presses, ricers, and squeeze-bottles of water.

- Fit gallon jugs of paint with gallon pumps (available from school supply catalogs). Place jugs with pumps where children can easily reach them and pump the paint they need (for example, into small yogurt cartons).

- Use heavy-duty materials when possible. Office-type tape dispensers and staplers, for example, last longer and are easier for young children to use than household-sized tape dispensers and staplers.

Creative Display Space

Chrissy has just spent work time on the art area floor making a long banner using the large, ink-filled roller-tipped markers adults use in bingo games, and a roll of shelf paper. "Bob," she says to her teacher, "Where can I hang this?"

"Well, I don't know, Chrissy, where do you think? It's very long." Bob admires her work and waits while Chrissy looks around the room at walls already covered with children's work.

"Up," she finally decides, pointing to the ceiling. Bob climbs on a chair and attaches one end of the banner to the ceiling. "What about this end?" he asks as they look together at the end still on the floor. "Over there." Chrissy indicates a spot on the wall across the room. Together they walk the free end over to see if it reaches. It does, so Bob climbs up on the chair again and fastens the free end to the wall. The next day Chrissy makes and hangs another banner. So do Lemar and Angie. The room looks quite festive!

Art Area Materials[5]

Paper
- White drawing paper, recycled computer/photocopying paper
- Graph paper, lined paper
- Newsprint
- Finger-paint paper
- Wrapping, butcher, or shelving paper (large roll)
- Tissue paper, wrapping paper, foil, cellophane
- Construction paper (many colors)
- Wallpaper samples
- Cardboard and mat board pieces
- Cardboard boxes and tubes (large and small)
- Contact-paper pieces and scraps
- Paper plates, grocery bags
- Used greeting cards, postcards, stationery
- Catalogs and magazines (with pictures reflecting the children and families in your program)

Painting and printing materials
- Tempera paints (primary colors, black, white, and brown)
- Paint pumps
- Watercolor paints
- Finger-paints (or liquid starch and soapflakes to add to tempera paints)
- Ink pads and stamps
- Paintbrushes (small ones for watercolors and large ones for tempera paints)
- Easels
- Jars with lids, squeeze bottles for mixing and storing paints
- Plastic plates or food tins to hold paint for printing
- Smocks or paint shirts
- Sponges, towels, newspaper

Fasteners
- Heavy-duty staplers, staples
- Hole punch
- Paste, liquid glue, glue sticks
- Masking tape, clear tape
- Paper clips, butterfly fasteners
- Rubber bands, elastic
- Pipe cleaners, wire
- String, yarn, ribbon, shoelaces
- Needles with big eyes, thread

Modeling and molding materials
- Moist clay, modeling clay
- Play dough (including black and shades of brown)
- Beeswax
- Plaster of Paris
- Modeling accessories — rolling pins, thick dowel rods, cookie cutters, plastic knives, hamburger or tortilla press

Collage materials
- Cardboard tubes, egg cartons, small boxes and cartons
- Empty thread spools, clothespins
- Wood and balsa pieces
- Cloth, felt, carpet scraps
- Old stockings and socks
- Feathers, cotton balls, fringe
- Buttons, straws, sequins
- Yarn, ribbon
- Styrofoam packing pieces
- Looms, weaving loops

Drawing and cutting materials
- Crayons (including a range of skin-tone colors)
- Block crayons
- Colored pencils
- Marking pens, markers (of varying sizes)
- Chalk
- Oil pastels
- Charcoal sticks
- Scissors

---
[5]Program staff should adhere to their state's licensing regulations when adding materials to the classroom.

This child hangs her painting to dry in the art area.

Sometimes adults look at the suggested list of art area materials and wonder whether it is wise to have all these things available for children on a daily basis. On one hand, like any other work area, the art area should provide a variety of materials to choose from. On the other hand, children also need time to work and experiment with particular art area materials in depth to discover their purpose and how they work best. Therefore, it makes sense to set up the art area with an initial supply of basic art materials and to supplement these with other materials as children become familiar with what is already there.

Accessible storage. Paper is best stored in a flat rack where it takes up little space, is somewhat protected and contained, and is easily reached by children. Small, loose items such as crayons, pencils, chalk, scissors, markers, paper clips, and toothpicks store well in clear plastic containers, lidless cigar boxes, or hanging shoe pockets.

Big art projects. Many art area experiences, such as drawing a picture or rolling play dough strands, involve working with fairly small objects in a relatively small space. This is enjoyable for many children, but here are some ideas to consider for those children who usually choose vigorous physical activity and who might be more inclined to work in the art area if they could be as vigorous there:

- Provide large appliance boxes and Styrofoam packing pieces for children to paint, decorate, and turn into houses, robots, dinosaurs, and so forth.

- Cover an art area wall with large sheets of butcher paper for large-scale painting, printing, and collage-making.

- Clear a tabletop for finger painting.
- Provide rope and large items for stringing, such as paper towel tubes, plastic pipe fittings, and funnels.

Outdoor art. The outdoors is a natural place for experimenting with art materials and working on large-scale art projects. Here children can paint with oversized paintbrushes and rollers on walkways, steps, fences, play structures, and tree stumps. They can paint with water or use paint, and then hose their creations away if necessary. Children can make footprints and handprints with paints or with mud on large paper or natural surfaces. They can also print with objects they gather, such as sticks, grass, leaves, flowers, stones, bricks, cans, and tires. Big looms strung from tree branches work well outside where children can weave in vines, sticks, hoses, long grasses, branches, and twine. Fences also make good "looms" for weaving things in and out.

One group of young children in Seattle worked outside each day for several weeks making a totem pole "about us." They decided to make the totem pole after looking at, touching, and hearing stories about real totem poles they had visited. One child reported that the city was cutting down damaged trees near her house "to make it more safe in the park." With the help of parents and a pickup truck, they got one of these "whole" tree trunks, stripped off the bark, and then set about adding things and painting. One section of the tree, for example, was a collection of wood pieces and bottle caps nailed in the pole. Another section was ringed with special "writing" that "helps us with magic." Another was wrapped with multicolored yarn and string. Pieces of clay made eyes and ears; yarn and ribbons streamed down for hair. One idea led to another, and everyone who was interested was able to contribute.

Art gallery art. Just as they like to sing and hear stories, children also enjoy looking at art created by others. Here are a few ways to bring young children and art together:

- Bring in masks, weavings, quilts, sculptures, carvings, baskets, pots, and mobiles for children to examine close up.

The outdoors is a natural place for experimenting with art materials and working on large-scale art projects.

- Hang paintings, prints, and photographs at children's eye level where they can look at them. Many museums and bookstores sell posters and prints, and some libraries lend framed prints.
- Include pairs of art-print postcards in the toy area for children to look at and match.
- Invite local artists to share their work with children. In one program, for example, a weaver brought in a multicolored hanging she had made, her table loom with a piece she was working on, and some very simple looms and thick yarns for the children to try on their own.
- Observe with children *natural outdoor art:* shadows, clouds, bare trees, rocks, leaves, flowers, birds, nests, insects.

The book and writing area

Here, children look at and read books, "read" books from memory and picture cues, listen to stories, and make up and write their own stories in their own way. For many children, this area is a cozy spot where they can look at books or magazines, either by themselves, with friends, or with an older person who has agreed to read aloud to them. Some children use story props to reenact and retell stories in their own words, while others write and illustrate their own books and stories. Although preschool children often "write" using scribbles, drawings, and letterlike marks rather than actual letters, expressing themselves in such unconventional forms is important because such experiences are the beginnings of literate behavior.

Location. The book and writing area is often near the art area so that children can easily obtain additional writing supplies whenever they need them. It is important that this area be located in a quiet spot away from areas of vigorous play. Windows add natural light and a window seat makes a cozy reading spot.

One team with limited space turned a storage closet into a book nook. They removed the door and the lower shelves, built forward-facing bookracks along the three closet walls, and covered the floor with pillows. They placed the writing table outside next to the nook. A sofa, forward-facing bookrack, large sturdy potted plants, and a low storage shelf for writing supplies can be used to serve as boundaries and make the area inviting. Another alternative, if there is limited space for a separate book and writing area, is to use the house area: put books next to the couch, beanbag chairs, or other comfortable reading spot; keep writing materials on or near a low table that children use as a "desk."

Materials. This area includes all kinds of commercially published, homemade, and child-made books along with magazines, photo albums, story props, and writing materials. As you select books from the library and bookstore, and make your own, look for the following:

- Books with illustrations (drawings, paintings, or photographs)
- Stories and pictures showing people of all races, ages, and physical abilities in positive, caring roles
- Stories and alphabet books in the languages spoken by the children in your program

It is important to create areas for reading books in quiet spots away from vigorous areas of play.

A Book Area at Home

"Sit, Mommy, sit," said Jamie, guiding her mom to the sofa. "Read, Mommy, read," she instructed, handing her mom the book *Caps for Sale*, by Esphyr Slobodkina, which she had selected from a collection of books on the coffee table. "Wait for me," called her sister Jessie, leaving her blocks and settling herself in on her mom's other side.

Preschoolers Jamie and Jessie McHugh, aged 2½ and 4 years, are part of a weekly home visit program. When Paula, their home visitor, first started visiting them and their mom, she ended each visit by asking Mrs. McHugh to read to the girls on the couch. Paula would then leave the book on the coffee table until her next visit. Between visits, Jamie and Jessie persuaded their mom to read them the story again and again. This led to a trip to the library where the girls were really excited about picking out their own books and having six books to choose from!

As their library visits continued and story-reading habits grew, Jamie and Jessie claimed the top of the coffee table for their books. If their mom put her magazine or coffee cup on their table, they reminded her, "No, Mom. This is where the storybooks go. You put your things over there." As their mom related this incident to Paula, she concluded, "Well, at first I was a little miffed, but then I thought how glad I am that the girls like stories so much they want their own library table. I never would have thought of such a thing when I was their age!"

Front-facing book racks make it easy for children to see and select books that interest them.

Book and Writing Area Materials[6]

Books

- Picture books, for example,
  - *Where the Wild Things Are* by Maurice Sendak
  - *Follow the Drinking Gourd* by Jeanette Winter
  - *Giberto and the Wind* by Marie Hall Ets
  - *When I Was Young in the Mountains* by Cynthia Rylant
- Wordless books, for example,
  - *Bored, Nothing to Do* by Peter Spier
  - *Anno's Counting House* by Mitsumasa Anno
  - *The Snowman* by Raymond Briggs
  - *Pancakes for Breakfast* by Tomie De Paola
- Folklore, for example,
  - *Gingerbread Boy, The Three Billy Goats Gruff, The Three Bears, The Three Pigs*, all by Paul Galdone
  - *Anansi and the Moss-Covered Rock* by Eric A. Kimmel
  - *The Tongue-Cut Sparrow* by Momoko Ishii
- Predictable-format books, for example,
  - *Brown Bear, Brown Bear, What Do You See?* by Bill Martin and Eric Carle
  - *Have You Seen Mr. Bear?* by Marjorie Flack
  - *"Pardon?" Said the Giraffe* by Colin West
- Poetry and song books, for example,
  - *Sing a Song of Popcorn: Every Child's Book of Poems* by Beatrice De Regniers
  - *The Three Bears Rhyme Book* by Jane Yolen
  - *Talking to the Sun* by Kenneth Koch and Kate Farrell
- Multicultural and bilingual books, for example,
  - *All Kinds of Children* by Norma Simon
  - *Shades of Black* by Sandra Pinkney
  - *Tortillas and Lullabies* by Lynn Reiser
- Nonfiction books, for example,
  - *The Story of Martin Luther King* by Johnny Ray Moore
  - *Dinosaur More!* by Henrietta Strickland
  - *Actual Size* by Steve Jenkins
- Concept books, for example,
  - *Rosie's Walk* by Pat Hutchins
  - *Mouse Numbers* by Jim Aronsky
  - *I Hate English* by Ellen Levine
- Alphabet books, for example,
  - *Alligators All Around* by Maurice Sendak
  - *Alligator Arrived With Apples: A Potluck Alphabet Feast* by Crescent Dragonwagon
  - *Eating the Alphabet: Fruits & Vegetables from A to Z* by Lois Ehlert
- Early mathematics books, for example,
  - *10 Little Rubber Ducks* by Eric Carle
  - *Round Is a Mooncake* by Roseanne Thong
  - *Roar! A Noisy Counting Book* by Pamela Edwards
- Homemade and child-made books
- Photo albums including photos of program children, their families and neighborhoods, children at work and play, field trips and special events
- Photo books, for example,
  - *Children of Many Lands, Children and Their Mothers, Children and Their Fathers*, all by H. Reich

Magazines and catalogs

- Magazines written for children, for example,
  - *Click*
  - *Faces*
  - *Cricket*
  - *Chickadee*
  - *Ladybug*
  - *Ranger Rick*
  - *National Geographic Kids*
- Old magazines donated by families and staff
- Old, donated catalogs

Storytelling props

- Characters and props (commercially available and/or homemade) for re-enacting stories, for example:
  - Three billy goats, a troll, a bridge
  - Three bears, their chairs, bowls, beds, a little girl
  - Max and the wild things

Writing materials

- Unlined paper of all colors, shapes, sizes
- Memo pads, notebooks, folders, envelopes
- Multicolored pencils, pens, markers, crayons
- Pencil sharpener
- Stickers, stamps and ink pads
- A sturdy, working typewriter
- Alphabet letter and numeral sets of wood, plastic

---

[6]Program staff should adhere to their state's licensing regulations when adding materials to the classroom.

- Stories and pictures reflecting the experiences of single-parent, two-parent, and extended families

Accessible storage. Forward-facing bookracks (as opposed to bookshelves) make it easy for children to see and reach books. Also accessible and inviting are book baskets or plastic milk crates on the floor that children can easily sort through. Writing materials can be stored and labeled in the same manner as art area materials.

The toy area

The toy area is a place where children play with simple games, puzzles, and sets of manipulatives that can be used in a variety of ways. Working on their own or near others, children use the materials in both simple and complex ways; they may explore new materials, fill and empty containers, put together and take apart small structures, sort and match, and make patterns. Some children spend time repeating and expanding new skills. Children who have mastered a puzzle may do it again and again, and then challenge themselves by putting the pieces together outside the puzzle frame. Some children play simple matching or make-believe games together. For example, they may use the pegs and pegboard to make a birthday cake, or build a fence of dominos for the rubber farm animals.

Location. Consider locating this area away from the house and block areas. While many children ignore the sounds of vigorous play, others are distracted by them, and almost all children need a relatively calm place to play sometimes. Although many of the materials in the toy area are small, children will still need ample space to spread out with their cards, beads, and interlocking shapes. Therefore, allow for plenty of comfortable floor space, especially next to the toy shelves where children often prefer to play. Where space permits, include a table and chairs as an alternative work surface.

Walls and low storage shelves help define the toy area. However, if this area is too enclosed,

For this child, the toy area is a place to work alone — with a set of wooden pieces that makes a castle.

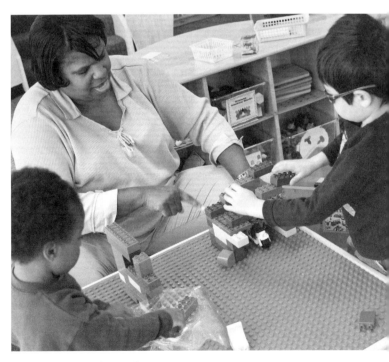

These children have choices among inviting items in the toy area to stack, sort, and manipulate.

Toy Area Materials[7]

Sorting and small building materials
- Beads (large and small) and strings
- Buttons, marbles, corks
- Shells, stones, pine cones, seed pods
- Bleached animal bones
- Building cubes
- Parquetry blocks
- Attribute blocks
- Nesting cups, boxes, rings
- Cuisenaire rods

Take-apart-and-put-together materials
- Washers, nuts, bolts
- Pegs and pegboards (large and small)
- Stacking rings and post
- Small Tinkertoys
- Interlocking blocks
- Interlocking shapes
- Connecting straws
- Puzzles (including ones with diverse images of people)
- Magnets

- Shape sorters and shapes
- Scales, balances
- Gear sets
- Sewing boards
- Geoboards and rubber bands
- Dowel rods with Velcro connectors

Pretend-play materials
- Counting bears
- Miniature animal collections
- Little people, gnomes
- Wooden village/city/farm sets
- Puppets (animals and multiracial people)
- Wooden train sets

Games
- Simple card games, such as Snap, Go Fish, Old Maid
- Memory card games
- Dominos (picture, texture)
- Picture lotto games
- Simple board games, such as "Candyland"

---
[7] Program staff should adhere to their state's licensing regulations when adding materials to the classroom.

children may tend to overlook it simply because they cannot see the small toys available. To avoid such situations, consider enclosing the toy area on three sides and leaving the fourth side open.

Space for explorers and pretenders. Sometimes the toy area becomes a supply area for role play initiated in another part of the room. Children come in to get beads for the "soup," pegs for their "birthday cake," cards for their "party," scales for their "store," and so forth. At other times, the toy area itself becomes the stage — for the dance program the children are putting on, for example, or for the "movie" for which they have made "tickets" and "popcorn." The actors may bring in extra chairs for the audience and large blocks for the stage. While all this activity is appropriate for the role players, it is also important to consider ways of preserving play space for children engaged in other activities in this area. Here are some strategies to consider:

- Include different toy area levels (lofts, platforms) that children can play under and on top of to help separate individual and social play.
- Include a toy area nook for individual play.

Toy Figures Attract Children

Ruth Strubank, a HighScope Certified Trainer, reported the following toy area experience when she was a teacher in the HighScope Demonstration Preschool:

"After noticing that our children were not paying any attention to the plants on a low table in the toy area, I asked a visiting six-year-old if she could think of a way to make the large and small pine cones, basket of rocks, aloe vera plant, and Norfolk Island pine plant more interesting to children. 'We have gnomes at my school,' she offered. Taking her advice, the next day I added nine small, flexible figures called Pocket Pals (made of wood, wire, and brightly colored felt) to the branches of the pine and aloe plants. I purposely did not introduce the new toy figures during the greeting circle because I wanted to see if and how the children would discover and use them on their own.

"Sure enough, when Maxwell finished in the computer area (next to the toy area), he noticed the Pocket Pals hanging from the plants. Discovering that they were flexible, he began bending them, hanging them in different positions, and making up conversations between them.

"Donnette and Christopher joined him, asking questions and offering suggestions. They used the rocks to make a path between the pine and the aloe plant and turned the rock basket over to make a house. They added a Tinkertoy pole so the Pals could slide from the table into their swimming pool on the floor. Will joined the play group, and gathering construction paper, tape, and scissors from the art area, built a bridge from the table to a chair. Maxwell brought over a basket of wood scraps, and Christopher colored two of them green for 'mean crocodiles' under the bridge.

"The children invited me to the toy area again and again as they added materials, expanded their ideas, and told stories aloud. I was very excited that such small additions made such a big impact on their play."

- Tip an appliance box on its side so children can work inside undisturbed.

Materials. An inviting toy area is amply stocked with fit-together-and-take-apart toys, sorting materials, small building materials, pretend-play materials, and games. As you select toy area materials, look for sets of things that children can use in a variety of ways. Since active learners are creative problem-solvers, a child in the toy area may make a house for counting bears by using a puzzle for the floor and dominos for the walls. Remember, too, that natural materials and homemade games are generally quite satisfactory and even preferable to some commercially made items. You can also save money by not buying battery-powered toys, which children tend to watch rather than manipulate.

Accessible storage. Sort sets of toys into suitable containers (clear plastic shoeboxes, baskets, food storage containers, silverware trays) and label each container with a picture or the actual object fastened to the outside of the container. Storing games in their original boxes works for as long as the boxes last. (It helps to reinforce the corners.) When the box falls apart, pictures from it make familiar labels for the new container. Puzzles store well in racks.

For objects such as pegboards, sewing boards, scales, and balances that simply rest on a shelf (rather than in a container), attach labels to the shelf to indicate where the object is stored.

Drawing children into the toy area. At the beginning of the year, many children tend to overlook the toy area, perhaps because the toys on the shelves are small and less immediately visible than the blocks, dolls, and easels. Here are some strategies to consider if this happens in your setting:

- Store some of the larger toy sets on the floor or on top of a low toy shelf where children can see them from different parts of the room.
- Add different levels to the toy area, both for storage and play. A loft works well. Using this

idea on a smaller scale, one teaching team added a low, carpeted platform with pillows to a corner of the toy area and stored the games there.

- If space permits, encourage children to use some of the large hollow blocks to arrange for their own play surfaces.
- Add other materials to the toy area (such as small figures) that will attract attention and that the children can incorporate into their play with the other toy-area materials.

The sand and water area

From infancy to adulthood, people enjoy sand and water. Young children like to play with sand and water and find such play satisfying. They enjoy mixing, stirring, heaping, dumping, digging, filling, emptying, pouring, patting, sifting, molding, and splashing, as well as making pretend cakes, houses, roads, and lakes for floating boats. Children in the sand and water area play by themselves, next to others, with a friend, or in a play group.

Location. Under the most natural conditions, the sand and water area is a shallow outdoor pond surrounded by sand where children can dig trenches, make mud pies, float sticks, wade, and splash. An outdoor sandbox and a hose or hand-pump serve the same purpose.

Indoors, the sand and water area generally centers around a table with its own water spigot, or a wheeled table lined with plastic with a stoppered hole for drainage. Locating this table close to a sink makes it easier for children to add water, and positioning it away from a wall allows children to play on all four sides. For an inexpensive alternative to a sand and water table, put several dishpans or baby bathtubs on a low table or on the floor. A tile floor aids cleanup. Otherwise, you can cover the floor with a sheet of heavy plastic or a shower curtain.

Children tend to work around the sand and water table with their backs to the surrounding

Young children enjoy playing with sand and water, both alone and with others.

Many different types of materials are suitable for children's enjoyment and exploration at the sand and water table.

Sand-and-Water-Area Materials[8]

Fill-and-empty materials
- Buckets
- Plastic food containers
- Plastic pump and squeeze bottles, poultry basters
- Measuring cups
- Plastic tubing
- Strainers, colanders, funnels
- Cake pans, muffin tins, plates, spatulas
- Shovels, trowels
- Scoops, spoons

Floating materials
- Corks, sponges
- Popsicle sticks, twigs
- Styrofoam bits and pieces

Pretend-play materials
- Rubber animals and people
- Plastic dishes
- Boats
- Cars, trucks, and construction vehicles

Alternatives to sand and water
- Chestnuts, leaves, pine needles
- Shells
- Pebbles and stones
- Pea gravel
- Marbles
- Snow
- Water and soap bubbles
- Shaving cream

Waterproof gear and cleanup materials
- Waterproof smocks
- Rubber boots and waders
- Towels, sponges
- Whiskbroom and dustpan
- Battery-operated hand-held vacuum

[8]Program staff should adhere to their state's licensing regulations when adding materials to the classroom.

---

play space. Therefore, physical boundaries are not essential to giving the children a sense of being in the area. On the other hand, low shelves on one or two sides of the table protect children from traffic interference and also provide storage space for sand and water play materials.

Materials. Sand and water play materials include containers, tools, and toys for filling and emptying, floating, and pretending; alternatives to sand and water (such as shells, pine needles, snow, shaving cream); waterproofing gear; and cleanup tools. Children will also bring things to the sand and water area from other areas, such as rubber dolls from the house area to bathe and boats they have made at the workbench.

Accessible storage. One of the easiest ways to store sand and water play materials is by sorting them into labeled tubs. Put the buckets and other containers in a tub labeled with a picture of containers, put the shells in a basket labeled with a shell, and so forth. If the sand and water table is next to a wall, it may be possible to hang some materials on hooks attached to the wall or a pegboard. For example, you might hang the whiskbrooms and dustpans over tracings of each one.

The woodworking area

Here, children can actually use the real tools they see adults and "big kids" using. They can exert real strength to pound a nail and saw through a piece

At the workbench, children use real tools to make their own creations.

> **Woodworking Area Materials**[9]
>
> **Tools**
> - Claw hammers (12-oz. heads)
> - Saws (crosscut, 10–12 teeth per inch, 16–18 in. blade)
> - Hand drill, brace, and bit
> - Screwdrivers (those with solid plastic handles are most durable)
> - Pliers (medium size)
> - Vises (mounted at either end of the workbench)
> - C-clamps
> - Sandpaper, sandpaper blocks
> - Safety goggles
>
> **Fasteners**
> - Nails
> - Golf tees
> - Screws
> - Nuts, bolts, washers
> - Wire
>
> **Wood and building materials**
> - Wood scraps and pieces (fir, white pine, balsa)
> - Styrofoam packing pieces
> - Bottle caps, jar lids (for wheels)
> - Dowel-rod pieces
>
> ---
> [9]Program staff should adhere to their state's licensing regulations when adding materials to the classroom.

of wood. Many children use the tools simply to understand how they work and for the satisfaction of pounding and sawing. Other children use the woodworking area to make things such as boats, walkie-talkies, guinea-pig beds, and birdhouses. In the process, they may incorporate such art area materials as glue and pipe cleaners; some children may carry their creations to the art area to paint.

Location. Locating the woodworking area near the art area makes sense, because children use both areas as they work on a project. Within the area, provide adequate space for a child-level workbench, tools, and wood storage. The woodworking area can also be located outdoors in an area removed from the path of wheeled toys and from general traffic patterns.

As you plan the area, keep in mind that children will tend to gather around the workbench, focusing on the immediate task at hand. Low shelves or boxes for wood and tool storage can also serve as protective boundaries on at least two sides of the workbench.

Materials. Woodworking materials include a variety of tools, fasteners, wood, and other building materials (such as Styrofoam packing pieces and dowels). You can buy tools and fasteners at discount stores, garage sales, auctions, and flea markets. Families may also be willing to donate spare items they no longer use at home. Just make sure that hammer heads and saw blades are securely fastened to their handles. Lumber yards generally have a bin of free scrap lumber you can rummage through periodically. Other sources of free or inexpensive wood scraps are furniture and cabinet makers, building sites, and ladder factories. You can also look for wooden packing crates discarded behind discount, hardware, appliance, and produce stores. And, you can buy a sturdy child-sized workbench or you can make one by bolting boards to low sawhorses or tree stumps.

Accessible storage. Hang the tools on pegboards with hooks, or store them on a low shelf or in a large toolbox with spaces for each kind of tool. Outlines and tracings make clear labels for tools. Fasteners store well in their own containers, labeled with pictures or with one of the actual fasteners. For example, you might store the medium-length nails in a butter tub, food container, small canister, or cookie tin. You can sort wood scraps and other building materials into labeled boxes, milk crates, ice-cream tubs, dishpans, or sturdy wastebaskets.

The music and movement area

Young children are music-makers. They like to sing, play musical instruments, make up songs, move to the beat, dance, and listen to music. Some children explore instruments, sounds, and motions, while others create their own songs, dances, and games: "You and Victor hold the scarves and move them up and down, okay? And me and Lolly go under them like this, see? Okay. Ready, go!"

Location. It makes sense to locate this area closer to the noisier areas, such as the house, block, and woodworking areas, and farther away from the book, writing, and art areas. If you can locate the music and movement area next to a central meeting area, music-makers can spread into this space to dance, play musical games, or engage in other movement activities. A nearby electrical outlet allows you to plug in CD or DVD players rather than rely on batteries. A carpet on the floor helps absorb some of the sound, as do pillows, wall hangings, and shelf backs covered with quilts, drapes, corkboard, egg cartons, or carpet squares. A protected outdoor music area is ideal. Walls, low storage shelves or cubbyholes, low pegboard partitions, and child-level potted plants make suitable boundaries.

These children enjoy having space to move through the classroom while making music.

> **Music and Movement Area Materials**[10]
>
> **Percussion instruments**
> - Drums, tambourines
> - Triangles
> - Maracas, gourds
> - Clavés, sandpaper blocks
> - Cymbals
> - Bells — handheld, or wrist and ankle bells
> - Xylophones, metalophones
> - Thumb pianos, keyboard
>
> **Simple wind instruments**
> - Whistles, slide whistles, kazoos
> - Harmonicas
>
> **Recording and music playing equipment**
> - Video cameras, digital recorders, CD players, or digital audio players
> - DVDs or CDs representing a variety of musical styles, traditions, and cultures
>
> **Dance props**
> - Scarves, ribbons
> - Hoops
> - Limbo sticks
>
> ---
> [10]Program staff should adhere to their state's licensing regulations when adding materials to the classroom.

Materials. The music and movement area includes percussion and simple wind instruments, recording equipment, and dance props. To maintain the sound quality and extend the life of these materials, it is important to clean the electronic equipment and wind instruments and to polish the wooden instruments regularly. Also, children need to know that while mallets are a must for the xylophone and metalophone, they will break the heads of drums and tambourines.

Accessible storage. Hang the instruments on pegboard hooks or store on low shelves, labeling the shelves or pegboard with line drawings or tracings of the instruments. Label the CDs and DVDs with pictures or drawings that children can identify — for example, a picture of people playing drums on a CD of African drum music or a picture of an Indian dance troupe on a CD of dance music from India.

The computer area

If your program has computers, choose a variety of computer programs designed especially for young children. Many software programs allow children to draw; make masks and jewelry; play matching, comparing, counting, and memory games; make up patterns; "drive" on-screen trains, cars, and boats; experiment with letters; and write their own stories. Don't forget that computers can also play music files, CDs, and DVDs. As you plan this area, keep in mind that social play is common at computers and that screens and keyboards should be arranged to permit more than one child to use a computer at a time. As children work at computers, they often share games, ideas, and discoveries, and rely on one another to solve problems (Clements, 1999).

Location. The computer area should be large enough to accommodate one to three computers, each on its own table. (Adjust the height of the table so the computer screens are at children's eye-level and the keyboards and touchpads are at children's elbow-level.) For example, with three computers, arrange the tables in a semicircle with the screens facing toward the center of the semicircle; with this arrangement, children can help one another while focusing on their own activity, and adults can easily see all the screens at once.

The computer area should allow children to work alone and together, with adults easily able to see all the screens at once.

A classroom corner and window help define this computer area.

Computers and Active Learning

When considering whether to use computer activities with young children, adults often find themselves caught up in a lively debate. At one extreme are those who believe that children must learn to use computers to ensure their place in tomorrow's labor force. At the other extreme are those who believe that exposing children to computers will inhibit, if not destroy, their creativity, thinking, and interpersonal communication skills. Both these viewpoints, fraught with powerful emotions and reflecting opposing world views, make it difficult to be objective about the use of computers in preschool settings. The ingredients of active learning, however, provide a more objective context in which to consider computer experiences and to decide whether to make them available to young children.

Because using computers has the potential to involve all the **ingredients of active learning — materials, manipulation, choice, child language and thought, and adult scaffolding** — the thoughtful use of developmentally appropriate computer activities can fit well in an active learning setting.

Materials. The computer (keyboard, touchpad, mouse, monitor, printer, and developmentally appropriate software) is a tool that can help children do things — find letters and numbers, draw, write stories, make masks, make birthday cards, drive cars through cities they have created, estimate distances and amounts. Children who see adults using computers are drawn to them just as they are drawn to telephones, music players, real kitchen utensils, vacuum cleaners, and hair dryers. While adults often feel intimidated by computers, children do not. Since everything in the world is new to children, they have not formed preconceived notions about computers and are as interested in computers as they are about anything else.

Manipulation. Because of its interactive character, a computer equipped with developmentally appropriate software allows children many opportunities to discover relationships by controlling events on the screen. When a child pushes a button on the keyboard or taps an arrow on the screen, something happens — the car turns a corner, the letter "A" appears, the triangle flips upside down, the printer prints out the child's mask or story. Many programs allow children to transform and combine colors, shapes, sizes, figures, facial features, articles of clothing, letters, numbers, and words to produce their own pictures, designs, cards, masks, crowns, and jewelry that they cut out, color, decorate, give away, or wear as they see fit.

Choice. First, as with any material in an active learning setting, children choose whether, when, with whom, and for how long to work with a computer activity. Given some initial adult guidance with each new piece of software, children are quite able to take care of their own needs at the computer. Generally, they can operate programs and print out the results on their own and at their own pace. As soon as they have a repertoire of programs, they can choose the programs that particularly interest them. Within each program, children can make things happen. Depending on the program they can, for example, choose to make a letter appear or disappear or decide whether to make the rider stay on his horse or fall off. In addition, some programs allow children to print out a product, such as a drawing, story, card, or mask, providing each child with the additional choice of deciding whether or not the product needs cutting, folding, coloring, painting, gluing, or other refinements.

Child language and thought. Children who choose to use the computer typically have as much to say about what they are doing as they would about any other activity they have chosen. Because the link between cause and effect is so immediate in appropriate programs, children are eager to tell others about the funny or surprising thing they just made the bird or the cat do, for example. Since children are just as likely to work with another child at the computer as they are to work by themselves, peer-to-peer conversations are common and children help one another solve problems (for example, "I got it to turn when I touched this arrow. You try it"). When computer programs involve simple writing tasks, children are also engaged in putting their own words into print and reading them back and/or in having someone else read them back.

Adult scaffolding. One of the surprising things about computers is the extent to which young children can work on them independently and successfully. Even though computers are complex machines, with developmentally appropriate software, they are easy to operate, quite robust, and tolerant of error. When a child makes a mistake, good software programs, like patient adults, give the child another chance, offer a clue, or simply present another problem.

As in any active learning situation, however, adult support is essential for computer activities. Adults provide and introduce developmentally appropriate software programs; they interact with children as they work at computers, using computers alongside children, observing what children are doing, conversing with children about their work, and referring one child to another. In other words, when interacting with children who are using computers, adults are guided by the same support strategies they use with other activities, such as building with blocks, playing with clay, or painting. Although the materials are different, the active learning process is the same.

It is important to locate the computer area where windows and lights do not create glare or reflection on the screens. Also, if the area is backed up against a corner, then wires, cables, power packs, and power cords will be safely out of the way. Since children often create things at the computer that they want to decorate, cut out, or add to, locating the computers near the art area facilitates the natural movement between these two areas. Since computer programs often involve "reading and writing," locating this area near — or as part of — the reading and writing area also makes sense.

In many cases, simply arranging the computer tables in a semicircle is adequate for defining the area for children. If you have fewer than three computers, however, you may wish to use low storage shelves or dividers for boundaries.

Materials. At a minimum, the computer area needs the following equipment:

- An up-to-date multimedia computer (with speakers)
- Software appropriate for young children
- A printer

Accessible storage. The computer, monitor (if separate from the computer), and printer are stationary pieces of equipment that should remain on their own tables. After program CDs are installed on the computer, they should be stored elsewhere in a safe space, unless they need to be inserted in the drive to run (use) the program.

The outdoor area

The outdoors is a wonderful place for children. Here they are free to run, ride wheeled toys, push and pull wagons, throw balls, roll down hills, dig, swing, slide, climb, and do all the other things adults caution them against when indoors. Children demonstrate different abilities in the outdoor setting than they do inside. They may show themselves, for example, to be skilled climbers and balancers, or imaginative large-scale builders. It is essential to young children's growth and development to have time each day to play in a safe place outdoors.

Most licensing regulations and professional organizations concerned with children's physical development recommend that the outdoor play area provide at least 75 square feet of space per child. A space of this size facilitates children's active and unimpeded movement, allows for the use of equipment (such as swings and tricycles) that develops large-motor skills, and minimizes the chance of collisions between children or children and objects. Ample outdoor space thus permits children to play in freedom and safety.

Location. Although children can play vigorously in a spacious gym, no indoor space can match the sounds, sights, smells, and textures of the natural world. Outdoor play areas are best located on open land or in a yard immediately adjacent to indoor play areas so that children can move quickly and safely from indoors to outdoors. In some urban locations, however, adjacent space may not be available for outdoor play. While there may be a public park within walking distance, this space will work only if children and adults feel safe. If there is no outdoor space available on ground level, consider the following:

- Develop a rooftop outdoor area with natural features such as sod and raised plant beds.
- Share an outdoor area with a nearby church, school, YMCA, or business.

Safety in the Outdoor Play Space

"The outdoor space should be designed for play value and safety," says pediatric health and safety expert Dr. Susan Aronson (2002, p. 120). Since many technical issues feature in the design of a safe playground, Aronson recommends that a Certified Playground Safety Inspector review existing facilities and plans to modify or build new outdoor spaces.

A significant concern in outdoor play areas is the safety of the surfaces and equipment. Since the majority of playground injuries are due to falls, the most important safety feature is an impact-absorbent surface that meets the standards of the American Society for Testing and Materials. The Consumer Product Safety Commission conducts tests on the shock-absorbing properties of common loose-fill surfacing material, including wood chips, shredded bark mulch, sand, pea gravel, and shredded rubber tires. Each has advantages and drawbacks, including the cost of periodic replacement due to weather-related deterioration. While commercially manufactured surface materials (also called unitary materials) may be more expensive initially to purchase and install, they require less maintenance and may save money in the long run.

In addition to protecting children from falls, outdoor play areas should guard against entrapment, tripping, and choking, and avoid exposure to excessive wind and direct sunlight. They should be separated from streets, traffic, and access by unauthorized persons, and be inspected daily to guarantee they are free of glass, litter, and other hazards, especially local public playgrounds used by the child care setting. (For more information on the safety of outdoor areas, see Aronson [2002] and the web sites of the organizations cited in this paragraph.)

You can define various parts of the outdoor area by changes in surface materials, such as hard surfaces for wheeled toys.

- Take a daily walk around the block with wagons, bikes, and strollers.

If you have your own ground- or roof-level outdoor space, consider planning the area so that children can explore and appreciate a variety of landscape elements (hills, valleys, sunlit areas, shaded areas, grass, rocks, gravel, water) and plant life (trees, shrubs, bushes, vines, and flowers). Include contrasts in shape, color, and texture — for example, a weedy area for exploration and a tilled bed for children's gardening. A fence or barrier around the entire perimeter of the outdoor area defines the play space, keeps children within safe limits, and provides a sense of security.

Within the outdoor area it is important to separate areas for physically vigorous play from areas of focused play — children should be able to dig in the dirt, for example, without having to watch out for children riding wheeled toys or children zooming off the slide. The sketch by Esbensen (1987, p. 12) presented on page 218 may give you some ideas for an outdoor area layout. You can define various parts of the outdoor area by

Outdoor Area Materials[11]

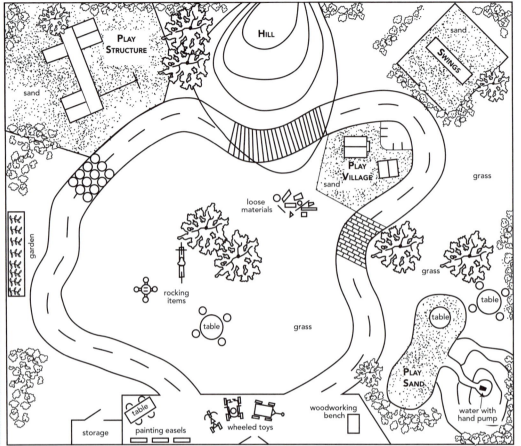

(This sketch originally appeared in Esbensen, 1987, p. 12)

Stationary structures
- Climbers
  - jungle gym, net climber
  - trees with low branches close together
- High places
  - raised platform, low tree house, sturdy crates
  - hills, boulders
  - tree stumps, snow piles
- Swings
  - commercial swing set, multiperson tire swing
  - rope swing from tree, low hammock
  - spring-based rocking toys
- Slides
  - commercial slide, hill slide
  - low ramp, low cable ride
  - firefighter's pole, sleds for winter
- Balances
  - balance beams
  - rows of railroad ties, bricks, or rocks arranged in rows (including parallel rows, curving, and zigzag rows)

Wheeled toys
- Tricycles
- Scooters
- Wagons
- Wheelbarrow
- Push vehicles with steering wheels
- Strollers, carriages

Loose materials
- Jumping equipment
  - inner-tubes, trampolines
  - old mattress, leaf piles
  - ropes (to jump over)
- Equipment for throwing, kicking, and aiming
  - balls (all sizes)
  - beanbags
  - low basketball hoop and net
  - pails, buckets, boxes, bull's-eye targets

- Building materials
  - boards of varying lengths
  - slotted plywood pieces (sanded smooth)
  - Styrofoam sheets, boards, packing pieces
  - cardboard boxes
  - twine, rope, pulleys
  - old sheets, blankets, tarps
  - small sawhorses
  - tires, inner-tubes
  - workbench and tools
- Sand and water materials
  - sand pit, box, table or tubs
  - sand, pea gravel, shells, sawdust, wood shavings, leaves, pine cones, snow
  - wading pool, spigot, hose, hand pump, flexible tubing
  - spoons, shovels, buckets
- Gardening equipment
  - garden plot, window boxes, tubs with soil
  - watering can or hose
  - gardening tools
  - seeds, bulbs, flowers, plants
- Pretend-play props
  - boat, car, plane, train, spaceship, tractor, hay wagon
  - dump trucks, bulldozers
  - mounted steering wheel
  - playhouse or enclosure (refrigerator box, dense shrubbery)
  - telephone in playhouse or booth, or on pole
  - mailbox
  - low clothesline, clothespins
  - small working flagpole with flags
  - gas pump handle and hose, empty oil can and spout
  - binoculars
  - helmets, hats, goggles
  - backpacks
- Musical instruments
  - pipe chimes, wind chimes
  - dinner bells, sleigh bells
  - trash-can drums, hollow-log drums
  - slatted fence (to run sticks across)
- Art materials
  - painting canvases made from old sheets, paints
  - paint rollers, large brushes
  - bubbles and bubble wands
  - large-scale weaving frame
  - multicolored chalk
  - clay for imprints of grass, stones, leaves, etc.
  - food coloring, sand tools, boxes, cans for snow sculpture

[11]Program staff should adhere to their state's licensing regulations when adding materials to the classroom.

Guidelines and Strategies for Arranging and Equipping Spaces for Children: A Summary

Organizing space

- The space is inviting to children. It includes
  - Softness
  - Rounded corners
  - Pleasing colors and textures
  - Natural materials and light
  - Cozy places
  - Purposeful sound
- The space is divided into well-defined and labeled interest areas to encourage distinctive types of play. A few basic areas plus a limited combination of other areas includes:
  - Block area
  - House area
  - Art area
  - Book and writing area
  - Toy area
  - Sand and water area
  - Woodworking area
  - Music and movement area
  - Computer area
  - Outdoor area
- The space incorporates places for group activities, eating, napping, and storing children's belongings.
- The space and materials accommodate children with special needs.

Establishing interest areas

- The interest areas are arranged to promote visibility and easy movement between areas.
  - The block and house areas are close to each other.
  - The art area is close to water.
  - The book and toy areas are located away from vigorous play areas.
  - The sand and water area is close to water.
  - The woodworking area is outdoors or near the art area.
  - The music and movement area is located close to other noisier areas.
  - The computer area avoids screen glare.
  - The outdoor area is close to indoor areas.
- The areas are flexible enough to accommodate practical considerations and children's changing interests.

Providing materials[12]

- The storage and labeling of materials promotes the find-use-return cycle.
- Similar things are stored together.
- Children can see into and handle containers.
- Labels make sense to children. They are made from
  - The materials themselves
  - Photographs, photocopies
  - Pictures
  - Line drawings, tracings
  - Written words in addition to any of the above
- Materials are plentiful and open-ended to support a wide range of play, and reflect children's family lives.

In the *block area*
  - Building materials
  - Take-apart-and-put-together materials
  - Fill-and-empty materials
  - Pretend-play materials
  - Reference photos

In the *house area*
  - Cooking and eating equipment
  - Pretending and role-play materials
  - Homelike materials reflecting children's family lives
  - Real cooking equipment (for use with adult supervision)
  - Reference photos and recipes

In the *art area*
  - Paper
  - Painting and printing materials
  - Fasteners
  - Modeling and molding materials
  - Collage materials
  - Drawing and cutting materials

In the *book and writing area*
  - Books
  - Magazines and catalogs
  - Storytelling props
  - Writing materials

In the *toy area*
  - Sorting and small building materials
  - Take-apart-and-put-together materials
  - Pretend-play materials
  - Games

In the *sand and water area*
- Fill-and-empty materials
- Floating materials
- Pretend-play materials
- Alternatives to sand and water
- Waterproof gear and cleanup materials

In the *woodworking area*
- Tools
- Fasteners
- Wood and building materials

In the *music and movement area*
- Percussion instruments
- Simple wind instruments
- Recording and music playing equipment
- Dance props

In the *computer area*
- Up-to-date multimedia computer
- Software appropriate for young children
- Printer

In the *outdoor area*
- Stationary structures
- Wheeled toys
- Loose materials

---

[12] Program staff should adhere to their state's licensing regulations when adding materials to the classroom.

changes in surface materials (pea gravel under climbers, hard surfaces for wheeled toys) or actual physical boundaries (low shrubs around the swings, railroad ties around the sand).

Materials. Outdoors, children enjoy stationary structures for climbing, swinging, and sliding; wheeled toys for pushing and pulling; and loose manipulative materials for exploring, pretending, and building. (See "Outdoor Area Materials" on pp. 218–219.) For the most up-to-date safety guidelines, consult the resources cited in "Safety in the Outdoor Play Space" on page 216.

Accessible storage. Wheeled toys need a safe, protected overnight storage space, preferably in an outdoor shed accessible to children (once it is unlocked). You can store loose materials in easy-to-carry tubs or buckets with handles. This enables children to readily locate and return these materials to their overnight storage space.

The relationship of arranging and equipping space to the rest of the curriculum

The way adults arrange and equip space for children is guided by the ingredients of active participatory learning and influences the way children and adults learn and teach. Because materials are plentiful and accessible, children can follow their own interests and intentions. A variety of well-organized, well-equipped interest areas lay the groundwork for the plan-work-recall segment of the daily routine (HighScope's plan-do-review process), and the other parts of the daily routine, which are discussed in the next three chapters. The interest areas are also equipped with materials that support the HighScope KDIs, discussed in the KDI books that accompany this manual (Epstein, 2012a–h), while the KDIs, in turn, inspire the addition of new equipment and materials.

CHAPTER 7

The HighScope Daily Routine: A Framework for Active Learning

Understanding the Daily Routine

"What happens now?"
"What do we do next?"
"When will we have time to...?"

The HighScope **daily routine** helps children answer these types of questions by providing them with a consistent schedule of events they can depend on and understand. It also helps adults organize their time with children to provide active, challenging learning experiences. In this sense, the parts of the daily routine are like stepping stones on a path. Along this path, children engage in a variety of adventures and experiences that interest them and suit their playful, inventive natures. A consistent daily routine allows enough time for children to pursue their interests, make choices and decisions, and solve the "child-sized" problems that arise.

Like all routines for children, the HighScope daily routine consists of specific time segments allotted to certain activities — times for children to plan and carry out their ideas, participate in group activities, play outside, and eat and rest. Yet, in the HighScope Curriculum, a consistent routine is much more than a set of labels for these daily activities. Each part of the day serves an important developmental purpose. *The daily routine provides a common framework of support for children as they pursue their interests and engage in various problem-solving activities.* Next, we describe some of the ways the HighScope daily routine supports children.

The daily routine supports child initiative

Just as the interest areas (as described in chapter 6) provide a structure *for the physical space* children use in HighScope settings, the daily routine provides a structure *for the events of the day* — a structure that loosely defines how children use the areas and what types of interactions children have with peers and adults during particular times.

> "The developmental potential of a day care or preschool setting depends on the extent to which supervising adults create and maintain opportunities for the involvement of children in a variety of progressively more complex (ongoing) activities and interpersonal structures that are commensurate with the child's evolving capacities and allow [the child] sufficient balance of power to introduce innovations."
>
> — Bronfenbrenner (1979)

The elements of the daily routine provide a common framework of support for children as they pursue their interests and solve problems throughout the day.

The daily routine supports a framework of relationships in which children and adults share control.

Though the routine breaks the day into recognizable blocks of time assigned to particular kinds of activities, it does not dictate the details of what children will do during each activity period. Instead, the routine is designed to support *child initiative*. As such, it provides time for children to express their goals and intentions; to follow through on these initiatives by considering their options, by interacting with people and materials, and by solving problems that arise; and to persist in these efforts until they are satisfied with the results.

In contrast to routines organized around an adult agenda of activities, the HighScope routine is organized to allow children to build on their own plans, interests, and strengths. This focus on children's initiatives frees adults from constantly supervising children to keep them "on track." Released from the necessity of managing and doing things for children, adults become fully engaged in supporting and encouraging children to do and say things for themselves.

The daily routine provides a social framework

As well as providing a structure for supporting daily events and activities, the HighScope daily routine provides a **social framework** that creates a community and sets the stage for the social relationships that develop. Social interactions, in turn, influence the ways learning experiences unfold. A HighScope routine encourages the formation of a **supportive community** in which relationships between adults and children are governed

This mother helps ease children's transition to school by reading with them at arrival time.

by the principle of **shared control.** This consistent commitment to shared control throughout the HighScope daily routine distinguishes it from routines in which adults are always in control and routines in which adults control some events and children control others. The HighScope daily routine both shapes and is shaped by all the persons participating in it. Such a daily routine relies on adults' careful team planning as well as their ability to respond quickly and appropriately to children's spontaneous interests and ideas.

The consistent social framework created by the HighScope daily routine provides children with a **psychologically safe and purposeful environment.** The parts of the routine — making a plan, playing outside, gathering for a snack or movement activity — break up the day into manageable blocks of time and provide children with a stable structure. Knowing what to expect during each part of the day helps children develop a sense of security and control. The daily routine also maintains a balance between limits and freedom for children. Children feel safe because of the daily routine's predictable structure and clear, appropriate limits within which they are free to work out their own ways of doing things. In an observational evaluation of a classroom that had been implementing HighScope for a year, educators Elizabeth Moore and Teresa Smith (1987) noted the impact of a consistent routine: "The general picture with HighScope is a sense of order and purpose — children taking a far more active part in their own learning, making their own decisions, and spending less time waiting to be told what to do, flitting, wandering aimlessly, or being disruptive" (p. 5). The HighScope daily routine thus provides children with the security of **predictable sequences of events, smooth transitions** from one activity period to the next, and **consistency in adult expectations and support** throughout the day.

The consistency of the routine is particularly important in early childhood settings because young children face, often for the first time, temporary separation from their parents or primary caregivers. This is a big step for children, and one that the HighScope daily routine is designed to assist with its predictable sequences, clear expectations and limits, and emphasis on adult support for children's initiatives. While they have little control over their parents' comings and goings, children have considerable control over what they themselves do in HighScope settings while their parents are away.

The daily routine eases children's transition from the home to the early childhood setting by building a *sense of community*. The *collective expectations and procedures* embedded in the daily routine create a *social network — we all make plans, we all have work time, we all talk about what we did*. In particular, for children whose families may be changing and re-forming, the orderly, communal aspect of the daily routine may serve as an important emotional anchor.

The daily routine provides a flexible structure

In the HighScope Curriculum, the daily routine provides an alternative to rigid structure on one hand and to randomness on the other. It is neither an unchanging sequence of events about which adults make all the decisions nor a series of randomly evolving daily activities. The daily routine segments do occur in a predictable sequence and adults make general plans for each part of the day. Nevertheless, the routine is flexible in that adults understand they can never predict with exactness what children will do or say, or how the decisions children make will shape each experience. Indeed, for children, the daily routine provides many opportunities for following and expanding their own interests. Consequently, the daily routine has the potential for teaching adults something new about each child every day.

> ### John Dewey on Community Life
>
> "Most children are naturally 'sociable.' Isolation is even more irksome to them than to adults. A genuine community life has its ground in this natural sociability. But community life does not organize itself in an enduring way purely spontaneously. It requires thought and planning ahead. The educator is responsible for a knowledge of individuals and for a knowledge of subject-matter that will enable activities to be selected which lend themselves to social organization, an organization in which all individuals have an opportunity to contribute something, and in which the activities in which all participate are the chief carrier of control."
>
> — Dewey (1938/1963, p. 56)

The daily routine supports curriculum values

As a series of experiences that are predictable in sequence but varied in content and shaped by suggestions from children, the HighScope daily routine framework enables adults to put into practice HighScope's curriculum values and educational philosophy. Our belief that children learn best by following their own interests and by constructing knowledge through personal experiences and our commitment to the ingredients of active learning (materials, manipulation, choice, child language and thought, adult scaffolding) shape the process of each daily routine segment.

In summary, the daily routine provides a stable framework within which children — assured of adults' full attention and supported by a secure social network — can safely initiate, reflect on, modify, repeat, and extend active learning experiences. While the HighScope interest areas

> **The HighScope Daily Routine: A Summary**
>
> The HighScope daily routine is an operational framework that defines and supports daily events in the early childhood setting. It provides a supportive educational and social framework that is an appropriate alternative to either rigid structure or random activity. It is a regular sequence of events that loosely defines the use of space and how adults and children interact during the time they are together. Content and process are of equal importance and reflect an educational philosophy that values active learning, shared control by children and adults, and adult support of child-constructed knowledge.

provide the *physical setting* for active learning, the HighScope daily routine provides the *operational framework* for setting active learning in motion.

General Guidelines for Organizing a Daily Routine

By using the following guidelines, you and your team can establish and maintain a daily routine that works well in your setting:

- A variety of active learning periods provide children with a range of experiences and interactions. These active learning periods include the plan-do-review sequence, small-group time, large-group time, outside time, transition times, and, if necessary, eating and resting times.
- Active learning periods occur in a reasonable, predictable sequence that meets the particular needs of the setting.
- Experiences take place in an appropriate physical setting.
- Each period involves children in active learning experiences within a supportive climate.
- The daily routine provides a range of learning experiences.
- The daily routine flows smoothly from one interesting experience to the next.

A variety of active learning periods provides children with a range of experiences and interactions

In a HighScope setting, teaching teams construct the daily routine from the following time segments:

Plan-work-recall

This three-part sequence is generally the longest and most intense time block of the day. While it can occur at any point during the daily routine, the three parts always occur in the same sequence. The plan-work-recall cycle (plan-do-review) is designed to build on and strengthen children's natural interests, capacity for initiative, and problem-solving skills.

Planning. Children gather in a small group with an adult for about 10 to 15 minutes, or until each child has planned and is ready to begin work time. (Children do not have to wait until everyone has planned; they can move to work time as soon as their own plans are complete.) Each child decides what to do and shares these ideas with the adult who watches and listens, asks for clarification or elaboration, and often records the child's plan in some way (for example, writing it down or putting an object in a container labeled with the interest area the child plans to play in). Planning by children encourages them to connect their interests with purposeful actions.

Working. Children immediately begin what they have chosen to do with the appropriate materials and people, and continue until they have completed their plans or changed them. Work time encourages children to focus attentively on both play and problem solving. As children work, adults pay close attention and move easily among the children — observing, supporting, and assisting them as needed. After about 45 to 55 minutes, children clean up by storing their unfinished projects

Sample Daily Routines

Children Arrive & Depart at the Same Time	Half Day	Full Day
	Greeting time, message board	Greeting time, breakfast, message board
	Planning, work, cleanup, recall	Large-group time
	Snack	Planning, work, cleanup, recall
	Large-group time	Small-group time
	Small-group time	Outside
	Outside time and departure	Lunch
		Books and rest
		Snack
		Outside time and departure
Staggered Arrivals & Departures	**Half Day**	**Full Day**
	Small-group time for early arrivers	Breakfast/free play/outside time at arrival
	Greeting time, message board	Greeting time, message board
	Planning, work, cleanup, recall	Planning, work, cleanup, recall
	Snack	Outside time and snack
	Outside time	Small-group time
	Large-group time	Large-group time
	Small-group time for late departers	Lunch
		Singing, rest
		Outside time and snack
		Planning, work, cleanup, recall with parents
Variations for	**Half Day**	**Full Day**
	Small-group time for early arrivers	Breakfast/free play/outside time at arrival
	Greeting time, message board	Greeting time, message board
	Ballet/outside time	Planning, work, cleanup, recall
	Snack and planning	Outside time and snack
	Planning, work, cleanup, recall	Visiting artists
	Large-group time	Large-group time
	Small-group time for late departers	Lunch
		Singing and rest
		Outside time and snack
		Planning, work, cleanup, recall with parents

Planning Time

Work Time

Recall Time

The plan-work-recall sequence (plan-do-review) builds on children's interests, capacity for initiative, and problem-solving skills.

These children plan what they will do at work time.

and putting away materials. **Cleanup** is thus part of the cycle. It can occur during work time — children may individually choose to put things away when they are finished using them — and/or as part of the classroom's transition between work time and recall time.

Recalling. Children meet with the same person and small group of children with whom they planned in order to share and discuss what they have done during work time. Recall lasts about 10 to 15 minutes, depending on how much detail children share (this increases with development). Adults listen carefully and converse with children about their work-time experiences. Other children may also ask questions or make comments. Recalling helps children reflect on, understand, and build on their actions.

This child puts his materials away at the end of work time.

This child recalls with her teacher what she did at the sand and water table.

During small-group time, adults encourage children to make choices about what they are doing and describe their activities in their own way.

Small-group time

This 15- to 20-minute time period is when children experiment with materials and solve problems in an activity adults have chosen for a particular purpose. Small groups of 5 to 10 children and one adult (the same groups that plan, recall, and eat together) meet to experiment with materials, pursue an expressed interest, or use materials to solve a problem. They gather in a regular location — on the floor, outdoors, or around a table — but may then move as a group depending on the planned activity. Although the adult introduces a common activity and associated set of materials, each child is free to work with the materials in whatever way he or she wishes. Adults encourage children to make choices and decisions about how to use the materials and describe in their own words what they are doing. In this small-group setting, children use materials and encounter problems they

"Let's dance!" At this large-group time, children try out their ideas for moving to music. Parents join in.

might not experience on their own, while adults have the opportunity to observe, join, and support children and learn new things daily about each child.

Large-group time

Large-group time, typically lasting 10 to 15 minutes, builds a sense of community for children. Children and adults come together for singing, movement and music activities, storytelling, and reenactments of familiar stories and meaningful events. While adults initiate many large-group experiences and maintain a fairly rapid sequence of events, children initiate countless variations as well as offer new ideas. "Now it's Susanna's turn to be the leader," "Let's try Tommy's idea," "Look what I can do," "Do my idea" are typical comments at large-group time. Participating in large-group time gives children and adults a chance to work together, enjoy one another, and build a repertoire of common experiences.

Outside time

This time of day is designed for vigorous, noisy, physical play. Children and adults spend at least 30 to 40 minutes outside once or twice a day. Without the restraint of four walls, many children feel freer to talk, move, and explore. Adults join in children's play, converse with them, and assist with pushes and pulls as needed. Outside time

At outside time, children have the opportunity for vigorous, noisy, physical play.

Children make the transition from home to school by looking at messages about the day on the message board at greeting time.

enables children to play together, invent their own games and rules, and become familiar with their natural surroundings. It also enables adults to observe and interact with children in what for many children is a very comfortable and stimulus-rich setting.

Transition times

Transitions are times when children move from one time period or experience to the next. Transitions occur as children move from home to the early childhood setting and back, and as they move through the segments of the routine in the classroom or center. Transitions are important because they create an atmosphere for the subsequent experience. Therefore, our goal is to make these potentially disruptive changes as peaceful and interesting as possible for children. For example, the day may begin with a greeting time that children join as they arrive. As they enter the group, they may share information from home, read a book with a parent or friend, or show a family member a special toy or picture. Message board lets them know about new materials, visitors, or special events that may be happening that day. Likewise, departure is a transition from the program day back to the world of home and family — or, for some children, to a second program setting for the remainder of the day. How children begin, move through, and end each day affects them, their peers, and the adults in their lives. Ongoing adult support and planning for transitions can increase the quality of these experiences.

Eating and resting

Meals and snacks are times for children and adults to enjoy healthy food in a supportive social setting. Resting is a time for sleeping, or quiet, solitary, on-your-own-cot play. These home-life activities, transported of necessity to the early childhood setting, are ones around which children and their families have built particular habits, customs, and preferences. While we recognize and respect family customs, our goal at these times is

Meals and snacks are times for children and adults to enjoy healthy food in a supportive social setting.

to ensure that children continue to experience, as much as possible, an active learning approach and sense of belonging in the classroom.

Quite simply, plan-work-recall time (plan-do-review), small-group time, large-group time, outside time, transition times, and eating or resting periods, are the building blocks of the HighScope daily routine. These time segments designate a *process* or *place* rather than specific *content* — "large-group time" rather than "story time" or "music time," for example, and "small-group time" rather than "table-toys time" — because the

Building Blocks of the Daily Routine

The time segments of the HighScope daily routine designate a *process* or *place* rather than specific *content*, because the content is set by both children and adults. For example, here is how Mrs. Ballou, Mr. Andrews, and their children included movement experiences throughout their daily routine one day in the fall.

Greeting time — Max shows Mrs. Ballou how he climbed up the ladder into his new bunk bed. Mrs. Ballou and the other children imitate his actions — stretching, reaching, lifting their legs and pretending to climb.

Message board — Looking at Mrs. Ballou's drawing, the children guess there is a new tricycle in the outdoor storage shed. "I know how to steer," says Gina, demonstrating with her arms.

Planning — Mr. Andrews and the group of children he plans with form a train and travel from area to area to have a look at all the choices before making their plans.

Working — The children in the house area have "sold" their "house." They fill a big carton so full of household goods that it takes all of them together to push it to their "new house."

Recalling — Mr. Andrews pats his knees to a steady beat and starts a recall chant: "I worked with the blocks today. This is what I have to say. I built them tall and that is all. Now it's Peter's turn to tell, what he did and did so well…."

Small-group time — Mrs. Ballou and the children in her small group use blocks to set up an obstacle course for the toy tumbling gnomes. She listens to children tell the gnomes where they should go and what they should do along the course: "Go up, up, up this side and then down to the bottom, right over here," Sophia tells her gnome.

Transition — After they put away their small-group time materials, the children "tumble" like gnomes to the next activity.

Large-group time — Each child and adult has a capped plastic milk jug partly filled with water, which they swing, push, and carry in many different ways. Everyone seems to have a new idea to demonstrate.

Eating — Children exercise their fine-motor skills at snacktime as they pour their own juice, spoon out fruit salad, and pass the pitcher and the salad bowl to one another.

Resting — As children settle down on their cots, Mr. Andrews has them close their eyes and then quietly asks them to move their arms or legs like a gentle wind…like rain softly falling…like a bird flying home to its nest…like a little bear curling up for a long winter's nap.

> ### When Can I Do…?
>
> Over the years, people have asked "If we follow a High-Scope daily routine, when can we do the XYZ program we're already committed to?" Special projects and experiences you want to provide for all the children generally fit well into small- or large-group times because these are times children are used to having the initial ideas come from adults. Even more important than how you fit these programs into the day, however, is how you *adjust them to include the ingredients of active learning.* **The challenge is to turn adult-initiated activities into experiences through which children can construct their own understanding of dance, art, mathematics, science, or whatever the subject of the special program is.**
>
> One center, for example, wrote a grant with the city ballet company and was funded to employ a ballet teacher for one hour each week. As it worked out, the ballet teacher came to the center from 9:00 to 10:00 on Wednesday mornings. Since this was generally the worktime segment of the daily routine, the first thing the staff did was adjust the Wednesday schedule by eliminating small- and large-group times and having plan-work-recall (plan-do-review) follow the ballet period.
>
> After the first two sessions, they realized that an hour was too long for the entire group of preschoolers to work together at the same thing, so they divided the group of children in half. From 9:00 to 9:30, the first group of children had ballet while the second group had outside time. At 9:30 the two groups switched. The early childhood staff also worked closely with the ballet teacher to reduce waiting time, change from French names for the movement patterns to names that made sense to the children, and give children time to try particular movement patterns and variations on their own. Through this give-and-take process, the ballet teacher began to focus on her young dancers' developmental levels and to adjust her expectations and teaching style accordingly. At the same time, the early childhood staff began to see opportunities throughout the week when they and the children could incorporate ballet movements into other parts of the daily routine.

content for each time period is set by children and adults. Consequently, children and adults read stories and become involved with art, music, movement, woodworking, computers, play acting, and building throughout the day in a variety of social and physical contexts. Rather than confining movement, for example, to a specific time of day, such as "exercise time," children and adults can build movement experiences into each part of the daily routine.

This is not to say that special activities — for example, an opportunity for a parent to visit and share an interest, or a local artist to host the class in his or her studio — cannot be incorporated into the daily routine. Rather, the daily routine provides a structure to include these adult-planned experiences in ways that allow children to take the initiative, use materials, interact with adults and peers, and construct knowledge in their own way.

Active learning periods occur in a reasonable, predictable sequence that meets the particular needs of the setting

The order of the daily routine — the sequence of the time segments — varies from setting to setting and team to team, depending on the length of the program day, children's arrival and departure patterns, program location, and climate. This section discusses how each of these factors may affect the team's decisions about the daily routine.

Program length

A major scheduling difference between half-day and full-day programs is the amount of time children spend eating and resting. Half-day programs generally include a snack and/or one meal and no time for rest, while full-day programs generally include 1–2 meals, 1–2 snacks, and an hour or so

An activity at arrival time, such as writing one's name on the sign-in sheet, helps children transition from home to school.

At departure time, teachers and parents share what children did during the day.

> **Beginning the Day With Support**
>
> "Though it is an inevitable part of becoming independent, the experience of separating from a parent can be very challenging....Here are some suggestions that will help.
>
> **"Reassuring greetings.** Plan for one teacher or caregiver to be at the door to greet children and their parents, and the other to be with the rest of the children. Greetings may seem like an obvious ritual, but being fully greeted in a conscious, sincere way sets a positive tone for each child's day....
>
> **"A predictable routine.** Each child's greeting should be followed by a predictable routine, which is calming for children because they know exactly what they will do next. For example, right after being greeted, children know they will hang up their coats and go to the breakfast table, where another teacher is offering cereal and milk and talking with children about their plans. Or, the routine may be to go to the book area where the other teacher is reading stories and exploring books with children, while the first teacher continues to greet children (and parents) as they come in. Parents who want to stay to read for a few minutes with children are welcome."
>
> — Evans (2005, pp. 50–51)

of rest. Full-day programs also permit more scheduling flexibility. A full-day program, for example, may include a longer plan-work-recall period in the morning and delay small-group time until after rest time. Or, a full-day program might include a plan-work-recall period in the morning and another one in the late afternoon. How much time you spend with children each day influences how much time you can allot for each type of experience.

Children's arrival and departure patterns

Many programs, especially half-day programs, have specific arrival and departure times so that most children arrive and leave at approximately the same time. This means that the children's day can officially begin and end at the same time for everyone and that all children can participate in each time period. In other programs, children's arrivals and departures are staggered over a one- to two-hour period so that the mid-part of the day is the only part that is common to every child. There are also programs for children whose parents are themselves in school or job-training programs. Many of these children participate in the early childhood setting only during the times their parents are attending classes or apprenticeships, so some may be there for plan-work-recall

Children's arrival and departure patterns can influence the structure of the daily routine.

while others are present only for small-group and outside time. They may not even be there every day. Children's arrivals and departures will therefore influence your plans for scheduling the beginning and end of the day, and how you help children transition into and out of the program setting.

Program location

For programs located in buildings serving a large number of children or adults, the arrangement of the daily routine may be influenced by the availability and location of the playground or gym, kitchen and cafeteria, or traffic patterns (for example, buses dropping off older children). If the outdoor play space is a public park, it may be important to plan to use it when traffic is light and older children are likely to be in school. Home settings often involve planning the daily routine around the work or school schedules of other members of the household.

Climate

In many climates, weather influences scheduling. In a half-day program, for example, it may make sense to begin or end the session with outside time during the winter to minimize the number of times the children have to deal with snowsuits and boots. In very warm climates, outside time may be scheduled during the cooler parts of the day, such as morning.

It is clear from this discussion that the daily routine *sequence* will vary from program to program. *Nevertheless, whatever order of events you and your team devise based on your particular situation, once a routine is established that works for your setting, it is important to maintain it.* A stable, predictable daily routine sequence gives children the sense that they have some control over what is going to happen next. They know, for example, that after recall time they will go outside, and that after large-group time they will go home. This consistency not only helps children feel secure but also assures children who are making a transition from one part of the routine to another that there will be time again tomorrow to play in the sand, hear a story, or swing. The cyclical nature of the daily routine allows children the opportunity to say "I can do the things I like again tomorrow."

Another advantage of a consistent daily routine is that children and adults can join the program at any point in the day, or year, and quickly make sense of how the day works. In this way, the daily routine is like a script for a play, with a certain number of acts each day. The standard "script" is repeated daily, enabling newcomers to quickly learn the order and requirements for each act or time block and to play their unique roles. Children whose first language is different from the setting's predominant language find the consistency of a daily routine an invaluable aid in understanding the program and what is expected of them.

Experiences take place in an appropriate physical setting

The room arrangement strategies presented in chapter 6 will help you establish appropriate settings for each segment of the daily routine. The plan-work-recall (plan-do-review) time block, for example, calls for interest areas that are well-stocked with organized and labeled materials that children can choose, use, and return on their own. Small-group-time works best when conducted in a cozy meeting place — with enough materials for each child and the adult. Large-group-time works best when conducted in a space that is large enough for the whole group to meet together and be active. Outside time requires a safe outdoor area equipped appropriately for vigorous play.

Each period involves children in active learning experiences within a supportive climate

A HighScope daily routine is distinguished by each time period's focus on the five ingredients of active learning — materials, manipulation, choice, child language and thought, and adult scaffolding. While the setting changes from indoors to outdoors, from large-group to small-group to individual play — and while the experiences change from quiet to noisy, from music to art, from exploration to pretend play — the interactions between children and adults, children and children, and children and materials all involve the ingredients of active learning. Throughout the day, children make choices and decisions about materials and actions, and they talk, in their own words, about what they are doing and experiencing. Adults attend and listen to, support, encourage, and gently challenge children as they move from one experience to the next.

This consistent approach to interacting with children throughout the daily routine distinguishes HighScope programs from programs in which the adult's role is not as clearly defined. In these programs, the adult's role shifts from monitoring, to teaching, to preparing for the next segment,

This child reads with an adult in a quiet area of the classroom.

to restoring order, to relaxing, to teaching again. As adults shift their roles, children's interactions reflect this inconsistency, as they shift from playing on their own and with peers to following (or not following) adult directions. The ingredients of active learning instead enable children and adults to act as *partners* throughout the day. Each daily routine segment provides adults with ongoing opportunities to engage children's natural interests and promote children's initiatives.

It is important to note that the *emotional climate* for each period is just as important in sustaining active learning as are the ingredients of active learning. Throughout the day, adults strive to maintain an atmosphere of trust in which children feel secure enough to try new things, speak their minds, identify problems, and attempt solutions. Adults set clear limits within which children are free to engage in purposeful, spontaneous, and inventive play. Rather than alternate between taking control of children's activities or turning away from them, adults *share control* with children during each time period so that children can assume increasing control of themselves and their learning within appropriate bounds of adult attention and support.

Attending to group dynamics is another important aspect of maintaining a supportive climate during each time period. For example, adult teams may put children who often play together in the same planning and recall group so that playmates can collaborate on developing and reviewing their plans. And, adults may put all the quieter children in one small group, as one team did, so that these children have an opportunity to speak up without being interrupted by their more assertive peers.

The daily routine provides a range of learning experiences

Assuring balance in the daily routine means assuring that children engage in a wide variety of learning experiences. Here are some examples of the kinds of experiences the daily routine should promote:

- Children interact with peers and adults in spontaneous groupings (at work time, outside time), in small groups (planning, recall, small-group time, snacktime), and in large groups (large-group time, cleanup time).

- Children play vigorously and quietly both indoors and outdoors.

- Children engage in activities that continue over time as well as those that end within the day.

- Children engage both in repetitive play and play that presents new challenges.

- Children are actively involved with sensory exploration, imitation and pretend play, stories, art, music, movement.

Maintaining this kind of balance in the daily routine also means balancing control between children and adults throughout the day. The overall concept to keep in mind, however, is that rather than taking control of certain parts of the daily routine and relinquishing control during others, adults in a HighScope setting strive to share control with children *throughout the day*.

In practical terms, this means that children initiate some experiences: "I'm going to the wood area and make a racer with fat wheels." Adults initiate some experiences: "Here are some shells and sand. What do you think you could do with them?" And children and adults jointly initiate some experiences:

Adult: Today I'm going to read the story about the three pigs.

Anton: Don't use the book. Tell it like you did that other time.

Valencia: Yeah, and we all be the pigs and the wolf.

Eddie: And we blow like this...

Whoever initiates the activity, both children and adults have the opportunity for the respectful addition of ideas and variations.

In a balanced daily routine, adults and children share control in activities during the day.

The daily routine flows smoothly from one interesting experience to the next

Moving smoothly from one part of the day to the next is also important so that children are neither hurried nor bored with waiting and pointless repetition. The general idea behind assuring smooth transitions is to recognize that when a daily routine on paper comes to life in an early childhood setting, different children will finish whatever they are doing at different times. Smooth transitions help to maintain flow and momentum, while respecting each child's individual pace and work style. When children recognize the consistency of the daily routine, they can anticipate upcoming events and move toward them. Therefore, it is generally important to start the next part of the routine while some children are still involved in the last, secure in the knowledge that they will join in as they are ready.

The daily routine thus provides a structure that is consistent with curriculum values and that supports children's initiative and development within the community of the classroom. In scheduling the daily routine, the teaching team plans a consistent sequence of events that provides a range of active learning experiences within a supportive and engaging setting. To help you make the most of the components of the HighScope daily routine, two chapters of this book focus specifically on the plan-do-review process (chapter 8) and group times in the other parts of the routine (chapter 9).

Daily Routine Basics: A Summary

The daily routine supports child initiative.
- Provides time for children to express and follow through on their goals and intentions
- Enables adults to become fully engaged in supporting and encouraging children to do and say things for themselves

The daily routine provides a social framework.
- Provides children with a psychologically safe and purposeful environment
- Eases children's transition between home and the early childhood setting by building a sense of community

The daily routine provides a flexible structure.
- Provides an alternative to rigid structure and randomness
- Has the potential for teaching adults something new about each child every day

The daily routine supports curriculum values.
- Enables children to construct knowledge
- Includes the ingredients of active learning in each segment

---

General Guidelines for Organizing a Daily Routine: A Summary

- A variety of active learning periods provides children with a range of experiences and interactions. These periods include plan-work-recall (plan-do-review), small- and large-group times, and outside time.
- Active learning periods occur in a reasonable, predictable sequence that meets the particular needs of the setting.
- Experiences take place in an appropriate physical setting.
- Each period involves children in active learning experiences within a supportive climate.
- The daily routine balances a range of learning experiences.
- The daily routine flows smoothly from one interesting experience to the next.

CHAPTER 8

The HighScope Plan-Do-Review Process

The **plan-do-review process** is the centerpiece of the HighScope active learning approach. It encompasses all the elements of active learning: materials, manipulation, choice, child language and thought, and adult scaffolding. Moreover, plan-do-review, also known as the plan-work-recall sequence, is the central element of the HighScope daily routine and is the longest segment of the day — lasting approximately one and one-half hours. Research confirms that opportunities to plan and recall, together with access to diverse materials during work time, are positively and significantly associated with early learning (Epstein, 1993). Children attending HighScope programs, with daily opportunities to express their intentions and reflect on their activities, score higher on observational measures of development than comparison children whose programs do not provide these opportunities.

In making daily plans, following through on them, and then recalling what they have done, young children learn to articulate their intentions and reflect on their actions. They also begin to realize they are competent thinkers, decision makers, and problem solvers. They will carry their self-confidence and independence into subsequent school settings and continue to benefit from these characteristics throughout their lives. *We cannot emphasize enough the importance of the plan-do-review process in the successful implementation of the HighScope Preschool Curriculum's active learning approach.*

This chapter highlights the three key elements of the sequence — **planning time** (plan), **work time** (do), and **recall time** (review) — and offers specific strategies adults can use to assist children in making the most of these important times in the daily routine. In addition, many scenarios are presented throughout this chapter to illustrate the dynamics of the plan-do-review process. These scenarios are based on actual events that have occurred in the HighScope Demonstration Preschool and in other early childhood settings that have adopted the HighScope approach.

> "One key feature of self-regulation is the ability to plan: Children who are able to plan, and carry out a plan, are more likely to develop advanced cognitive skills."
> — Hyson (2008, p. 24)

Understanding Planning Time

In a HighScope setting, children plan every day, both at the designated time for planning and throughout the day as they think about what they want to do. Thus, it is important that adults understand all aspects of the planning process: the role planning plays in an active learning setting, where planning occurs, what children do as they plan, and how best to support children at this time. The following plans, made by three- and four-year-olds in HighScope programs, illustrate ways young children typically express their intentions:

Point to the house area.

Bring a block from the block area to the planning table.

"Me and Justin are building a road so our racing cars can go really fast!"

"Make a mask. On the computer."

"Dance in the big skirts for Cinco de Mayo."

"Make a cream factory with sticks and glue like Chris did. It will be real big for lots of cream. I'll show you how."

What is planning?

Planning is a thought process in which internal goals shape anticipated actions. When young children plan, they start with a personal intention, aim, or purpose. Depending on their age and capacity to communicate, they express their intentions in actions (getting a block), gestures (pointing to blocks), or words ("I'm going to play with blocks"). Because they participate in the planning process each day, children grow accustomed to indicating their intentions before acting on them. This helps children become conscious of their capacity to shape and control their own actions.

The roots of planning

The HighScope practice of encouraging young children to make and carry out plans is based on the theories and observations of researchers (Berry & Sylva, 1987; Bullock & Lütkenhaus, 1988; Case, 1985), child development and educational theorists (Dewey, 1933, 1938/1963; Erikson, 1950; Piaget, 1951/1962; Piaget & Inhelder, 1966/1969; Smilansky, 1971; Smilansky & Shefatya, 1990) and our own experience in preschool education (Epstein, 2003) over the past 50 years. Recent theory and research on the role of planning in children's *self-regulation* (Bodrova & Leong, 2007) and *executive functioning* (Rothbart, Sheese, & Posner, 2007; Zelazo, Muller, Frye, & Marcovitch, 2003) also support the importance of this ability in early development. HighScope was the first comprehensive curriculum model to include planning by children as a major component.

Today, planning is recognized as an important activity in the Head Start Performance Standards (US Department of Health and Human Services, 2002) and best practices advocated by the National Association for the Education of Young Children (2005), as well as state early childhood learning standards (Gronlund, 2006). The child's capacity to plan emerges during what Erikson (1950) calls the stage of "initiative versus guilt" about self-initiated actions (p. 255). This means that preschoolers have many ideas they want to try out. When they are able to follow through on their intentions successfully, they develop a sense of initiative and enterprise. When their attempts to follow their interests are regularly thwarted, however, young children may feel guilty about taking the initiative, and their energy and enthusiasm for doing so wanes.

The ability to plan develops along with the young child's growing capacity to use language and form mental pictures of actions, people, and materials that are not actually present. Preschoolers are able to imagine and talk about something they want to do but have not yet begun. So planning in the HighScope daily routine builds on what developmental psychologist Robbie Case (1985) describes as the child's *executive control structures:* "By definition, an executive control structure is an internal mental blueprint that represents [the child's] habitual way of constraining a particular problem situation, together with his or her habitual procedure for dealing with it" (p. 68).

Plan-Do-Review: A Summary

Planning time (plan)
- Each child states, in gestures or words, a plan of action.

Work time (do)
- Children carry out their initial plans and other self-initiated activities, working and playing alone or with others.
- Adults interact with children to scaffold (support and gently extend) their activities.
- At the end of work time, children put away materials.

Recall time (review)
- Children reflect on, share, and discuss their work-time experiences.

The plan-do-review sequence enables children to act with purpose and to re-create their most memorable experiences.

For this child, one day's sequence involves making a plan by "driving" the airplane to the art area on the classroom map made from blocks, drawing and coloring a picture and discussing it with a classmate, and recalling the highlights of her picture-making with the aid of classroom area signs.

Current research supports the importance of *executive functioning* in the young child's ability to successfully complete tasks and solve problems (Rothbart et al., 2007; Zelazo et al., 2003). The ability to plan, that is, to anticipate what needs to be done and how to do it, helps young children remain engaged in the goals they set for themselves. Likewise, planning helps children with emotional self-regulation, which researchers Elena Bodrova and Deborah Leong (2007) describe as children's "ability to act in a deliberate planned manner in governing much of their own behavior" (p. 127).

Strikingly, the ability to plan appears to have lifelong implications. The Longevity Project — an 80-year study that followed the lives of 1,500 boys and girls — found that being planful in childhood and adulthood was associated with living longer and enjoying better physical and psychological health (Friedman & Martin, 2011). In fact, a measure of being prudent, persistent, and planful was the strongest individual difference or personality predictor of longevity.

Psychologist Sara Smilansky and educational theorist John Dewey have also commented on the important roles planning and reflecting on actions play in learning and development. Dewey (1938/1963) articulates the view that education revolves around *goal-directed activity* and the *child's participation* "in the formation of the purposes which direct his or her activities in the learning process" (p. 67). In 1964, Smilansky, a close observer and longtime proponent of the value of children's play and a consultant to the HighScope Perry Preschool Project, urged HighScope curriculum developers to incorporate a *recall process* into the planning and work time sequence to strengthen children's ability to reflect on their plans and actions.

The process of planning

When children make plans, they undertake a variety of mental tasks. Next we describe some of these tasks, or components, of the planning process.

> "A child whose self-directed learning is encouraged will develop a sense of initiative that will far outweigh a sense of guilt about getting things started. On the other hand, a child whose self-directed learning is interfered with, who is forced to follow adult learning priorities, may acquire a strong sense of guilt at the expense of a sense of initiative."
>
> — Elkind (1987, p. 111)

Establishing a problem or goal. Children decide what they are going to do based on their own interests:

- "I'm going to make a boat…."
- "I wonder what's in that box…."
- "I want to find my mom…."

For Case (1985), "the overriding image of the young child [is of one who] is endowed with certain natural desires, encounters certain natural barriers to their realization, but who also has the capability for overcoming these barriers" (p. 59), a capability HighScope early childhood educators support and encourage. Planning raises this sequence — expressing a desire or identifying a problem, imagining the outcome, and deciding on a strategy to achieve it — to the level of consciousness. Once children become consciously aware of their capacity to plan, they begin to see themselves as active agents in their own lives.

Imagining and anticipating actions. As children plan, they imagine something that has not yet happened, and they begin to understand that some set of their own actions can make it happen. The child who wants to make a boat says, "I'll get some wood and nails and a hammer." The child who wonders what is in the box thinks, "If I push the stool right next to the box, I might be high enough to see in." The child who wants her mom says to herself, "I heard singing on the porch. I'll look for Mom there." Thus, children

begin to see their own actions as a means to an end. They also develop the desire and ability to resist distractions, overcome obstacles, and remain task oriented long enough to act on their desires (Bullock & Lütkenhaus, 1988).

Expressing personal intentions and interests. It is important to emphasize that it is children's own intentions — their interests and desires — that impel them to engage in a series of actions that lead them toward a goal. This is true whether their intentions are relatively simple (to pick up the stuffed rabbit under the chair) or fairly complex (to build an outdoor pen for a real bunny). When children act on their intentions, they generally exhibit the energy, enthusiasm, and desire that make effective teaching and learning possible. *Children become most involved in learning experiences when adults acknowledge and support children's intentions rather than attempt to stifle or divert them.* Effective planning starts with children's spontaneous interests — it comes from within the child. As Dewey (1938/1963) reminds us, "interests are the signs and symptoms of growing power. I believe that they represent dawning capacities. Accordingly, the constant and careful observation of interests is of the utmost importance for the educator" (p. 14).

Shaping intentions into purposes. As Marilou Hyson stated in the quotation that begins this chapter, a child's ability to plan ties directly to his or her ability to self-regulate. When a child plans, he or she pauses between impulse and action to shape an intention into *purposeful* action. Appropriate adult support at planning time helps children formulate such purposeful plans.

Deliberating. Young children are initially more concerned with success (having their ideas work) than with efficiency (having their ideas work the best way possible). As young children develop their capacity to plan, however, they learn from experience: "The last time I rolled a ball at my stuffed rabbit, it hit the rabbit but the rabbit didn't move very much…." Through this type of deliberation, children's actions become more strategic and

Planning is a thought process in which internal goals shape anticipated actions. "I'm going to build a house with Charlie," this child tells his teacher during planning time, and then he does so.

efficient as they become increasingly able to build on previous actions and their outcomes.

Making ongoing modifications. Children make initial plans ("I'm going to play in the rocking boat with Kevin. We're catching fish!") and then often modify their plans as they play ("Let's pretend crocodiles are all around. We better make a bridge or they'll bite our legs off!"). Children construct new ideas and encounter unforeseen problems as they play. Therefore, planning is a *flexible process* that occurs both *before* and *during* the play sequence.

Because planning is a process, it involves imagination, deliberation, and ongoing modifications through which children turn intentions, desires, and interests into purposeful actions. Planning is well within the range of what young children can do because they have the requisite capacities to solve problems, form mental images, express intentions, deliberate, and make changes. Planning on a conscious level, however, is not something that most young children are in the *habit* of doing. Therefore, it is a process that requires daily adult support and attention. When adults do not support planning, children's actions may be impulsive or lack purpose. With adult-supported planning, children express their intentions and purposefully act in ways that help them achieve their goals.

Why is planning important?

In any setting, there are many reasons for adults to encourage young children to express their intentions before carrying them out.

Planning encourages children to articulate their ideas, choices, and decisions

Putting their plans and observations into their own words helps children think about and clarify their intentions. Articulating their plans also enables children to add detail to the mental pictures they are forming of what they are about to do. Further, children who articulate and act on their interests, choices, and plans gradually come to realize that they are ultimately responsible for their own decisions and actions.

Planning promotes children's self-confidence and sense of control

By planning, children come to rely on their own capacities to make choices and decisions and on their own ideas and direction. In contrast, psychologist Daniel Jordan (1976) points out that "children who grow up having no experience in setting their own objectives and pursuing the steps required to achieve them never become fully independent, responsible, and self-reliant human beings" (p. 294). Clearly, planning gives children opportunities to experience in concrete terms the relationship between their intentions and actions and the results of their actions. They see themselves as people who can do things and make things happen. Jordan (1976) describes the benefits of child planning this way:

> Being able to decide what it is one wants to accomplish and then being able to achieve it are vital to the maintenance of mental health and stability of personality. It is the wellspring of reality-based confidence, one of the fundamental sources of self-encouragement. (p. 296)

Parents of children in HighScope settings report that their children have become "more independent, self-confident, and less subject to frustration or temper tantrums" (Moore & Smith, 1987, p. 9). In a study of the plan-do-review process in HighScope settings conducted in Great Britain, psychologists Carla Berry and Kathy Sylva (1987) found a relationship between child planning and children's increased sense of efficacy, control over events, and self-worth.

Planning leads to involvement and concentration on play

Psychologist Thomas Lickona (1973) stresses that much social and educational literature supports the notion that people become more committed to and involved in tasks they choose for themselves.

The Impact of Planning on Children's Actions

	Internal intentions and interests	Thought processes	Child actions	Outcomes
Child has no plan	The child does not form a particular interest or intention; he or she may be impulsive and act on whatever comes to mind at the moment.	The child does not think through what he or she will do during work time.	The child may be aimless and wander around the room or wait to be told what to do.	The child either does exactly what the adult says to do or moves from one impulsive activity to the next.
Child creates a plan	The child forms internal intentions and interests and expresses them to an adult and/or to other children.	The child • Is deliberate. • Can see a goal and means of reaching it. • Imagines the whole and can select a part to start on. • Is able to connect internal ideas with actions. • Anticipates problem(s) and alternatives.	The child • Carries out a purposeful sequence of actions. • Concentrates on tasks. • Overcomes obstacles. • Encounters and solves problems. • Deals with contingencies. • Persists until reaching goals.	The child • Experiences achievement of an internal goal. • Has feelings of success. • Achieves a satisfying experience. • Has a process or product which can be shared.

Further, Berry and Sylva (1987) found that children who planned concentrated on their play for longer periods than did children in settings where they did not plan. They were engaged in what they were doing and excited about the possibilities brought about by their own actions. "Planning is not a promise to 'do something acceptable'....It's an exciting opportunity to form a mental model to guide future activity" (Berry & Sylva, 1987, p. 34).

Planning supports the development of increasingly complex play

In their study of the plan-do-review process, Berry and Sylva (1987) found that "children played with more imagination, concentration, and intellectual complexity during the time they carried out their plans than during more spontaneous, unplanned play" (p. 34). Planning, therefore, has the potential for drawing children into increasingly complex and more challenging activities characterized by novelty, imagination, systematic and goal-oriented actions, thoughtful mental effort, and purposeful social interactions. By contrast, the ordinary play typically found in programs that do not promote planning is characterized by routine or repetitive actions, aimless behavior, and lack of intention.

While children need opportunities to engage in both challenging and ordinary play, one goal

> ### Challenging Versus Ordinary Play
>
> **Challenging play is…**
>
> "Novel, creative, imaginative, productive
>
> Cognitively complex, involving the combination of several elements, materials, actions, or ideas
>
> Carried out in a systematic, planned, and purposeful manner
>
> Structured and goal-directed — working toward some aim, whether the result is a tangible end-product or an invisible goal
>
> Conducted with care and mental effort; the child devotes a great deal of attention, is deeply engrossed, takes pains
>
> Learning a new skill, trying to improve an established one, or trying novel combinations of already familiar skills"
>
> **Ordinary play is…**
>
> "Familiar, routine, stereotyped, repetitive, unproductive
>
> Cognitively unsophisticated, not involving the combining of elements
>
> Performed in an unsystematic, random manner with no observable planning or purposefulness
>
> Not directed toward a new, challenging goal, 'aimless' and without structure
>
> Conducted with ease, little mental effort, and not much care; the child is not deeply engrossed, his attention may not be entirely on that task
>
> Repeating a familiar, well-established pattern without seeking to improve upon it and without adding any new component or combination"
>
> — Sylva, Roy, & Painter (1980, p. 60)

of the HighScope Curriculum is to encourage children to take on appropriate challenges that stimulate and support their emerging capacities. Child planning enables children to remain in control of the challenges they take on and the manner in which they deal with them.

What children do as they plan

Understanding what children do as they plan helps adults appreciate and support the wide range of planning behaviors children develop over time. These behaviors include expressing their intentions as indicated through gestures, actions, and words; making vague, routine, and detailed plans; making a variety of plans over time; and even making plans at home as they anticipate what they will do at school that day or the next.

Children develop the capacity to express their intentions

Children are natural planners and problem solvers. Infants face and overcome problems in a world where everything is new to them. As Case (1985) notes, "The 2-month-old infant who has just experienced the sensation of having its finger in its mouth will actively work towards reinstating this pleasant state, experimenting with various possible arm movements that might enable it to do so" (p. 273).

Toddlers are increasingly able to work toward a goal without becoming distracted. Psychologists have noted that toddlers begin by focusing "more on the flow of activities than on the ends or consequences their activities lead to" (Bullock & Lütkenhaus, 1988, pp. 671–672). By the age of two,

When children plan and have the opportunity to fulfill those plans, they have an increased sense of control and become more independent.

> **Planning — What and Why: A Summary**
>
> **What planning is**
> - Establishing a problem or goal
> - Imagining and anticipating actions
> - Expressing personal intentions and interests
> - Shaping intentions into purposes
> - Deliberating
> - Making ongoing modifications
>
> **Why planning is important**
> - Encourages children to articulate their ideas, choices, and decisions
> - Promotes children's self-confidence and sense of control
> - Leads to involvement and concentration on play
> - Supports the development of increasingly complex play

most children begin to shift their attention toward attaining outcomes that require some effort. They may decide to use blocks, for example, to make a stack and stop when they have a stack that satisfies them. They may knock their stack down and build it again, but if stacking is their intention, two-year-olds remain quite determined to create stacks and are not easily distracted by other possibilities.

Preschoolers can solve problems by planning a course of action in advance. While three-year-olds can keep a goal in mind, they generally work their way toward it one step at a time and deal with problems as they encounter them rather than anticipating and planning for them in advance. Very gradually, however, children between the ages of three-and-a-half and five-and-a-half gain the ability to plan a more complex course of action. They foresee problems and ways around them before they launch into action, rather than dealing with each problem along the way in a trial-and-error fashion.

Being aware of how children's planning capacities develop helps adults see that planning takes on various forms and is present in a variety of behaviors, depending on each child's growing capacity to identify, mentally picture, and work toward the solution of personally interesting problems. For example, for some children, planning consists of simply indicating a starting point: "Play over there." "Play with play dough." Other children plan by listing several beginning points: "Read in the cozy area, paint, and play with magnets." Others plan by outlining several steps beyond the beginning of their plan: "Make a robot. Get a big box. Tape on a smaller one for the head. Find something long for the arms." Still other children can envision a fairly complex sequence of events: "We're putting on a show so we need to make a stage with the big hollow blocks, and make tickets, and put chairs up in front so people can see. And we need to practice our dance, and then everybody can get their tickets and watch." Once adults understand that children's capacity to plan develops with time and experience, they can support all sorts of planning in ways that make the most sense to each child.

Children indicate their intentions through gestures, actions, and words

From the outset it is important to realize that young children indicate their plans both nonverbally and verbally. Many people associate planning solely with talking, and they view planning time as an opportunity for children to build expressive language skills. For many children this is the case, but, for others, planning begins with nonverbal communications.

Expressing intentions through gestures and actions. When asked what they would like to do, some young children respond by pointing to someone or something, looking at a friend or toy, or simply starting their activity (e.g., going to the block area, touching a red cardboard block, and looking back for adult acknowledgment). Other children may bring the animals or truck they want to play with back to the person they are planning with. They may also take that person by the hand and lead him or her over to the desired play area. These are all legitimate expressions of intent, conveyed by gesture and action, that adults can duly acknowledge and support as shown in the following examples:

"Oh, you're pointing to the book and writing area, Katie. What will you do there?" Katie gets the book Mr. Gumpy's Motor Car. *"You're going to read* Mr. Gumpy's Motor Car." *Katie nods and heads back to the book area to begin.*

Often, when nonverbal children feel assured that adults understand their gestures and are not pressuring them to talk, they begin to add words on their own:

Vanessa points to the block area and after a second shouts out, "Block area!" with great gusto. "What

> **The Development of Young Children's Planning**
>
> - **Infants:** Work to repeat pleasant random actions.
> - **Toddlers:** Follow their intentions but focus on doing rather than on outcomes.
> - **2-year-olds:** Focus increasingly on outcomes; not easily distracted.
> - **3-year-olds:** Work purposefully toward a goal one step at a time.
> - **3½- to 5½-year-olds:** Gradually gain the ability to plan a multistep sequence of actions to reach a goal.

will you do in the block area?" Karl asks. Vanessa acts out building a tower and then raises both arms and says "Big!"

Six children in Andrea's child care home gather around Andrea on the living room rug. After the preschool- and kindergarten-aged children plan, two-year-old Tessa makes her plan. To an outsider, her speech would sound like babbling, but her brother Rusty interprets: "She's saying she's going to play with the blocks." Tessa babbles her assent and toddles off to the block corner.

In a center for preschoolers with special needs, a group of children sit at a table with a clear view of their newly arranged interest areas stocked with toys, blocks, and books. Most of them cannot talk and many of them have trouble moving, but when Mrs. Manet asks them what they would like to play with, they have no trouble indicating their choices with gestures, sounds, and actions.

Children with even limited ability or no ability to talk prove to be enthusiastic choice makers and planners.

Expressing intentions in words. Most children respond to the question "What would you like to do?" by saying aloud what they intend to do. They describe their plans in single words ("Cars" or "Hammer"), in phrases ("With the glitter and glue" or "Over there by David"), in brief sentences ("Make something for my mom" or "I'm going to play the ducks game on the computer"), or in whole paragraphs ("First me and Lena are going to play dentist again. I'm being the dentist and she's the little girl. She doesn't want her teeth fixed because she thinks it's going to hurt, but, see, I'm the Doc, and I give her special stuff in her mouth. Then I read her a story…"). Whether young children plan in words, phrases, sentences, or paragraphs is not as important as the fact that they are putting anticipated actions into their own words. Whatever language children use and however they speak, it is our job to listen attentively, asking for clarification if necessary.

While language is highly important (language from children is an essential ingredient of active learning), it is also important to build on children's other skills and dispositions. If we equate planning solely with talking, we may bypass many *nonverbal* planners. For most children, planning ultimately does become a springboard for thoughtful conversation, but we must take our cues from children and value planning in both its nonverbal and verbal forms.

Children make vague, routine, and detailed plans

In the study cited earlier, Berry and Sylva (1987) noted that the clarity of children's plans depends on the extent to which they can mentally picture what they are about to do. Their classification of children's plans as "vague," "routine," or "detailed" (pp. 9–10) is useful for adults to keep in mind as they listen to children plan.

Vague plans. These are minimal plans in which children just barely indicate a choice or beginning point in response to the question "What are you going to do today?" Children might answer, for example, "Go over there," "House area," or "Make something."

> **"What Would You Like to Do?" Typical Children's Responses**
>
> - Pointing to an object, place, or person
> - Looking at an object, place, or person
> - Touching an object
> - Bringing a toy or other object back to the person with whom they are planning
> - Taking an adult to a place or thing
> - Acting out the intended action
> - Talking about intended actions in their own words, phrases, sentences, or paragraphs
> - Any combination of the above

Children who make such ambiguous plans seem to have an unclear picture in their minds of what they actually want to do. They often end up doing one of three things: (1) going to a safe, unoccupied spot, picking up something such as a doll or stuffed animal, and watching other children; (2) wandering from place to place; or (3) seeking out an adult to join and follow. These children may be indicating that they need time to take in all the possibilities, time to see what other children are doing, or time to grasp the fact that they can make choices. In their own way, they may be trying to tell us, "I want to watch for a while before I decide what to do" or "I want to do something really safe before I risk something new."

Routine plans. These are simple plans in which children mention an activity, process, or material as a beginning point. Children might say, for example, "Play with blocks," "Cutting…lots," or "Wear the bells. I'll be jingling!"

These children seem to have a clear picture in mind of themselves engaged in a particular experience or with a specific material. They have a clear place to begin and generally get started right away unless someone else is using the equipment they have in mind.

Children may plan by using a classroom "map" their teacher has created with blocks and area signs. This child expresses her plans by pointing to where she would like to go; her teacher supports her by acknowledging her gestures and naming the area where she plans to play.

Detailed plans. These are more complex plans in which children mention an activity, process, or material as a beginning point, goal, or outcome and often outline one or more steps or accessories for getting from beginning to end as shown in the following examples:

- "Make a Robin Hood hat. With a feather, a real one like Michael's."
- "Be a doggie with Gutrune in the house area. I'll have a bowl for drinking and food."
- "Use the Construx. Make a telephone truck with a very tall ladder...and I think I'll put balancers on the sides so it won't tip over, and a cab for the driver."
- "I saw birds at the beach with my dad. Hey, I bet I could make a beach with birds on it! Three birds — the mama, the dad, and the little boy bird...and a nest for them...oh, yeah, and some water too. You want to see it? I'll tell you to come over and look, okay?"

These children seem to have quite an extensive mental picture of what they want to accomplish and how they plan to go about it. They are generally quite persistent in spite of problems that arise, and they make modifications as necessary along the way.

Children make a variety of plans over time

Children's plans change as they become familiar with available materials, their peers, and their own ability to make plans and think about how to carry them out. Here are some examples of how specific children's plans changed over time:

Teri: Planning Theme and Variations

September:

- "Make a house with blocks."
- "Make a house with long blocks and cardboard blocks."
- "Play with Cassie in our house. Use the big pillows for beds."

October:

- "Make a house with the giant Tinkertoy building blocks. It will have a roof too."
- "Build a big Tinkertoy house and put sheets over it so no one can see us."
- "Me and Cassie are going to make another house with sheets and Tinkertoys, and the gate will be the door."

November:

- "Paint in the art area. Make a picture of a house. It's for my grandma. She's at my house."
- "Look at my box from my new shoes my grandma got me! I'm going to cut holes for windows and doors. One of those tube things for a chimney. Then I'm going to paint it blue."

January:

- "Make a birdhouse at the workbench like Joey's."
- "Still working on my birdhouse. Put on the roof, but I need a big enough board or something else big."
- "Paint my birdhouse in the art area. One color for one side and another color for the other side, and one for this side, and one for this side, and then on the top. That's one color, two colors, three colors, four colors, and five colors!"

William: From Nonverbal to Verbal Planning

August:

- Looks at the boys playing in the block area.
- Points to the block area.
- Goes to the block area next to Ricky and Joey, and looks back with a smile.

September:

- Brings a car from the block area back to the planning table.
- Brings a car and long block back to the planning table and inclines his head toward the boys in the block area.
- Brings a long block back and moves his hand up and down the blocks, making a very quiet "rrum, rrum" noise.

October:

- Says very quietly, "Blocks and cars" and points to the block area.

November:

- Brings the container of small metal cars from the toy area and says quietly to the teacher, "Make a road."

Children engage in the planning process at home

Over the years, parents with children in High-Scope preschool and child care programs have been reporting on their experiences at home with the child planning process. Here are some parents' reports of these experiences:

What Children Do As They Plan: A Summary

- Children develop the capacity to express their intentions.
- Children indicate their intentions through gestures, actions, and words.
- Children make vague, routine, and detailed plans.
- Children make a variety of plans over time.
- Children engage in the planning process at home.

- "Tina told me her plan while she was getting dressed this morning."
- "Ricky made his plan in the car. He already knows what he wants to do."
- "When she came home yesterday, Tanya told me her plan was to look at books during her nap, and then after nap to play in the sandbox with Teri. I said, 'What about going to see Grandma?' 'We'll do that after the sand,' she said. She was very firm about it. And that's exactly what she did. Read the books, played in the sand with her friend, and then we went to my mother's. This child knows her mind!"

- "On Saturdays we all have to make a plan. Klenton is so used to planning each day with you, Ruby, that I guess he just brings it home with him. So now we *all* plan! Even Mona who has always been so scatterbrained. I think she does it because she is so surprised her little brother would come up with such an idea. It's fun to find out what everyone has in mind."
- "The other day, I heard Ollie telling his friend Fred, 'Okay, first we have to make a plan. Then we'll get all the stuff we need.' I don't think Fred even knows about planning, but he went along with it!"

When children become more confident planners, their plans often become more elaborate. Using the classroom "map" the teacher has drawn, this young child tells her teacher about her plans for work time: She's starting off in the woodworking area, then to the sand and water area, and finally to the house area for dress-up.

How Adults Support Children's Planning

It is planning time at the beginning of the program year. Ruth, an adult, is sitting at the child-sized house-area table with a group of nine children. She holds a cardboard tube to one eye as a spyglass, looks around the areas, and says:

Ruth: I see blocks. I see books. I see paints on the easel. I see a computer. I see dolls and a small crib in the house area. I see lots of things to play with! *(Looks at the children through her tube.)* I have a spyglass tube like mine for each of you, so you can look for things you'd like to play with today at work time. *(Ruth gives a tube to each child, and they all begin to look through their tubes. Some stand up for a better view; others comment spontaneously on what they see.)*

Chris D.: Steering wheel.

Ruth: You see the steering wheel.

Chris D.: I'm going to use it.

Ruth: What will you use it for?

Chris D.: A fire truck! *(He leaves to get started.)*

Kathryn: *(Looks toward the art area.)* Ruth, I'm going to make two things. A birdhouse with scissors and paper and then a wasp nest. *(Kathryn heads for the art area without waiting for Ruth's response.)*

Colin: *(Swings his tube toward the art area.)* I'm going to make a wasp nest — with baby wasps.

Ruth: You made some baby snakes yesterday.

Colin: Yes, but the wasps will be paper. *(Colin goes off to join Kathryn.)*

Ruth: What do you see, Will?

Will: Blocks!

Ruth: What will you do with the blocks?

Will: Build a boat. *(Leaves to get started.)*

Ruth: Caroline, I see you're looking at lots of different things.

Caroline: Well, I'm going to the computer to make a crown first. Then I'm going to color it with the pastels, and then be a princess.

Ruth: You'll be the princess with the pastel crown!

Caroline: No, it will be gold with jewels!

Ruth: Oh, gold with jewels. *(Caroline heads for the computers.)* What about you, Chris?

Chris W.: Sand area.

Ruth: You see the sand area.

Chris W.: Yep, I'm going to use the tubes to make poison, and I'm giving it to you! *(He grins.)* Then I'm going to the computer. *(He leaves for the sand area, taking several tubes with him.)*

Sara: *(Puts her tube down.)* Ruth, that's where *I'm* going.

Ruth: You're going to the sand area, Sara?

Sara: No, silly, the computer. I'm playing the playroom game.

Ruth: Oh, the program where you make the animals move.

Sara: I'm going to do that and that other room where the letters come up. *(Sara heads for the computers.)*

Ruth: What do you see through your tube, Max?

Max: I see Will. I'm playing with him.

Ruth: Why don't you find out what Will is doing? Perhaps you can make your plan with him. *(Max joins Will.)*

Donnette: Ruth, I'm reading you a story in the book area!

Ruth: Okay! *(They move toward the books.)* I wonder which story it will be.

Donnette: It's a surprise! Close your eyes.

As this scenario illustrates, planning time is a fairly brief period that involves focused, enjoyable exchanges between each child and an adult. It is important for adults to conduct planning as Ruth did, in ways that engage children and encourage them to make their plans as completely as possible. Adults can support children's planning in four important ways:

- Planning with children in an intimate setting
- Providing materials and experiences to maintain children's interest at planning time
- Conversing with individual children about their plans
- Anticipating changes in children's planning over time

Adults plan with children in an intimate setting

Children plan with the adult and their group in the same place each day, but that can occur in a variety of settings — at the art area table, in the block area, in a circle on the floor, in the middle of the room. Intimate settings such as these will help the planning process.

Plan in a place where intimate conversations can occur

Wherever it occurs, planning should involve a thoughtful conversation between the child planner and a supportive adult. The child gestures, talks about, or in some way indicates an intention, and the adult enters into a dialogue with the child about how to carry out the intention. Since planning with a group of children involves a series of such one-to-one conversations, the smaller the number of children in each group sharing their plans with one adult, the more intimate and unhurried each planning exchange will be.

In their study of the plan-do-review process, Berry and Sylva (1987) indicate that children in smaller, more intimate planning groups tend to make more detailed plans:

Number of children in planning group	Percentage of detailed plans
1–4	60%
5–7	42%
8–10	15%

"We wonder," the authors relate, "whether the staff become more concerned in larger planning groups with 'getting through' and not losing the attention of the group than with the quality of each child's plan" (p. 16). Nevertheless, Berry and Sylva also point out that group size is not the only factor that influences the quality of children's plans: "Staff expectations and priorities also influence the sophistication of the planning process and the children's plans which emerge from it" (p. 16).

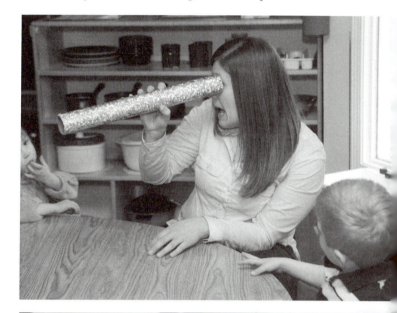

Here the teacher demonstrates an I spy planning game using a cardboard tube. The children then have a chance to peer through the tube to look at the areas and decide what they want to do at work time.

In other words, while planning in a small group contributes to intimacy and detail and is therefore preferable, teachers may have little control over group size (the number of teachers and children is typically set by agency-level policies). Therefore, it is important to know that an atmosphere of intimacy is one that adults can foster regardless of planning-group size. For example, one way to foster intimacy is to converse with children at their physical level. Another is to provide interesting materials for the whole planning group to use while you converse with each child in turn. In the scenario at the beginning of this section, for example, the adult (Ruth) planned with nine children. As she planned with each child, the remaining children were engaged looking through their spyglass tubes and thinking about what they wanted to do at work time.

Plan in a stable pair or group

Planning flourishes in a secure setting in which the adult, the other children in the group, and the actual physical space remain fairly constant. Such stability gives children the feelings of security and internal control they need to take on the challenge of planning. When changes do occur, it helps to alert children in advance: "Tomorrow, Bob and I are going to switch planning groups so we have a chance to plan with everyone. Bob is coming to the house area to plan with you, and I'm going to plan with the children in the art area."

Plan where people and materials are visible

The younger the planners, the more they need to be able to see the materials available to them. When materials are easy to see, children are reminded of all the objects they can choose from as they formulate their plans. For example, planning in a place that allows children to easily see the materials in the house area helps them to imagine what they might do with the dress-up clothes. In most early childhood settings, however, there will be some materials children cannot see as they plan, no matter where planning occurs.

Adults can overcome limited visibility problems during planning by changing the planning setting from time to time and by having children tour the areas just before they make their plans.

Adults provide materials and experiences to maintain children's interest at planning time

The challenge we accept at planning time is to keep a small group of young children engaged so that we can plan individually with each child. When children have interesting materials to use, they do not mind waiting for their turn to plan. Once children are engaged, adults feel less pressure to rush through planning and are comfortable taking the time needed to talk with each child in turn.

Provide special games and experiences

A variety of special games and experiences have evolved over the years as ways to provide an enjoyable group setting for planning. These include *visibility games, group games, props and partnerships,* and *representations* (see "Planning Games and Experiences" on pp. 262–263). Such activities rely on playfulness and novelty to keep planning from becoming routine, and they challenge children to stretch their abilities to picture and describe their intended actions as completely as possible. They also help children see the many possibilities of planning time.

Allow children to take charge

As children become familiar with the planning process, they are able to assume increasing control over planning time. They do this by adding their own spontaneous variations to planning games; taking over the adult role of plan elicitor; and planning on their own, in pairs, or in small groups. For example, when one adult introduced the "Jingle, jingle, jingle" name rhyme at planning time ("Jingle, jingle, jingle, Jallie. It's your turn to plan if your name is Callie!"), the children in her planning group made it more fun and more active by pounding on the table to the beat, anticipating the name from the initial rhyme, and pointing with great gusto to the child with the rhyming name. Because the adult listened to and appreciated their ideas, the children expanded a planning rhyme into a playful movement experience.

Children also become quite adept at planning with each other, whether they are using props such as phones or simply planning face to face. Often, children who tend to make fairly vague plans with an adult will make more detailed plans with another child, and the two will often end up carrying out their plans together.

Over time, children assume as much control over making plans as adults are willing to relinquish. Ultimately, as children take more control, adults become less central to setting the planning process in motion and more important as attentive resource persons and facilitators.

Adults converse with individual children about their plans

After they have set a playful context for planning, adults focus on *one-to-one planning conversations* with each child. In these intimate conversations, adults elicit children's plans, listen attentively, converse sensitively with both nonverbal and verbal planners, encourage coworkers to plan together, value children's plans, and note the connections between children's plans and actions. In the planning-time scenario on page 258, for example, the adult gives each child a spyglass and then converses with each child in turn, using the strategies described next.

Elicit children's plans by asking "what" questions

To begin, put yourself at the children's physical level to engage in a real dialogue about an important subject. Then, the most direct way to elicit a child's plan is simply to ask, "What would you like to do today?" This open-ended question invites many possible responses, and a child can answer it without prior understanding of the meaning of the word *plan*.

A Caution About Asking "Where" Questions

Encouraging children to describe the actions they intend is at the very heart of the HighScope planning process. Questions such as "*What* will you do?" and "*How* will you do it?" encourage children to anticipate their actions. Conversely, asking "*Where* are you going to work?" may help adults monitor children's use of the interest areas at work time, but it does not encourage them to anticipate and describe a plan of action. Here is an example of what can happen:

Adult: Where are you working today, Nick?

Nick: In the block area.

Adult: *(Later during work time)* Nick, what are you doing in the house area? Your plan is in the block area and that's where you belong!

This last statement is not appropriate. Perhaps Nick was finished in the block area or was consulting a friend. Perhaps he was getting something from the house area he needed for his block play. Planning is meant to help children picture and think about what they want to do before they do it, not to confine them to a particular area.

In their study of the HighScope plan-do-review process, Berry and Sylva (1987) found that asking "Where?" and leaving planning at that level leads to fairly minimal plans. If you do initiate planning by asking "Where will you play?" be sure to follow the child's response with "*What* will you do there?" Furthermore, if you ask "Where?" be prepared for answers such as "All over the place" and "In a whole bunch of places."

Planning Games and Experiences

Visibility games

These games can help young planners see the choices available to them. They can also help children feel comfortable in a new setting or understand a change in the interest areas.

Guided tours

Children tour the interest areas in pairs; a child familiar with planning and with the setting is paired with a new child. When they find something interesting, they begin playing. *Variation:* Pairs of children tour the interest areas, bring something they have found back to an adult, and have a brief planning conversation.

Displays

Display a variety of materials gathered from the interest areas at the planning table (or spot), and encourage the children to handle the materials and talk about which ones they would like to play with. When they have made a choice, they get started.

Train

Make a train with the children and "chug" to all the interest areas, looking at the materials and the play possibilities as they move about the room. Have children leave the train as they see things that interest them. *Variations:* (1) Children take turns being the leader of the train. (2) The train travels around all the interest areas once with everybody on it. As the train makes its second tour, children "disembark" when the train arrives at the interest area and materials they want to explore.

Collections

Ask each child, "What are you going to do today?" Instead of pursuing planning conversations at this point, give each child a bag, basket, or box and ask the children to collect some of the things they need to carry out their plans. As children return with their unique collections, continue planning conversations with each child about the materials in the bags and how he or she will use them. *Variation:* Offer collection containers of varying sizes (from cups to boxes) and ask children to select the specific container they think will best suit the materials they will be using.

Group games

Games that involve suspense about who will plan next can hold children's interest in anticipation of their turns to plan.

Hula-Hoop

Mark one spot on a Hula-Hoop by wrapping it with a piece of colored tape or masking tape. Five or six children sit in a tight circle, each one holding on to the hoop with both hands. As everyone sings a short song, the children turn the hoop in a circle so that the marked spot passes from hand to hand. When the song ends, the child whose hand is either touching or closest to the marked spot plans with the adult. Repeat until all children have planned. *Variation:* In place of a Hula-Hoop, tie several scarves together end to end and then tie one large knot (looped three or four times over) to join the endmost scarves together into a circle. Have children close their eyes and sing a familiar song. At the end of the song, the child holding the scarf with the large knot plans.

Ball

Children sit in a circle. A child or adult rolls the ball to a child who then plans with the adult. When the child has finished planning, the child rolls the ball to another child who then plans, and so forth, until every child has made a plan. *Variation:* Do the same thing with a ball of yarn.

Spinner

Children sit in a circle. Using a bottle or block for a spinner, one child gives it a spin. When it stops spinning, the child it points to plans with the adult. Upon completing the planning conversation, the child spins the spinner to designate which child will plan next.

Playing games helps keep planning fun. During this planning time, each child unwrapped a block with a letter die. The teacher called out a letter, and the child whose letter matched the teacher's letter told his or her plan.

Symbols or letter links

Put each child's symbol or letter link in a box or bag. A child draws a symbol or letter link from the box without looking. The child whose symbol or letter link is drawn plans with the adult, then draws the symbol or letter link of the next child to plan, and so forth.

Rhymes

Make up a name rhyme, for example: "Jingle, jingle, jingle Jerry. It's your turn to plan if your name is Kerry." Kerry then discusses her plan. When she has finished, repeat with another child's name: "Jingle, jingle, jingle jax. It's your turn to plan if your name is Max."

Props and partnerships

Using a variety of props and forming planning pairs helps to hold children's attention while other children are planning.

Spyglasses

Give each child a cardboard tube, and have them look around the play space to see things they might want to do or play with. As children are spying and talking among themselves, plan with each child. (See example on p. 258.)

Phones

Using two phones, the adult "calls up" a child, and they have their planning conversation over the phone. At the end of the conversation, the child gives his or her phone to another child. The adult calls that child (or that child calls the adult), they plan over the phone, and so forth until each child has planned. *Variations:* (1) Have two children on the phones (one child plans and the other takes the adult role of supporter and questioner). (2) Have enough phones for each child so the other children can converse with one another while one of them is talking with the adult.

Puppets

The adult wears a hand puppet who converses with each child in turn about his or her plan. After a child has planned, he or she tells the puppet which child to plan with next. *Variations:* (1) The adult uses one puppet and the children use another puppet so that planning takes place between two puppets. (2) Each child has a puppet.

Child pairs

Two children plan together. One describes a plan while the other takes the support role. Then they change roles. This works well once young children have planned enough with adults to understand the planning process.

Representations

Sometimes photos, pantomime, drawing, and writing can help children *represent* (i.e., visualize and describe) their plans more fully. These strategies also give each child something to do or explore while others are planning with the adult.

Pictures

Put together a collection of clear, contact paper–covered or laminated photos, catalog pictures, and drawings of all the materials in your setting, sorted into boxes by area. First, ask each child a quick "What are you going to do today?" Then ask children to select pictures of the materials they will be using. Finally, talk with each child in turn about the pictures and how they relate to his or her plan. *Variations:* (1) Have the children tape their pictures onto their symbols to refer to at recall time. (2) Have the children sequence the pictures in the order in which they think they will be using the materials.

Pantomime

Ask each child, "*Show* me what you plan to do today. Pretend with your body but do not use any words. The rest of us will try to guess." After the child has acted out some or all of his or her plan, converse with the child about details and then move on to the next child's pantomime.

Map

This strategy calls for a large map of the interest areas, including pictures or drawings of some of the materials in each area. Ask each child, "What are you planning to do today?"; give the children a plastic bear or other play figure; and then ask them to walk their bear to the places on the map where they plan to play. You might say, "Show and tell me with your bear on the map what you plan to do." This strategy is appropriate for children who are experienced planners who can interpret such a map. *Variation:* For children not ready for a map, try a planning path — a length of fabric or butcher paper divided into sections representing each interest area. Children stand on the interest area they would like to work in and then plan what they will do among themselves or with an adult.

Drawing and writing

Provide paper and a variety of drawing and writing tools, ask children to draw or write what they plan to do, and talk with each child in turn about his or her plan. This strategy works well when adults anticipate and appreciate a variety of drawing and writing styles, including scribbles, tracings, figures, symbols, and letters in any combination.

Other variations include:

- "What would you like to do during work time?"
- "What are you going to do next?"
- "Tell me about what you're going to do today, Bill."
- "I see you have some magnets, Sharee. What are you going to do with them?"
- "Your dad told me that you already know what you're going to do today, Kwame!"
- "Yesterday you said you wanted to work on your house again today, Teri. What do you think about that idea today?"

Once children become familiar with planning and understand the meaning of the word *plan* through their own experiences, you can use this word in opening questions and statements. For example:

- "What is your plan today, Omondi?"
- "Tell me about your plan, Cindy."
- "Your mom said you already made your plan at home, Jeff. What do you plan to do?"
- "What are you planning to do today, Joseph?"
- "I see you've brought something with you that you plan to work with, Angie. How will you use it?"
- "Joanie, you started to talk about your plan at breakfast. What else have you thought about it?"

Note that "what" and "how" questions leave it open to children to describe their intentions and elaborate their plans as much as they want or are able to. By contrast, "where" questions ask only that children name an interest area but do not encourage them to offer further details. They also do not open the possibility that children may choose to work in more than one area as they carry out their plans, for example, moving materials from the block area to the house area to make a bed for the baby.

Watch and listen attentively to children's responses

Give each child ample time to respond. Whatever a child does or says tells you something about that child's planning process. Listen for and be aware of both nonverbal and verbal planning. This tells you whether you will be translating the child's nonverbal communication into words (e.g., naming a toy the child points to) or engaging in a

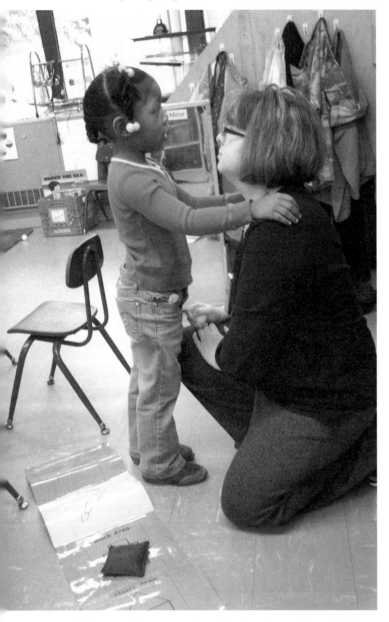

Wherever it occurs, planning involves a thoughtful conversation between the child planner and a supportive adult.

dialogue about the child's intentions (e.g., talking about what the child wants to do with the toy). Listen for vague, routine, and detailed plans to gain some idea of how much the child is able to imagine an action sequence and to what extent you might be able to help him or her picture it more completely.

Watching and listening carefully to children as they plan allows you to respond appropriately to each child. As you become familiar with the High-Scope **key developmental indicators (KDIs)** in early learning, which are described in the KDI books that accompany this manual, you will add a new dimension to your understanding of each child's plans. The KDIs will shed light on how the activities children choose and their particular ways of thinking about their plans relate to the important abilities they are developing.

Converse in a turn-taking manner with nonverbal and vague planners

After an adult elicits a child's initial plan and listens to his or her response, the next step is to continue the conversation. With nonverbal and vague planners, who do not state an initial plan in words or who do so only sketchily, the main idea is to explore the child's plan as far as possible without pressuring the child. The conversational turn-taking strategies, illustrated in examples that follow, are useful for gently eliciting more detailed plans. Using this turn-taking approach, the adults in the examples make a statement and then pause for the child to respond. After the child responds, the adults comment on the *child's* idea, rather than introduce new ideas of their own. The strategies illustrated here enable adults to share control with children during planning conversations.

Interpret gestures and actions. With nonverbal planners, one effective strategy is for the adult to translate the child's gestures and actions into words. This calls for close attention to the child and verbal restraint. We are often tempted to jump in with our suggestions rather than wait patiently and respect the child's ideas, as this adult does:

Adult: What are you going to do today, Katie?

Katie: *(Points to the book and writing area.)*

Adult: You're pointing to the book and writing area.

Katie: *(Nods yes.)*

Adult: Show me what you'll do there, Katie.

Katie: *(Goes to the bookshelf and brings back* Mr. Gumpy's Motor Car.*)*

Adult: Oh, you're going to read *Mr. Gumpy's Motor Car.*

Katie: *(Nods yes and heads over to the beanbag chair with her book.)*

Ask an initial, open-ended question. This strategy works well with very young planners if the adult listens and offers comments afterward instead of responding with another question to each statement the child makes, as shown in this example:

Adult: How about you, what's your plan today, Pattie?

Pattie: Make something.

Adult: You're going to make something.

Pattie: Like hers. *(Points to Donna.)*

Adult: Like Donna's.

Pattie: A crown. On the computer.

Adult: You'd like to make a crown like the one Donna made on the computer.

Pattie: But I don't know how to do that one.

Adult: Well, I bet Donna would help you get started on the crown-making program.

Narrate what you see and comment on what the child says. This strategy helps slow the adults to the child's pace of communication. Also, as with the previous strategy, it allows the child to direct the conversation. The inexperienced planner feels less pressure and anxiety because the adult simply makes comments rather than asks questions that demand an answer. Here is an example:

"Hello, what would you like to do today?" is a straightforward way to begin a one-to-one planning conversation with a child.

Ike: *(Pounds on the table.)*

Adult: I saw you pound like that yesterday.

Ike: Play dough. I pounded it real hard.

Adult: Hard and loud!

Ike: Yeah, it was loud. I made it flat all right!

Adult: Flat as a pancake!

Ike: Flat as *two* pancakes even! I'll show you how I can do it.

Adult: All right. I'll be over to see how flat you can pound the play dough.

Offer alternatives when the child does not respond. As you get to know each child, you will be able to offer alternatives suited to each child's particular interests. The adult cited here (on three different days) knows that Wendy has played with beads and dolls. The adult offers these materials, and her own presence, as secure and familiar starting points for Wendy's planning. Also, when questions and comments fail, she offers actions:

Adult: What would you like to do, Wendy?

Wendy: *(Long pause. No response.)*

Adult: Yesterday you strung lots of beads.

Wendy: *(Nods and smiles slightly.)*

Adult: *(Waits.)*

Wendy: *(Takes adult's hand and heads to the toy area.)*

Adult: Let's see what we can find.

Adult: What would you like to do, Wendy?

Wendy: *(Long pause. No response.)*

Adult: Sometimes you point to something you'd like to work with.

Wendy: *(Sits in adult's lap.)*

Adult: Maybe you'd like to stay with me and watch for a while.

Wendy: *(Nods yes.)*

Adult: What would you like to do, Wendy?

Wendy: *(Watches children playing with dolls.)*

Adult: Jill and Anna are playing with the doll babies.

Wendy: *(Continues to watch.)*

Adult: I'm going to feed my doll baby in the house area. You can help me if you'd like.

Wendy: *(Nods yes.)*

Converse with routine and elaborate planners

Routine planners, who state simple but clear plans, and elaborate planners, who articulate plans of more complexity, also need adult support to continue the planning dialogue. Sometimes, however, in an effort to finish planning time, adults rush through planning conversations with such children and then try to talk and ask questions during work time. At planning time, children are generally willing to stop and think about what they are going to do because they have not yet started to play. During work time, however, in the midst of their play, questions may disrupt what children are doing. Therefore, it is important to converse with these able planners at *planning* time, to engage them in the challenge of thinking *before* doing.

Interestingly, Berry and Sylva (1987) report that while adults tend to question nonverbal and vague planners extensively, they seldom question routine and elaborate planners. Their findings suggest that adults tend to persist in questioning vague planners until they arrive at a more complete picture of what they might do, but pass up the opportunity to converse with and question children who have the potential for thinking through and articulating even more elaborate plans. Perhaps this tendency stems from a focus on what children *cannot* do rather than on what they *can* do. Whatever the cause, it is also important to encourage both routine and elaborate planners to think through their plans as much as they can. Respectful listening and turn-taking strategies are important for these more experienced planners, just as they are for nonverbal and vague planners. In addition, using the following strategies will help routine and elaborate planners further develop their ideas. As you review the strategies and accompanying conversational examples, note again how the adults work to give the child control in each planning dialogue by asking an opening question, waiting for a response, and reflecting children's ideas in their comments and responses.

Converse about space and materials. This can help children anticipate and solve problems that might otherwise prevent them from carrying out or even getting started on their plans:

Adult: What's your plan today, Pete?

Pete: Make a really big monster house. Really big!

Adult: How will you make a really big monster house?

Pete: With all the blocks. The cardboard ones, the big wooden ones, and those other ones you can reach inside of.

Adult: That sounds like almost all our blocks to me.

Pete: Yep! I'm using all of them.

Adult: You know, I see some other kids already using the big hollow blocks and some of the big wooden blocks.

Pete: Aw, darn it! I need those!

Adult: Well, there are still some blocks left.

Pete: *(Looks around.)*

Adult: Sometimes people make houses out of other things.

Pete: I could use the pillows.

Adult: The pillows.

Pete: Maybe those boxes we had yesterday!

Adult: The boxes we used at small-group time.

Pete: Yeah, they're even bigger than the blocks. Ha! I'm going to have an even bigger monster house now!

❖

Adult: How about you, Maria, what's your plan?

Maria: Paint at the easel. Make a rainbow.

Adult: Paint a rainbow at the easel.

Maria: But there's no room!

Adult: There are already some kids using the easel.

Maria: Well, but I want a big paper.

Adult: Yes.

Maria: And room for all the colors.

Adult: You need room for all the colors and a big piece of paper.

Maria: I could put it on the table.

Adult: Yes, you could. There's no one using the table.

Talk about details. Talking about details gives a child the opportunity to put a fairly extensive mental picture into words and to think through and describe some of the steps needed to accomplish the task he or she has in mind:

Adult: What will you do today, Jeff?

Jeff: Make an exercise machine.

Adult: Oh, an exercise machine. That sounds like a hard thing to do.

Jeff: Well, I'm going to use the big giant Tinkertoys and make some of those lifter things.

Adult: A lifter thing like a bar with weights on the ends?

Jeff: Yeah, I'll get a long Tinkertoy for the lifter and then put the round wheel things on for the weights.

Adult: So your exercise machine will have a lifter with weights.

Jeff: I'll make a part for your feet where you put them under and then lift them like this. *(He lies on the floor and shows where the bar goes over his feet.)*

Adult: I see.

Jeff: I'll have to make a holder for it, maybe with blocks…some on one end and some on the other.

Talk about sequence. Sequence conversations allow children to organize multiple intentions. Such children generally follow these "maps across time" quite rigorously once they have described them in their own words and set themselves the challenge, as Mira does after she explains her plan to an adult:

Adult: Well, Mira, what's your plan?

Mira: Play in all the areas.

Adult: All the areas. That's a lot of places. What will you do first?

Mira: Go to the art area. Make a card for my mom.

Adult: Ah, make a card.

Mira: A happy birthday card because it's her birthday. It's going to have flowers.

Adult: First you're making a birthday card with flowers for your mom.

Mira: Then put it in my cubby and read a book.

Adult: Make a card, put it in your cubby, read a book.

Mira: Then I think…the block area. Yeah, make a house in the block area and then go to the house area for some stuff for soup.

Adult: I don't know if I can remember all that.

Mira: Write it!

Adult: You tell. I'll write.

Mira: First, card for my mom, put it in my cubby, then read, then make a house and soup. *(Adult writes down Mira's words.)*

Adult: You're going to all do those things, Mira!

Remind children about related prior work. Reminders help children build on their previous play and begin to see that the plans they make from day to day can be related. In this dialogue, the adult adds a few reminders to help Tonio build on his plan:

Adult: Hi, Tonio. What do you think you'll be doing today?

Tonio: Being a policeman.

Adult: You made some policeman things yesterday.

Tonio: Yep. I made me a police badge. I have to get some tape to hold it on my jacket. And handcuffs too.

Adult: I remember you tied two bracelets together with yarn for handcuffs.

Tonio: Now I need a belt because when you're carrying the handcuffs you put them over your belt.

Adult: Today you need a belt?

Tonio: There's that one in the house area. And I need a map that says where to go. You know, one of those folding ones.

Adult: We have some maps in the book area.

Tonio: Okay! And I'm going to make a police car with the steering wheel and blocks and put all my stuff in it.

Encourage playmates to plan together

When children play together, it often makes sense for them to plan together. This gives them a real-life setting for teamwork and cooperative problem solving as shown in this exchange between Linda and her teacher:

Adult: What will it be for you today, Linda?

Linda: Play with Jan and Rita.

Adult: Play with Jan and Rita.

Linda: Play with the dress-ups like we did the other day.

Adult: Maybe you and Jan and Rita can make a plan together.

Linda: We'll tell you!

Value children's plans

Adult interest and responsiveness support children's development. While children are highly self-motivated, they are more likely to express and carry out their intentions when adults value their efforts to do so. Use the following strategies to show the value you place on children's plans.

Encourage rather than praise children's ideas. Adults can more appropriately communicate the value they place on children's intended actions through interest and specific encouragement rather than praise. HighScope field consultant Mark Tompkins (1996) explains:

> Praise, well-intentioned as it might be, has been shown through research and practice to invite comparison and competition and to increase the child's dependence on adults. Too much praise can make children anxious about their abilities, reluctant to take risks and try new things, and unsure of how to evaluate their own efforts. (p. 16)

During a planning dialogue, an adult works to give a child control by asking an opening question, waiting patiently for a response, and then reflecting the child's ideas in her comments.

Adults are attentive to children's desire to get going on their plan. This child knows that she is going to take apart the phones in the woodworking area and is eager to get going there as soon as she tells her teacher.

Adult *encouragement,* however, puts children in control and makes them the evaluators of their own work. (For more on the use of encouragement instead of praise when interacting with children, see chapter 2.)

At planning time, adults encourage children's ideas by attending to them and by commenting specifically on some aspect of a particular plan. Here are some examples:

Barry: I wish my cousin's dog didn't run into that dangerous street. *(Pause.)* Well, maybe I'll make a house with a big fence around it. Yeah, that's what I'll do.

Adult: Building a fence will keep a dog safe. So that's your plan, Barry, to make your house with a big fence around it?

❖

Adult: Ah, make a card.

Mira: A happy birthday card because it's my mom's birthday. It's going to have flowers.

Adult: A card with flowers you draw is a way to tell your mom happy birthday.

❖

Adult: Sometimes people make a house out of other things.

Pete: Maybe I could use those boxes we had yesterday.

Adult: Yes, the boxes we used at small-group time are big and sturdy.

Pete: They're even bigger than the blocks!

❖

Linda: Play with the dress-ups like we did the other day.

Adult: Linda, you made some very colorful hats with the scarves and feathers.

Linda: Maybe we'll use some ribbons this time too.

Write down children's plans. Writing down a child's plan is another way adults show they value children's planning. This act says to the child, "Your plan is so important that I'm going to save it by writing it down." Some adults write down what each child says, word for word, while others take notes. Whatever the method, children see adults writing and know that adults value their ideas and intentions. By writing down children's plans, adults also encourage children interested in writing to write their own versions of their plans.

Even as adults value children's plans, they may sometimes wonder if they need to more actively "guide" them to ensure that children experience the full range of options the program has to offer. Common concerns are what to do if all the children choose to play in the same area or with the same materials and how to support children who seem to make the same plan every day, play with the same materials, or show no interest in trying new materials. These concerns can generally be addressed, respectively, by arranging for sufficient space within and between areas in the classroom, introducing new materials at small-group time (which the child can then choose to use — or not use — at planning time), and noticing and supporting even small variations in how children carry out their plans from day to day. All these strategies respect children's individual plans and allow them to be in charge of their learning experiences. (For further details on how to address these questions, see "Common Adult Concerns About Planning Time" on p. 272.)

Note the connection between children's plans and actions

Planning time ends for children when they have reviewed their plans with an adult and leave the planning group to get started. At this point, adults note the connection between the child's actions and what he or she has just planned. Does Katie read *Mr. Gumpy's Motor Car*? Does Ike get started with the play dough? Does Pattie get help from Donna starting up the crown-making program? Briefly observing each child as he or she leaves the planning group gives adults a clue about the child's understanding of the planning process and who might need some help getting started at the beginning of work time.

Adults anticipate changes in children's planning over time

The dynamics of planning time change as children and adults get to know one another, become familiar with the interest areas, and become increasingly confident in their abilities to make and support choices and plans. From a quiet, low-key beginning, planning time grows into an exciting time when children talk with assurance about their ideas and ways of carrying them out.

Ruth Strubank, former head teacher at the HighScope Demonstration Preschool, contributed the following account of how planning changes over time:

Beginning the Planning Process

In the beginning, it is very important not to make planning time difficult for children or adults. For many children, the concept of making choices is new. Therefore, we (my team member Ann and I) focused on helping children become familiar with materials and the interest areas where they were located. The children needed to know what materials were available before they could tell us what they planned to do with them. With this in mind, these are some of the ways we initiated planning with children:

- *On the first day, we involved new planners with experienced planners by asking each experienced child to take a new child to an interest area to look at what was available. Our subsequent planning conversations with new children were quite informal and occurred after the children had started to play. Generally, we said something like "Max, I see you've decided to play with the trucks in the block area." New planners simply told us what they were going to play with and where they were going to play.*

Common Adult Concerns About Planning Time

What if all the children plan to play in the block area?

Adults new to the planning process worry that if they allow children to decide for themselves what to do during work time, the children will all choose the most popular area and chaos will ensue. First, be assured that, when given a choice, most children will follow their own interests. When the interest areas are well stocked, children plan to work with a variety of materials, not just with those in one area. If, for some reason, a number of children plan to play in the block area and it does become crowded, they have the opportunity to solve a real problem. Among themselves or with adult support, if needed, they will figure out ways to share space and materials or move some of their block play to a less crowded spot. Adults can alleviate their fears of overcrowding by having faith in the breadth of children's interests and their ability to solve their own problems.

Adults can also make sure that all the interest areas are arranged and equipped so that children will want to do things in every area. If the block area is full of interesting materials but the house area consists of one table and one doll, most children will choose the block area over the house area. To avoid overcrowding in one area, make all the interest areas irresistible!

One strategy we do not advocate is setting limits on the number of children who can play in an area at one time. This "administrative" approach to potential overcrowding deprives children of opportunities to solve real space and material problems, and it allows adults to ignore play space arrangement issues. Furthermore, limiting access to interest areas undermines the child planning process.

What if some children never make a plan to work with certain materials?

When you give children choices, some children will want to try everything, and eventually they will, while other children will prefer to stay with a favorite material or activity for extended periods of time. Ricky, for example, may build with blocks, boxes, Tinkertoys, Legos, and sand but will never plan to paint, draw, cut, or glue. While we want children to work with a variety of materials, including art materials, planning time is not the time to force choices on children or manipulate their choices to fit our expectations. For example, we do not want to say to Ricky, "Ricky, today you have to make a plan to paint or glue before you can build with blocks." Giving children planning choices means respecting their ideas and interests. Nevertheless, we can make sure that Ricky works with art materials by using them at small-group time and providing them at outside time. Using art materials at other times of the day gives Ricky the chance to see their potential for his work-time projects, and gradually he will incorporate them into his plans. He may begin, for example, by using paper, tape, and crayons to make road signs.

What if a child makes the same plan every day?

Noting the connection between plans and actions is important. While children may say the same thing over a period of time at planning time, careful observation generally reveals that, in fact, children vary and build on what they do from day to day. For a number of days, Margo, for example, planned to be a doggie with Donna. While they did play doggie each day, their role play expanded to include making dog dishes with dog food, reading stories before dog naps, making dog jewelry and dog toys, making dog houses from large boxes, and so forth. Although her plans remained rather brief, at recall time Margo talked about the new things she had done each day.

For other children, play variations are less dramatic. Michael, for example, often planned to play in the sand and water area. Once there, however, he used a variety of containers and scoopers for filling and emptying and imitated other children who also played there. Some days he concentrated on molding; on other days, Michael worked to keep the water in his sand holes. One day, he brought the small plastic animals over for a swim and a "jungle farm." While children may say the same thing at planning time, it is up to adults to look for, appreciate, and acknowledge the variety in their actual play.

Even though the "beauty salon" is very popular, these children have figured out how to share materials, space, and the customer!

- *On the second day of planning, we all sat down in a circle together. Ann and I had gathered things from all the interest areas and put them in the middle of the circle. As children handled and talked about the materials, they got ideas about what they would like to do. Some children shared their ideas with Ann or me at this point, while others simply went to the areas to get started. We talked with these children as soon as we could get to them. Since most children didn't know the word* plan, *we asked, "What would you like to do today?" or "You're holding a paintbrush. There are paint and paper in the art area if you'd like to paint today." We also referred new planners to experienced planners for help in getting started. The experienced children felt good about knowing where things were and how to use them, and we relied on their help.*

- *By the end of the first week of planning, we divided the children into two planning groups, one with me and one with Ann. We put their [letter link] signs around the two planning tables to help them find the planning group they belonged to. In these small groups we played a variety of visibility games — a train to the interest areas, walking tours of the interest areas, displays of new and familiar materials from each area. Planning conversations with each child were simple and brief.*

One key to introducing planning time is finding a balance between visibility games and planning conversations. On one hand, we often get so carried away with making a train, or playing with materials from the interest areas, that we lose sight of planning conversations. On the other hand, planning conversations in the absence of materials and knowledge of what is available make little sense. We need to take our cues from the children, doing things that help them become aware of materials and choices, and conversing with children in a way that is supportive rather than burdensome.

When children are new to planning, they tend to plan fairly rapidly. Children often have little to say until they become familiar with the interest areas, the materials, and the other children. They will often simply indicate one thing they want to use, one person they want to play with, or one place where they want to work. Many children make similar plans at first because they like the comfort of repetition and familiar things. Their experience with materials is limited, and they need additional opportunities to use the materials in different ways.

Planning After Two Months

By now, planning time is part of the routine children anticipate and expect. Children are ready for more planning games and longer planning conversations. They often arrive at planning time with a plan in mind; make plans for more than

Visibility games and props (such as "fishing" for which area you are going to work in) can make planning less routine and more exciting; however, it is important to remember that the focus is on the planning conversations rather than the props.

one activity; describe in some detail what they are going to do; and as a group, make a greater variety of plans.

Planning After Five or Six Months

By this time, children often describe what, how, where, and with whom they will work and are apt to make several connected plans. Christopher, for example, planned to make a screwdriver using the pegs in the toy area and then to get dressed up and use the screwdriver to repair the house area's refrigerator and stove. He did all this, and went on to repair the boat Will had made in the block area.

Because children now feel more competent about making decisions and have had more experience using materials in several different ways, they are making a wider variety of plans. Planning time also lasts longer because children are more involved with their ideas at this stage and have more details to share, and sometimes more than one plan to consider. They are also more aware of one another and may engage in cooperative or team planning. With five or six months of planning experience, children can plan in pairs rather successfully and enjoy adding to each other's ideas.

How Adults Support Children's Planning: A Summary

Adults plan with children in an intimate setting.
- Plan in a place where intimate conversations can occur.
- Plan in a stable pair or group.
- Plan where people and materials are visible.

Adults provide materials and experiences to maintain children's interest at planning time.
- Provide special games and experiences: visibility games, group games, props and partnerships, representations.
- Allow children to take charge.

Adults converse with individual children about their plans.
- Elicit children's plans by asking "what" questions.
- Watch and listen attentively to children's responses.
- Converse in a turn-taking manner with nonverbal and vague planners.
  - Interpret gestures and actions.
  - Ask an initial, open-ended question.
  - Narrate what you see and comment on what the child says.
  - Offer alternatives when the child does not respond.
- Converse with routine and elaborate planners.
  - Converse about space and materials.
  - Talk about details.
  - Talk about sequence.
  - Remind children about related prior work.
- Encourage playmates to plan together.
- Value children's plans.
  - Encourage rather than praise children's ideas.
  - Write down children's plans.
- Note the connection between children's plans and actions.

Adults anticipate changes in children's planning over time.
- Recognize that planning is a child-adult partnership.
- Recognize that planning is just a beginning.

Recognize that planning is a child-adult partnership

Child-adult cooperation is the key to successful planning experiences. The child supplies the intentions and ideas for carrying them out; the adult encourages the child to think about and discuss his or her plans. In their study of early education programs, Rheta DeVries and Lawrence Kohlberg (1987) make this observation about the importance Piaget placed on child-adult cooperation: "Piaget emphasized that ego development necessitates liberation from the thought and will of others. Lack of this liberation results in the inability to cooperate. How does this liberation come about? For Piaget, it is through the child's experience of being respected by the adult who offers to cooperate with the child. Learning to understand others begins as [adults] show that they understand the child's inner feelings and ideas" (p. 35).

Recognize that planning is just a beginning

The whole point of making a plan is to carry it out — turning intentions into actions. Now that we have looked closely at what it means to plan, we are ready to move on to **work time,** the "do" part of the HighScope plan-do-review process.

Understanding Work Time

Work time is the time of day during which children carry out their intentions, play, and solve problems. In this section, we explain why work time is such an important part of the HighScope daily routine, where children play during this time, what children do during work time, and how adults support them effectively. The following re-creation of several minutes of an actual work time in one HighScope preschool program illustrates the dynamics of this part of the plan-do-review process.

It is work time. Donnette is "reading" a story to Ruth, an adult. Kathryn is folding a cardboard roof for her birdhouse. Nearby, Colin searches for just the right paper for creating baby wasps, while Dom "writes" out tickets for a show Linda and Kerry are staging in the block area. Will and Max have converted the rocking boat into a "net fishing" boat, and they are talking with Ann, an adult, about what they might use for their net. "It's got to have holes," Will says, "but not too big holes or the fish will get out."

Joseph adds more blocks to his house. "No fire, yet," he tells Chris D. and Athi. "It's not ready." Athi and Chris D. have propped the steering wheel between three cushions for their fire truck. Since Joseph's house isn't ready for a fire, they consult a roadmap for other fires. Over in the sand, Ali pauses to watch Chris W. fill cardboard tubes.

"Hey! Watch this, Caroline!" Caroline turns from her computer screen to Sarah's and laughs with Sarah as she makes a balloon come out of a drawer pictured on the screen. Hearing their laughter, David and Chris M. look up from arranging their small blocks. In doing so, David glances at a set of tumbling gnomes, decides to use them in his play, and then gathers up some pipe cleaners and a kaleidoscope to complete his selections.

What is work time and why is it important?

At work time children carry out a *purposeful sequence of actions* they have thought about and described during planning time, while also following through on new ideas and plans that arise as they play. As they work independently and with other children and adults, children play with purpose and concentration, solve problems they encounter, and engage in the HighScope KDIs.

Children carry out their intentions

Work time in the HighScope Curriculum is the "doing" part of the plan-do-review process. Children transform their initial plans into concrete

At work time, children carry out their plans ("We are going to play mommy!"), play, and solve problems ("What do we do if the baby is sick?"). Here the mommies are taking care of their sick baby. They are using a real stethoscope on her chest and wrapping her in paper to "keep her warm."

actions, discover new ideas, make choices, select materials, and finish what they have started. The most obvious reason for work time is to provide children with the immediate opportunity to put into action the ideas they have indicated at planning time. Making plans is just the beginning; at work time, children select materials, find a place to start, and get started, critical steps that lead children to view themselves as *doers*.

Children play with purpose

While work time is *purposeful*, it is also *playful*. Dewey (1933) recognized the value of playfulness in the education process: "To be playful and serious at the same time is possible, and it defines the ideal mental condition" (p. 286). Similarly, educator Michael Ellis (1988) discussed the significance of play as a medium for learning and development:

The propensity to play is a biological system for promoting rapid adaptation to threats to survival that cannot be predicted....Playfulness is a critically important characteristic of humans....Play has brought us to where we are now both as a species and as individuals and will be the basis for our future adaptation to the unpredictable future. (pp. 24–25)

With the emphasis on academic preparation in the last two decades, the benefits of play in the early years have been overshadowed. Recently, however, prominent organizations such as the American Academy of Pediatrics (2006) and the National Research Council and the Institute of Medicine (2000) have emphasized the vital role of play in children's social and emotional development. The eager learning that occurs during purposeful play in turn provides a foundation for children's explorations and discoveries in every content area.

It is clear that children discover and make sense of their world through playful pursuits. HighScope's work time promotes children's innate desire and need to explore, experiment, invent, construct, and pretend — in short, *to play*. Through the HighScope planning process, children give conscious direction to their play. When children carry out their plans at work time, their activities have both the concentration and seriousness of work and the enjoyment and spontaneous creativity of play.

Children participate in a social setting

The social context of work time becomes evident as we observe children working in self-selected pairs and groups. Even children working alone are generally aware of others. Because of its social nature, work time may be noisy, even boisterous, at times. As children carry out their plans and comment on the pursuits of their peers, there is a constant, comfortable hum of conversation, laughter, and noise brought about by children's industrious use of materials.

Children solve problems

Children's work-time pursuits are self-generated, influenced by new ideas, and likely to lead to unforeseen events and problems — the baby doll is too big for the bed, the paint drips, the sand runs out through the holes in the cup, the blocks topple. Further, what children *think* is going to happen often does not — the marker will not mark on foil; the roof board that fits over one part of the house does not fit over another; Betty wants to be the doctor, not the mommy, in a pretend-play scenario. Encountering and dealing with such unexpected difficulties can lead children to a new and more complete understanding of physical and social realities.

Children construct knowledge as they engage with content (reflected in the KDIs)

The HighScope KDIs for early learning fall under eight major categories (also called content areas), which include Approaches to Learning; Social and Emotional Development; Physical Development and Health; Language, Literacy, and Communication; Mathematics; Creative Arts; Science and Technology; and Social Studies. The KDIs are described fully in the companion books that accompany this manual (Epstein, 2012a–h), but what is important to note here is that they generally occur as a natural part of children's self-initiated activities at work time. The KDIs reflect what children are learning about themselves and the people, materials, ideas, and events that make up their world:

- "I think I need the really strong tape to make it stick." (KDI 5. Use of resources [Approaches to Learning content area])
- "He's crying because Ellie's got the truck, and he wants it for his garage." (KDI 10. Empathy [Social and Emotional Development content area])
- "I put together the puzzle with all the little pieces." (KDI 17. Fine-motor skills [Physical Development and Health content area])
- "I think that fox is going to get Rosie. Turn the page!" (KDI 28. Book knowledge [Language, Literacy, and Communication content area])
- "Look where I climbed. I'm taller than even you!" (KDI 36. Measuring [Mathematics content area])
- "Let's pretend I'm the mom and you're the baby, and we're going to the farmers' market." (KDI 43. Pretend play [Creative Arts content area])
- "I think it's going to turn green when I add blue." (KDI 48. Predicting [Science and Technology content area])
- "I'm going to save the rest and put it back in the paper tray. Maybe someone will want to draw on it." (KDI 58. Ecology [Social Studies content area])

In other words, at work time preschool children construct their own knowledge. They initiate active, hands-on experiences that enable them to construct the kinds of knowledge and capacities represented by the HighScope KDIs.

During work time, children construct their own knowledge, represented by the HighScope KDIs. These three children are putting together a puzzle (KDI 17. Fine-motor skills and KDI 35. Spatial awareness).

> **Work Time — What and Why: A Summary**
>
> - Children carry out their intentions.
> - Children play with purpose.
> - Children participate in a social setting.
> - Children solve problems.
> - Children construct knowledge as they engage with curriculum content (as reflected in the KDIs).
> - Adults observe, learn from, and support children's play.

Adults observe, learn from, and support children's play

By observing, supporting, and entering children's play in the appropriate spirit, adults have the opportunity to discover the special interests of individual children: how they think and reason, whom they like to play with, how they use what they know to solve problems. *In fact, the insights adults gain about children at work time guide them in their interactions with children throughout the day.* By watching and listening to children, adults learn about their level of development and their understanding of the world. Adults are then able to scaffold learning — through supporting and gently extending children's play — in meaningful ways.

What children do at work time

To support children appropriately at work time, it is important for adults to understand what children *do* in relation to plans, social settings, types of play, and conversations.

Children initiate, work on, modify, complete, and change their plans

After children have indicated a choice or talked about a plan with an adult, they are very likely to get started immediately. The transition from gestures or words to action marks the beginning of work time for each child.

The way young children carry out their plans varies from child to child. Some children stay in one spot, while others move from place to place. For example, Kathryn works very intently at the art table making a wasp's nest, while Kevin sits on the floor putting together a puzzle. They work for a long time at their projects until each is satisfied with the results. Other children make plans that take them from area to area: "We made cookies, and now we're taking them around to everybody." Still other children start working in an interest area that does not have many children in it but move when they feel crowded. Darien, for example, lines up all the animals in the block area but moves to the animals in the toy area when several other builders enter the block area.

Some children begin to carry out their ideas — making a sailboat, for example — but then run into a problem, such as what to use for a sail. They may modify their original idea ("Let's pretend it's a *row* boat and use the long blocks for oars") or they may figure out how to make a sail. Depending on how long it takes them to come up with a satisfactory sail, children may or may not get to use it on their sailboat that day. They may decide to use the sail another day or be satisfied with the process of making the sail as an end in itself and never play "boat" with it.

Some children start working on their plans, stop to watch or join another child or group, and then return to what they were doing originally. For example, when Linda, Kerry, and Dom are ready to put on their show, they recruit an audience of children who obligingly interrupt their own plans to watch and applaud. Some then go back to what they were doing before the show, while others join in an extended pretend-play scenario with Linda, Kerry, and Dom.

Watching young children pursue their plans at work time, we can often see that while choices and plans shape children's initial actions, they can also lead children to actions and problems they did not anticipate. One experience leads to another, and children's play expands beyond their initial plans. Athi and Chris D., for example, planned to put out the fire in Joseph's house, but when Joseph's house was not ready for the fire, they returned to the "planning roadmap" to choose another place to put out a fire. Colin could not find any "wasp" paper that suited him, but he found some great "bee" paper, so he decided to make bees instead.

Children spend varying amounts of time executing their initial plans — from 2 minutes to 15 minutes, to all of work time, or to two or three consecutive work times. During one work-time session, some children may make and complete several related plans. Caroline, for example, made a crown, colored it, and then assumed the role of a princess. Other children may begin and complete their initial plan and then go on to something entirely different. Donnette, for example, read a book to Ruth, joined Ali in the sand, and then painted. Observed as a whole, a classroom full of children at work time can exhibit what looks like a lot of random movement. Observed individually, however, each child's actions generally fit an internal logic that is related to the child's particular purpose. So while children move from place to place and talk with one another other along the way, their actions more often than not serve some purpose they have set for themselves — to get a book to "read" to their "sick baby," to take play dough cookies to everybody, to get the right kind of paper or fabric for their sail, to gather up an audience, to put the birdhouse outside for the birds, to find something to stand on to tie the streamers up over their house.

Research and experience have shown that once children start their plans, they are very likely to complete them. In their study of the plan-do-review process, Berry and Sylva (1987) report that "31 of the 34 children who made plans completed them (91%). Furthermore, of these 31 children, 30 immediately started an activity related to their stated plan. Thus, children are purposeful and get down to work right away" (p. 20).

The insights adults gain about children at work time guide them in their interactions with children throughout the day.

Children play in a variety of social contexts

During work time, children are involved with others to varying degrees. They watch others, play by themselves, play next to others, and play in pairs and groups. These categories of social interaction are similar to those described decades ago in a classic study by Mildred Parten (1932). Parten reported that young children are involved in *onlooking, solitary play, parallel play, associative play,* and *cooperative play.* She observed that younger preschool children tend to watch and play by themselves, while older preschool children tend to play with others. The research of Kenneth Rubin, Greta Fein, and Brian Vandenberg (1983) supports Parten's finding that as preschool children grow older, solitary play tends to decrease while interactive play tends to increase. In the face of these important observations, adults must recognize that "solitary play does not necessarily mean a child lacks social ability" (Sponseller, 1982,

p. 218). It may simply mean that the older preschool child sometimes chooses to play alone and has the confidence to do so.

It is also interesting to note that playing in pairs seems to lead preschool children into more complex play. For example, early childhood researchers have noted that "4½- to 5½-year-old children achieve their highest levels of play when in the company of adults, whereas younger children (3½ to 4½ years old) have higher proportions of challenging play when playing in child-child pairs or in parallel to others. In the company of adults, children in both age groups are more likely to engage in complex play when the adult is actually interacting with them rather than merely being present" (Sylva, Roy, & Painter, 1980, pp. 71–73). Further, children playing alone rarely change their level of play, but each child in a pair is more likely to shift toward more complex play, while a child playing in a group is more likely to shift toward simpler play.

Children engage in different types of play

Based on their emerging capacities and interests, children play with people and materials in ways that involve a range of interactions, from simple exploratory manipulation to complex social and imaginative play. While all animal species play, humans play most of all. Our brains shape how we play, and play in turn shapes our brains (Brown & Vaughan, 2009). The types of play that preschoolers are typically involved in include *exploratory play, constructive play, pretend play,* and *games.*

Exploratory play. This relatively simple type of play involves manipulating materials, trying out new actions, and repeating them, all of which enable the child to practice what Smilansky and Shefatya (1990) describe as "physical capabilities and the chance to explore and experience the material environment" (p. 2).

At work time, children involved in exploratory play spend time manipulating materials to see what will happen — squishing and patting play dough, filling and emptying containers, cutting paper into little strips, standing all the blocks on end, running their hands through a tub of buttons, smearing glue all over a piece of paper. In these explorations, many KDIs can be seen, including KDIs 1. Initiative, 3. Engagement, 5. Use of resources, 8. Sense of competence, 17. Fine-motor skills, 33. Part-whole relationships, 35. Spatial awareness, 40. Art, 47. Experimenting, 48. Predicting, 49. Drawing conclusions, and 52. Tools and technology.

Constructive play. The development from exploratory play to constructive play is "a progression from manipulation of a form to formation; from sporadic handling of sand and blocks to building something which will remain even after the child has finished playing. The child expresses activity through these 'creations' and recognizes himself or herself as 'creator'" (Smilansky & Shefatya, 1990, p. 2).

Children involved in constructive play build towers, roads, bridges, and buildings; make birthday cakes out of clay and pegs; hollow out rivers in the sand; make up songs and dances; nail together boats and birdhouses; create structures and figures out of Tinkertoys, straws, pipe cleaners, and wire; cut out, staple, glue, and tape together kites, hats, masks, and collages; and draw and write pictures, designs, cards, and books. As they do these things, children exhibit a variety of KDIs, such as KDIs 4. Problem solving, 16. Gross-motor skills, 18. Body awareness, 28. Book knowledge, 29. Writing, 32. Counting, 36. Measuring, 37. Unit, 38. Patterns, 40. Art, 41. Music, 42. Movement, 51. Natural and physical world, 56. Geography, and 58. Ecology.

Pretend play. This type of play involves pretending and acting out "what if" situations, for example, "What if I were the mom and you were the baby?" Children imitate the actions and language of others, using objects as make-believe props and taking on a variety of roles. One child puts on a chef's hat and says to himself, "I'm making burgers." Another group of children play dentist. As the mommy and daddy drive their baby to the dentist, their car (made of blocks) has a flat

Children involved in constructive play use materials to create things, such as blocks to make an elaborate roadway for cars (and people).

tire. While mommy and daddy change the tire, the dentist drills and brushes the baby's teeth with dental equipment made from Tinkertoys. "Now sit real still and this won't hurt," the "dentist" advises.

Many KDIs are seen in children engaged in pretend play, including KDIs 6. Reflection, 7. Self-identity, 9. Emotions, 10. Empathy, 12. Building relationships, 13. Cooperative play, 15. Conflict resolution, 22. Speaking, 23. Vocabulary, 26. Reading, 53. Diversity, 54. Community roles, and 57. History.

Games. Preschoolers enjoy playing conventional games such as dominos, cards, board games, hide-and-seek, and catch. Generally, they play games cooperatively rather than competitively and with little concern for sticking closely to the rules. Their aim is not to win but to have a good time hiding and looking for people, spinning the spinner and moving the pieces around the board, or picking up and trading cards with one another. Preschoolers are also beginning to invent their own simple games, such as "jumping bears," where one child pushes a plastic counting bear off the big block into the box and then another child pushes another plastic bear off the block into the box. They take turns repeating this pattern until all the bears have "jumped." As children play these simple games, many KDIs occur, including KDIs 11. Community, 14. Moral development, 18. Body awareness, 21. Comprehension, 31. Number words and symbols, 37. Unit, 46. Classifying, 50. Communicating ideas, 55. Decision making, and 56. Geography.

When preschool children can freely choose their play activity at work time, they are most likely to be involved in constructive play; followed by exploratory and pretend play; and finally, by simple games whose rules they adjust or invent to suit themselves (Bergen, 1988a, 1988b).

Children carry on conversations

The characteristic elements of work time — intimate settings, pretend play, shared goals, a common focus, and sympathetic partners — encourage children to converse with peers and adults. When children converse among themselves at work time, they often talk in quiet, enclosed spaces, for example, under a blanket draped over two chairs that then becomes a tent or secret hiding place. Many conversations between children at work time occur when children are involved in pretend or role play, which by its very nature depends on dialogue and shared imagination.

What Children Do at Work Time: A Summary

- Children initiate, work on, modify, complete, and change their plans.
- Children play in a variety of social contexts.
- Children engage in different types of play.
- Children carry on conversations.

How Adults Support Children at Work Time

What adults do at work time is based on what children do, their understanding of these actions, and the questions these actions raise: "What is Christopher doing with the blocks? Does he need my support? What should I do?" Supporting children at work time is both an active and a reflective process. In addition to providing appropriate work spaces and materials and recording their observations of children for planning and assessment, adults use the following seven strategies to support active learning at work time:

- Scanning the interest areas to find out what children are doing
- Choosing children to observe, gaining children's perspectives, and forming on-the-spot interaction plans
- Offering children comfort and contact
- Participating in children's play
- Conversing with children
- Encouraging children's problem solving
- Bringing work time to an end

Adults scan the interest areas to find out what children are doing

Sometimes adults begin work time by joining a child who requests help in getting a plan started: "I want to make a dinosaur out of big boxes, but I need you to help me make some of that sticky paste stuff to hold the newspaper on" or "Come on, Ruth, I'm reading you a story!"

To identify children who do not make such clear requests, adults should periodically scan the interest areas and check the status of children's plans. They should also take note of the social interactions, types of play, or the KDIs in which children are involved. In effect, as they scan, adults are thinking, "I am going to interact with children in a supportive way. I need to decide whom to interact with and how. Scanning will

As she scans the interest areas during work time, Sarah (the teacher) realizes that Ethan is stuck. He is making a home for Valentine, the classroom guinea pig, with the big wooden blocks and newspaper. He's not sure what to do about the hole in the hollow block along the wall that Valentine could escape through. Sarah supports Ethan as he figures out how to rotate that block so the hole is facing upward. Valentine can now come into his new home and play.

help me find out what children are doing, what plans and play I might support, and who might be most open to support at this moment."

Look for the status of children's plans

As you scan the play space, look at each child and ask yourself these kinds of questions:

- Is Jimmy starting a plan?
- Does he have a plan well under way?
- Is he focused on what he is doing?
- Has he interrupted his work on his plan? If so, why? To watch or join someone else? Because he is stuck? To get something he needs?
- Is he completing a plan? Changing his plan?

Answers to such questions will help you decide which children need support. For example, you may notice that Jimmy has stopped working on his "space machine" because he has used up all the available shiny cardboard. He may be willing to consider alternative materials, if prompted.

Look for children's individual and social interactions

As you scan, ask these kinds of questions:

- Which children are watching others play?
- Which children are engaged in solitary play?
- Which children appear to be playing next to someone else without any particular association with them?
- Which children are playing in pairs? In groups?

The answers to these questions may lead you to a child such as Crystal, who seems to be hanging about the fringes of a group of children who are playing beauty parlor. Perhaps she could use your support to join the beauty parlor play.

Look for specific types of play

To identify specific types of play, scan the setting and ask yourself such questions as these:

- Who is exploring, manipulating, or practicing something?

Scanning the Interest Areas: What to Look for at Work Time

KDIs	Play types	Social contexts	Children's plan status
Approaches to Learning	Exploratory play	Onlooking	Starting a plan
Social and Emotional Development	Constructive play	Solitary play	Continuing a plan
Physical Development and Health	Pretend play	Parallel play	Interrupting a plan
	Games	Group play	Completing a plan
Language, Literacy, and Communication			Changing a plan
Mathematics			
Creative Arts			
Science and Technology			
Social Studies			

- Who is constructing or making something?
- Who is pretending, carrying out a role, or role playing with others?
- Who is playing a game of some sort?

These questions may lead you to a child like Sammy, who is filling sand containers. Perhaps if an adult plays next to Sammy, she or he will find out more about Sammy's play and thinking.

Look for the HighScope KDIs

Scanning for HighScope KDIs involves asking such questions as these:

- Is there anything going on right now that could be identified as a KDI?
- How are children using KDI 17. Fine-motor skills (or KDIs 32. Counting, 40. Art, 46. Classifying, or 55. Decision making, to name a few) as part of their play?
- What KDIs might be occurring as Brenda builds at the workbench?
- Might Leroy be feeling frustrated because he needs more pegs that match the ones he has been using?
- Might Cerise be looking for someone to share her conclusions with as she experiments with the soap bubbles?

The answers to these and similar questions about the KDIs might lead you to give Leroy an additional box of pegs so that he can continue his pegboard pattern or to make eye contact with Cerise to acknowledge that you would like to hear what she is doing with and concluding about the soap bubbles.

Adults choose children to observe, gain children's perspectives, and form on-the-spot interaction plans

Scanning helps you select children to observe. *Close observation* helps you understand children's perspectives and development, so you can decide on an *interaction plan* to scaffold their learning.

Choose children to observe

As you periodically scan the interest areas, particular children and play situations may draw your attention, such as a child hesitating at the beginning of his plan, a child who is stalled in her work, a child changing his plan, a child soliciting help, a child carrying out a novel or long-term plan, a child enjoying what she is doing, a child watching others for a lengthy period, a child talking to himself, a child repeating the same activity, a child hesitating near or trying to join ongoing play activity, a child exploring materials, a child making something complex, a child playing a game others can join, a child clearly having an experience that you recognize as a KDI, a quiet or withdrawn child, or an upset or frustrated child.

Observe to gain each child's perspective

Once you have selected a child with whom you might interact in a supportive manner, move closer to the child. Put yourself on the same physical level, for example, on the floor if the child is on the floor, on the climber if that is where the child is playing, or on your knees by the sand table. Positioning yourself at the child's level enables you to see what the child sees and establishes you as an available partner. Maintaining silence enables you to listen carefully and give your full attention to the child's actions and words. It also allows the child to be aware of your interest and support without being interrupted by your unsolicited questions, comments, and suggestions.

Form on-the-spot interaction plans

As you observe, focus your full attention on the child to find out more about the situation that first caught your attention — the child's plan, social interactions, play type, or particular KDI. Your interaction plan starts with what you already know about (1) the child you are observing; (2) what typically happens at work time; and (3) what is possible at work time, given the available play space, materials, and human support systems. An interaction plan includes a hoped-for goal or outcome (such as finding out what the child is doing and thinking; supporting the child's plan, play, or train of thought; or gently scaffolding the child's knowledge or skills) and possible steps for reaching it. Following are sample work-time interaction plans, as formulated throughout work time by one adult in the HighScope Demonstration Preschool. Although the sample interaction plans are in written form (for the sake of illustration), note that your actual interaction plans will be the ideas you formulate "on the spot" in your head based on your observations.

Brent seems hesitant to begin his plan to play with the Legos because the box of Legos isn't on the shelf where he thought it would be. I remember that yesterday Shasha put the Legos in the refrigerator to represent ice cubes. I'm going to suggest to Brent that he look there so that he can find and play with them as he planned.

Jimmy has been working very intently on his "space machine," but now he is hitting a juice can with a block, and he seems to be trying to get the metal bottom separated from the cardboard. If I say to him, "Jimmy, you're banging that can pretty hard," maybe he will tell me what he is trying to do and if and how it is related to his "space machine."

Crystal seems to be hanging about the edges of the beauty parlor play as if she would like to join in. She's holding a purse and some rollers, and she's watching the "beauty lady" and the lady in the chair getting her hair done. Maybe if I get a purse and some rollers I could say to her, "Hi. I'd sure like to get my hair fixed up too." Depending on her response, maybe we could go together to the beauty parlor so that she could become part of the play.

Sammy seems to be enjoying himself in the sand area. He started filling a baby bottle using his hand as a scoop and then a cup as a scoop; then he turned the baby bottle over and used it as a scoop. Now he is using a funnel as a scoop and noticing that the sand can run out both ends of the funnel into the bottle. Maybe if I get a container and funnel and use them in the same way, he will say something to me about his play.

❖

Brenda seems very intent on sawing pieces of wood. After she cut the first piece, she laid it on top of the length of wood she was cutting from as if to guide where she wanted to make the next cut. I'm going to watch for when she finishes sawing and then say something like "Brenda, you were cutting your wood pieces very carefully" to see if she might explain to me in her own words what she was doing.

We can summarize these five on-the-spot interaction plans in this way: Once adults have scanned the interest areas, observed a child to gain the child's perspective, and formed an on-the-spot plan of interaction, the next step is to join a child or play group and to use the interaction strategy that is appropriate by offering comfort and contact, playing with children, conversing with children, or encouraging children's problem solving. These strategies are discussed next.

Adults offer children comfort and contact

There are times when children need immediate adult reassurance and acknowledgment of their feelings or efforts. Here are some strategies to help you identify and work with such children so they can regain their composure.

Look for children in need of comfort and contact

Children will express their need for comfort and contact in a variety of ways. Barry, for example, was not able to talk about his plan until he talked about the death of his cousin's dog. Some children are more subdued than usual. When Billy's parents were getting divorced, he tended to work quietly by himself. He barely acknowledged other children, as if focusing all his attention on materials over which he had control could temporarily make up for his lack of control over his home life. Other children become less focused, finding it difficult to concentrate on one activity for long. After her baby sister was born, Laura began to move from one material to the next, giving up any sustained activity in favor of being with adults. Some children may pout and wait for an adult to notice their feelings, while others call out incessantly — "Look it!" "Come here!" — as if to reassure themselves that the adults in this setting are still present and responsive.

It is important to recognize and respond to all types of requests for comfort and contact, even if we are sometimes reluctant to do so for fear of "spoiling" children, "giving into" their bids for attention, or preventing their learning how to do something "on their own." Children are not being manipulative when they seek adult comfort and contact in various ways. In fact, by meeting children's emotional needs, you enable them to get past what is upsetting them and move on to purposeful, gratifying play.

As you scan the interest areas, you might identify children who need comfort and contact by observing those children who are expressing anxiety or discomfort through looks, actions, or words; watching others play or being by themselves; moving rapidly from one material to another; asking frequently for adult acknowledgment; or needing ongoing adult presence to start and continue plans.

Offer reassuring physical contact

Sitting next to Kristina, waiting quietly in the same spot for Kwame to return from saying good-bye to his mom, touching Chavon's hand or Misao's cheek, rocking Jodi — such reassuring physical contacts are sometimes the most important interactions an adult can have with a child. While it is important to respect children's growing need for independence and autonomy, it is equally important to be there when children need a hand to hold or a lap to curl

Nobody Paid Attention to Me When I Pouted!

From a distance, Michael, a preschooler, watches some children playing with blocks. He has an unhappy expression on his face. Seeing him, an adult remarks, "He's just pouting to get attention!"

While young children sometimes need comfort and contact, adults are often reluctant to give it for a variety of reasons. Here are some examples:

- "I don't like pouting. I wasn't allowed to pout when I was a child, so I'm going to ignore him when he pouts."

- "Her pouting is annoying. I know she wants me to feel sorry for her, but I'm not going to be manipulated by her needs. She needs to learn to overcome self-pity."

- "She's just being stubborn. She could talk if she wanted to. If she wants me to talk to her, she has to talk to me."

- "He could join in the block play if he really wanted to. He just wants me to help him, but I'm not going to because he has to learn to be independent."

- "I'm not her mom! Pulling a long face may work at home, but it won't work here. That's a habit she'll have to break if she wants to succeed here."

- "He can sulk all he wants as long as he's quiet and not causing trouble. I see no reason to interact with him at this time."

Many young children rely on nonverbal communication to convey their need for comfort and contact. Such children may not yet be able to verbalize their feelings or describe what is bothering them, but they can perceive whether an adult is willing to comfort them through their own ups and downs. As mature professionals committed to supporting children, it is up to us to be aware of our own prejudices and to set them aside so that we may provide children with the support they need to carry out their intentions.

The supportive touch of a friendly adult helps give this child confidence to join his classmate in building with the blocks.

up in. Experiencing a moment or several minutes of physical comfort seems to "refuel" some children, enabling them to reenter the more autonomous world of plans and play.

Some children will signal their need for your warmth and comfort by clinging to your leg, tugging at your arm or sleeve, hugging you, or climbing into your lap. Other children will not initiate physical contact so overtly but will ask for reassurance through their expressions and postures, responding positively when it is offered. And some children pull away from physical contact but respond well to an adult who is calm and nearby. Keep in mind that the type of contact that feels comfortable to adults and is well received by children varies from adult to adult, child to child, and situation to situation.

Offer simple acknowledgments

Sometimes children need adult acknowledgment of their efforts:

"Look it! Look it!" Vanessa calls out every few minutes. "I see, Vanessa," an adult responds each time with a smile, looking at Vanessa's block pile or line of animals or painting. Vanessa quickly returns to her play.

William stands quietly at Mrs. Elkin's side. She puts her arm around him; he smiles and returns to his building. A little while later he is back, she gives him a hug, and he returns to his tower. The next time he seeks her out, he says quietly, "Come here." He takes her hand and leads her to his tower. She kneels down next to him. He leans against her. "It's tall," William says. "Yes, it is," she agrees. He begins to build another tower next to the first. Mrs. Elkin watches for a while before joining a child at the workbench.

Adults participate in children's play

Participating in children's play is one way adults can demonstrate that they value and support children's interests and intentions. Sometimes adults feel uncomfortable about "playing," which is typically thought of as an activity for children. However, participating in children's play not only respects and supports them but also provides adults with a window into children's thinking. When children are playing or starting to play and are receptive to other players, adults can sometimes join them in a nondisruptive, respectful manner. They can do this by looking for natural play openings, joining children on *their* physical level, engaging in parallel play with children, playing as a partner, referring one child to another, and suggesting new ideas within children's ongoing play activities.

Look for natural play openings

In general, it is easier for adults to join some types of play than others. For example, an adult can usually join children's exploratory play without disrupting it simply by exploring the same materials in a similar manner. Moreover, pretend play, by its very nature, depends on others joining in and taking on supportive roles. And children's games also require more than one player. *Generally, it is more natural and less disruptive to join children's exploratory play, pretend play, or games, rather than their constructive play.* (Constructive play may include building a Tinkertoy house, painting,

What? Me Play! You've Got to Be Kidding

Playing with children does not come easily for some adults. Wood, McMahon, and Cranstoun (1980) report that reluctant adults come up with all kinds of reasons to avoid playing with children:

- Play is for children, not adults.
- Adults upset the delicate balance of children's play.
- It is wrong for adults to intrude. They spoil things.
- Playing with children is too repetitive and boring.
- Adult ideas destroy children's creativity.
- It is more important for children to play with other children than with adults.
- It is too embarrassing. What if someone sees me!
- I would lose my authority with children if I did what they wanted me to do.

It is important for adults who are uncomfortable playing with children to be aware of their feelings and weigh them against the benefits of playing respectfully and joyfully with children. When adults play with children, the children experience adults as supporters and resources, people who want them to succeed.

or making a birthday card. In these types of activities, children focus so much energy on the task at hand that they have little left for adults.)

In scanning the interest areas for children whose play you might join, look for children creating and experiencing collaborative play; pretending and role playing; moving to music; looking to join others' play; engaging in parallel play; exploring, manipulating, or repeating actions; playing games; having difficulty starting a plan; or having their plan interrupted.

Join children's play on the child's level

Joining children's play successfully depends on seeing it from the child's perspective and allowing the child to retain control over the play situation. Here are some examples:

A child is sitting on the floor, beating a tambourine and singing "Hopa, hopa, hopa." You sit on the floor near her, hold a tambourine, and wait for her signal to play your tambourine and sing "Hopa, hopa, hopa." When she gives you the go-ahead, you play and sing softly enough so that you can hear her voice and tambourine above your own. When she signals you to stop, you stop.

"Here's some hay for you, horse," says a child walking a rubber horse to a green bead of "hay" he has put in a "stall" built of cardboard tubes and Lincoln Logs. Sitting near the child, you make your rubber horse "walk" near the stall and then quietly whinny "Neigh, neigh."

Sometimes children invite adults to join their play, and sometimes adults take the initiative: "I am going to join the beauty parlor play to see if I can help Crystal participate." The success of the adults' initiatives, however, depends on their responsiveness to the specific play situation: "Since Crystal is holding a purse and some rollers, I'll take my cue from her. I'll get a purse and rollers and pretend I want to go to the beauty parlor too." Interestingly, the more adults take the initiative for joining children's play in a respectful manner, the more children are apt to invite them in. Researchers report that when children see adults assume the role of players, they learn that adults are willing to play: "The children learn that the adult is approachable and not a remote authority figure, and they may come to trust her more" (Wood et al., 1980, pp. 157–158).

Play in parallel with children

This strategy can be effective with children who are involved in exploratory play; that is, using materials for their own sake without really trying to make something or pretend with them. These children often play by themselves but are receptive to the supportive presence of others. In fact, having an adult play alongside them may lead to longer and more complex interactions with the materials they are using (Kindler, 1995).

In parallel play, adults play near the child using the same materials the child is using in the same or a very similar manner:

Child: *(Fills a bucket with sand, empties it out, fills it up again, and empties it into a bowl.)*

Adult: *(Fills a margarine tub with sand, empties it, fills it again, and empties it into a saucepan.)*

The adult may introduce variations in the play; for example, she may fill a sieve or funnel with sand. It is important for the adult to realize, however, that the child may not notice these variations. And, furthermore, if the child does notice them, he or she may or may not incorporate them into the play.

Conversation in parallel play may be minimal, as shown here:

Child: I need that *(indicating the saucepan the adult is using)*.

Adult: *(Hands the saucepan to the child.)*

On the other hand, because exploratory play is relatively undemanding, the presence of an adult may inspire child-initiated chats about personally meaningful topics, not necessarily related to the materials at hand, as in this example:

This adult joins a child on the floor so she can see the road and tunnel for the cars from the child's point of view.

Child: My mommy's picking me up.

Adult: Yes, she is.

Child: Not my daddy like the other days.

Adult: Usually your daddy comes, but not today.

Child: He's at his work.

Adult: He's at his work so your mommy's coming.

Child: Yep! We're going someplace too, and I know where!

Adult: You're going someplace with your mom.

Child: Yeah, my Grammy's!

Play as a partner with children

This strategy can work well with children involved in pretend play and games, play that by nature depends on more than one person. The key is *partnership*: adults functioning as equals and followers rather than leading or taking over the play. As partners, adults enter into the spirit of the play, adjust their speech and actions to the pace and theme of the play, accept or assume a play-related role, follow rules established by the children, and take direction from children. Here are two brief examples:

(Two boys stand in front of the mirror putting on and taking off their sunglasses.)

First child: Cool.

Second child: Bad! Real bad.

Adult: *(Puts on a pair of sunglasses.)*

First child: *(To adult)* Hey, you bad! *(Both children giggle.)* Look at you in the mirror! *(Adult moves in front of the mirror.)*

Second child: *(To adult)* Hey, man, want to see our stuff?

Adult: Okay, man, sure.

Second child: Come on. *(Takes adult by hand.)* Sit here. We'll get the stuff. *(Adult sits on the pillow as indicated.)*

First child: Close your eyes. Don't open till we tell you.

Adult: *(Closes eyes.)* I'm scared!

First child: Don't worry. We'll be right back!

(The children return with a grocery bag full of picture books and small, multicolored blocks.)

(Two children are playing with hand puppets.)

First child: *(Lowers puppet behind shelf, then raises puppet up.)* Boo!

Second child: *(Repeats same actions with her puppet.)* Boo!

First child: *(Repeats actions.)* Goo!

Second child: *(Repeats actions.)* Woo!

Adult: *(Does the same thing with her puppet.)* Moo!

Second child: *(Repeats actions.)* Achoo!

First child: *(Repeats actions.)* Boo hoo!

Adult: *(Repeats actions.)* Garoo!

First child: *(Repeats actions.)* Kangaroo! Hey, I know. Let's each have two puppets!

Sometimes adults feel uncomfortable with — or even disapprove of — the types of pretend play that children engage in. A typical example is superhero play when children act out or imitate the aggressive actions of characters they learn about through the media. (See "Ban It, Ignore It, or Join It? What to Do About Superhero Play" on pp. 294–295.) However, by using a variety of active learning strategies, such as providing related materials, joining as a play partner, offering gentle extensions, and planning related experiences, such as field trips, any play theme that is generated from the children's own interests can become the basis for meaningful interactions and learning.

Refer one player to another

In the role of partner or follower in play rather than boss or leader, the adult should, whenever possible, refer one child to another for play support and expansion. This enables children to recognize each other's strengths, regard each other as valuable resources, use their abilities for the benefit of others, and play cooperatively as seen in this dialogue:

Tim: *(To adult)* How do you get these all mixed up? *(Tries to shuffle a deck of go fish cards.)*

Adult: Joe had a good way to do it.

Joe: *(Takes a few cards.)* See. First, you have to put them all like this. *(He stacks the cards carefully.)*

Suggest new ideas within ongoing play situations

Adults working with young children often express a desire to extend children's play. In a sense, playing respectfully in parallel and as partners with children can and often does extend the length and even the scope of some play episodes. Beyond this, however, adults may also wish to challenge, in a gentle way, young children's thinking and reasoning to expand the breadth of their play, and, consequently, their understanding. When adults attempt this type of play extension, it is important that they offer new ideas within the context of the ongoing play. Based on her classic long-term study of dramatic and sociodramatic play, Smilansky (1971) suggested some effective strategies for doing this, followed by examples that demonstrate the strategies:

Offer suggestions within the play theme.

Adult: I brought my baby's thermometer. *(Hands the "doctor" a wooden Tinkertoy.)*

Address the role person rather than the child.

Adult: Doctor, can you check my neighbor's arm? She hurt it at the fire. *(Rather than saying, "Sandy, let Gina play with you.")*

Respect the child's reaction to your idea.

Adult: Doctor, her temperature is going up. She's warm.

Child: I'll check her after lunch. Here. *(Hands her a magazine.)* Look at this till I get back.

Adult: Thanks.

Child: Want me to bring her some milk and fries?

Adult: Yes, please, doctor.

Adults converse with children

There are moments when conversation is a natural outgrowth of children's work or play. Adults look for these opportunities to converse with children as partners, following their leads and asking questions sparingly so that children retain control of the dialogue. The more children converse, the more they put into words their own thoughts and experiences and the more involved they are in interpreting and understanding their world.

Look for natural opportunities for conversation

The relative simplicity of exploratory play sometimes inspires young children to talk either about what they are doing or about an apparently unrelated topic. Pretend play relies heavily on role-related conversation, and games often involve verbal negotiations over rules and process. There are times during constructive play when children pause to take a look at what they have done so far

---

Sharing Conversational Control

Based on their observations of adults and children, Wood et al. (1980, p. 73) devised a framework for identifying who controls a conversation. In conversational moves 1–3 below, the speaker retains control of the conversation. In moves 4–5, the speaker offers control to the listener.

Who controls the conversation?

Speaker retains control
1. Enforced repetition ("Say 'Night, night' to baby.")
2. Closed question ("Is your baby crying?")
3. Open question ("Where are you taking your baby?")

Speaker passes control to listener
4. Contribution ("I used to take my baby to the park.")
5. Acknowledgment ("I see.")

Why it matters

As they observed, taped, and analyzed recordings of adult-child conversations, the researchers came to these conclusions:

- "The adult with the least controlling style on our particular measure asked relatively few questions and made a high proportion of contributions."

- "The adult who exercised least control over children was much more likely to be questioned and to hear unsolicited ideas from children, and was far more likely to have her questions not simply answered but elaborated upon."

- "Generally speaking, all children followed contributions and phatics [acknowledgments] with contributions of their own. In other words, each child responded conversationally to non-controlling adult moves, so adult questions are not the only device for keeping a child involved in dialogue."

- "By leaving the child more turns that are not directly controlled, the adult provides an opportunity for the child to put his own ideas into words and, on occasion at least, a chance to ask the adult questions."

- "By leaving the child time to think and periodically taking the pressure off to reveal something of her own thoughts, she is most likely to see the child at his or her linguistically most active." (pp. 79–81)

Ban It, Ignore It, or Join It? What to Do About Superhero Play

Reflecting on the impact of her early training, Early Childhood Director Beth Marshall describes how using the philosophy and practices of the HighScope Curriculum helped turn children's superhero play into a gratifying learning opportunity for both the children and the adult:

Like many preschool teachers, I can trace my career by naming the superhero characters I've seen children transform themselves into, beginning with the Incredible Hulk and memories of children with glazed expressions and puffed-up chests stomping around the playground. New characters would take the Hulk's place, but children's interest in power-oriented play persisted.

Over the years, I have tried several methods for dealing with this challenging play. First, I tried banning it, telling children they couldn't play that way at school. However, this approach wasn't very satisfying, for me or for the children. It felt like I'd turned into a classroom policeman, constantly on the lookout for superhero characters. Rather than comply with my new rule, the children became more deceptive about their superhero pretending, quickly changing their roles and their props if I came near. Next, I tried just ignoring it, letting children pretend to be those characters if they chose but not doing much to support it either. Unfortunately, this didn't work either; I still wasn't comfortable with children's actions. As children ran through the classroom and high-kicked other children (we were into Ninja Turtles by now), I wondered what my next move should be.

Fortunately, around that time I started to attend a HighScope Training of Trainers course. I began the process of reexamining all my practices and beliefs, measuring them against the new concepts I was learning. Although my problems with superhero play didn't magically disappear, at least now I had an educational philosophy to help me make some decisions about what to try next. I found the following general strategies for supporting pretending to be particularly helpful for my classroom Power Rangers.

1. Observe children's play over time.

Document your observations to help evaluate children's superhero play. Watch for actions and details that seem to be important to the children. For example, Jennifer seems to enjoy running. Mark seems to love dressing up in a cape, boots, and long gloves. Next, observe how the play changes or develops over time, if at all. What variety occurs with characters, their actions, the story, or the materials? For example, I noticed that Jack and Raina planned each day to be Batman and Robin, and the resulting play mainly consisted of putting on scarves and darting back and forth across the room. Over time, this play stayed pretty much the same; in other words, it was *imitative* in nature. On the other hand, when Rachel pretended to be a Power Ranger, she made a "hiding spot" under the table and stocked it with pretend food. She added *representational* variation to her pretend play.

2. To encourage more complex play, add related materials.

Be flexible in how and where these materials are used. HighScope field consultant Betsy Evans (1996) recommends that teachers develop a list of the characteristics of superheroes that children find appealing and then list materials that could be added to the classroom that correspond to each characteristic:

- *Strength:* hammers, wood, heavy blocks, stumps
- *Speed:* ramps, balls, cars, trikes
- *Appearance changes:* scarves, headbands, sparkly or shiny clothes
- *Scary situations:* books, music, flashlights
- *Emergencies:* hospital or fire station materials, emergency rescue props

When I evaluated my own classroom in terms of Evans's list, I decided to add more materials for *appearance changes* and *scary situations*. I started by adding some long, brightly colored gloves, donated by a local bridal shop, and some colorful lengths of fabric that children often used as capes. When I saw children often incorporating hiding and finding into their play, I added flashlights that really worked to the house area. We also added a recording of the *Jurassic Park* soundtrack that had some eerie-sounding selections. Children often chose this scary music as a backdrop for their play. Other teachers have found that children use the materials they have provided (such as masks, paper towel rolls, and tin foil) to make their own superhero costumes and props as they begin to focus on the details of the characters. This tends to slow down the play, and children move more carefully. As a result, rougher play diminishes. In addition, the ensuing superhero play is more complex, lasts longer, and involves more conversation among the children.

3. Enter children's superhero play as a coplayer, just as you would with any other type of play.

This allows you to experience this play through the eyes of a child, rather than as an adult looking on. When I tried this with my superhero preschoolers, I found that their play was not as wild and violent as it looked when I observed from the outside. When coplaying with children, remember these three important guidelines: *Imitate the child's actions at first, take your cues from the child about how to play,* and finally, **make sure the child retains control of the play.** It was important for me to follow and respect what the children were doing. Once they were comfortable with me as a coplayer, I could try the next strategy.

4. Add to the complexity of superhero play by offering ideas for extensions.

If you find that children's superhero play is very imitative, you may want to try extending it. Staying within your role as a player, try *posing a problem to extend children's thinking*. When I was the "bad guy," I kept escaping from jail. James ("Batman") had to do some problem solving about how to keep me in there. He decided to make some paper handcuffs he called "bat cuffs." Now, in addition to pretending, he was cutting paper strips, taping them around my wrists, and figuring it out how to make the cuffs the right size (so I couldn't escape again). You can also *make a comment that extends children's ideas*. At one of the rare times I was allowed to pretend to be Batgirl, I yawned and said to my coplayers, "I'm rather sleepy." They jumped on the idea and told me it was nighttime and we all had to go to bed. Where do Batman, Robin, and Batgirl sleep? Why, in the Bat Cave, of course! By now we were making a bat cave out of large hollow blocks and stocking it with pillows and blankets and food. Once children had this new idea, their play spiraled in all kinds of directions.

When making suggestions for play extensions, remember to *respect children's responses to your ideas*. One time, when children were running down the hill outside, I ran with them for a while. When I asked where our bat cave was (thinking perhaps we might construct one outdoors), I was told, "Beth, we're just running and flying now." Remembering that children should retain the control of their play, I went right back to running and flying with them.

5. Add to the children's store of related real-life experiences by planning field trips and inviting visitors to the classroom.

Although there are no superheroes in real life, there are field trips or visitors that build on the interests children are expressing through this kind of play. Decide what seems to be most interesting to your children and look around your community for inspiration. If your children seem to be interested in the rescuing aspect of superhero play, invite an emergency medical technician to visit your classroom or go on a field trip to the fire station. If you think it's the changes in appearance that interest children most, arrange a visit to the local community theater and look at its costume collection.

— Adapted from Marshall (2001, pp. 43–52)

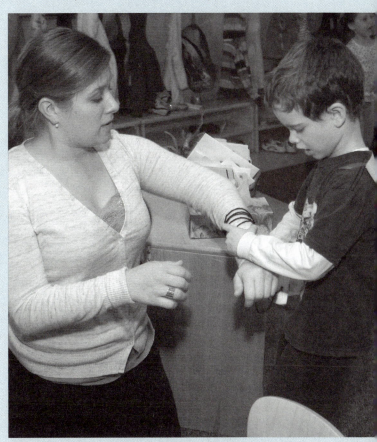

This teacher is a coplayer in this child's superhero play. He is taking her to jail, because she has been a "bad doggie."

or to consider a problem. A conversation is more likely to occur at these times than when children are wholly involved in making something. Also, children who have interrupted, completed, or are changing their plans may find that conversing with an adult can help them clarify what they have done or intend to do next. Such conversations are most likely to occur during work time when children are describing what they are doing; pretending and role playing; exploring, manipulating or repeating actions; pausing during play; talking during games; and interrupting, completing, or changing plans.

Join children at their level for conversation

At its best, conversation is an intimate exchange between trusting people. For such conversations to occur, adults position themselves near the child *at the child's physical level* so that children are not "looking up" to adults and adults are not "looking down" on children. For the most part, this means that adults spend a lot of time squatting, kneeling, sitting, and occasionally even lying on the floor. Adults must "shrink" to the children's size so that children and adults can converse easily and comfortably.

Respond to children's conversational leads

When adults make themselves available for conversation with children during natural pauses in their play, and when they are silent yet attentive, listening patiently and with interest to ongoing conversations, children are likely to address adults directly or make the first move toward involving them in conversation:

Child: *(Wipes hands on smock and studies collage she is making.)*

Adult: *(Squats down next to child and looks at collage.)*

Child: This is for my mom.

Adult: Ah, something for your mom.

Child: It's a...it's not done.

Adult: Oh.

Child: I'm going to put some of that twisty stuff on right here and those things he's got.

Adult: You mean acorn tops like Ryan is using?

Child: Yeah! Acorn tops. We picked them up, didn't we?

Adult: Yes. We found the acorn tops on our walk.

Child: And Linda found that stick, and you jumped over it!

Adult: You did too!

Child: Yep! *(Pauses)* I'm going to put a stick on and those tops. A lot! *(Turns back to her work.)*

Adult: I'll come back to see what it looks like with the twisty stuff and the stick and the acorn tops. *(Moves toward another child.)*

Converse as a partner with children

As partners in dialogues with children, adults resist taking control of the conversation. Instead, they try to pass conversational control back to the child at every opportunity. Adults do this by sticking to the topic the child raises, making personal comments or affirmative utterances that allow the conversation to continue without pressuring the child for a response, waiting for the child to respond before taking another conversational turn, and keeping their comments fairly brief.

Adults often wait for the child to open the conversation but may also initiate conversation, leaving it up to the child to decide whether to continue the exchange. An appropriate way to open a conversation with a child is to begin with a comment or an observation. This gives the child control over his or her response and, consequently, over the direction of the conversation. In the following examples, note how the adults give conversational control to the child by opening with an undemanding comment and then leaving the direction of the conversation to the child:

Child: *(Brushes the coat of a fluffy stuffed dog.)*

Adult: My dog Stanley likes to have his coat brushed.

Child: So does my doggy. He hates baths.

Adult: Stanley doesn't like baths, either.

Child: Sometimes I have to put him in the tub.

Adult: I bet he tries to get out.

Child: He tries to get over the side, and then he shakes the water all over the place!

❖

Tyson: *(Standing at the workbench with a car he has made.)*

Adult: You made a very long car, Tyson.

Tyson: I got this long piece and this other piece on top.

Adult: Yes.

Tyson: These are the wheels.

Adult: They really turn.

Tyson: It's going to be a speed racer.

Adult: A speed racer.

Tyson: It's going to have speed racer stripes right here and here.

Adult: Then it will really go fast.

Tyson: Yeah. Red stripes. That's the fastest color.

Adult: I didn't know that.

Tyson: Yeah, because my brother's is red, and it's the fastest one.

Adult: I see.

Tyson: I'll show you how fast when I put on the red.

Adult: Okay!

Ask questions responsively

While asking questions is a commonly accepted teaching method with older children, questioning younger children can be tricky. Our questioning styles can either dampen conversations or stimulate them, depending on how responsive our questions are to young children's play and interests. Questions that dampen conversation tend to be questions about facts that are obvious ("What color is that?" "Which board is longer?" "Is that a house?") and questions unrelated to the situation at hand (such as asking a child who is coloring, "Have you had your juice yet?"). According to Wood et al. (1980), these "test-type questions are a violation of normal conversational etiquette and the child seems intuitively aware of this fact. Adults tend to resort to test-like questions when they focus on topics and tasks beyond the child's comprehension or interests. Furthermore, in a drive for answers, they fail to share their own views and reactions with the child" (p. 178).

A string of adult questions also tends to put the adult in control of the conversation. As Wood et al. (1980) point out, "if the adult maintains the dialogue largely through questions, children's answers tend to be terse. [In such cases,] once the adult has the conversational bit between her teeth, her questions may even override the spontaneous offerings of the children. Indeed, the tendency

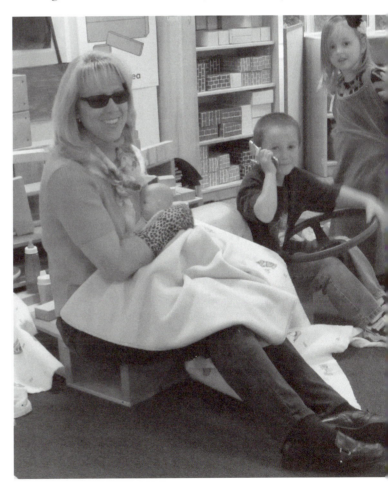

As a partner in play, this adult goes along for the "bus ride." Her job: to comfort and hold the baby.

to ignore children, talk over them, and generally dominate the proceedings prevents rather than encourages children's thought and conversation" (p. 65).

On the other hand, questions that tend to stimulate conversation have the following characteristics: *They are used sparingly, they relate directly to what the child is doing, and they ask about the child's thought process.*

Ask questions sparingly. Adult questions are a conversational tool to be used with care. Such questions can help children contemplate, describe, and become more aware of their own thought processes. Nevertheless, it is important to remember that our main purpose is to support the children's desire to ask and answer *their own questions.*

An adult may ask a question to start a conversation but then should follow the course set by the child. Wood et al. (1980) characterize this style as "asking a question to get the child to say something, and then stepping back, taking the pressure off, either by making a contribution or by making an utterance that effectively fills your turn in the dialogue. [This style enables the child to]… elaborate on the theme and to take off in a direction that he chooses himself, presumably along the line he feels most interesting" (pp. 67, 69). In the following dialogue, the adult opens with a question but then repeats, rephrases, or reacts to what the child says. This lets the child know the adult is listening and interested and spurs more conversation from the child.

Child: *(Watching the fish in the fish tank.)*

Adult: *(Watches next to the child for a while.)*

Child: *(Points to one fish.)*

Adult: What's that fish doing?

Child: He's waiting for his daddy.

Adult: Oh, he's waiting.

Child: See that big one down there? He's the daddy, and he's waiting for him so they can go around together.

Adult: I see.

Child: They both have those tails like that. Kind of pointy. That's how you know.

Adult: Oh, the pointy tails mean they go together.

Child: Yeah, that means they're the boy and the daddy. Once I got lost.

Adult: Oh, dear!

Child: I couldn't find my daddy. He found me.

Adult: He didn't want to lose you.

Child: *(Pointing to fish.)* Now they're together.

Adult: Like you and your daddy.

Child: Uh-huh. There they go.

Curiously enough, the fewer questions we ask young children and the more we listen and converse with them as partners, the more likely they are to see us as sympathetic listeners and, hence, to ask *us* questions of particular interest to them as shown in this conversation:

Child: *(Rocks her stuffed dog.)*

Adult: *(Rocks a stuffed dog next to child.)*

Child: Does your father live with you?

Adult: No, he lives in Canada with my mom.

Child: Well, does that man Bill live with you?

Adult: Yes, Bill is my husband. He lives with me and Stanley.

Child: Stanley is a boy dog, right?

Adult: Right!

Child: My doggy is a boy dog too. His name is Sky Star.

Relate questions directly to what the child is doing. This strategy is another way of following the child's lead. Even though the adult is asking the question, it is based on everything she understands about the child at that moment. When the question grows out of the immediate situation, it is more likely to add to (rather than take away) from the conversation. For example, in the conversation about fish, the adult asks about the fish the child is pointing to. As the conversation continues, the adult asks another question that grows out of the exchange:

After the teacher asks who she is calling on the telephone, the child answers that she is calling her grandmother who is visiting for the week.

Child: That fish only has one eye.

Adult: How can you tell?

Child: Because look. That's all you can see.

Adult: I see. You can see only one eye.

Child: Yeah, one eye right on the side up by his nose.

Ask questions about the child's thought process. Questions that stimulate conversation focus on *thought processes* rather than *facts:* "How many eyes does the fish have?" demands a factual answer, which by the way, the adult already knows. In contrast, the question "How can you tell?" is asked in response to the child's observation that the fish has one eye and encourages the child to describe how he arrived at the conclusion. *Only the child has the answer to this question, so it is a question well worth asking.* Furthermore, in the process of answering the question, the child has the opportunity to consolidate what he knows and recognize how he knows it. Questions that inquire about children's thinking and reasoning include these:

- "How can you tell?"
- "How do you know that?"
- "What do you think made that happen?"
- "How did you get (the ball) to…?"
- "What do you think would happen if…?"

Again, ask these questions sparingly and in relation to what the child is doing. Also, be alert for answers the children give to their own unspoken questions:

Child: *(Building a block tower.)* It's getting higher!

Adult: *(Watches and nods in agreement.)*

Child: It's higher than even me!

Adult: Yes, it is!

Child: It's moving. *(Tower falls.)* Oh, no!

Adult: Uh-oh!

Child: *(Studies the fallen tower.)* It was too heavy. Up there. *(Holds hand out, indicating where the top of the tower had been.)*

Adult: *(Supplying what she thinks might be the child's unspoken question.)* That's why it fell?

Child: Yeah. It couldn't keep that big block up.

Adult: It couldn't keep the big block up.

Child: It wasn't strong enough. I know what! *(He begins to rebuild.)*

Adults encourage children's problem solving

Throughout the day in any stimulating environment, young children encounter physical problems ("This piece won't fit!") and social conflicts ("He took my truck!"). Adults who support children's active learning encourage them to grapple with child-sized problems rather than give up in frustration or turn to adults to patch things up.

Not all adults encourage young children to solve their own problems. In fact, some adults attempt to provide a trouble-free environment. They admonish children not to argue and step in at the first sign of trouble to provide whatever direction is needed to keep things running smoothly. For example, a child making a book hits the stapler, but no staples come out. Noticing the situation, a nearby adult says, "Here, let me fix that for you." She opens up the stapler, sees that the staples are jammed, and pulls out the jammed staples. She then hands the stapler back to the child and says, "Now it will work."

Some adults attempt to mediate disputes and problems so that wrongs are recognized and punished. In such a setting, when a child making a book hits the stapler and no staples come out, a nearby adult says, "You've hit the stapler so hard, the staples are jammed." She then proceeds to unjam the stapler and puts it up on a shelf beyond the child's reach. "Maybe you can have another try with it tomorrow after you've had time to think about using it properly," she says to the child.

In a HighScope setting, adults encourage children to solve their own problems. They believe that as young children work through the problems they encounter, they learn firsthand about how things work, begin to see things from a variety of perspectives, and develop self-confidence. Consider this example: In a HighScope setting, a child making a book pounds on the stapler and notices that no staples come out. He shakes the stapler and tries again without any luck. He leans on the stapler with both hands but it still doesn't work:

Child: *(Addressing a nearby adult)* Hey, this thing is not working.

Adult: Sometimes, if you open it up, you can see what's the matter. *(The child does this.)*

Child: They're in there, but this one is…is… is going the wrong way. *(He tries to pull out the jammed staple with his fingers, then gets a pair of blunt-edged scissors, which he uses to pry off the staples.)* There. I got it! Now let's see. *(He tries the stapler once again. This time it works.)*

Look for children involved in problem situations

Problems may arise in any type of children's play, and it is important for adults to be looking for children in need of support. In particular, children involved in constructive play, more so than children engaged in exploratory play, may encounter problems simply because they generally have a clear goal in mind and may have to overcome unexpected obstacles to achieve it. Also, children who have stopped working on their plans may have done so because they are having difficulty solving a problem. Children recognizing and solving problems (e.g., "How many do I need?" "What will fit?" "What goes next?"), children developing strategies for dealing with social conflict, children whose project is not working, and children who have interrupted or are changing their plans are examples of some problem solvers in work-time situations who may need your assistance and support.

Allow children to deal with problems and conflicting viewpoints

Children are, by nature, problem setters and problem solvers. They can and do solve many problems on their own. Sometimes adults, who are more efficient problem solvers than children, have to restrain themselves from interfering prematurely with children's problem-solving attempts. Here are some strategies to help practice such restraint.

Sit down with children. Do this as often as possible rather than remaining highly mobile throughout work time. While you must remain alert to what is going on in as much of the play space as possible, by having to get up and walk over to the problem solvers, you give children more time to sort things out on their own or generate their own solutions to try.

Give children time to use their own problem-solving skills. Even if you move close to problem solvers, wait to offer assistance until children ask or until they have made an attempt at a solution and seem about to abandon the effort.

Refer one child to another. Whenever possible, refer problem solvers to other children who have the skills to help them at the moment. This empowers the child who assists and enables the problem solver to view peers as resources as seen in this example:

Child: Darn! I can't get this open!

Adult: Yesterday, I saw Reeny open her glue bottle. Maybe she could help.

Child: Hey, Reeny! How do you do this?

Reeny: I'll help you. See, you push this up like this.

Listen to conflicting viewpoints. Children frequently disagree with one another. Some adults may want to keep children from arguing, but a more appropriate response would be to listen to the conflicting views and encourage children to elaborate these views as this adult does:

Adult: *(Reading the story of how the elephant got his trunk. Stops to look at the picture.)*

As often as possible, sit down with children during work time. Even if you are sitting close by, observe children and wait for them to use their own problem-solving skills before you offer assistance.

First child: He's a nice elephant.

Second child: No, he's not. He's bad.

Adult: What makes you say that?

Second child: Because he went down to the river when he wasn't supposed to.

Adult: Yes, he went down to the river.

First child: No, he's nice. He's just a nice little baby elephant.

Adult: Yes, he's a baby.

Second child: Read some more.

Adult: Okay. Let's see what else we'll find out about the baby elephant at the river.

Interact with rather than manage children

When adults *interact* with children, they play and converse with them as partners. When adults *manage* children, they retain the upper hand by passing out instructions and warnings: "You need to go wash your hands." "You need to find something else to do. It's too crowded for you to play here." "That's too much glue. Take just a little bit." "Three more minutes till you have to get off the trike." Not only does adult management prevent children from confronting and working with child-sized problems, it also limits or curtails more beneficial and enjoyable adult-child interactions.

Here is an example of two adults approaching the same situation in different ways, the first through interaction and the second through management:

First child: Yip, yip, yip.

Second child: *(Pretends to eat out of "dog" dish.)*

First adult: *(Patting both "dogs.")* Nice doggies.

First child: *(Sits up and "begs.")* Yip, yip.

First adult: Let me see if I have a bone for you. *(Finds a pretend bone in her pocket.)* Here, doggie. (Several other "dogs" join the play in the house area. After eating, the dogs decide they want to go to sleep in their "doggie beds." However, after two children lie down, there is not enough room for the others. The children rearrange themselves closer together so there is room for each doggie, as well as several more who come over from other areas of the room.)*

Second adult: *(Across the room, flicks lights off and on.)* There are too many children playing dogs and there's too much yipping. You two can stay in the house area, but the rest of you will have to find something else to do.

The children who are encouraged to work together to find space for their dog beds have a very different experience from those being shooed out of their play space. While prevention of the problem may be a more efficient short-term approach, encouraging children to solve the problem for themselves accomplishes more in the long run because of the opportunities it provides. However, supporting children through the problem-solving process will require a greater degree of adult involvement than solving the problem for them.

Furthermore, as Wood et al. (1980) noted, "[adult] management seemed to breed more management, [adult] interactions, more interactions. Where an adult herself usually initiated contact with children for purposes of management, children often came to her for similar purposes. Their spontaneous overtures took the form of requests for turns and arbitration, questions about when story time was and other basically managerial functions. However, where the adult was holding a conversation with children or playing with them, the opening from a 'new' child was much more likely to be a request for her to play with them, help them with something, or simply to talk" (pp. 47–48).

Calmly assist with unresolved conflicts

When conflicts arise that children are not able to resolve on their own, adults use the following six-step approach to conflict resolution (see also KDI 15. Conflict Resolution in *Social and Emotional Development*, Epstein, 2012g):

1. Approach calmly.

Adult: *(Kneeling beside the children and using a calm voice)* We seem to have a problem here.

First and second child: *(Nod.)*

2. Acknowledge children's feelings.

Adult: You both look pretty upset.

First child: I'm pretty steamed!

Second child: This is getting me mad!

Adult: So you're steamed and you're mad.

3. Gather information.

Adult: *(Pause)* Tell me what's happening here.

First child: I need that big, big box.

Second child: I had it first.

To help these children with a conflict they cannot resolve on their own, this teacher begins by approaching calmly, getting on the children's level, and gathering information from both of them about what happened.

First child: You weren't using it.

Second child: I was going to use it.

4. Restate the problem.

Adult: It seems that both of you need a box.

First child: I need it for my house so I can get into it.

Second child: Well, I need a big box to put all these papers in.

Third child: Box! Me!

Adult: *(To third child)* You need a box too.

Third child: *(Nods in agreement.)*

5. Ask for ideas for solutions, and choose one together.

Adult: So we have one big box and each of you wants to use it. How can we solve this problem?

First child: *(Thinks.)* I could use it first and you could use it the other days.

Second child: I need it now.

Third child: No. Mine.

Adult: Everybody needs the box now, today.

Second child: We could all get in.

First child: Yeah!

Second child: But don't sit on my papers.

First child: We could put them in a bag and then put them in.

Third child: Me, bag.

Second child: Let's all have bags, okay? *(The other children nod yes.)*

Adult: So you're all getting in the box, and each person has a bag to put papers in. *(Again, the children nod yes as they move into action.)*

6. Be prepared to give follow-up support.
Adult: *(Checks periodically from across the room for the next 5–10 minutes and observes the three children playing without conflict in the box and bringing in a variety of materials.)*

Adults bring work time to an end

Adults alert children a few minutes before the end of work time so children can come to a natural stopping place in their play and prepare to return materials to their labeled storage places. Putting away toys and materials creates a transition from work time (do) to recall time (review) in the plan-do-review process. Cleanup time, as with the rest of work time, is a time for problem solving, playfulness, and realistic expectations.

Encourage problem solving

At the end of work time, some children deal with the problem of how to continue play that is not quite finished. They figure out on their own, or with the support of adults, how to complete what they are doing — either at the moment, later on in the day, at home, or during work time the next day. For example, at the end of one work time, two children continue working on a large puzzle they have almost finished so that they can bring it to recall. Then they help put other puzzles and toys away. Another child puts the special materials he needs to finish his dinosaur inside the box he is using so he can continue to work on it at home. He puts some of the paper he has been using in his dinosaur box and then puts the rest on the art shelf. Yet another child gets a work-in-progress sign (with a crossed-out drawing of a hand for the universal do-not-touch message), clips it to her drawing, and stores her picture on a shelf with a plan to complete it the next day.

Figuring out how to save what they are working on is another problem some children face at the end of work time. For example, several children have built a "cave" out of blankets and rocks. Instead of taking it down and putting the blankets away, they want to save it to play in after naptime. They discuss their plan to save the cave with an adult who supports their idea; then they make a "Please do not disturb" sign to hang on their cave.

Putting toys and materials back in their containers or on the shelf so they can find them the next time they need them is another problem children solve at the end of work time — a problem-solving situation that generally calls upon their sorting and matching skills.

Children enjoy figuring out how to use mops, vacuum cleaners, brooms, and sponges because they get to use the real tools that grown-ups use. For example, two young children run a tank-type vacuum cleaner. One guides the hose while the other pushes the tank. Although it takes some time for them to coordinate their efforts, the two children are pleased with their accomplishments, and the house-area floor is free of the pinecone bits and sand left over from "dinner."

Play put-away games

Some children derive a great deal of satisfaction out of stacking blocks back on a shelf, hanging up dress-up clothes, washing paintbrushes, and sorting stones and shells; other children do not. At the end of work time these children are ready for a change of pace. They see no particular problems to solve, they have completed their plans to their satisfaction, and now they are happy to cruise the areas and engage in rough-and-tumble play with other like-minded children. Sometimes these children will join and contribute enthusiastically to physically active put-away games such as tossing all the inch cubes into the inch-cube box, seeing how many big blocks can be carried at once, racing against

At cleanup time, these two children work together to put away the large blocks.

the sand timer to put all the dollhouse furniture back on the shelf, setting up a "bucket brigade" line in which items are passed from child to child until they reach their shelf or container, or playing peddler and gathering stray toys into a sack.

Maintain realistic expectations

For many adults, cleanup time is not a favorite part of the day. They worry that materials will not be put away; that some children will not help; that putting away toys will take too long; that they will tend to direct rather than interact with children; and that if another adult is observing this time of day, that person will find fault in all these areas of concern. Some or all of these situations probably will occur on any given day. Here are some strategies to help you cope with them:

- Focus on supporting children's problem solving and play. Approach cleanup time, like any other time of the day, from the child's viewpoint.

- Remain calm and optimistic. Generally, within 10 minutes the interest areas will be in decent shape.

- Work along with the children to put away toys and materials and to keep the spirit of play and problem solving alive. Enjoy children's energy and ingenuity.

- Begin recall time even if there are still materials left to put away. It makes more sense to go on to recall than to prolong the end of work time. Sometimes the remaining materials can serve as useful recall reminders.

How Adults Support Children at Work Time: A Summary

Adults scan the interest areas to find out what children are doing.
- Look for the status of children's plans.
- Look for children's individual and social interactions.
- Look for specific types of play.
- Look for the HighScope KDIs.

Adults choose children to observe, gain children's perspectives, and form on-the-spot interaction plans.
- Choose children to observe.
- Observe to gain each child's perspective.
- Form on-the-spot interaction plans.

Adults offer children comfort and contact.
- Look for children in need of comfort and contact.
- Offer reassuring physical contact.
- Offer simple acknowledgments.

Adults participate in play with children.
- Look for natural play openings.
- Join children's play on the child's level.
- Play in parallel with children.
- Play as a partner with children.
- Refer one player to another.
- Suggest new ideas within ongoing play situations.
  – Offer suggestions within the play theme.
  – Address the role person rather than the child.
  – Respect the child's reaction to your idea.

Adults converse with children.
- Look for natural opportunities for conversation.
- Join children at their level for conversation.
- Respond to children's conversational leads.
- Converse as a partner with children.
- Ask questions responsively.
  – Ask questions sparingly.
  – Relate questions directly to what the child is doing.
  – Ask questions about the child's thought process.

Adults encourage children's problem solving.
- Look for children involved in problem situations.
- Allow children to deal with problems and conflicting viewpoints.
  – Sit down with children.
  – Give children time to use their own problem-solving skills.
  – Refer one child to another.
  – Listen to conflicting viewpoints.
- Interact with rather than manage children.
- Calmly assist with unresolved conflicts.
  – Approach calmly.
  – Acknowledge children's feelings.
  – Gather information.
  – Restate the problem.
  – Ask for ideas for solutions, and choose one together.
  – Be prepared to give follow-up support.

Adults bring work time to an end.
- Encourage problem solving.
- Play put-away games.
- Maintain realistic expectations.

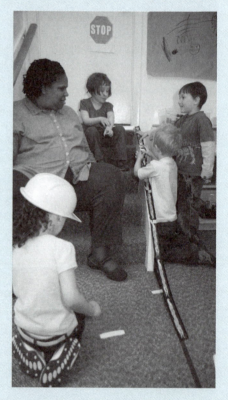

Understanding Recall Time

Recalling takes place both in the *recall* (also called *review*) segment of the daily routine — the final element in the plan-do-review process — and throughout the day as children reflect on their work. Just as planning is more than simply choosing — it is making a purposeful or intentional choice — recall is more than simply remembering — it involves purposeful memory (Norman, 1982). The purpose of recall is to help children think about what they have done in their interactions with materials, people, and ideas and reflect on what they want to take away from these experiences. This part of the chapter examines the recall process: why it is important, where it occurs, what children do at this time, and how adults can best support them.

The following examples from an actual recall time in a HighScope program illustrate the various ways preschool children talk about what they have done.

"I got dressed up and went to a wedding! Scott went. Kelly went. They got dressed up."

"Me. Baby," says Carol, thumping her chest with the flat of her hand on each word.

(Jessa brings a plate to Becki, an adult.) "I saw you using that plate today, Jessa," Becki says. *"It looked like you were cooking." (Jessa nods in agreement.)*

"French fries. We cooked lots. I took some to the block area and gave them to Linda to eat!"

"See this!" (Shows a toothpick and clay structure.) "This keeps the giants out. And the ugly trolls. Dogs bark down here. The princess locks the door. Up, up to the top of the tower. Faster than a motorcycle. 'You leave me alone, you bad giants.' *That's why she has this tower."*

What is recall and why is it important?

During recall time, children reflect on, talk about, and exhibit what they have done at work time. While the *planning process* helps children form a purpose and anticipate a course of action that leads to active learning experiences, the *recall process* helps children make sense of these actions. At recall, children are involved in several important processes — drawing on memories, reflecting on experiences, associating plans with outcomes, and talking with others about their discoveries and actions.

Remembering and reflecting on actions and experiences

For young children, the recall process involves much more than the straightforward retrieval of facts and figures stored away in the brain. During recall children engage in an active, story-forming process. They literally *construct* memory, which in the words of Edmund Bolles (1988) "is a living product of desire, insight, and consciousness" (p. xiv). When children recall their work-time experiences, they form a mental version of their experiences based on their ability to understand and interpret what they have done. They select and talk about the parts of their experiences that have a special meaning to them: "We made mud! We love mud, don't we, Jeff!" As psychologist Roger Schank (1990) points out, "We need to tell someone else a story that describes our experiences because the process of creating the story also creates the memory structure that will contain the gist of the story for the rest of our lives. Talking is remembering" (p. 115).

As children engage in this process of selecting events to talk about and then interpreting what happened, they develop a better understanding of their experiences. Writing, talking, storytelling, painting, sculpting, dancing, composing music — these are all ways we as adults organize and make sense of what we know. We have an experience, feeling, or idea that we attempt to give form to or describe by using words, notes, numbers, formulas, brush strokes, or movements.

Preschoolers have the same need as the rest of us to remember and make sense of what they know. In fact, their own words and gestures are their primary tools for shaping and understanding past events, as shown in the following example:

Reeny: I was…I was playing in the sand but…it was too dry!

Adult: Too dry?

Reeny: It wouldn't stay in a cake so I…I…um… made it very muddy!

Adult: Oh….How did you do that?

Reeny: I put in lots of water!

Adult: I saw you put in lots of water.

Reeny: Then it sticked in a cake…and…it sticked *(looks at hands)* on me too!

As children reflect on what they have done, they begin in their own deliberate fashion to consider the meaning of their experiences and ideas, turning them over in their minds. They thus begin to think about what they have done *in the abstract*. Moreover, by thinking things through, they begin to understand that they can make things happen, learn new things, and solve their own problems: "The paint knocked over. I put my hand down fast to catch it. I held it on the edge of the table. [The child demonstrates.] Then Timmy got paper towels. It didn't even go on the floor, only just a little bitty drop."

Berry and Sylva (1987) underscore the importance of recall time for young children's development in this succinct observation: "Recall provides a rich potential for language use, discussing means-ends relationships, and exploring connections" (p. 35).

Associating plans, actions, and outcomes

As children recall their work-time experiences, they gradually begin to associate what they did with the plans they made before they started. They begin to develop a consciousness of purpose, realizing that planning prior to doing gives them control of their actions through the entire

At recall time, children reflect on and talk about what they did at work time. This child (first picture), a beginning planner, points to show his teacher that he worked in the woodworking area. He then says, "I broke it," recalling how he had used a hammer to take apart an old watch (as illustrated in the second picture).

plan-do-review process: "I planned to be a kitty with Sabrina. And we were kitty cats all the whole time. Even at cleanup time!"

Talking with others about personally meaningful experiences

Recalling involves social interaction on a very personal level — reflecting on experiences and finding the words, actions, and gestures to convey their meaning to others: "I made a…a…paper with lots [acts out squeezing a glue bottle]…lots of drippy glue! I'll show you. [Gets paper.] It's here [points to patches of glue] and here. It's…it's… you can touch it. It's not sticky!" The very process of talking about their intentions and actions helps children actually create or construct meaningful memories (Bolles, 1988).

Such recall experiences are an opportunity for children to engage in personal storytelling in which they, as narrators, are the major characters. The dramatic, exciting, or puzzling aspects of work-time experiences provide the raw materials that children use at recall time to construct a story for others. Clearly, the social aspects of planning, doing, and recalling directly support children's emerging literacy. Through this process, children become conscious of themselves and their peers as people with interesting thoughts to relate. This awareness contributes to their readiness to relate their experiences in emerging print forms and to interpret the printed narrations created by others.

Put another way, *during planning time children turn their interests into purposeful actions, while at recall time children turn their purposeful actions into narratives that capture the striking features of those actions*. Educators who help children capture these moments meet the educational challenge described by educator Elliot Eisner (1990) as "finding a way of helping children acquire the language they need while at the same time keeping a playful attitude toward language alive" (p. 47).

Recalling also makes children's experiences public. Since recalling is a social phenomenon taking place between two or more people, it has the effect of opening up personal experiences to public scrutiny. Children have the opportunity to present their experiences in such a way that others not only listen to them but also add their observations and ideas:

Carlie: I played with Jack.

Kevin: You played with me too.

Tim: And you drove me, remember?

Carlie: We all played and played!

Public discourse, even at this very simple level, is an essential part of any culture. Eisner (1990) explains this function in these terms: "The public representation of ideas and images is a way to share them with others. We usually take this function for granted, but unless the private is made public there is no way to participate in the experience of others….The process of representation is a way to enter the lives of others and to begin to understand what others have thought and felt. Without representation, culture itself would not be possible" (pp. 53–54).

Children who engage in the recall process are offering their experiences for public examination. Catherine, for example, displays the banner she has made, and over the next week or so, other children, intrigued with the idea, experiment with banner making in a variety of forms. Clearly, as children become interested in and experiment with one another's projects and experiences, these ideas and ways of doing things gradually are assimilated into the culture of their early childhood setting.

Forming and then talking about mental images

Preschoolers have the capacity to picture in their minds real and imagined past and future experiences. This capacity for using mental pictures and symbols enables them to use both language and movement to recall, imagine, talk about, and describe people and objects in forms that others can comprehend. In other words, they can *represent* experiences. The recall process provides an

As children recall, they search for images and words to express their interpretations of their immediate past. This child talks about the pocketbook she made at work time.

opportunity for children to exercise their emerging representational abilities. As they turn their memories into concrete words and gestures, children form their own understanding of their work-time experiences: "I, um [gestures with hands as if using the mouse] worked in the computer…area today. I made pictures! Then I cut…a, um [holds an imagined page with one hand and makes scissor-like motions with the other], I cut a, um… the…pictures apart!"

Expanding consciousness beyond the present

In their newfound capacity for engaging in pretend play with others, preschoolers use what educator Anthony Pellegrini (1986) describes as the "language of absence": "Language that takes people away from their immediate surroundings" (p. 83). Children also use the language of absence as they recall their work-time experiences: "I got Will money and that's all I can tell. And I played with those two guys. And I drove the cars and they broke out our windows!" As children recall, they consciously look back in time and search for the images and words to express their interpretation of their immediate past:

Adult: What happened when you broke out the windows?

Kyle: We'd be dead!

Adult: You were dead, Kyle?

Ben: Me too!

Thus, as they recall, children come to understand what they have done and develop the ability to relate their actions and outcomes to others who can then explore and modify them. Remembering and reflecting on their original intentions, associating plans with actions and the outcomes of these actions, and talking with others about meaningful experiences are important to the intellectual and social-emotional development of all of us, not just children. These mental and social processes allow us to search through the past for clues to the present and future. Recalling events and experiences is a skill that will benefit children throughout their lives. For this reason, the recall process is an essential element of the HighScope daily routine.

What children do as they recall

As fledgling storytellers, preschoolers recall in unique ways. Adults should be aware of the characteristics of preschoolers' personal storytelling styles to understand what to expect during their recall conversations with children.

Children grow in their capacity to recount past events

As toddlers, children develop the capacity to talk about the past. In one study, Peggy Miller and Linda Sperry (1988) observed two-year-old children to find out how they talked about past events they had personally experienced. The authors found that during this period (2.0–2.6 years of age), the children talked mostly about negative experiences, such as instances of physical harm that caused them pain or confusion. The amount of such talk doubled during these months, and the children were increasingly able to describe the

> **Recalling — What and Why: A Summary**
>
> - Remembering and reflecting on actions and experiences
> - Associating plans, actions, and outcomes
> - Talking with others about personally meaningful experiences
> - Forming and then talking about mental images
> - Expanding consciousness beyond the present

order in which events occurred. They were also five times as likely to use descriptive words and report their emotional reactions to these upsetting events as they were in other instances of speech. These results show that by the time children pass the age of two and a half, telling stories of personal experiences is meaningful to them. Moreover, it is the emotional significance of the events, not just their social or cognitive aspects, that determine the amount and nature of the language they use.

In examining three- and four-year-olds' ability to recall work-time experiences, Miller and Sperry (1988) note that "preschool-aged children also tell stories about events that happened to them or their associates — a fight with another child, a ride at the Fair, an accidental injury, a trip to the swimming pool" (p. 294). Berry and Sylva (1987) found that "children [in HighScope programs] were able to recall what they had done, and often with considerable detail. They frequently included comments indicating that they were aware of the difference between activities they had planned and others they had not planned" (p. 16).

Clearly, while the ability to talk about their own experiences is evident very early, children are often able to add more details to these discussions as they grow older. The more they understand about what they have done, the more they are able to talk about it in detail, as shown by Ben and Linda during one recall time:

Ben (three years old): *(Pretends to type.)* I played with the computer.

Linda (four years old): Me and Chelsea played wedding. We danced on the steps and then we went home. And then we had dinner…and had dessert…and then pretended that we were playing downstairs…and then…and then we played again!

A common thread that seems to run through most stories about the past is a personal emotional investment in the original experience. Children, indeed persons of all ages, are most apt to recall experiences in which they themselves were actively and emotionally engaged.

Children select experiences to recall

Throughout most of work time, four-year-old Trina was engaged in an elaborate role-play sequence that eventually involved several other children. The children decided to dress up as ballerinas. Once dressed in their tutus, the children built a stage for their show, set up chairs for the audience, made tickets, and recruited everyone they could to sit in the chairs and watch. At recall time, the adult recalling with Trina anticipated a detailed report, because Trina had been so focused on the play sequence that had involved almost every other child and adult at one time or another. What Trina actually talked about at recall, however, had nothing to do with dressing up, building a stage, or dancing. Instead, she told about something she had done after the show, in the last 10 minutes of work time: "I made a card for my Daddy…for his birthday. It's this day!…I sent him one card but…but this card's for when…for when…he's home!"

It is often difficult to predict what, out of all the things they have done at work time, young children will choose to talk about at recall time. What impresses an adult about a child's work-time experiences may or may not be what a child decides to share. Children rarely give a strictly chronological account of their work-time experiences. Instead, they tend to select one or two things that are of particular significance to them, regardless of how much time they actually have spent on the activities. They may talk about the last thing they did during work time. They may show a picture that took them five minutes to paint or a workbench construction that took all of work time to complete. They may simply recount whom they played with, if playing with their friends was more significant than anything they actually did together. The point is that recalling is a selective experience. Children choose what they want to talk about based on their own interests and ideas. Having the opportunity to say something about their own experiences is more important than which experience they actually recall.

Children construct their own understanding of what they have just done

"We remember things according to our understanding of what happened, not according to the way something really occurred" (Bolles, 1988, p. 72).

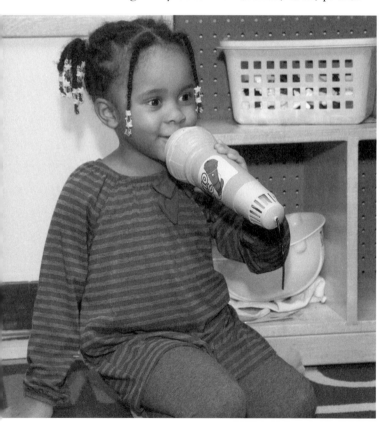

This child recalls by talking through a play microphone.

For example, the child in this anecdote describes splashing water as "jumping" out of a hole, which is how his animistic (or "it's alive") way of thinking perceives it.

First child: We made mud. The water…it jumped out…out of the hole…so we made mud.

Adult: It jumped out of the hole!

First child: Yeah, just like this. *(Makes a jumping motion with his hand.)*

Second child: We love mud, don't we, Jeff?

First child: Yeah, we love mud!

As children's understanding of experiences increases, they are able to construct memories that are closer to actuality. When children understand what they have done, the recall stories they construct are fairly accurate and straightforward, as this child demonstrates in his description of making tin-can stilts:

Child: *(Shows a pair of tin-can stilts.)* These are my stilts. I made them.

Adult: I saw you pounding holes in the tops.

Child: Well, I pounded…I pounded a nail…one here…here…here, here *(points to four holes)*. It's hard to poke this string through…it kept slipping back out. I stopped it with this tape, see, right here…you can walk on them. Like this. *(Demonstrates.)*

Children recall experiences in a variety of ways

While the recall process generally involves discussions, young children also use motions and gestures, reenactments, drawings, and written accounts to describe their work-time experiences.

Gesture and reenactment. Some children, especially young children who are new to the plan-do-review process, simply point to a person or object they played with or to one of the places where they played. They may also get something they used or act out something they did. Three-year-old Tara, for example, uses all of these strategies:

> **What Children Do as They Recall: A Summary**
>
> - Children grow in their capacity to recount past events.
> - Children select experiences to recall.
> - Children construct their own understanding of what they have just done.
> - Children recall experiences in a variety of ways.

Adult: What did you do today, Tara?

Child: *(Points to the sand and water table.)*

Adult: Ah, you played in the sand.

Child: *(Nods in agreement.)*

Adult: I saw you.

Child: *(Gets a bucket from the sand table.)* This!

Adult: This bucket.

Child: *(Makes scooping motions.)*

Adult: *(Makes scooping motions.)*

Child: *(Laughs and turns bucket over.)* All gone!

Adult: All gone!

Talking. It is very common for preschoolers to talk as they recall. As they remember and construct past events, their speech is often punctuated by pauses during which they search their minds for words to express their understanding. Older, more experienced recallers will include more details in their stories and are also likely to add to other children's recall narratives.

Drawing and writing. As noted earlier, children also draw and write about their experiences in a variety of forms, including scribbles, simple and more detailed drawings, letters, and words. While some children can write and draw about their work-time experiences from the image they have in their minds, other children need the actual object to trace or refer to (e.g., a small metal car they used during work time).

How Adults Support Children at Recall Time

Adults support children at recall time by using many of the same open-ended strategies they use at planning time. In the following example, it is recall time in Becki's program, and Becki and the children have been planning and recalling for about three months. Five of the nine children in the recall group talk with Becki about what they have done, with one of the children (Linda) listening closely and occasionally commenting as Becki recalls one-on-one with another child. (Note that Becki's recall interchange with each child is quite short, lasting from 35 to 50 seconds):

Becki: Scott, what did you do at work time?

Scott: Ah, I played with....Will played with me.

Becki: Will played with you.

Scott: And I played with Will.

Becki: And you played with Will.

Scott: We were robbers.

Becki: You guys were robbers?

Scott: Yeah, we took all the food!

Becki: You took all the food from there.

Linda: Did you guys all give it back?

Scott: No.

Becki: You took it all from off that shelf?

Scott: Yeah...and even that basket.

Becki: Even that basket. You sure did.

Scott: Even the chocolate milk!

Becki: Even the chocolate milk! And what happened when you were done robbing the house?

Scott: We cleaned it up!

Becki: You cleaned it up. *(To the other children)* You know what, guys? They surprised me. They cleaned up after they robbed the house. I turned around, and it was like magic. It was all clean!

During this recall time, the children and adult gather around on the carpet and use a Hula-Hoop as a turn-taking device.

Becki: What did you do, Chelsea?

Chelsea: Ummm…played with all these things.

Becki: You played with all those what?

Chelsea: Fruit.

Becki: All that fruit. What did you do with all that fruit?

Chelsea: I ate it all up.

Becki: All by yourself?

Chelsea: Yeah.

Becki: You ate it all up all by yourself! Did you do anything else?

Chelsea: Nope.

Becki: Nope.

Chelsea: That's all I did!

Becki: That's all you did!

❖

Linda: Me!

Becki: Linda, what did you do today?

Linda: Me and Chelsea played wedding. We danced on the steps and then we went home. And then we had dinner…and had dessert…and then we pretended that we were playing downstairs… and then…and then we played again.

Becki: You did all that, and then you played wedding again!

Linda: And lots of kids danced on the steps.

Becki: I saw you on the steps. There were lots of kids on the steps today.

❖

Becki: Ben, your plan was to work with blocks.

Ben: I worked with Kyle.

Linda: *(Making a rhyme)* Kyle and style.

Becki: What did you do with him?

Ben: I worked with um…*(talking among children)* Callie was with me. And I worked with Will.

Kyle: Callie worked with me.

Becki: *(To Ben)* And you worked with Will. What did you do when you worked with Kyle and Callie and Will?

Ben: I got Will money and that's all I can tell. And I played with those two guys. And I drove the cars, and they broke out our windows.

Becki: They broke out your window?

Ben: Me and Kyle.

Becki: You broke out of the windows in the car?

Ben: Uh-huh.

Becki: What happened when you broke out of the windows?

Kyle: We'd be dead.

Becki: You were dead, Kyle?

Ben: Me too!

Becki: And you were dead too! Oh, dear!

❖

Becki: Callie, what did you do in the block area?

Callie: Played with stacks.

Becki: Played with stacks.

Callie: *(Talks with other child in the group.)*

Becki: You played with Kyle too?

Callie: *(Points.)*

Becki: You played in that area.

Callie: Block area.

Becki: You played in the block area.

Callie: We played.

Becki: You played.

Callie: And that's it!

Becki: That's it!

In HighScope active learning environments, the adults' role at recall time is similar to the adults' role at planning time and grows out of their work-time observations, conversations with children, and participation in children's play. These shared work-time experiences become the basis for recall stories and conversations. As at planning time, adults can best support children's recall by adopting the following four strategies:

- Recalling with children in a calm, cozy setting
- Providing materials and experiences to maintain children's interest at recall time
- Conversing with children about their work-time experiences
- Anticipating changes in the way children recall over time

Adults recall with children in a calm, cozy setting

Effective recall experiences are more likely to occur in calm, cozy settings under the guidance of adults who are willing to follow the child's lead.

Recall in intimate groups and places

Young children seek out and benefit from full adult attention as they try to recall and describe their activities in their own words. Thus, small and intimate recall groups result in more satisfying recall times for both preschool children and adults (although five- and six-year-old children are increasingly able to recall in whole-group settings, especially if their peers are willing to listen to them with genuine interest). While adults cannot always control the size of recall groups, they can make them as intimate as possible by adopting the following practices, some of which are also used at planning and work times:

- Converse with each child at the child's physical level.

- Provide materials at recall time to engage all children as each child recalls individually (see ideas for props in "Recall Games and Experiences" on p. 317).

- Physically separate recall groups as much as possible so that the natural noise and enthusiasm of one group does not distract another.

- Consider cozy alternatives to sitting in chairs around a table. For example, recall in a block building made during work time, under a table draped with a blanket, outside under a tree, or on cushions in the book area.

Recall with those who shared the experiences children are recalling

Because preschoolers are relatively new at consciously constructing memories and expressing their thoughts in ways that are comprehensible to others, they appreciate recalling with adults who know what occurred at work time. As children recall, particular objects, sounds, smells, and actions may suddenly remind them of work-time experiences. These spontaneous recollections may often seem out of context to listeners who have not shared the same experiences unless they realize that the child has linked the present with the past. Berry and Sylva (1987) confirm the value of shared experiences at recall time: "Recall was especially detailed when it was conducted by the staff person who had been in the activity area where the child worked, rather than by an adult who had participated in planning but was ignorant of what the child actually did during work time" (p. 18). Consider these examples of recalling shared experiences:

Recalling child: I played with Callie.

Adult: You played with Callie.

Recalling child: Played baby.

Adult: I saw you had a crib over there.

Contributing child: I played baby too!

Recalling child: We went to the store…we…we went…hunting.

Adult: You went hunting?

Recalling child: For toys! Baby toys!

Adult: I saw you hunting for toys in the toy area.

Recalling child: Yeah, we got lots. We had to have a bag to carry them all! That many!

Adults provide materials and experiences to maintain children's interest at recall time

When recalling with more than three or four children at a time, it is important to provide materials that children can use during one another's recall narratives or to play games that make waiting for a turn to recall enjoyable rather than tedious for children.

The ideas presented in "Recall Games and Experiences" (p. 317) are similar to those for planning time (pp. 262–263) because they serve a similar purpose: to hold the interest of small groups of children while one child recalls. When trying out these ideas, be alert to the possibility that the game or material may take over, rather than support, the recall process. Sometimes, for example, children using phones may recall in a fairly perfunctory manner because what they really want to do is choose the next person to use the phone and dial their number, as shown in this example:

Adult: Hello, Ivan. What did you do today?

Ivan: I made a boat and played diver. Now I'm calling Yuri. Get ready, Yuri, I'm calling…one…two…two…four…that's your number…. Ring…ring…ring!

Sometimes, too, if the recall materials or game require much adult explanation, the game itself may command all the children's attention and interest and recalling may feel to them like an imposition. If these types of situations occur, take note, follow the children's interests, and try simplifying the strategy the next time you use it.

Adults converse with children about their work-time experiences

Once adults have incorporated materials and games that engage all the children in their recall group, they can turn their attention to conversing with individual children about what they have done. The following suggestions are similar to the suggestions we offer for conversing with children about their plans. In planning, however, children look forward to what they *might do;* in recalling, the children reflect on some aspect of what they *have done*. In either case, adults support children's anticipated actions and construction of memory in the same attentive, responsive fashion.

Take an unhurried approach to recall

In their observations of recall time, Berry and Sylva (1987) note that the benefits of recall are often missed in the daily pressure on the adult to get through all the members of the group. One way to avoid rushing is to recall in small groups of three or four children. If this is not possible, it may be more relaxed for children and adults to recall with half the children in each recall group each day. One benefit of slowing down appears to be that by recalling with fewer children each day in a more leisurely fashion, children feel less pressured and more inclined to add to one another's narratives, as shown here:

Recalling child: We were movers!

Adult: You guys were movers?

Recalling child: Yeah, we moved all the food!

Adult: You moved all the food from there.

Recall Games and Experiences

Tours

The games and experiences presented here allow children to go to places where they have played and to things they have made during work time. Thus, children can move around for recall rather than being confined to one place.

Visits to structures

The recalling child leads the rest of the group to a structure he or she has made (and that has not been taken apart and put away during cleanup). Gathering around a block house, for example, reminds the recalling child of what she did and the adventures she had. In addition, the rest of the children may become very interested too, because they can see and touch the structure for themselves. Often they ask their own questions (e.g., "How do you get inside, Malek?").

Gallery visits

Similar to visits to structures, during gallery visits the recalling child leads the rest of the group to a picture on a wall, artwork drying on a rack, or a workbench piece in process.

Collections

At the beginning of recall, all the children gather one or two things they have played with during work time and bring them back to the recall place. Children take turns talking about and demonstrating what they have chosen to gather.

"Let's be..." or "Let's take the..."

This strategy changes with children's interests. If children have been playing ghost, for example, you might say, "Let's be ghosts and fly with Amir to something he played with at work time." Or, if children are spending a lot of time building police cars you might say, "Let's drive in our police cars, following Nikki to something she wants to tell us about."

Group games

These recall games provide children with enjoyable things to do or anticipate while other children are recalling.

Photographs

During work time, take and print a number of digital photographs of each child in your recall group. At the beginning of recall, spread the photos out on the floor and have each child collect the photos in which he or she appears. As children talk among themselves about what they see, move from child to child for individual recall conversations.

Musical chairs or carpet squares

Set up a circle of chairs, carpet squares, or blocks. Mark one seat as the recall seat (e.g., the seat with the red bow). Play music, stopping the music at unexpected intervals. The children walk (or crawl or hop) around the circle until the music stops and then sit on the nearest seat. The child who sits on the recall seat has a turn to talk about work time. If you have the children move around the inside of the circle, they will end up facing toward the center of the circle and one another as they recall.

Hula-Hoop, ball, spinner, symbols or letter links, and rhymes

See the descriptions of these games on pages 262–263. Modify them for recall time by substituting the word *recall* for *plan*.

Props and partnerships

These recall experiences center around materials children can use as they recall and as they await their turn to recall.

Spyglasses, phones, and puppets

See the descriptions of these games on page 263 and modify for recall time. Or modify them by giving one spyglass, phone, or puppet to each child so that children can talk with each other as you move from child to child for individual recall conversations.

Representations

Pantomime, mapping, and drawing enable children to construct and represent recall memories in media other than words.

Pictures, pantomime, maps, and drawing and writing

See descriptions of these strategies on page 263. Modify them for recall time.

Group work-time story

Hang up or lay out a long piece of butcher paper. Ask each child to use a part of it to draw and write about what he or she did at work time. Children who played together may wish to share a space or work next to each other.

Recall books

Sometimes children enjoy collecting their recall drawings and writings into a book they can take home. For example, if you ask children to draw and write their recall stories once a week, at the end of a month, you might bring all their drawings to recall time along with different fasteners children can use to make them into a book.

These ideas for tours, group games, partnerships, and representations at recall time are just a beginning. As you recall with children, you and your team will devise your own strategies for making recall time an active learning experience for the children in your care.

At recall time, this adult listens very carefully to this child's description of how she and her classmate played with the Duplos during work time.

Contributing child: Did you guys put it back?
Recalling child: No.

Invite children to talk about what they have done

After putting yourself at or below the child's eye level, there are several ways to begin the recall experience.

Pick up on children's opening comments. Sometimes a child begins a recall conversation with a comment he or she is eager to share, or one that is inspired by a particular material:

Child: *(Looking at a work-time photo)* That's me… over at the…the…the books!

Adult: That's you over at the books!
Child: The story about the trees.

Comment on a child's play. An adult can also begin a recall conversation with a personal comment or observation about a child's work-time experience:

Adult: I saw you driving, Denise.
Denise: Marshall didn't want to go to the clinic, but I told him, "You get in that car!"

Ask an open-ended question. For example, "What did you do today, Sam?"; "What happened with you and Ricky in the sand, Lenore?"; or "What were you doing with all that tape, Larry?"

Opening questions are fine as long as children respond to them with interest, but try to avoid an overdependence on adult questions to begin recall conversations. Note which children respond most naturally to comments and which children respond to open-ended questions.

Watch children and listen attentively

When you take time to recall with children in an unhurried manner, you will often be surprised by what children choose to talk about and how they construct their memories in words:

Adult: What did you do, Namen?

Namen: Oh, I went to…. I played next to…. I was in the water table!

Adult: You were in the water table.

Namen: I worked with…with sand…and water.

Adult: It looked like you took about three or four bottles of water over there.

Namen: Uh-huh. I took tons of it.

Adult: You took tons of it!

Some children may use gestures and actions rather than words. By watching carefully and knowing what the child was doing at work time, you can incorporate these actions into your conversation, as this teacher does with Bethany:

Adult: I saw you with lots of stuffed animals, Bethany.

Bethany: *(Giggles. Gets as many stuffed animals as she can carry and brings them back to the group.)*

Adult: Here they are!

Bethany: *(Makes each animal lie down. Pats each one.)*

Adult: *(Pats an animal.)*

Bethany: *(Smiles. Puts her finger to her lips.)* Shh!

Adult: Shh!

As with planning, it is important to follow the child's lead in recall conversations whether or not they are related to a work-time experience, as demonstrated in this dialogue:

Child: I'm not telling what I did.

Adult: Oh?

Child: That boy messed with me.

Adult: That boy messed with you at work time?

Child: No! That…that big boy…on the bus.

Adult: A boy on the bus. This morning?

Child: No, that other day…tomorrow.

Adult: Oh, the other day.

Second child: Did you tell your momma?

Child: I told my momma. She said, "You quit messing with little kids." Then she told his daddy, and he gave him a whooping.

Adult: He got a whooping, and he didn't bother you today.

Child: He looked at me…but he's scared of his daddy.

Adult: Getting whooped is scary.

Child: I don't want him messing with me. He pushed me down.

Adult: Being pushed on the bus is scary too.

Sometimes, particularly after three or four other children have recalled, children who were eager to recall at the beginning of recall time are ready to move on. Consider this recall time during which the children are talking to one another through a pretend television screen:

Adult: Chris, you've been waiting to talk on the television.

Chris: I don't want to anymore.

Adult: You don't want to talk on the television anymore. Do you want to recall some other way?

Chris: No.

Adult: No…. What do you want to tell us?

Chris: I want to do snack! I want to pass out the cups and the napkins!

Adult: Okay! We'll start with you tomorrow at recall time. But now it's time for you to pass out the cups and napkins for snack.

Contribute observations and comments to keep recall narratives going

Some children rely on responsive adult contributions and acknowledgments to help them spin their narrative thread. Note how the adult's neutral comments help this child keep his recall narrative going:

Antoine: I worked on the computer.

Adult: I saw you.

Antoine: I worked on the mask program.

Adult: Oh! The mask program.

Antoine: I made it again and again and again…on the printer.

Adult: You made it again and again and again!

Antoine: Yeah, a big long…banner…for the school.

Adult: For the school.

Antoine: You could hang it from the ceiling.

Angelette: I know. We could hang right…up…there! *(Points above their heads.)*

Children: Yeah, let's.

Use questions thoughtfully and sparingly

While you may use a question to begin a recall conversation, it is important to remember that, in general, when an adult asks a child a question, the adult rather than the child retains control of the conversation. When you do ask questions during recall, ask them sparingly rather than bombarding the child with one question after another. Also, ask questions that encourage children to describe and explain, such as "How did you do that?" and "Why did you decide to add the string?" as the adult does in the following example:

Adam: I made it real, real tall.

Adult: It was tall. How did you get it to stay up?

Adam: We put that big board up and…and Brian stood on the other side like this. *(Demonstrates.)* And I put that other board on. And then he didn't have to stay there anymore.

Adult: Brian didn't have to stay on the other side any more.

Adam: No, because then it stood up, and he didn't even have to hold it!

Support children's co-narratives and conflicting viewpoints

When children share their work-time experiences and adults listen and contribute, other children often add their own questions, observations, and opinions. These extended conversations can be very enjoyable, even though they may become heated at times and stray from the original topic. Here, for example, is the full conversation that followed from Bethany's rather brief recall narrative presented on page 319:

Adult: I saw you with lots of stuffed animals, Bethany.

Bethany: *(Giggles. Goes to the house area, gets as many stuffed animals as she can carry, and brings them back to the group.)*

Adult: Here they are!

Bethany: *(Makes each animal lie down. Pats each one.)*

Adult: *(Pats an animal.)*

Bethany: *(Smiles. Puts her finger to her lips.)* Shh!

Adult: Shh!

Markie: She's putting them to sleep!

Other children in the group: Shh! They're sleeping. *(Whispering)* We better whisper, okay?

Adult: *(Whispering)* Bethany played with the animals and put them all to sleep.

Bethany: And I gave them peaches. *(Pretends to feed a cat.)*

Joey: *(Out loud)* Cats don't like peaches. They like cat food!

Bethany: Peaches!

Erika: My dog likes bananas.

Joey: That's dumb. Dogs aren't supposed to eat bananas. They like bones.

This teacher uses a chart with the children's names and sticky notes labeled with the classroom area signs for recall time, which encourages other children to add in their own contributions.

Margo: My cat likes chicken bones, but my mom says he'll choke. But he just coughs up hair. Like this. *(Demonstrates.)*

Joey: Yeeck! That's gross.

Adult: Some cats like peaches, some like cat food. Some dogs like bananas, some like bones.

Margo: And chicken bones.

Adult: And chicken bones. Some cats like chicken bones.

Bethany: Peaches.

Joey: Oh, brother!

Acknowledge (rather than praise) children's work-time experiences

It is important to acknowledge children's work-time experiences rather than praise them. It is more beneficial to children in the long run if we *avoid phrases* such as "I *liked* the way you…" or "You really did a *good job* on…" however well intentioned these comments may be. Instead, comment on a specific aspect of a child's play, as shown in this conversation:

Adam: We put that big board up and…and Brian stood on the other side like this. *(Demonstrates.)* And I put that other board on. And then he didn't have to stay there anymore.

Adult: Brian didn't have to stay on the other side anymore.

Adam: No, because then it stood up and he didn't even have to hold it!

Adult: Your tower stayed up because Brian held it up while you leaned the long board against it.

Adam: Yeah! That's how we did it!

Writing down what children say as they recall is another way to acknowledge the importance of children's recall narratives. Recording recall narratives serves the same purpose and also allows adults to listen to themselves. As they listen, adults can evaluate which conversational strategies (such as contributing, commenting, repeating, acknowledging, and questioning) they use most often in recall conversations and how children are responding. While recordings take time to transcribe, once you hear what you have said, you can gain a clearer picture of how effectively you are supporting children's construction of memory.

Note connections between children's recall narratives and plans

It is instructive for adults to note connections between children's plans and what they choose to talk about at recall time. Often, experienced planners and recallers make these connections on their own — "I planned to play with Barbara, and we played baby with Gwen and Eva." Other children make a plan, complete it, and move on to something else. They may talk about this second activity in their recall narrative rather than discuss the activity they first anticipated and carried out. This is perfectly natural. As children grow in their ability to articulate what they want to do and construct memories in words, their understanding of the connections between their plans and recall narratives becomes increasingly apparent.

Adults anticipate changes in the way children recall over time

Over time, bolstered by daily experience, children's ability to recall increases. While preschoolers may still need to see or hold on to something they used at work time to spur their memories, they also

- Become increasingly able to add detail to their recall stories: what they used, how they worked or played, and with whom they played.

- Tell longer stories: "First we played wedding, and then...."

- Add to the recall narratives of their friends.

- Become aware of similarities between what they did at work time and what others did: "I did that too!"

- Include more detail in drawings of what they did.

- Anticipate how the activities of one work time might lead to further play at work time the next day.

It is noteworthy, too, that once children become accustomed to talking about what they have done at work time, they depend on the recall process to give a sense of closure to their work-time experiences.

In the following chapter, which concludes our discussion of the HighScope daily routine, we examine the purpose and meaning of other parts of the day — group times, outside time, and transitions — and offer suggestions to help adults make the most of these important active learning experiences.

How Adults Support Children's Recall: A Summary

Adults recall with children in a calm, cozy setting.
- Recall in intimate groups and places.
- Recall with those who shared the experiences children are recalling.

Adults provide materials and experiences to maintain children's interest at recall time.
- Tours
- Group games
- Props and partnerships
- Representations

Adults converse with children about their work-time experiences.
- Take an unhurried approach to recall.
- Invite children to talk about what they have done.
  - Pick up on children's opening comments.
  - Comment on a child's play.
  - Ask an open-ended question.
- Watch children and listen attentively.
- Contribute observations and comments to keep recall narratives going.
- Use questions thoughtfully and sparingly.
- Support children's co-narratives and conflicting viewpoints.
- Acknowledge (rather than praise) children's work-time experiences.
- Note connections between children's recall narratives and plans.

Adults anticipate changes in the way children recall over time.

This teacher uses a drum as a prop during recall time. The child with the drum can pat the drum and recall what he or she did during work time before passing it along to the next child.

CHAPTER 9

Group Times, Outside Times, Transitions

Although the **plan-do-review** process is the centerpiece of the HighScope daily routine, regular times are also allotted for other important experiences. These regularly scheduled events include:

- Small-group time
- Large-group time
- Outside time
- Transitions

Each of these times has distinctive features that create special opportunities for active learning.

At **small-** and **large-group times,** children participate in adult-initiated experiences in which they encounter new activities, concepts, and materials. These group activities also offer special opportunities for social interaction.

At **outside time**, children have access to a range of play experiences that differ from those available in the indoor setting. During this time, children can experience the sights and sounds of the outdoors, use outdoor play materials and equipment, and play vigorously and noisily (or quietly, if they prefer).

During **transitions,** children move from one activity to the next. Rather than regarding transitions as incidental events, adults in HighScope programs use these times to provide children with opportunities for choice-making, movement activities, and a variety of learning experiences.

Though these special times have distinctive features, they share a common goal: to encourage children's active involvement with materials, people, ideas, and events. During group times, outside time, and transitions, active learning is the guiding philosophy, just as it is during plan-do-review. Throughout these activities, children make choices and decisions, learn through direct experience, and talk about what they are doing.

This chapter presents the unique features of each of these parts of the daily routine and the ways adults implement an active learning philosophy throughout small- and large-group times, outside time, and transitions.

> "Why do small groups seem to work so well — for people of all ages? People process information better and seem to stay more attentive, focused, and engaged when they are part of a small group in which everyone has a chance to contribute and to hear what others think. Even nonverbal children are able to observe others' work in a small group and get ideas from their peers."
>
> — Hyson (2008, p. 88)

Special Features of Group Times

Small- and large-group times are adult initiated — they are planned and set in motion by the adult. At small-group time, an adult meets with 5 to 10 children each day for about 15 to 20 minutes. The adult provides common sets of materials children can use for exploring, creating, experimenting, or building. At large-group times, adults meet briefly with the entire group of children for about 10 to 15 minutes to sing songs, do fingerplays, tell and reenact stories, move to music, or participate in action games or other group activities.

Because these group times are initiated by adults, they present an opportunity to introduce various concepts, activities, and materials to children. At large-group time, for example, the adult might interact with children to create a new variation of a familiar song or game. At small-group time, the adult might introduce new materials or new combinations of materials to children — a computer program, counting bears and small blocks, or toy farm animals. Sometimes, the materials the adult sets out at small-group time have already been available in the classroom; the small-group time, however, allows children who have not yet used the materials to explore them in a comfortable setting.

Group times also offer special social opportunities. During the child-initiated parts of the routine, children can choose how solitary or sociable they wish to be — working by themselves, with a friend or adult, or with a group. Since some children will choose not to play with others during these times, the group times offer additional opportunities for them to participate in a social experience. At small-group time, for example, where everyone is working with the same materials, children often share and discuss what they are doing, learn from one another, and help one another. At large-group time, where everyone is engaged in a common action game or song (all of which are safe, low-risk social experiences), children have opportunities to contribute and demonstrate their ideas to the group as well as to imitate and learn from their peers.

Briefly, then, group times in HighScope settings are not times for rigid routines, complicated games, or teacher-led lessons. Instead, the hallmarks of group activities are the ingredients of active learning (materials, manipulation, choice, child language and thought, adult scaffolding); flexibility; and openness to children's signals, interests, initiatives, and ideas.

Scaffolding Children's Learning at Group Times

In the HighScope Curriculum, scaffolding means to both

- *Support* children at their current developmental and ability level.
- *Gently extend* children's learning as they move to the next level.

Group times provide many opportunities to scaffold children's learning in every area of the curriculum. The challenge is how to do this in ways that incorporate active learning and take into account how children learn.

Young children learn in a sequential process; they build on their existing knowledge and skills to acquire new concepts and abilities. For example, in mathematics, children must understand the concepts of longer and shorter before they can measure and compare two lengths. Beginning readers must know the sounds of individual letters before they can blend two or more letters to make a word. In the area of physical development, children use two hands to manipulate objects before they can do things one-handed. A child must have the fine-motor control to handle a crayon before using it as a drawing tool. This type of sequencing is found in virtually every domain of development.

In designing group activities, there are two ways to approach the sequential nature of learning. Most curriculum models sequence the learning *across* activities. All the children in a class participate in the same activity in the same way as they move through a fixed sequence of activities over time. The disadvantage to this approach is that children at different developmental or ability levels may be lost or left behind if the class proceeds to the next activity before they are ready. If some children are more advanced than their peers, they may become bored and disinterested.

A contrasting approach — the one used in the HighScope Curriculum — is to sequence the learning *within* each activity. Children participate together in the same activity, but it is open ended to accommodate a range of developmental and ability levels. This allows children to engage with the materials and ideas according to their current knowledge and skills and enables teachers to individualize their scaffolding strategies. Children of all backgrounds and ability levels can therefore enjoy the activity and experience success. See "The Four Steps in Scaffolding Children's Learning" on page 329 for a more detailed description on how teachers can incorporate scaffolding into their teaching.

The daily group times described in this chapter encourage teachers to use the ingredients of active learning to scaffold development for individual children and for the class as a whole. For further information on scaffolding learning in the specific curriculum content areas, see the scaffolding charts in the **key developmental indicator (KDI)** books that accompany this manual. The charts in those books contain ideas to help teachers sequence learning for children at earlier, middle, and later levels of development.

Understanding Small-Group Time

In the HighScope Curriculum, small-group times are adult-initiated activities during which children explore materials in their own way with the adult sharing the excitement of their discoveries. As they experiment with the materials, children talk about their observations and discoveries and solve the problems they encounter. *Adult-initiated* means the teacher plans the materials and the learning experience based on the curriculum content, children's interests, and children's developmental and ability levels. To illustrate the dynamics between adults and children during small-group time, we have re-created two actual small-group times from HighScope preschool programs.

The "Pineapple Connection"

Carol and Elaine have taken their children to a farmers' market where the children are particularly intrigued by a basket of pineapples. The adults buy four of the pineapples, and the next day these pineapples become the focus of Carol's and Elaine's small-group times. Here is a sample of what happened in Carol's group:

Carol cuts one pineapple into slices and gives a slice to each child. Joanie licks her slice. Antoine watches her intently and then takes a tentative lick of his own slice. Jeff matter-of-factly takes a bite: "I like it. It's...sweet."

"I'm going to cut the stickers off mine," announces Teresa.

"Me, too," says Felix. They go to the house area for some table knives. This idea catches on and soon many children are cutting their pineapple pieces, "making juice," and examining the "pineapple string."

"Watch out. It sticks. It's tangled into my teeth!" warns Jeff.

Carol leaves the second uncut pineapple in the middle of the table.

"I don't want to touch that. It's got stickers," says Teresa.

"Let me feel it. Let me feel it," says Sammy. "Ouch!" He draws his hand back.

"It's prickery to me too," says Pepe.

"Look at me! I'm holding it by the leaves! It's not prickery to me!" says Jennifer.

"I can make it roll," says Kadith. "See?" She rolls it across the table to Pepe.

"It goes kind of crooked," Pepe notices.

All the Colors of the Rainbow

Becki has prepared materials for the children in her small group to color eggs. The table is covered with newspaper, and a plastic cup holding a small amount of vinegar awaits each child.

"What is this?" someone asks.

"Well, see if you can tell by using your nose," Becki replies.

In the HighScope Curriculum, learning is sequenced within each activity, so children can engage with materials according to their current knowledge and skills.

"It's gross!"
"If you drink it you'll get sick!"
"Mine spilled!"
"Just what happened with mine."
"It stinks, yewee! It stinks!"
"It does stink," says Becki. "It's vinegar."
"Vinegar, yuck!"

"I'm giving you each a color tablet, then water and a spoon, then eggs," Becki says, giving each child a tablet. The children drop their tablets in their vinegar.

"Colors!"
"It turned a color!"
"Mine is turning green, Becki!"
"It is turning green," Becki acknowledges.
"Mine is coming into orange!"
"Mine is turning to yellow."
"Mine is turning to red."
"Mine turned to orange."
"Watch that. That turned to yellow!"
"Does the green really go even to the bottom?"
"It's spreading."

"It is spreading," Becki says to Catherine who has been looking at the bottom of her cup.

"It's really, really green! Even on the bottom."

The children talk excitedly about the colors they see emerging and pour water from a small pitcher into their colored vinegar. Becki gives each child three hard-boiled eggs in a small berry basket. "When you put them in gently," she says, "they won't crack."

"Drop it in gently!"
"Mine's on top."
"Look, I did it gently."

There's a lull in the conversation as children concentrate on putting their eggs into the dye. Some use their hands while others use spoons.

"I think I need a little bit more water," Amy says.

"You get it on your fingers," says Boomer.

"I'm keeping mine in for a long time!" says Namen.

"What will happen to it in a long time?" Becki asks.

"It'll catch more color," Namen answers.

The Four Steps in Scaffolding Children's Learning

Step 1. Identify the content area and materials to be used.
- What is the content focus?
- What materials are the children interested in using?

Hint: These can come in either order (content or materials first) as you think about small-group time, as long as you take both into consideration.

Step 2. Consider children's developmental range.
- Think in terms of three broad ranges of development: earlier, middle, and later.
- How are the children in each range likely to respond to the content and materials?

Hint: Expect children to use materials in their own unique ways. Anticipate how they *might* respond but support what they *actually* do.

Step 3. Provide support at each child's current developmental level.
- Imitate the child's actions.
- Label the child's actions.
- Introduce additional vocabulary to describe what the child is doing.
- Ask the child to describe his or her actions.

Hint: Pause to see how the child responds to what you are saying. This will give you clues about whether to continue with step 3 or try step 4.

Step 4. Offer gentle extensions.
- Comment on what another child is doing.
- Ask the child to explain his or her thinking.
- Gently introduce a new idea or material.
- Pose a new challenge.

Hint: Carefully observe how children respond to your extension. Pushing them to advance before they are ready can make them lose interest, discourage their initiative, and weaken their trust in your dependability to support their efforts.

"Oh, the egg catches the color," Becki says.

"Yeah, if you put it in just a little bit, just a little bit gets on there," he answers.

"Would you like to trade colors?" Catherine asks Caleb.

"Mine turned something…red!" Kyle says.

"Mine spilled again," says Namen. Becki passes him some towels.

"Becki, I need another color," says Namen.

"Catherine and Caleb traded colors," Becki says. "Maybe someone will trade with you."

"Can I use your color?" Namen asks Amy.

"Want to trade colors?" she replies.

"Here, guys, blue!" Max says.

"I'm gonna make mine two different colors, red and yellow!" Namen says.

"I want red now," Catherine says to Kyle. "Can I have your spoon too?"

"Look at mine, look at mine!" says Namen.

"Look at yours, Namen!" Becki says.

"I need orange," Boomer says.

"Kyle has orange," says Max.

"Becki, don't take it out. It needs more green," Caleb advises.

"Okay," Becki agrees.

Two children pour their dyes together. "It looks like dog doo but it isn't. I made mine all different colors."

"I need more eggs!" says Catherine.

"We only cooked enough eggs for each person to have three," Becki says.

"Mine cracked," Boomer says.

"Sometimes that happens," Becki says.

"But that's okay," Max says.

"It sure is!" Becki agrees.

"I'm done," Catherine says. She goes to the window ledge and gets another basket she has decorated (at an earlier small-group time) with real grass (planted several weeks before). She puts her three colored eggs on top of the grass.

"Look what Catherine did," Becki says, holding up Catherine's basket. "Here's her basket with her grass and her three eggs."

In this small-group time, children use eyedroppers and colored water to make new colors.

The children talk together as they add their eggs to their baskets. "We can take them home today, can't we Becki?"

"You sure can," she agrees.

The children admire their baskets, help clean up the table, and gather with Becki again for planning time.

What is small-group time?

As illustrated in the previous examples, at small-group time the same group of children meets each day with the same adult for about 15 to 20 minutes. In this intimate setting, children are given their own materials, make choices about how to use them, and talk with one another and the adult about what they are doing.

An unchanging group of children with the same adult

Small groups should be created with *consistency* and *composition* in mind. To keep small groups consistent

- Small groups should meet at the same time each day, each group of children with their same classroom adult.
- Groups (children and their teacher) should stay together for two to three months.
- Groups should always meet in the same place. Sometimes, however, groups may need to meet in a different place (e.g., the block area or outdoors). At these times, the group should meet in its normal spot first and then move to the other location.
- Adults should post a list of the group members' names and their letter-linked symbols by their meeting place.

To create the composition of a small group, adults should

- Determine group size by dividing the number of children by the number of classroom adults. For example, in a class with two adults (one teacher and one assistant teacher) and 18 children, each group has 9 children. In a class with three adults (one teacher and two aides) and 21 children, each group has 7 children.
- Balance groups by gender, age (developmental and/or ability level), and temperament.
- Place children who play together in the same group.

Active learning in a supportive setting

At small-group time, adults introduce the activity but then allow children to work with materials in their own way and at their own rate. Children make choices and decisions about what to do with the materials, talk with one another and the adult about what they are doing, and receive appropriate adult support and encouragement. Small-group time provides children with the daily opportunity to try out their own ideas as well as the ideas of others, and children often carry small-group ideas into their work-time play. Attentive adults create this safe setting and are close by to act as partners in children's discoveries. All the ingredients of active learning are present:

Materials: Children use their own set of materials.

Manipulation: Children experiment with the materials, using them in ways that make sense to them (which may or may not be what the teacher originally had in mind).

Choice: Children choose what to do with the materials offered, based on their personal interests and ability levels.

Child language and thought: Children talk about their ideas and discoveries.

Adult scaffolding: Adults support and gently extend each child's learning.

An adult-initiated learning experience based on children's interests and development

While adults plan and introduce small-group-time learning experiences, such as building with blocks, working in the garden, and making collages from materials collected on a walk, their inspiration for

Small-group time introduces children to active learning experiences, such as exploring and "painting" with shaving cream on a plastic table.

each small-group experience comes from their understanding of what children learn (based on the curriculum content in the KDIs and COR Advantage) and what children like to do as they pursue their interests. Small-group times also provide an opportunity to introduce new materials or allow children to use familiar materials in unexplored ways. Family and community traditions that children are familiar with and interested in also provide ideas for planning small-group times.

Here are some examples of how small-group time originates:

Several children were very enthusiastic about tossing blocks into the block box at cleanup time, so Beth planned a small-group time around beanbags and baskets that built on this interest, KDI 16. Gross-motor skills, and COR Advantage Item I. Gross-motor skills. Some children stood very close to their "targets" while others challenged themselves by tossing their beanbags into the box from farther and farther away.

Knowing how excited children were about Halloween and realizing that many would stay up late that night, Becki and Beth planned a small-group time for the day after Halloween that involved using play dough and "slime." They had decided that this tactile experience would satisfy the children's interest in Halloween-related play without taxing their patience. Indeed, after their trick-or-treating adventures, the children were happy to return to a familiar material they could easily shape and control. While exploring their enduring

interest in these materials, the children were also engaging with several Science and Technology KDIs (45. Observing, 47. Experimenting, 49. Drawing conclusions, and 50. Communicating ideas) as well as COR Advantage items in Science and Technology (BB. Observing and classifying and CC. Experimenting, predicting, and drawing conclusions).

Since the children in her small group often requested the story Caps for Sale and were also involved in role play at both work time and outside time, Becki planned a small-group time around reenacting the story using different colored caps for props. This involved KDIs in Creative Arts (43. Pretend play) and Language, Literacy, and Communication (21. Comprehension and 28. Book knowledge) as well as COR Advantage Item BB. Observing and classifying. The children took turns being "the peddler," but their favorite role was "being monkeys." They decided the hollow blocks could be their tree "because we need to climb up and throw the caps down."

For more information and examples on ideas for small-group times, see "Ideas for Small-Group Times" on pages 334–335.

Why is small-group time important?

Small-group time builds on children's strengths, introduces children to materials and experiences they might otherwise miss, and provides adults with an intimate setting in which to observe and learn about individual children on a daily basis.

An opportunity to build on children's strengths

By planning small-group activities around children's emerging abilities, adults can help children consolidate what they are learning and develop related skills. Shannon, for example, observed her children and discussed her ideas during team planning: "Alex, Audie, and Sarah are really involved in cutting, so I'm going to plan a small-group time using scissors and construction paper. It's not too thick and it's not too flimsy, so everyone in my group can be successful." Small-group times planned with children's interests in mind encourage children to do things they can and like to do. As they gain confidence in their abilities, children are willing to take on new challenges: "I don't want this paper," says Julia. "I'm going to get some magazines to cut."

An opportunity to provide new materials and experiences

"Kacey, Frances, and JoJo like to play in the water. I'm going to plan a small-group time with water and introduce turkey basters and short lengths of hose," Sue says to her coteacher Becki. At small-group times adults can present children with new materials — a computer program, saws and wood, a set of interlocking blocks — as well as "old" materials children may be overlooking — toy farm animals and blocks, beads and strings, sticky-backed foam scraps and paper towel tubes. Thus, for children who choose to play with blocks at work time, small group may be a time to try out scissors, musical instruments, or sand and water. For children who choose to draw and paint at work time, small group may be a time to build with blocks, act out stories, and wash bicycles. In this manner, children discover new ideas to incorporate into their play at work time, outside time, and home.

An opportunity for regular peer contacts and interactions

Small-group time draws a little band of children together to explore the same materials. Because of their close proximity, children have lots of opportunities to interact and communicate with one another. Children who play by themselves at work time will play next to other children at small-group time. In fact, children may team up to help each other out: "Megan, will you take the wrappers off my Band Aid?" Alex asks. "Namen, can I use your orange egg dye?" Kyle asks.

Ideas for Small-Group Times

Where do adults get ideas when planning small-group times? Here are four sources you can use and several examples of activities that originated with each one.

Content area

- Think about what content area(s) will be supported by a small-group time (appropriate content areas include the KDIs and items from COR Advantage).
- Plan around the content areas that you see emerging in children's play.
- Plan around content areas you have not yet observed to get more information about children's developmental and ability levels.

Examples:

- Noting children's interest in playing musical instruments at work time and parading with them at outside time, Beth planned a small-group time around KDI 41. Music and COR Advantage Item U. Measurement. Each child chose an instrument and together the group played along to fast and slow musical selections. Midway through the activity, one child requested, "Let's play another fast song." Another child said, "After that, do the slow song again."
- Interested in KDI 38. Patterns and COR Advantage Item V. Patterns, Ann provided each child in her small group with lengths of wide, flat ribbon in several colors along with paper and a glue stick. "What could you do with these ribbons?" she asked. She then watched to see if any patterns emerged in the children's creations. Amy made a border on her paper that repeated the pattern red-white-red-white-red-white. Namen made a "wild man" with alternating green and blue ribbon hair. Claire announced, "I'm making a flower with three colors." She arranged a circle of yellow, green, and purple ribbon "petals" in an ABC-ABC-ABC pattern.
- Keeping in mind the KDI 16. Gross-motor skills and COR Advantage Item I. Gross-motor skills, Sam planned an outdoor small-group time around walking on tin-can stilts. He provided children with a choice of stilts in a variety of heights (from tuna cans to coffee cans) so that each child could find a comfortable height, and fastened them securely to the children's feet with thick elasticized bands. The children found it was easier to walk on the paved area (where they rode their tricycles) than on the grass where, according to Jeremy, "the stilts sink in the dirt." They tried walking, stomping, hopping, and skating on the stilts. "I can march lifting my knees real high," said Bella, demonstrating. "Me too," said Felicity, copying her movements.

Children's interests

- Think about what children like to do, the materials they like to use, and how they interact and play with one another; planning small-group times around children's interests can motivate their initial engagement with the materials.
- Always layer children's interests into the content area you focus on (i.e., do not consider content without also taking children's interests into account).

Examples:

- At outside time, Betsy helped four children figure out together how to push a wagonload of sticks and tires around the playground. As she described their interaction at team planning, Betsy decided to plan a cooperative-play small-group time using long planks and boards that were too heavy for one child to manage alone. The children worked in twos, threes, and fours to carry the planks and boards from one place to another and to lift them to make steps, ramps, and other constructions. Betsy added to the children's vocabulary by commenting that they were working *together*, *cooperating*, and acting as a *team*.
- Becki noticed that the children in her small group liked to say rhymes, so she planned a small-group time around reading a picture book that repeated several short rhymes the children could easily anticipate and learn by "reading" the pictures. When they were familiar with the book, several children added their own rhymes, using real and made-up words.

- At work time, Ann noticed that several children working in the art area were really involved in squeezing glue on to pieces of construction paper. This prompted her to plan a "squeezing" small-group time using plastic ketchup and mustard bottles at the water table. She filled some of the bottles with plain water, others with colored water, and still others with liquid dish soap (that made bubbles) so the children could see different liquids emerge when they squeezed them. Ann also provided deep and shallow containers for the children to practice squeezing the liquid into.

New and unexplored materials

- Introduce materials new to the classroom during small-group time, which gives children a chance to try out the materials and help decide where they should be stored.

- Observe materials children do not use; that is, have never used or stopped using. Reintroducing these materials at small-group time may reawaken children's interest in them. You might also consider combining familiar materials in new ways, for example, using animal figures with blocks.

Examples:

- Linda planned a small-group time around the materials children had gathered on a walk around the block — stones, chestnuts, leaves, twigs, an old windshield wiper, a hubcap, and hedge clippings. In response to Linda's question, "What can we do with these things we found on our walk?" children got tape and clay and made musical instruments, collages, animals, dog and cat houses, "soup" and "pizza," and people.

- Becki introduced nine new rubber playground balls at a small-group time she held outside. The children rolled, kicked, threw, and bounced their balls. Carlos tried to walk cradling a ball under his arm, and Marcy and Rose sat opposite each other and rolled a ball back and forth between the V they made with their legs. At the end of small-group time, they put the balls in the storage shed "for outside time."

- One team introduced children to a new combination of materials — golf-ball tees (which the children had been inserting in play dough) and pieces of Styrofoam (which they had been using at the workbench). Some children filled pieces of Styrofoam with golf-ball tees, randomly or in patterns. Others made "cakes" (using the tees as birthday candles) and "walkie-talkies" (pretending the tees were buttons they pushed to make calls and send messages).

Local traditions

- Occasionally look to local traditions and community events that children are familiar with and interested in. These can include festivals, holidays, or seasonal activities that are part of their lives, for example, collecting fall leaves, decorating pumpkins, or sprucing up the playground for a community cleanup day.

- Invite family members to join small-group times and share their traditions.

Examples:

- After Mardi Gras, a major community celebration, Helena and Sarah noticed that their children were very interested in costumes, so they planned costume-making small-group times. They provided children with butcher-paper smocks (with head and arm holes), crepe paper, scissors, and tape so they could make their own colorful cos-

tumes like the ones they had seen in the parade. Some children taped small pieces of crepe paper to their smocks while others preferred long streamers. As backup materials, Helena and Sarah also set out feathers and ribbons for the children to decorate their costumes.

- In a center where one of the children's parents was a weaver, the teaching team planned a small-group time around outdoor weaving. The weaver mom set up two simple outdoor looms and went back and forth between the two groups helping children weave in streamers and materials they found outside, including sticks, leaves, plant stalks, grass, and even a sandbox shovel and a plastic snake.

- After a trip to a nearby pumpkin patch, Ruth and Ann planned their small-group time around exploring the pumpkins the children had gathered. Since the weather was still nice, they spread newspapers outside, helped the children cut the tops off their pumpkins, and provided spoons for "scooping out the insides." Many children preferred to use their hands to dig out the "yucky slime and seeds." They washed the seeds, let them dry, and toasted them for a healthy snack.

Small-group time also provides children with the opportunity for *immediate feedback from peers* on their work: "Hey, look what Louie did!" "See, mine stays up all by itself!" In this way, children comment on one another's discoveries and learn from their peers. Such interactions are important, report developmental psychologists Rheta DeVries and Lawrence Kohlberg (1987): "When the child has the experience of others who react to what he says, he begins to feel that the truth is important" (pp. 30–31). The consistency of the small-group-time community provides a *social anchor* for children and an important contrast to the openness of work time when children play alone or in spontaneous groups throughout the interest areas.

An opportunity for adults to observe and interact daily with the same children

Adults can observe children's development over time, appreciate individual differences, and begin to predict how children in their groups will respond to small-group experiences adults plan. As Linda plans a small-group time using glue, for example, she imagines how each child in her group might respond: "I think Corey and Joanie will just want to squeeze their glue bottles and watch the glue dribble out on the paper. Lynnette and Tracy will probably glue scraps and shapes to their paper, and Wendy and Erica may have a plan in mind of a particular thing they want to

---

The Importance of Small-Group Time

Builds on children's strengths
- Small-group times are planned around children's emerging abilities.
- Adults support and extend each child's learning.
- As children gain confidence in their abilities, they are willing to take on new challenges.

Provides new materials and experiences
- Small-group times can introduce children to materials and experiences they might otherwise miss.
- Children can incorporate new materials and ideas into their play at other times of the day.
- Teachers can use small-group times to appropriately build in content experiences.

Provides regular peer interaction
- Small-group times provide children with the opportunity to form stable relationships.
- Children begin to appreciate the qualities and strengths of others in their group.
- Children can develop confidence speaking to this smaller group of peers.
- For these reasons, HighScope recommends children stay in the same small groups for two to three months.

Enables adults to learn more about their group.
- Adults have the opportunity to observe and interact daily with the same children, learning more about their abilities and interests.
- Adults can observe children's development over time.
- Adults can anticipate how individual children might react to the small-group experiences they plan (but are prepared to be surprised).

Gives adults an opportunity to use support strategies.
- Small-group times give teachers the opportunity to practice their adult-child interaction skills in a stable setting.
- Adults can refer children to one another for ideas and help.

Small-group times enable adults to observe, interact, and learn more about children's abilities and interests.

represent. Wendy has been drawing horses lately, so she might try to make a horse out of shapes and scraps. I'll have some yarn available too. She might use it for a tail or mane."

An opportunity for adults to practice support strategies in a stable setting

Watching and listening to children at small-group time gives adults an excellent opportunity to practice support strategies. In the following example, Mrs. L., aware that her habit of asking too many questions sometimes inhibits children's conversations, practices repeating and commenting on children's observations as an alternative to questioning:

Rita: See my play dough. It's flat.

Mrs. L.: Your play dough is flat.

Rita: I know. My hands are stronger…stronger than play dough.

Mrs. L.: Oh, your hands are stronger than play dough.

Rita: Yeah. That's why it squeezes out. See, I'll show you.

Mrs. L.: I see.

Rita: And if you stand up it's even stronger!

Another adult, Mr. P., takes the opportunity to practice referring one child to another rather than doing things for them:

Alice: *(Says to Mr. P.)* How do you get this…all…all spread on the table?

Mr. P.: It looks like Rahima has figured out a way.

Alice: *(Watches Rahima)* How do you do that?

Rahima: Like this. *(She demonstrates.)*

Where small groups meet

When planning a place for each small group to meet, designate a consistent gathering place, but do not confine yourself to experiences that can only be done in that place. Be willing to move to wherever the relevant materials are located.

Gather together in a consistent place

Pick out places in your setting where each small group can gather and work comfortably — on the floor in the block area, at the table in the art area, or outside under a tree. A designated gathering place for each small group gives children a sense of belonging and control. If Anna knows that her small group gathers at the house-area table, she can go there every day on her own at small-group time and know that she will meet with Beth, her teacher, and the same seven children.

Go to the relevant materials

While a consistent gathering place is important, it is equally important not to be limited by your location. Often, you will spend small-group time in the place where you gather, but other times, after gathering, you will go together as a small group to the sandbox, the garden, the workbench, the butcher paper on the floor, or the totem pole outside.

At the beginning of the year, teachers Beth and Becki chose the art- and house-area tables as their small-group-time gathering places. As they talked with children at planning time, they realized that many of the children were not aware of what was in each interest area and their lack of knowledge limited their work-time plans. Therefore, the adults planned small-group times that would explore the interest areas. For example, after Becki's group gathered at the house-area table, they went together to the block area "to find all the things there are to play with." There, Becki's children discovered the steering wheel and the large blocks. Meanwhile, Beth's group gathered at the art-area table: "Let's 'sneak' to the house area (her children liked to 'sneak') and see what we can find to play with." They found poker chips, bottle caps, and chestnuts inside canisters, a stack of diapers, and dishes for setting the table. Later, the children incorporated some of these "new" materials into their work-time play.

What children do at small-group time

The discussion of small groups began with examples of small-group times in which children cut up pineapples and colored eggs. Here is another account of the egg-coloring small-group time from the perspective of one child, Catherine:

*Catherine is one of the first children to arrive at her teacher Becki's small group. Catherine converses with Amy across the table. Then she listens as the other children talk about the smell of the vinegar, and she watches Namen mop up his spill. Catherine is very interested in watching what happens when the children add their pellets to their vinegar. When she adds her own pellet she says, "Mine is turning green, Becki!" "It **is** turning green," Becki acknowledges. After watching the color spread through the vinegar, Catherine asks, "Does the green really go even to the bottom?" She lifts her cup over her head to look at it from the bottom. "It's spreading," she says. "It is spreading," Becki acknowledges. "It's really, really green! Even on the bottom," Catherine says.*

Next, Catherine pours water into her cup of green-colored vinegar, watches Becki balance an egg on a spoon, and then puts her first egg into the dye using her fingers. Her hands get a little wet and green. She shakes the water drops off, and then leaves the table to get a towel from the bathroom. When she returns, she takes her egg out with a spoon, looks at it, returns it to the dye solution, takes it out again after a short while, puts it on the table in front of her, and wipes her fingers on the newspaper covering the table. Turning to her peer Boomer, she asks, "Would you like to trade?" Boomer doesn't respond, so she turns to Caleb, and asks, "Would you like to trade colors?" "Sure!" Caleb takes her green solution and she takes his yellow solution. Catherine tries to explain to Caleb

After meeting at their usual gathering place, this small group moved together to the butcher paper on the floor where they could explore paint and a new material — sponge paint wands.

that the spoon goes with the dye, but he wants his original spoon, so she keeps her "green-dye" spoon. Suddenly, Caleb understands the purpose of the exchange request, gives Catherine the yellow-dye spoon, and takes the spoon for the green dye.

Catherine stirs the yellow dye, adds her second egg, turns it over occasionally with her spoon, watches Caleb spoon the green-dye solution over his yellow egg, and then takes out her yellow egg, placing it on the table next to her green egg. "I want red now," she says to Kyle. "Can I have your spoon too?" They make the trade. She dyes her last egg. "I need more eggs!" she says. "We only cooked enough eggs for each person to have three," Becki tells her.

Catherine informs Boomer that one of his eggs is cracked, then says, "I'm done." She goes to the window ledge, gets her grass basket, and carefully puts in her three dyed eggs, parting the grass for each egg. She then takes the basket to Becki. "Look what Catherine did," Becki says to the other children, who are still working. "Here's her basket with her grass and three eggs." As they finish dying their eggs, the other children follow Catherine's lead. While Catherine watches, Amy fills her basket with three colored eggs and they talk about their worktime plan to play together with Sarah.

Children explore, play, work with materials, and talk about what they are doing

Catherine's varied experiences and interactions during this one small-group session illustrate the diverse learning opportunities these times offer. To support children appropriately at small-group time, it is important for adults to realize that children use small-group time to explore, play, work with materials, and converse. Thus, small-group time offers a range of active learning experiences. Children use materials in a variety of ways guided by their imagination, creativity, and personal intentions. They explore with all their senses ("This pineapple tastes yucky!"), discover relations through direct experience ("Look, it's yellow! Mine turned yellow!"), transform and combine materials ("I'm going to put some beans in my dough"), and acquire skills with tools and equipment ("This beater makes the bubbles really big. Bigger than ever!"). They make choices about what to do with materials ("I'm pushing down on my pineapple; the juice comes out") and materials to add ("This glue doesn't stick — I'm getting some tape"). They talk about what they are doing with other group members ("Hey, everybody, there's a worm in my dirt!"), and they think and reason out loud ("It won't bounce because…because it sticks to the floor!"). Each small-group time presents many active learning challenges as children work with materials, select additional materials, talk about their work, solve problems, and comment on the work of others.

Children solve problems they encounter

As they work with materials, solving a problem presented by an adult (e.g., "Let's see what we can do with these tubs full of snow"), children also form their own goals and discover problems they need to solve to accomplish them: "I'm making my snow into a house…. But the roof?… It has to go over this hole…I know. Sticks!" In the anecdote about coloring eggs, Caleb and Namen decide to make their eggs two different colors. Caleb does this by dying his egg yellow and spooning green dye over it. Namen goes about it a different way. He dips one end of his egg in green dye and the other end in orange dye. For young children, solving small-group problems means looking to see

These children at small-group time use cloth elastics, homemade geoboards, and people figures to play "family" — the geoboards and the cloth elastics are the house and the people are mom, dad, and the sisters.

what other people are doing and experimenting with their own ideas.

When small-group time involves a new material, such as chestnuts picked up on a walk, cardboard packing boxes, or a set of large Tinkertoys, children also solve the problem of where these materials should be stored so that they will know where to find them at work time: "I know…let's put these [chestnuts] in a can over there [points to the house area]…then we can make soup!"

How Adults Support Children at Small-Group Time

Above all, small-group time is supposed to be an enjoyable event in which an adult brings a small group of children together to use a common set of materials according to the children's interests and understanding. Adults support children at small-group time by using the following strategies:

- Preparing for small groups *before* the children arrive
- Setting small groups in motion: The beginning
- Scaffolding children's ideas and use of materials: The middle
- Bringing small-group time to a close: The end

Adults prepare for small groups *before* children arrive

Once adults have a plan firmly in mind, small-group time requires adult preparation before the children arrive. Two strategies that help adults get ready are gathering materials for each child and putting them within easy reach of children.

Gather materials for each child and adult

Since children learn from their own interactions with materials (as opposed to watching someone else), small-group time works best when each child has a set of materials to use. This means providing children with their own collection of small blocks and cars, paintbrushes and jars of paint, slices of pineapple, play dough and cookie cutters, rocks and magnifying glasses, or whatever materials the small-group experience involves. Adults should also have a set of materials so they can play alongside the children, imitating their actions and trying out the children's ideas.

Have materials ready

Gather materials before children arrive and put them in a spot close to your small-group meeting place. This allows you to get small groups started as soon as children gather. One team started the day with small-group time, setting out materials on the table in the art and house areas each day before the children arrived. Another team scheduled small-group time right after recall time. In the morning, before the children arrived, they sorted small-group materials into bags, boxes, or baskets that they stored close to their meeting places so that they could pass them out quickly at the beginning of small-group time. (See "Preparing for Small-Group Time" on p. 342.)

Adults set small groups in motion: The beginning

Children come to small-group time eager to begin. Here are two strategies that allow them to get started with a minimum of delay.

Give children materials as they arrive

Often adults set small-group time in motion simply by having materials out when children assemble. When presented with a pile of blocks, markers, and paper, or a hat full of little animals, a child will generally begin to build, draw, or play.

Make a brief opening statement to introduce the activity

Opening statements serve to introduce the activity to the children. They capture the children's attention and get them engaged with the materials. Statements should be brief so the children can begin to work with the materials and carry out their own ideas as soon as possible. There are

Preparing for Small-Group Time

Review your plan.
- Anticipate children's reactions but be prepared to be flexible and follow in whatever directions the children's interests take them. *Reminder:* Each small group in the classroom will do its own activity, based on the children in that particular group.

Gather a set of materials for each child and for yourself.
- For example, for an art-focused small-group time, you might include scissors, glue stick, and paper scraps in each basket.

Sort the materials into individual containers.
- Use small baskets, yogurt containers, trays, lunch bags, shoeboxes, and so on to hold a set of materials for each child and for you.

Have backup materials ready.
- Backup materials are extra materials that you may distribute to help extend the small-group activity, for example, more paper scraps, yarn, and feathers for the art-focused small-group time.

Place materials within easy reach of your small-group meeting place.
- Distribute materials shortly after you introduce the activity so children do not have to wait to get started.

The benefits of preparing ahead of time
- Cuts down on wait time
- Makes materials easy to distribute to children
- Ensures that each child will have what he or she needs

four types of opening statements typically used at small-group time. You can

- Describe the materials.
- Connect the materials to children's previous play or interests.
- Tell a short and simple open-ended story using the materials (called a *story starter*).
- Make a statement that draws children's attention to a content focus (KDI or COR Advantage item).

Adults scaffold children's ideas and use of materials: The middle

Once children have their materials and are involved cutting paper, stacking blocks, filling and emptying squeeze bottles, cutting and tasting pineapples, or pounding nails into soft pine, it is up to adults to support their efforts. The following strategies will help you do so.

Move to the children's physical level

If children are sitting on the floor, sit on the floor with them. If they are kneeling around a large piece of butcher paper, kneel around it with them. If they are marching in a parade, march with them. Joining children at their physical level gives you an idea of what they are seeing and experiencing and makes you easily accessible for conversation and play.

Watch what children do with materials

This gives you an idea of how each child interprets the initial challenge. Frances fills her whole pegboard with pegs, Kacey makes a pattern, Julia counts her pegs, and Douglas sees how high he

Opening Statements for Small-Group Times

Opening statements help to focus the children's attention on the small-group activity. Below are four types of opening statements, each used to illustrate the same small-group activity: writing with markers on dry-erase boards.

Simply describe the materials.
"In your baskets, you'll find some special markers and white drawing boards. When you are done drawing, see what happens when you wipe your board with your cloth."

Connect the activity to the children's interests.
"Yesterday, during work time, Amaia and Jordyn wrote some letters on our message board. Today, I thought it would be fun for us to write on our own message boards. Let's see what you can do."

Tell a short and simple open-ended story (also called a *story starter*).
"Once upon a time, there were some letters playing on a board. Soon, more and more of their letter friends joined them. Here are some markers and boards you can use to make your own letter stories."

Draw attention to a content focus.
"We always have drawings on our message board, and sometimes we also have letters. Today, for small-group time, you each have your own message board. I'm curious to see what letters you write."

can stack his pegs. Adults will observe a range of responses within their groups — from Megan who watches other children get started before painting with her water colors to Alex who covers his paper with green and blue to Julia who mixes colors for "pea soup." Adults will also see various KDIs emerge as Audie counts the number of steps he takes on his stilts (KDI 32. Counting), Sarah talks about the noise the stilts make (KDIs 46. Classifying and 50. Communicating ideas), and Amos fills his stilt cans with pea gravel (KDI 35. Spatial awareness). Using this kind of information, adults can begin to see how they might interact to support each child appropriately. Occasionally, adults will also introduce backup materials if children seem interested. For example, if Amos is curious about the sound that pea gravel makes in his stilt cans, the teacher might have a few different filler materials on hand for him and others to try.

Listen to what children say

By listening attentively to children, you learn what they find interesting and what they are thinking about, as you might hear the children say, for example: "Mine is coming into orange!" "I'm keeping mine in [the egg dye] for a long time." "How do you keep the can part on?" Their language gives you a clue about what the small-group experience means to them and what they might find meaningful to talk about.

Move from child to child so that all children receive attention

Even with a small group of children, it is difficult to attend to every child at once. By moving from child to child, you will see and hear each child and, by your actions, show children you will come to them when they need you. Your willingness to move about allows children to focus exclusively on their work; they can just call you over if they need your assistance.

Imitate children's actions

Often at small-group time, children's intense focus on materials takes up all their energy and

Adults support children's ideas and use of materials by working alongside them, listening to them, and using the materials in similar ways.

conversation takes a back seat to action. At these times, adults may wish to join in and support children's work by using a set of materials themselves and imitating what children are doing. Imitation puts adults into partnership with children without interfering with children's intentions.

Converse with children, following their leads

When children are ready to talk, follow their conversational leads. In this way, you operate at their level of understanding:

Catherine: Mine is turning green, Becki!

Becki: It is turning green.

Catherine: It's spreading. *(She looks at her cup from the bottom.)*

Becki: It is spreading.

Catherine: It's really, really green! Even on the bottom.

Encourage children to do things for themselves

Children learn through their own actions, so the more they can do for themselves at small-group time, the more opportunities they have for learning and gaining a sense of their own competence. When children spilled their dyes, Becki handed them a towel. They matter-of-factly wiped up their spills and went on with their egg coloring. Their own experiences enabled them to sympathize with other spillers: "Just what happened with mine!" When Catherine got dye on her fingers, she went to the sink, washed her hands, then returned to color her other two eggs.

Even though we may like to do things for children at small-group time, we will be more effective teachers if we allow children to do things for themselves.

Refer children to each other for ideas and assistance

This helps children learn that other children are valuable resources. Small-group interactions such as the following can strengthen children's beliefs in themselves and their peers:

Namen: Becki, I need another color.

Becki: Catherine and Caleb traded colors. Maybe someone will trade with you.

Namen: *(To Amy)* Can I use your color? *(Amy and Namen exchange colors.)*

Ask questions sparingly

In general, the most relevant questions are the ones children ask themselves: "Does the green really go even to the bottom?" Catherine wonders, after she drops her color pellet in the vinegar. When you do ask a question at small-group time, make sure it is part of an ongoing conversation and is directly related to what the child is doing or thinking. Questions that probe the child's thought process are useful, as shown in this dialogue:

Namen: I'm keeping mine in for a long time!

Becki: What will happen to it in a long time?

Namen: It'll catch more color.

Becki: Oh, the egg catches the color.

Namen: Yeah, if you put it in just a little bit, just a little bit gets on there.

Adults bring small-group time to a close: The end

Adults strive to bring small-group time to a close without rushing children or holding them to a task in which they are no longer interested. The following are some strategies that can help.

Realize that children finish at different times

In an active learning small-group experience, children proceed at their own pace and finish at different times. While all the children in Becki's small group received their egg-coloring materials at the same time, Catherine finished first. She stayed with the group, put her materials away, and helped Amy clean up. Namen, on the other hand, was still coloring his last egg as the other children put their colored eggs in their baskets. Becki began planning time with the children who were finished. Namen continued working and was the last person to plan.

In another preschool setting, large-group time followed small-group time. Children joined the large-group activity individually, as they finished with small group. Basically, one adult started large group as soon as several children gathered. This accommodated children who finished small-group time early and allowed others to take the time they needed to carry out their small-group ideas.

Give children a warning near the end of the session

Give children a warning several minutes before they need to stop working and put materials away (e.g., "In three minutes, it will be time to put our things back in the basket"). Advance notice lets children know ahead of time that they may have to stop working before they are finished. It gives them an opportunity to modify their plans so they can come to a natural stopping point or make plans to continue what they are doing during the next work time.

Support children's concluding observations

Children often like to share their work or observations about what they have done. This happened in Becki's egg-coloring group as the children gathered around the window ledge, gently parted the grass to make a place for their eggs, and talked together about their eggs and baskets. Becki joined them to hear and take part in the conversation: "We can take them home today, can't we Becki?" "You sure can," she assures them.

Tell children that materials will be available at work time

This strategy enables children to incorporate small-group-time ideas into their play at other times of the day. It also assures children who may not have finished that they can return to these materials at work time or outside time. Children may also suggest where new materials can be stored and even make labels for them.

Ask children to put away materials

As children finish, ask them to put their materials away. Give them concrete suggestions about where to put materials and/or what they can do to help clean up (e.g., "Let's put our pegs in the basket"; "Here are some sponges to wipe off the table"). Have a trash can handy for scraps and newspaper table coverings, a bucket for emptying containers of liquids, a box for the scissors (or other loose materials), and sponges or cloths for wiping the table.

Plan how the children will transition to the next part of the daily routine

It is easier for children to leave what they are doing at small-group time and move to the next

When this child completes her picture, her teacher talks with her about what she has done. The teacher listens carefully to what the child says and follows her conversational lead. The teacher uses these strategies so she can support the child's thinking rather than impose her point of view.

part of the day if they are actively engaged in the transition process. Plan a transition related to the small-group time activity or something else of interest to the children. As with all transitions, build in child choice; for example, after a painting small-group time, you might say, "Let's move like the paintbrushes to the rug for large-group time. I wonder how you're going to move."

By planning and thinking through the beginning, middle, and end of small-group time, you can ensure that children have an active learning experience during this part of the daily routine.

For a personal reflection on small-group time, see "One Teacher's Thoughts About Small-Group Time: Using Found Materials" on page 348. For sample small-group-time plans, see pages 349–352.

The Components of Small-Group Time

Beginning: Getting small-group time started
- Have the materials ready ahead of time.
- Use a brief opening statement to introduce the activity or materials to the children.
- Give children their own set of materials and let them begin working immediately.

Middle: Scaffolding active learning during small-group time
- Get on the same physical level as the children.
- Watch what individual children do with the materials.
- Listen to what children say about what they are doing.
- Move from child to child.
- Use your own set of materials to imitate what the children do or to try out their ideas.
- Talk with children about what they are doing.
- Encourage children to do things for themselves.
- Refer children to one another for ideas and assistance.
- Ask questions sparingly.
- Bring out backup materials as needed.

End: Bringing small-group time to a close
- Understand that children finish at different times.
- Give children a warning before ending the activity.
- Support children's concluding observations.
- Remind children where they can find the materials if they want to use them at work time.
- Encourage children to help you clean up the materials.
- Plan a way for the children to transition to the next part of the daily routine.

During smalll-group times, teachers support and gently extend children's learning. This teacher encourages the child to read the letters in her name.

One Teacher's Thoughts About Small-Group Time: Using Found Materials

In the following account, former HighScope teacher Ruth Strubank discusses a small-group time she planned around new collage materials from a local recycling center. She thought these materials might encourage children to experience and describe the positions of things (KDI 35. Spatial awareness and COR Advantage Item T. Geometry: Shapes and spatial awareness).

I made a trip to The Scrap Box where I found laminated pieces of white cardboard with four holes in them. I also picked up some cardboard tubes and some two-sided plastic stickers. Back at the preschool, I stapled each laminated cardboard piece with holes to a sheet of green construction paper using four staples, one in each corner. I also filled a baggie of stickers for each child in my small group.

At small-group time, I gave each child a cardboard/green paper piece and a cardboard tube and asked them what they could do with them. I thought they might try to fit the tubes into the holes, but basically, they ignored the tubes and began by putting their hands through the holes and opening up the sides of the paper. When I gave them the two-sided stickers, some children used them to stick the green and white sheets together, some stuck them through the holes onto the green paper, some stuck them on the back (the green side without holes). Children said things like "Look, I sticked mine together"; "Now it won't open, see?"; "I put mine in the middle"; "Mine are side by each."

Eventually, Joseph pulled the sides of his paper open and put the paper over his head. He looked out the holes one at a time. Chris watched and then tried the same thing, except that he pulled the narrow sides of his cardboard piece open. When his head didn't fit he said, "My head is too big!" Then Joseph showed him how to turn the paper around the long way so it would fit on his head. Chris then looked through the holes in his paper so that he had one hole in front of each eye. "I am a robot," he said in a robot-like voice. "Put a sticker on this white part," he continued. "It's the on/off button. Push it to make me walk." I followed his instructions and pushed his "on button." He began to move around the table making stiff, jerky movements. This inspired Kerry, Caroline, and Noah. They, too, became robots, only Kerry said her button meant "hot and cold." Meanwhile, the rest of the children continued filling up their papers with stickers.

At outside time, Chris and Kerry took their creations outside and continued to play robots until it was time to go home.

While I had hoped the children would become involved in describing where they were placing their stickers, which they did, I was amazed at their ability to turn an experience I had seen only for its spatial potential into one of pretend play (a KDI in Creative Arts) and pretending (a COR Advantage item in Creative Arts).

After a small-group time in which children did not use cardboard tubes in the way the teacher had planned, the children took a new interest in using the tubes at work time to build towers and to look through as spyglasses.

A Sample Small-Group-Time Plan: Making Play Dough Models

Originating idea:
Content area — KDI 40. Art (Creative Arts) and COR Advantage Item X. Art (Creative Arts).

The children in my small group often make block models of houses and things, but I have never seen them make clay or play dough models.

Materials for each child and teacher:
A sizable piece of homemade play dough, a heavy piece of cardboard to work on and save the model on, uncooked spaghetti and noodles in various sizes and shapes sorted onto Styrofoam trays

Possible KDIs:
F. Creative Arts: 40. Art
E. Mathematics: 34. Shapes

Beginning:
Give each child a lump of dough and a cardboard base. Say "Here's some play dough and a board to work on. I wonder what you could make that would fit on your board." As children begin, put trays of noodles in the center of the table where everyone can reach them.

Middle:
Watch to see what children do with their dough. Some may make "cakes." Perhaps the children who usually draw people will make people. Move from child to child to watch and listen.

End:
Have each child share what he or she has done, take it to the window ledge to dry, and help put remaining noodles back in the trays.

Follow-up:
- Add noodle collection to the art area.
- At next small-group time, have children check to see if their models are dry.
- When they are dry, have children put their models in boxes to take home.

The children continued to use play dough and clay during work time after this small-group time. This child used a wooden tool to carve out eyes for her puppy.

A Sample Small-Group-Time Plan: "Writing" Thank-You Cards

Originating idea:
Local traditions — After a trip to a local dairy farm, we need to thank Farmer Gerry.

Materials for each child and teacher:
Farm-visit photographs, construction paper, markers in a basket, large manila mailing envelope addressed to Farmer Gerry

Possible KDIs:
D. Language, Literacy, and Communication: 29. Writing
F. Creative Arts: 40. Art
H. Social Studies: 54. Community roles

Beginning:
Have photos on the table for children to view. Listen briefly to what children say. Then say "Today we need to make Farmer Gerry thank-you cards for all the things he showed us at his farm." Bring out paper and markers. Say "Whatever you draw and write to Gerry, I'll send to him in this big envelope so he'll know how much we liked our visit."

Middle:
Move from child to child as they draw and/or write. Watch and listen. Some children may want to give dictation. Others will want to do their own form of writing.

End:
Have children "read" their cards, put them in the envelope, put the caps back on their markers, and put their markers back in the basket.

Follow-up:
- Tomorrow walk to the mailbox around the corner at the beginning of outside time.
- Put dairy farm photos in an album in the book area. Write a message on the message board to remind the children that it is there to view.

A Sample Small-Group-Time Plan: Exploring Coconuts

Originating idea:
New materials — The children have been reciting a rhyme about coconuts but are not sure what coconuts are. (You can do this activity with other fruits and vegetables, such as pomegranates, as shown in the photo below.)

Materials for each child and teacher:
Coconuts, plastic tablecloth, board with a coconut-sized hole in it, hammer, goggles, table knives, one coconut with two holes pounded in it for pouring out "milk," cups, plastic bucket

Possible KDIs:
G. Science and Technology: 45. Observing, 51. Natural and physical world

D. Language, Literacy, and Communication: 23. Vocabulary

C. Physical Development and Health: 17. Fine-motor skills

Beginning:
Have children help spread the plastic tablecloth on the floor and sit around the edge. Give each child a coconut and ask "What can you find out about your coconut?"

Middle:
Listen to and support children's observations. When children mention juice or milk, show them the coconut with the holes and have them pour a little bit into their cups to taste. Have one child try opening her coconut by putting on the goggles, putting her coconut in the hole board, and hammering it until it splits open. Pass board, goggles, and hammer around until everyone who wants to open a coconut has the opportunity to do so. Have table knives available for children with open coconuts.

End:
Collect coconut pieces in the plastic bucket and ask children, "What could we do with these pieces tomorrow at work time?" Listen to children's ideas. Together gather up the plastic tablecloth so the coconut milk stays in the middle. Have children take cups and knives to the dishpan next to the sink and wash their hands before outside time.

Follow-up:
- "Write" a message on the message board about coconut pieces to remind children of their work-time ideas.
- Bring a grater and some big coconut pieces to snack-time tomorrow.
- Recite the coconut rhyme at large-group time. Listen for children's comments about real coconuts.

A Sample Small-Group-Time Plan: Jumping

Originating idea:
Children's interests — For several days, Ricky, Joey, Markie, and Lynnette have been playing "monster" at work time, jumping off blocks, chairs, and the sofa.

Materials for each child and teacher:
Tire-swing pit (since it is a safe jumping place). The pit is filled with pea gravel and surrounded by rubber-padded ledges of varying heights — from just about ground level to about three feet.

Possible KDIs:
C. Physical Development and Health: 16. Gross-motor skills

E. Mathematics: 35. Spatial awareness, 36. Measuring

Beginning:
Meet in the block area as usual. Say "Today we're having small-group time outside so we can do some jumping. Think of how you could jump all the way from the block area to the tire swing." Jump with children to the tire-swing pit. At the pit say "When nobody is swinging, this is the place for jumping. You can jump from a low ledge or a high one."

Middle:
Stay in the middle as children jump. Listen for their comments and observations. They may mention distance, direction, height, and how they are going to jump. Some children may want to jump to you and give instructions about how close to them you should stand.

End:
Give a warning, for example: "Two more jumps, and then it's time to go in for large-group time." Ask children to think of a way to jump back to large-group time.

Follow-up:
- At outside time, some children may want to jump while others may want to swing on the tire swing. Since jumping can only happen when no one is swinging, listen for and be ready to support children as they work to solve this problem.
- Listen to and support children as they think of other places to jump to and from at outside time.

After this small-group time, children's interest in jumping continued, both outdoors and inside.

Understanding Large-Group Time

In the HighScope Curriculum, large-group times are adult-initiated activities during which all children and adults participate in singing, movement experiences, or reenacting stories. Adults plan and initiate participatory large-group experiences that are active rather than passive, move swiftly from one experience to the next, involve brief rather than lengthy introductions, and accommodate children's interests and initiatives. To illustrate the dynamics of large-group time, we have re-created an actual large-group time from a HighScope preschool program.

Moving and Singing Together

The entire group gathers in the middle of the block area for large-group time. As the children arrive, Sam, a teacher, sits down and leans back on his hands, bending his knees and lifting his feet up and down. "Tap, tap, tap your feet, tap them on the rug," he sings to the tune of "Row, Row, Row Your Boat." "Tap, tap, tap your feet, tap them on the rug." The children join in sitting like Sam, singing, and tapping their feet.

"I've got an idea," says Anna at the end of the verse, "your nose!" She sings and demonstrates, "Tap, tap, tap your nose, tap it with your fingers."

Sam, Beth (also a teacher), and the other children join in. Petey, Callie, and Bryant offer variations for everyone to try — "Pound your hands," "Clap your knees," and "Shake your head."

After the last variation, Beth says, "I've got a new song with four movements. The first one is marching. See if you can do some marching." The children and Sam march in various directions about the block area.

"Okay, marchers," says Beth. "The next movement is up. Try stretching up tall."

The children try this out on their own. "Look, I can go really high," says Kenneth. "Me too!" "Me too!"

After the children have tried stretching up, Beth says, "The next movement is down. Try bending and reaching way down to the floor." Some children bend and touch the floor; others crouch.

"The last movement is halfway up," Beth says. "It's in between down and up. See if you can make yourself halfway up." She waits to see how children will interpret this idea. When some have decided on a crouching stand and others are bending over, Beth says, "Here's the song that goes with these movements," and she sings "The Noble Duke of York." The children and Sam join in with words and phrases on the next several times through the song. The last time, they try out the movements as they sing.

When they are finished singing "The Noble Duke of York," Sam says, "When I turn on the 'boing-boing' music, you can move any way the music makes you want to move." He turns on a musical selection that sounds like rubber bands stretching and contracting.

"This is the funny jumping music," Kenneth says, as the children laugh and bounce, bend, jump, and stretch.

When the music ends, several children say, "Let's do it again."

"Okay," says Sam, "but this time, think of a way to move to the coat rack so we can put on our coats for outside time." He plays the music again, and he, Beth, and the children hop, bounce, stretch, and "boing" over to the coat rack.

What is large-group time?

Since ancient times peoples of all cultures have gathered around fires, on hilltops, in clearings, or along the shore to sing, dance, tell stories, and exchange information. In a similar spirit, children and adults in a HighScope preschool program gather together at large-group times for about 10 to 15 minutes each day for companionship, the sharing of creative movement and music ideas, and the enjoyment of doing things together as a community.

Children and adults together

Large-group time involves the entire group of children and all the members of the adult teaching team. Everyone participates in singing, movement experiences, and reenacting stories. Large-group time is active learning in a whole-group setting. The focus is on an enjoyable experience that everyone in the classroom can share together.

Active learning in a communal setting

At large-group time, adults introduce the activity but then the children make choices about what song to sing, how to change the words or gestures of a song or chant, whether and how to play musical instruments, how to move their bodies, what animals to pretend to be, how to use balls or scarves to accompany their movements or instrumental music, or what storytelling props to use. Children share their ideas and observations and receive adult support for their initiatives. All the ingredients of active learning are present:

Materials: Children can use their bodies, voices, or props.

Manipulation: Children use their bodies, voices, or props in ways that make sense to them.

Choice: Children decide how to move, what to sing, and when and how to participate or offer ideas.

Child language and thought: Children share ideas, express choices, and figure out how to respond to movement and music suggestions.

Adult scaffolding: Adults use nonverbal and verbal strategies to support and extend children's intentions.

Five Types of Large-Group-Time Activities

1. Easy-to-join activities
- Use few or no directions.
- Enable children to participate actively and immediately.
- Include frequent opportunities for children to add their ideas.

2. Songs, fingerplays, chants, and poems
- Maintain a slow tempo.
- Keep hand motions simple.
- Build in children's choices and ideas.
- Use a song book.

3. Storytelling and reenacting stories and nursery rhymes
- Make up simple stories based on children's interests.
- Reenact simple stories and nursery rhymes.
- Have only a few roles or one role that all children can act out.

4. Movement activities (with or without music or objects)
- Give children opportunities to move their bodies, developing coordination skills.
- Explore moving with objects first, and then layer on music.
- Occasionally be specific when asking children for their ideas (e.g., "How else can we move our arms?" "What other ways can we walk?").
- Always use instrumental music so children can hear the beat and aren't distracted by the words.

5. Cooperative games
- Do not have winners and losers — the fun is playing the game!
- Maintain reasonable expectations.
- Be flexible so children can respond at their own level — games with few or no rules work the best.
- Remember, even with games, always build in choices for children!

Singing together during large group builds a sense of "we" and "us."

My Window." Carole, another adult, and the children join in by running around in a circle and singing: "Run around, run around, run around the circle. Run around, run around, run around the circle. Run around, run around, run around the circle. Run around and stop." "I've got an idea. Jump!" says Joey. Everyone begins the action song again, this time substituting jumping for running. The children suggest and try out other actions including marching, flying, popping, and wiggling.

At the beginning of winter, the children are very interested in figuring out how to put on their warm outside clothes. Thinking of this interest, as well as KDIs 19. Personal care and 43. Pretend play and COR Advantage Items K. Personal care

An adult-initiated experience based on children's interest and development

Just as with small-group times, adults plan and introduce large-group times, but their ideas come from their understanding of what children learn (the curriculum *content* in the KDIs and COR Advantage) and what children like to do as they pursue their *interests*. For inspiration, they also turn to the *five types of large-group-time activities* (see facing page) and *events and traditions* that are meaningful to the children. Here are some examples of how large-group time originates:

Lately at outside time, the children have enjoyed running around the circular grassy area. Thinking of KDIs 16. Gross-motor skills, 41. Music, and 42. Movement and COR Advantage Items I. Gross-motor skills and Y. Music. Linda, an adult, begins singing the "Run Around the Circle" song to the tune of "Bluebird, Bluebird, Fly Through

and healthy behavior and AA. Pretend play, their teacher Beth tells a story called "The Mitten," about forest creatures who huddle inside a mitten to stay warm in the winter. A large red sleeping bag serves as the mitten. Children get into and out of it as they pretend to be the mice, chipmunks, hedgehogs, squirrels, rabbits, foxes, and bears in the story. At the end, everyone "pops" out when the mitten finally bursts at the seams.

Aware of children's interest in number words and symbols (KDI 31) and thinking of KDIs 17. Fine-motor skills and 32. Counting, Becki, an adult, initiates a fingerplay based on the rhyme "Five Little Monkeys Jumping on the Bed." Everyone says the first verse together: "Five little monkeys jumping on the bed. One fell off and bumped his head. The

To share control with children during large-group time, adults plan the activities and children contribute their ideas. In this large-group time, the adults planned to play instrumental music and to offer the children fabric pieces while the children choose how to use those fabric pieces.

doctor came and this is what he said, 'No more monkeys jumping on the bed!'" Before the next verse Becki asks, "How many monkeys this time?" "Lots," says Alana. "What are lots of monkeys doing?" Becki asks. "Climbing up a tree," suggests Andrew. The next verse goes like this: "Lots of monkeys climbing up a tree. One fell off and bumped his head [some children said "knee" to rhyme with "tree" — an example of KDI 24. Phonological awareness]. The doctor came and this is what he said, 'No more monkeys climbing up a tree.'" The fingerplay continues with "Seven little monkeys making popcorn soup," "Two little monkeys playing in the mud," and "Twenty-seven monkeys knocking on the door." The children use their fingers to express their idea of "lots"; 7, 2, and 27; and also make up hand motions for climbing, making soup, playing in mud, and knocking on the door.

For more information and examples on ideas for large-group times, see "Ideas for Large-Group Times" on pages 358–359.

Shared control

Shared control is the mutual give-and-take between teachers and children. At large-group time, both children and teachers take turns being the leader and follower, the speaker and listener. Teachers plan activities that allow for children's input, choices, and ideas. In shared control, teachers make adult-sized decisions (e.g., planning to move to music with children). Children make child-sized choices (e.g., deciding how to move their arms to that music). To share control with children, adults use the following strategies:

Plan ways to build in choices for children. Children are more likely to become engaged in the activity when they can contribute ideas.

Take cues from children. Following children's cues gives them opportunities to express their own ideas.

Participate with children as partners. As partners, adults can share in children's interests, delights, and creativity.

By using these strategies, children will become active participants — and enjoy opportunities to lead and follow the ideas of their peers — during large-group times.

Why is large-group time important?

Large-group time brings children and adults together for brief periods to exchange information and do things as a group. This experience builds a sense of "we" and "us."

A repertoire of common experiences

Children draw on large-group experiences as they play at other times of the day. For example, outside on the tire swing, Julia and Andrew sing "The Mud Song," then change some of the words, making up their own variations: "Ponds, ponds, we love ponds for floating boats and floating on." "Listen to this," Jalessa says, joining Julia and Andrew when the swing comes to a halt: "Dirt, dirt, we love dirt, on your face and on your shirt." Singing together as they swing is a natural expression for these children because all three have learned and sung "The Mud Song" many times at large-group time. They are comfortable singing together and readily accept new singers and new verses to their songs.

A sense of community

Large-group time briefly draws everyone together — to look at new instruments, try out a new way of moving, sing a favorite song, or act out a story. The underlying message of this time of day is togetherness. It is a time to sing, dance, pretend, and talk with everyone. When the day begins or ends with large-group time, parents can also participate. When their parents are present, children often nestle in their parent's laps. In fact, one-child-one-lap is probably a preschooler's ideal for singing and storytelling at large-group time.

Group membership

At large-group time, children have many opportunities to participate as a member of the group. They express their own ideas and listen to those of others. Children may observe one another and use what they see and hear to copy, modify, or spur their own innovative ideas. They participate in the activities as group members working in parallel or in collaboration with others.

Children can also work as a group to solve the specific problems that arise during large-group time. For example, sometimes children have more ideas for songs to sing than time allows. In such instances, an adult might say, "Three of you have suggested songs but there's only time for one before the bus comes. What should we do?" A child responds, "I know. Close my eyes and pick." A child may also be disappointed if time runs out before he or she suggests a song verse or movement. The group may decide that that child should be first to suggest an idea the following day. "Write that on the message board," someone may add, "so we don't forget!" Actively moving children may also inadvertently bump into one another. With adult help, the group can solve the problem of how to move freely while respecting one another's personal space and safety.

Child-sized leadership roles

In a HighScope large-group time, it is common for children to say, "I've got an idea!" and then assume a leadership role to change a song, introduce a movement, add to a story, or modify a game. Children are never required to lead, but even children who hesitate to speak up at other times of the day may be eager to offer an idea for others to copy. Sometimes two or more children want to lead at the same time. When this happens, adults facilitate the process with statements such as "We'll try your idea, James, after Erica's and Trey's ideas."

Ideas for Large-Group Times

Where do adults get ideas when planning large-group times? Here are three sources you can use, and several examples of activities that originated with each one:

Content

Look at KDIs and COR Advantage items in the following areas in particular:

- F. Creative Arts (KDI); Creative Arts (COR Advantage)
- C. Physical Development and Health (KDI); Physical Development and Health (COR Advantage)
- D. Language, Literacy, and Communication (KDI); Language, Literacy, and Communication (COR Advantage)
- E. Mathematics (KDI); Mathematics (COR Advantage)

Examples:

- After several children expressed an interest in pickup sticks, Yvonne and Karen thought of KDIs 16. Gross-motor skills (Physical Development and Health) and 42. Movement (Creative Arts), and COR Advantage Item Z. Movement (Creative Arts). They planned a large-group experience around moving with large Tinkertoy sticks. At large-group time they asked the children to select a large Tinkertoy piece to hold as they moved to music, but in such a way so that the Tinkertoy did not touch anybody. When the music stopped, they asked the children to put the sticks down and walk to the music around the block area without touching the sticks as they walked.

- Linda and Carole played a simplified version of hot potato with their children. At large-group time, each child selected a potato. When the music played, they passed the potatoes around the circle; when the music stopped, they held on to their potatoes. Some children talked to their "potato babies" during the pauses. After several rounds, one child had the idea of passing potatoes with his feet, which everyone tried with much laughter and lots of straying potatoes. This camaraderie engaged children in KDI 11. Community (Social and Emotional Development) and COR Advantage Items B. Problem solving with materials (Approaches to Learning) and AA. Pretend play (Creative Arts).

- Thinking of KDI 40. Art (Creative Arts) and COR Advantage Item X. Art (Creative Arts), Cindy and Bob planned a large-group time around making a mural together. They laid a long piece of butcher paper on a paved part of the playground. At large-group time, each child selected a brush and a jar of paint, and everyone gathered around the paper and painted a mural to hang on the playground fence. To get the project started, Bob said, "Paint any way you want to make a big picture to hang on our fence."

Children's interests and development

During different parts of the day

- Watch how children like to move (e.g., prowling like jungle cats, galloping like horses).

- Listen to what they enjoy singing (e.g., singing lullabies while rocking babies in the house area, singing "The Eensy Weensy Spider" when rolling strands of clay to make "spaghetti" in the art area).

- Take note of play experiences that lend themselves to a large-

group-time activity. Puppy play, for example, might lend itself to reenacting a simple puppy story. A child dancing in front of a mirror in the house area during work time might lend itself to moving to music at large-group time.

Examples:

- Erin and Markie had new baby sisters at home and played "babies" a lot at work time, so teachers Linda and Carole planned a large-group time around being "tiny babies who can't crawl yet." They asked the children to lie on their backs and move their arms and legs around "like tiny babies" to a slow musical selection and then to one with a faster tempo.

- One spring day, Ruth and Ann observed that several of their children liked to play tag, so they planned an outdoor game of tree tag for large-group time. They made the rules very simple: When the drum is beating, run. When the drum stops, run to a tree for "safety." No one was "it," and adults and children took turns beating the drum.

- Teachers Peter and Becki watched Audie and L.J. throw beanbags to each other, so they planned a large-group time with beanbags. The next day at large-group time the adults gave a beanbag to each pair of children to toss and catch. Some children stood very close to each other while tossing their beanbags, while other more experienced throwers stood farther apart.

Events currently meaningful to the children

- Seasonal holidays or special events (large-group activity could include dancing like snowflakes, falling leaves, or singing a birthday song)
- Field trips (large-group activity could include moving like the fish the children saw on a trip to the fish store or doing stop, drop, and roll after their trip to the fire station)
- Local traditions (large-group activity could include moving like some of the animals at the county fair or pretending to have a parade [for July 4th or other local celebration])

Examples:

- In the days following Halloween, Helena and Sarah observed that several children continued to play trick-or-treat. They then planned a stopping-and-starting large-group experience in which the children trick-or-treated using an instrumental music selection. When the music stopped, the children knocked on any surface they could find and said "Trick or treat." The children enjoyed finding different places to knock on (blocks, windows, shelves, tables).

- One weekend, the streets of the town where most of Gwen and Betsy's children lived were "taken over" by a basketball tournament that raised money for local charities. On Monday, the adults observed the children talk about the tournament and decided to incorporate basketball into large-group time the next day. Using duct tape, they securely taped hoops at fairly low levels along the fence on the playground. Each child selected a rubber playground ball and had the opportunity to shoot baskets. Several children invented a game of standing inside the hoops, catching the balls, and throwing them back to "their team." The teachers left the hoops up so that children could continue to use them at outside time.

- After a trip to the corner gas station, Carole and Elaine planned a large-group time to make up a song about what the children saw on their trip. Elaine played a simple tune on her guitar while the children made up words and motions for the verses. The children's verses included "We saw the windshield wipers," "We saw the car go up," "We saw the candy machine," "We saw the piles of tires," "We saw the mom and her baby," and "We saw the dog digging."

Here are the five types of large-group activities and examples of activities that originate with each one:

Easy-to-join activities

- While Shannon helped children clean up after snacktime, Sue sat on the rug and began patting her knees to the beat of a familiar song. As children finished washing up, they came to the rug and began patting their knees too. When all the children and Shannon had arrived at large-group time, Sue asked the children for their ideas on where to pat to the beat.

Songs, fingerplays, chants, and poems

- Teachers Barbara and Michelle heard Julia sing "Do Your Ears Hang Low?" several times during work time, so they planned to have Julia help them teach this song and its movements the next day at large-group time.

Storytelling and reenacting stories and nursery rhymes

- Helena and Sarah used a group storytelling idea with their children that involved musical instruments. They made up simple stories with lots of sounds in them to mimic: crying babies, barking dogs, walking up stairs, ringing telephones, and running water in the bathtub. As they told the story at large-group time, the children provided the sound effects, using their voices, as well as instruments from the music area.

Movement activities

- Sam and Peter planned a large-group experience around dancing with wrist and ankle bells. At large-group time, the children chose how to wear their bells and danced to the drum beat Peter played. He was ready to trade the drum for bells so that other children could play the drum, but that day all the children wanted to dance with their bells.

Cooperative games

- Karen and Jeanne planned a cooperative large-group time around Maypole dancing. Since their children enjoyed dancing to music with streamers, they thought this idea might work, but first they needed to find a sturdy pole. They finally decided to tack nylon streamers to a pole outside that held up their bird feeder. At large-group time, everyone went outside, found the end of a streamer, and danced around the pole to different selections of music. "Look what's happening to the pole!" the children exclaimed when the music stopped. "It's getting colors!"

> **Making Large-Group Activities More Child Centered**
>
> Use the following strategies to make large-group activities more child centered:
>
> **1. Separate: Separate the words (say) from the actions (do).**
> - Show the motions OR describe the motions.
> - Don't talk and show at the same time.
> - For a song or fingerplay, introduce the motions first and then layer on the song or words.
>
> *Hint:* If you find this is hard for you, try keeping your hands in your pockets.
>
> **2. Simplify: Simplify the words and/or actions so they make sense to children.**
> - If the song or activity involves a movement sequence, present each motion individually before putting the sequence together.
> - Use words the children understand (e.g., say "one hand" and "the other hand" rather than "left hand" and "right hand").
> - Use actions that children can do (e.g., rather than snapping fingers, try wiggling them or patting knees).
>
> **3. Facilitate: Support children's choices, actions, and language.**
> - Comment on what you see children doing.
> - Imitate children's actions and use their words.

Where large groups meet

Large-group meetings call for a space flexible enough for both vigorous action and cozy intimacy as well as the enactment of young children's ideas about when and how to move and where and how to sit.

Gather in a spacious location

Large-group meetings often take place in the most spacious interest area. To make enough space available, you may have to move a shelf or a large piece of equipment. One teaching team used the block area for large-group meetings. When they added a music area at one end of the block area, they moved the instrument shelf each day for large-group time to make enough space for everyone to move freely. In warm climates and seasons, large-group time might take place outside under a tree or on a patio or deck.

Let the large-group-time experience determine the formation of the group

Some large-group games call for a circle formation. Some movement activities confine children to individual carpet squares or the inside of their hoops. In other experiences, children move about the whole area. When they reenact stories, children like to build and perform on a platform stage assembled out of blocks. For important information, children draw as close as they can to the speaker or object of interest. Rather than expecting children to always sit in a circle for large-group time, adults in a HighScope program understand that the positions children assume will vary depending on what they are doing.

What children do at large-group time

Returning to the account of Sam and Beth's large-group time (see p. 353), let us observe the experiences of one child, Kenneth:

Kenneth joins the singing game in progress at the end of the "tap your feet" verse. He has just gotten his feet going when Anna changes the verse to "tap your nose." He keeps his feet tapping for a few beats and then switches to tapping his nose with three fingers on each hand while looking at his friend Bryant. "What if a giant tapped his nose!" Kenneth says to Bryant, as Petey talks to Sam about changing the verse to "pounding the floor." When Petey's verse begins, Kenneth leans over and pounds the floor with both fists. At the end of this verse, he and Bryant continue their conversation about giants: "A giant could pound through the floor." "And he wouldn't get hurt." "Yeah, he has special powers." For the "clap your knees" verse, Kenneth pounds his knees, then shakes his head "like a giant" from side to side during the last verse.

Kenneth is still shaking his head as Beth encourages the group to try the marching movement for the new song. When other children begin to march, Kenneth gets up and marches after Bryant. "We're giants, aren't we Bryant," he says. They lift their legs as high as they can as they weave in and out among the other marchers. "Look, I can go really high," Kenneth tells Beth after she describes the second movement, "Go high." He stands on his toes and stretches toward the ceiling. Beth nods and smiles in acknowledgment and then asks the children to go down. *Kenneth falls to the floor on his hands, then crouches with his arms wrapped around his knees. For* halfway up, *he watches Bryant and then assumes a standing crouch. When Beth begins to sing, Kenneth falls to the floor on his hands again, crawls over to Beth, sits down, and leans comfortably against her, singing along from time to time. When it is time to sing and move, Kenneth jumps up and marches with Bryant, reaches up, falls to the floor, then stands in a crouch. He sings some of the words and goes back to marching until Sam puts on the "boing-boing" music. "This is the funny jumping music!" Kenneth says, as he jumps up and down. "Let's do it again," he says when the music stops. Kenneth is the first to reach the coat rack when Sam plays the music a second time. As soon as he gets his coat on, he resumes jumping until the music stops. "Bryant," he says on the way out the door. "Let's be giants, okay?"*

As Kenneth's experiences illustrate, in an active learning setting, children's actions and ideas play a major role in shaping the content and process of large-group gatherings.

Children actively participate

At large-group time, as at other times of the day, children use both materials and their own bodies in creative ways. For example, they march, fall to the ground, wave and jump over streamers, dance their own interpretation of popcorn popping, line up blocks for a stage, shake tambourines and hit them against different parts of their bodies, make up movements for others to try, and assume the shape and motions of characters to act out familiar stories (e.g., the monsters in *Where the Wild Things Are*). They make choices about how to move, what songs to sing, what stories to reenact, what words and actions to change, what music to dance to, what instruments to play first, what games to play, and whom to sit near. In the process, they voice their own opinions ("A giant could pound through the floor!") and observations:

The Importance of Large-Group Time

Gives all children a repertoire of common experiences
- Children draw on large-group experiences as they play together at other times of the day.
- Children readily accept new children into their spontaneous movement, music, and pretend play activities.

Builds a sense of classroom community
- The underlying message of large-group time is togetherness.
- Parents can also join in large-group-time activities.

Encourages all children to be members of the group
- Children can participate by joining in the ideas offered by others.
- Children figure out what to do when there is not enough time for everyone's ideas.

Provides opportunities for children to take child-sized leadership roles
- Children can choose to lead and contribute their own ideas.
- Children experience the satisfaction of having others carry out their ideas.

Adult: *(Telling a story)* And he cried and cried and cried.

First child: Whaaaaa, whaaaa.

Second child: Maybe he cried "Boo hoo, boo hoo."

Third child: My baby cries like this, "Eeeeee, eeeee."

Fourth child: "Maaa, maaa, maaa," he wanted his mom.

They also tell their own stories ("Once there was an old man and he walked around with his hands in his pockets, like this…") and make up their own songs ("The bird flew up the tree, the bird flew up the tree, the bird flew up the tree, and then it went to sleep").

Children initiate ideas, offer suggestions, and generate solutions

Throughout large-group gatherings, children initiate their own ideas ("We're giants and we take really big steps all the way across the room"; "Let's sing that donkey song!"). They make suggestions about what the group might say and do ("We could jump way up high and go 'Boo!'").

Children also offer solutions to the problems that inevitably arise when many people share one space and juggle competing ideas ("I know — if you want to come back to your same square, just tell everybody, and they won't get on yours. But the other kids can change, because they like to go to different squares"). In a HighScope large-group time, adults and children both shape what happens.

The large-group-time activity determines the formation of the group. In this activity, children gather around a parachute to "pop" homemade sponge balls.

How Adults Support Children at Large-Group Time

The adults' role at large-group time is similar to their role at small-group time — adults initiate experiences and support children's initiatives. The following strategies help them do this:

- Preparing for large groups before the children arrive
- Setting large groups in motion: The beginning
- Scaffolding children's ideas and initiatives: The middle
- Bringing large-group time to a close: The end

Adults prepare for large-group time *before* children arrive

Active large-group experiences like the ones just described require well-prepared adults. Here are some strategies that help adults plan for these sessions.

Modify songs and games to fit children's development and specific events

For example, in singing games like hokey pokey, change references from "right foot" and "left foot" to "one foot" and "the other foot" (preschool children do not know the difference between their right and left foot). In musical chairs, do not remove any chairs so that all children can participate throughout the game (there should not be "winners" and "losers"). After a trip to the farmers' market, change the words of "Old MacDonald Had a Farm" to "Farmer Karpo went to market…. In the market he had some apples…" (i.e., match the words of the song to children's actual experience).

Practice ahead of time

At daily team planning, sing "Farmer Karpo Went to Market" or "The Noble Duke of York" with your team member so that you both know the words, the tune, and the motions (if there are any). Listen to the "boing-boing" music, "Popcorn," "O, How Lovely," or whatever musical selection(s) you plan to use during a movement activity. Find and listen to the fast and slow selections you plan to play for "pretending to be babies lying on their backs." Practice the story you plan to tell about Little Red Riding Hood and the wolf, and so forth.

Have materials ready

Before the children arrive, draw messages on the message board, put the music you plan to use on or in the audio player, or gather the streamers you need for dancing and put them on a shelf near your large-group meeting place. Having materials gathered and ready ahead of time allows you to start large-group time as soon as children begin to gather.

Adults set large groups in motion: The beginning

Here are some strategies for getting large-group time off to a smooth start.

Draw children to the group with a simple, easy-to-join activity

Plan to begin large-group time with an enjoyable activity children can easily join. Easy-to-join activities

- Have few or no directions.
- Are active.
- Include frequent opportunities for children to add their ideas.

This might be moving to a song such as "Run Around the Circle"; singing a favorite song, such as "Jingle Bells" or "Row, Row, Row Your Boat"; or doing an often-requested fingerplay such as "Five Little Monkeys" variations. By going to the large-group meeting spot and starting an activity, adults (and children) signal that large-group time has begun. When adults consistently start large-group time with an easy-to-join activity, children will begin to imitate the adults, as Vanessa did one day when she came to the circle first and began singing "Row, Row, Row Your Boat."

Preparing for Large-Group Time

Review your plan.
- Anticipate children's reactions but be prepared to be flexible and follow in whatever directions the children's interests take them.

Practice ahead of time.
- Practice with your team member so you both know the words, tune, and motions (if any). Practice the story you plan to tell. Know which team member will do which part.

Have the materials ready.
- Cue up the music.
- Have the songbook ready.

Gather props for each child and for yourself.
- Make sure you have enough props for each child and teacher before large-group time starts (e.g., have plenty of scarves and streamers for a large-group time to move to music).

Have backup materials ready.
- Have backup materials readily available to distribute to help extend the large-group activity (e.g., paper plates for the large-group time to move to music).

Place materials within easy reach of your large-group meeting place.
- Distribute materials shortly after you introduce the activity so children do not have to wait to get started.

• • • •

The benefits of preparing ahead of time
- Cuts down on wait time
- Makes materials easy to distribute to children
- Ensures that each child will have what he or she needs

Start right away with the children who have gathered

This strategy minimizes delays for the children who arrive first and encourages children who are still busy with the previous activity (snack, small-group time, or hanging up their coats) to finish so they can join the fun. As you begin, do not worry about children who linger at the previous activity; they will participate more readily when they do arrive if they can join at their own pace. Some children, for example, find particular satisfaction in watching large-group time begin while they finish snack. This brief observation period gives them extra time to think about what they might want to do (e.g., how to move) or ideas to share with others if they want to be the leader (e.g., a movement for others to copy).

Adults scaffold children's ideas and initiatives: The middle

Once you begin a large-group experience and involve children in singing, moving, or storytelling, they will offer their own variations and modifications. Here are ways you can support children's ideas and initiatives at large-group time.

Make a brief opening statement to introduce the next experience

At the conclusion of the activity you have used to draw children to large-group time, go right on to the next experience you have planned. Give a *brief* explanation if one is needed to catch the children's attention and get them engaged in the activity:

- "I'm going to put on some music. Listen to the music, and then you can move your body the way the music sounds."
- "Today we have balls to take outside for shooting baskets."
- "We're going to tell a story about rabbits and pretend to act like them."
- "Let's see all the ways we can move in and out of these hoops."

Turn props and materials over to children

When your large-group experience involves storytelling props, such as Little Red Riding Hood and wolf puppets, or materials, such as musical instruments, streamers, balls, potatoes, cloths, or rubber bands, get them into the children's hands as soon as possible. If you spend a long time passing out the props and materials, children will become distracted. Worse, if adults are the only ones using them, children will rapidly lose interest.

Participate on the children's physical level

If the children are sitting on the floor, sit on the floor with them. If they decide to crawl to the music, crawl to the music along with them. If they are dancing around a Maypole, grab a streamer and join the dance. Being at the children's physical level gives you a better idea of what the children are saying and seeing. Trying out their suggestions lets them know that you value their ideas and initiatives.

Watch and listen to children

Observing children gives you an idea of how each child is making sense of the experience you have planned. During the pass-the-potato game, teachers Carole and Linda noticed that Joanie and Corey, two of their youngest children, did not pass their potatoes, although they passed along the potatoes that others passed to them. In musical carpet squares, their teachers recalled, Joanie and Corey were also the children who stayed on or next to their own squares the whole time. Linda and Carole understood that hanging on to "their" possessions was still very important to Corey and Joanie and that both activities could accommodate their particular requirements.

Attending closely to children also gives you a clue about how they are fitting the experience into the context of their own lives. For example, when teachers Becki and Peter played the "Popcorn" music and Alana requested salt, they later heard L.J. say, "Give me some hot sauce"; Nathan say, "Give me some pepper"; and Julia say, "I need

Knowing the song and the beat before large-group time begins helps ensure that children will be actively involved.

some cheese." They sprinkled on these toppings and were pleased at the range and flexibility of the children's thinking.

Follow up on children's suggestions and modifications

While adults plan for large-group time each day, they are also prepared to modify their plans to accommodate children's ideas. This is a way to support and encourage children's thinking, creativity, and initiative. Generally you can incorporate children's suggestions ("Let's do it again fast!" "I know! We all live in a yellow school bus!") into the activity you are already doing. Other times children suggest favorite activities you have not planned for that day ("Let's play that game where we pretend to be different animals"; "Let's play that tree game again"). If there really is no time to accommodate children's suggestions, write them down on the message board to remind you and the children that you will do them the next day at large-group time. Flexibility is a hallmark for adults conducting large-group meetings with active learners.

The teacher here turns the straws and balls over to the children as soon as she begins large-group time and gets down on their level to try her hand at blowing the ball with a straw.

Let children be the leaders

Children can stop and start the music for a game, tell a story, demonstrate a movement for others to try out, and suggest a song to sing. Being the leader puts children in the position of thinking clearly about what they are doing so that other children can do it as well. In addition, the other children are usually very responsive to peer leaders. To make sure the other children have understood what the leader is suggesting, you may need to repeat, rephrase, or demonstrate it for them. This not only helps everyone pick up on the idea but also makes the leader feel his or her idea is valued.

Plan one long or two shorter activities

Depending on the length of the activity, you may plan one long activity or two shorter activities for large-group time. For example, the children may play duck, duck, goose the entire time or sing two songs and then move with streamers to the beat of the music. Whatever you have planned for large-group time, be prepared to switch to another activity if the children lose interest, or conversely, to extend a short activity into a longer one if the children remain engaged.

Adults bring large-group time to a close: The end

By planning large-group time ahead of time, adults can end the session with a transition to the next part of the daily routine.

Warn children when the activity is ending

As with any other part of the day, it will be easier for children to let go of what they are doing and move on to the next activity when they know what to expect.

Make the final large-group experience a transition to the next part of the daily routine

Before Sam, an adult, played the "Popcorn" music for the last time, he said, "I'm going to put on the 'Popcorn' music for the last time. This time, move like popping corn to the coat rack so we can put on our coats for outside time." The children had been moving around the block area. Now they used the same music and movement ideas as a transition to outside time.

When teachers Beth and Becki sang "Yellow Submarine" with their children, they used the last variation ("We all live in a red choo-choo train") as a transition idea. "This time, think of a way you could drive your red choo-choo trains to outside time," said Beth. After children pretended to be "tiny babies," Carole said to them, "This time, pretend you have grown into crawling babies. When I put the music on, see how you can move like a baby to small-group time!"

Put materials away as part of the transition activity

Give children concrete suggestions for where to put away materials and what to do as part of the transition. For example, after teachers Helena and Sarah played the scary music for flying ghosts, they put on a lullaby and asked the children to fly their ghosts to snacktime and "put them to bed" in the "ghost basket" on their snack table. After "Jingle Bells" and several other songs with bells, Peter, an adult, asked the children to "jingle over to the door for outside time and put your bells in the box by the door." Linda and Carol had the children toss their potatoes into a basket and then move to small-group time like "hot potatoes."

By planning and thinking through the beginning, middle, and end of large-group time, you can ensure that children have an active learning experience during this part of the daily routine. For more information about large group, see "One Teacher's Thoughts About Large-Group Time" on pages 368–369 and sample large-group time plans on pages 370–373.

The Components of Large-Group Time

Beginning: Getting large-group time started

- Draw children to the group with a simple, easy-to-join activity.
- Begin immediately with the children who have gathered, even if others are still transitioning from the previous part of the day.

Middle: Scaffolding active learning during large-group time

- Once all the children gather, give a brief opening statement designed to catch their attention.
- Turn the props and materials over to the children.
- Participate on the children's physical level.
- Watch and listen to the children to observe how they interpret the activity.
- Imitate what the children do, and try out their ideas and suggestions.
- Let children be the leaders.
- Depending on the activity length, plan one longer activity or two shorter activities.

End: Bringing large-group time to a close

- Warn children when the activity is ending.
- Plan a transition to the next part of the daily routine that incorporates the activity.
- Put away any props or materials as part of the transition activity.

One Teacher's Thoughts About Large-Group Time: Planning All the Components

In the following statement, HighScope teacher Beth Marshall (now Director of Early Childhood) reflects on how she considered all the components of large-group time — beginning, middle, end, and transition to the next part of the daily routine — when planning with her co-teacher.

When planning large-group times, I think about the beginning, the middle, and the end with a transition to the next activity, which in our daily routine is outside time. For the beginning of today's large-group time, I planned to start playing the "Run Around the Circle" singing game with the children who finished their snacks first. I think it is important to begin large-group time with an active experience because (1) the children have been sitting for snack and (2) large-group time should be attractive to children who are still eating. My co-teacher, Becki, agreed that I would start large-group time and that she would stay with the children still eating snack and join the large group when most of the children were finished.

For the middle of large-group time, I wanted to sing "The Depot Town Song" we had written with the children earlier in the week at large-group time after walking to our neighborhood farmers' market (located in a part of the city called Depot Town). As the children suggested ideas for verses, we recorded them on a sheet of butcher paper using words, drawings, and the children's letter links. Becki and I both noticed that the children went to the song sheet to "read" and sing "The Depot Town Song" during work time the next day. "Great," we said to each other, "they're reading, a Language, Literacy, and Communication KDI" (and also a COR Advantage item).

Finally, I wanted to end large-group time with a child's work-time idea. During our daily team planning session, Becki and I discussed and recorded an anecdote about Anna's "hopping stones." Anna had taken several sheets of colored paper from the art area and placed them on the floor in the block area. She then hopped from paper to paper, going back to the art area several times to get more paper to add to her spreading collection. When Callie and Ben asked her what she was doing, she said the floor was "hot lava," and she could only step on "these safe hopping stones." Ben and Callie quickly stepped on a piece of paper so they would be "safe" and joined her game. I decided to incorporate this new play into large-group time by using paper plates and adding some hopping music.

I was interested in two things: Would children pick up on Anna's hopping from "stone" to "stone" idea, and what movement ideas would children come up with? (Movement is a Creative Arts KDI as well as a COR Advantage item under Creative Arts.)

Thinking about the transition to outdoor time, I wanted to end the stone activity and get the children across the room to the door. I thought that if Becki picked up her paper plate toward the end of the hopping music and hopped with it over to the door, perhaps the children would follow her lead. They could then stack the plates by the door and go outside.

Today, before the children arrived, I prepared for large-group time by putting the instrumental musical selection I had chosen in the audio player and making sure we had enough paper plates for each child (plus a few extra). When snack was almost over, I joined the children who had already gone to the large-group-time space. We sang and moved to the "Run Around the Circle" song we made up:

> *"Run, run, run around the circle.*
> *Run, run run around the circle.*
> *Run, run, run around the circle,*
> *Until you want to stop."*

The children suggested other ways to move — tiptoeing, rolling, walking backward, and jumping. As we sang and moved, the rest of the children joined us as they finished snack.

When all of the children were present, we sat down and sang "The Depot Town Song." The children enjoyed "reading" and singing each verse. When we got to Becca's butterfly letter link, Becca patted herself on the chest and said "That's me! I did the train," as the rest of the group sang "Becca saw the fast train." When we sang the verse "Alana saw a bunch of carrots," Alana ran to the house area and got the plastic carrots!

After "The Depot Town Song," I got a paper plate from the pile and said that I had some "hopping stones" for everyone. The children quickly helped themselves to the paper plates, and Becki spread out the rest while I turned on the music.

I was amazed at the variety of things the children did. Brian hopped from the rug to his plate to the rug over and over again. Rachel hopped on her plate from corner to corner. Chelsea got a scarf, stood on her plate, and slowly moved the scarf to the music. Ben sat by the window and watched what the other children were doing. Deola hopped all over the large-group area, landing sometimes on paper plates, sometimes on the rug. Mikey ran around his paper plate. Anna and most of the other children hopped from plate to plate, even hopping to "the really 'farest' one." We noticed that some children hopped to the steady beat of the music.

Becki and I supported what individual children did by imitating their actions. We also mentioned what some children were doing when it seemed appropriate. "Alana, Chelsea's doing something different with her hopping stone," I said. As we neared the end of the song, Becki picked up a plate and hopped toward the door. I told the children that when they were ready to go outside, they could hop to the door with a "hopping stone," and we hopped to the door, stacked our plates, and hopped outside.

A Sample Large-Group-Time Plan: Being Horses

Originating idea:
Children's interests — Wendy, Erin, Scott, and Troy have been playing "horses" at work time, walking about on all fours, rearing up on their "hind legs," neighing, and pawing the air.

Materials:
No materials are needed.

Possible KDIs:
F. Creative Arts: 42. Movement , 43. Pretend play

D. Language, Literacy, and Communication:
   21. Comprehension

Beginning:
Start with a variation of "Run Around the Circle":

"Horses run, horses run, run around the circle.
Horses run, horses run, run around the circle.
Horses run, horses run, run around the circle.
Horses run, then stop."

Ask children for other ways horses can go around the circle. Sing and do these variations.

Middle:
Tell a simple, repetitive story about horses that the children can act out along the way. To introduce it, say "Here's a story about horses just like you who have been running around the circle" before beginning a story such as the following:

Once upon a time there were 18 little horses who had run about all day long, so they walked slowly to their barn and went to sleep. Good night, horses (pause for the horses to go to sleep). The next morning they woke up refreshed and rested. They stretched their long legs (pause for leg stretching). They stretched their long necks (pause for neck stretching). They felt hungry so they went out to the pasture to eat grass (pause for grass eating). They ate grass all day long (pause for more grass eating). When nighttime came, they were tired, so they walked slowly back to their barn and went to sleep. Good night, horses (pause for sleeping).

The next morning the 18 little horses woke up refreshed and rested. They stretched their long legs (pause for leg stretching). They stretched their long necks (pause for neck stretching). They felt like neighing and pawing their feet in the air, so they went out to the pasture to rise up on their back legs and neigh (pause for neighing and pawing). They neighed and pawed their feet in the air all day long (pause for more neighing and pawing). When nighttime came, they were tired, so they walked slowly back to their barn and went to sleep. Good night, horses (pause for sleeping).

The next morning the 18 little horses woke up refreshed and rested. They stretched their long legs (pause for leg stretching). They stretched their long necks (pause for neck stretching). They felt like — what did they feel like doing? (get action from children) — so they went out to the pasture to _____ (pause for action children suggest). They _____ all day long (pause for more of the action children suggest). When nighttime came, they were tired, so they walked slowly back to their barn and went to sleep. Good night, horses (pause for sleeping).

(Repeat as long as the children are involved and offer actions.)

End:
End the story with a transition to outside time, for example:

The next morning the 18 little horses woke up refreshed and rested. They stretched their long legs (pause for leg stretching). They stretched their long necks (pause for neck stretching). They felt like playing outside like girls and boys so they trotted over to the coat rack to put on their girl and boy coats for outside time. (Trot over to the coat rack with children.)

Follow-up:
- Continue to watch children's "horse" play for other actions to build into this story.
- Plan a field trip to a local horse farm to see what horses do and how they move.

A Sample Large-Group-Time Plan: Singing Favorite Songs

Originating idea:
Content area — KDIs 41. Music and 42. Movement (Creative Arts) and COR Advantage Items Y. Music and Z. Movement (Creative Arts).

The children know more songs than they probably realize.

Materials:
Song cards, masking tape, message board, bag of children's letter links, instrumental music selection

Possible KDIs:
F. Creative Arts: 41. Music, 42. Movement
E. Mathematics: 32. Counting

Beginning:
Play an instrumental music selection and sway to the beat as children arrive. They will probably think of other ways to move on their own. Follow children's movement ideas. To get in position for singing, initiate a sitting movement on the final time through.

Middle:
Spread out the song cards face up. Ask a nearby child to pick a child's letter link out of the bag, and then say to the child whose letter link has been drawn, "Devon, it's your turn to pick the first song we're going to sing." Tape the song card Devon chooses and his letter link next to each other on the message board.

Have another child draw a second letter link from the bag. Have the second child drawn pick the second song and tape that song card and child's letter link next to each other on the board underneath the first song card and letter link. Repeat this process until there are five song cards on the board.

Point to and count the songs together with the children, and say "Let's start with the first song." Sing the songs in order, and transition to the next song by saying something like "Now we'll sing the second song." Have the child who chose the song pick a way for everyone to move to the beat as they sing (e.g., rocking, swaying, tapping a body part).

End:
Ask children to think of a way to move to small-group time humming the last song they just sang.

Follow-up:
- Leave the song cards and letter links up on the message board and repeat this process at large-group time later in the week until the children have sung all the songs they know so they can see how many songs they can sing.
- Watch to see if the children stop to "read" the song list on their own during the day.

In this preschool classroom, the children choose their favorite songs from a song book, which is a collection of song cards.

A Sample Large-Group-Time Plan: Moving Sand

Originating idea:
Cooperative play and projects — We have a new sandbox with no sand in it and a pile of sand that was just delivered and dumped about 20 feet away from the sandbox.

Materials:
Sand, shovels, good-sized buckets with handles, camera

Possible KDIs:

B. Social and Emotional Development: 13. Cooperative play

E. Mathematics: 35. Spatial awareness

A. Approaches to Learning: 4. Problem solving

Beginning:
As children gather, to the tune of "Row, Row, Row Your Boat," sing "Fill, fill, fill your buckets, fill your buckets with sand. Fill, fill, fill your buckets, fill your buckets with sand." Do filling motions along with the song. Sing other verses (e.g., "Carry, carry, carry your buckets…" "Dump, dump, dump your buckets…"). Ask children for additional ideas.

Middle:
Say something like "For large-group time, we're going outside to move the sand from the sand pile into the sandbox. Here are some buckets and shovels we can use." Respond to children's comments and questions.

Distribute buckets and shovels and go outside. Watch to see how children fill the buckets, what they do when they find that a full bucket is too heavy for one person to carry, and if they think of using other containers such as the wagon. Support children's problem solving and observations about this task. Take pictures so that later the children can see themselves at work, and they can see the sand pile growing smaller and the pile in the sandbox getting bigger.

End:
When all the sand is in the sandbox, go to the sandbox and start singing (to the tune of "Row, Row, Row Your Boat"), "We moved all the sand, we moved all the sand. We moved all the sand, we moved all the sand." Ask children for additional verses and sing them. Conclude with a statement such as "Now it's outside time and we can play in the sand or anything else on the playground."

Follow up:
- Leave buckets and shovels out for sand play.
- Print the pictures and introduce them at morning greeting time or small-group time.

After moving the sand into the sandbox, these children enjoy the fruits of their labor by playing in it.

A Sample Large-Group-Time Plan: Exploring Helium Balloons

Originating idea:
Currently meaningful events — Since Sanna brought balloons for everyone on her birthday, the children have been exploring balloons (blowing them up, tying off some, and releasing others so they zoom around the room). They have been wondering how those other kinds of balloons stay up in the air.

Materials:
Heavy-duty balloons, long strings with loops on one end to fit over children's wrists (if they want to use the strings), a small tank of helium

Possible KDIs:
G. Science and Technology: 47. Experimenting, 51. Natural and physical world

F. Creative Arts: 41. Music, 42. Movement

D. Language, Literacy, and Communication: 22. Speaking

Beginning:
Fill balloons with helium, tie on long strings, and distribute to children as they gather. Listen for and support children's observations and conversations.

Middle:
When everyone has a balloon, say "See how many things you can do with your helium balloons. Then when you hear the music, bring your balloons back to the circle." Watch and listen to the children. Support their experiments. (They may let their balloons go up to the ceiling and pull them back down. They may try tying them to various objects around the room to see if they will lift them.)

End:
Ask the children to wear the loops at the end of their balloon strings over their wrists. Put on a lively instrumental musical selection.

Put the loop of your balloon on your wrist, tap your head with both hands to the beat of the music, and watch balloons move to the beat with the children. Ask children for other body parts or things to tap to the beat and continue to watch the balloons move.

At the end of musical selection, ask "Where can we park our balloons for the night before we go home?" Once children settle on a balloon storage location, say "When you hear the music, put your balloon in _____ and move any way you like to the music to get your things for going home." Play another instrumental musical selection as children park their balloons and get ready to go home.

Follow-up:
- Talk with children at greeting time tomorrow about what they notice about the balloons.
- Let children know that the balloons are available for them to use at work time.

Understanding Outside Time

At outside time in a HighScope program, children pursue active physical play with the support of attentive, playful adults. Adults and children alike enjoy the sights, sounds, and vigor of play and exploring on the playground, at a nearby park, or in neighboring woods. To illustrate the dynamics of outside time, we have re-created a portion of an actual outside time from a HighScope program.

"Mud, mud, we love mud," sing Julia, Andrew, and Jalessa swinging together on the tire swing.

L.J. and Nathan hit Wiffle balls with short plastic Wiffle bats. Becki, an adult, is their pitcher. Brianna picks up the third bat and joins "batting practice." "What a hit," Becki says. "That was right to me!"

Mikey, Audie, and Brian are riding tricycles and watching the pinwheels they have taped to the handlebars.

"Look, Beth," says Brian to the other adult on the playground, "they're turning!"

"I see," Beth calls from under the climber, where Kacey, Erica, and Chrysten have placed her "under a magic spell." They are "good witches," protecting the children from "bad witch" Beth.

Trey and Douglas fill buckets with pea gravel and dump them into Alana's wagon. "I got more stones," Alana calls to Sarah, who is on the climbing net. They are dropping the pea gravel through the cracks in the tree-house deck.

What is outside time?

Outside time is a daily opportunity for children to engage in vigorous, noisy outdoor play. Children continue their indoor play in a more expansive setting, examine their natural surroundings, gain a sense of their immediate neighborhood, and experience changing weather conditions and seasons. Adults join children's play and gain a broader understanding of children's interests and abilities.

Energetic outdoor play

Outside, children have room to run, jump, throw, swing, climb, dig, and ride. Their pretend play ranges all over the play area: under the slide, up the climbing net into the tree house, down the hill in the wagon, and over to the sandbox. They can be galloping horses or rocket ship explorers. They have space to make big paintings and chalk drawings, weave streamers into the fence, pound nails into a tree stump, and make forts from big cardboard boxes.

Opportunities for social play

Outdoor play often brings young children together. Large pieces of equipment, such as slides, climbers, and tree houses, have a socializing effect because they accommodate more than one child at a time. Children try to do what they see others doing — sliding backward, climbing up the cargo net, twirling on the trapeze. Sandboxes also draw children together for filling and emptying activities and all kinds of pretend play. Even bike riding and swinging seem to invite conversational exchanges. While children also play by themselves, an expression such as "Look what I found!" from a lone explorer can attract curious children playing nearby.

An outdoor setting for learning

At outside time, children construct and test knowledge about people, things, and actions in their immediate world. Studies show that some children, for example, boys and those from low-income families, actually play longer and with greater complexity outdoors, creating many opportunities for learning (Heidemann & Hewitt, 2010). As further evidence of the learning potential outside, see how these examples of outdoor activities readily fit the KDIs:

Group Times, Outside Times, Transitions | 375

At outside time, children pursue active physical play with the support of attentive, playful adults.

- KDI 4. Problem solving — "I added water to the [sand] tower and then it didn't fall down."
- KDI 13. Cooperative play — Jonah and Alyssa each hold one end of a heavy board to carry it across the play yard.
- KDI 16. Gross-motor skills — "Run, Erica, she's going to get you!"
- KDI 23. Vocabulary — "I know. Let's do different words to the mud song, Julia!"
- KDI 32. Counting — "You need leaves! Two handfuls!"
- KDI 43. Pretend play — "We're ninja guys. Follow me because I'm the leader."
- KDI 46. Classifying — "This house is for cats. No people allowed!"
- KDI 54. Community roles — Misha is the bus driver who takes Tomas, Lena, and Julio to the movies after they get on board and pay their fare.

Why is outside time important?

Outside time allows children to express themselves and exercise in ways that are generally not available to them in indoor play. Although children in active learning settings move throughout the day, outside they engage in more invigorating, noisy play.

Healthy, unconstrained play

Children breathe fresh air; absorb vitamins from the sun; exercise their hearts, lungs, and muscles; and see broader vistas. Children who are quiet and shy inside often become more talkative and adventurous outside. Some children play with children outside whom they may not play with inside.

And children who like to make noise feel free to do so outside.

Contact with nature

At outside time, children experience the natural world in ways that make sense to them. They collect flowers, leaves, and nuts. They see the sky darken as the sun goes behind a cloud. They watch the motions of insects, birds, and squirrels. They dig in the dirt for worms and turn over logs and tires to find bugs. They hang wet things in the sun to dry, feel the wind, and see rain making puddles. They make observations ("This bug's carrying something") and draw conclusions ("He must be moving to a new house").

An opportunity for adults to learn more about children

At outside time, adults observe, converse, and play with children to learn more about what children can do and what attracts their interest. "I had no idea Brianna was so interested in batting," Becki reported to Beth during daily team planning after the outside time described earlier. "She was very persistent and by the end of outside time she was hitting the ball on almost every swing." Another team of teachers noted that as their children planted and tended a garden, they became increasingly attuned to seasonal changes: "Look! It's a baby flower!" "This is bigger than me!" "The flowers are changing. They're turning brown!" "Look inside! Tiny seeds!" The children demonstrated a true interest in time and the changing seasons, more than they would have if the teachers had attempted to do a daily calendar or weather time in the classroom.

Where children play outside

On a playground designed for young children

In most cases, children in active learning settings play on a playground designed and equipped to meet their particular needs and interests. In such an environment they are safe, secure, and stimulated to try things that suit their inclinations ("I'm going to swing!") and challenge their physical abilities ("Let's hang upside down from the net!").

In a neighborhood park

When programs do not have playgrounds of their own, children often play in neighborhood parks, taking loose materials, bikes, and wagons along to supplement the equipment that is already there.

What children do at outside time

At one outside time, Douglas plays by himself because his best friend is absent. He climbs to the top of the tire tree. "I just like to look around from up here," he remarks to Beth, one of his teachers. After a while, Douglas climbs almost all the way down and then jumps to the ground. He walks to the tire swing where Alana is swinging, balances on the ledge that surrounds the tire swing pit, walks around the ledge, hangs from the tire arm, and jumps down into the pea gravel.

From here he makes his way to the Wiffle ball and bat. Becki, his other teacher, pitches and he hits or throws the ball back to her. After batting, he moves onto the scooter, pushing himself swiftly with one foot, then balancing on both feet for the glide. Finally, he climbs up the cargo net, carefully placing each foot until he reaches the tree house. He climbs onto the deck and scoots down the tree-house stairs, holding on to the handrails for balance. "Hi, Daddy!" he calls, seeing his dad and little brother who have come to take him home.

To support children at outside time, it is important for adults to understand that children take on physical challenges and continue indoor types of play in a vigorous way.

Children play, converse, and solve problems they encounter

Children engage in *exploratory* play — digging, looking under logs for bugs, figuring out how to bounce balls, and hanging upside down from the trapeze. They engage in *constructive* play — making a tire tower, decorating the sidewalk or fence, making a pile of leaves or snow — and in *pretend*

Children get to experience firsthand the changing seasons during outside time.

play — making sand and stick "cakes," playing "monster," giving people "taxi" rides.

Children also invent games like toss and catch, galloping horses, and streamer parades. They play alone, in pairs, and in groups. They carry on conversations:

"Don't get in there."

"Why not?"

"There's a spider."

"Let's put grass on the spider."

"They like grass."

And they solve problems they encounter, such as drying a wet climber, stopping the bikes before running into the fence, and carrying the tires up the slide.

Children try out and practice climbing, pumping, pedaling, jumping, steering, throwing, hitting, and catching

Children take on these challenges inspired by their access to climbers, swings, pedal toys, sleds, and balls, as well as natural features such as hills, boulders, and tree stumps. They approach experiences on their own time at their own pace. For example, on the swings, Callie likes gentle pushes, Julia likes strong pushes, and Alana prefers to pump for herself. In one center, at the beginning of the year, the children found the slight incline on their bike path too steep to ride down. However, over time and with daily bike-riding experiences, the incline gradually became a challenge of just the right size, and finally it became just another bike path: "I wish we had a big hill," one bike rider said in the spring.

How Adults Support Children at Outside Time

The adults' role at outside time is very similar to their work-time role. They focus all their attention on children so they can understand and support children's outdoor initiatives in a playful, nonmanagerial way. Adults support children during outside time with these strategies:

- Helping children obtain the materials they need
- Using work-time support strategies
- Observing nature with children
- Bringing outside time to a close

Adults help children obtain the materials they need

While swings, climbers, slides, and tree houses are permanently situated, other materials, such as bicycles, sandbox dishes and shovels, scarves, pinwheels, chalk, paints, hammers and nails, balls and bats, and wagons, are usually stored in a protected storage area or shed. It is up to adults to devise ways of getting these materials in and out of the storage area on a daily basis so that children have a rich variety of props and objects to inspire and support their outdoor play. Here are some ideas to consider:

- As a team, take loose materials outside before the children arrive. Include early-arriving children and parents as helpers in this task.
- Store loose materials in milk crates or baskets with handles that children can easily carry outside by themselves or in pairs.
- Involve children (and parents) in gathering up loose materials at the end of the day.
- Place locked storage containers around the playground — one for balls, bats, and ropes; one for sand toys; one for dress-up materials; and so on. Unlock the containers at the beginning of outside time and have children help with cleanup at the end of the session.

Adults use work-time support strategies

Once children are outside with the materials they need, adults use the same support strategies as used at work time. These strategies are described in chapter 8 and are summarized below:

Participate in children's play

To support children's outdoor play, treat it with the same attention and respect you grant to children's indoor play at work time. Consider the following strategies:

Look for natural play openings. Observe children filling and emptying buckets at the sandbox, singing on the swings, playing "rocket ship" on the climber, and chasing one another in a game of tree tag or hide-and-seek.

Join children's play at the children's levels. Slide with children on the slide, climb up and under the climber, roll down the hill, and jump in the leaf pile.

Play in parallel with children. Fill and empty your own container with water or nuts, run with a pinwheel, or jump over sticks.

Play as a partner with children. Play toss and catch with a child, join a streamer parade, or look at things from the top of the climber with a child who is already up there.

Refer one player to another. Help children help each other. For example, Robert asked his teacher, "How do you do that?" She replied, "Ask Brandon. He's the one who wove all these streamers into the fence."

Suggest new ideas for ongoing play. Offer suggestions to children as part of a natural conversation about their play. Julia, for example, was playing race car driver and had lost her "starter flag."

Julia: Where's my starter flag. It's gone!

Adult: Here's a starter flag you could use. *(Hands her a large fallen leaf.)*

Converse with children

Children who are quiet inside often find lots to say at outside time. Here are some conversational strategies you can use to converse with children:

Look for natural opportunities for conversation. Conversations occur when children are engaged in repetitive play such as swinging, filling cups with sand, or digging in the garden. Sometimes, children come up to you with a discovery to share: "Hey Beth, look at this!"

Join children at their level for conversation. Sit with children on the climbing net, under a tree, on the tire swing; stand on the slide ladder or wherever the children are.

Respond to children's conversational leads. This allows you to pursue the child's topic:

Child: *(Digging)* My daddy has a shovel.

Adult: Your daddy likes to dig and so do you.

Converse as a partner with children. Offer comments and observations so that the child retains control of the conversation. Here is how the digging conversation continued:

Child: I can get a lot of sand in my shovel.

Adult: Yes, you can.

Group Times, Outside Times, Transitions 379

To support children's outdoor play, look for a natural play opening and play as a partner with children.

Child: I can fill up this whole bucket…but it's going to take a lot of shovels.

Adult: Yeah, that's a pretty big bucket.

Child: We have a really big one at home. It's for horses.

Adult: I didn't know you had horses at your house.

Child: No. It's for my sister's horse at Karen's barn.

Ask questions sparingly. Use occasional questions to clarify your understanding of the child's thinking:

Adult: You mean your sister has a horse but it lives in Karen's barn?

Child: Yeah, lots of horses live there. But you have to go and feed them and stuff.

Encourage children's problem solving

As children play outside, they encounter all kinds of problems to solve, such as how to keep the balls inside the tires while they are rolling and how to keep the "robot sticks" on their backs while running. To encourage children's independent problem solving, try these strategies:

Encourage children to deal with problems and conflicting viewpoints. Rather than solving things for children (e.g., taking away the toy that

> **How Adults Support Children at Outside Time**
>
> **Adults help children obtain the materials they need.**
>
> **Adults use work-time support strategies.**
> - Participate in children's play.
>   - Look for natural play openings.
>   - Join play on children's levels.
>   - Play in parallel with children.
>   - Play as a partner with children.
>   - Refer one player to another.
>   - Suggest new ideas for ongoing play.
> - Converse with children.
>   - Look for natural opportunities for conversation.
>   - Join children at their level for conversation.
>   - Respond to children's conversational leads.
>   - Converse as a partner with children.
>   - Ask questions sparingly.
> - Encourage children's problem solving.
>   - Encourage children to deal with problems and conflicting viewpoints.
>   - Interact with children rather than manage them.
>   - Calmly assist with unresolved conflicts.
>
> **Adults observe nature with children.**
>
> **Adults bring outside time to a close.**

several children want), encourage children to find a way to share it. Working out a system for sharing the job of steering the taxi is as important as the task of learning how to steer.

Interact with children rather than manage them. Playing and conversing with children supports children's learning more effectively than spending outside time "policing" the use of the bikes and the swings.

Calmly assist with unresolved conflicts. When children seek your assistance or seem to need your support, listen to their descriptions of the issue and ask them for their ideas about what to do. Do as little of the talking as possible. They are the ones who need the experience of putting their own thoughts and feelings into words.

Adults observe nature with children

Several children are smelling, holding, looking at, and breaking apart seed pods they have discovered. Julie, an adult, joins them and begins breaking apart seed pods herself and listening to the children's conversation. They all continue to collect and study the pods for about 15 minutes.

Adults like Julie remain alert to natural things that attract children's attention — bugs and spiders that cross their paths, worms they dig up in the garden, playground plants and animals that catch their eye, birds that fly overhead, puddles, the sound of the wind. Adults look for opportunities to join children as they observe, experiment with, and draw conclusions about the natural and physical world. For example, in even the most urban areas, planting a garden of any size — an 8' by 12' plot on the playground, containers on the roof, milk crates (lined with plastic bags) in the sun, window boxes, hanging pots — draws children, adults, and nature together to dig, plant, weed, water, make mud, pick, smell, eat, and observe. Flowers attract butterflies. Trees and bushes are home to insects, birds, and squirrels. A water garden, watercourse, swamp, or wetland area provide children with plant and creature life to watch; sticks to float; water to enjoy; and stones and rocks to gather, examine, carry, and rearrange. Such experiences shared with supportive adults encourage children to love, appreciate, and care for the earth and living things.

Adults bring outside time to a close

Before the end of outside time, adults give children a warning so that they have a chance to bring their play to a timely end. "Five more minutes till it's time to put the bikes and toys away and then go inside for lunch," Julie says to each group of players as she tours the playground.

Adults also engage children in gathering up and storing the loose balls, sand toys, streamers, bikes, wagons, and scooters. When the day ends with outside time, storing loose materials can be a leisurely activity for everyone — children, parents, and teachers.

In sum, outside time has the same elements of active participatory learning as work time and other indoor activities. Children engage with one another and with adults, with the natural and physical world, and with all the content areas in the KDIs.

How Adults Support Children During Transitions[1]

Throughout the day in every early childhood setting, there are many transitions for children — when a parent drops a child off in the morning, when children and adults walk down the hall on their way to the playground, when a small group of children stops recalling and starts eating their snacks, when the parent picks up the child at the end of the day. At these times, children experience one or more changes — of activity, location, caregiver, or playmates. Adults may think of these changeover times as incidental parts of their routine, but they are crucial events for children who often react strongly to them ("I want my mommy!" "I don't want to cleanup!"). Well-planned transitions are often the difference between a "bad day" and one that goes smoothly

---

[1] The section on transitions was adapted from Perrett (1996).

Outside Time: A Summary

What outside time is
- Energetic outdoor play.
- Opportunities for social play.
- An outdoor setting for learning.

Why outside time is important
- Outdoor play is healthy and unconstrained.
- Children have contact with nature.
- Adults continue to learn about children.

Where children play at outside time
- On a playground designed for young children.
- In a neighborhood park.

What children do at outside time
- Children play, converse, and solve problems they encounter.
- Children try out and practice climbing, pumping, pedaling, jumping, steering, throwing, hitting, and catching.

for both children and adults. The following strategies help adults do this:

- Adjusting transition times to suit children's developmental needs
- Planning for transitions with individual children in mind
- Planning for cleanup, the longest transition

Adults adjust transition times to suit children's developmental needs

To ease transition times for children, start by thinking about preschoolers' need for active learning and a climate of support. Consider ways to adjust transitions to fulfill these needs.

Establish a consistent daily routine

Transitions go more smoothly for children when they know the daily routine and can prepare themselves for what comes next. A consistent daily routine not only helps children feel secure but also assures children, as they make the transition from one part of the routine to the next, that there will be time again the next day to continue their play.

Keep the number of transitions between activities, places, and caregivers to a minimum

In discussing the daily routine as a team, ask yourselves the following questions: Are there too many transitions? Can we coordinate our daily routine so there are fewer changes and smoother transitions? For example, adults in one Head Start program reduce the number of transitions in their day by having children plan individually as they finish breakfast, instead of regrouping children in another location to make their plans. In this program, an adult asks for each child's plan at the breakfast table, as soon as the child has finished eating. Then the child moves directly into work time. This way, children make only one shift in location (from the breakfast table to the chosen play area) instead of two (from the breakfast table to the planning table to the play area). In addition, the children do not have to wait for others to finish eating before they can make their plans. As this example shows, reducing the number of changes children have to make and eliminating waiting time are key principles for planning successful transitions.

Start new activities right away

At the beginning of small- or large-group times, for example, children can become distracted if they have to wait — as the teacher prepares materials or as all the children gather. Therefore, it makes sense to start a new activity even if all the children are not finished with the one before it. At the HighScope Demonstration Preschool one year, large-group time followed snacktime. The children were assigned to two groups for snack, one group with each teacher. Children moved to the large-group meeting place one by one as they finished eating. As soon as a few children had gathered, the adult designated to lead the large-group activity that day would join them and start right in with a song, active game, or fingerplay. This way, adults did not have to tell children, "Let's wait until everyone is finished eating."

When waiting time cannot be avoided, plan ways to keep children actively involved

Waiting time can be reduced, but it cannot always be eliminated. If children have to wait for the school bus at the end of the day, plan to use this time with them for singing songs, learning fingerplays, and talking or reading books together. Remember that children of this age do not like to sit still and keep quiet.

Plan enjoyable ways for groups of children to move from place to place

Keeping children mentally and physically active when they have to walk from place to place makes these transitions pleasant for children and adults. Instead of asking children to walk quietly, single file, with their hands at their sides, encourage them to move in creative ways. For example, you might ask, "Which animal can we move like as we walk down the hall to the bathroom?" Each child can then choose an animal to imitate. (For further discussion of this topic, see "Sharing of control between adults and children" on p. 68.)

Adults plan for transitions with individual children in mind

The strategies just described usually make transitions go smoothly for the group as a whole. There may be some children, however, for whom transitions are particularly stressful. These children may find it difficult to get involved in cleaning up after work time, resist leaving the playground when everyone else is going inside, or "hide" under the table at the beginning of small-group time. As you develop strategies for these children, it is especially important to keep in mind two of the ingredients of active learning — **choices** and **adult scaffolding.**

Decide where to position adults during transition times

During daily team planning, decide where adults can best position themselves as children change from one part of the routine to the next. At times, it may be helpful to designate a team member to assist a particular child. For example, if Jessica has trouble getting started with cleanup, choose an adult to be near her at the end of work time.

Offer appropriate choices to individual children before a transition

Choices may help children focus on a particular action they can take during an upcoming transition. Here are two examples:

"Mikey, when you finish your snack, it will be large-group time. Is there someone you want to sit next to when we sing?"

"Chelsea, it is almost time to go inside. Show me how you are going to move to get to the door."

Alert children to the upcoming change

If the end of work time or some other part of the routine is near and a child shows no sign of completing his or her activity, alert the child to the upcoming change. At the same time, give the child some control in deciding what to do. Here is an example:

"Deola, work time is almost over. When you finish the face on your drawing, it will be time to clean

Changeover times, such as arrival, are crucial events for children. Well-planned, comfortable transitions can make the difference between a difficult day and one that goes smoothly for children, parents, and teachers.

up. *[Pause. Deola quickens the pace on her drawing.]* Where can you put your drawing so you can finish it tomorrow?"

Adults plan for cleanup, the longest transition

Cleanup time is often the longest transition of the day. Further, cleaning up is an emotional issue for many adults who judge themselves by how clean and orderly their homes are. Teaching teams too may measure the day's success by how smoothly cleanup time goes. Following are strategies that can help adults relax in the face of this potentially stressful time.

Maintain realistic expectations of children

Cleanup is an adult-initiated activity, yet a child's need at cleanup is often to continue to play. Though we as adults may hate to clean, we expect children to clean up willingly and are surprised when this does not happen.

While it is natural for children to resist cleaning up, cleanup is a valuable learning experience. As they put toys and materials away, children are developing self-help skills and a sense of responsibility for their environment. In addition, they are engaging in many activities that are KDIs. For example, they are classifying (KDI 46) as they sort spoons from forks and place the utensils on the shelves; they are involved in pretend play (KDI 43) as they zoom like pilots "flying" the toys to their boxes; and they are developing a sense of ecology (KDI 58) as they put paper into the recycling bin.

Label containers and shelves to indicate where materials are stored

Cleaning up is a lot easier if adults and children know where materials belong. Therefore, it makes sense to label shelves and containers with developmentally appropriate labels. Use *concrete labels* — the actual objects taped to the sides of their containers (e.g., a Lego block); *pictures of the materials* — drawings, catalog pictures,

Children love to use things they see their parents use at home, and child-sized cleaning tools, like this broom and dustpan, can help children maintain their interest in cleanup.

photocopies, or photos taped to the containers or shelves; *tracings* — outlines of objects taped to the exact places where the objects go on shelves, pegboards, or racks; and simple *letters and words* — such as ART AREA — that children will be able to read as they acquire literacy skills. (Chapter 6 contains more information on arranging, equipping, and labeling your classroom or center.)

When possible, clean up throughout work time

Encourage children to put away the materials they are using before they start a new activity: "Tiffany, you're done playing in the house area. Let's put away the dishes and then you can tell me your

"Ready or Not!" Cleanup-Time Games

Once cleanup has begun, *look for ways to make the process active and enjoyable* for children. Here are some ideas to try:

Imitation
Sometimes children enjoy carrying toys in unique ways. If you see a child carrying something behind his or her back, try imitating the child as you carry a toy to its place on the shelf. This will probably catch the attention of other children who will then imitate what they see the two of you doing.

Beat the clock!
Encourage children to clean up an area quickly before the sand in the sand timer runs all the way to the bottom, the timer (set for three to five minutes) rings, or the big hand on the clock gets to the four.

Paper bag
Give each child a lunch sack or grocery bag. Ask the children to move around the room, filling up their bags with toys that are out. When the bags are full, ask them to return the toys to their places in the room.

Football game
An adult pretends to be a football player, "hiking" a toy between her legs to a child behind her. The child then puts that toy away and returns for another one. Children will often line up behind the adult to play this game.

Statues
Play music as children clean up, stopping the music occasionally. When the music stops, children pose as statues, resuming cleanup when the music begins again.

Music cleanup
Music can be used in a variety of other ways during cleanup. For example, sing a cleanup song, with or without children's names in it. It is also fun to play selections at different tempos as children put things away — ask children to match their pace to the music, speeding up or slowing down as the music changes. Another idea is to play a familiar song on your audio player and ask children to clean up the room before the song is over.

These suggestions are intended merely as examples — the same principles of adult support and active learning can be used in many other ways at cleanup time. Use these strategies as a starting point for brainstorming ideas of your own.

next plan." This strategy reduces classroom clutter, making it easier for children to see the choices available to them. And there is less to do later at cleanup time if children pick up as they go along. There are occasions, however, when it is not appropriate for children to clean up immediately after they finish doing something. For example, if five children have built a stage out of blocks for a "concert" and one of them decides to paint, the block stage should be left out for the other children to use. Deciding if and when children should be expected to "clean as you go" is an issue for the teaching team to resolve through discussion.

Further, encouraging children to put toys away throughout work time should not take precedence over playing and conversing with children and supporting problem solving.

Follow children's interests at cleanup time
Use what you know about individual children and build on it. If Petey loves to pretend he is a basketball star, hold out the trash can and encourage him to "shoot baskets" with paper scraps and other litter. Another way to follow children's interests at cleanup time is to extend their work-time activities. If children are pretending to be

Transitions: A Summary

Adults adjust transitions to suit children's developmental needs.

- Establish a consistent daily routine.
- Keep the *number* of transitions between activities, places, and caregivers to a minimum.
- Start new activities right away.
- When waiting cannot be avoided, plan ways to keep children actively involved.
- Plan enjoyable ways for groups of children to move from place to place.

Adults plan for transitions with individual children in mind.

- Decide where to position adults during transition times.
- Offer appropriate choices to individual children before a transition.
- Alert children to the upcoming change.

Adults plan for cleanup, the longest transition.

- Maintain realistic expectations of children.
- Label containers and shelves to indicate where materials are stored.
- When possible, clean up throughout work time.
- Follow children's interests at cleanup time.
- Remain flexible.

dogs during work time, encourage the "dogs" to clean up: "Doggie Ben (hand the child a toy), here is a bone for you to put away." You might follow this by saying, "Can *you* find another bone to put away?"

Remain flexible

Just because cleanup (or some other transition) is not going as smoothly as it might does not mean it cannot result in a worthwhile experience for children. See "'Ready or Not!' Cleanup-Time Games" on page 385 for more strategies for making cleanup an effective learning experience for children.

Nevertheless, dealing with children's approaches to cleanup can push adults to the limits of their patience. We offer the following two vignettes of cleanup times from the HighScope Demonstration Preschool to show how adults can respond calmly to unexpected cleanup-time situations, helping children learn about the natural consequences of their actions.

Responding to the Unexpected

During one day's cleanup time, Sam, a teacher, asked three children to wash paintbrushes. They took the brushes into the bathroom, and Sam got involved with several other children putting blocks away. Shortly afterward, a child ran to Sam, reporting, "The kids are painting the bathroom!"

Sam walked into the bathroom. The children had indeed painted the toilets and the linoleum walls with red, green, and blue paint. Resisting the temptation to get angry, Sam calmly asked the children what happened. "We're painting just like my dad does at home," Max said. Sam asked the children what they needed to do and several answered, "Clean up the bathroom." Sam found sponges and the children washed off all the paint.

Later, at their daily planning session, Sam and Becki decided to support the children's interest in painting by making large paintbrushes and buckets of water available at outside time the next day. They also decided to confine paintbrush-washing to the sink in the art area to help limit the temptation for children to paint the bathroom walls.

The next day, the children enjoyed "painting" the climber, the surface of the playground, and the building with water. They never again tried to paint the bathroom.

One day at the beginning of the school year, Kenneth decided it might be fun to make a pile of toys in the house area. The idea was contagious, and soon a small group of children were pulling toys off the shelves and adding them to the rapidly growing pile.

When it came time to clean up, Beth reminded the children that it was their job to put the pile of toys away. It took 45 minutes for the children who had made the pile to put the toys in their places. The teachers supported them throughout this process, using all the active learning strategies they could muster to help keep them involved in their task.

The next day, the teachers overheard Petey asking Kenneth if he wanted to make a pile again. "No way!" they heard Kenneth reply. "If we dump out all these toys, we'll be cleaning up forever!"

In both these situations, which occurred early in the school year, children were "testing the boundaries" of appropriate behavior by making bigger-than-usual messes. However, in both cases adults resisted the temptation to scold children. Instead, they stepped back and looked for ways to turn the situations into active learning experiences with a lasting impact. Instead of squelching children's initiatives, they built on them but still made it clear they expected the children to clean up after themselves. These cleanup experiences gave children opportunities to learn about the natural consequences of their actions.

In this section we have presented ideas for smoothing transition times for children. You have probably noticed that we approach transitions with the same general teaching approach we use during other parts of the daily routine. During transitions, just as at work time or small-group time, *remember to use the principles of active participatory learning and the elements of support and to build on children's interests.*

Understanding Other Group Times

The HighScope daily routine also includes other group times when children socialize and share food and information with adults (teachers and parents) and one another. These times — meal- and snacktime, greeting and departure, and message board — are each described here.

Meal- and snacktime

In most part-day programs, children and adults share a snack, while full-day programs have both meal- and snacktimes. Eating together is generally done in small groups, preferably with the same children who gather together for planning, recall, and small-group time.

The emphasis during snacks and meals is on social interaction. It is important for adults to eat with children, both as a natural social situation and as an opportunity to share relaxed conversation and to support children's ideas. Teachers should not have a hidden agenda for teaching specific academic skills during mealtimes, although opportunities for teaching and learning often occur naturally. For example, a list indicating whose turn it is to set out the plates and cups can help children develop literacy skills, and children taking a turn will be involved in one-to-one matching of utensils and people who will be eating, which helps develop mathematics skills. Snack and mealtime are also occasions when children enjoy practicing self-help skills such as pouring their own juice, cutting things into portions, folding napkins, and wiping up spills. Note that plastic knives work well for spreading but they are often too flimsy for cutting and may frustrate children. Regular (metal) butter knives, however, work well for cutting and are safe.

Greeting and departure time

You will find that elements of both individual and group activities are characteristic of greeting and departure times. These periods are also transitions, and you can use the transition strategies described previously to help children make the shift from home to school and back again. For arrivals, it is important that each child be welcomed every day by a teacher. When an adult brings a child to school (as opposed to the child's arriving by van or bus), that adult should also receive a personal *hello* from a staff member. The same holds true for saying *good-bye* on a daily basis.

If arrival and departure times are staggered, the adult helps each child enter into or finish up whatever part of the routine is underway. For example, you may plan with a child so he or she can begin working, or you may help a child put things away and get dressed shortly before a parent is due to pick up the child. If children arrive at the same time, greeting takes on more of the character of a group event; however, it also may happen in various pairings and small groups. For example, children, along with parents who can stay a while, may look at books until the rest of the children arrive. When most of the children depart from the program at the same time, departure is still likely to be more individualized since parents rarely come at the same moment. Nevertheless, since a child is leaving the group as well as the current activity, adults help the child bring his or her day to a close with a sense of completion.

Message board

Gathering at the message board is a large-group activity that generally takes place once everyone has arrived. This is a time to share announcements and let children know about things that are happening that day or that are coming up soon. For example, visitors may be expected (such as a local artist or a prospective student and parent), perhaps new material or equipment introduced the

During message board, children and adults share important information, such as new materials for outside time and the art area.

day before can now be found in a specific area of the room, or perhaps a field trip is planned for the next day. You can also use this time as an opportunity for the whole class to solve a problem that affects everyone. For example, if running through the classroom poses a safety hazard, the children might brainstorm possible solutions and choose one or two to try out. A few days later, during message board time, they may review the situation and decide if the problem is solved or whether they need to try a different approach. To illustrate the types of interactions that occur around the message board, we have re-created an actual message board time from a HighScope preschool program.

The Information Exchange

It is the beginning of the day. Two adults, Beth and Sam, and 16 children, gather in the middle of the toy area and together "read" the messages for the day "written" by adults and children on the message board that hangs on the wall low enough for everyone to reach and see:

The first message leads to a discussion about the friendly neighborhood kitty that has been joining the children at outside time. Yesterday, the children had asked about bringing the kitty inside with them. Beth had promised to talk with their neighbor, "the kitty's mom."

"We can't bring him inside," Beth tells the children, "because if we let him in, he won't go back to his house at night for food. But our neighbor says we can play with him when we're outside."

"He's a nice kitty."

"I wish he could come inside."

"My kitty at home is orange…with stripes."

Next, the group talks for a few minutes about Becki, another adult, who is away. They count the number of balloons left on the wall, one for each day Becki will be absent. Then Alana pops today's balloon. Before she does, however, several children note that the "pop's gonna be loud. I'm covering my ears!" Others announce, "Not me." "It's not too loud for me."

The third message, written and read by Max, leads to a brief discussion about the fact that Sam is the teacher while Becki is away.

The last message on the board focuses the attention of all 16 children on Beth, who is holding a cell phone (an old one donated by a parent). She pushes some buttons to demonstrate.

"Can you call somebody?" one child asks.

"No, it is no longer working."

"But we can pretend to call someone!" says Callie.

Beth agrees, and everybody announces at once that they want to use the phone at work time.

"What can we do so everyone can have a turn?" Beth asks.

Several children understand that some kind of turn-taking will be necessary, but it takes the group another five minutes of discussion to finally put the turn-taking steps together: a list of people who want to use the phone and a timer to tell how long each turn is. Throughout this discussion, the children remain huddled around Beth, leaning in, intently focused on the phone, which is obviously of great interest to them. Once the phone-using problem is solved and the list is actually started, the children pull back, and Beth asks Ben how they should move to small-group time. "Like this!" he says,

> **Other Group Times: A Summary**
>
> **Meals and snacktimes**
> - Adults and children eat together, usually in the same group used for planning, recall, and small-group time.
> - Emphasis is on social interaction.
> - Children have many opportunities for developing self-help skills (e.g., pouring liquids, wiping up spills) as well as skills in literacy (e.g., writing turn-taking lists), mathematics (e.g., matching napkins to the number of people at the table), and other content areas.
>
> **Greetings and departures**
> - Teachers welcome and say good-bye to each child (and any accompanying adults) individually.
> - Adults help children enter into the program day and bring closure to ongoing activities when it is time to leave.
>
> **Message board**
> - Messages are "written" using pictures, symbols, and words so children of all literacy levels can "read" them.
>
> - Adults share announcements and let children know about upcoming special events, new materials, visitors, and so on.
> - Class may engage briefly in group problem-solving discussions.
> - Time at the message board creates a sense of "community" in the classroom.
>
>

holding his hand to his ear as though he is talking on the phone, and everyone holds one or both hands to their ears on the way to small-group time.

Teachers "write" these messages — on a dry-erase board, easel pad, chalkboard, or similar surface — using pictures, symbols, and words. Writing messages in various ways allows children of all literacy levels to "read" them, know what to expect, and participate in the discussion. It is also an opportunity for children to recognize letters and words (especially their own and others' names) and for adults to introduce language and literacy games, such as rhyming and alliteration.

Finally, the message board helps to create a sense of community before children proceed to the next part of the day.

Throughout the daily routine, HighScope teachers are continually aware of what children are experiencing and learning. To guide their planning and interactions with children, teachers keep in mind the KDIs that are important in the early years. These essential indicators — in all content domains of learning — are described in the next chapter of this book.

CHAPTER 10

Introduction to HighScope's Curriculum Content

What are young children like? What kinds of play experiences and activities do they seek out, no matter where they live? How do they make discoveries and achieve an understanding of their world? What kinds of support do they need to grow and prosper? As early childhood educators, our answers to these questions are embodied in the HighScope Curriculum's **content areas** and **key developmental indicators (KDIs).** These guideposts define both our *beliefs* about how children develop and the *actions* we must take to support that development.

HighScope is a comprehensive curriculum model — it addresses all areas of development. In the HighScope Curriculum, the *content of* children's learning is organized into eight major divisions that are easily aligned and consistent with the Head Start Child Development and Early Learning Framework, Common Core Standards, and other national and state early learning standards (Gronlund, 2006; National Association for the Education of Young Children & National Association of Early Childhood Specialists in State Departments of Education, 2002). HighScope's eight curriculum content areas are

> "All children — not simply some — are entitled to early experiences that will foster their optimal development."
> — National Education Goals Panel (Kagan, Moore, & Bredekamp, 1995, p. 1)

A. Approaches to Learning

B. Social and Emotional Development

C. Physical Development and Health

D. Language, Literacy, and Communication

E. Mathematics

F. Creative Arts

G. Science and Technology

H. Social Studies

The National Education Goals Panel (NEGP; Kagan et al., 1995) emphasizes the interdependence of these areas and the importance of addressing them all at every age and grade level. It is also valuable to note that children's development varies widely within and across content areas. No two children are alike, and any individual may be more or less advanced from one domain to another. The objective of early childhood programs is to provide the kinds of experiences that support and nurture all of these areas of learning and development in every child. Adults scaffold children's learning when they support them at their current level and gently extend their knowledge and thinking as they progress along a developmental trajectory.

With the KDIs as a guide, educators can be sure they are providing the essential learning experiences that all children are entitled to, in this case opportunities to use gross-motor skills (KDI 16) and experience cooperative play (KDI 13).

HighScope is also committed to the idea that education does not end with childhood. When individuals actively engage with objects, people, events, and ideas, they continue to learn from infancy through adulthood. The early childhood curriculum framework can thus apply to working with older students and is even applicable to adult learners. Specific content areas may vary in significance at different developmental stages. Physical development, for example, is a greater concern at younger ages while science and technology may grow in importance over time. However, in a comprehensive approach to learning, every content area affects thought and behavior. It is widely accepted that children learn through play. It is equally true that adults learn through the playful exploration of ideas, and are most effective when they draw simultaneously on many areas of knowledge. HighScope therefore sees play and work as part of a lifelong continuum of learning.

The content areas and KDIs help adults plan comprehensively around the skills and abilities children are developing in preschool. This simple graphing activity is built around KDI 39. Data analysis in the Mathematics content area.

KDIs — Guideposts for Child Development

Within each content area, HighScope identifies the key developmental indicators[1] that are the building blocks of thinking and reasoning. The KDIs are based on current child development research and national and state early learning standards but also reflect HighScope's educational philosophy and teaching practices. KDIs pave the way for later schooling and entry into the adult world. In terms of the two major types of learning objectives used by many educational theorists, the indicators include both *knowledge* and the application of this knowledge in *thinking* (Marzano, 2001). For example, preschoolers need to know color names (knowledge) in order to sort objects by color (thinking).

The term *key developmental indicators* encapsulates HighScope's approach to early education. The word *key* refers to the fact that these are the meaningful ideas children should learn and experience. HighScope acknowledges that young children need to master a wide range of specific knowledge and thinking skills — the list could be almost endless in scope and detail. To avoid losing sight of what is essential and important, the content captured in the individual KDIs stresses the broader areas of knowledge and skills that lay the foundation for further learning.

The second part of the term, *developmental,* conveys the idea that learning is gradual and cumulative. Learning follows a sequence, generally moving from simple to more complex knowledge and skills. Moreover, the word *developmental* emphasizes that it is inappropriate, not to mention futile, to expect preschoolers to behave and learn as kindergarten or first-grade students

---

[1] Key developmental indicators were formerly called *key experiences,* and these differed both in organization and content from the current KDIs. For a discussion of the curriculum's evolution from key experiences to key developmental indicators, see Hohmann, Weikart, and Epstein (2008, pp. 300–303).

HighScope Preschool Curriculum Content
Key Developmental Indicators

A. Approaches to Learning
1. **Initiative:** Children demonstrate initiative as they explore their world.
2. **Planning:** Children make plans and follow through on their intentions.
3. **Engagement:** Children focus on activities that interest them.
4. **Problem solving:** Children solve problems encountered in play.
5. **Use of resources:** Children gather information and formulate ideas about their world.
6. **Reflection:** Children reflect on their experiences.

B. Social and Emotional Development
7. **Self-identity:** Children have a positive self-identity.
8. **Sense of competence:** Children feel they are competent.
9. **Emotions:** Children recognize, label, and regulate their feelings.
10. **Empathy:** Children demonstrate empathy toward others.
11. **Community:** Children participate in the community of the classroom.
12. **Building relationships:** Children build relationships with other children and adults.
13. **Cooperative play:** Children engage in cooperative play.
14. **Moral development:** Children develop an internal sense of right and wrong.
15. **Conflict resolution:** Children resolve social conflicts.

C. Physical Development and Health
16. **Gross-motor skills:** Children demonstrate strength, flexibility, balance, and timing in using their large muscles.
17. **Fine-motor skills:** Children demonstrate dexterity and hand-eye coordination in using their small muscles.
18. **Body awareness:** Children know about their bodies and how to navigate them in space.
19. **Personal care:** Children carry out personal care routines on their own.
20. **Healthy behavior:** Children engage in healthy practices.

D. Language, Literacy, and Communication[2]
21. **Comprehension:** Children understand language.
22. **Speaking:** Children express themselves using language.
23. **Vocabulary:** Children understand and use a variety of words and phrases.
24. **Phonological awareness:** Children identify distinct sounds in spoken language.
25. **Alphabetic knowledge:** Children identify letter names and their sounds.
26. **Reading:** Children read for pleasure and information.
27. **Concepts about print:** Children demonstrate knowledge about environmental print.
28. **Book knowledge:** Children demonstrate knowledge about books.
29. **Writing:** Children write for many different purposes.
30. **English language learning:** (If applicable) Children use English and their home language(s) (including sign language).

---

[2]Language, Literacy, and Communication KDIs 21–29 may be used for the child's home language(s) as well as English. KDI 30 refers specifically to English language learning.

E. Mathematics

31. **Number words and symbols:** Children recognize and use number words and symbols.

32. **Counting:** Children count things.

33. **Part-whole relationships:** Children combine and separate quantities of objects.

34. **Shapes:** Children identify, name, and describe shapes.

35. **Spatial awareness:** Children recognize spatial relationships among people and objects.

36. **Measuring:** Children measure to describe, compare, and order things.

37. **Unit:** Children understand and use the concept of unit.

38. **Patterns:** Children identify, describe, copy, complete, and create patterns.

39. **Data analysis:** Children use information about quantity to draw conclusions, make decisions, and solve problems.

F. Creative Arts

40. **Art:** Children express and represent what they observe, think, imagine, and feel through two- and three-dimensional art.

41. **Music:** Children express and represent what they observe, think, imagine, and feel through music.

42. **Movement:** Children express and represent what they observe, think, imagine, and feel through movement.

43. **Pretend play:** Children express and represent what they observe, think, imagine, and feel through pretend play.

44. **Appreciating the arts:** Children appreciate the creative arts.

G. Science and Technology

45. **Observing:** Children observe the materials and processes in their environment.

46. **Classifying:** Children classify materials, actions, people, and events.

47. **Experimenting:** Children experiment to test their ideas.

48. **Predicting:** Children predict what they expect will happen.

49. **Drawing conclusions:** Children draw conclusions based on their experiences and observations.

50. **Communicating ideas:** Children communicate their ideas about the characteristics of things and how they work.

51. **Natural and physical world:** Children gather knowledge about the natural and physical world.

52. **Tools and technology:** Children explore and use tools and technology.

H. Social Studies

53. **Diversity:** Children understand that people have diverse characteristics, interests, and abilities.

54. **Community roles:** Children recognize that people have different roles and functions in the community.

55. **Decision making:** Children participate in making classroom decisions.

56. **Geography:** Children recognize and interpret features and locations in their environment.

57. **History:** Children understand past, present, and future.

58. **Ecology:** Children understand the importance of taking care of their environment.

The KDIs apply to the activities of children in all early childhood settings. In every country and culture, for example, children enjoy imitating, pretending, and using items they see adults using.

do. Whatever level we are addressing, from infancy through adulthood, the curriculum must be consistent with what we know about human development at each stage of life.

Finally, *indicators* was chosen to emphasize that educators need evidence that children are developing the knowledge, skills, and understanding considered important for school and life readiness. To plan appropriately for students and to evaluate program effectiveness, we need observable indicators of our impact on children. Further, by defining these child outcomes in measurable terms, we can develop assessment tools that are consistent with the curriculum. In other words, an assessment system tied to the KDIs should *indicate* whether the program is meeting its goals.

The continuity across content areas and KDIs allows for the fact that development occurs along a continuum and children of different ages and abilities cannot be pigeonholed into a single age-based category. This book focuses on the 58 KDIs that make up the HighScope Curriculum's content for preschoolers, that is, children aged three to five. However, some children in this age range may exhibit behaviors characteristic of older toddlers or of early elementary students. For this reason, the discussion of each KDI in the eight books that accompany this manual (Epstein, 2012a–h) includes a chart containing behavioral examples of that KDI and related teaching suggestions for children at a wide range of levels. (See the discussion of scaffolding charts at the conclusion of this chapter.) Furthermore, children with special needs can fall at different points along the learning continuum, without regard to age, so this flexible system for presenting the content helps practitioners understand and plan for their development as well.

For children to learn the content contained in the KDIs, it is not enough for adults to simply pass along information. Children must experience the world firsthand. Moreover, true learning takes time and repeated exposure. Therefore, the discussion of each KDI includes multiple strategies that adults can use to support each child's current level of understanding, and scaffold his or her progress to a new level of knowledge, skill, and insight.

The KDIs are also written to be universal in their application to diverse early learning settings. Teachers and caregivers from different cultures in the United States and countries all over the world report that they see children engaging in these developmentally important behaviors. Researchers also confirm these commonalities among children of all backgrounds. For example, children everywhere sort objects into containers and take things apart and put them together. The exact materials used may vary from culture to culture (plastic containers, woven baskets, shoeboxes, dried gourds), but the activity and the resulting learning about the nature of things is essentially the same.

Teachers use the KDIs to guide all aspects of their program. They set up the classroom, plan the day, observe children and extend their thinking, and measure children's progress based on the general principles of active learning and the specific content in the indicators.

The rest of this chapter explains why the KDIs are an important curriculum component and how adults use them as they work with young children. The eight KDI books that accompany this manual present a more detailed examination of the KDIs in every area of children's early learning and explain the thoughtful and practical strategies HighScope teachers use to promote them.

The Significance of the KDIs

The eight content areas and 58 KDIs within them are significant for adults using the HighScope Preschool Curriculum because they provide a framework for supporting children's *real* activities. When children are actively engaged with people and materials, they naturally encounter these key concepts and skills. As children play — build with blocks, look at books, draw pictures, pretend to be firefighters — they construct knowledge and gain a sense of competence. For adults, the KDIs give meaning to what children are doing. Adults who understand the importance of the KDIs as tools for observing, describing, and supporting children's development can use them to shape their work with children — in the ways outlined next.

KDIs focus adults' observations and interpretations of children's actions

Curriculum content provides adults with a child development "filter" for observing children and for choosing appropriate interactions. For example, through the filter of the KDIs, an observation such as "Johnny is playing in the sand" might expand to "Johnny is playing in the sand filling pots and colanders (KDI 35. Spatial awareness) and watching to see what happens to the sand in each case (KDIs 45. Observing and 46. Classifying)." KDIs can help adults interpret what children do and say throughout the day and can shape adults' support strategies: "Perhaps if I sit down next to Johnny and start filling and emptying the sieve, he might begin to put his observations about the sand into words;" or, "At recall time, I'll ask Johnny if he can show us what happened to his sand."

KDIs serve as a cross-cultural reference for observing and interpreting children's actions

As mentioned earlier, practitioners from many different cultures around the world report that they see their children doing such things as playing with the sounds of language (KDI 24. Phonological awareness), comparing the length of two sticks (KDI 36. Measuring), looking intently at plants (KDI 51. Natural and physical world), and acting out familiar scenarios from home (KDI 43. Pretend play). Each child is an individual and each culture and community is unique, yet child development occurs in similar progressions everywhere. For example, children like to build things. Although they may use different materials depending on what is available (mud, twigs, blocks, shells, empty food containers), given the opportunity they will spend considerable time making various structures with them, using them to stand for whatever they need in their play and describing in their own words what they are doing with them.

KDIs help adults maintain reasonable expectations for children

Adults who understand how specific skills develop are more likely to provide appropriate support and less likely to either underestimate what children can do or push them to achieve beyond their abilities. For example, adults familiar with the KDIs in Language, Literacy, and Communication know that many young children are intrinsically motivated to write, and that this process emerges slowly through a series of imitations — drawing, scribbling, and making letterlike forms — that are themselves as valuable and necessary as children's later attempts to make conventional letters. These adults understand that imitation is a part of learning to read as well. Therefore, they are happy to provide Rachel with writing tools and listen to her "read" her story about a storm, even though what she has written looks to the adults like a series of squiggles and blobs. They are not concerned that Rachel does not yet make conventional letters or decode actual text because they understand and expect her to be engaged in the kind of "writing" and "reading" that are appropriate to her level of development.

Also, the KDIs can put children's mishaps into perspective for adults. Pouring juice at snack time, for example, becomes a valuable experience for children because it gives them a real-life opportunity to develop *spatial awareness* (KDI 35) and use their *fine-motor skills* (KDI 17). However, pouring is an emerging capacity that takes lots of practice, since children in their excitement about pouring sometimes forget to stop. But that is a valuable experience, too, because cleaning up spilled juice provides children with an opportunity for *problem solving* (KDI 4) and sharing responsibility for the classroom *community* (KDI 11).

KDIs answer questions about the legitimacy of children's play

Play is a legitimate and necessary activity for young children. However, for adults who may be concerned that play prevents children from engaging in the "real work" of learning, the KDIs identify 58 concrete and meaningful learning experiences. Moreover, the words used to identify the content areas (such as *mathematics, creative arts, science, technology*) and to label the KDIs (such as *empathy, vocabulary, history*) are the same terms that appear in national and state early learning standards. Using the KDIs can therefore deepen adults' appreciation of the complexity of children's play, and the wide range of knowledge and skills they acquire through it.

KDIs guide decisions about materials and the daily routine

The broad content areas and specific KDIs provide adults with a comprehensive set of criteria for selecting appropriate materials in an active learning environment. They encourage teaching teams to ask themselves questions like these: What kinds of materials can we add for children to rearrange and reshape as they develop *spatial awareness* (KDI 35 in the content area of Mathematics)? Would children engage with *music* (KDI 41 in Creative Arts) more often if we added relevant sound-making materials to different areas of the room? Since many children have been involved in "building the longest train in the world," how can we rearrange the block area to make more

KDIs help teachers plan for the segments of the daily routine. This large-group movement and music activity is planned around KDIs in Creative Arts and Physical Development and Health.

floor space and promote *gross-motor skills* (KDI 16 in Physical Development and Health) and *cooperative play* (KDI 13 in Social and Emotional Development)?

The KDIs also provide a window on the daily routine, that is, some indicators may tend to occur more often or more readily at certain times of the day. For example, in a well-organized setting, there are days when cleanup time is characterized by concentrated *classifying* (KDI 46) as children sort and match toys before putting them away. After children decipher a message board announcement about a new material in the classroom, they may enjoy participating in *decision making* (KDI 55) about which area of the room to store it in. On the other hand, if the need for *conflict resolution* (KDI 15) tends to escalate right before lunch, this may indicate that a change in the daily routine is in order.

KDIs enable adults to recognize and support children's emerging capacities

Knowledge of the content areas and KDIs guides adults in planning activities and supporting children's play. For example, Lisa made "pizza" in the house area and invited Beth, her teacher, to "sample" a piece. Beth exclaimed that the pizza was delicious and asked Lisa for the recipe. Hurrying to the art area, Lisa chose some writing materials and returned to the house area to write her recipe in scribble form. Beth knew from her previous observations that Lisa was beginning to *write* (KDI 29) and, by asking her for the recipe, was able to create an occasion for her to use her emerging skill.

In summary, the HighScope content areas and KDIs can broaden adults' understanding of what children do, say, think about, and enjoy. This appreciation of the complexity of children's pursuits enables adults to support children's emerging capacities with appropriate materials and interactions rather than to focus on children's mistakes and deficits. KDIs help adults recognize all the ways children learn and how to support their development.

Using the KDIs to Support Teaching and Learning

For all the reasons discussed thus far, the content areas and KDIs are useful tools for adults working with young children. Their daily usefulness, however, depends on accessibility. Since few people are likely to memorize the entire list of KDIs, it is important to keep the list where adults can easily refer to it. For example:

- Post a large-print version of the KDI list in a central location where adults can glance at it throughout the day.

- Keep one-page lists of KDIs in places where team members can refer to them as needed — for example, with the daily team planning log, child anecdotal records, and parent conference folders; and on the parent announcement board. Lamination extends the lifetime of each list.

To order KDI posters, laminated lists, and other related materials from HighScope Press, visit the Foundation website at www.highscope.org.

Some adults are hesitant to use the KDIs because they are not familiar with them. However, the best way to become familiar with the KDIs is to *use them*. Following are six ways to get started.

Use the KDIs as a basis for assessing the materials available to children

To begin this process, select the entire group or a subgroup of KDIs in one content area (for example, the content area Mathematics or the KDIs 34. Shapes and 35. Spatial awareness). Identify materials in the interest areas and on the playground that currently support those KDIs. If you come up with few items or none at all for one particular KDI, brainstorm a list of materials to add. For more ideas for materials, you might also skim the corresponding KDI chapter in the *Mathematics* companion book (Epstein, 2012d) and ask the children for their ideas as well. Repeat this process periodically over the course of the year to systematically assess and provide materials related to each of the eight curriculum content areas and their KDIs.

For example, one teaching team, while evaluating the materials available to support the Creative Arts content area, particularly KDI 43. Pretend play, made a list of what they had and what they wanted to add (see below). They also decided to consult their children. At greeting circle the next day, they asked, "What do you think our house area needs that would make more children want to play there?" "A dog!" was the children's immediate response (a surprise to the adults). Nevertheless, taking their children's interests to heart, one team member arranged to bring her gentle family dog, Daisy, into the house area for several days along with her water and food dishes, leash, grooming brush, and bed. During her visit, Daisy was well cared for, and after she left, the children continued to play doggy, making their own beds and dishes from blocks, boxes, and blankets.

Using Content Areas and KDIs to Choose Materials

Here is a form one teaching team devised to assist with materials selection. They photocopied a batch of these forms, kept them in the daily planning log, then filled in the content area heading and particular KDI that was relevant. Below is one of the forms as they filled it out.

Content area: *Creative Arts*

KDI: *43. Pretend play*

Area	Materials We Already Have	Materials We Want to Add
Book Area	catalogs, maps	puppets
Block Area	steering wheel, small vehicles	vinyl strips for roads
House Area	dress-up clothes, pots and pans, dolls, phones, food containers, hair salon props	stuffed animals, dog accessories
Art Area	yarn, glitter	twine, leather scraps
Toy Area	dollhouse and toy people, counting bears and cats, train set	tumbling monkeys
Sand/Water Area	coffeepot, dishes	rubber animals
Outside	boxes, streamers, sand toys	rowboat, gardening tools

Realizing that they needed to make more materials available related to KDI 44. Appreciating the arts, teachers introduced a book about Picasso's paintings at snack time and then added the book to the classroom bookshelf.

Use the content areas and KDIs to organize and interpret observations of children

As you interact with children throughout the day, jot down specific, short observations about what they do and say. During daily team planning, share these anecdotes and decide together which of the KDIs they most closely illustrate. Then save the anecdote, for example, by creating a separate page or file for each curriculum content area. Then you can refer to the anecdotes during subsequent planning sessions, when filling out assessments such as COR Advantage (Epstein et al., 2014) and in meetings with parents.

More lengthy anecdotes of specific events are also useful for staff planning. One adult, for example, made the following observation of Jonah during work time:

At work time in the toy area, Jonah selects all the black chess pieces from the box and puts them next to one side of the chess board. Then he goes to the other side of the board and dumps all the white pieces out. He returns to the first side and places all the black chess pieces on the black squares and then moves to the other side of the board and places all the white pieces on the white squares.

As the adult discussed this anecdote with her team member during daily team planning, they were both struck by the precision with which Jonah sorted the chess pieces by color and matched them with squares of the same color, and by his desire to place all the black pieces on one side of the board and all the white pieces on the other. They interpreted Jonah's actions as relating to his interest in and ability to group things together and explore the relationships between

Using Content Areas and KDIs to Take Anecdotal Notes

Child: Jonah   **Observers:** Betsy and Merrilee

Date all entries, indicate the part of daily routine,[3] and (for work time) the room area.[4]

Approaches to Learning

01/6   At PT, Jonah says, "Make a bow and arrow with pipecleaners and tape. Then a boat, but the boat will have sticks and paper and tape."

01/28   At WT in the BL area, Jonah plays with blocks and bears, then puts the blocks away and says, "Now I'm going to use these bears with play dough."

02/25   At WT in the BL area, Jonah says to Colin, "Are you using this truck?" Colin says he is. Jonah looks around for another truck like Colin's. He can't find one so he asks Merrilee if there are any more. She suggests he look in the TY area. Jonah goes there, finds a truck, and returns with it to his play.

02/28   At RT, Jonah says he made a rocket ship with a lift-off pad.

03/1   At WT in the BL area, Jonah and Jason tie ropes to chairs, then climb up the climber as they hold the free ends of their ropes and begin pulling in an attempt to hoist the chairs onto the climber.

Social and Emotional Development

01/6   At OT, Jonah whispers to Evan, "Do you want to come to my house sometime?" Jonah runs over to Merrilee. "He said YES!" he tells her.

01/13   At WT in the BK area, Jonah sees Ashley crying for her mom. In the AR area, he makes her some "gold" and then draws a picture of her smiling.

01/21   At WT in the BL area, Jonah pushes Owen very hard against the shelf. When Betsy asks, "What's the problem here?" Jonah says, "He knocked over my magic tower."

02/11   At SGT, Jonah says, "Claire! She hates me. Why did she give me a Valentine?" He shakes his head.

03/18   At SK, Jonah tells Jason, "You can have the last one [apple slice]. I think you are more hungrier than me!"

Physical Development and Health

01/12   At WT in the AR area, Jonah tells Nicholas how to use the stapler, demonstrating and describing the movement. "You push on it till you hear a big click. Like this."

02/11   At LGT, Jonah marches to the beat of the music.

02/28   At SK, Jonah says, "Cheese makes your muscles grow strong."

03/1   At OT, Jonah gets on the trapeze by himself, gets down, twirls, and tries swinging sideways.

03/15   After SK, Jonah wipes the table and then washes his hands.

03/16   At SGT, held on the playground, Jonah weaves a scarf in and out of the chain link fence. When he is almost done, he uses his right index finger to poke the short end of the scarf through the last opening.

Language, Literacy, and Communication

01/8   At OT, Jonah tells Betsy, "I jumped up and down and you know what I said? 'Bang-a-wang!'"

01/22   At GC, as Merrilee reads Rosie's Walk, Jonah says, "That fox will never catch her! He'd better watch out!"

02/24   At WT in the AR area, Jonah tells Colin about the garlic press he's using with play dough. "It's a special tool. Close it and push it. Then it comes out like this."

03/22   At WT in the HO area, Jonah tapes a tag to his shirt and asks Betsy to write on it, "I am the king of the puppies."

03/28   At RT, Jonah says to Merrilee, "Nobody is stronger than Cathy. Cathy can pick up a whole house. She's stronger than anybody. Isn't she amazing! She's one of my invisible friends."

03/29   At LGT, when it's his turn to suggest a way to move that begins with the same sound as his name, Jonah says, "Let's jump!"

---

[3] Abbreviations for parts of the daily routine: GC=greeting circle, PT=planning time, WT=work time, RT=recall time, SK=snacktime, SGT=small-group time, LGT=large-group time, OT=outside time
[4] Abbreviations for play areas: HO=house, BL=block, BK=book, AR=art, TY=toy, SW=sand and water

Mathematics

01/13   At WT in the AR area, Jonah draws a picture of himself and says, "I have a lot of teeth, more than my mom. And lots of mouths. Now I can talk a lot of times."

01/29   At WT in the AR area, Jonah draws a spiral that starts out large and gets smaller and smaller. Several children ask how he does it. Jonah shows them how to "start big and then small and smaller."

02/1   At SGT, Jonah counts six sticks on his collage and seven pieces of foam. "There are more of those," he says, pointing to the foam pieces.

02/1   At WT in the TY area, Jonah strings beads and counts them up to 25, then counts "27, 29, 50, 60, 66."

02/16   At WT in the TY area, Jonah fits Lincoln Logs together to make a tower.

03/10   At SGT, Jonah looks for triangle on a shape hunt. "I'm looking for the ones with three sides," he says.

03/12   At OT, Jonah and Colin use five lengths of string to measure from the climber to the sandbox, and eight lengths to measure from the climber to the picnic table. Jonah says it is "longer" to get from the climber to the table.

Creative Arts

01/8   At WT in the HO area, Jonah puts on a wool cap. "This is a fire cap," he tells Betsy, then shows her a picture in a book of a firefighter wearing a similar cap.

02/7   At WT in the BL area, Jonah and Jason, both "puppies," crawl together, then stop. "Pretend I'm sad because my parents died," Jonah says to Jason. "They were killed by a hunter."

02/8   At OT, Jonah spins around on the trapeze and chants, "I'm going down the drain. I'm going down the drain!"

02/11   At WT at the SW table, Jonah sings "Dee, dee, dee" as he sifts sand.

03/11   At WT in the AR area, Jonah and Rachel stand side by side at the easel. On his half of the paper, Jonah makes up-and-down strokes that all run together, using a brush full of black, then red, then white paint. On her side, with a brush in each hand, Rachel makes distinct green lines.

03/24   At SGT, Jonah sorts postcards of the paintings the class saw on their field trip to the museum. "I like the ones with red in them," he tells Merrilee.

Science and Technology

01/12   At WT in the TY area, Jonah builds an oval track and says, "I think the marble is going to stop at the corner."

02/10   At SGT, Jonah uses a magnifying glass to study the vein patterns on the leaves the class collected the day before.

02/24   At WT in the TY area, Jonah selects all the black chess pieces from the box and puts them next to one side of the chess board. Then he goes to the other side of the board and dumps all the white pieces out. He returns to the first side and places all the black chess pieces on the black squares and then moves to the other side of the board and places all the white pieces on the white squares.

03/4   At RT, Jonah tells Merrilee, "You know what? If you only mix in a little white paint, the colors don't change."

03/13   At WT in the AR area, Jonah shakes a cup he has filled with paper and cloth pieces and taped closed. "It doesn't make a sound. It has quiet things in it," he says.

Social Studies

01/22   At RT, Jonah shows and talks about four drawings he made. "This one isn't a picture. It's a map."

01/26   At SK, Jonah says to Amanda, "We get candy on Hanukkah, Shabbat, and I think on Friday and Saturday."

01/26   At SGT, Jonah says to Jacob, who is drawing next to him, "My sister's older than both of us. She's seven!"

01/29   At WT in the TY area, playing with bears, Jonah says, "This bear is getting ready for war. He's going to fight the bad guys." When Betsy asks why, Jonah says, "The bad guys want to get the Jews. The Jews need to protect themselves."

02/9   At GC Jonah says, "I only need one more day. One more day after today and I get a toy. I'm going to get a ninja guy. I make them fight and kill all the bad guys."

02/14   At SGT, as the group decides where to store the new shells and twigs, Jonah suggests the house area. "So we can use them to make soup," he explains.

03/11   At SK, Jonah says, "When the snow melts, it will be my birthday."

03/15   At the end of WT in the AR area, Jonah puts newspaper scraps in the recycling bin.

As she observes and interacts with a child during a bookmaking activity, the teacher jots down brief anecdotal notes. Later, she will interpret what the child did using the KDIs in Language, Literacy, and Communication and/or items on an assessment instrument such as COR Advantage.

objects in the same and different categories. They therefore recorded this incident as an example of KDI 46. Classifying under the Science and Technology content area.

Use KDI-based child observations as a basis for daily team planning

After you have discussed your observations of children's actions during various times of the day and interpreted them in light of the KDIs, use what you learn from your observations and discussions to plan support strategies and experiences to use with children the next day. You can also use these notes as part of the COR Advantage assessment process as described later in this chapter and detailed in chapters 4 and 5.

For example, after discussing Jonah's "chess playing," his teachers went on to consider how they could build on this insight about Jonah in their interactions with him the next day. If Jonah planned to play with the chess pieces again, they decided that one of them would try to be near him to see if he said anything about what he was doing and to be available if Jonah asked her to play. They also decided to add a set of colored marbles and a Chinese checkers game board to the toy area next to the chessboard to provide another game-like classifying opportunity. For small-group time, Jonah's small-group teacher decided to bring in enough checkerboards for each pair of children in her group to have one. For game pieces, she planned to provide a box of small varicolored plastic counting bears to see what kinds of "chess games" the children might make up. She was particularly interested in seeing what Jonah would do with colored bears that were not the same color as the squares on the board. (For another discussion of the adult planning process based on child observations, see the story of Vanessa on pp. 131–134.)

Use the KDIs as a guide to planning small-group and large-group times

Building on your observations of what interests children, you can introduce activities at small- and large-group times that provide opportunities for children to engage in activities related to specific KDIs. For example, if box elder bugs are swarming outside and have attracted the children's attention, you might plan for children to observe the bugs and draw them at small-group time (Science and Technology: KDI 51. Natural and physical world; Creative Arts: KDI 40. Art). Or, if some children have recently talked about seeing circus clowns walking on stilts at a community festival, you might plan an outdoor large-group time in which children try walking on tin-can stilts tied to their shoes (Physical Development and Health: KDI 16. Gross-motor skills) or look at and read a picture book about the circus at small-group time

(Language, Literacy, and Communication: KDI 26. Reading).

Use the content areas and KDIs to guide on-the-spot interactions with children

As you talk with children and support their problem-solving efforts, observe what children are doing in terms of curriculum content. This type of observation will often give you ideas for ways to support and extend their play. Asking yourself, "What is Sally doing? What is she involved in at this moment? What KDIs are at work here?" will often yield cues about ways to enter children's play without disrupting it. Here are some examples of how this process works:

Marco is in the art area having trouble using the tape dispenser. Your first impulse is to go over and get the tape untangled for him and into position over the cutting edge. But then you think of KDI 4. Problem solving (in Approaches to Learning). So instead you sit down next to him. He stops and you think he has given up, but then he comes back with a pair of scissors, cuts off the tangled part, and carefully puts the straight edge of the tape in place over the cutter. "There!" he says with obvious satisfaction. "You fixed the tape," you agree.

At greeting circle, Sandra brings over a book and sits down in your lap, but instead of opening the book, she starts to tell you about the groundhog her father caught in a trap and how she and her brother and father "took the groundhog in the truck to a big, big field and then we let him go." Several nearby children join the conversation with questions ("Did it get bloody?" "How did it get in there?"), comments ("I'm glad it was okay," "It would be sad if it got its leg hurt"), and their own animal stories. Although this is not a discussion you had planned on, and greeting circle is therefore taking longer than usual, you listen to and participate in the children's conversation about traps and animals because they are so earnestly involved in speaking to one another and using their vocabulary (two Language, Literacy, and Communication KDIs). They are also expressing emotions and showing empathy toward the animals (two Social and Emotional Development KDIs).

Jessa and Anna are building an elaborate "beehive" in the block area with blocks of all sizes and colored scarves. Later they come over to the art area (where you and several other children are working with play dough) and press a small triangle block into your arm. Giggling, they wait for your response. At first you are taken by surprise, but then you remember the "beehive" and think of KDI 43. Pretend play (in the content area Creative Arts). "Ouch, bees," you reply. "Please don't sting me!" The two giggling "bees" fly back to their hive. You have understood and entered into the spirit of their play.

Use the curriculum-based planning and assessment tool, COR Advantage

Drawing on your ongoing observations of children and the anecdotes recorded daily on the KDIs you observe, you will have the information needed to use COR Advantage (Epstein et al., 2014) with each child in your program. COR Advantage is a validated assessment instrument, based on the HighScope preschool curriculum content, that reflects the strands of development seen in all early childhood programs. To use COR Advantage to assess child development, early childhood staff draw on the information gathered from daily child observations. The process of filling out COR Advantage based on anecdotes gathered and recorded over several months will give your team an idea of where each child is developmentally in terms of many of the KDIs, and will let you chart each child's growth from one part of the year to another. For more information about COR Advantage, see coradvantage.org.

Through the lens of the KDIs, an ordinary childhood activity such as swinging takes on more meaning: the child is developing body awareness (KDI 18) as she moves steadily to an internal beat and senses how her body position changes in relation to her surroundings.

The HighScope curriculum content areas and KDIs are a set of tools designed to help adults understand young children and to use this understanding in their daily interactions with children. As adults use the KDIs to assess materials, interpret observations of children, plan for the next day, guide on-the-spot interactions, and assess children's development, they begin to appreciate their children's strengths and capacities, and to expand their own repertoire of support.

More information on using the KDIs to support learning can be found in the eight KDI books that accompany this manual (Epstein, 2012a–h). These books are organized according to the HighScope curriculum content areas: Approaches to Learning; Social and Emotional Development; Physical Development and Health; Language, Literacy, and Communication; Mathematics; Creative Arts; Science and Technology; and Social Studies. Each of these books begins with a chapter summarizing the literature on why that content area is important, followed by a chapter discussing general teaching strategies to support early learning in that area. Following this overview are chapters focusing on the individual KDIs in that area. Each KDI chapter includes a detailed discussion of that KDI, including children's developmental progress in acquiring the relevant knowledge and skills, anecdotal examples of children's behaviors and supportive adult-child interactions, and specific strategies adults can use to support their development. Each KDI chapter concludes with a scaffolding chart with examples of what children at three developmental levels (earlier, middle, and later) might do and say as they engage with that KDI, and how adults can support and gently extend learning at each level. Teachers can use the ideas in these charts to carry out the strategies described in the text as they play and interact with children throughout the program day.

Using the HighScope Preschool Curriculum content areas and KDIs, presented in this chapter and detailed in the accompanying eight content area books, teachers will be able to understand early development, plan and carry out active learning experiences, and support and assess young children as they progress through these exciting years.

References

Ainsworth, M., Salter, D., Blehar, M. C., Waters, E., & Wall, S. (1978). *Patterns of attachment: A psychological study of the strange situation.* Hillsdale, NJ: Erlbaum.

American Academy of Pediatrics. (2006). *The importance of play in promoting healthy child development and maintaining strong parent-child bonds* (Clinical report). Elk Grove Village, IL: Author. doi:10.1542/peds.2006-2697

Aronson, S. S. (Ed.). (2002). *Healthy young children: A manual for programs* (4th ed.). Washington, DC: National Association for the Education of Young Children.

Baker, A. C., & Manfredi/Petitt, L. A. (2004). *Relationships, the heart of quality care: Creating community among adults in early care settings.* Washington, DC: National Association for the Education of Young Children.

Barnett, W. S., Epstein, D. J., Carolan, M. E., Fitzgerald, J., Ackerman, D. J., & Friedman, A. H. (2010). *The state of preschool 2010.* New Brunswick, NJ: National Institute for Early Education Research.

Bereiter, C., & Engelmann, S. (1966). *Teaching the disadvantaged child in the preschool.* Englewood Cliffs, NJ: Prentice Hall.

Bergen, D. (1988a). Methods of studying play. In D. Bergen (Ed.), *Play as a medium for learning and development* (pp. 49–66). Portsmouth, NH: Heinemann.

Bergen, D. (1988b). Stages of play development. In D. Bergen (Ed.), *Play as a medium for learning and development* (pp. 27–44). Portsmouth, NH: Heinemann.

Berry, C. F., & Sylva, K. (1987). *The plan-do-review cycle in HighScope: Its effect on children and staff.* Unpublished manuscript. Available from HighScope Educational Research Foundation, Ypsilanti, MI.

Bodrova, E., & Leong, D. (2007). *Tools of the mind: The Vygotskian approach to early childhood education* (2nd ed.). New York, NY: Prentice Hall.

Bolles, E. B. (1988). *Remembering and forgetting: An inquiry into the nature of memory.* New York, NY: Walker and Company.

Bowlby, J. (1969). *Attachment: Attachment and loss* (Vol. 1). New York, NY: Basic Books.

Bredekamp, S., & Rosegrant, T. (Eds.). (1992). *Reaching potentials: Appropriate curriculum and assessment for young children* (Vol. 1). Washington, DC: National Association for the Education of Young Children.

Bronfenbrenner, U. (1979). *The ecology of human development: Experiments by nature and design.* Cambridge, MA: Harvard University Press.

Brown, S., & Vaughan, C. (2009). *Play: How it shapes the brain, opens the imagination, and invigorates the soul.* New York, NY: Penguin Group.

Bruner, J. S. (1986). *Actual minds, possible worlds.* Cambridge, MA: Harvard University Press.

Bullock, M., & Lütkenhaus, P. (1988). The development of volitional behavior in the toddler years. *Child Development, 59*(3), 664–674. doi:10.2307/1130566

Buysse, V., & Boyce, L. (2003). Evaluating programs that serve infants and families: The quest for quality. *Zero to Three, 23*(6), 4–5.

Case, R. (1985). *Intellectual development: Birth to adulthood.* Orlando, FL: Academic Press.

Center for the Child Care Workforce. (2001, April). *Then and now: Changes in child care staffing, 1994–2000.* Washington, DC: Author.

Clements, D. H. (1999). The effective use of computers with young children. In J. V. Copley (Ed.), *Mathematics in the early years* (pp. 119–128). Reston, VA: National Council of Teachers of Mathematics and Washington, DC: National Association for the Education of Young Children.

Clements, D. H. (2004). Major themes and recommendations. In D. H. Clements, J. Sarama, & A.-M. DiBiase (Eds.), *Engaging young children in mathematics: Standards for early childhood mathematics education* (pp. 7–72). Mahwah, NJ: Lawrence Erlbaum.

Copple, C., & Bredekamp, S. (2006). *Basics of developmentally appropriate practice: An introduction for teachers of children 3 to 6.* Washington, DC: National Association for the Education of Young Children.

Copple, C., & Bredekamp, S. (Eds.). (2009). *Developmentally appropriate practice in early childhood programs serving children from birth through age 8* (3rd ed.). Washington, DC: National Association for the Education of Young Children.

Curry, N. E., & Johnson, C. N. (1990). *Beyond self-esteem: Developing a genuine sense of human value.* Washington, DC: National Association for the Education of Young Children.

Dalton, J. (1991). *State of affairs report of Clayton Thinkers.* Denver, CO: The Clayton Foundation.

Derman-Sparks, L. (1989). *Anti-bias curriculum: Tools for empowering young children.* Washington, DC: National Association for the Education of Young Children.

DeVries, R., & Kohlberg, L. (1987). *Programs of early education.* New York, NY: Longman.

Dewey, J. (1933). *How we think: A restatement of the relation of reflective thinking to the educative process.* Boston, MA: Heath.

Dewey, J. (1938/1963). *Experience and education.* New York, NY: Macmillan.

Dowling, J. L., & Mitchell, T. C. (2007). *I belong: Active learning for children with special needs.* Ypsilanti, MI: HighScope Press.

Eisner, E. W. (1990). The role of art and play in children's cognitive development. In E. Klugman & S. Smilansky (Eds.), *Children's play and learning: Perspectives and policy implications* (pp. 43–58). New York, NY: Teachers College Press.

Elias, M. J., Zins, J. E., Weissberg, K. S., Frey, M. T., Greenberg, N. M., Kessler, R.,… Shriver, T. P. (1997). *Promoting social and emotional learning: Guidelines for educators.* Alexandria, VA: Association for Supervision and Curriculum Development.

Elkind, D. (1987). Early childhood on its own terms. In S. L. Kagan & E. Zigler (Eds.), *Early schooling: The national debate* (pp. 98–115). New Haven, CT: Yale University Press.

Ellis, M. J. (1988). Play and the origin of species. In D. Bergen (Ed.), *Play as a medium for learning and development* (pp. 23–25). Portsmouth, NH: Heinemann.

Epstein, A. S. (1993). *Training for quality: Improving early childhood programs through systematic inservice training.* Ypsilanti, MI: HighScope Press.

Epstein, A. S. (2003). How planning and reflection develop young children's thinking skills. *Young Children, 58*(5), 28–36.

Epstein, A. S. (2007). *Essentials of active learning in preschool: Getting to know the HighScope Curriculum.* Ypsilanti, MI: HighScope Press.

Epstein, A. S. (2012a). *Approaches to learning.* Ypsilanti, MI: HighScope Press.

Epstein, A. S. (2012b). *Creative arts.* Ypsilanti, MI: HighScope Press.

Epstein, A. S. (2012c). *Language, literacy, and communication.* Ypsilanti, MI: HighScope Press.

Epstein, A. S. (2012d). *Mathematics.* Ypsilanti, MI: HighScope Press.

Epstein, A. S. (2012e). *Physical development and health.* Ypsilanti, MI: HighScope Press.

Epstein, A. S. (2012f). *Science and technology.* Ypsilanti, MI: HighScope Press.

Epstein, A. S. (2012g). *Social and emotional development.* Ypsilanti, MI: HighScope Press.

Epstein, A. S. (2012h). *Social studies.* Ypsilanti, MI: HighScope Press.

Epstein, A. S., Gainsley, S., Hohmann, M., Jurkiewicz, T., Lockhart, S., Marshall, B., & Montie, J. (2013). *Program Quality Assessment Form B — Agency Items for infant-toddler and preschool programs.* Ypsilanti, MI: HighScope Press.

Epstein, A. S., Marshall, B., & Gainsley, S. (2014a). *COR Advantage: Information for families.* Ypsilanti, MI: HighScope Press.

Epstein, A. S., Marshall, B., & Gainsley, S. (2014b). *COR Advantage: User guide.* Ypsilanti, MI: HighScope Press.

Epstein, A. S., Marshall, B., & Gainsley, S. (2014c). *COR Advantage 1.5: Scoring guide.* Ypsilanti, MI: HighScope Press.

Epstein, A. S., Marshall, B., Gainsley, S., Red-e Set Grow, Albro, C., Claxton, J.,…Smith, E. V. (2014). *COR Advantage 1.5* [Computerized assessment system]. Online at http://www.coradvantage.org.

Erikson, E. (1950). *Childhood and society.* New York, NY: Norton.

Esbensen, S. B. (1987). *The early childhood playground: An outdoor classroom.* Ypsilanti, MI: HighScope Press.

Evans, B. (1996). "Super strategies" for superheroes. In N. A. Brickman (Ed.), *Supporting young learners* (Vol. 2, pp. 53–56). Ypsilanti, MI: HighScope Press.*

Evans, B. (2002). *You can't come to my birthday party! Conflict resolution with young children.* Ypsilanti, MI: HighScope Press.

---

*Also available at the HighScope *Extensions* archive at highscope.org.

Evans, B. (2005). "Bye Mommy! Bye Daddy!" — Easing separations for preschoolers. In N. A. Brickman, H. Barton, & J. Burd (Eds.), *Supporting young learners* (Vol. 4, pp. 49–57). Ypsilanti, MI: HighScope Press.*

Filcheck, H. A., McNeil, C. B., Greco, L. A., & Bernard, R. S. (2004). Using a whole-class token economy and coaching of teacher skills in a preschool classroom to manage disruptive behavior. *Psychology in the Schools, 41*(3), 351–361. doi:10.1002/pits.10168

Flavell, J. H. (1963). *The developmental psychology of Jean Piaget*. Princeton, NJ: D.Van Nostrand.

Friedman, H. S., & Martin, L. R. (2011). *The Longevity Project: Surprising discoveries for health and long life from the landmark eight-decade study*. New York, NY: Hudson Street Press.

Fromberg, D. P. (1987). Play. In C. Seefeldt (Ed.), *The early childhood curriculum: A review of recent research* (pp. 35–74). New York, NY: Teachers College Press.

Gelman, R., & Baillargeon, R. (1983). A review of some Piagetian concepts. In P. H. Mussen (Ed.), *Handbook of child psychology* (pp. 167–230). New York, NY: Wiley.

Gelman, R., & Brenneman, K. (2004). Science learning pathways for young children. *Early Childhood Research Quarterly, 19*(1), 150–158. doi:10.1016/j.ecresq.2004.01.009

Gelman, R., & Gallistel, C. R. (1986). *The child's understanding of number*. Cambridge, MA: Harvard University Press. (Original work published in 1978)

Gilliam, W. S., & Leiter, V. (2003). Evaluating early childhood programs: Improving quality and informing policy. *Zero to Three, 23*(6), 4–5.

Goleman, D. (1989, March 28). The roots of empathy are traced to infancy. *The New York Times*, pp. B20–B21.

Gonzalcz-Mena, J. (2007). *Diversity in early care and education: Honoring differences* (5th ed.). New York, NY: McGraw-Hill and Washington, DC: National Association for the Education of Young Children.

Gopnik, A. (2011, March 16). Why preschool shouldn't be like school: New research shows that teaching kids more and more, at ever-younger ages, may backfire. *Slate*. Retrieved from http://www.slate.com/

Goswami, U. (Ed.). (2002). *Blackwell handbook of child cognitive development*. Malden, MA: Blackwell.

Greenspan, S., & Greenspan, N. T. (1985). *First feelings*. New York, NY: Viking Press.

Gronlund, G. (2006). *Making early learning standards come alive*. St. Paul, MN: Redleaf Press and Washington, DC: National Association for the Education of Young Children.

Hamre, B. K., & Pianta, R. C. (2007). Learning opportunities in preschool and early elementary classrooms. In R. Pianta, M. Cox, & K. Snow (Eds.), *School readiness and the transition to kindergarten in the era of accountability* (pp. 49–84). Baltimore, MD: Brookes.

Hauser-Cram, P., Pierson, D. E., Walker, D. K., & Tivnan, T. (1991). *Early education in the public schools: Lessons from a comprehensive birth-to-kindergarten program*. San Francisco, CA: Jossey-Bass.

Heidemann, S., & Hewitt, D. (2010). *Play: The pathway from theory to practice* (2nd ed.). St. Paul, MN: Redleaf Press.

HighScope Educational Research Foundation. (2003a). *Preschool Program Quality Assessment (PQA)* (2nd ed.). Ypsilanti, MI: HighScope Press.

HighScope Educational Research Foundation. (2003b). *Preschool Program Quality Assessment (PQA): Administration manual*. Ypsilanti, MI: HighScope Press.

HighScope Educational Research Foundation. (2003c). *Youth Program Quality Assessment (PQA)*. Ypsilanti, MI: HighScope Press.

HighScope Educational Research Foundation. (2006). *Ready Schools Assessment*. Ypsilanti, MI: HighScope Press.

HighScope Educational Research Foundation. (2009). *Family Child Care Program Quality Assessment (PQA)*. Ypsilanti, MI: HighScope Press.

HighScope Educational Research Foundation & Red-e Set Grow. (2012). *OnlinePQA* [Computerized assessment system]. Online at http://www.onlinepqa.net/

Hills, T. W. (1992). Reaching potentials through appropriate assessment. In S. Bredekamp & T. Rosegrant (Eds.), *Reaching potentials: Appropriate curriculum and assessment for young children* (Vol. 1, pp. 43–65). Washington, DC: National Association for the Education of Young Children.

Hohmann, M., Lockhart, S., & Montie, J. (2013). *Infant-Toddler Program Quality Assessment*. Ypsilanti, MI: HighScope Press.

Hohmann, M., Weikart, D. P., & Epstein, A. S. (2008). *Educating young children: Active learning practices for preschool and child care programs* (3rd ed.). Ypsilanti, MI: HighScope Press.

Honig, A. (2002). *Secure relationships: Nurturing infant/toddler attachment in early care settings*. Washington, DC: National Association for the Education of Young Children.

Hunt, J. M. (1961). *Intelligence and experience*. New York, NY: Ronald Press.

Hyson, M. (2008). *Enthusiastic and engaged learners: Approaches to learning in the early childhood classroom*. New York, NY: Teachers College Press and Washington, DC: National Association for the Education of Young Children.

Jablon, J. R., Dombro, A. L., & Dichtelmiller, M. L. (2007). *The power of observation for birth through eight*. Washington, DC: National Association for the Education of Young Children.

Jalongo, M. R. (2008). *Learning to listen, listening to learn: Building essential skills in young children*. Washington, DC: National Association for the Education of Young Children.

Jordan, D. C. (1976). The process approach. In C. Seefeldt (Ed.), *Curriculum for the preschool-primary child: A review of the research* (pp. 273–303). Columbus, OH: Merrill.

Kagan, S. L., Moore, E., & Bredekamp, S. (Eds.). (1995, June). *Reconsidering children's early development and learning: Toward common views and vocabulary* (Goal 1 Technical Planning Group Report 95-03). Washington, DC: National Education Goals Panel.

Keyser, J. (2006). *From parents to partners: Building a family-centered early childhood program*. St. Paul, MN: Redleaf Press and Washington, DC: National Association for the Education of Young Children.

Kindler, A. M. (1995). Significance of adult input in early childhood artistic development. In C. M. Thompson (Ed.), *The visual arts and early childhood learning* (pp. 1–5). Reston, VA: National Art Education Association.

Kohn, A. (1993). *Punished by rewards: The trouble with gold stars, incentive plans, A's, praise, and other bribes*. Boston, MA: Houghton Mifflin.

Kohn, A. (2001). Five reasons to stop saying "Good job." *Young Children, 56*(5), 24–28.

Lewis, M. (1986). The role of emotion in development. In N. E. Curry (Ed.), *The feeling child: Affective development reconsidered* (pp. 7–22). New York, NY: Haworth Press.

Lickona, T. (1973). The psychology of choice learning. In T. Lickona, R. Nickse, D. Young, & J. Adams (Eds.), *Open education: Increasing alternatives for teachers and children* (pp. 65–77). Cortland, NY: Open Education Foundation, State University of New York.

Likert, R. (1967). *The human organization: Its management and value*. New York, NY: McGraw-Hill.

Lippitt, G. (1980). Effective team building develops individuality. *Human Resource Development, 4*(1), 13–16. doi:10.1108/eb002336

Mahler, M., Pine, F., & Bergman, A. (1975). *The psychological birth of the human infant*. New York, NY: Basic Books.

Manlove, E. E., Frank, T., & Vernon-Feagans, L. (2001). Why should we care about noise in classrooms and child care settings? *Child and Youth Care Forum, 30*(1), 55–64.

Marshall, B. (1996). Classrooms that reflect family experiences. In N. A. Brickman (Ed.), *Supporting young learners* (Vol. 2, pp. 137–142). Ypsilanti, MI: HighScope Press.*

Marshall, B. (2001). Ban it, ignore it, or join it? What to do about superhero play. In N. A. Brickman (Ed.), *Supporting young learners* (Vol. 3, pp. 43–52). Ypsilanti, MI: HighScope Press.*

Marshall, B. (with Lockhart, S., & Fewson, M.). (2007). *HighScope step by step: Lesson plans for the first 30 days*. Ypsilanti, MI: HighScope Press.

Marzano, R. (2001). *Designing a new taxonomy of educational objectives*. Thousand Oaks, CA: Corwin Press.

Maxwell, L. E., & Evans, G. W. (n.d.). *Design of child care centers and effects of noise on young children*. Retrieved from http://www.designshare.com/research/lmaxwell/noisechildren.htm

Meisels, S. J. (2001). Fusing assessment and intervention: Changing parents' and providers' views of young children. *Zero to Three, 21*(4), 4–10.

Miller, P. J., & Sperry, L. (1988). Early talk of the past: The origins of conversational stories of personal experience. *Journal of Child Language, 15*(2), 293–315. doi:10.1017/S0305000900012381

Moore, E., & Smith, T. (1987). *HighScope Report 2: One year on*. London, England: Volculf.

---

*Also available at the HighScope *Extensions* archive at highscope.org.

National Association for the Education of Young Children. (2005). *Early childhood program standards and accreditation performance criteria*. Washington, DC: Author.

National Association for the Education of Young Children & National Association of Early Childhood Specialists in State Departments of Education. (2002, November). *Early learning standards: Creating the conditions for success — Joint position statement*. Retrieved from http://www.naeyc.org/files/naeyc/file/positions/position_statement.pdf

National Education Goals Panel. (1998). *Principles and recommendations for early childhood assessments*. Washington, DC: Author.

National Research Council. (2001). *Eager to learn: Educating our preschoolers*. Washington, DC: National Academies Press.

National Research Council. (2005). *Mathematical and scientific development in early childhood: A workshop summary*. Washington, DC: National Academies Press.

National Research Council & Institute of Medicine. (2000). *From neurons to neighborhoods: The science of early childhood development*. Washington, DC: National Academies Press.

Newcombe, N. (2002). The nativist-empiricist controversy in the context of recent research on spatial and quantitative development. *Psychological Science, 13*(5), 395–401.

Norman, D. A. (1982). *Learning and memory*. San Francisco, CA: W. H. Freeman.

Parten, M. B. (1932). Social participation among preschool children. *Journal of Abnormal and Social Psychology, 27*(3), 243–269.

Pellegrini, A. D. (1986). Communicating in and about play: The effect of play centers on preschoolers' explicit language. In G. Fein & M. Rivkin (Eds.), *Reviews of research* (Vol. 4, pp. 79–91). Washington, DC: National Association for the Education of Young Children.

Perrett, B. (1996). Shifting gears smoothly: Making the most of transition times. In N. A. Brickman (Ed.), *Supporting young learners* (Vol. 2, pp. 87–96). Ypsilanti, MI: HighScope Press.*

Phillips, C. B. (1988). Nurturing diversity for today's children and tomorrow's leaders. *Young Children, 43*(2), pp. 42–47.

Phyfe-Perkins, E., & Shoemaker, J. (1986). Indoor play environments: Research and design implications. In G. Fein & M. Rivkin (Eds.), *The young child at play: Reviews of research* (Vol. 4, pp. 177–193). Washington, DC: National Association for the Education of Young Children.

Piaget, J. (1951/1962). *Play, dreams, and imitation in childhood*. New York, NY: Norton.

Piaget, J. (1972). *To understand is to invent*. New York, NY: Viking Press.

Piaget, J., & Inhelder, B. (1966/1969). *The psychology of the child*. New York, NY: Basic Books.

Piscatelli, B. (2000). Practicing what we preach: Active learning in the development of early childhood professionals. In N. J. Yelland (Ed.), *Promoting meaningful learning: Innovations in educating early childhood professionals* (pp. 37–45). Washington, DC: National Association for the Education of Young Children.

Rogers, C. R. (1983). *The freedom to learn for the 80's*. Columbus, OH: Merrill.

Rothbart, M. K., Sheese, B. E., & Posner, M. (2007). Executive function and effortful control: Linking temperament, brain networks, and genes. *Child Development Perspectives, 1*(1), 2–7.

Rowe, S. M., & Wertsch, J. V. (2002). Vygotsky's model of cognitive development. In U. Goswami (Ed.), *Blackwell handbook of child cognitive development* (pp. 539–554). Malden, MA: Blackwell.

Rubin, K. H., Fein, G., & Vandenberg, B. (1983). Play. In E. M. Hetherington (Ed.) & P. H. Mussen (Series Ed.), *Socialization, personality, and social development: Handbook of child psychology* (Vol. 4, pp. 698–744). New York, NY: Wiley.

Satir, V. (1988). *The new peoplemaking*. Mountain View, CA: Science and Behavior Books.

Schank, R. C. (1990). *Tell me a story: A new look at real and artificial memory*. New York, NY: Scribner.

Schmoker, M. (1989, September 6). The sentimentalizing of "self-esteem." *Education Week*, p. 34.

Schweinhart, L. J., Montie, J., Xiang, Z., Barnett, W. S., Belfield, C. R., & Nores, M. (2005). *Lifetime effects: The HighScope Perry Preschool Study through age 40*. Ypsilanti, MI: HighScope Press.

---

*Also available at the HighScope *Extensions* archive at highscope.org.

Schweinhart, L. J., & Weikart, D. P. (1997). *Lasting differences: The HighScope Preschool Curriculum Comparison Study through age 23*. Ypsilanti, MI: HighScope Press.

Sears, P. S., & Dowley, E. M. (1963). Research on teaching in the nursery school. In N. L. Gage (Ed.), *Handbook of research on teaching* (pp. 814–864). Chicago: Rand McNally.

Shore, R. (2003). *Rethinking the brain: New insights into early development* (Rev. ed.). New York, NY: Families and Work Institute.

Smilansky, S. (1971). *Play: The child strives toward self-realization*. Washington, DC: National Association for the Education of Young Children.

Smilansky, S., & Shefatya, L. (1990). *Facilitating play: A medium for promoting cognitive, socio-emotional and academic development in young children*. Gaithersburg, MD: Psychosocial & Educational Publications.

Smith, L. (2002). Piaget's model. In U. Goswami (Ed.), *Blackwell handbook of child cognitive development* (pp. 515–537). Malden, MA: Blackwell.

Sponseller, D. (1982). Play in early education. In B. Spodek (Ed.), *Handbook of research in early childhood education* (pp. 215–241). New York, NY: Macmillan.

Strayer, J. (1986). Current research in affective development. In N. E. Curry (Ed.), *The feeling child: Affective development reconsidered* (pp. 37–55). New York, NY: Haworth Press.

Sylva, K. (1992). Conversations in the nursery: How they contribute to aspirations and plans. *Language and Education, 6*(2), 141–148. doi:10.1080/09500789209541333

Sylva, K., Roy, C., & Painter, M. (1980). *Childwatching at playgroup and nursery school*. Ypsilanti, MI: HighScope Press.

Talbot, J., & Frost, J. L. (1989). Magical playscapes. *Childhood Education, 66*(1), 11–19.

Tegano, D., Moran, J., DeLong, A., Brickley, J., & Ramanssini, K. (1996). Designing classroom spaces: Making the most of time. *Early Childhood Education Journal, 23*(3), 135–141. doi:10.1007/BF02364747

Thompson, R. A., & Nelson, C. A. (2001). Developmental science and media: Early brain development. *American Psychologist, 56*(1), 5–15. doi:10.1037/0003-066X.56.1.5

Tompkins, M. (1996.) In praise of praising less. In N. A. Brickman (Ed.), *Supporting young learners* (Vol. 3, pp. 15–22). Ypsilanti, MI: HighScope Press.*

US Department of Health and Human Services, Administration for Children and Families, Head Start Bureau. (2002, October). *Program Performance Standards and other regulations*. Washington, DC: US Government Printing Office.

US Department of Health and Human Services, Administration for Children and Families (2003, May). *Head Start FACES 2000: A whole-child perspective on program performance* (Contract No. HHS-105-96-1912). Retrieved from http://www.acf.hhs.gov/programs/opre/hs/faces/reports/faces00_4thprogress/faces00_title.html

Veen, A., Roeleveld, J., & Leseman, P. (2000, January). *Evaluatie van Kaleidoscoop en piramide eindrapportage* [Evaluation of Kaleidoscoop and final reporting pyramid]. SCO Kohnstaff Institute, University of Amsterdam.

Vogel, N. (2001). *Making the most of plan-do-review*. Ypsilanti, MI: HighScope Press.

Vygotsky, L. S. (1934/1962). *Thought and language*. Cambridge, MA: MIT Press.

Waters, E., & Cummings, E. M. (2000). A secure base from which to explore close relationships. *Child Development, 71*(1), 164–172. doi:10.1111/1467-8624.00130

Williams, L. R., & De Gaetano, Y. (1985). *ALERTA: A multicultural, bilingual approach to teaching young children*. Menlo Park, CA: Addison-Wesley.

Wood, D., McMahon, L., & Cranstoun, Y. (1980). *Working with under fives*. Ypsilanti, MI: HighScope Press.

Zelazo, P. D., Muller, U., Frye, D., & Marcovitch, S. (2003). The development of executive function. *Monographs of the Society for Research in Child Development, 68*(3), Serial No. 274.

Zill, N., Resnick, G., Kim, K., O'Donnell, K., & Sorongon, A. (2003, May). *Head Start FACES (2000): A whole-child perspective on program performance: Fourth progress report* (Contract No. HHS-105-96-1912). Administration for Children and Families, US Department of Health and Human Services, Washington, DC.

---

*Also available at the HighScope *Extensions* archive at highscope.org.

Photo Credits

Betsy Evans — 85

Bob Foran — Front cover, 1, 3, 6, 12, 13, 15, 16, 18 (bottom), 19, 22 (middle, bottom), 23 (top), 25, 36, 41 (right), 44, 45, 49, 53, 54 (top), 55, 80, 82, 96, 97, 98, 114, 122, 137, 144, 149, 151, 156, 164, 173, 174, 176, 182, 186, 188, 193, 196 (top), 199 (right), 201, 203 (top right), 208 (left), 215, 217, 219 (left), 223, 224, 230 (top right), 234 (right), 240, 252, 262, 264, 273, 283, 303, 310, 318, 325, 328, 332, 336, 342, 346, 347, 350, 358, 362, 366, 375, 379, 388, 393, 401, back cover

Gregory Fox — 7, 8, 18 (top), 20, 22 (top), 23 (middle, bottom), 24, 27, 30, 31, 32, 34, 35, 38, 40 (top left, top right), 43, 46, 47, 54 (bottom), 57, 60, 61, 63, 67, 69, 71, 73, 74, 76, 87, 91, 94, 99, 101, 106, 111, 116, 119, 121, 124, 130, 132, 136, 148, 152, 154, 155, 161, 171, 178, 180, 181, 184, 185, 189, 191, 196 (bottom), 197, 199 (left), 200, 205, 208 (right), 210, 211, 213, 219 (right), 225, 230 (top left, bottom left), 231, 232, 233, 234 (left), 235, 237, 238, 239, 243, 246, 248, 257, 259, 261, 266, 269, 270, 272, 276, 277, 279, 288, 295, 299, 301, 305, 306, 308, 312, 314, 321, 323, 334, 337, 339, 343, 352 (right), 356, 365, 367, 368, 369, 371, 372, 381, 383, 384, 385, 386, 390, 391, 392, 396, 404, 406

Pat Thompson — 5, 41 (left), 255, 291, 330, 344, 355, 398

HighScope Staff — All other photos

Index

A

Abstract thought and recall time, 308
Acceptance and building relationships, 112
Accommodation in developmental theory, 16
Accountability, 59, 152. *See also* Assessment, program
Accreditation. *See also* Licensing
    parent involvement, 93
    PQA, 166
Achievement
    gap, xii, 2
    longitudinal studies, 8, 9
Ackerman, D. J., 93
Acknowledgment
    children's choices and actions, 42–43
    for comfort and encouragement, 78, 287–288
    in conversation, 70
    feelings in conflict resolution, 81, 82, 302
    vs. praise, 321–322
    repeating and restating, 79
Acoustics of learning environment, 176
Active learning, 12–53
    beliefs about, 21, 24
    benefits, 48–50
    child choice, 27–30
    child initiative and intention, 4, 26–27, 42–45
    child's activities in, 26–27, 30–37
    cleanup time, 387
    complexity of, 16–20
    computers, 214–215
    conversations, 36–37
    curriculum principle, 3, 16–17
    daily routine, 239–240
    defined, 17
    development and, 14–16
    elements of, 17–20
    gross-motor skills, 34, 35–36
    ingredients, 51–53
    interest areas, 172–173
    KDIs as framework, 25–26, 28–29
    learning environment, 172–174
    overview, 26–27, 30–37
    parent involvement, 94, 96–99
    PQA, 146–147
    problem solving, 17, 20
    reflection and, 4, 17–18, 36–37
    relationships between things, 31, 32
    spontaneous learning, 33
    summary, 54
    support activities, 20–24, 37–48 (*See also* Adult-child interactions; Climate, supportive; Scaffolding)
    teamwork, 120
    tool and equipment use, 34–35
    transformation of materials, 31–33, 340
    in Wheel of Learning, 4
Active learning environment. *See* Learning environment
Active participatory learning. *See* Active learning
ADA (Americans With Disabilities Act), 175
Administrators
    COR Advantage use, 160
    curriculum criteria, 3
    PQA use, 165
    program assessment, 6

Adult-child interactions. *See also* Climate, supportive; Conversation with adults; Plan-do-review process; Play, adult; Scaffolding
    adult *vs.* child thinking, 19
    beliefs, 59
    child's intentions, 248
    conflicts, 48
    consistency, 239
    curriculum principle, 5, 46–48
    family and culture, 95–96
    learning environment, 190
    management *vs.* interaction, 57, 302, 380
    PQA category, 164, 169–170
    in Wheel of Learning, 4
    zone of proximal development, xii, 26
Adult-initiated activities. *See* Initiative, adult
Ainsworth, Mary, 56–57
Allergies, 188
American Academy of Pediatrics, 175, 276
American Society for Testing and Materials, 216
Americans With Disabilities Act, 175
Anchor points, 84
Anecdotal notes. *See also* Observations of child
    COR Advantage/assessments, child, 155, 156, 157–161
    curriculum overview, 6
    examples, 402–403
    KDIs, 401–403
    photos, 130
    PQA, 145, 165
    sharing with families, 109, 110, 156
    sharing with team, 130–131, 136
    in Wheel of Learning, 4
Announcements, classroom, 388
Anticipating
    actions, 247–248
    excellence, 103, 113–114
Appliances, child-sized, 194
Approaches to Learning KDIs and content area, 26, 28, 392, 394
Aronson, S., 179, 216
Arrests, research, 8–10
Arrival patterns, 237–238. *See also* Greeting time
Art
    artist visits, 202
    Creative Arts KDIs and content area, 26, 29, 392, 395
    display, 21, 198
    gallery art, 201–202
    recall time, 308
Art area, 185, 197–202, 210, 215, 219
Articulation, child's. *See also* Communication
    nonverbal, 253–254, 256, 264–267
    planning time, 244, 248, 249, 251–257
    recall time, 308, 309–310
    repeating and restating, 79, 303
Assessment, child, 151–161. *See also* COR Advantage
    authentic, 153–155
    with COR Advantage, 152–153, 155–161, 401, 404, 405
    curriculum principle, 6–7
    defined, 152
    disadvantages, 153–154
    with KDIs, 396, 401, 404, 405
    literacy and reading to children, 92
    parent involvement, 93
    summary, 167
    uses, 152

validity, xiii, 153, 155, 167
in Wheel of Learning, 4
Assessment, classroom materials, 399–400
Assessment, program, 151–153, 160–167. *See also* **Preschool Program Quality Assessment (PQA)**
about, 152–153
curriculum principle, 6
examples, 162
KDIs, 396
parent involvement, 93
Perry Preschool Study, xi, 2–3, 7–9
with PQA, 152–153, 162–168
Preschool Curriculum Comparison Study, 3, 7, 8–9
quality components, 160–163
summary, 168
supportive climate, 86, 88–89
Training of Trainers Evaluation, 7, 9–10
validity, xiii, 153, 162–164, 168
in Wheel of Learning, 4
Assessment, staff
self-assessment, 162, 165, 166
teacher, 143–148
teams, 129
Assimilation, 16
Assistive devices, 188
Associative play, 279
Attachment, 56–57
Attentiveness. *See also* **Listening to children**
family and parents, 114
planning time, 264–267, 270
recall time, 319
supportive climate, 74
teamwork, 121
work time, 278, 296
Authentic assessment, 153–155
Authentic relationships
family and parents, 100–101, 106
respecting differences, 127
supportive climate, 68, 72–75
transitions, 84
Autonomy. *See also* **Independence**
authentic relationships, 73
and interest areas, 177
relationship-building, 58
vs. shame and doubt, 56
supportive climate, 67, 77

B

Background noise, 176
Backup materials, 342, 343, 364
Baillargeon, R., 14
Baker, A., 93, 120
Balances, 218
Balloon activity, 373
Balls, 218
Barnett, W. S., 7–8, 93
Belfield, C. R., 7–8
Beliefs
adult-child interactions, 59
adult play, 289
comforting and contact, 287
family and culture, 103–104
learning, 21, 24
superhero play, 292, 294–295
Belonging, sense of, 120, 122
Bereiter, C., 9
Bergen, D., 282
Bergman, A., 57

Bernard, R. S., 78
Berry, Carla
benefits of planning time, 245, 249, 250
completion of plans, 279
complexity of plans, 254
intimacy, 259
questions in planning time, 264, 267
recall time, 308, 311, 315–316
"Best practices" and PQA, 166
Bilingual learners. *See* **Language, home**
Blaming, 126
Blehar, M. C., 56–57
Block area, 185, 190–193
Bodrova, E., 245, 247
Body-awareness skills, 34, 35–36
Bolles, Edmund, 307, 309, 312
Book and writing area, 172, 185, 202–205, 215
Books
house area, 195, 202
recall, 317
special needs, children with, 188
types, 204
Bowlby, J., 56–57
Boyce, L., 153
Brain research
curriculum basis, 3
empathy, 61
play, 280
support for active learning, 15, 16
Bredekamp, Sue
assessment, 152, 172
encouragement *vs.* praise, 78
families and communities, 2
foreword by, xi–xiii
inclusivity, 392
learning environment, 179
Brenneman, K., 14
Brickley, J., 177
Bronfenbrenner, Urie, 70, 224
Brown, S., 280
Bruner, J., 26
Building materials
block area, 192, 193
outdoor area, 219
toy area, 206, 207
woodworking, 210
Bullock, M., 245, 248, 251
Buysse, V., 153

C

Carolan, M. E., 93
Case, R., 245, 247, 251
Catalogs, 199, 204
Cause-and-effect relationships, 32, 33, 35
Center for the Child Care Workforce, 93
Certification, 166. *See also* **Accreditation; Licensing**
Certified Playground Safety Inspectors, 216
Changeover times. *See* **Departure time; Greeting time**
Chants, 354, 359
Child and Adult Care Food Program guidelines, 175
Child assessment. *See* **Assessment, child**
Child-initiated activities. *See* **Initiative, child**
Child language and thought. *See also* **Articulation, child's;** *entries beginning with* **Conversation; Language, home**
active learning ingredient, 51, 52
child thinking *vs.* adult thinking, 19
computers, 215
large-group time, 354, 360

learning environment, 172
plan-do-review process, 244
questions, 299–300
recall time, 308
small-group time, 331
supportive climate, 77
Child Observation Record (COR). *See* **COR Advantage**
Child's intentions. *See also* **Planning time**
commenting, 43
curriculum principle, xii, 23, 24, 42–45
development, 60
questions, 43, 254, 298–299
work time, 275–276
Child's interests. *See also* **Planning time**
authentic relationships, 74
cleanup, 385–386
daily routine, 228, 230
focus on strengths, 71–72
large-group time, 355, 358–359
outside time, 376
small-group time, 333, 334, 343–344
Child's perspective. *See also* **Physical level of child**
focus on strengths, 71–72
work time, 285
Child thought. *See* **Child language and thought**
Choice, adult
to collaborate, 127, 128
teamwork, 120
Choice, child. *See also* **Plan-do-review process; Planning time**
acknowledging, 42–43
active learning ingredient, 27–30, 51, 52
beliefs, 21
cleanup, 385–386
computers, 215
conflicts, 48
daily routine, 225, 239
exploratory play, 282
interest areas, 177–178
large-group time, 354, 356–357, 360, 361–362
learning environment, 5, 172–173, 177–178, 181
materials, 27–30, 37, 172–173, 272
recall time, 311–312
reflecting family life, 97–98
small-group time, 331, 339–340
toy area, 205
transitions, 83–84, 346, 383
Classroom Assessment Scoring System (CLASS), 86, 88–89
Classrooms. *See* **Learning environment**
Clay. *See* **Modeling and molding materials**
Clayton Kids Study, 50
Cleanup
daily routine, 228–231
examples, 386–387
find-use-return cycle, 183
games, 304–305, 385
labels, 186, 384
large-group time, 367
musical instruments, 212
outside time, 381
planning, 382, 384–387, 386
recall during, 305
sand and water area, 209
small-group time, 345
during transitions, 231, 382, 384–387
work time, 304–305, 384–385
Clements, D. H., 212
Climate, supportive, 55–89. *See also* **Adult-child interactions; Scaffolding**
active learning, 20–24, 239–240
authentic relationships, 68, 72–75

benefits, 65–67
CLASS framework, 86, 88–89
commitment to support play, 68, 75–78, 84
control, shared, 63, 64, 68–70, 83
daily routine, 239–240
directive climate, 62–67
encouragement *vs.* praise, 68, 78–79, 84–85
family involvement, 100–102, 106
focus on strengths, 68, 70–72, 84
inclusivity, 392
laissez-faire climate, 62–67
management *vs.* interaction, 57, 302, 380
problem solving and social conflicts, 68, 79–83, 85–86
program assessment, 86, 88–89
relationships, 57, 58–62, 65–66, 68, 72–75
sense of self, 56–58
shifting, 64–65
social interactions, 22, 24
strategies, 67–83
summary, 87
teamwork, 120, 129
trust, 67, 77
Climbers, 218
Close-ended materials, 182–183
Coconuts sample plan, 351
Cognitive development research, 3, 10, 11, 14–15
Collaboration. *See* **Partnerships; Teamwork**
Collage materials, 199, 348
Colors in learning environment, 175
Comforting, 282, 286–289
Commenting
child's intentions, 43
large-group time, 360
planning time, 265–266, 267, 269, 270
play extension with, 295
recall time, 318, 320
specificity, 79
work time conversations, 296–297
Common Core Standards, 392
Communication. *See also* **Articulation, child's;** *entries beginning with* **Conversation**
barriers, 128
building relationships, 113
developing intentional, 56
and program assessment, 162, 163
teamwork, 126–127
Community, sense of
daily routine, 225–226, 227
large-group time, 233, 355, 357, 361
message board time, 390
Community involvement
context of child learning, 2
insight into child's culture, 184
materials, 94–95
by teachers, 94, 108
Competence
from active learning, 48
assumption of, 113
learning environment, 172
special needs, children with, 188–189
supportive climate, 60, 62
Completion of plans, 278–279
Complex play, 250–251, 280, 294
Computer area, 212–216
Computers, 38, 214–215
Computing (communication), 126–127
Concentration on play, 249–250
Concrete labels, 176, 186, 384

Confidence
    active learning, 48
    family and culture, 96
    parent-teacher, 93
    plan-do-review process, 244
    planning time, 249
    relationships, 58, 61–62, 73
    supportive climate, 60, 67, 77

Conflict resolution
    child's choice, 48
    outside time, 379–380
    problem-solving approach, 68, 79–83, 85–86, 301–304, 379–380
    teacher-parent, 114–115
    teams, 129
    transitions, 85–86
    in Wheel of Learning, 4
    work time, 300–305

Consciousness and recall time, 310

Consistency
    daily routine, 224, 226, 238, 239, 241, 382
    interest areas, 177
    large-group time, 363
    planning time, 260
    small-group time, 331
    storage, 186
    teamwork, 122
    transitions, 241, 382

Constructive play
    adult participation, 289–290, 293–296
    conflicts, 300
    outside time, 376
    work time, 280, 281, 282, 300

Constructivist model, 3, 16, 312
Consumer Product Safety Commission, 216
Contact, physical, 282, 286–289
Control, child. *See also* **Control, shared**
    conflict resolution, 81
    daily routine, 5–6, 238
    need for, 24
    planning time, 249, 260–261, 267, 269
    play, 295
    questions and, 297–298

Control, shared. *See also* **Control, child**
    community, sense of, 225–226
    conversation, 70, 265, 293, 296
    culture and family, 100
    daily routine, 225–226, 239–240
    large-group time, 356–357
    materials, 59
    with parents, 106
    planning time, 70
    supportive climates, 63, 64, 68–70, 83
    teamwork, 121, 122
    transitions, 83–84
    work time, 296–297

Conversation with adults
    adult participation in play, 293–300
    authentic relationships, 74–75
    child's cues, 68, 378
    child's intentions, 43
    component of active learning, 36–37
    control, shared, 70, 265, 293, 296
    daily routine, 239
    encouraging, 79
    home language, 98
    intimacy, 259–260
    outside time, 376, 378–379
    parallel play, 290–291
    partnership and, 47
    planning time, 254–257, 259–260, 261–270
    recall time, 230, 309–310, 313, 315, 316–322
    reflection, 43–45
    small-group time, 331, 343, 344–345
    work time, 282, 293–300

Conversation with parents and family, 106, 109–110, 114, 184
Conversation with peers. *See also* **Peer relations**
    computers, 214
    meals, 387
    outside time, 377
    small-group time, 331, 338–340
    work time, 282

Conversation with supervisors, 144, 145
Cooking and eating equipment, 97, 195
Cooperative games, 354, 359
Cooperative play, 193, 279
Cooperative relationships, 149. *See also* **Teamwork**
Coordination skills, 34
Copple, C., 78, 172, 179

COR Advantage
    about, xiii, 152–153
    assessment with, 152–153, 155–161, 401, 404, 405
    categories, 156–157
    curriculum overview, 6
    large-group time, 355, 358
    parent involvement, 94, 156, 157, 160
    planning with, 131, 134, 136, 138, 159–160
    samples, 158–160
    small-group time, 332, 334, 342

Council for Exceptional Children, 189
Coziness, 175–176, 315–316
Cranstoun, Yvonne
    adult-child interaction, 57, 302
    adult play, 289, 290
    conversation, 293, 297, 298

Creative Arts KDIs and content area, 26, 29, 392, 395
Creative Curriculum, 11
Crime, research, 8–10
Cues, child
    conversation, 68, 378
    large-group time, 357
    nonverbal, 99
    outside time, 378
    supportive climate, 68

Cues, parent, 106
Culture
    beliefs about, 103–104
    commonalities across cultures, 396
    defined, 95
    family, 94, 95–96, 99, 103–110, 184
    fear of differences, 100–101
    and KDIs, 396, 397
    small-group time, 335
    social climates, 62–67

Cummings, E. M., 56–57
Curriculum
    changes to fourth version, xi–xiii
    CLASS framework, 86, 88–89
    comparison studies, 3, 7, 8–9
    content areas, 391–406
    Creative Curriculum, 11
    daily routine, 5–6, 227–228
    decisions, 125, 140–141
    effectiveness, 7–11
    Head Start alignment, 392
    KDIs framework, 4, 25–26, 392–406
    overview, 2–11, 390–406
    parent involvement, 93

planning and assessment PQA category, 147, 169–170
principles, 3–7
unified approach, 120, 122
validity, xiii
Wheel of Learning, 3, 4
Curriculum Comparison Study, 3, 7, 8–9
Curry, N., 56, 61, 74, 81
Cutting materials, 199, 263

D

Daily planning. *See* **Planning (by teachers), daily**
Daily routine, 222–241. *See also* **Planning time; Recall time; Work time;** *specific periods, e.g.,* **Large-group time**
about, 224–228
benefits, 224–228
consistency, 224, 226, 238, 239, 241, 382
curriculum principle, 5–6, 22, 24, 227–228
flexibility, 227–228
KDIs, 398–399
large-group time in, 39–42, 228, 233, 235
learning environment, 226–227, 239
meals, 228, 234–235
message board time in, 235
organization, 22, 39–41, 228–241
outside time in, 42, 228, 233, 238
plan-do-review process in, 39, 228–231
planning time in, 228, 230, 235
PQA category, 147, 164, 169–170
predictability, 236–238
process or place *vs.* content, 235–236
recall time in, 230–231, 235
sample, 229, 235
small-group time in, xiii, 4, 39, 228, 232–233, 235
social framework, 225–227
special events and activities, 236
summary, 228, 241
supportive climate, 239–240
transitions in, 227, 228, 234, 235, 238
in Wheel of Learning, 4
work time in, 228, 231, 235
Deficit-based approach, 70–71. *See also* **Focus on strengths**
De Gaetano, Y., 95, 103
Deliberation, 248–249
DeLong, A., 177
Denver Project, 50
Department of Agriculture Child and Adult Care Food Program guidelines, 175
Departure time. *See also* **Transitions**
about, 387–388, 390
conversations with parents, 109–110
daily routine, 234
patterns, 237–238
teamwork, 123
Derman-Sparks, L., 183
Detailed planners, 255–256, 257, 265, 267–269, 274
Development, child. *See also* **Key developmental indicators (KDIs)**
about, 14
appropriate practices, 14, 166
beliefs, 21
child's intentions, 60
cognitive, 3, 10, 11, 14–15
comparison studies, 10, 11
computer programs, 214
continuum, 396
differences in child and adult thinking, 19
emotional, 56, 57, 276
framework for education, 14–16
importance of play, 276
large-group-time activities, 358–359, 363
motor, 10, 11
planning, 245, 247, 251–253
recall skills, 311–312, 315, 322
reflection, 247
relationships, 58–62
sense of self, 56–58
sequencing in learning, 327, 329
social, 56, 57, 58–62, 276
and sounds, 176
supportive climate, 66, 67, 392
trajectories, 15
transitions, 382–383, 386
zone of proximal development, xii, 26
Development, professional. *See* **Professional development**
Developmentally appropriate practice, xi, xiii, 14, 48, 51, 127, 166, 172, 214–215, 384
DeVries, R., 275
Dewey, John
adult's role, 26
child's interests, 248
community, 227
curriculum basis, 3
developmental theory, 14–15
importance of play, 276
observation, 129
planning, 247
Dichtelmiller, M. L., 154
Direct action on objects, 17
Direct experiences, 4, 31, 32
Direct instruction
comparison study, 3, 9, 10
disadvantages, 31, 33
passivity, 27
Directive climate, 62–67
Discipline, 59, 66
Discovery. *See* **Exploration**
Display space for art, 21, 198
Distracting (communication), 126–127
Distractions, 248
Diversity, 95, 183, 184, 185
Documentation of observations, 129, 130–131, 138. *See also* **Anecdotal notes**
Dolls, 183, 184, 195
Dombro, A. L., 154
Doubt *vs.* **autonomy, 56**
Dowley, E. M., 9
Dowling, J. L., 189
Dramatic play, 76, 77
Drawing, 199, 263, 313
Dress-up clothes, 195, 196
Dropoff time. *See* **Departure time; Greeting time**
Drying space for art, 198
Dual language learners. *See* **Language, home**

E

Earnings, 8, 9
Easy-to-enjoy activities, 359, 363, 367
Easy-to-handle materials, 39, 41
Eating. *See* **Meals**
Economic status, 8
Educational performance, 8, 9
Eisner, E., 309
Elaborate planners. *See* **Detailed planners**
Elementary school. *See* **School achievement; School readiness**
Elias, M. J., 92

Elkind, D., 247
Ellis, M., 276
Emotional development, 56, 57, 276
Empathy
    attachment, 57
    authentic relationships, 73
    as building block of relationships, 58, 60–61
    conflict resolution, 81
    modeling, 66
    supportive climate, 67, 77
Encouragement. *See also* Climate, supportive; Scaffolding
    adult play as, 78–79
    adult support, 5, 23, 24
    child's description, 79
    planning time, 269–270
    vs. praise, 68, 78–79, 84–85, 269–270
    transitions, 84–85
    in Wheel of Learning, 4
Engelmann, S., 9
English language leaners. *See* Language, home
Environment. *See* Learning environment
Epstein, Ann
    conflict resolution, 302–304
    curriculum books, xi, 2
    curriculum history, 3
    KDIs, 393
    plan-do-review process, 244
    planning, 245
    Training of Trainers evaluation, 9–11
Epstein, D. J., 93
Equipment. *See also* Materials
    age-appropriate, 34–35
    health and safety standards, 175
    outdoor area, 216, 376
Erikson, Erik, 56, 245
Errors. *See* Mistakes and mishaps
Esbensen, S. B., 217–218
Evaluations. *See* Assessment
Evans, Betsy, 80–83, 237, 294
Evans, G. W., 176
Events, special, 236, 355, 359
Excellence, anticipating, 103, 113–114
Executive control structures, 245
Executive function and planning, 245, 247
Exercises, beliefs, 21, 59
Expectations
    collective, 227
    of excellence, 103, 113–114
    teamwork, 129
Exploration. *See also* Exploratory play; Play
    and autonomy, 58
    cultural and family differences, 102
    developmental theory, 56
    importance of, 30–34
    of materials, 30–31, 34, 280
    small-group time, 338–340
Exploratory play. *See also* Exploration
    adult participation, 47–48, 77, 289, 290
    child choice, 282
    defined, 280
    outside time, 376
    toy area, 206–207
Extension
    of learning, 327, 329
    of play, 292–293, 295, 378
Eye contact, 99

F

Falling in love, 56
Family and parent involvement, 90–117
    active learning, 96–99
    anecdotal note sharing, 109, 110, 156
    anticipating excellence, 113–114
    benefits, 92–94, 102–103
    books and reading, 92, 203
    child's choices, 97–98
    context of child learning, 2, 95–96
    COR Advantage, 94, 156, 157, 160
    culture, 94, 95–96, 103–110, 184
    gatherings, 109
    Head Start standards, 92, 93, 124
    home visits, 94, 104–108, 123–124, 184, 203
    inspired play, 100, 101–102, 106
    large-group time, 357
    materials that reflect, 96–97, 174, 183, 185
    Perry Preschool Study, 8
    PQA category, 147, 164, 168, 170
    small-group time, 335
    strategies for, 93–96, 103–116
    summary, 117
    supportive climate, 100–102, 106
    teacher-parent relationships, 72, 92–95, 114–115
    teamwork, 124
    transitions, 96, 103, 107–108, 109–110, 226
    trust, 58
    valuing families, 102–103, 108–109, 183
Fasteners, 199, 210
Fears of differences, 100–101, 103, 112
Feedback
    authentic relationships, 74, 106
    observation/feedback (O/F), 144–145
    program quality measures, 163
Feelings
    acknowledging in conflict resolution, 81, 82, 302
    and empathy, 61
    recall time, 311
Fein, G., 279
Field trips, 110, 112, 295, 335, 359
Filcheck, H. A., 78
Fill-and-empty materials, 192, 193, 209
Find-use-return cycle, 172, 183. *See also* Cleanup
Fine-motor skills, 34
Fingerplays, 354, 359, 360
Fitzgerald, J., 93
Flavell, J. H., 17
Flexibility
    cleanup and transitions, 386
    daily routine, 227–228
    house area, 194
    large-group time, 365, 366
    learning environment, 174, 180–182
    materials storage, 172
    planning time, 249
Floating materials, 209
Flooring, 198, 208, 212
Focus on strengths
    culture and differences, 102–103
    parents and family, 104, 105, 106, 112–113
    small-group time, 333, 336
    supportive climate, 68, 70–72
    teachers', 104, 121, 138
    transitions, 84
Follow-up in conflict resolution, 81, 82, 304
Food. *See also* Meals
    health and safety standards, 175
    as play material, 39, 195

Found materials, 38, 39, 40, 182, 348
Frank, T., 176
Frey, M. T., 92
Friedman, A. H., 93
Friedman, H. S., 247
Friendships. *See* Peer relations
Fromberg, D. P., 77–78
Frost, J. L., 182, 196
Frye, D., 245, 247
Funding, 160
Furniture
    art area, 198
    block area, 192
    book and writing area, 202
    computer area, 212, 215
    health and safety standards, 175
    house area, 194, 195
    inviting, 175–176
    multiple usage, 182
    sand and water area, 208
    toy area, 205
    woodworking area, 210

G

Gallistel, C. R., 14
Games
    adult participation, 289, 291–292, 293
    cleanup, 304–305, 385
    cooperative, 354, 359
    group games, 260, 262, 317
    large-group time, 354, 359, 363
    message board time, 390
    outside time, 377
    planning time, 259, 260, 262–263, 273
    recall time, 315, 316, 317
    with rules, 77
    types, 206, 207
    work time, 281–282
Gardening, 219
GED (General Education Development certificate), research, 8
Gelman, R., 14
Generativity, 17, 18–20
Gestures. *See also* Nonverbal communication
    planning time, 253–254, 265
    recall time, 308, 312–313, 319
Gilliam, W., 161
Glue, 198
Goals. *See also* Planning (by teachers), daily; Planning time
    child's, 247–248
    program goals and PQA, 166
    setting by teams, 129, 136
    small-group time, 340
Goleman, D., 61
Gonzalez-Mena, J., 95
Gopnik, A., 31, 33
Goswami, U., 14
Graduation rates, 8, 9
Greco, L. A., 78
Greenberg, N. M., 92
Greenspan, Nancy, 56
Greenspan, Stanley, 56
Greeting time. *See also* Transitions
    about, 387–388, 390
    arrival patterns, 237–238
    conversations with parents, 109–110
    in daily routine, 234, 235
    reassurance during, 237
    teamwork, 123

Gronlund, G., 245, 392
Gross-motor skills, 34, 35–36
Group decisions
    about children, 126, 129, 131–134
    about teamwork, 126, 136, 138–141, 143, 145
    curriculum, 125, 140–141
Group dynamics, 240
Group games, 260, 262, 317
Group times. *See* Large-group time; Message board time; Outside time; Small-group time; Transitions
Guilt *vs.* initiative, 56, 245, 247

H

Hamre, B. K., 86
Hauser-Cram, P., 50
Head Start
    Child Development and Early Learning Framework, 157, 392
    Child Development and Early Learning Outcomes, 138
    Child Outcomes Framework, 157
    Family and Child Experiences Survey, 10–11, 92
    health and safety standards, 175
    HighScope curriculum alignment, 392
    parent involvement, 93, 124
    planning with standards, 245
    PQA alignment, 164
Health
    planning skills, 247
    special needs, children with, 189
    standards, 175, 179, 189
Hearing impairment, children with, 188
Heidemann, S., 374
Hewitt, D., 374
HighScope Preschool Curriculum. *See* Curriculum
HighScope Preschool Curriculum Comparison Study, 3, 7, 8–9
HighScope Preschool Wheel of Learning, 3, 4
HighScope Training of Trainers Evaluation, 7, 9–10
Hills, T. W., 154
Hohmann, Mary, 3, 393
Holidays, 335, 359
Home
    -based programs, 123–124, 238
    book and writing area at, 203
    materials from, 96–97, 195, 196–197
    ownership, 8
    planning at, 256–257
    visits, 94, 104–108, 123–124, 184, 203
Home Link Book, 110
Home-school connection. *See* Parents and family involvement
Honesty, 75, 113, 121
Honig, Alice, 56–57, 93
Horses large-group activity, 370
House area, 185, 193–197, 202
"How" questions, 264
Hunt, J. M., 2
Hypotheses, child, 20, 44–45
Hyson, M., 244, 248, 326

I

IDEA (Individuals With Disabilities Education Act), 189
IDEA Infant and Toddler Coordination Association, 189
Imagining actions, 247–248
Imitation of child's actions
    cleanup, 385
    large-group time, 360, 367
    small-group time, 329, 343–344
Inclusion programs, 187

Independence. *See also* **Autonomy**
    child choice, 97–98
    computers, 214
    development, 58
    importance of, 24
    learning environment, 190
    plan-do-review process, 244
    planning time, 249
    problem solving, 17, 45–46, 50
    small-group time, 344
Individual play, 191–192, 193, 205, 206–207
Individuals With Disabilities Education Act (IDEA), 189
Infant and Toddler Coordination Association, 189
Infants
    empathy, 60
    planning, 251, 253
Information gathering
    in conflict resolution, 81, 302–303
    teamwork, 126, 129–131, 143
Information sharing
    with parents, 94, 109, 110
    PQA, 166–167
    teamwork, 122, 125, 126, 136
Inhelder, B., 14, 245
Initiative, adult
    active learning principle, 46–47
    vs. child initiative, xii
    defined, 328
    directive climate, 63–64, 66
    large-group time, 233, 353, 354, 355–356
    play, 289, 290, 292–293
    small-group time, 232, 328, 331–333
    special events and activities, 236
    supportive climates, 64
    teamwork, 121, 149
    in Wheel of Learning, 4
Initiative, child
    active learning, 4, 26–27, 46–47
    vs. adult-initiative, xii
    authentic relationships, 73
    child choice, 51
    comparison studies, 10, 11
    in conflict resolution, 81
    daily routine, 224–225, 240
    vs. guilt, 56, 245, 247
    laissez-faire climates, 62–63, 66
    large-group time, 233, 365
    learning environment, 177–178, 190
    partnerships with adults, 47
    planning time, 245, 247
    recall time, 319
    relationships, 58, 60
    supportive climate, 24, 67, 77
    in Wheel of Learning, 4
    work time, 278–279
Initiative, family, 94
Institute of Medicine, 276
Instruments, musical, 211–212, 219
Intentions, child. *See* **Child's intentions**
Interactions. *See also* **Adult-child interactions; Peer relations**
    daily routine, 225
    and learning, 15, 16–20
    vs. management, 57, 302, 380
    on-the-spot, 285–286, 405
    outdoor time, 380
    partnerships, 57
    strategies, 4, 5
    styles and culture, 99

Interest areas. *See also* **Learning environment; Outdoor area**
    active learning principles in, 172–173
    adding new, 177
    art area, 185, 197–202, 210, 215, 219
    block area, 185, 190–193
    book and writing area, 172, 185, 202–205, 215
    computer area, 212–216
    curriculum overview, 5
    flexibility, 174, 180–182
    house area, 185, 193–197, 202
    labeling, 174, 177, 186–187
    music and movement area, 185, 211–212
    organization, 174, 176–182
    outdoor area, 175, 198, 201, 202, 215–221, 360, 376
    overcrowding, 272
    sand and water area, 208–209
    size of, 177
    strategies for arranging, 190–221
    summary, 220–221
    toy area, 185, 205–208
    visibility, 174, 179–180, 181
    in Wheel of Learning, 4
    woodworking area, 209–211
Interpreting
    by child, 19
    child's actions, 23, 24, 397, 401–405
    gestures, 253–254, 265, 308, 312–313, 319
Intimacy, 259–260, 261, 315
Intrinsic motivation, invention, and generativity, 17, 18–20, 27, 51. *See also* **Child's intentions; Initiative, child**
Intuitive thought, 19
Invention
    active learning component, 17, 18–20, 47–48
    by adults, 47–48
IQ scores, 9

J

Jablon, J. R., 154
Jargon, 126, 162, 163
Johnson, C., 56, 61, 74, 81
Jordan, D., 249
Judgments
    about children's actions, 130–131
    child's, 19, 97–98
Jumping sample plan, 352

K

Kagan, S. L., 2, 392
KDIs (Key developmental indicators). *See* **Key developmental indicators (KDIs)**
Kessler, R., 92
Key developmental indicators (KDIs)
    about, xii, 4, 25–26, 393–395
    assessment with, 396, 401, 404, 405
    cleanup time, 384
    companion books, xii, 405
    content areas, 28–29, 392–406
    curriculum basis, 4, 25–26, 392–406
    importance of, 397–399
    interpreting children's actions, 23, 24
    large-group time, 327, 355, 358, 368, 404
    learning environment, 25
    list, 28–29, 394–395
    materials, 183, 398–400
    outside time, 374–375
    planning time, 265
    planning with, 134, 136, 138, 396–397, 398–399, 404

play types, 280–282, 398
revised, xi–xii
scanning during work time, 282, 284
small-group time, 327, 332, 334, 342, 343
special needs, children with, 396
support strategies, 399–406
in Wheel of Learning, 4
work time, 277–278, 280–282, 284, 285

Key experiences, 393. *See also* **Key developmental indicators (KDIs)**
Keyser, J., 92–93
Kim, K., 11
Kindergarten. *See* **School readiness**
Kindler, A. M., 290
Kohlberg, L., 275
Kohn, Alfie, 78

L

Labels
avoiding labeling children, 113
avoiding labeling team members, 121
block area materials, 193
child belongings, 179
children's actions, 329
cleanup and, 186, 384
comparison studies, 10
concrete, 176, 186, 384
curriculum overview, 5
find-use-return cycle, 183
home language, 102, 196
house area, 196–197
interest areas, 174, 177, 186–187
music and movement area, 212
picture, 176, 186, 384
"readability," 176, 186–187, 384
sand and water area, 209
toy area, 207
types, 384
woodworking area, 211

Laissez-faire climate, 62–67
Language, home. *See also* **Language skills**
book and writing area materials, 202
consistency in daily routine, 238
KDIs, 394
labels, 102, 196
supporting, 98, 102, 103

Language, Literacy, and Communication KDIs and content area, 26, 28, 392, 394
Language skills. *See also* **Language, home**
language of absence, 310
message board time, 390
noise and, 176
recall time, 308, 309

Large-group time, 353–373
about, 328, 353–357
activities' length, 366, 367
activity types, 354, 359
benefits, 326–327, 357, 361
child's activities in, 360–362
choice, child, 354, 356–357, 360, 361–362
components, 353–357, 367, 368–369
control, shared, 356–357
curriculum overview, 6
in daily routine, 39–42, 228, 233, 235
defined, 39–42, 326, 353
ending, 366–367
examples, 353, 358–359, 360–361, 370–373
forming, 360

ideas, 358–359
importance of, 357, 361
KDIs, 327, 355, 358, 368, 404
learning environment, 174, 178–179, 239
location, 360
message board time, 388–399
planning, 368–369, 404
preparing, 363, 364
problem solving, 357, 362, 389
scaffolding, 327, 329, 354, 364–366, 367
special events and activities, 236, 355, 359
support strategies, 363–373
in Wheel of Learning, 4

Leadership, child, 21, 357, 366, 367
Learning, active. *See* **Active learning**
Learning environment, 170–221. *See also* **Outdoor area**
acoustics of, 176
active learning principles in, 172–174
art area, 185, 197–202, 210, 215, 219
block area, 185, 190–193
book and writing area, 172, 185, 202–205, 215
choice, child, 5, 172–173, 177–178, 181
computer area, 212–216
curriculum principle, 5, 6, 22, 24, 39–42
daily routine, 226–227, 239
flexibility, 174, 180–182
group activities, 174, 178–179
guidelines for organizing, 174–187, 190–221
house area, 185, 193–197, 202
inviting to children, 174–176
maps and planning time, 255, 257
movement between areas, 174
music and movement area, 185, 211–212
outdoor area, 175, 198, 201, 202, 215–221, 360, 376
outside time, 239
PQA category, 164, 169
sand and water area, 208–209, 219
shared spaces, 181–182, 216
special needs, children with, 187–189
summary, 220–221
supporting KDIs, 25
toy area, 185, 205–208
visibility, 174, 179–181
in Wheel of Learning, 4
woodworking area, 209–211

Learning pathways. *See* **Development**
Leiter, V., 161
Leong, D., 245, 247
Leseman, P., 10
Lesson plans. *See* **Planning (by teachers), daily**
Letter links
labels, 179
large-group time, 371
planning time, 262, 263
recall time, 317
small-group time, 331

Leveling, 126–127
Lewis, M., 57
Licensing
learning environment, 174
outdoor area, 216
parent involvement, 93
space requirements, 179
special needs, children with, 189

Lickona, T., 51, 249
Lighting, 175, 198
Likert, R., 123, 127
Limits, setting, 114–115
Lines, walking in, 84

Lippitt, G., 127, 142
Listening to children. *See also* **Attentiveness**
    authentic relationships, 74
    beliefs, 59
    conflict resolution, 81, 82, 301, 303
    large-group time activities, 365
    planning time, 264–267
    recall time, 319
    reflection, 43
    repeating and restating, 79, 303
    supportive environment, 77
    work time, 278
Literacy. *See also* **Language skills; Writing**
    labels, 384
    message board time, 390
    reading to children, 92, 203
    recall time, 309
Lofts, 193, 194, 206, 207–208
Longevity Project, 247
Longitudinal studies, 7–10
Lunch, family participation, 110
Lütkenhaus, P., 245, 248, 251

M

Magazines, 199, 202, 204
Mahler, M., 57
Management
    vs. interaction, 57, 302, 380
    social climates, 66
Manfredi/Petitt, Lynn, 93, 120
Manipulation
    active learning ingredient, 51, 52
    computers, 215
    exploratory play, 280
    large-group time, 354
    learning environment, 172
    plan-do-review process, 244
    small-group time, 331
    supportive environment, 52, 77
Manlove, E. E., 176
Maps and planning time, 255, 257, 263
Marcovitch, S., 245, 247
Marriage, research, 8
Marshall, B., 184, 294–295, 368–369
Martin, L. R., 247
Marzano, R., 393
Materials. *See also* **Storage**
    active learning ingredient, 51, 52
    adult use, 42–43
    amount, 174, 182
    art area, 197–202, 219
    avoiding, 272
    backup materials, 342, 343, 364
    block area, 192–193
    book and writing area, 202–205
    building, 192, 193, 206, 207, 210, 219
    child choice, 27–30, 37, 172–173, 272
    collage, 199, 348
    community involvement, 94–95
    comparison studies, 10
    complex play, 294
    computer, 214, 215
    control of, 59
    curriculum overview, 5, 6
    direct action on objects, 17
    drawing and cutting materials, 199, 263
    easy-to-handle, 39, 41
    exploration, 30–31, 34, 280
    fill-and-empty materials, 192, 193, 209
    find-use-return cycle, 172, 183
    found, 38, 39, 40, 182, 348
    heavy, 39, 41
    homelike, 96–97, 195, 196–197
    house area, 194–195
    KDIs, 183, 398–400
    large-group time, 354, 363, 364, 365, 367
    learning environment, 172
    maps and planning time, 263
    mathematics and science, 190
    messy, 38, 39
    modeling and molding, 199, 349
    music and movement area, 212
    natural, 38, 39, 40, 175, 207
    open-ended, 174, 182–183
    organization and provision, 22, 37–42
    outdoor area, 218–219, 221
    outside time, 377–381
    parent involvement, 94–95, 96–97
    plan-do-review process, 244
    planning time, 260–261, 267–268
    practical, everyday, 38, 39, 40
    pretend play, 192, 193, 195, 206, 207, 209, 219, 282
    "realness," 196
    for recall time, 315, 316
    reflecting diversity, 185
    reflecting family lives, 96–97, 174, 183, 185
    sand and water area, 208, 209
    small-group time, 331, 333, 335, 336, 338–340, 341–347
    sorting, 206
    special needs, children with, 187–189
    supportive climate, 77
    take-apart-and-put-together, 192, 193, 206, 207
    toy area, 206–207
    transformations, 31–34, 340
    types, 38–41
    visibility, 260, 273
    in Wheel of Learning, 4
    woodworking area, 210–211
    writing, 52, 172, 202–204, 263
Mathematics
    books, 204
    exploration, 32
    KDIs and content area, 26, 29, 392, 395
    materials, 190
Maxwell, L. E., 176
McMahon, Linnet
    adult-child interaction, 57, 302
    adult play, 289, 290
    conversation, 293, 297, 298
McNeil, C. B., 78
Meals
    allergies, 188
    in daily routine, 228, 234–235, 387, 390
    food program guidelines, 175
    and length of program, 236–237
    parent involvement, 110
    space for, 174, 178–179
Meisels, Sam, 152, 167
Memory creation and recall time, 246, 307, 312
Mental images
    planning time, 249
    recall time, 307, 309–310, 311
Message board time, 234, 235, 388–390
Messes, 38, 39, 45–46. *See also* **Mistakes and mishaps**
Miller, P., 310–311

Mistakes and mishaps
    corrections, avoiding, 44, 48
    KDIs, 398
    learning opportunities, 20, 44–45, 61–62
    problem solving, 61–62
Mitchell, T. C., 189
Modeling and molding materials, 199, 349
Modifications to child's plans, 249, 278–279, 284
Montgomery County Community Action Agency (MCCAA) Head Start Program, 124
Moore, E., 2, 226, 249, 392
Moran, J., 177
Motivation. *See also* **Child's interests; Initiative, child**
    and focus on strengths, 70–71
    intrinsic, 17, 18–20, 27, 51
Motor development, 10, 11
Movement
    between interest areas, 174, 180
    large-group time, 354, 359
    and music area, 185, 211–212
    outside time, 377
    skills development, 34, 35–36
Muller, U., 245, 247
Music
    background, 176
    cleanup time, 385
    instruments, 211–212, 219
    large-group time, 354
    and movement area, 185, 211–212
    outdoor area, 219

N

NAEYC. *See* **National Association for the Education of Young Children (NAEYC)**
Naptime
    in daily routine, 228, 234–235, 236–237
    planning during, 123
    space for, 174, 178–179
Narrating as planning-time strategy, 265–266
Narrative/Notes form, 144
National Association for Family Child Care, 175
National Association for the Education of Young Children (NAEYC)
    assessment, 152, 155
    curriculum alignment, 392
    health and safety standards, 175
    parent involvement, 93
    planning, 245
National Association of Early Childhood Specialists, 392
National Education Goals Panel, 2, 392
National Information Center for Children and Youth With Disabilities, 189
National Institute for Early Education Research, 93
National Research Council, 92, 160, 276
Natural materials, 38, 39, 40, 175, 207
Nature, observing, 376, 377, 380
Nelson, C. A., 15
Newcombe, N., 15
Newsletters, 110
Noise, 176
Nonverbal communication
    comfort and contact, 287
    culture and family, 99
    planning time, 253–254, 256, 264–267
    recall time, 308, 312–313, 319
    small-group time, 326
Nores, M., 7–8
Norman, D. A., 307

Notes. *See* **Anecdotal notes**
Nursery rhymes, 354, 359

O

Observation/feedback (O/F), 144–147
Observations by child
    as active learning component, 37
    large-group time, 361–362
    small-group time, 345
Observations of child. *See also* **Anecdotal notes; COR Advantage**
    assessments and, 6, 154–156
    child's intentions, 43
    comparison studies, 10
    family culture, 184
    focus on strengths, 70–72
    KDIs, 397, 401–405
    large-group time, 365, 367
    materials use, 43
    outside time, 376
    parent and family involvement, 94, 108–109, 110, 115–116
    participant-observers, 17, 20–24
    photo notes, 130
    planning, daily, 120, 122, 124, 129–131
    recall time, 319
    small-group time, 336–337, 342–343
    supportive environment, 23, 24, 77
    work time, 278, 282–286, 296–297
Observations of teacher, 143–148. *See also* **Assessment, staff**
O'Donnell, K., 11
Onlooking play, 279
One-thing-at-a-time thinking, 19
Open-ended materials, 174, 182–183
Open-ended questions, 10, 261, 265, 313, 318–319, 323
Open-ended stories, 342, 343
Open floor plan, 179–180
Open houses, 109
Opening statements for group activities, 341–343, 364, 367
Outdoor area
    arranging and equipping, 175, 215–221, 376
    art materials, 198, 201, 202, 219
    large-group time, 360
    music and movement area, 212
    sand and water area, 208, 219
Outside time, 374–381
    about, 374–375
    child's activities in, 376–377
    components, 374–375
    conflicts, 379–380
    in daily routine, 42, 228, 233, 238
    defined, 42, 326, 374
    ending, 377, 381
    importance of, 375–376
    learning environment, 239
    location, 376
    summary, 381
    support strategies, 377–381
    weather, 238
Overcrowding, 272

P

Pace, child's, 31, 345. *See also* **Patience**
Painter, M., 280
Painting and printing materials, 199
Parallel play, 279, 289, 290–291, 378
Parent Involvement and Family Services PQA category, 147, 163, 167, 169

Parent Education Participation Program (PEPP), 124
Parent and family involvement, 90–117
    active learning, 96–99
    anecdotal notes, sharing, 109, 110, 156
    anticipating excellence, 113–114
    benefits, 92–94, 102–103
    books and reading, 92, 203
    child's choices, 97–98
    context of child learning, 2, 95–96
    control, shared, 100, 106
    COR Advantage, 94, 156, 157, 160
    culture, 94, 95–96, 103–110, 184
    gatherings, 109
    Head Start standards, 92, 93, 124
    home visits, 94, 104–108, 123–124, 184, 203
    inspired play, 100, 101–102
    large-group time, 357
    materials that reflect, 96–97, 174, 183, 185
    Perry Preschool Study, 8
    PQA category, 147, 163, 167, 169
    small-group time, 335
    strategies for, 93–96, 103–116
    summary, 117
    supportive climate, 100–102
    teacher-parent relationships, 72, 92–95, 110–113, 114–115
    teamwork, 124
    transitions, 96, 103, 107–108, 109–110, 226
    trust, 58
    valuing families, 102–103, 108–109, 183
Parks as outdoor area, 216, 238, 376
Parten, M., 279
Participation, adult
    on child's terms, 68–69
    constructive play, 289–290, 293–296
    exploratory play, 47–48, 77, 289, 290
    family-inspired play, 101
    games, 289, 291–292, 293
    large-group time, 357, 365, 366
    materials use, 42–43
    outside time, 378
    participant-observers, 17, 20
    pretend play, 289, 291–292, 293–296
    work time, 282, 289–293
Partnerships. *See also* **Adult-child interactions**
    adult-child, 47, 57, 68–69, 239, 290–292
    conversations, 296–297, 378–379
    large-group time, 357
    outside time, 378
    planning time, 260, 263, 275
    supportive climates, 64
    teachers, administrators and researchers, 3
Patience
    authentic relationships, 74, 75
    nonverbal children, 265
    planning time, 267
    recall time, 316–318
    teamwork, 121, 128
Peer conflict. *See* **Conflict resolution**
Peer relations. *See also* **Referring children to each other; Social interactions**
    empathy, 60
    family and culture, 95
    large-group time, 326–327, 357, 361
    planning time, 261, 269
    recall time, 320–321
    sharing recall time, 315–316
    small-group time, 326–327, 333–336
Pellegrini, A., 310
PEPP (Parent Education Participation Program), 124

Performance standards. *See* **Standards**
Perrett, B., 381
Perry Preschool Study, xi, 2–3, 7–9
Phatics, 293
Phillips, C. B., 95
Photos, 109, 130, 192, 195, 202, 204
Phyfe-Perkins, E., 57, 176, 178
Physical Development and Health KDIs and content area, 26, 28, 392, 394
Physical level of child
    adult play, 289, 290, 296, 365, 366, 367, 378
    conversation, 260, 261, 296, 315, 378
    large-group time, 365, 366, 367
    outside time, 378
    partnership and, 47
    planning time, 260
    recall time, 315
    small-group time, 342
    work time, 285
Physical setting. *See* **Learning environment**
Piaget, Jean
    adult-child cooperation, 275
    adult's role, 26
    child's choice, 51
    curriculum basis, 3
    developmental theory, 14–15, 16
    planning, 245
Pianta, R. C., 86
Pickup time. *See* **Departure time**
Picture labels, 176, 186, 384
Pierson, D. E., 50
Pine, F., 57
Piscatelli, B., 14
Placating, 126
Plan-do-review process, 242–323. *See also* **Planning time; Recall time; Work time**
    benefits, 244
    comparison studies, 10
    curriculum overview, 5–6
    daily planning, 134–136
    in daily routine, 39, 228–231
    development of child planning, 245, 247, 251–253
    importance of, xi, 244
    independence, 244
    learning environment, 239
    overview, 244
    parent involvement, 94
    problem solving, 230, 244
    summary, 245
    in Wheel of Learning, 4
Planning (by teachers), daily
    with COR Advantage, 131, 134, 136, 138, 159–160
    examples, 131–133, 135, 139
    focus on child's strengths, 72
    KDIs, 134, 136, 138, 396–397, 398–399, 404
    large-group time, 368–369, 404
    plan-do-review process, 134–136
    role in supporting active learning, 6, 23, 39–42
    scheduling, 123–124, 134
    teamwork, 126, 131–138
    in Wheel of Learning, 4
Planning time, 244–275. *See also* **Recall time; Work time**
    about, 244–246
    benefits, 249–251
    child's activities in, 247–249, 251–257
    concerns about, 271, 272
    control, shared, 70
    conversation, 254–257, 259–260, 261–270
    in daily routine, 228, 230, 235

detailed plans, 255–256, 257, 265, 267–269, 274
development, 271–275
examples, 256
games, 262–263
at home, 256–257
importance of, 10, 249–251, 252
intimacy, 259–260, 261
materials, 260–261, 267–268
nonverbal children, 253–254, 256, 264–267
problem solving, 248, 249
routine plans, 254, 265, 267–269
size, 259–260
starting, 271
summary, 245, 252, 257, 274
support strategies, 258–274
vague plans, 254, 265
writing down, 271
Plants, 175, 188, 195, 202, 211
Plan-work-recall process. *See* **Plan-do-review process**
Play. *See also* **Play, adult; Play, constructive; Play, exploratory; Play, pretend**
associative, 279
challenging *vs.* ordinary, 250–251
commitment to support, 68, 75–78, 84
complex, 250–251, 280, 294
cooperative, 193, 279
cues, 68
disquieting, 77
dramatic, 76, 77
effects of child planning on, 249–250
family-inspired, 100, 101–102, 106
importance of, 75–76, 276, 398
individual, 191–192, 193, 205, 206–207
KDIs, 280–282, 398
natural openings, 289–290, 378
onlooking, 279
in pairs, 280
parallel, 279, 289, 290–291, 378
repetitive, 240, 272, 273
role play, 193, 194, 195, 206–207
social, 191–192, 206, 212, 213, 374, 381
solitary, 279–280
superhero play, 292, 294–295
in transitions, 84
variety in, 240
vigorous, 217, 233–234, 239, 374, 375–376
Play, adult
child's control, 295
constructive play, 289–290, 293–296
conversation, 293–300
as encouragement, 78–79
family-inspired, 101
initiative, 289, 290, 292–293
outside time, 378
parallel, 289, 290–291, 378
parent involvement, 106
partnership, 47
supportive climate, 77–78
work time, 282, 289–293
Play, constructive
adult participation, 289–290, 293–296
conflicts, 300
outside time, 376
supportive climate, 76, 77
work time, 280, 281, 282, 300
Play, exploratory. *See also* **Exploration**
adult participation, 47–48, 77, 289, 290
child choice, 282
defined, 280

outside time, 376
toy area, 206–207
Play, pretend
adult participation, 289, 291–292, 293–296
conversation, 293
materials, 192, 193, 195, 206, 207, 209, 219, 282
outside time, 219, 376–377
recalling, 310
toy area, 206–207
work time, 280–281, 282
Play areas. *See* **Interest areas**
Play dough. *See* **Modeling and molding materials**
Play extension by adults, 292–293, 295, 378
Poems, 354, 359
Policymakers and assessment tools, 160, 166–167
Portfolios and assessment, 154
Posner, M., 245, 247
Potlucks, 109
Pouting, 287
Power-oriented play. *See* **Superhero play**
PQA. *See* **Preschool Program Quality Assessment (PQA)**
Praise
vs. acknowledgment, 321–322
disadvantages, 62, 78
vs. encouragement, 68, 78–79, 84–85, 269–270
transitions, 84–85
Predictability and daily routine, 228, 236–238
Preschool Curriculum Comparison Study, 3, 7, 8–9
Preschool Program Quality Assessment (PQA)
about, 152–153
categories, 169–170
curriculum overview, 6
Head Start alignment, 164
parent involvement, 93
supportive climate, 86
teacher assessment, 144, 145–148
using, 164–168
Preschool Wheel of Learning, 3, 4
Pretend play. *See* **Play, pretend**
Print materials. *See* **Book and writing area; Books; Writing**
Problem solving
active learning principle, 17, 20
by adults, 59
cleanup time, 304–305
confidence, 61–62
daily routine, 225
in elementary school, 50
importance of, 17, 20, 57
large-group time, 357, 362, 389
message board time, 389
outside time, 379–380
plan-do-review process, 230, 244
planning time, 248, 249
referring children to each other, 46, 301
small-group time, 340–341
social conflicts, 68, 79–83, 85–86, 301–304, 379–380
supporting, 5, 24, 45–46, 61–62
teamwork, 121, 122–123, 136, 149
tools and technology, 35
transitions, 85–86
in Wheel of Learning, 4
work time, 276, 277, 278–279, 282, 300–305
Professional development
HighScope, xiii
observation and supervision, 143–148
PQA, 146, 165
program quality measures, 163
rotating tasks, 137, 138
Program assessment. *See* **Assessment, program**

Program Management PQA category, 147, 163, 169
Program quality. *See* Assessment, program
Props
    book and writing area, 202, 204
    dance, 212
    house area, 194, 195, 196
    large-group time, 364, 365, 367
    outdoor area, 219
    planning time, 260, 263, 273
    recall time, 315, 317
Public discourse and recall time, 309
Puzzles, 188

Q

Quality measures. *See* Assessment, program; Preschool Program Quality Assessment (PQA)
Quality rating and improvement system (QRIS), 86, 88–89
Questions
    authentic relationships, 75, 106
    avoiding, 79
    beliefs about, 59
    from child, 46, 59
    child's intentions, 43, 254, 298–299
    control, 70
    for curriculum decisions, 140–141, 146
    "how" questions, 264
    for observing children, 129–130
    open-ended, 10, 261, 265, 313, 318–319, 323
    outside time, 379
    parents, 106
    planning time, 261, 264, 265
    recall time, 318–319, 320
    small-group time, 344–345
    "what" and "where" questions, 261, 264
    work time, 267, 284, 297–300

R

Ramanssini, K., 177
Reading to children, 92, 203
Realistic expectations
    cleanup time, 304, 305, 384, 386
    KDIs, 397–398
Recall time, 307–323. *See also* Planning time; Reflection; Work time
    about, 307
    child's actions in, 310–313
    during cleanup, 305
    conversation, 230, 309–310, 313, 315, 316–322
    in daily routine, 230–231, 235
    defined, 307
    development, 311–312, 315, 322
    examples, 307, 313–315
    games, 315, 316, 317
    group activities, 315
    importance of, 10, 246, 247, 307–310
    intimacy, 315
    materials, 315, 316
    memory creation, 246, 307, 312
    nonverbal communication, 308, 312–313, 319
    summary, 245, 311, 313, 323
    supporting, 313–322
Reciprocal relationships
    authenticity, 73
    importance of, 47
    sharing control, 68–70
Recycled materials, 198, 210–211
Reenactments, 312–313, 354, 359

Referring children to each other. *See also* Peer relations
    large-group time, 329
    outside time, 378
    play, 289, 292
    problem solving, 46, 301
    small-group time, 329, 336, 344
Reflection. *See also* Recall time
    active learning component, 4, 10, 17–18, 36–37
    adult, 122, 131–132
    child's intentions, 43
    curriculum overview, 6
    development, 247
    encouraging, 24, 43–45, 79
    plan-do-review process, 244
Regulation. *See* Self-regulation
Relationships, human
    adults' effect on children, 120, 149
    authentic, 68, 72–75, 84, 100–101, 106, 127
    and development, 58–62
    reciprocal, 47, 68–70, 73
    supportive climate for, 57, 58–62, 65–66
    teacher-parent, 72, 92–95, 110–113, 114–115
    teamwork, 121, 126–129, 142–143
Relationships between things
    cause-and-effect, 32, 33, 35
    direct experience, 31, 32
    planning time, 249, 271
    recall time, 308–309, 322
Reliability of assessments, 155
Remembering. *See also* Recall time
    memory creation, 246, 307–308, 312
    reminders of previous work, 268–269
Repetition
    child's words, 79, 303
    in play and planning, 240, 272, 273
Representations
    planning time, 260
    recall time, 309–310, 317
Research, HighScope Curriculum effects
    independent, 10–11
    Perry Preschool Study, xi, 2–3, 7–9
    Preschool Curriculum Comparison Study, 3, 7, 8–9
    Training of Trainers Evaluation, 7, 9–10
Resnick, G., 11
Respect
    adult play, 293, 295
    family and culture, 96, 102
    planning time, 275
    teamwork, 120, 121–122, 127
Responsibility
    cleanup time, 384
    longitudinal studies, 8–9
    teams, 136, 140
Restating child's words, 79, 303
Rest time. *See* Naptime
Review time. *See* Recall time
Roeleveld, J., 10
Rogers, Carl, 72–73
Role play, 193, 194, 195, 206–207
Roles, team, 125, 136, 137, 138–141
Rosegrant, T., 152
Rotating tasks, 137, 138
Rothbart, M. K., 245, 247
Routine. *See* Daily routine
Routine plans, 254, 265, 267–269
Rowe, S. M., 15
Roy, C., 280
Rubin, K., 279

S

Safety
    learning environment, 172, 173, 174, 175
    outdoor area, 216
    outside time, 376
    sense of, 226–227
    sources for health and safety standards, 175, 216
    special needs, children with, 189

Salter, D., 56–57
Sand activity, 372
Sand and water area, 33, 208–209, 219
Satir, Virginia, 126
Scaffolding. *See also* **Plan-do-review process**
    active learning ingredient, 51, 52
    adult's role, 26
    computers, 215
    defined, 25, 26
    development and, 392
    example, 52
    focus on child's strengths, 72
    group times, 327, 329
    interaction plan, 285–286, 405
    large-group time, 327, 329, 354, 364–366, 367
    learning environment, 172–173
    parents and family, 95, 99
    small-group time, 327, 329, 331, 342–345
    supportive climate, 77
    transitions, 383
    work time, 278, 285–286
    zone of proximal development, xii, 26

Scanning
    children in need of comfort, 286–289
    playing with children, 290
    work time problems, 282–285

Schank, R., 307
Scheduling
    active learning periods, 228
    daily planning, 123–124, 134
    home visits, 106
    special events and activities, 236, 355, 359

Schmoker, M., 62
School achievement, xii, 2, 8–9
School readiness
    adjusting to school, 48–50
    Clayton Kids study, 50
    parent involvement, 92
    pressure for, 21, 31, 33, 276

Schweinhart, L. J., 7–8, 9
Science and Technology KDIs and content area, 26, 29, 392, 395
Science materials, 190
Scientific thought, child's, 19
Sears, P. S., 9
Self, sense of, 56–58
Self-confidence. *See* **Confidence**
Self-directed learning, 247. *See also* **Initiative, child**
Self-esteem, 62. *See also* **Confidence**
Self-help skills, 384, 387
Self-knowledge, adult, 103–104
Self-regulation
    development, 56–57
    and planning, 244, 245, 248
    supporting, 59

Self-understanding, 56–58
Senses and exploration, 30
Sequences
    learning and development, 327, 329
    planning time, 268

Shame and doubt *vs.* **autonomy, 56**
Sharing control. *See* **Control, shared**
Sharing space with other organizations, 181–182, 216
Sheese, B. E., 245, 247
Shefatya, L., 245, 280
Shoemaker, J., 57, 176, 178
Shore, R., 15, 16
Shriver, T. P., 92
Siblings, 60, 98
Sign language, 98
Signs for interest areas, 177, 186–187. *See also* **Labels**
Sinks, 194, 208
Size
    block area, 192–193
    planning time groups, 259–260
    play areas, 177
    recall time groups, 315

Slides, 218
Small-group time, 328–352
    about, 328, 331–333
    benefits, 326–327, 333–337
    child's activities in, 338–341
    choice, child, 331, 339–340
    components, 331–333, 347
    creating groups, 331
    curriculum overview, 6
    in daily routine, xiii, 4, 39, 228, 232–233, 235
    defined, 39, 326, 331
    ending, 345–347
    examples, 328–331, 332–333, 334–335, 348–352
    ideas for, 334–335
    importance of, 333–337
    KDIs, 404
    learning environment, 239
    location, 331, 338
    nonverbal children, 326
    planning, 404
    preparation, 341, 342
    problem solving, 340–341
    scaffolding, 327, 329, 331, 342–345
    special events and activities, 236
    support strategies, 341–346
    in Wheel of Learning, 4

Smilansky, S., 245, 247, 280, 292
Smith, L., 15
Smith, T., 226, 249
Snacks. *See* **Meals**
Social and Emotional Development KDIs and content area, 26, 28, 392, 394
Social conflict. *See* **Conflict resolution**
Social development
    building blocks of relationships, 58–62
    importance of play, 276
    theory, 56, 57

Social experiences of learning, 14
Social framework of daily routine, 225–227
Social interactions. *See also* **Adult-child interactions; Peer relations**
    comparison studies, 10, 11
    daily routine, 225–227
    and interest areas, 177–178
    large-group time, 326–327
    meals, 387, 390
    outside time, 374
    recall time, 309–310
    small-group time, 326–327, 333–336
    social play, 191–192, 212, 213, 374, 381
    supportive climate, 22, 24
    work time, 276, 279–282, 284

Social play, 191–192, 206, 212, 213, 374, 381
Social responsibility, 8–9
Social Studies KDIs and content area, 26, 29, 392, 395
Solitary play, 279–280
Songs, 354, 357, 359, 360, 363, 365, 371
Sorongon, A., 11
Sorting materials, 206
Sounds in learning environment, 176
Space. *See also* Learning environment
    block area, 191–192
    distribution of, 177
    house area, 194
    large-group time, 360
    for materials, 39–42
    outdoor area, 216
    per child, 99, 179, 216
    toy area, 205, 206–207
Special needs, children with
    Americans With Disabilities Act, 175
    anticipating excellence, 113–114
    Individuals With Disabilities Education Act, 189
    KDIs, 396
    labels, 186
    learning environment, 187–189
Speech development. *See* **Language**
Sperry, L., 310–311
Spills, 45–46. *See also* Mistakes and mishaps
Spoiling, 287
Sponseller, D., 279–280
Spontaneous learning, 33
Stability, 93, 260. *See also* Consistency
Staff. *See also* **Teachers**
    health and safety, 174
    hiring, 125
    new, 142–143
    sharing child's interests, 72
    supervision, 143–148, 163, 169
    support staff, 124–125, 167
    turnover, 93
Staff Qualification and Staff Management PQA category, 147, 163, 169
Standards
    Common Core Standards, 392
    COR Advantage alignment, 157
    Head Start, 92, 93, 124, 175, 245
    health and safety, 175, 179, 189
    HighScope curriculum alignment, 392
    parent involvement, 92, 93, 124
    planning time, 245
    PQA alignment, 164, 165
    special needs, children with, 189
Stationary structures, 218
Storage. *See also* **Labels**
    art area, 200
    block area, 193
    book and writing area, 202, 205
    child choice, 172
    child's belongings, 174, 178–179
    computer area, 215–216
    containers, 186
    curriculum overview, 5
    find-use-return cycle, 172, 183
    house area, 196–197
    music and movement area, 212
    outdoor area, 221, 378
    sand and water area, 209
    shared spaces, 181–182
    small-group time, 341
    strategies, 183–186

    toy area, 207
    in Wheel of Learning, 4
    woodworking area, 211
Story starters, 342, 343
Storytelling
    by child, 309, 310, 362
    large-group time, 354, 359
    props, 202, 204
Strayer, J., 60
Strengths, focus on. *See* **Focus on strengths**
Strubank, R., 207, 271–274
Success, assuming, 113–114, 121
Superhero play, 292, 294–295
Supervisors
    program assessment, 6, 163, 169
    staff support and supervision, 143–148
Support, adult. *See* **Adult-child interactions; Climate, supportive; Planning (by teachers), daily**
Support staff, 124–125, 167
Supportive climate. *See* **Climate, supportive**
Swings, 218
Symbols, 186, 262, 263, 309, 317, 331, 390. *See also* **Labels; Letter links; Signs for interest areas**
Sylva, Kathy
    benefits of planning time, 10, 245, 249, 250
    completion of plans, 279
    complexity of plans, 254
    complex play, 280
    intimacy, 259
    questions in planning time, 264, 267
    recall time, 308, 311, 315–316
Sympathy, 57

T

Take-apart-and-put-together materials, 192, 193, 206, 207
Talbot, J., 182, 196
Tasks, rotating, 137, 138
Teachers. *See also* **Adult-child interactions; Participation, adult; Play, adult; Scaffolding; Teamwork**
    assessment, 143–148, 162, 165, 166
    belief exercises, 21, 59
    certification and PQA, 165
    community involvement, 94, 108
    family and culture beliefs, 103–104
    feedback, 163
    health and safety, 174
    hiring, 125
    as learners, 69, 123
    new team members, 142–143
    -parent relationships, 72, 92–95, 110–113, 114–115
    partnerships with administrators, 3
    professional development, xiii, 137, 138, 143–148, 163, 166
    program assessment, 6
    recognition, 120, 122
    sharing experiences, 74
    Training of Trainers evaluation, 7, 9–10
    turnover, 93
Teaching theory, 3. *See also* **Curriculum**
Teamwork, 118–149. *See also* **Planning (by teachers), daily**
    about, 120–123
    active learning in, 120
    benefits, 120, 122–123, 142
    characteristics of effective teams, 129
    curriculum decisions, 125, 140–141
    in curriculum overview, 6
    forming teams, 123–125
    gathering information, 127, 129–131, 143

generating strategies, 132–134
group decision making, 126, 131–141
large-group time, 357
new team members, 142–143
problem solving, 121, 122–123, 136, 149
relationships, 121, 126–129, 142–143
staff support and supervision, 143–148
strategies and elements, 125–134, 149
summary, 149
in Wheel of Learning, 4

Tegano, D., 177
Testing, 153–154, 155, 297. *See also* **Assessment, child**
Thank-you card activity, 350
Thinking. *See also* **Child language and thought**
abstract, 308
adult *vs.* child, 19
emotional, 56
intuitive, 19
questions about child's, 299–300

Thompson, R. A., 15
Time
exploration, 31, 34
materials, 39–42
problem solving, 46, 301
recall, 316–318
work time, 279

Tivnan, T., 50
Toddlers
autonomy, 58
empathy, 60
planning, 251–252, 253
recall, 310–311
trust, 58

Tompkins, M., 269
Tools
types, 38, 39
use in active learning, 34–35
woodworking, 209–211

Touch
comforting, 282, 286–289
and culture, 99

Tours, planning, 317
Toy area, 185, 205–208
Traditional nursery schools, 3, 9, 10
Traditions, 335, 355
Training of Trainers Evaluation, 7, 9–10
Transformations, 31–34, 340
Transitions. *See also* **Departure time; Greeting time**
activities for, 382–383
arrival and departure, 237–238, 383
child choice in, 83–84, 346, 383
and cleanup, 231, 382, 384–387
consistency, 241, 382
control, shared, 83–84
daily routine, 227, 228, 234, 235, 238
defined, 326
development, 382–383, 386
family and culture, 96, 103, 107–108
home visits, 107–108
importance of, 234
large-group time, 364, 366–367
minimizing, xii–xiii, 382
outside time, 377
parent involvement, 109–110, 226
planning for, 382–384, 386
small-group time, 345–346
smooth, 241
summary, 386
support strategies, 83–86, 381–387

team roles, 123, 141
walk example, 83–86
work time, 304–305

Traveling. *See also* **Transitions**
field trips, 110, 112, 295, 335, 359
supportive climate, 83–86

Trust
authentic relationships, 73
conflict resolution, 81
daily routine, 239
development, 56
leveling, 126
relationship building, 58, 112
supportive climate, 67, 77
teamwork, 120

U

US Consumer Product Safety Commission, 175
US Department of Agriculture Child and Adult Care Food Program guidelines, 175

V

Vague planners, 254, 265
Validity
active learning, 15
assessment, xiii, 153, 155, 160–162, 167

Valuing
differences, 112
families, 102–103, 108–109, 183

Vandenberg, B., 279
Vaughan, C., 280
Veen, A., 10
Vernon-Feagans, L., 176
Visibility
games, 260, 262, 273
interest areas, 174, 179–181
materials, 260, 273
planning time, 260
toy area, 205–206

Visitors, 94, 108, 110, 295
Visits, home, 94, 104–108, 123–124, 184, 203
Visual impairment, children with, 186, 188
Vogel, N., 187
Volunteers, parents as, 94, 95, 98, 124
Vygotsky, Lev, xii, 3, 15, 26

W

Waits, limiting, xii–xiii, 382
Walker, D. K., 50
Walks, 83–86, 217
Wall, S., 56–57
Warnings, 345, 366, 383–384
Water
art area, 197–198
sand and water area, 33, 208–209, 219

Waters, E., 56–57
Weather, 182, 238
Weikart, David P., 2–3, 7–8, 9, 393
Weissberg, K. S., 92
Wertsch, J. V., 15
"What" questions, 261, 264
Wheelchairs, 188
Wheeled toys, 218, 221
Wheel of Learning, 3, 4
"Where" questions, 261, 264
Williams, L., 95, 103

Wood, David
    adult-child interaction, 57, 302
    adult play, 289, 290
    conversation, 293, 297, 298
Woodworking area, 209–211
Work time, 275–306. *See also* **Planning time; Recall time**
    about, 275
    adult play, 282, 289–293
    child's activities during, 278–282
    cleanup during, 304–305, 384–385
    comforting and contact, 282, 286–289
    conversation, 282, 293–300
    in daily routine, 228, 231, 235
    defined, 275
    ending, 304–305
    examples, 275
    importance of, 10, 275–278
    interactions, on-the-spot, 285–286, 405
    observations, 278, 282–286, 296–297
    problem solving, 276, 277, 278–279, 282, 300–305
    questions, 267, 284, 297–300
    scanning, 282–285
    small-group-time materials, 345
    summary, 245, 278, 282, 306
    support strategies, 282–306, 377, 378–380
Writing. *See also* **Book and writing area**
    materials, 52, 172, 202–204, 263
    message board time, 390
    planning time, 271
    recall time, 313, 322
    small-group-time sample plan, 350

X

Xiang, Z., 7–8

Z

Zelazo, P. D., 245, 247
Zill, N., 11
Zins, J. E., 92
Zone of proximal development, xii, 26. *See also* **Scaffolding**